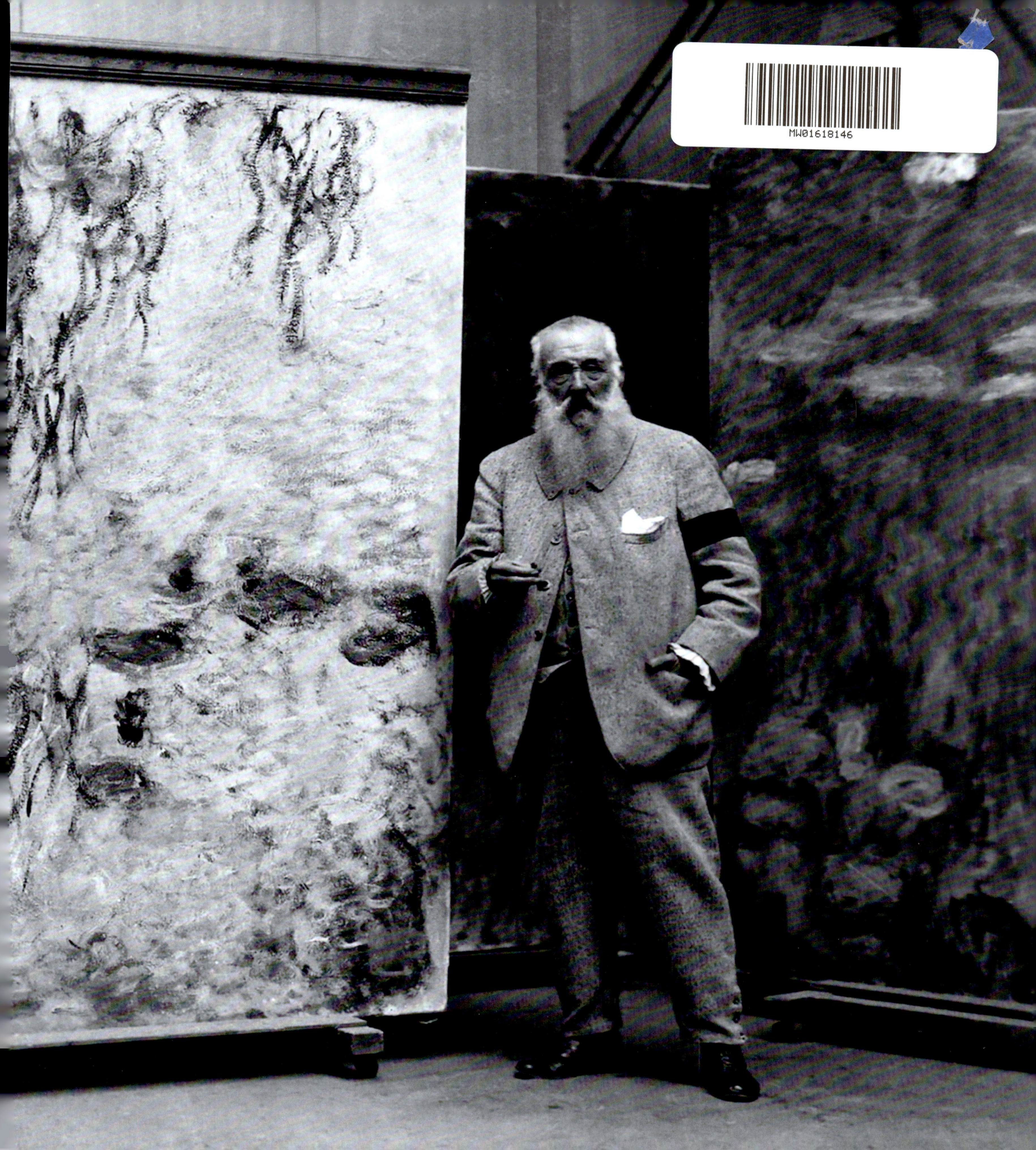

The exhibition is organized by the Kimbell Art Museum, Fort Worth, and the Fine Arts Museums of San Francisco, with the exceptional support of the Musée Marmottan Monet, Paris.

The Fine Arts Museums of San Francisco's presentation of the exhibition at the de Young is made possible by presenting sponsors John A. and Cynthia Fry Gunn and Diane B. Wilsey.

Lead support is provided by the Clare C. McEvoy Charitable Remainder Unitrust and Jay D. McEvoy Trust and the San Francisco Auxiliary of the Fine Arts Museums.

Major support is provided by the Ray and Dagmar Dolby Family Fund and Barbara A. Wolfe.

Significant support is provided by The Art Party, the Diana Dollar Knowles Foundation, Carole McNeil, and MaryBeth and David Shimmon.

Generous support is provided by Denise Littlefield Sobel and David A. Wollenberg.

Additional support is provided by Mrs. George Hopper Fitch, Bob and Jan Newman, Marianne H. Peterson, Maria Pitcairn, and Andrea and Mary Barbara Schultz.

The exhibition is supported by an indemnity from the Federal Council on the Arts and the Humanities.

Exhibition dates:
Fine Arts Museums of San Francisco, February 16–May 27, 2019
Kimbell Art Museum, June 16–September 15, 2019

Kimbell Art Museum
3333 Camp Bowie Boulevard
Fort Worth, Texas 76107-2792
www.kimbellart.org

Yale University Press
302 Temple Street
P.O. Box 209040
New Haven, Connecticut 06520-9040
www.yalebooks.com/art

Produced by the Publications Department of the Kimbell Art Museum
Megan Smyth, Manager of Publications
Juan Gonzalez, Designer

Printed in Canada by Friesens

ISBN
Softcover: 978-0-91280-456-9
Hardcover: 978-0-300-24325-3

Details:
Front cover: *Water Lilies* (cat. 12); Back cover: *Weeping Willow* (cat. 44); Frontispieces: *Water Lilies* (cat. 11) and Claude Monet in his third studio at Giverny, 1923; Pages 106–7: *The Japanese Bridge* (cat. 36); Page 215: *The Japanese Bridge* (cat. 33)

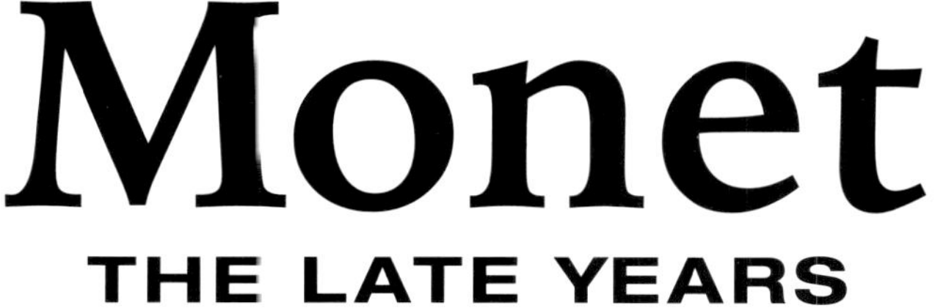

George T. M. Shackelford

With essays by
Claire M. Barry
Simon Kelly
Emma Cauvin
Marianne Mathieu

Kimbell Art Museum
Fine Arts Museums of San Francisco

Distributed by Yale University Press, New Haven and London

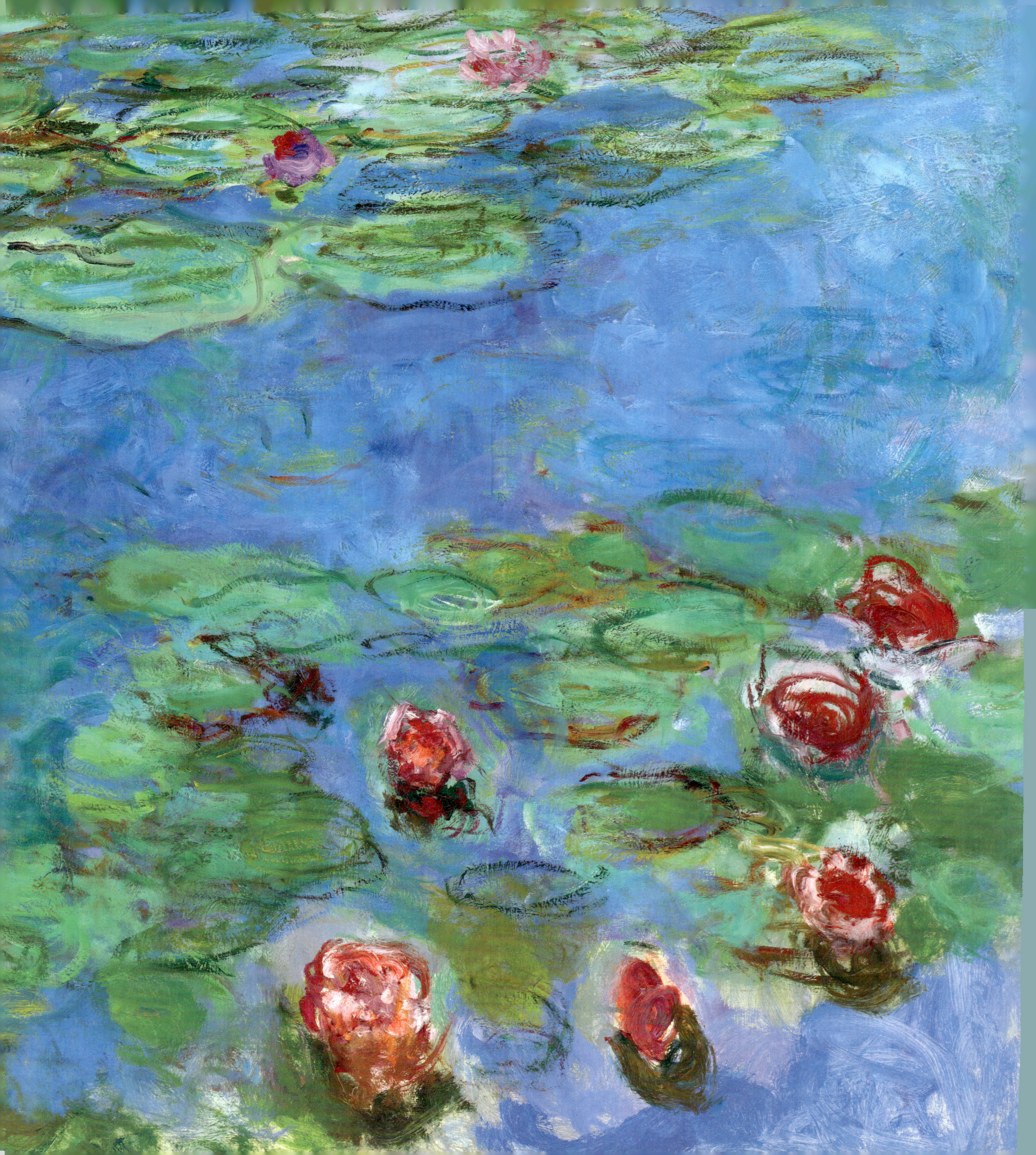

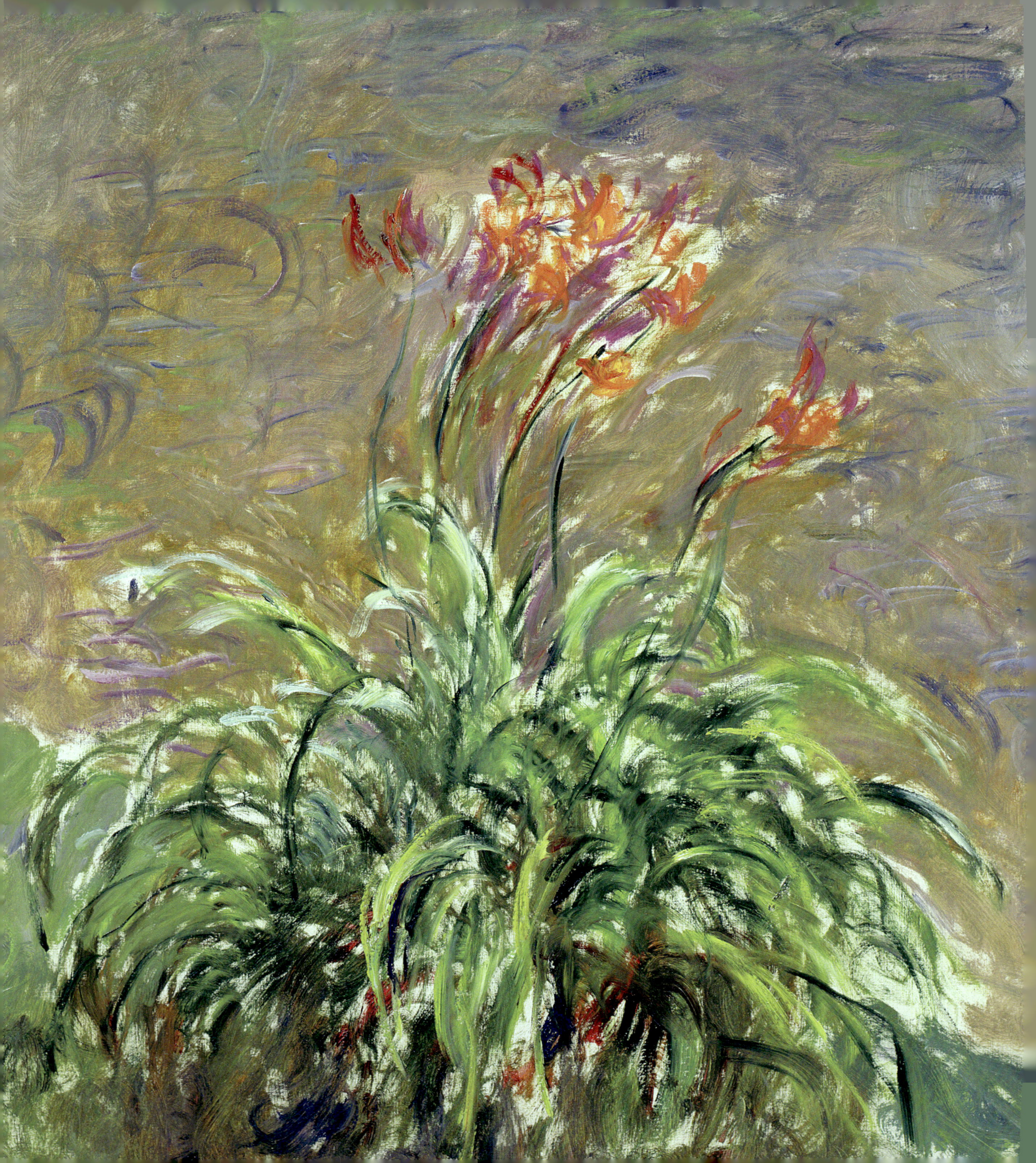

Foreword

Inspired by Claude Monet's masterpieces in the museum's collection, the Kimbell Art Museum decided in 2014 to present two exhibitions investigating the chronological extremes of the artist's long career, both in partnership with the Fine Arts Museums of San Francisco. *Monet: The Early Years* surveyed the painter's evolution during his twenties. *Monet: The Late Years* focuses on the painter at work in his seventies and eighties, exploring the series that Monet invented and reinvented in his Giverny garden, including the Kimbell's *Weeping Willow* and San Francisco's *Water Lilies*. Through some fifty paintings, marked by bold methods of paint application, surprising harmonies or clashes of color, and imposing scale, *Monet: The Late Years* will demonstrate to our visitors the radical nature of the painter's late works.

We would like to thank George T. M. Shackelford, deputy director of the Kimbell Art Museum, organizing curator of both this exhibition and *Monet: The Early Years*. With the collaboration of colleagues at the Fine Arts Museums, including former curators Esther Bell and James A. Ganz, and Melissa Buron, director, art division, George has selected the works on view and has secured the cooperation of people across the world to bring the show and its catalogue into being. To them, to their many colleagues at both our museums, and to the scholars who have contributed to this impressive volume, we offer our profound thanks.

The Kimbell would like to thank Kay and Ben Fortson, Kimbell Fortson Wynne, and the Board of Directors of the Kimbell Art Foundation for their unfailing support of the project. The Fine Arts Museums of San Francisco would like to thank presenting sponsors John A. and Cynthia Fry Gunn and Diane B. Wilsey. The Museums also gratefully acknowledge lead support from the Clare C. McEvoy Charitable Remainder Unitrust and Jay D. McEvoy Trust and the San Francisco Auxiliary of the Fine Arts Museums; major support from the Ray and Dagmar Dolby Family Fund and Barbara A. Wolfe; significant support from The Art Party, the Diana Dollar Knowles Foundation, Carole McNeil, and MaryBeth and David Shimmon; generous support from Denise Littlefield Sobel and David A. Wollenberg; and additional support from Mrs. George Hopper Fitch, Bob and Jan Newman, Marianne H. Peterson, Maria Pitcairn, and Andrea and Mary Barbara Schultz. Further, thanks are graciously extended to the Museums' Board of Trustees for its unwavering support.

Deepest appreciation is extended to the Federal Council on the Arts and the Humanities, which granted the exhibition an indemnity; special thanks are given to Patricia Loiko, indemnity administrator.

Our utmost debt of gratitude is owed the lenders—both public institutions and private collectors—of the magnificent artworks on view. Most especially, we would like to recognize the outstanding support of the Musée Marmottan Monet in Paris, which is lending twenty of its superb paintings to the show. Without their generosity, an exhibition of this quality would never be possible. Thanks to all of them, the brilliant, inventive works of Monet's last years can be explored anew.

Eric M. Lee
Director
Kimbell Art Museum

Thomas P. Campbell
Director and CEO
Fine Arts Museums of San Francisco

Claude Monet, *Day Lilies* (detail), cat. 20

Acknowledgments

I would like to first extend my deepest gratitude to the collectors, directors, curators, and scholars who have so generously facilitated the loans of the works that have made this beautiful and groundbreaking exhibition possible, and who have graciously shared their knowledge of Monet and his world. A special note of gratitude must go to Patrick de Carolis and Marianne Mathieu of the Musée Marmottan Monet for their willingness to collaborate with us on this project.

In addition, I would like to thank William Acquavella, Richard Aste, Helga Aurisch, Joseph Baillio, Christoph Becker, Greg Bell, Brent Benjamin, David Bomford, Richard Brettell, Caroline Campbell, Dawson Carr, Keith Christiansen, Cyanne Chutkow, Stephane Cosman Connery, Mary McDermott Cook, Barbara and Ronald Cordover, Laurence des Cars, Frouke van Dijke, Benjamin Doller, Ann Dumas, Kaywin Feldman, Brian Ferriso, Gabriele Finaldi, Michael Findlay, Gloria Groom, Josef Helfenstein, Christoph Heinrich, Kimberly Jones, Sam Keller, Brian Kennedy, Marine Kiesel, Azu Kubota, Ulf Küster, Teresa Krasny, Marc Larock, Patricia Loiko, Akiko Mabuchi, Nannette V. Maciejunes, the late Margaret McDermott, Olivier Meslay, Adrien Meyer, Mary Morton, Nicole Myers, all members of the Nahmad Family, David Nash, Lawrence Nichols, Patrick Noon, Theresa Papanikolas, Sylvie Patry, Romy Peires, Paul Perrin, Joachim Pissarro, Lionel and Sandrine Pissarro, Clarissa Post, Earl A. Powell III, Eva Reifert, Christopher Riopelle, James Rondeau, Timothy Rub, Simon Shaw, Olivier Simmat, Timothy Standring, Susan Alyson Stein, Charles F. Stuckey, Benno Tempel, Jenny Thompson, Gary Tinterow, and Guy Wildenstein. I am grateful as well to those who wish to remain anonymous and to those who have been inadvertently omitted.

At the Kimbell Art Museum, I want to thank the Board of Directors, led by Kimbell Fortson Wynne and Kay and Ben Fortson, for their support of the exhibition. In addition, thanks are due to our museum director, Eric M. Lee; Brenda Cline, executive vice president and chief financial officer of the Kimbell Art Foundation; Susan Drake, deputy director of finance and administration; Claire Barry, director of conservation, with Peter Van de Moortel and Candace Carlisle Vilas; Patricia Decoster, collections manager and registrar, with Samantha Sizemore and Shelly Threadgill; Jessica Brandrup, head of marketing and public relations, with Madison Ladd and Alex Conger; Robert McAn, membership and special events manager; Angie Bulaich, head of corporate partnerships; Larry Eubank, operations manager, with Jesse Hernandez, Bert Herrington, Cory Ottinger, and Rickey Honaker; Connie Hatchette-Barganier, education manager; Liz Johnson, executive assistant to the director; Robert LaPrelle, photographer; Gary Yawn, visitor services manager; Megan Smyth, manager of publications; Juan Gonzalez, designer; Regina Palm and Katherine Stephens, curatorial assistants; and fellow curators Jennifer Casler-Price, Nancy E. Edwards, and Guillaume Kientz.

The Fine Arts Museums of San Francisco wish to thank the president of the Board of Trustees, Diane B. Wilsey, along with all of the other members of the Board; Thomas P. Campbell, director and CEO, and Max Hollein, former director and CEO; Melissa E. Buron, director, Art Division; and former curators Esther Bell and James A. Ganz. We also acknowledge Krista Brugnara, director of exhibitions; Kimberley Montgomery, chief registrar; Shannon Anandasakaran, exhibitions manager, and Caroline McCune, senior exhibitions coordinator; Elise Effmann Clifford, head paintings conservator; Christopher Busch, senior exhibition designer; Linda Butler, director of marketing, communications, and visitor experience; Amanda Riley, director of development; Sheila Pressley, director of education, and Emily Jennings, director of school and family programs; Abigail Dansiger, head of library and archives; Leslie Dutcher, director of publications; Stuart Hata, director of retail operations; and all of their talented staffs. Our presentation has been graciously supported by John A. and Cynthia Fry Gunn and Diane B. Wilsey, our presenting sponsors.

The exhibition at both venues is further supported by an indemnity from the Federal Council on the Arts and the Humanities.

I owe an enormous debt of gratitude to my friends Paul Hayes Tucker and MaryAnne Stevens, with whom I was privileged to work on the exhibition *Monet in the 20th Century* some twenty years ago. I have been lucky to share the Monet pathway with them, and with Robert Gordon, Richard Kendall, Richard Thomson, Charles F. Stuckey, the late John House, and the late Charles Moffett. Finally, I would like to thank the scholars who have contributed such insightful and engaging essays to the catalogue: Claire Barry, Emma Cauvin, Simon Kelly, and Marianne Mathieu, as well as Philippe Piguet, who gave particular assistance with photographs. Their writing enriches this exhibition and gives form to the genius and powers of reinvention of one of the world's best-known artists.

George T. M. Shackelford
Deputy director, Kimbell Art Museum,
and curator of the exhibition

Lenders to the Exhibition

France
Musée Marmottan Monet, Paris
Musée d'Orsay, Paris

Japan
The National Museum of Western Art, Tokyo

Switzerland
Fondation Beyeler, Basel
Kunstmuseum Basel

United Kingdom
The National Gallery, London

United States
The Art Institute of Chicago
Columbus Museum of Art, Ohio
Denver Art Museum
Fine Arts Museums of San Francisco
Honolulu Museum of Art
Kimbell Art Museum, Fort Worth
The Metropolitan Museum of Art, New York
Minneapolis Institute of Art
Museum of Fine Arts, Houston
National Gallery of Art, Washington, DC
Philadelphia Museum of Art
Phoenix Art Museum
Portland Art Museum, Oregon
Saint Louis Art Museum
The Tobin Theatre Arts Fund, courtesy of the McNay Art Museum, San Antonio
Toledo Museum of Art, Ohio

Private Collections
Collection of Diane B. Wilsey, San Francisco
Private collection, Dallas, in honor of Kay Fortson
Private collection, London
Private collection, courtesy Benjamin Doller, New York
Private collection, courtesy Christie's, New York
Private collection, courtesy Helly Nahmad Gallery, London
Private collection, courtesy Sotheby's, New York
Collectors who wish to remain anonymous

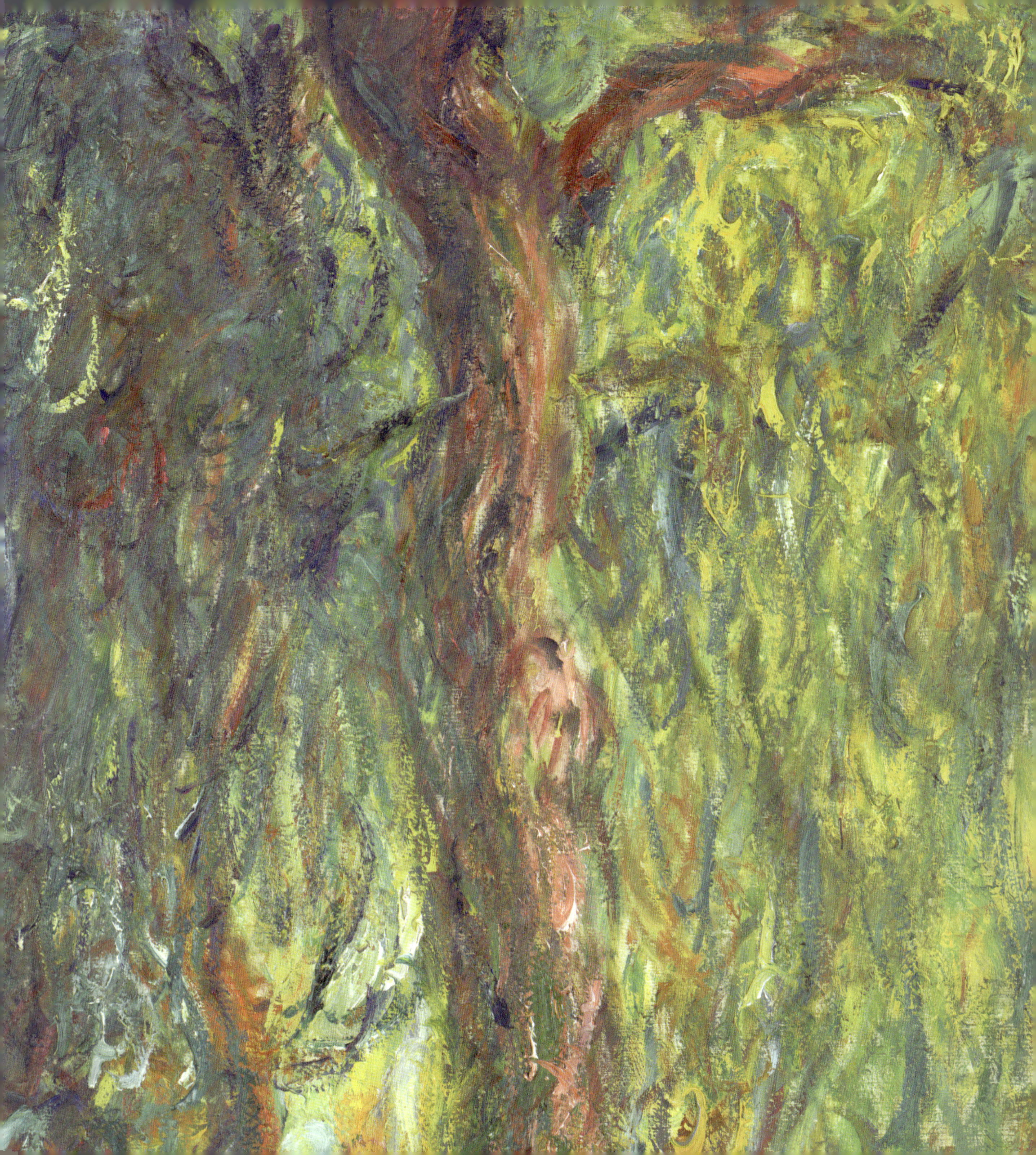

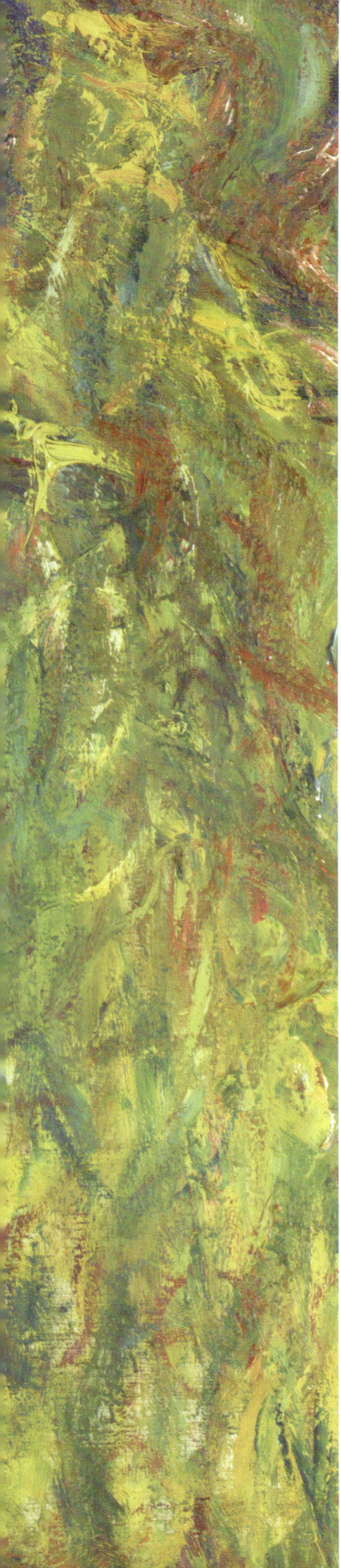

Introduction: The Reinvention of Monet

George T. M. Shackelford
Deputy director, Kimbell Art Museum

In 2016 and 2017, the Kimbell Art Museum and the Fine Arts Museums of San Francisco presented *Monet: The Early Years*, an exhibition of more than fifty paintings that surveyed the artist's work from a picture exhibited in 1858—when he was seventeen years old—to a group of paintings from the summer of 1872—completed when he was still just thirty-one. *Monet: The Late Years* returns to take up the story of Monet's art at the very end of his career—after the heady days of the explosion of Impressionism in the 1870s; after his exultant mastery of his medium in the 1880s and his recognition as chief of the Impressionist landscape painters; after the momentous decision, in the 1890s, to work in series; and after the first decade of the twentieth century, which saw the debut of his views of the Thames in London in 1904 and his triumph with the *Water Lilies* exhibition of 1909. This exhibition—though it opens with a prologue of works painted at the very end of the 1890s, a selection of the classic water-lily paintings of 1904–7, and the two views of his garden painted around 1913—begins in earnest with Monet's return to painting in the late spring of 1914, tracing his career until his death in 1926.

The spring of 1914 was a turning point for the artist. On April 30, Monet wrote to his friend Gustave Geffroy, an art critic as well as a novelist, that he was "doing wonderfully and am obsessed by the desire to paint; I've been prevented from doing so during the last, very beautiful, days, but I should have got myself back to work yesterday, everything was ready for me, and then voilà, time wasted, false start."[1] A month later, Monet was back to painting in earnest, as he told the critic Félix Fénéon that he was "working at full speed, and no matter what the weather, I paint." He went on to say that he was beginning "a huge labor, I am passionate about it."[2]

His joy at painting once more was all the more intense because, in the years 1909 to 1914, he experienced some of the most difficult times in his life. He had begun the century with a successful exhibition including many views of his Giverny garden, held at the Galerie Durand-Ruel, whose proprietor, Paul Durand-Ruel, had been his

Claude Monet, *Weeping Willow* (detail), 1918–19, cat. 44

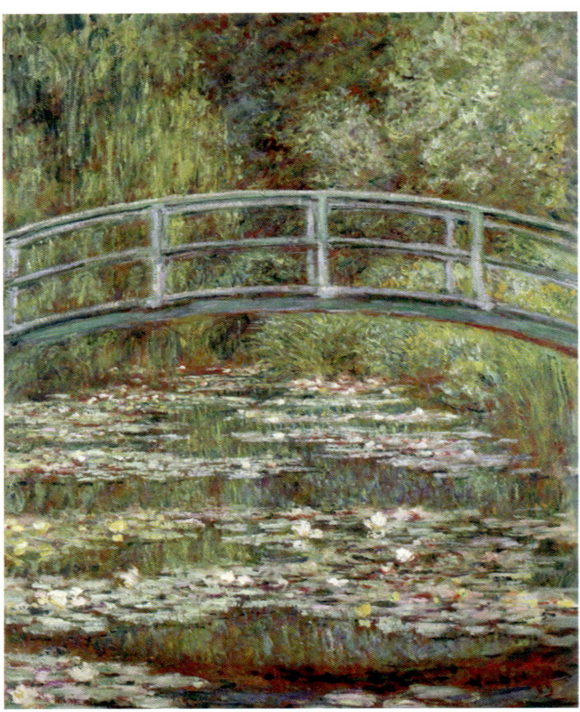

Fig. 1. Claude Monet, *Bridge over a Pond of Water Lilies*, 1899. Oil on canvas, 36 ½ x 29 in. (92.7 x 73.7 cm). The Metropolitan Museum of Art, New York. H. O. Havemeyer Collection. Bequest of Mrs. H. O. Havemeyer, 1929, 29.100.113

champion and dealer since the Impressionist exhibitions of the 1870s (see cat. 3). His simultaneous trips to London had yielded a series of canvases showing the Waterloo and Charing Cross Bridges as well as the Houses of Parliament at different times of day and under different weather conditions. In the years following the exhibition of his London views in 1904, he was both a celebrity and something of a mystery, as he mostly held back from public view the new, radical paintings of the water lilies floating on the surface of his garden pond (see cats. 4–8). Something of their qualities—or perhaps those of an earlier view of the garden—had been revealed to Marcel Proust, however, who in 1907, in *Le Figaro*, wrote a text entitled "Splendors."

> [If] I can someday see M. Claude Monet's garden, I feel sure that I shall see something that is not so much a garden of flowers as of colors and tones, less of an old-fashioned flower garden than a color garden, so to speak, one that achieves an effect not entirely nature's, because it was planted so that only the flowers with matching colors should bloom at the same time, harmonize in an infinite stretch of blue or pink. This clearly manifest painterly intent has neutralized, to a certain extent, everything that is not the same color. The picture consists of land flowers as well as of water flowers, those soft white water lilies that the master has depicted in sublime canvases, of which this garden is like a first and living sketch, or at least, like the palette already artfully made up with the harmonious tones required to paint it. The garden itself is a real transposition of art, rather than a model for a painting, for its composition is right there in nature itself and comes to life through the eyes of a great painter.[3]

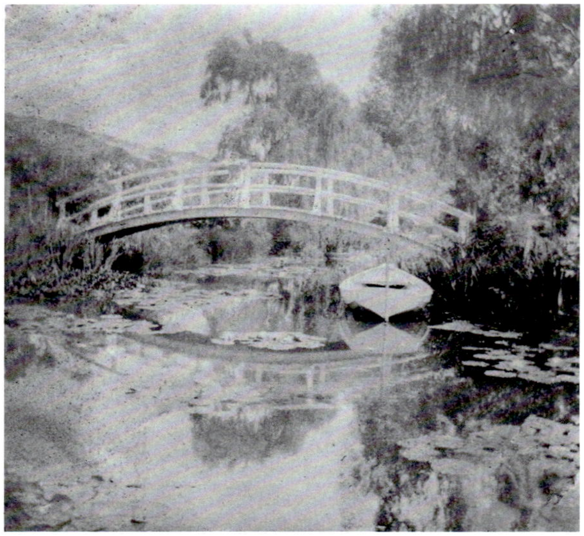

Fig. 2. View of the water-lily pond and the Japanese bridge with Jim Butler, Giverny, c. 1900. Collection Philippe Piguet

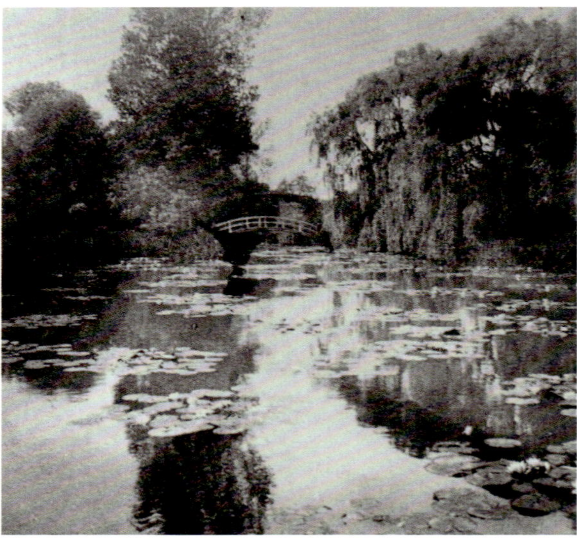

Fig. 3. View of the water-lily pond and the Japanese bridge topped by its metal structure, Giverny, c. 1915–20. Collection Philippe Piguet

Since the exhibition of his views of the pond beneath the Japanese bridge in 1900, Monet had been hard at work on the garden. The limited water surface visible in the paintings (fig. 1) and in contemporaneous photographs (fig. 2) had proved far too limited for the painter's ambition, and in 1900 he had decided to enlarge the eastern end of the pond. The greater surface (fig. 3) allowed many more lilies to be planted, created larger spaces of clear, mirror-like water, and inevitably provided new and more numerous points of view. The westward-looking viewpoint that was to become so important for the water lilies of 1907 (fig. 4) was created at this time and would again inspire many of the views of the pond that the artist undertook more than a decade later.

The work leading up to the exhibition of the water lilies exhausted Monet. A large number of paintings were available to be chosen from in March 1908, when the Durand-Ruels came to Giverny, attempting to organize a selection (fig. 5). In the end, however, Monet wanted to add another year's worth of paintings to the series, further delaying the dealer's plans. When the last of the canvases were put away at the end of the blooming season in 1908, he took a trip to Venice with his wife, Alice, to bolster his spirits and to give him a respite from the garden, that he might return to the paintings once more with a fresh eye before their presentation to the public (see fig. 6). Unable to travel without painting, he began a new series in Venice, regretting that it had taken him so long to visit the city so beloved of his idol William Turner and his friend James Whistler (fig. 7). When the water lilies were shown to the public in the next spring, the reaction was sensational (see Emma Cauvin's essay in this catalogue).

At the end of 1909, however, Monet stated to his friend Geffroy that bad weather, generally declining health and crippling headaches, the frustrations that attended his exhibition, and "the sadness and petty miseries that come with getting old" had meant that "since my return from Venice, a year ago, I have done nothing, haven't touched a brush."[4] Alice's rapidly declining health, beginning with her diagnosis of leukemia in February 1910, caused still greater worry, and the whole of 1910 went by without a return to work. When Alice died in May 1911, Monet entered a period of deep mourning. "I must admit to you," he wrote in September to Julie Manet Rouart, the daughter of Berthe Morisot, that "shut up in my sadness, I no longer even have the courage to go out."[5] At the beginning of 1912, he rallied briefly to be able to complete the paintings of Venice that had gone untouched since his return three years before; they were exhibited in late May and June with the Galerie Bernheim-Jeune. The success of the exhibition, which Monet inwardly doubted, was followed by another setback—the diagnosis of cataracts in both his eyes, the source of the vision problems he had been experiencing already for some time. He nonetheless was able to paint, around 1912 and in 1913, a handful of pictures of his house and garden (cats. 9 and 10) and to receive a journalist in November—however

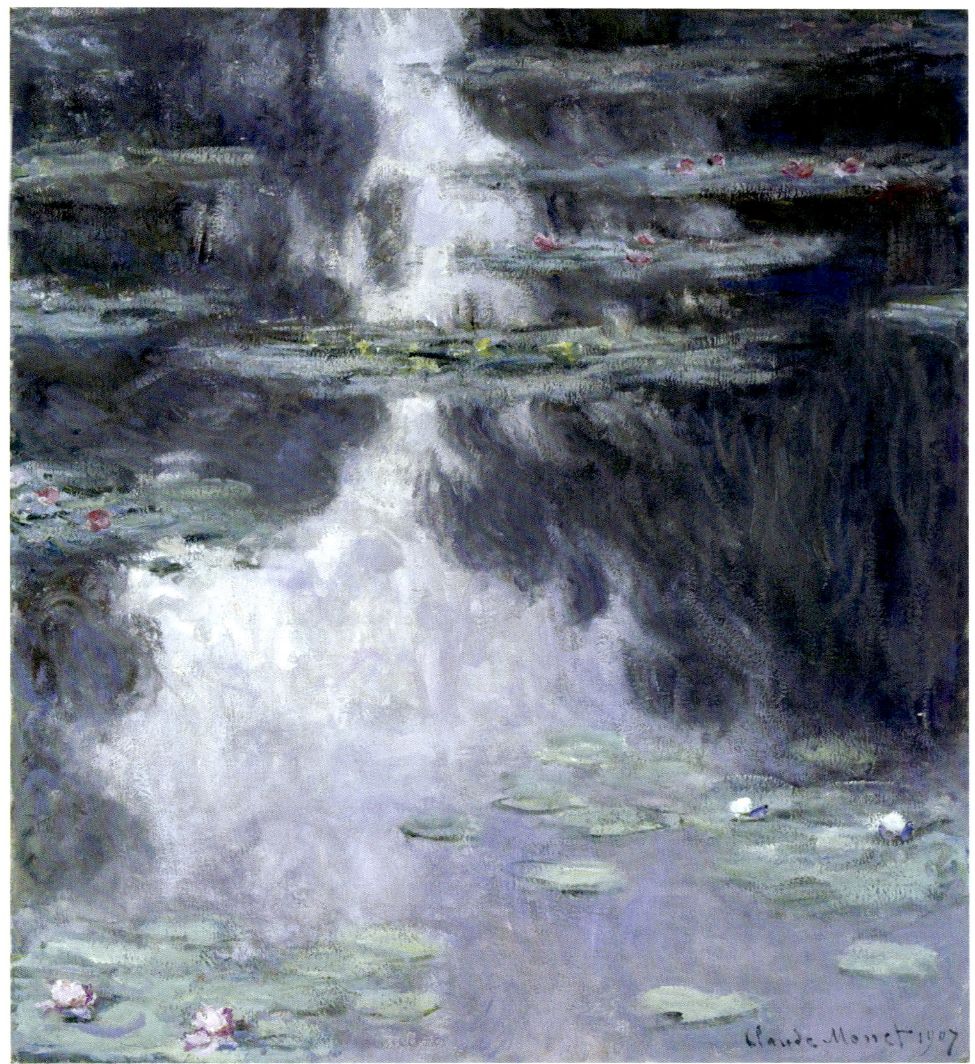

Fig. 4. Claude Monet, *Water Lilies*, 1907. Oil on canvas, 36 1/4 x 31 7/8 in. (92 x 81 cm). Museum of Fine Arts, Houston. Gift of Mrs. Harry C. Hanszen, 68.31

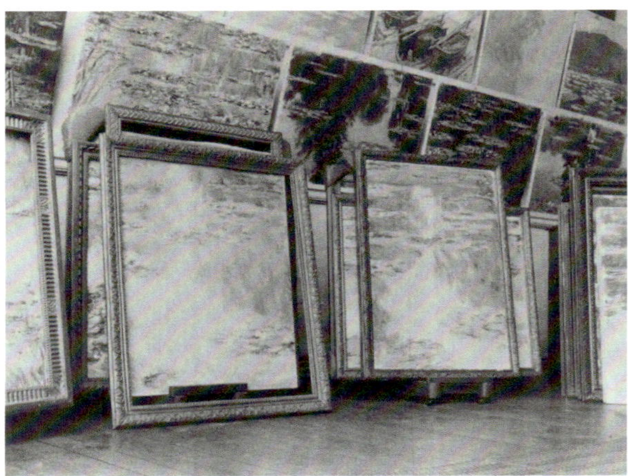

Fig. 5. Monet's second studio with the *Nymphéas, Paysages d'Eau* paintings, March 1907. Galerie Durand-Ruel, Paris

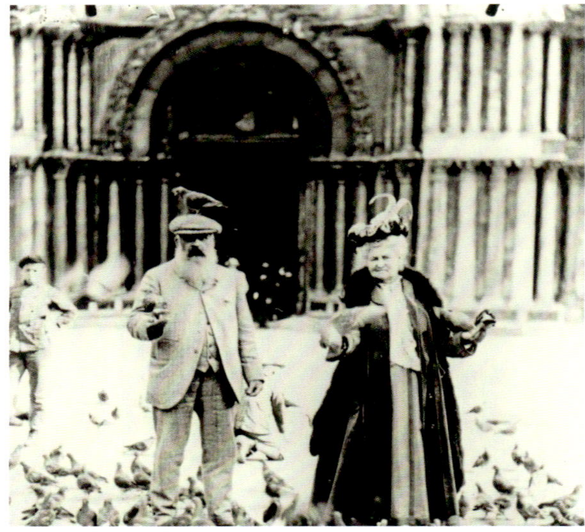

Fig. 6. Claude Monet and his wife Alice in St. Mark's Square, Venice, October 1908. Musée Marmottan Monet, Paris

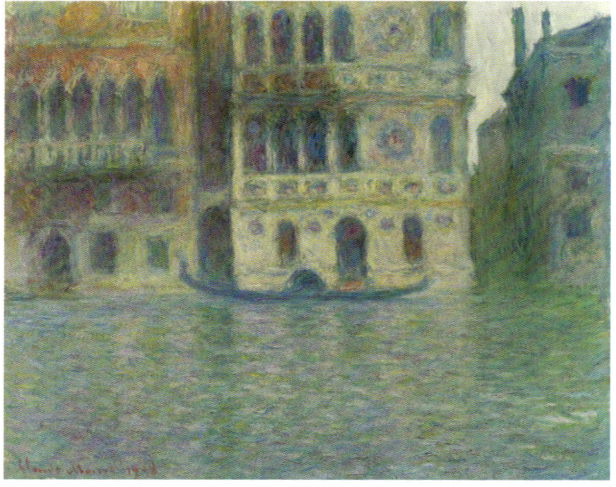

Fig. 7. Claude Monet, *Venice, Palazzo Dario*, 1908. Oil on canvas, 26 1/8 x 32 ¼ in. (66.2 x 81.8 cm). The Art Institute of Chicago. Mr. and Mrs. Lewis Larned Coburn Memorial Collection, 1933.446

reluctantly—for an article to appear in the popular press, illustrated with large-scale photographs showing him at work on one of the garden paintings and posing at the center of his studio-salon (figs. 8 and 9). By the time the article appeared in *Je Sais Tout* in January, however, the state of health of Monet's eldest son, precarious since the previous summer, had become acute; Jean Monet, born to the painter and his first wife Camille in 1867, died on February 9, 1914. He left behind his wife, Blanche, the daughter of Alice Monet and her first husband, Ernest Hoschedé; his younger brother Michel; and, of course, his father, who was for a second time plunged into mourning.

It was, then, with some surprise that his friends were informed that the painter was returning to painting in his garden some three months later. The signs of interest in working again, briefly manifest the year before, had even deeper roots. In the photograph of Monet standing in his studio in 1913, displayed among paintings from many periods in his career—going back to the 1860s, with a portrait of Camille Monet—were two unusual paintings, images of water lilies that were not like those he had painted between 1900 and 1908. On the wall at left, and behind him at right, these were, in fact, the earliest studies of water lilies, which he had shown to one critic in 1897 (see pp. 109–10). In the letter he wrote to Geffroy, among the earliest to communicate his newfound energy, he said "I am even counting on taking up big things, of which you will see the previous attempts that I found in the basement. Clémenceau has seen them and is impressed."[6]

The moment of Monet's "rediscovery" of the 1897 water-lily canvases—among them the painting from the National Gallery of Modern Art, Rome (fig. 10) and the large panel in this exhibition (cat. 1)—cannot be precisely fixed. He had mentioned them to Claude Roger-Marx, who in his lengthy review of the 1909 *Water Lilies* exhibition had made reference to Monet's embryonic idea, from a past time, of a decoration based on water-lily paintings.[7] They had not, therefore, been long forgotten; but it must be sometime before the end of 1913, when the photograph was made, that they were brought into view once more. Seeing them again would have returned his thoughts to his first approach to the subject of his water-lily garden, made before the enlargement of the pond just after the turn

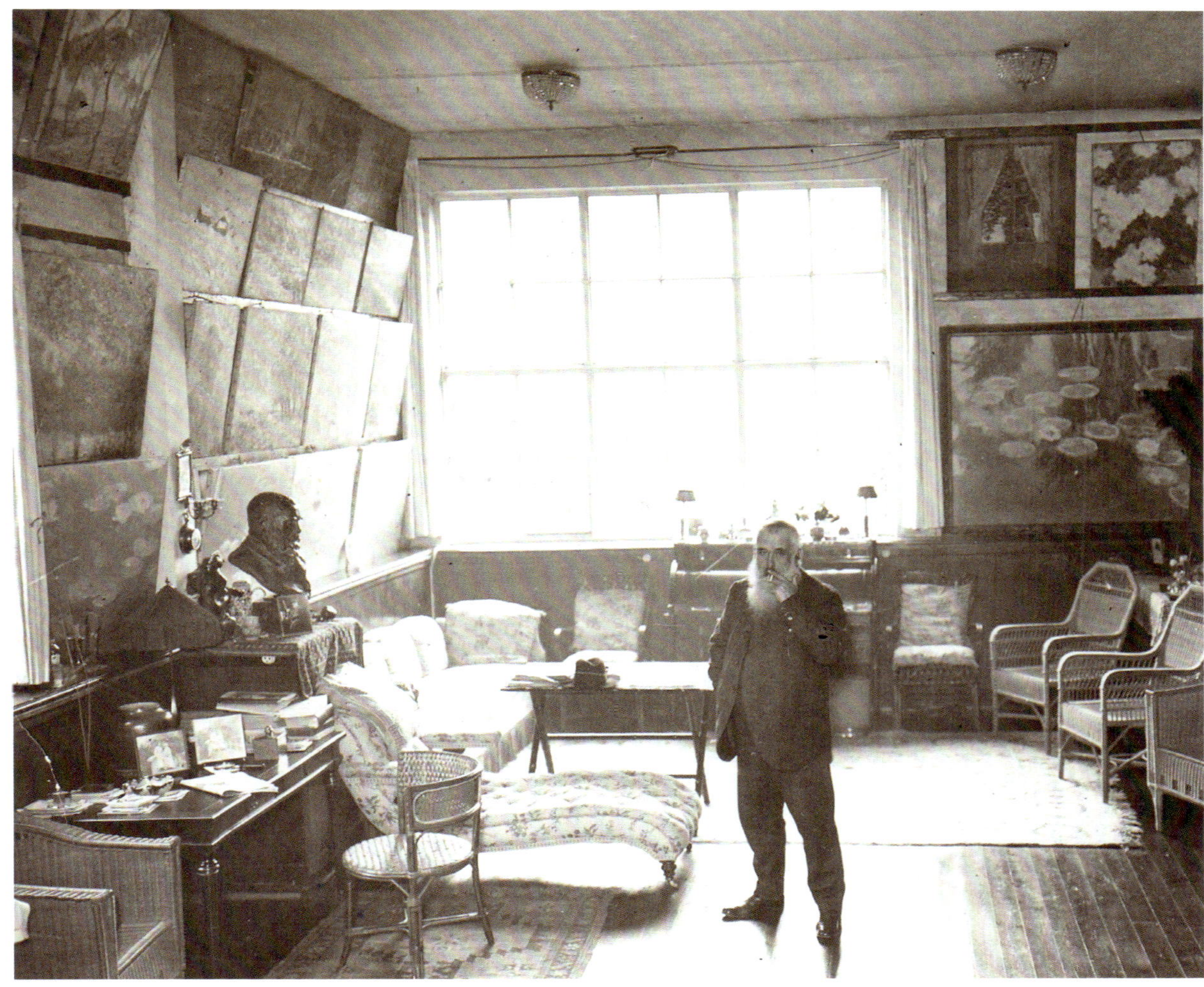

Fig. 9. Claude Monet in his salon-studio in Giverny, November 1913. Collection Philippe Piguet

of the century. One of the features of this group of canvases is their overhanging, almost plunging, point of view—exactly the same angle and attitude shown in the early photograph of the pond surface, a tiny contact print from a tiny negative, traditionally dated to about 1905 but made potentially as early as the 1890s (fig. 11).[8] Like *Water Lilies and Reflections of Grasses*, the photograph plays with this vertiginous angle of view, and likewise with the varying reflectivity of the water in bright sunlight and deep shadow—including the shadow of the photographer's head and hat.

A related quality of the 1890s *Water Lilies* was the way they had shown surface and depth. The challenge of painting the reflective surface of the water, of making its planar recession clear, while simultaneously looking beneath the surface—through the looking-glass, as it were—was one that Monet had relished in the 1860s, studying the Seine at La Grenouillère

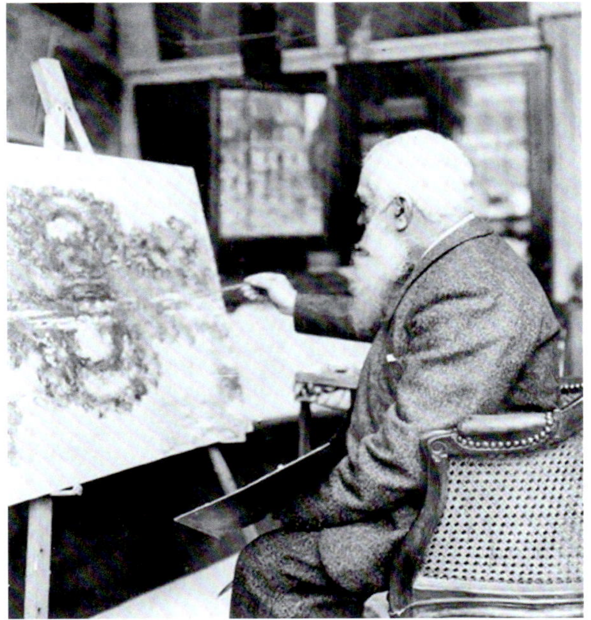

Fig. 8. Claude Monet painting *Flowering Arches, Giverny*, November 1913

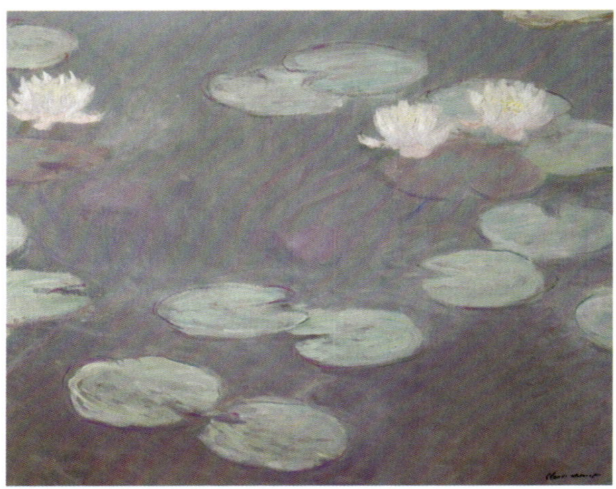

Fig. 10. Claude Monet, *Water Lilies*, 1897–99. Oil on canvas, 31 7/8 x 39 3/8 in. (81 x 100 cm). Galleria Nazionale d'Arte Moderna, Rome, inv. 5163

(see fig. 119).[9] In the 1880s, painting the water grasses undulating under the surface of the water beneath a rowboat near Giverny (fig. 12), he could not rely on either reflective ripples or floating lilies to define the surface, which is therefore more felt than seen, more implied than depicted. Several of the canvases Monet worked on in 1914 and 1915 take up this idea, among them the large panel from the Portland Museum of Art (fig. 13; cat. 12), which Monet was painting when photographed in 1915 (fig. 14), and the remarkable canvas from the Wilsey collection, with its undulant vertical reflections (cat. 13). Similarly, some of the large paintings begun in 1914 to recapitulate ideas first expressed in 1904–6. The Fine Arts Museum of San Francisco's canvas, for example, is essentially an enlargement of the earlier picture from the Art Institute of Chicago (cats. 11 and 6). But others, such as the

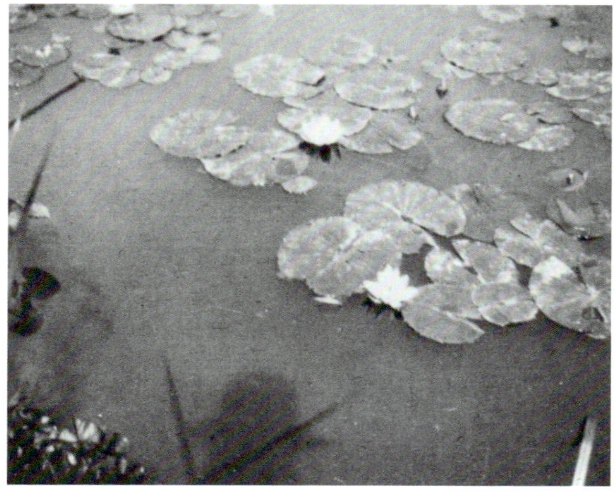

Fig. 11. Claude Monet, *Self-Portrait in the Surface of the Water-Lily Pond, Giverny*, c. 1905. Collection Philippe Piguet

2 meter tall canvases from the Musée Marmottan Monet and the Fondation Beyeler (fig. 15; cats. 14, 15), have fewer parallels in earlier work. In such paintings, the artist tries to look down, to look across, and to look up at the same time—seeking the panoramic view that follows a vertical, rather than horizontal, axis.

The work Monet began in 1914 was exhausting. As he wrote to his dealer Durand-Ruel, "you know that when I set myself to something, I set myself to it seriously, so much so that waking up at 4 o'clock in the morning, I labor all day and, come nightfall, I collapse with fatigue."[10] The artist was anxious to share his new work with his friends. "It would be a great pleasure to

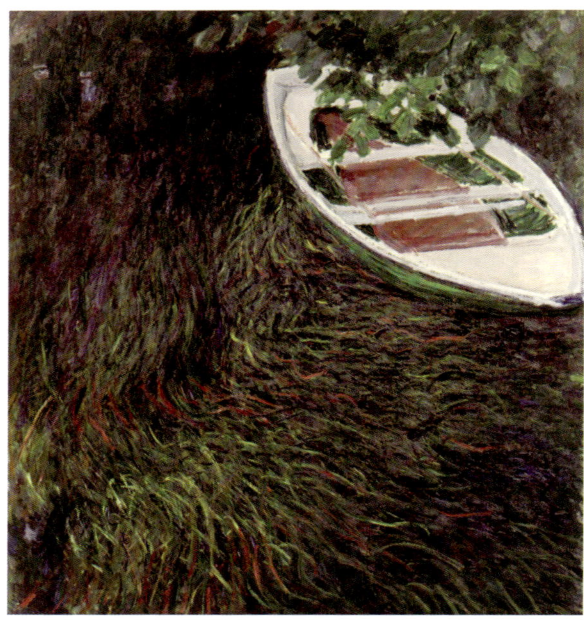

Fig. 12. Claude Monet, *The Rowing Boat*, c. 1889–90. Oil on canvas, 57 ½ x 52 3/8 in. (146 x 133 cm). Musée Marmottan Monet, Paris

see you," he told Geffroy, "and also to show you the beginnings of the great work that I have begun, for you know that for the last two months I have been working nonstop."[11] The work Monet began in 1914 was also revolutionary, a transformation that amounted to a break with the past and a new beginning. He had decided to accomplish, on a huge scale, the long-considered idea for a water-lily decoration, the great work of his old age, the *Grandes Décorations*, installed in the Orangerie of the Tuileries Gardens after his death. Even without this perspective, those who saw the new paintings in 1914 and 1915 would have realized two things: Monet the creator was obsessed with his "great

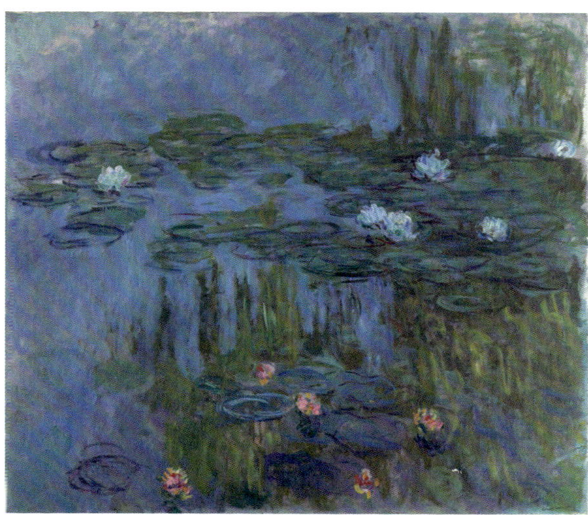

Fig. 13. Claude Monet, *Water Lilies*, 1914–15. Oil on canvas, 63 1/4 x 71 1/8 in. (160.7 x 180.7 cm). Portland Art Museum. Museum purchase, Helen Thurston Ayer Fund

work"; and Monet the seventy-three-year-old master was setting about to reinvent himself.

There was, above all, the new scale of the paintings. Such works as the *Water Lilies* from Portland were more than 5 feet tall by nearly 6 feet wide. Sitting before them in the garden, perched on a high chair, Monet seems small by comparison (see fig. 14). And soon he had obtained canvases that measured 2 meters in height, approximately 6 and a half feet. Not since he had painted the *Luncheon on the Grass* and *Women in the Garden* in 1865 and 1866 had Monet put his brush to a stretched canvas that was taller than he.[12] By 1915, of course, he needed a greater space to work in—though the second studio he had built, detached from his house, in the 1880s could hold many of the vertical canvases, he would need much more room to take the 2 meter tall canvases into the broad horizontal panels measuring more than 4 meters in width that he had in mind. Construction of the third studio began in July of 1915, and by the autumn Monet was able to move into the new space, which measured 23 meters long on the north-south axis and 12 meters wide. A roof fitted with large skylights rose high above the floor, supported off the long wall by metal struts, and was fitted with canvas shades that could be moved to adjust the intensity of the light.

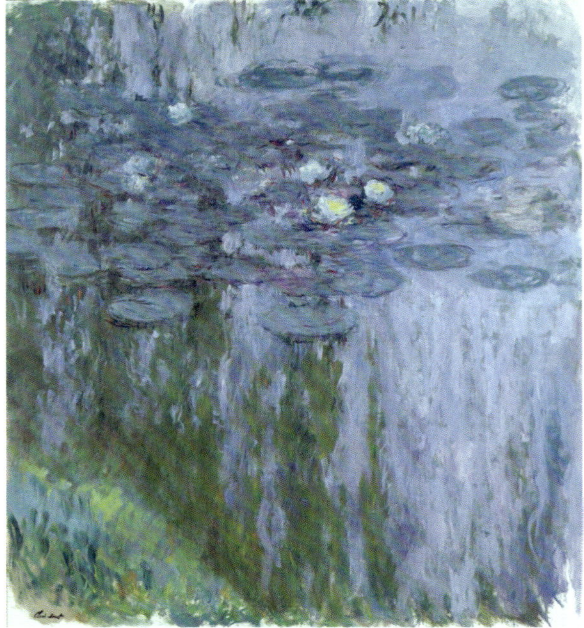

Fig. 15. Claude Monet, *Water Lilies*, 1916–19. Oil on canvas, 78 3/4 x 70 7/8 in. (200 x 180 cm). Musée Marmottan Monet, Paris. Michel Monet Bequest, 1966, inv. 5119

"I speak as if I had much ahead, which is pure folly, like taking up such an endeavor at my age and throwing myself into gigantic construction projects," he wrote to Jean-Pierre Hoschedé, his son-in-law, who like his son Michel had been away in the army since the previous August, when war had been declared with Germany. Perhaps to give Jean-Pierre a lighter view of what was going on at home, he added, "Yes, it's crazy, very crazy, all the more so because it is horribly expensive. The said Lanctuit [the contractor] has moreover constructed something ignoble, and I'm ashamed to have built it, I who am always yelling at those who make an ugly mess of Giverny" (fig. 16).[13]

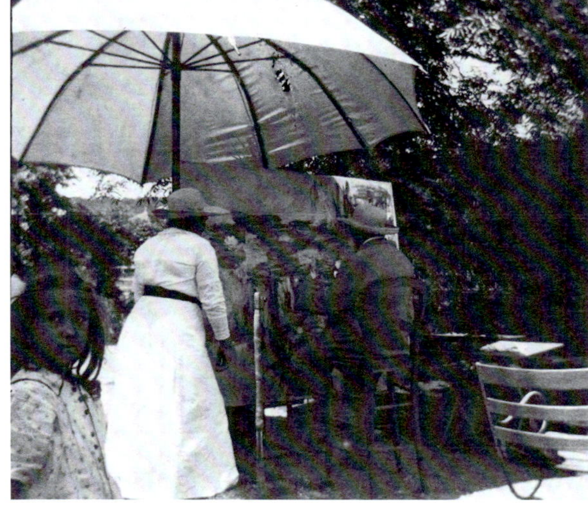

Fig. 14. Claude Monet next to the water-lily pond during a working session at 1 p.m. Next to him, his daughter-in-law (and stepdaughter) Blanche Hoschedé-Monet and one of his step-granddaughters, Nitia-Dominique Salerou, Giverny, July 1915. Collection Philippe Piguet

As war raged at the front, Monet's work proceeded apace at Giverny. Consuming meter after meter of canvas and massive quantities of paint—"Money is rare and painting pays it out rather than bringing it in," he had written to Jean-Pierre—he proceeded to assemble groupings of the wide canvases that, side by side, formed continuous views of the water-lily pond (see Simon Kelly's essay in this volume). He invited his closest friends to see the work—Geffroy and Georges Clémenceau, his friend since the 1860s and as of 1917 France's prime minister—and a few

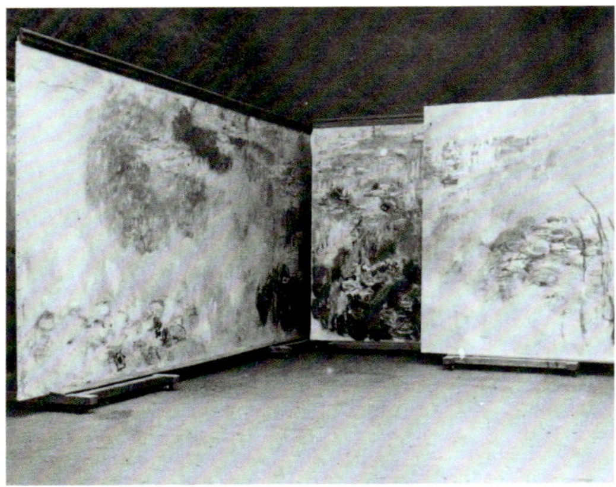
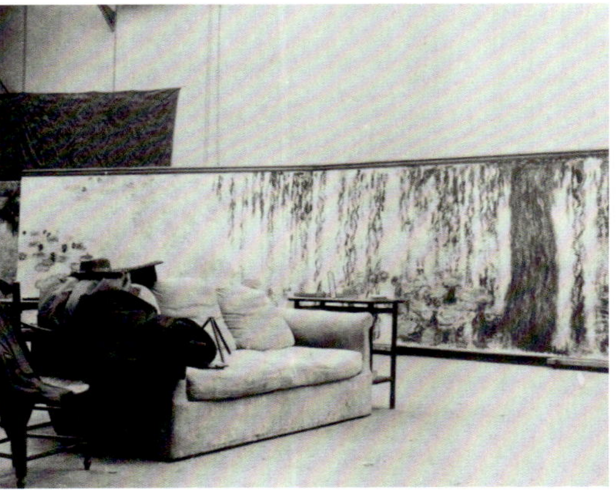
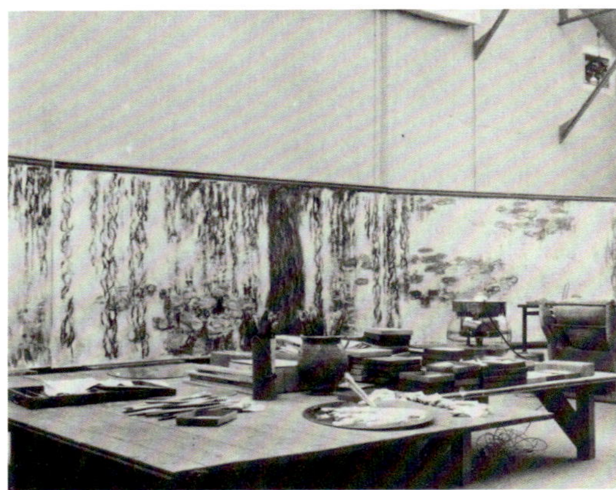

Figs. 17–19. *Water-Lily* paintings for the *Grandes Décorations* in Monet's third studio at Giverny, Sunday, November 11, 1917. Galerie Durand-Ruel, Paris

interested art dealers, the young Georges and Joseph Durand-Ruel and Gaston and Josse Bernheim-Jeune. He also invited artists to visit—younger painters, as by the mid-teens his surviving contemporaries, Degas and Renoir, no longer were able to travel. The Nabi painters Édouard Vuillard and Pierre Bonnard, whose view of bathing children Monet had acquired, came to visit him. After 1912, when Bonnard bought a house in the outskirts of Vernon, across the Seine from Giverny, Monet often went to visit him there.[14] Henri Matisse and Albert Marquet—whose work Monet had also purchased—paid a visit to Monet in May 1917; a previous visit by Matisse had been arranged with the Bernheim brothers but was cancelled when Monet found himself preoccupied. "Just now I have thrown myself into transformations on my large canvases and my mood is foul," he explained.[15]

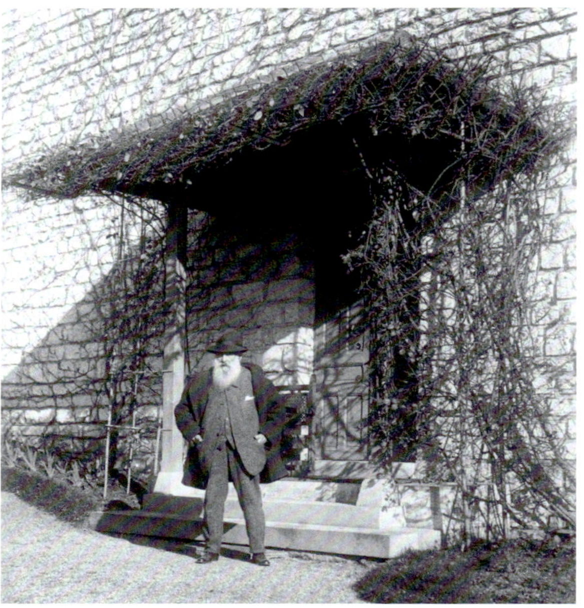

Fig. 16. Claude Monet in front of his third studio, Giverny, 1926. Photograph, 5 1/8 x 7 in. (13 x 18 cm). Agence de presse Meurisse

From time to time, Monet allowed his visitors to photograph the works in progress in the studio. The Durand-Ruels had long made a practice of taking photographs of Monet's works in the second studio, making records of them in advance of arranging exhibitions (see fig. 5), but in 1917 they brought with them a professional photographer who made a series of six views of large panels standing side by side around the studio (figs. 17–22). The panels were fitted to rolling supports that allowed them to be moved from one wall of the studio to another; some were finished with a cornice-like molding at top that must have added protection against the great rectangles flexing while being moved.

Standing with his back to the north wall of the room, the photographer took views of the northeast corner, the east wall, the south wall, and part of the west wall of the studio. In the northeast corner stood one panel that is probably an early stage in the development of the right part of the composition now called *Clouds* at the Musée de l'Orangerie, Paris.[16] Moving clockwise, a second photograph showed two panels of willows; the righthand canvas now forms the leftmost panel of *Bright Morning with Willows* at the Orangerie.[17] Three more views continue to show aspects of *Bright Morning with Willows*. In the last of these, the rightmost panel seems to have been shifted westward, towards the corner; behind it can be seen the reverse of another canvas, and then at right, and continuing into the sixth view, are the central and righthand panels of the *Agapanthus* triptych. (see cat. 28 and Simon Kelly's essay).

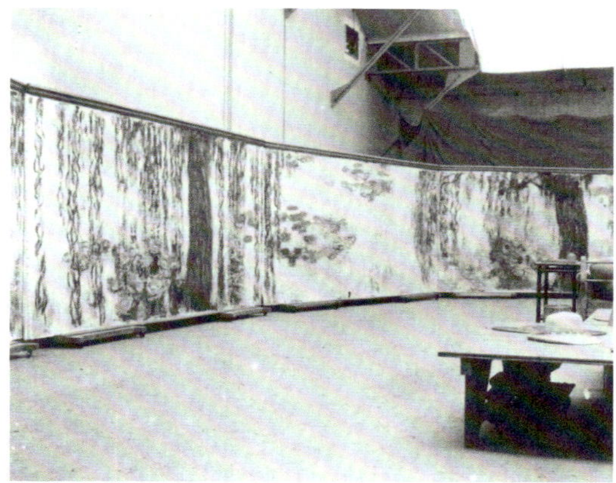
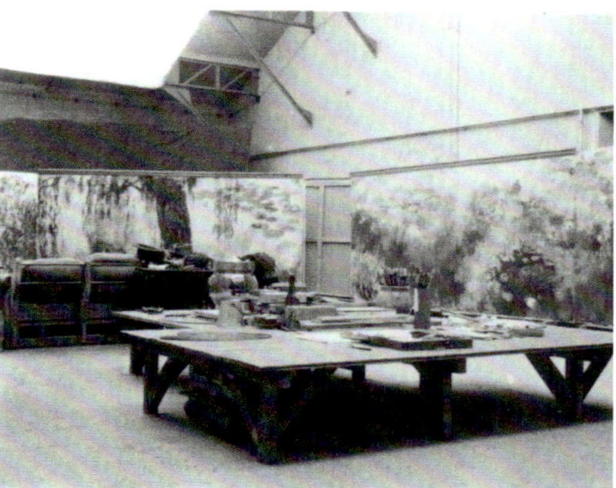
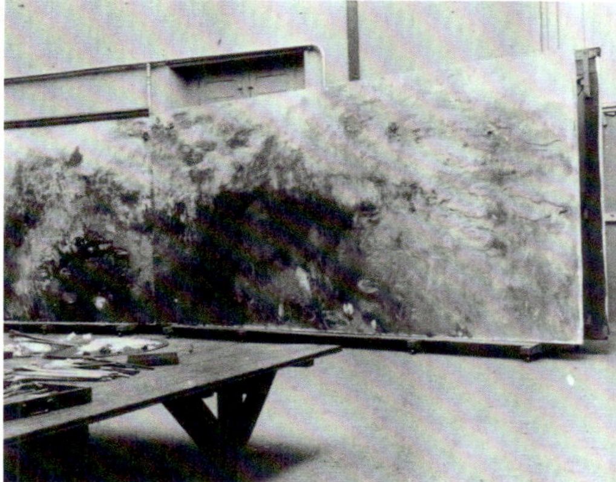

Figs. 20–22. *Water-Lily* paintings for the *Grandes Décorations* in Monet's third studio at Giverny, Sunday, November 11, 1917. Galerie Durand-Ruel, Paris

The unwieldy paintings were physically mobile, capable of being shifted into new relationships if the painter's ideas should change, but their vast surfaces were equally mutable: even accounting for the inaccuracies of color that might register on 1917 film stock, none of the paintings photographed in 1917 remained the same thereafter. Painting indoors, using studies made in nature but relying in large part on memory and fantasy, Monet was increasingly becoming a tinkerer, never quite satisfied with the correctness of the effects he had invented as the painting progressed. "I am in a very bad phase of work and in a state of impossible irritation," he complained to Sacha Guitry, the actor and dramatist. "I have lost some good things that I wanted to improve and that I must at all costs find again."[18]

Comparison of photographs of the *Grandes Décorations* in progress almost always reveals major shifts on the way to the paintings' final states—"final," rather than "finished," inasmuch as a composition may have been deemed finished at some point in its development, only to be largely reworked (see cat. 28). An autochrome photograph taken in the third studio shows two 4 meter panels standing on their easels, isolated against the west wall of the room (fig. 23) identifiable as such by the placement of the piping for electrical wires; see figs. 21 and 22). Although at first glance it might appear to be a nascent stage of development in the *Agapanthus* triptych, comparison with the finished decorations in the Orangerie shows that the two panels in fact make up the complete composition now called *Reflections of Trees*.[19]

As Claire Barry shows in her essay in this volume, the scale of the work at hand changed Monet's working methods. Not only did he go through much more paint in a matter of weeks than he ever had before, he applied the massive quantities to the large canvases with brushes larger than he had ever used previously. And, as she discusses, Monet wished the surfaces of the *Grandes Décorations* to have a particular dry, matte

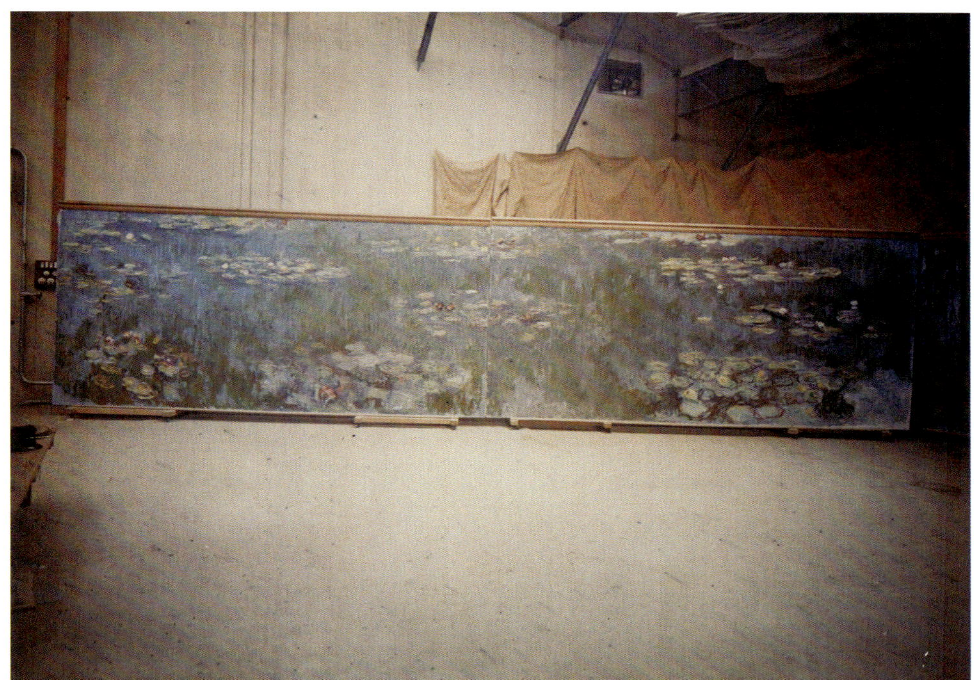

Fig. 23. Autochrome photograph of an early stage of the composition now called *Reflections of Trees* and in the Musée de l'Orangerie, Paris

quality, which he sometimes achieved by soaking oil binder from his paint, squeezed from the tube onto felt blotters. When, after 1918, he returned to the practice of easel painting, he found the transition difficult to make; in February 1920 he would tell the dealer René

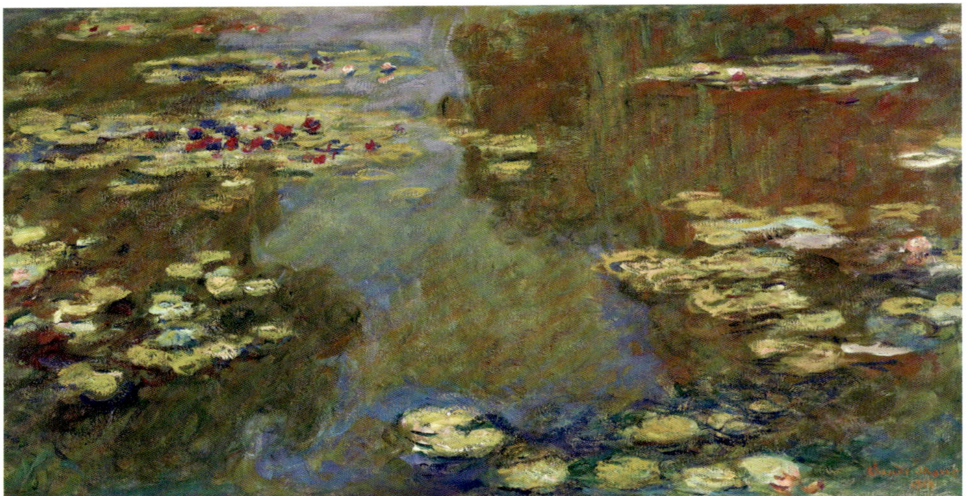

Fig. 24. Claude Monet, *Water-Lily Pond*, 1919. Oil on canvas, 39 ½ x 79 in. (100.3 x 200.7 cm). Paul G. Allen Family Collection

Gimpel that he was frustrated with the technical aspects of creating the smaller paintings, having "become used to painting broadly and with big brushes."[20] His 1918 order for twenty 1 x 2 meter canvases—large as easel paintings go, but much smaller than the decorations—marked the point at which we can assume he began his parallel exploration of garden motifs on a smaller scale, sometimes less than one meter square (see, for instance, the paintings of the water-lily pond, cats. 23–27, or the Japanese bridge, cats. 32–38).

The year 1918 marked another critical moment in the development of the *Grandes Décorations*. On November 11, an armistice was announced to call an end to the war that had devastated the populations of the Allies and the German forces alike. The next day, Monet wrote to his friend the prime minister, Georges Clémenceau, a letter of congratulations, containing the offer of a great gift to the people of France:

> Great and dear friend, I am on the verge of finishing two decorative paintings that I want to sign on the day of Victory and have you offer to the State on my behalf. It's not much, but it's the only way I can take part in the Victory. I want the two panels placed in the Musée des Arts Décoratifs and would be happy if you chose them. I admire you and embrace you with all my heart.[21]

The gesture of thankfulness at the end to conflict, of pride in victory and in his native land, of recognition of the leadership that Clémenceau, his "great and dear friend," had brought to the nation in time of trial, would change forever the meaning of the *Grandes Décorations*. Before November 12, they were a great project undertaken by an old man for his own ends; afterwards, first on a modest scale and then, as time went by, growing more and more grandiose, they became a great personal statement of ambition in the public space.

Monet's grand gesture, his offer to the state of a highly symbolic gift, must be seen against a more complex background involving not only the multiplicity of the painter's artistic preoccupations but also the facts of his daily life. Throughout the teens, Monet sold paintings from his inventory of older works to dealers, usually Durand-Ruel and Bernheim-Jeune, for the simple reason that, as he had told Jean-Pierre Hoschedé, money was hard to come by, he was spending lots of it, and the huge paintings he was in the process of painting did not bring money in. Paintings from the 1870s through the 1890s were regularly sent to Paris against payments by the dealers; at the end of 1918 and into 1919, however, Monet began to sell some of his latest canvases, all of them—like the earlier work—on smaller-sized stretchers. The 1913 *Flowering Arches, Giverny* (cat. 10) was sold in 1917; a *Weeping Willow* (cat. 43) was one of two sold late in 1918; Durand-Ruel and Bernheim-Jeune jointly purchased *The Water-Lily Pond* (cat. 34) in January 1919; and in November 1919, the Bernheim-Jeune brothers bought five paintings, four 1 x 2 meter *Water-Lily Ponds* (see fig. 24) and a view of the *Japanese Bridge* (cat. 34).[22] As Marianne Mathieu has shown (see pages 78–80), these sales, with the 1922 sale of three late works to the Baron Kojio Matsukata, represented the few recent works released from Giverny before Monet's death (and until long after, as it turned out). Attempts to buy the large decorations, coming from Martin Ryerson of Chicago and the Bernheim-Jeune brothers failed, as Monet was unwilling to be parted from his last great work.

His dealer's adverse reaction to, and unwillingness to purchase, the majority of the easel-scale paintings Monet produced in the years between 1918 and 1922 is almost certainly due to the huge changes in the appearance of Monet's paintings occasioned by changes in his eyesight. Diagnosed with cataracts in 1912, the painter had sought opinions from a large number of doctors, hoping to find relief to the blurring of vision and shifts in color perception that he was experiencing. By the end of 1919, he felt, as he explained to Geffroy, that his situation was a "complete disaster."

> My sight has altered once more, and I have had to give up painting and must leave aside so much work I'd begun and which I could never have made good on. What a sad end for me, and yet, all summer, I was working beautifully, fervently, but it must be noted that this beautiful fervor was hiding powerlessness. I shall not leave my garden; it will soon be three years that I haven't been to Paris, and I don't think I'll ever go again.[23]

Monet's complaint of poor vision may have been exaggerated in 1919—at the beginning of the letter he thanks Geffroy for the gift of a book and says that he has enjoyed reading his friend's preface. He had been able for some time to compensate for shifts in his perception of color by carefully arranging his palette so as to be able to make paintings that, for all their exaggeration of chromatic effects, do not seem incoherent to modern eyes. As Claire Barry observes, close examination of the brushwork of his *Weeping Willows* or *Japanese Bridges* reveals sophisticated juxtapositions of hues and tones, delicate and precise brushwork, including a considerable amount of mixing of color on one brush. That such paintings looked very strange to the young Durand-Ruels and Bernheim-Jeunes must have been in part a result of the dealers' realization that such paintings had little or nothing to do with what collectors were looking for in a work by Monet. The artist's reinvention, largely accomplished in private, had progressed beyond his time; the new Monet was, in fact, too ambitious for his public.

Such a painter as Pierre Bonnard, however, could have appreciated what Monet was doing as he reached his eightieth year. Bonnard, after all, like his Nabi cohorts Vuillard and Maurice Denis, had begun to paint decorative cycles in the 1890s; by the time Monet began his *Grandes Décorations*, Bonnard had already completed his own garden decoration, a cycle of pictures completed in 1911 and 1912 for the Russian collector Ivan Morosov. The first element, a Mediterranean triptych that was installed in the spaces between four columns, was followed by a pair of almost-square canvases filled with harmonies of color taken from the north of France—blues, greens, and yellows (figs. 25 and 26). Measuring more than three meters on each side, these panels are massive pastorales, as befitted the program of Morosov's Moscow palace.[24] Monet would not have seen these works on his visits to Bonnard's house in Vernonnet, but he would have seen the large-scale depictions of the Normandy landscape that Bonnard painted steadily there in the late teens and into the twenties; and Bonnard's experience with mural

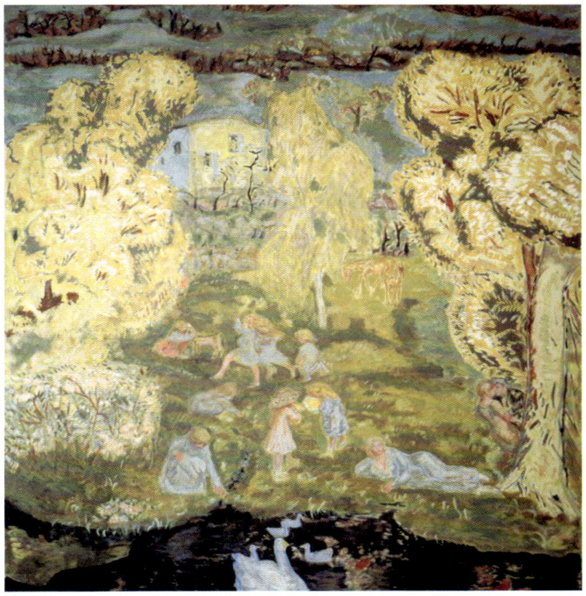

Fig. 25. Pierre Bonnard, *Autumn, The Grape-Harvest*, 1912. Oil on canvas, 145 ¼ x 137 ⅜ in. (368.8 x 349 cm). The Pushkin State Museum of Fine Arts, Moscow

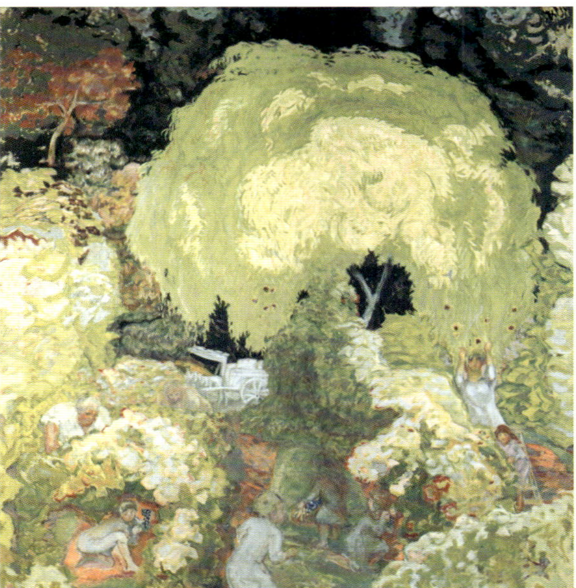

Fig. 26. Pierre Bonnard, *Beginning of Spring in the Village*, 1912. Oil on canvas, 145 x 137 in. (368.5 x 348 cm). The Pushkin State Museum of Fine Arts, Moscow

commissions had given him the acumen to understand the challenge and ambition of his neighbor and mentor.

The photograph of Monet with Bonnard taken around 1926 shows the two artists in the garden at Giverny; the season must be summer since sunflowers are in bloom in the distance (fig. 27). Monet is characteristically dressed in his custom-made vested tweed suit, his ruffled linen shirt, his cashmere sweater over his shoulders, and his straw hat atop his head. In addition, he is wearing a pair of tinted glasses, provided to him to protect his eyes from excessive light and to correct both his focus and his color sense. By autumn 1922, Monet had realized that the cataracts in his eyes had thickened to such an extent that he was hardly able to see. Seeking the advice of Charles Coutela, a leading Parisian ophthalmologist, he was first prescribed eyedrops that temporarily improved his vision. Surgery, however, was deemed the only practical solution to his problem, and with great trepidation the artist allowed Coutela to operate on his right eye in early January 1923. Returning to Coutela's clinic, Monet had a second operation on the same eye at the end of the month; a third was performed at Giverny in the summer (fig. 28). There followed, over the course of the next months and years, a succession of medications and eyeglasses that attempted to fine-tune the artist's sight, to give him the ability to see distances as well as things nearby, and above all to respond to his complaints about color perception. The experts were frustrated, however, by their patient's changing litany of complaints. As Ross King explains:

> Making Coutela's task difficult was the fact that Monet's claims about his disordered color perception were ambiguous and sometimes contradictory. . . . Monet's statement to Clémenceau about seeing only two colors, yellow and blue, had originally read "yellow and green" before Monet struck out "green" and wrote "blue," while a few days later he wrote to Coutela that he saw "yellow as green and everything else more or less blue."[25]

This ambiguity persists in modern interpretations of the ways in which Monet's very real and very persistent problems of vision affected the appearance of his paintings. With meager evidence and only the artist's complaints and a series of undated paintings as guideposts, it is nearly impossible to assign cause and effect—the more so because there is, experientially, no way to measure the correspondence between what Monet's eyes registered as he looked at the motif and

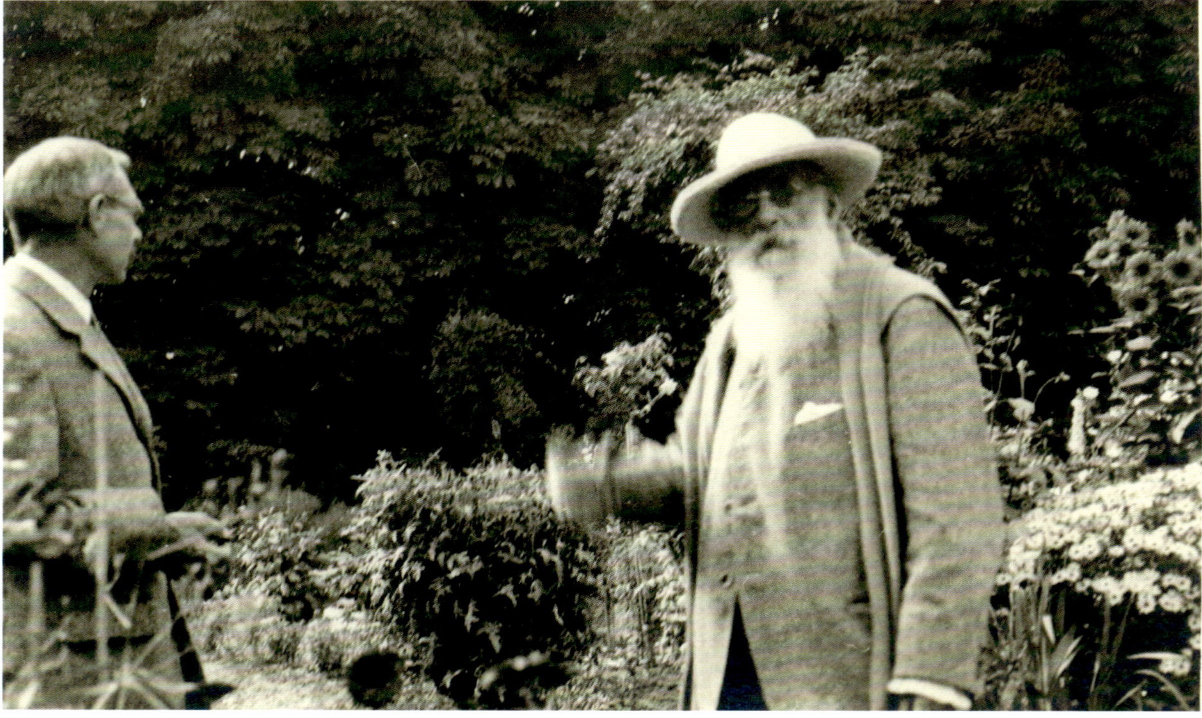

Fig. 27. Reine Natanson, *Pierre Bonnard with Claude Monet in Giverny*, 1926. Enlarged silver print, 4 3/8 x 6 7/8 in. (11.2 x 16 cm). Private collection

then looked at the work of art.

The testimony of contemporary witnesses, whether frustrated dealers or amateurs, nonetheless registers surprise at the changes that Monet's paintings revealed in the early 1920s. His biographer Thiébault-Sisson initially doubted Monet's claims of fading vision, believing that the aging painter was exaggerating the degree to which his art was affected by his vision.

> I was to find proof to the contrary, however, when I accompanied him to his everyday studio and examined twenty-five or thirty works he had cast aside, works dating back to the time when, after having experienced the onset of his infirmity, he had still attempted to go on working. Their color notations were horribly out of tune, and although the artist was still present in the drawing, the talent for composition and the overall appeal of the work, the colorist seemed to have disappeared.[26]

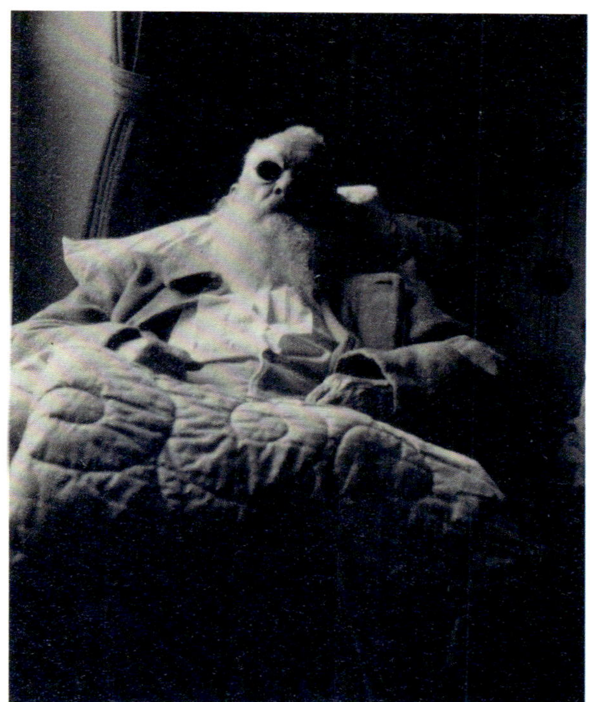

Fig. 28. Claude Monet after his cataract surgery, 1923. Photograph possibly by Michel Monet. Collection Philippe Piguet

There is ample evidence for Monet destroying many works of art he deemed substandard, building a fire and throwing the offending paintings into it. Were the dozens of paintings that Thiébault-Sisson found "horribly out of tune" the pictures now admired—the highly charged depictions of the Japanese bridge, for instance—or did he see a group of works that do not survive?

What can be said is that despite his compromised vision, Monet found ways of continuing to work. And there is evidence that the painter considered even the most challenging paintings admirable. In the famous photograph of Monet with the Duc de Trévise in the second studio (fig. 29), Monet gestures to one of the most remarkable of his early works, the picnic in the forest of Fontainebleau that he had begun to paint for the Salon of 1866 but had left unfinished. Beside him, on the floor, are stacks of paintings, including *Water Lilies* from his first series and a view of Charing Cross Bridge at extreme right. But other paintings are there, placed in gilded frames as if for exhibition. They include three works of the past decade: *The Artist's House at Giverny* is there, between Monet and his visitor (cat. 9); at the far left is one of the variants of the *Corner of the Water Lily Pond* (cat. 31); and beneath a classic water-lily composition (closely related to cat. 5) can be seen the Kimbell Art Museum's *Weeping Willow*, the last of those that would be released from the studio in the artist's lifetime (cat. 44). Yet another photograph, taken in the salon studio that was part of the main house, shows even more recent paintings hanging among pictures dating back to the 1880s (fig. 30). They include one of the 2 meter *Japanese Bridge* compositions at upper left (cat. 33); a *Weeping Willow*, probably the Kimbell Art Museum painting; and to either side of the door leading into the foyer and the dining room beyond, two paintings of the bridge—at left, a very close variant of the blue-green bridge from the Fondation Beyeler (cat. 38) and at right, yet another, a painting now known only through a black and white photograph.[27] Among the canvases on view, beside a view of Venice on the left wall, is one from the series Monet devoted to his house seen from the rose garden, the group that the poet Paul Valéry saw under way in 1925. "He showed us his latest paintings," Valéry wrote. "Strange clumps of roses captured under a blue sky. A dark house."[28]

These paintings, like the series of four paintings of *The Artist's House Seen from the Rose Garden* from the Musée Marmottan Monet, exhibited here, are among the artist's last works, painted in the summer of 1925, when the artist found his "vision completely improved."[29] A great struggle over the *Grandes Décorations*, their

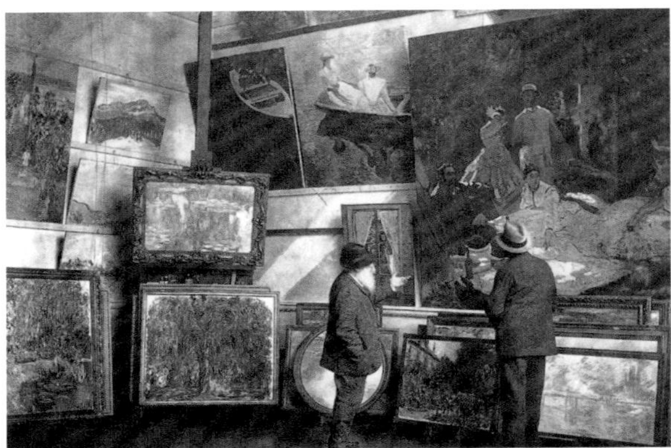

Fig. 29. Claude Monet in his second studio in Giverny with the Duc de Trévise, c. 1920. Musée du Louvre, Paris

placement in Paris, their number, the building in which they eventually would be housed—an ongoing struggle that had begun almost as soon as Monet had offered two panels to the state in 1918—was over, and the twenty-two panels, grouped into eight majestic compositions, were slated to be installed in two specially constructed rooms in the Orangerie of the Tuileries Gardens as soon as Monet would consent to release them.[30] He was fiddling with them still in 1926, when the painters Édouard Vuillard and Ker-Xavier Roussel came to visit him and witnessed him preparing paint for further use.[31]

Twelve years before, in 1914, Monet had set out to change his art. Deciding to return to ideas he had first explored at the end of the 1890s, he had come to the decision to begin his great project, the series of huge paintings, the most exhaustive he had ever attempted, on the theme of his water-lily pond. With the new project came a new way of working, a shift in the scale of every component of his art-making. Going large, he found it difficult to scale his art back again, yet he did so brilliantly, transforming his way of painting at the same time to overcome the barriers placed in his way by his fading vision. The "impressive yet fragile deity of the Seine" had, in the end, become something of a giant, even as his body and his physical capacities had steadily diminished.[32]

In August 1926 doctors diagnosed, through an X-ray scan, that Monet had developed pulmonary sclerosis, a scarring and hardening of the lung tissue, certainly exacerbated by the artist's incessant use of tobacco. A mere three months later, on December 5, Monet died, and was buried three days later in Giverny, his funeral attended by a crowd of mourners, with Georges Clémenceau at the head (fig. 31). In the following spring, beginning on May 16, 1927, the *Grandes Décorations* were revealed to the public, standing as the testimony of Monet's reinvention (see fig. 151).

In the century since Monet announced his gift of his great project to the people, the meaning of Monet's art, and perhaps particularly the works produced in his late years, has undergone enormous change. The changes that the water-lily cycle underwent in its birth

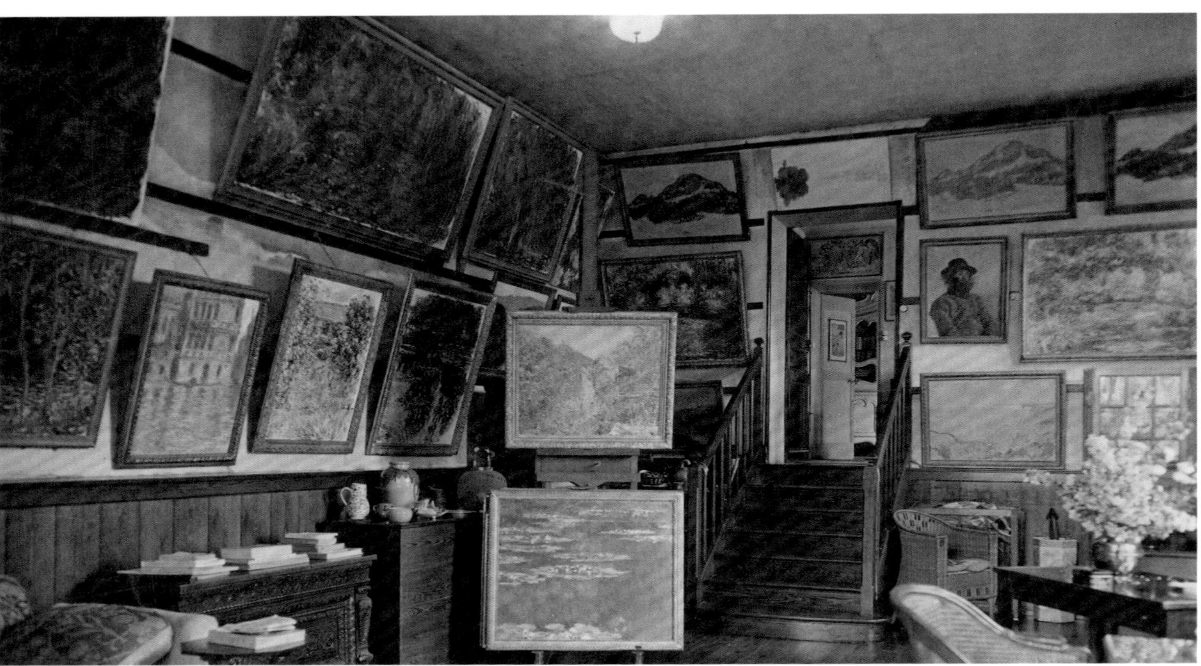

Fig. 30. View of Claude Monet's salon-studio, Giverny, c. 1920. Collection Philippe Piguet

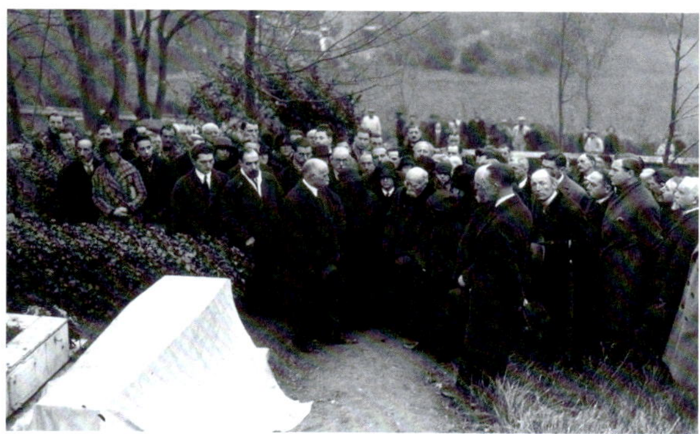

Fig. 31. The funeral of Claude Monet, Giverny, 1926. Bibliothèque nationale de France

Fig. 32. Ellsworth Kelly, *Tableau Vert*, 1952. Oil on wood, 29 ¼ x 39 ¼ in. (74.3 x 99.7 cm). The Art Institute of Chicago. Gift of the artist, 2009.51. © Ellsworth Kelly

and in the years after its inauguration have revealed the vulnerability of the project and of the artist's reputation, as documented here by Simon Kelly and Emma Cauvin. Beginning in the 1950s, as Marianne Mathieu recounts, a revival of interest in Monet led audiences in Europe and America to discover the large-scale paintings that were not part of the Orangerie decoration, and led artists as diverse as Ellsworth Kelly and Milton Resnick to radically different responses to Monet's example (figs. 32 and 33). The artist's methods, as described by Claire Barry, made him a convenient "ancestor" for action painting, the "all over" compositions of his reinvention held up as a vindication of and inspiration for a new art; critics and historians then reinvented Monet to suit their own needs, and will do so again. Exhibitions such as this one have been mounted in order to give the public the chance to see the works themselves at first hand and to understand, through looking closely, the evolution of Monet's reinvention of his art. We should be careful, however, to remember that Monet saw his last works, however radical they might have become, as a continuation—we might now say a culmination—of a lifetime of studying nature. The attitude towards the natural world that gave the works of his youth their magic was, in the artist's late years, the same. As the artist himself said:

> My sensitivity, far from diminishing, has been sharpened by age, which holds no fears for me so long as unbroken communication with the outside world continues to fuel my curiosity, so long as my hand remains a ready and faithful interpreter of my perception.[33]

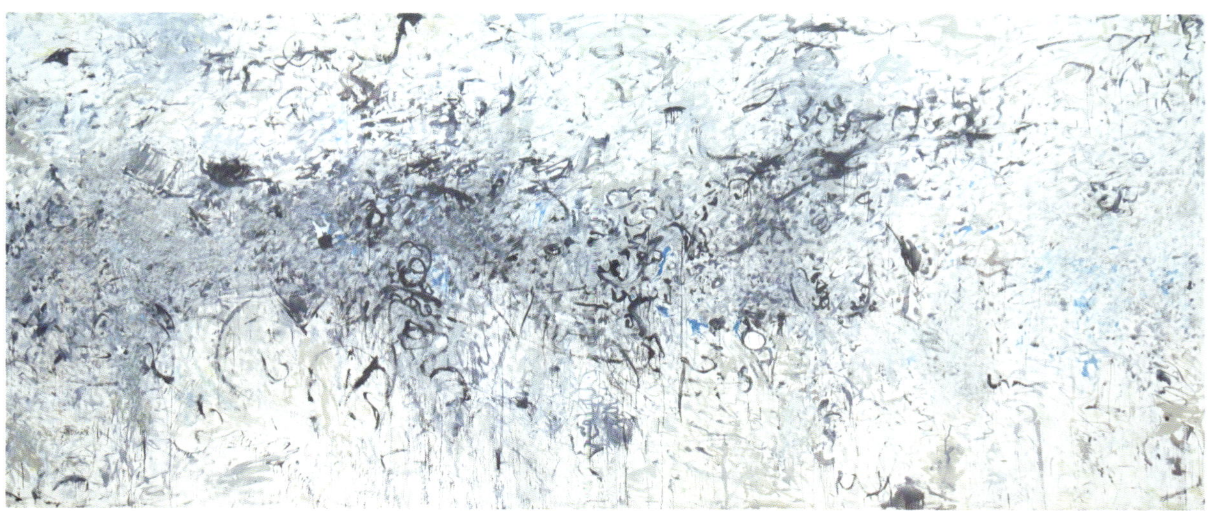

Fig. 33. Milton Resnick, *Swan*, 1961. Oil on canvas, 116 ¾ x 273 ⅝ in. (296.5 x 695 cm). The Modern Art Museum of Fort Worth, Museum purchase, The Benjamin J. Tillar Memorial Trust. © The Milton Resnick and Pat Passlof Foundation

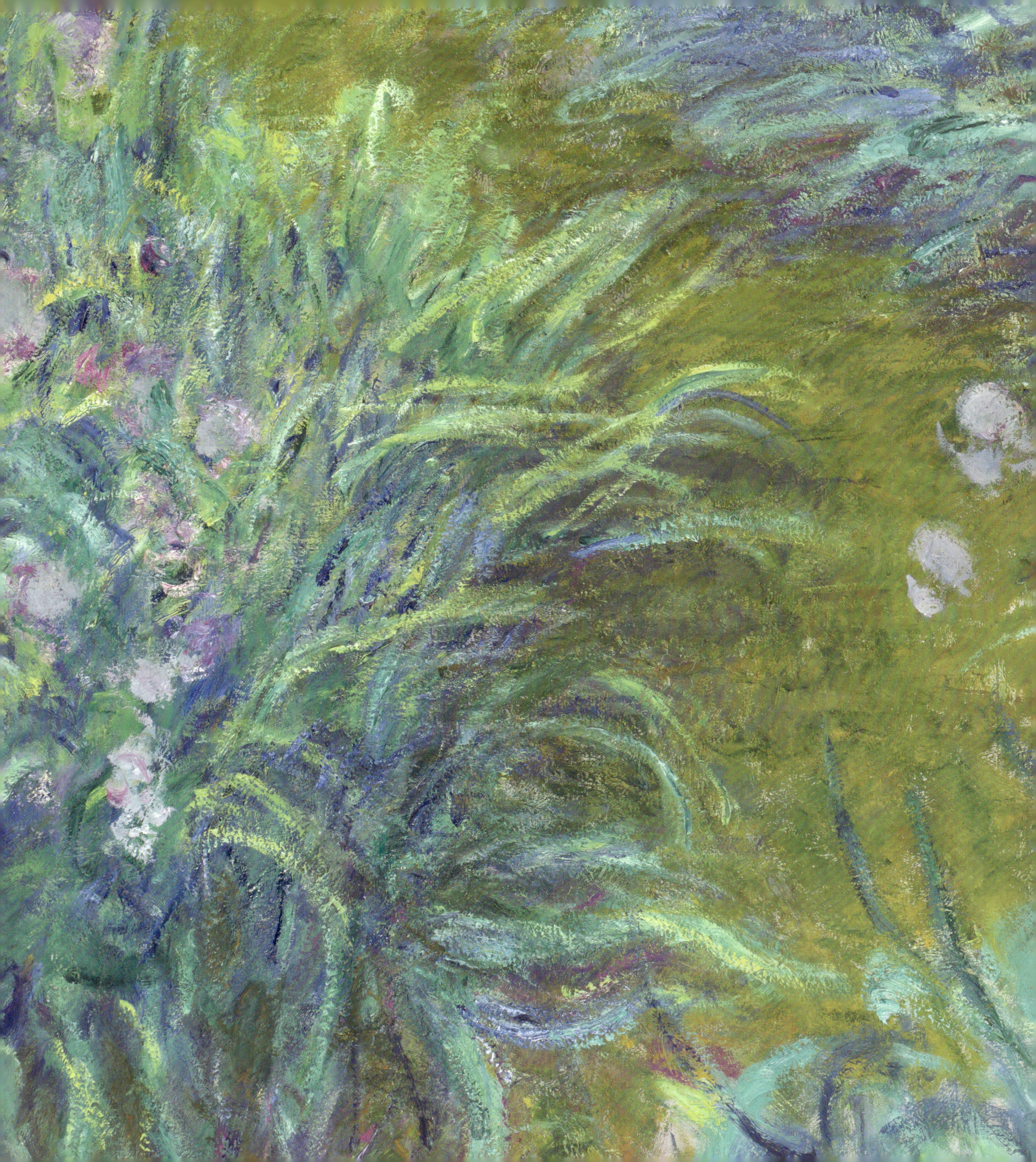

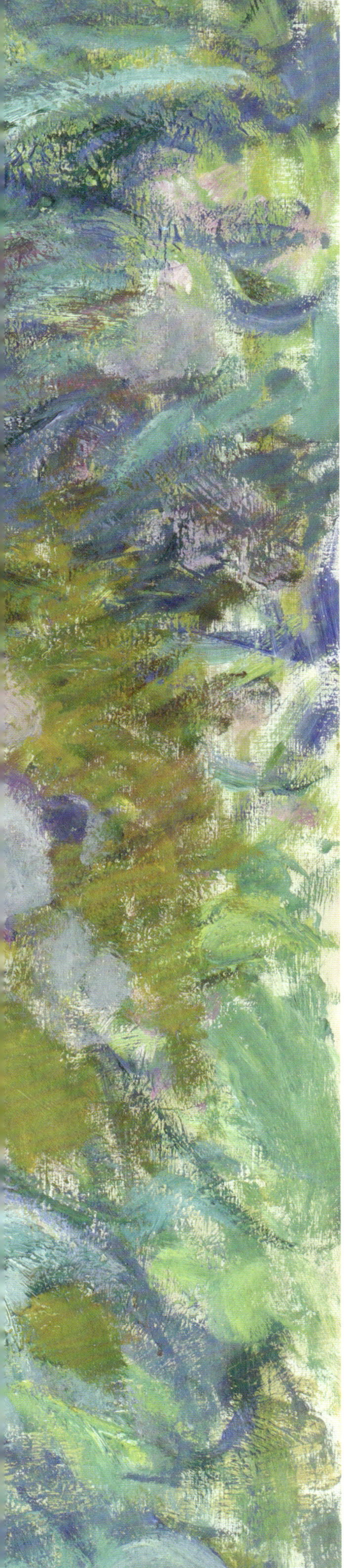

"Color is my day-long obsession": Monet's Late Painting Materials and Techniques, 1914–1926

Claire M. Barry
Director of conservation, Kimbell Art Museum

Introduction

Nothing in the whole world is of interest to me but my painting and my flowers.[1]

From 1914 to 1926, Claude Monet painted with the principal goal of creating *Grandes Décorations* in the form of murals for France, now in the Musée de l'Orangerie. In the controlled environment of his self-designed studios and gardens at Giverny, he created dozens of oversized panels for the series, of which twenty-two were selected for the final cycle. He also painted several études (paintings from nature left in an incomplete state) in preparation for the series, as well as smaller easel canvases of subjects from his Giverny garden intended for sale, with themes ranging from water lilies, weeping willows, Japanese bridges, and irises to the ephemeral reflections upon the surface of his water-lily pond.

In 1914, the seventy-three-year-old artist had only recently returned to painting following a prolonged hiatus after the death of his beloved second wife, Alice Hoschedé, in May 1911. His reengagement with painting inspired significant changes in his use of materials and techniques. These occurred as the aging Impressionist grappled with the issues of painting on a grand scale and with overcoming the limiting effects of cataracts, which compromised his finely tuned sense of color. Examination of the artist's paint surfaces from this period suggests that not only did Monet surmount these challenges, but he also retained his exceptional inventive powers until the end of his life.

For this analysis, numerous works dating from 1914 to 1926 were examined under magnification, and conservation files were consulted when available. Following an overview of the artist's painting environment and materials, two case studies each take a deeper look at paintings closely related in subject and date to the *Grandes Décorations*. The first study compares the Kimbell Art Museum's *Weeping Willow* of 1918–19 (cat. 44), an easel painting of conventional dimensions, to the National Gallery's *Irises* of c. 1914–17 (cat. 17), an overscale study, or étude, made in the manner of

Claude Monet, *Irises* (detail), c. 1914–17, cat. 17

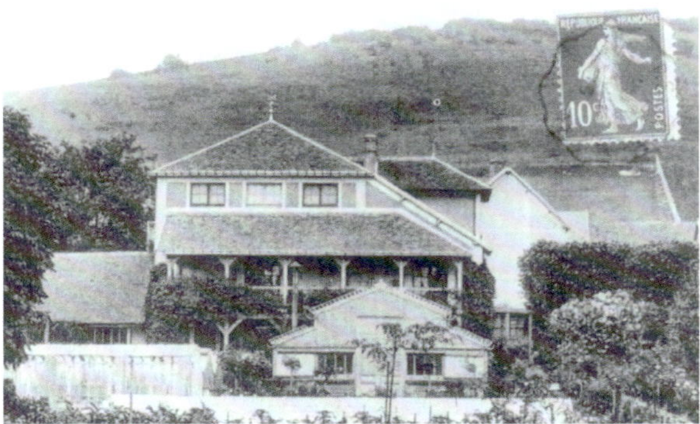

Fig. 34. Postcard of Claude Monet's second studio in Giverny with greenhouses in the foreground

the water-lily studies that preceded the longer *Grandes Décorations* panels. The second examines three closely related paintings of the water-lily pond's surface, each a pronounced horizontal in format. The goal of these studies is to evaluate Monet's materials, his use of color, brushwork, and texture, and his varying notions of finish in his late paintings.

Portrait of the Artist's Studio and Painting Materials

I can no longer work outside because of the intensity of the light.[2]

When Monet moved to his Giverny estate, called Le Pressoir, in 1883, he rented the property as a tenant and converted a dirt-floor barn into his first studio.[3] The next iteration of his studio came when he purchased the property in 1890 and built a two-story pavilion (fig. 34). There, the artist worked in a high-ceilinged, skylit room on the building's second floor.[4] The studio was accessible through a staircase on the ground floor, which housed a garage for his motorcars, a darkroom, and an aviary—trappings of the success his art had brought.[5]

By 1914, Monet was even more famous, successful, and well-connected. Despite France entering into war with Germany in August of that year, and though trains carrying troops to the front passed directly by his property, Monet was able to continue his work, overcoming the challenges of obtaining art materials and other essential supplies in large part through his powerful political allies. For example, he kept in close touch with Georges Clémenceau, France's prime minister from 1917 to 1920 (fig. 35), and other influential politicians who advised him and granted him favors to support his painting. Monet repeatedly petitioned the minister of commerce, Étienne Clémentel, to overcome administrative obstacles to transport art supplies to Giverny (fig. 36).[6] Clémentel even released the artist from wartime railway freight exemptions so that Monet could receive shipments of oversized, pre-stretched canvases (measuring 2 meters in one direction by 1, 1.3, and 1.5 in the other) from Le Besnard, his supplier in Paris, at his Giverny studio.[7]

In addition to art supplies, Monet welcomed a steady stream of friends—including many of these politicians, like Clémenceau, as well as artists like Henri Matisse—to Le Pressoir. Eventually, Monet transformed his second-floor studio into a showroom, furnished with wicker chairs, a banquet, a chaise longue, desks, and tables covered with photographs, vases of flowers, and Auguste Rodin's bust of Monet—and positively crowded with paintings. Canvases were hung salon-style on the studio walls, with recent works propped up on the floor (fig. 37).

In 1915, Monet constructed his final studio in Giverny to accommodate the massive canvases he was creating, which had begun to overfill the second-floor studio. With a ceiling height of fifteen meters (forty-nine feet), the studio's raking, pitched roof towered above the artist's house. This newest studio was

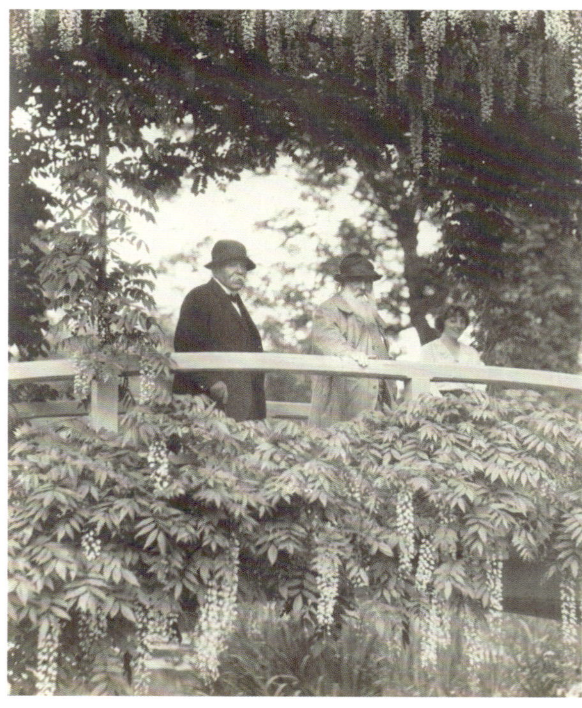

Fig. 35. Georges Clémenceau, Claude Monet, and Lily Butler on the Japanese bridge in Monet's garden, Giverny, c. 1921, gelatin silver print. Photo attributed to Henri Martinie

flooded with natural light, emitted through a skylight and two rows of windows. Monet could control the overhead light with the aid of fabric panels, which could be drawn across the skylight with pulleys. At about 24 x 12 meters, the studio was large enough to accommodate a ring of twelve murals, each supported by a rolling chassis that allowed Monet to reposition panels as needed.[8] There was ample room for the artist to step back from his paintings to evaluate his progress on the overall series. "I'll finally be able to judge what I have done," Monet declared.[9]

Photographs of Monet in Giverny after 1914 provide further insights into his studio and working practices.[10] Monet carefully managed his image, just as he assumed full control over the universe he created in Giverny. In a series of photographs from 1920, Monet, smartly attired in a three-piece suit complete with pocket square, poses for the camera in his new, custom-built studio (fig. 38). (Fittingly, his late wife Alice Hoschedé had called him *le marquis* because of his lordly manners and taste for dressing in fine English tweeds.[11]) The image of Monet standing in front of his enormous water-lily panels, placed side by side in a continuous series, communicates the magnitude of his ambitions.[12] In the photograph, he grasps with his left hand a massive palette smeared with paint and long-handled brushes: it is the picture of a resilient artist at the height of his powers. It was paradoxical to see an Impressionist who had made his reputation painting *en plein air* occupy such a large studio; in the 1880s or 1890s canvases would be painted in nature and only given finishing touches indoors. But by this point, Monet frequently finished paintings begun out-of-doors in the studio or even executed murals entirely indoors, less than a quarter mile away from the motif.[13] The comfortable, well-appointed space, containing expansive work tables laden with art supplies, was furnished over the years with sofas, end tables, and moveable chairs. The working studio doubled as a showroom, providing a setting for discussions between Monet and others as his work on the water-lily series slowly progressed over the years. His ongoing dialogue with select visitors about his *Grandes Décorations* became an integral part of Monet's creative process as the series evolved.

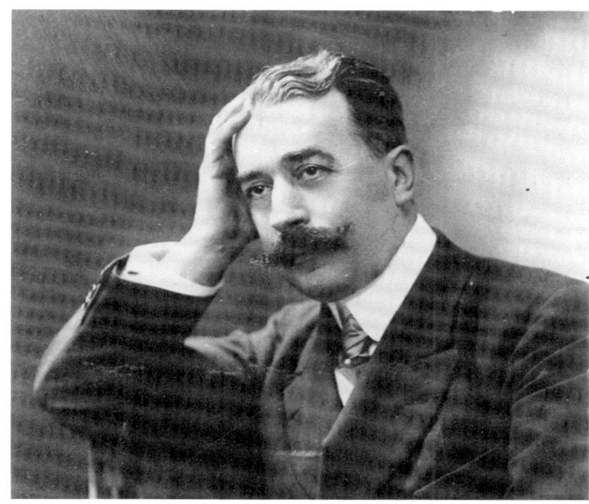

Fig. 36. Étienne Clémentel, c. 1924. George Grantham Bain Collection, Library of Congress Prints and Photographs Division, Washington, DC

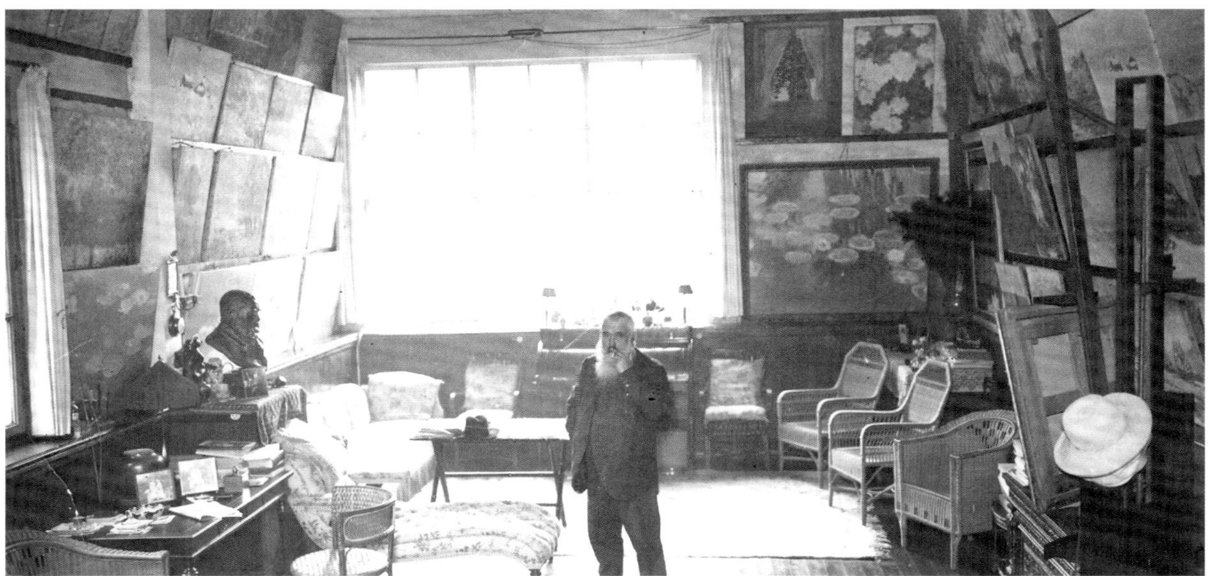

Fig. 37. Claude Monet in his second Giverny studio, mid-November 1913. Published in *Je sais tout*, January 14, 1914, p. 35

The artist lived at Le Pressoir surrounded by an entourage of family and staff, including up to eight gardeners. They formed the infrastructure he required to be able to paint as well as sustain the enchanting gardens he had created. In a photograph taken near the water-lily pond in July 1915, Monet paints beneath a large umbrella, wearing a hat, the former to control the bright sunlight and the latter to reduce glare (fig. 39). By this time, the artist's cataracts had made him more sensitive to light, and its reduction enabled him to see more clearly.[14] Hovering directly to his left, Monet's daughter-in-law (also his step-daughter) Blanche Hoschedé Monet leans forward as if anticipating a pending need.

Her presence denotes a change from Monet's earlier practice, in which he generally preferred to work alone or, rarely, with a fellow painter such as Pierre-Auguste Renoir for company.[15] Monet now had assistants that he utilized in his day-to-day painting practice. The devoted Blanche, herself a painter, occasionally helped the artist by applying grounds over his stretched canvases and, in later years, assisted him in editing his copious body of work by destroying paintings that he rejected as unsuitable.[16] Additionally, Monet's gardeners aided the elderly painter in the practical task of carrying his easels and canvases between the garden and his studio. From 1914 to 1926, the artist regularly shifted his painting sessions between these two settings. His choice of locations would be dictated by the time of day, the season, the size of his canvases, and, not least, his failing eyesight. To accommodate his cataracts, Monet often painted outdoors in the mornings and moved into the studio for afternoon sessions.[17]

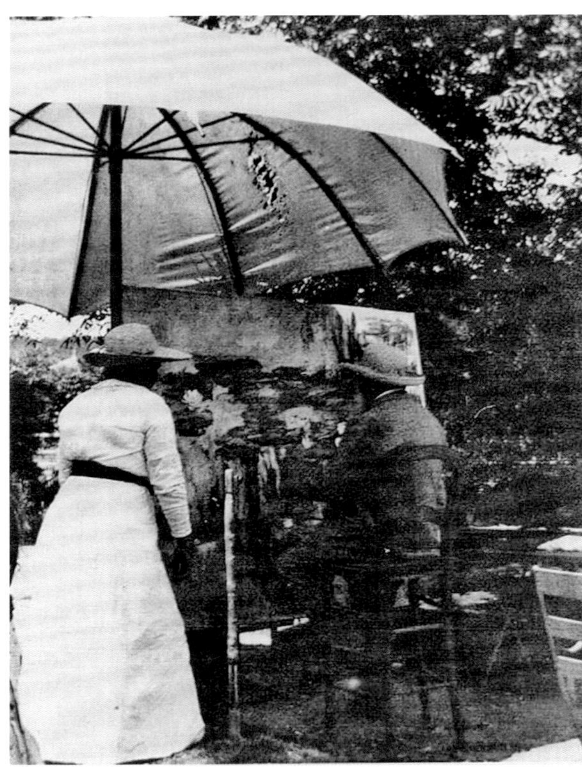

Fig. 39. Claude Monet at work in the garden at Giverny, July 1915, with Blanche Hochsedé Monet

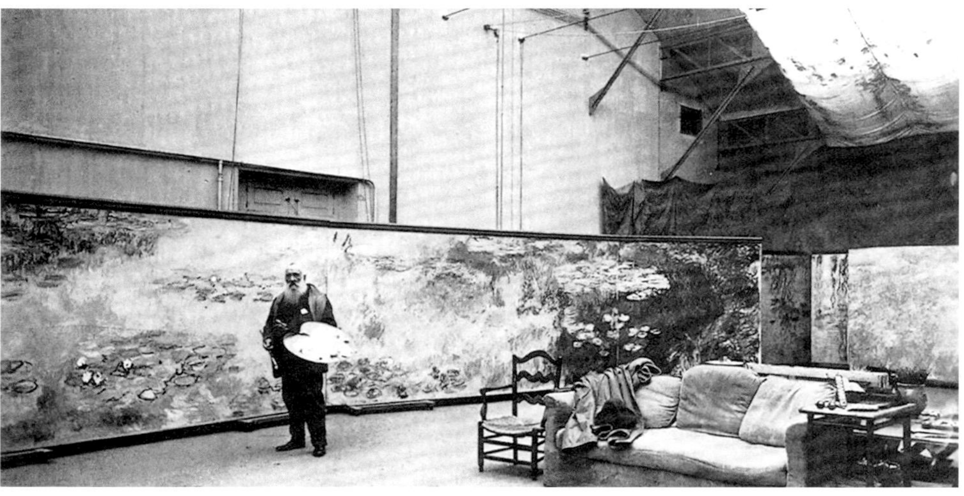

Fig. 38. Claude Monet in his third studio at Giverny, 1920, gelatin silver print. Photo by Henri Manuel

He continuously revised his paintings over a prolonged period of time while working on several canvases at once.[18] The artist depended on his staff to bring him one painting after another as he labored throughout the day. As he explained on August 19, 1918: "In the atmosphere a color reappears that I found and sketched on one of the canvases yesterday. Quickly I am passed the painting and I try my best to put down this version definitively, but usually it disappears as quickly as it came into view to make room for another color already rendered several days before on another study which is almost instantly placed before me . . . and so on all day."[19]

As this working method suggests, Monet was more obsessed with color than with the subject he was depicting. Evoking the notion of the "innocent eye," he once advised a visiting American painter to "try to forget what objects you have before you . . . Merely think, here is a little square of blue, here an oblong of pink, here a streak of yellow."[20] Monet described the pain he experienced in chasing the "merest sliver of color" as he strove to grasp the "intangible." He mused, "Color, any color, lasts a second, sometimes three or four minutes at most. What to do, what to paint in three to four minutes?"[21]

The artist's preoccupation with color extended to the quality and stability of his paints. After visiting Monet's studio in 1918, the French art dealer René Gimpel recorded in his journal: "Monet is very concerned with the chemical evolution of his colors, and he admits that he thinks about it constantly while he's painting."[22] The Parisian color merchant Moisse, previously from the renowned Maison Edouard, supplied Monet's paints during the First World War. He recorded the artist's purchases as follows: "flake white, cobalt violet pale, viridian green, extra-fine ultramarine. Sometimes—rarely—vermilion. Then a trinity of cadmium yellows: pale, deep, and lemon. I also sold him an ultramarine lemon yellow."[23] (This last is a fanciful misnomer for strontium chromate yellow.)

In February of 1918, Monet explained to a visitor his habit of arranging his pigments in a particular order on his palette. This fastidious practice had become essential for Monet when his color perception was diminished by his cataracts. His claimed that by carefully reading the paint tube labels and consistently organizing the colors on his palette, he could avoid making mistakes.[24] As Monet explained in an interview with the journalist François Thiébault-Sisson at Giverny: "If I have regained my sense of color in the large canvases I've showed you, it is because I have always adapted my working methods to my eyesight and because most of the time I have laid down the

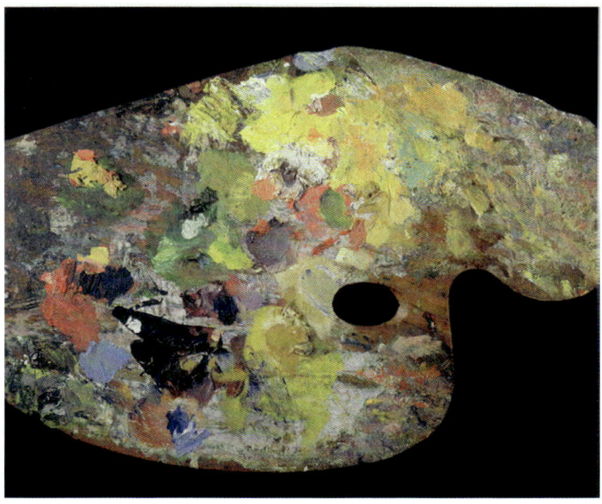

Fig. 41. Claude Monet's palette. Musée Marmottan Monet, Paris

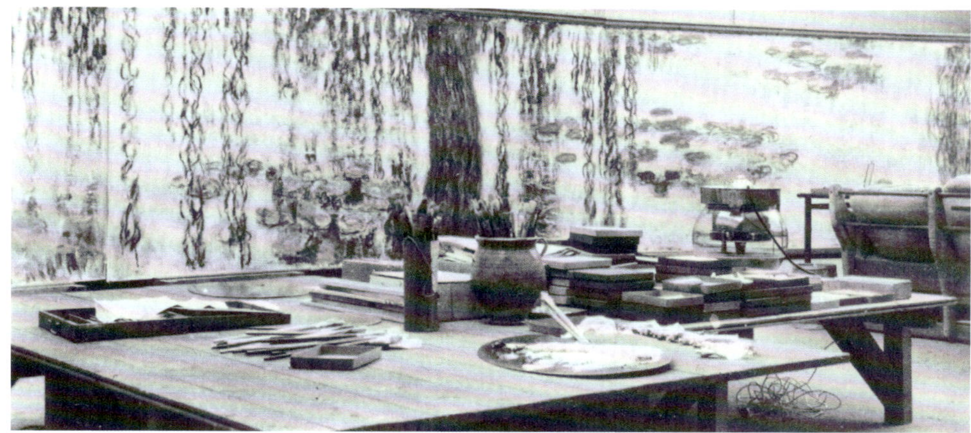

Fig. 40. Claude Monet's work table laden with art supplies and examples of the *Grandes Décorations* in the background, November 1917. Photograph by Joseph Durand-Ruel. Archives Durand-Ruel

color haphazardly, on the one hand trusting solely to the labels on my paint tubes and, on the other, to force of habit, to the way in which I have always laid out my materials on my palette. I soon grew used to it, and I've never made a mistake. I should add that my infirmity had sometimes gone into remittance and that on more than one occasion my color vision has come back as it was before, and I have profited from those moments to make the necessary adjustments."[25]

The meticulous order with which Monet organized his art materials in his studio helped him identify different tubes of paint more readily, thereby helping the artist to compensate for his compromised sensitivity to color. Following his visit to Giverny, Gimpel described the art supplies that he had seen spread out on Monet's work tables. Gimpel noted "some forty cardboard boxes, each containing a dozen large tubes of paint of the same color . . . laid out very precisely. There were more than fifty very clean brushes in a glazed earthenware pot, and perhaps twenty-five others in a second pot. Still more were lying about, all three-quarters of an inch to an inch wide. There were two palettes, remarkably clean; they looked like new. One was covered with colors in little spaced-out daubs: cobalt, ultramarine blue, violet, vermilion, ocher, orange, dark green, another very clear green, and lastly a lapis lazuli yellow [strontium chromate yellow]" (fig. 40). Gimpel's description of Monet's palette parallels the blue to red to yellow color sequence found on one of the artist's palettes, now in the Musée Marmatton Monet (fig. 41).[26]

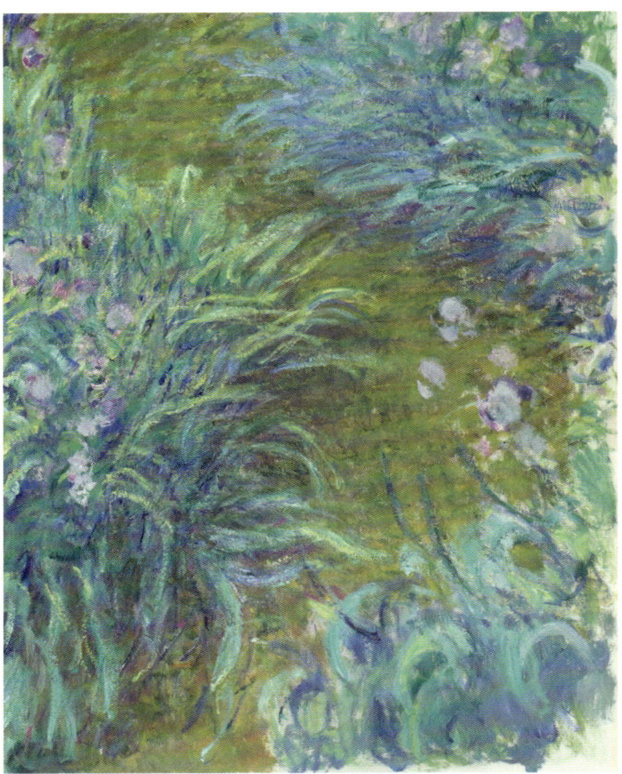

Fig. 42. Claude Monet, *Irises*, c. 1914–17. Oil on canvas, 79 x 59 in. (200.7 x 149.9 cm). The National Gallery, London. Cat. 17

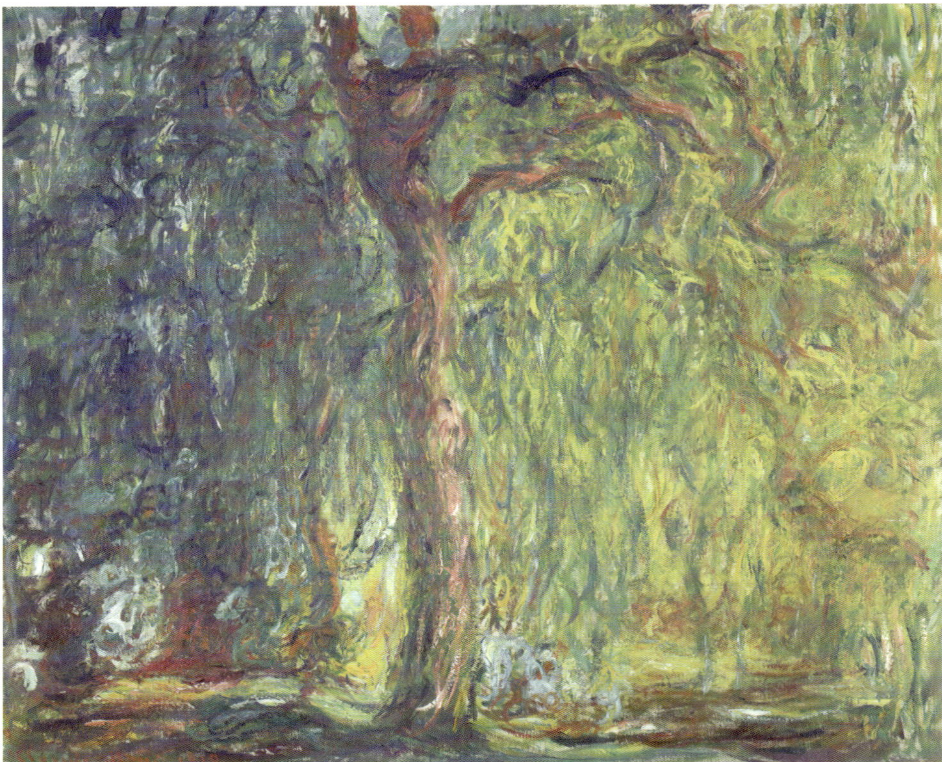

Fig. 43. Claude Monet, *Weeping Willow*, 1918–19. Oil on canvas, 39 ¼ x 47 ¼ in. (99.7 x 120 cm). Kimbell Art Museum. Cat. 44

Two Case Studies of Monet's Painting Process, 1914–1926

Color is my day-long obsession, joy, and torment.

I: Étude versus Easel Painting

Two case studies were conceived to closely examine different aspects of Monet's late painting process. The first case study compares *Irises*, a large étude now in the National Gallery, London (fig. 42), with *Weeping Willow*, an easel painting now in the Kimbell Art Museum, Fort Worth (fig. 43). The artist painted the unsigned *Irises* as an exercise in preparation for his *Grandes Décorations* cycle of water lilies. Because its height corresponds to that of the cycle, Monet could view *Irises* alongside other canvases as he developed the overall composition of the series. This practice, which he adopted in his late period, is illustrated in his studio photographs (fig. 44), which show square paintings on display that closely resemble the Toledo Museum of Art's *Water Lilies* (cat. 16). *Weeping Willow*, by contrast, is considered an easel painting due to its smaller size and the fact that Monet produced it to sell on the market. One of a series of approximately a dozen canvases of weeping willows that he likely painted in the spring and summer of 1918—though two, including the Kimbell's, were signed and dated "1919" before being sold—it represents the artist's return to easel painting near the end of the First World War. In fact, the twisting, distorted tree trunk and branches and densely cascading foliage are thought to symbolize the anguish of war itself. [27]

Color

Recent investigation of Monet's use of pigments in *Weeping Willow* expands our awareness of the artist's twentieth-century palette, elaborating upon Gimpel's 1918 firsthand account and Ashok Roy's 2007 pigment study of *Irises*.[28] Conservation scientist John Twilley analyzed numerous minute samples of *Weeping Willow* in 2017–18 using scanning electron microscopy, polarized light microscopy, and Ramen spectroscopy, and Richard Newman, head of scientific research at the Museum of Fine Arts, Boston, carried out analysis of the binding medium in four paint samples that were provided by Twilley. These results were compared with Roy's earlier findings. A majority of the pigments identified were shared by *Weeping Willow* and *Irises*, including lead white, French ultramarine, cobalt blue, cobalt violet, cadmium orange, cadmium yellow, zinc-potassium chromate yellow, and barium chromate yellow and viridian.[29] Hyperspectral photography of *Weeping Willow* by John Delaney confirmed that cobalt blue was the primary blue used; Monet applied it extensively, especially throughout the gray and dark blue areas (fig. 45).[30]

Scholarship has traditionally suggested that Monet abandoned chrome yellow due to its instability and tendency to fade. Lead chrome yellow had developed a poor reputation among artists for noticeably darkening after exposure to light; for example, the appearance of several of Van Gogh's paintings was altered due to his use of this pigment.[31] Nonetheless, chromate yellows were, in fact, found in both Monet paintings.[32] Comparing the results of the London and Fort Worth studies exposes some key differences in the way Monet used these yellows, however. In *Irises*, Monet used mixtures of zinc-potassium chromate yellow and barium chromate yellow, which are among the more stable chrome yellows.[33] By contrast, in *Weeping Willow*, Monet applied these chromate pigments separately in trace amounts but opted for cadmium yellow, a brilliantly colored yellow with good covering power and excellent light-fastness, as his primary yellow throughout the painting.[34] Monet's preference for cadmium yellow is supported by his color merchant's account that the artist purchased "a trinity of cadmiums: pale, deep, and lemon."

As this example demonstrates, although *Weeping Willow* and *Irises* are based on many of the same pigments, Monet used them differently to construct distinct color schemes in each work. Monet created *Weeping Willow* using a vibrant palette of saturated hues; strong color contrasts animate broad areas of light and shadow separated by the central tree trunk, with a cooler blue area of foliage on the left and fiery yellow foliage at right. The trunk itself is formed from a colorful network of curving, interlocking, and crisscrossed brushstrokes (fig. 46). Monet's interweaving strokes of complementary colors—green with pink and blue with orange—provide classic illustrations of Chevreul's theory of simultaneous contrast. This theory, often demonstrated by the Impressionists in their painting, suggests that placing complementary colors side by side enhances the luminosity of each. *Irises*, by contrast, is based on a cool palette of greens, blues, and violets within a close range of tones, which imparts a more muted coloring overall. Monet highlights the cool lavender irises on the right by overlaying them on the warm yellow-green pathway, which provides the only significant tonal shift within the painting (fig. 47). As in *Weeping Willow*, the painter contrasted warm and cool complementary hues in *Irises* but here used a more nuanced and subtle approach.

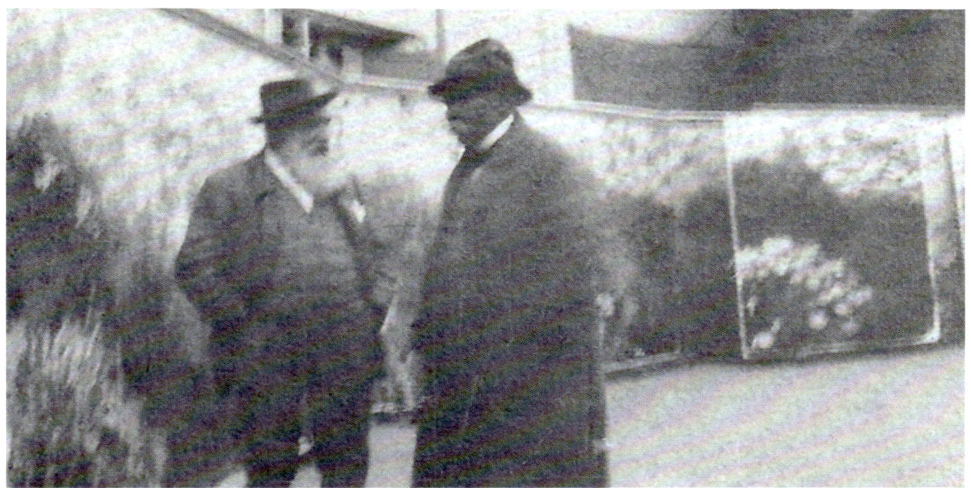

Fig. 44. Claude Monet and George Clémenceau in Monet's large studio, showing an étude placed alongside *Grandes Décorations* canvases. Collection Philippe Piguet

The étude, a broadly-conceived exercise, displays less complicated paint mixtures and purer applications

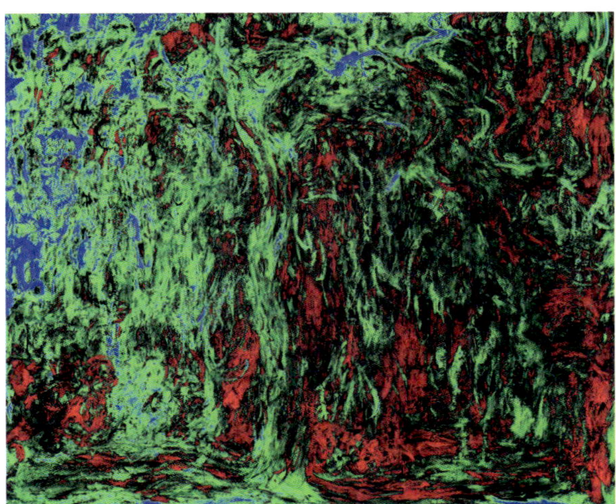

Fig. 45. Hyperspectral image of the Kimbell's *Weeping Willow* illustrating Monet's use of cobalt blue. Green represents cobalt blue pigments, blue represents dark cobalt blue pigments, and red represents white pigments.

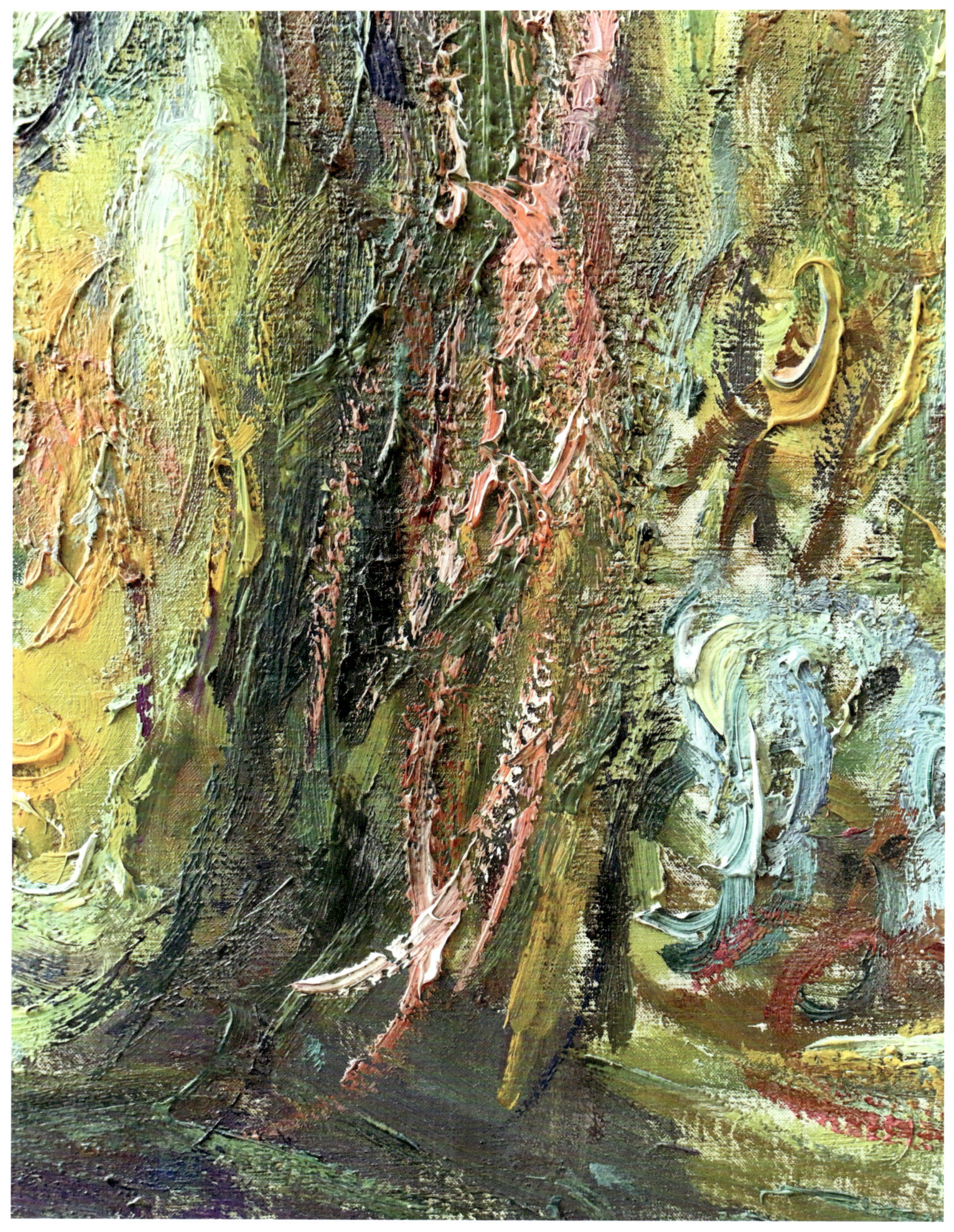

Fig. 46. Detail of the trunk in the Kimbell's *Weeping Willow*

of color than the signed easel painting made for the market.[36] In *Irises*, Monet's brushstrokes typically consisted of either single pigments or just two colors mixed together (either wet-in-wet or blended), often with lead white (fig. 48). This finding previously led to the hypothesis that Monet simplified his pigment mixtures in his late work.[37] In *Weeping Willow*, on the contrary, more complex pigment mixtures were discovered. Monet also employed wet-in-wet mixing of more colors than were found in *Irises*.[38] One sample consisted of a mixture of four pigments—violet, orange, medium blue, and darker blue—while another cross section contained up to nine layers: white lead ground, yellow-green, yellow-orange, pale blue, violet, blue-violet, rose and green, warm white, and violet lake (figs. 49, 50). This suggests that differences in the complexity of Monet's color mixing should be considered not just in terms of date but also in terms of the painting's scale and intended purpose.

Although Monet did not use zinc white paint in the two works examined, zinc did, unexpectedly, appear in most of the spectra in the analysis for *Weeping Willow*.[39] This anomaly may be explained by the knowledge that small amounts of zinc were sometimes added as low-cost extenders to provide added weight or bulk to paints. The addition of zinc, however, can lead to the formation of zinc soaps beneath the surface of the painting.[40] Fortunately these lumpy particles have not yet appeared on the surface of *Weeping Willow*.

Variations in Monet's use of red pigments also came to light in the study of the two canvases. Red lake was identified in both paintings, but with significant chemical differences.[41] Vermilion and cadmium red, a pigment introduced to the market in 1910 and known for its improved light-fastness, appear in *Weeping Willow* but are missing in *Irises*.[42] Monet witnessed a great deal of industrial change and experienced the arrival of several such new pigments in the marketplace during his lifetime.[43] In *Weeping Willow*, he prioritized stable pigments with good covering power such as cobalt blue and cadmium red, orange, and yellow—all of which were newer and missing from many of his earlier paintings.[44]

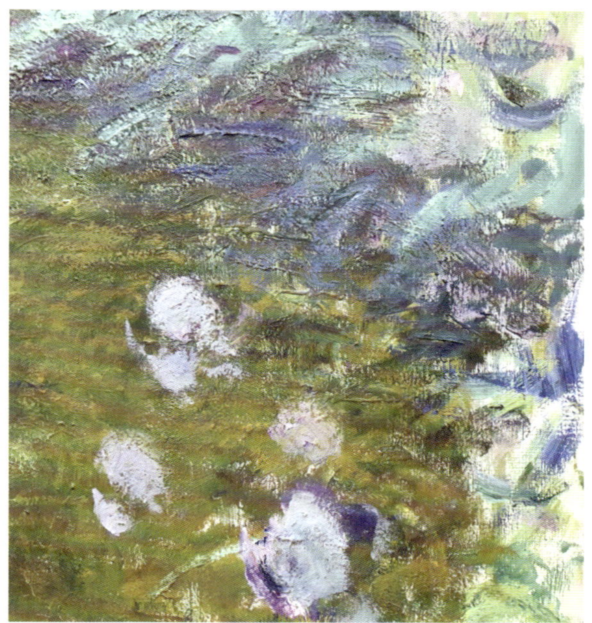

Fig. 47. Detail from the National Gallery's *Irises* showing irises overhanging the pathway

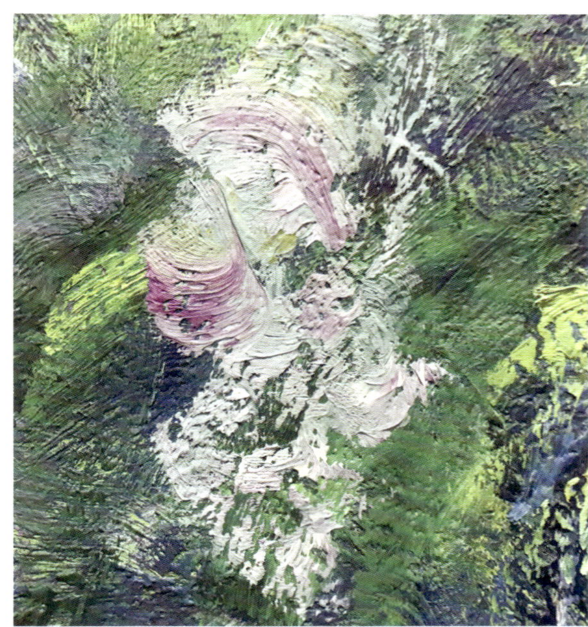

Fig. 48. Detail of lavender pigment mixed with lead white in *Irises*

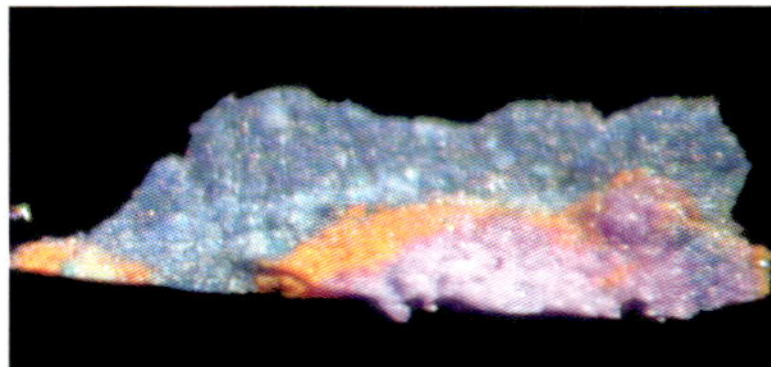

Fig. 49. Paint fragment from *Weeping Willow* displaying layers of violet, orange, medium blue, and darker blue

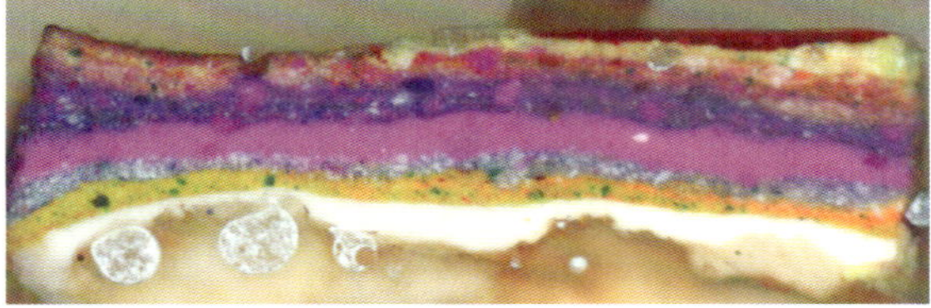

Fig. 50. Cross section, orthogonal view, from *Weeping Willow* showing nine layers of paint on top of the white lead ground

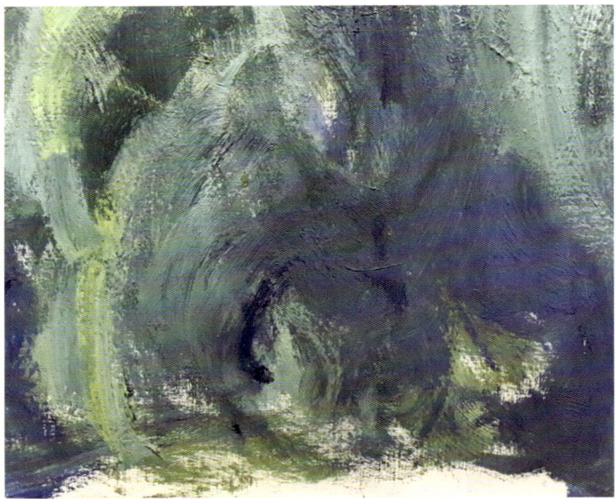

Fig. 51. Detail of *Irises* showing white ground along edge where brushwork tapers off

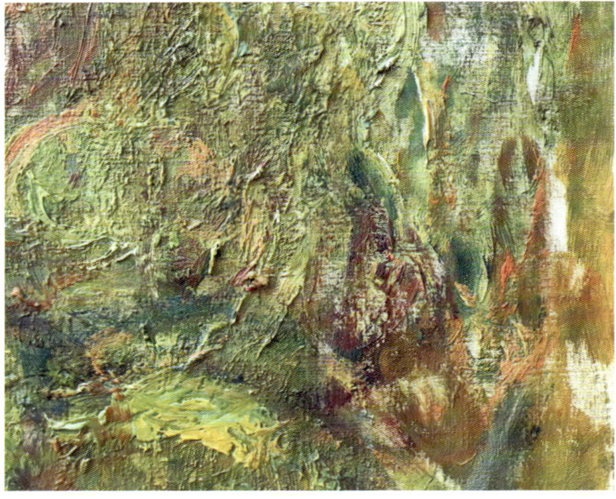

Fig. 52. Detail of *Weeping Willow* showing areas of exposed white ground along right edge

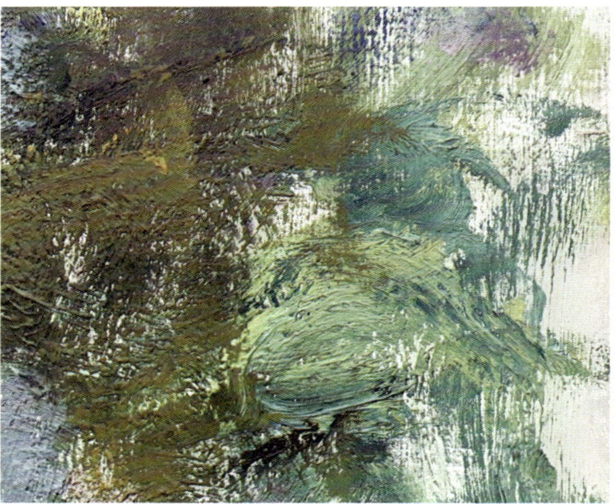

Fig. 53. Detail of *Irises* showing Monet's initial sketching-in of the motif along right edge where white priming is exposed

Brushwork, Texture, and Paint Surface

Both the large *Irises* and the smaller *Weeping Willow* are executed on pre-primed, lead-white grounds over similar plain-weave canvases.[45] Their differing dimensions reflect their separate functions as an easel painting and étude. *Weeping Willow* is painted on a single-layer, bright-lead-white ground, while *Irises* is executed on a double-layer lead-white-in-oil ground consisting of a lower, creamy layer followed by a cooler, possibly leaner, upper layer, most likely applied in Monet's studio.[46] These findings align with Monet's stated preference for painting on white-primed canvases in order to establish the scale of his values.[47]

Poppy-seed oil has been identified as the medium in numerous samples from *Irises*.[48] This slow-drying oil was the principal binding medium for Impressionists.[49] It enabled Monet to extend his work sessions over a period of several days: an advantage for an artist who consistently reworked his canvases over time.[50] Furthermore, since poppy-seed oil yellows less than linseed oil, it was an appropriate choice for the light, refined color harmonies Monet sought. This particular binder produces a thick, buttery paint ideally suited for the type of dense impasto, bravura brushwork, and wet-in-wet paint handling that characterize Monet's late paintings.[51]

Medium analyses of four samples from *Weeping Willow*, on the other hand, were inconsistent for poppy-seed oil. Two of the samples, one lead white and the other a yellow orange consisting predominantly of a mixture of cadmium yellow and orange and lead white, showed a range typical of walnut oil.[52] The two other samples, one a thick red lake comprised of a predominantly alumina-based red lake(s) with minor vermilion and the other a deep cobalt blue aluminate,[53] appeared to consist of a mixture of linseed oil and walnut oil.[54] Three of the samples (thick red lake, deep blue, and white) also showed traces of conifer resin (probably pine). Conifer resin was fairly commonly found in the binding media of several Impressionist paintings examined at the National Gallery, London. Newman found that a sample of the deep blue paint also indicated fatty acids and hydrocarbons characteristic of beeswax, which was sometimes added to the medium to stabilize certain pigments.[55]

This variability in the choice of medium should not come as a surprise: in a survey of fifteen Impressionist paintings at the National Gallery, London, every painting contained mixtures of different drying oils, indicating the variety of oil-paint media then available through artists' colormen.[56] The study found mixtures of both linseed and poppy-seed oil and walnut and poppy-seed oil in four early works by Monet.[57] Although these oils possess diverse working properties, it is difficult to know whether Monet selected particular drying oils intentionally. Nevertheless, it is interesting to note that, at least in this case, Monet chose differently drying oils for the large étude, *Irises*, and *Weeping Willow*, the painting intended for sale.

Walnut oil, which was significantly more expensive than linseed or poppy-seed oil,[58] has been used as a paint medium (either pure or mixed with linseed oil) since the Renaissance. In his sixteenth-century book *Lives of the Painters, Sculptors, and Architects*, Giorgio Vasari cited the advantages of walnut oil over linseed oil as yellowing less over time. But walnut oil also dries faster than poppy-seed oil and retains a brilliant gloss, imparting excellent saturation and depth to colors.[59] Monet's use of walnut oil as a medium for *Weeping Willow* undoubtedly enhanced the painting's jewel-like color contrasts of blue and yellow, pink and green.

Both *Irises* and *Weeping Willow* reflect Monet's late practice of concentrating his painting activity at the center of the composition. Their white grounds are visible along the edges of the canvases as Monet's brushwork tapers off (figs. 51, 52). Parts of Monet's initial sketching-in of the motif are visible along the right and lower-right sides of *Irises*, where the white priming layer is exposed (fig. 53). Monet started with dry applications of a dilute paint before eventually building up the final paint surface to a crisp impasto. Initially, Monet left an unpainted margin around the perimeter of *Weeping Willow*, as well. A photograph of Monet in his second studio in Giverny, standing beside the painting, which had been temporarily fitted into a gold frame, shows its still-unpainted borders (fig. 54). At a later stage, possibly before he sold the painting to Kojiro Matsukata, Monet covered the exposed borders with haphazard, rapidly applied, lean brushwork, then added his signature and date at the lower left on top of the filled-in border (fig. 55).

Although Monet began the compositions for both *Irises* and *Weeping Willow* similarly, with a rough, underlying, painted sketch, he adjusted his brushwork in the final paintings in response to their respective scales and purposes. The surface of *Weeping Willow* exhibits a higher degree of finish and a greater diversity of brushwork than that of the larger, broadly painted étude. This variety enlivens the appearance of *Weeping Willow*—from the fluid, sweeping strokes of impasto to the crumbly brushwork that skips across the uneven surface of underlying paint (fig. 56). The repeated layering of such fragmented brushstrokes created a corrugated surface texture that became a distinctive feature of many of the artist's late canvases. At the same time, much of the surface of *Weeping Willow* displays Monet's wet-in-wet mixing of colors (fig. 57). He worked up the trunk and willow branches using narrow, flat brushes measuring about a quarter- to a half-inch wide to apply a complex web of diagonal, swirling, and comma-like brushstrokes (fig. 58). In a final stage of painting, the artist applied medium-rich white and yellow impastoed highlights to the willow fronds. The delicacy of Monet's touch is seen in the tapering of yellow highlights into tendrils of paint no thicker than an eyelash (fig. 59). To perceive the full array of Monet's brushwork in *Weeping Willow* at close range—from areas of primed, unpainted canvas to

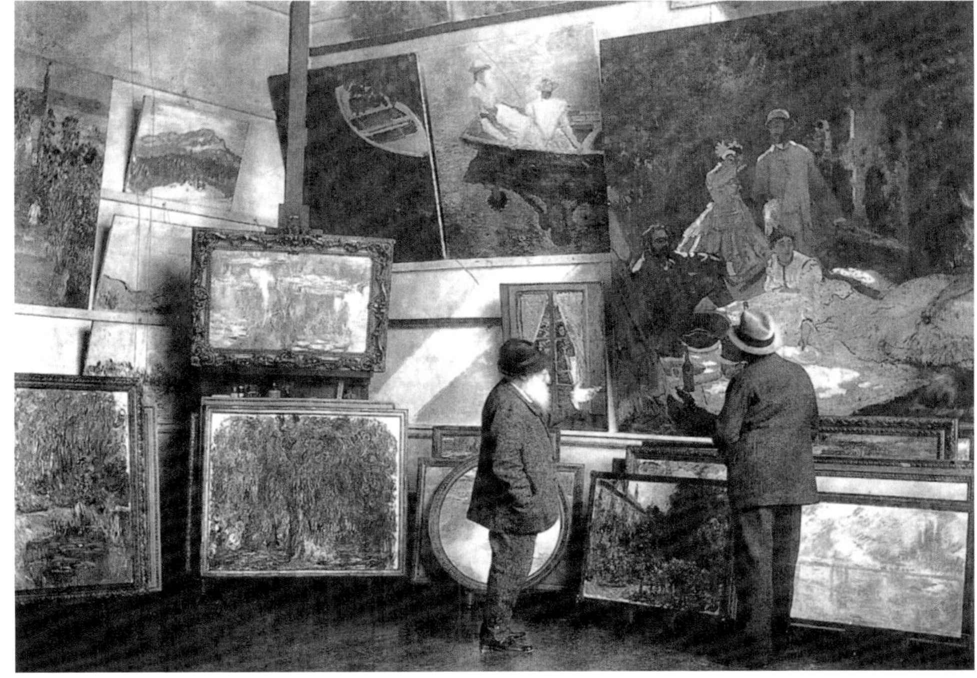

Fig. 54. Claude Monet in his second studio in Giverny with the Duc de Trévise, c. 1920. *Weeping Willow*, with unpainted borders, is visible near the bottom left. Musée du Louvre, Paris

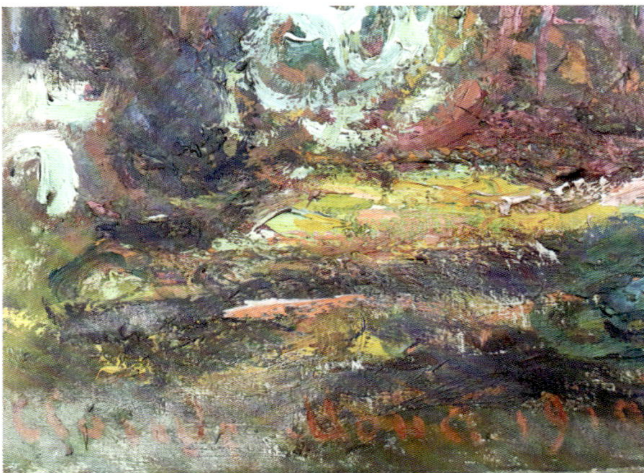

Fig. 55. Detail of the filled-in border of *Weeping Willow*, lower left, with Monet's signature and the date in red paint.

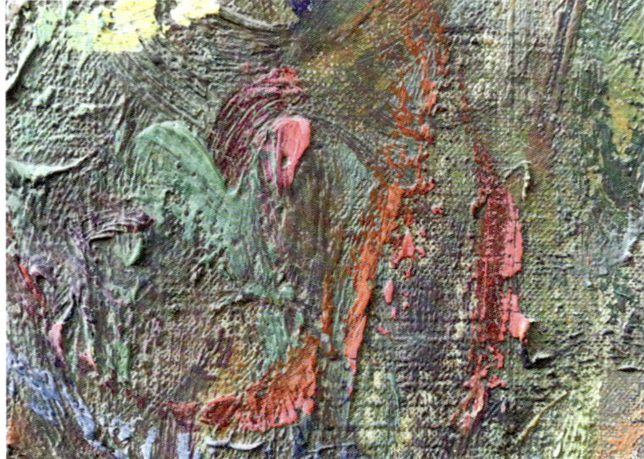

Fig. 56. Detail of *Weeping Willow* showing fragmented red and fuchsia brushstrokes

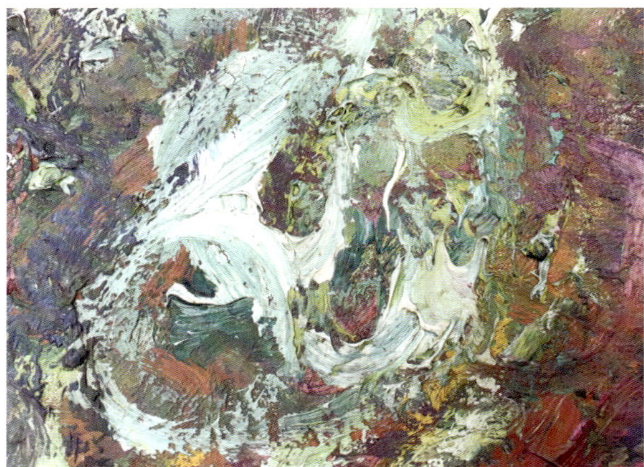

Fig. 57. Detail of *Weeping Willow* showing wet-in-wet mixing of colors

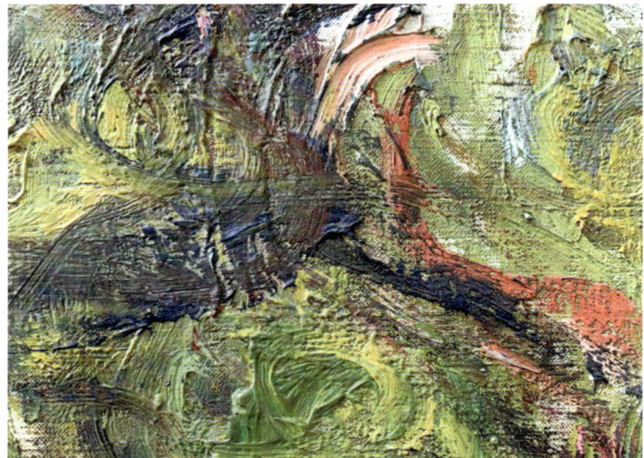

Fig. 58. Detail of *Weeping Willow* showing diagonal, swirling, and comma-like brushstrokes

mounds of thick impasto—is to experience a sculpture in low relief.

While *Irises* also shows strong variation in the thickness of paint, its buildup creates a distinctive effect. Monet presents the subject from a different, closer vantage point than the immersive frontal perspective of the *Weeping Willow*. In the étude, the viewer looks down at the garden path from above. The bird's-eye view in a vertical format with little sense of spatial recession exemplifies the influence of Japanese systems of perspective in Monet's work. Monet greatly simplified his palette for the étude, which appears more pastel than the vibrant *Weeping Willow*. For *Irises*, he often mixed just one or two colors with white wet-in-wet in a single brushstroke (fig. 60). As he developed his composition, Monet employed broad, energetic dry brushwork, using flat brushes of varying widths to apply his color with swirls, dashes, and dabs and curved, slashed, comma-like strokes. After building up the surface with several layers of color, many of Monet's final brushstrokes break up as they skip over the texture of the underlying paint. This is especially evident in the linear yellow-green and white highlights that the artist added to the foliage in a final stage of painting (fig. 61)—so different from the delicate tendrils of impasto left by the oil-rich paint of the highlights in *Weeping Willow*. Monet's layering of dry brushwork in *Irises* imparts a crusty, corrugated texture to the painting overall that is very distinct from the more intricately wrought surface of *Weeping Willow*.

Monet often strived for a lean, chalky paint surface. He intentionally leached his oil paints—a widespread practice among the Impressionists, including Renoir and Edgar Degas, and Post-Impressionists.[60] One of the most surprising discoveries about *Weeping Willow* was that parts of its surface—notably the willow leaves—

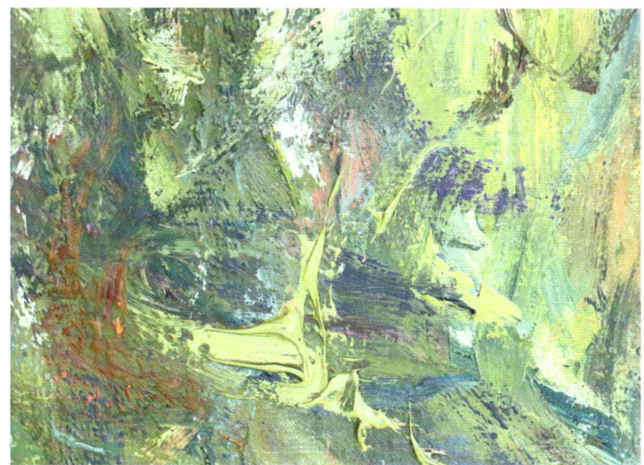

Fig. 59. Detail of *Weeping Willow* showing impastoed yellow highlights.

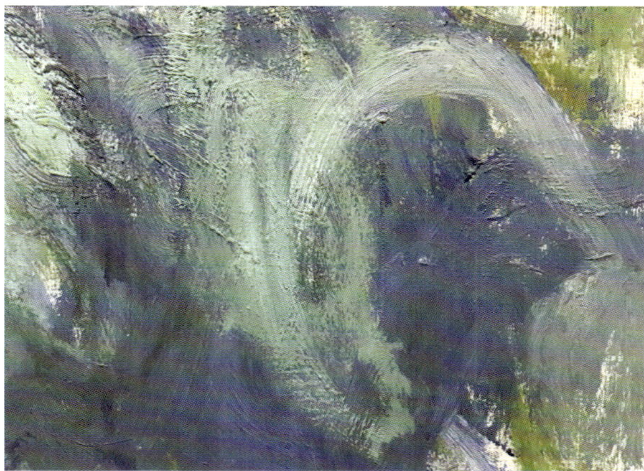

Fig. 60. Detail of *Irises* illustrating Monet's mixing of one or two colors with white wet-in-wet in a single brushstroke

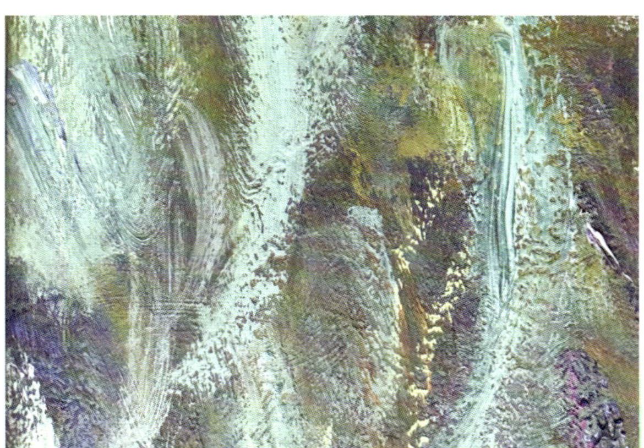

Fig. 61. Detail of linear, fragmented yellow highlights in *Irises*

are covered with a loose granular wash consisting entirely of paints from Monet's palette, including lead white, cadmium yellow, minor chrome oxide, cobalt violet, and traces of ultramarine (fig. 62).[61] There is no indication that these unbound pigments resulted from shedding or some form of degradation. Rather, it appears that in a final stage of painting, Monet applied a thin tonal layer of leached oil paint to emulate the matte surfaces of the foliage he perceived in nature.[62] When Édouard Vuillard and a group of visitors once questioned Monet about a large sheet of absorbent paper in his studio in June 1926, the artist explained that it was for his tube paints, which contained more oil than he desired.[63]

Fortunately, the surfaces of both *Irises* and *Weeping Willow* are unvarnished, reflecting their intended dry, matte appearances.[64] The surface of *Irises*, in particular, exhibits a parched quality. Monet's preference for unvarnished paintings naturally went hand in hand with his desire to create matte surfaces. This was not unique to his late canvases, since he had decided not to varnish his paintings beginning in the mid-1870s, if not earlier.[65] As someone who obsessed about color, Monet was also worried by the inevitable yellowing of natural resin varnishes. In the later works, any varnish would have been quickly absorbed by the leached paint, saturating the dark blue pigments in a manner that Monet never intended, emphasizing the illusion of depth and diminishing the sense of atmosphere.[66] Furthermore, a glossy surface coating would have reflected and scattered light, detracting from the nuanced handling of the heavily impastoed surface. While both *Irises* and *Weeping Willow* are united by their shared matte surfaces, however, comparison of these works highlights the variation in Monet's paint media, brushwork, and even the complexity of his paint mixtures in two paintings created for different purposes.

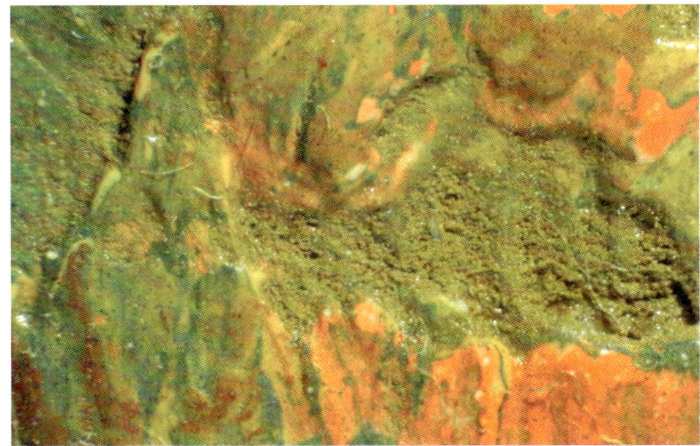

Fig. 62. Heavy accumulation of loose granular pigments on the surface of *Weeping Willow*, 7x magnification

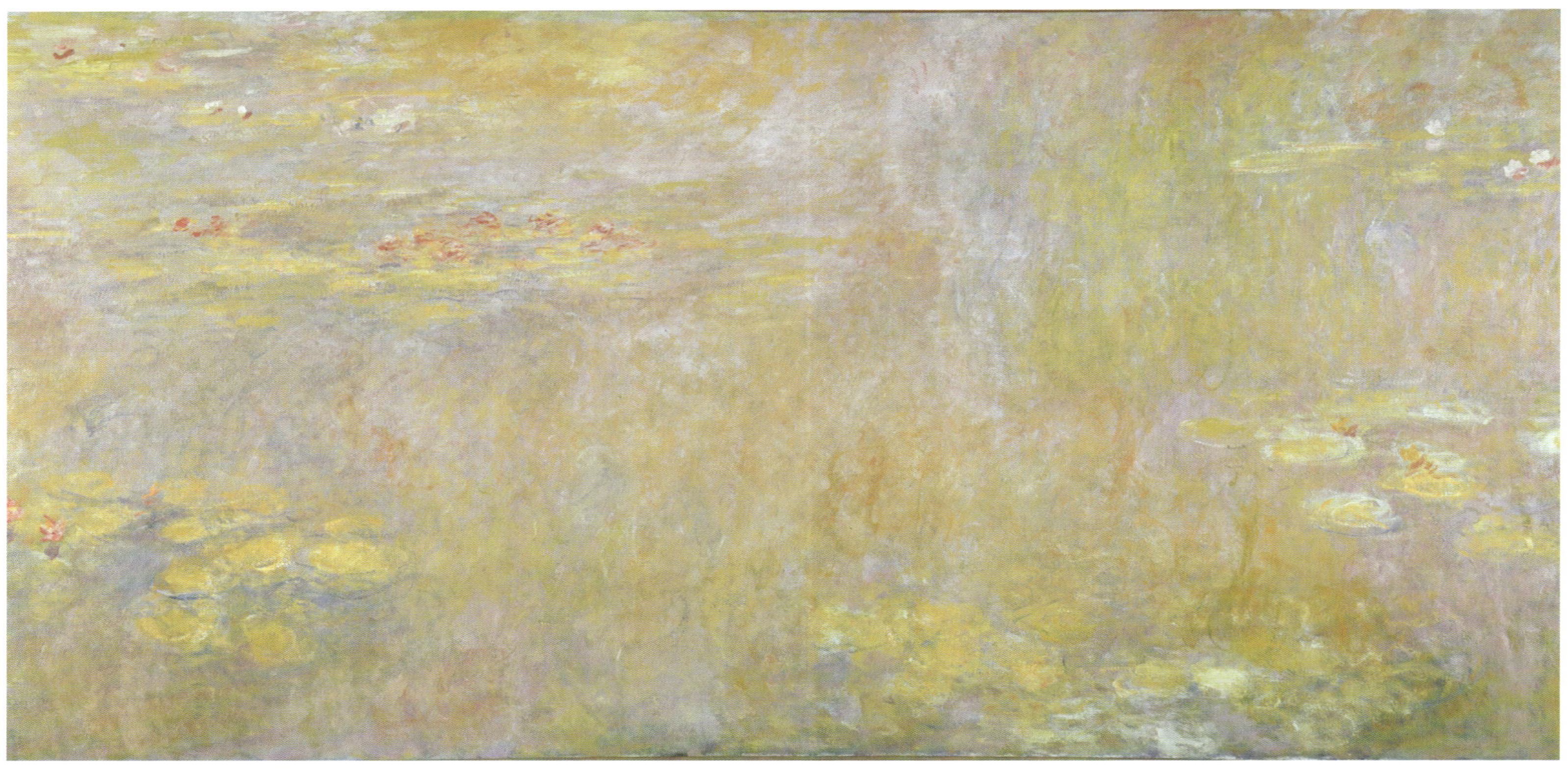

Fig. 63. Claude Monet, *Water Lilies*, after 1916. Oil on canvas, 79 x 168 in. (200.7 x 426.7 cm). National Gallery, London. Bought, 1963

II: Notions of Finish in the *Water Lilies*

I'm not performing miracles, I'm using up and wasting a lot of paint.

For the *Grandes Décorations*, Monet painted his water-lily garden on horizontal canvases all measuring about two meters in height but varying in width and in the number of panels per series. Of the forty-one canvases that survive, Monet selected twenty-two for the final installation of the cycle in the Orangerie. Working through his ideas by painting an abundance of canvases was central to Monet's creative process. The National Gallery's *Water Lilies* (fig. 63) was one such work painted for the Orangerie cycle and depicts water lilies floating on the pond with reflections of the sky and foliage mirrored on its surface. It is closely related in subject and composition to the well-known *Agapanthus Triptych* of 1915–26 (see fig. 73),[67] but it is characterized by a more muted color scheme, a different surface texture, and a densely worked-up level of finish. The total number of panels that Monet painted in preparation for the *Grandes Décorations* is unknown, since he repeatedly slashed and burned canvases that didn't measure up to his expectations.

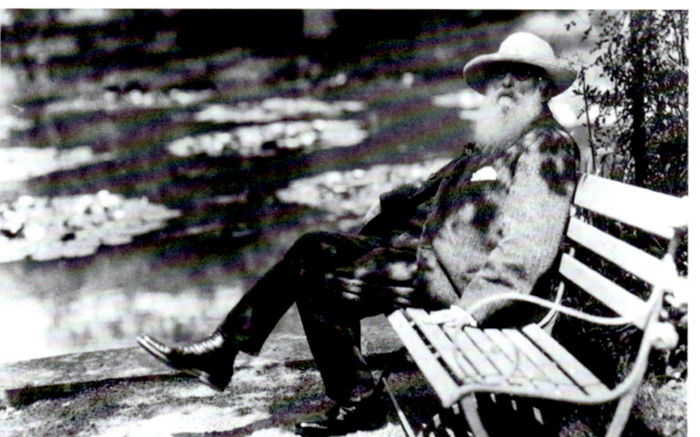

Fig. 66. Claude Monet beside the water-lily pond, summer 1926

In addition to the two-meter-high canvases, Monet explored the water-lily subject in a series of smaller horizontal canvases measuring approximately one by two meters—about one quarter the size of the Orangerie cycle panels. On April 30, 1918, Monet ordered twenty stretched horizontal canvases of this smaller format from Le Besnard, his Parisian supplier.[68] Similarly sized pictures still in existence include *Water Lilies* (fig. 64), in the collection of the Metropolitan Museum of Art, and *Water-Lily Pond* (fig. 65; cat. 25), in a private collection. These provide insights into the smaller-format series that Monet created of water lilies floating amidst mirrored

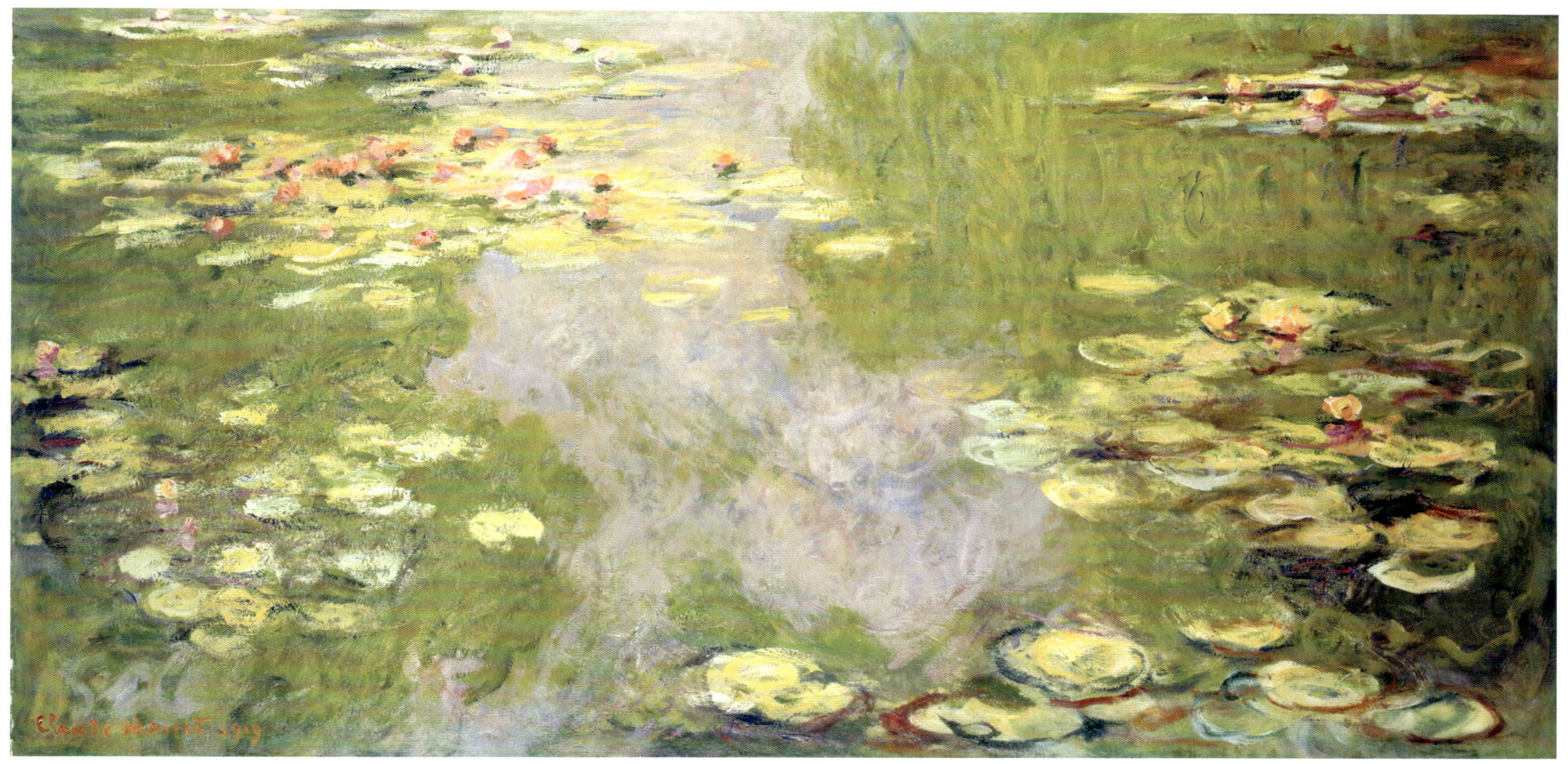

Fig. 64. Claude Monet, *Water Lilies*, 1919. Oil on canvas, 39 ¾ x 78 ¾ in. (101 x 200 cm). The Metropolitan Museum of Art, New York. The Walter H. and Lenore Annenburg Collection, Gift of Walter H. and Lenore Annenburg, 1998, Bequest of Walter H. Annenberg, 2002.

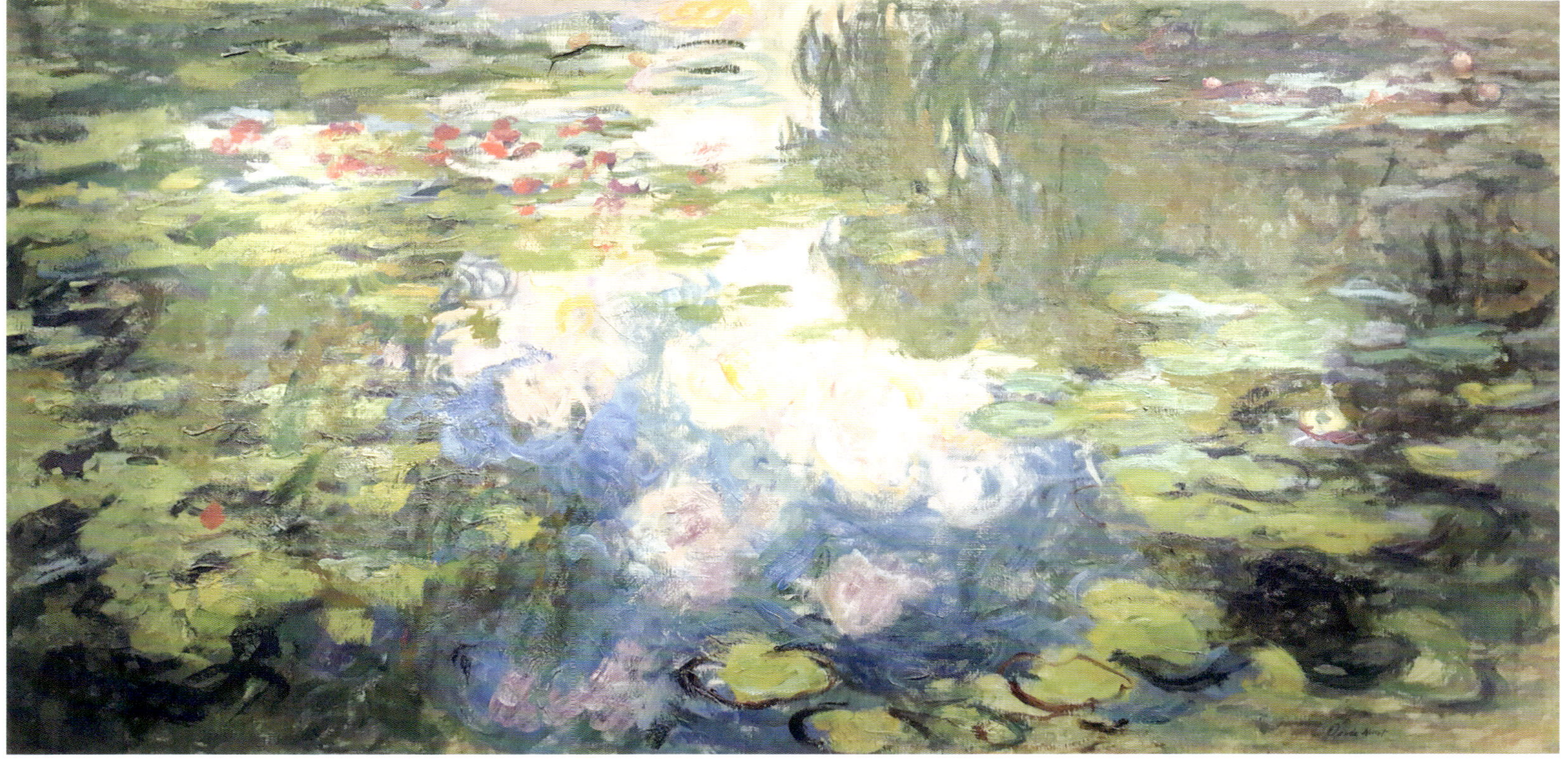

Fig. 65. Claude Monet, *Water-Lily Pond*, 1917–19. Oil on canvas, 39 3/8 x 78 3/4 in. (100 x 200 cm). Private collection. W1897. Cat. 25

reflections on the pond's surface. Monet signed and dated the Met's *Water Lilies* when he sold it, in 1919, to the Galerie Bernheim-Jeune. Other canvases from the series, including fig. 65, were left in varying states of finish in his studio at his death. Some were almost sketch-like in their execution, with large areas of untouched canvas, while others, more densely worked, could have served as preparatory studies for the *Grandes Décorations*.

Color

Typical of other Monet series, the three pictures being analyzed depict the same composition painted at different times of day and in diverse weather conditions, which is reflected by their distinct colors. It is impressive that Monet painted these canvases at a time when his worsening cataracts were impeding his color perception (fig. 66). He became more concerned about his color acuity than the clarity of his forms. He complained in 1918, "I no longer perceived color with the same intensity, I no longer painted light with the same accuracy. Red appeared muddy to me, pinks insipid, and the intermediate or lower tones escaped me. As for forms, they always appeared clear, and I rendered them with the same distinction."[69]

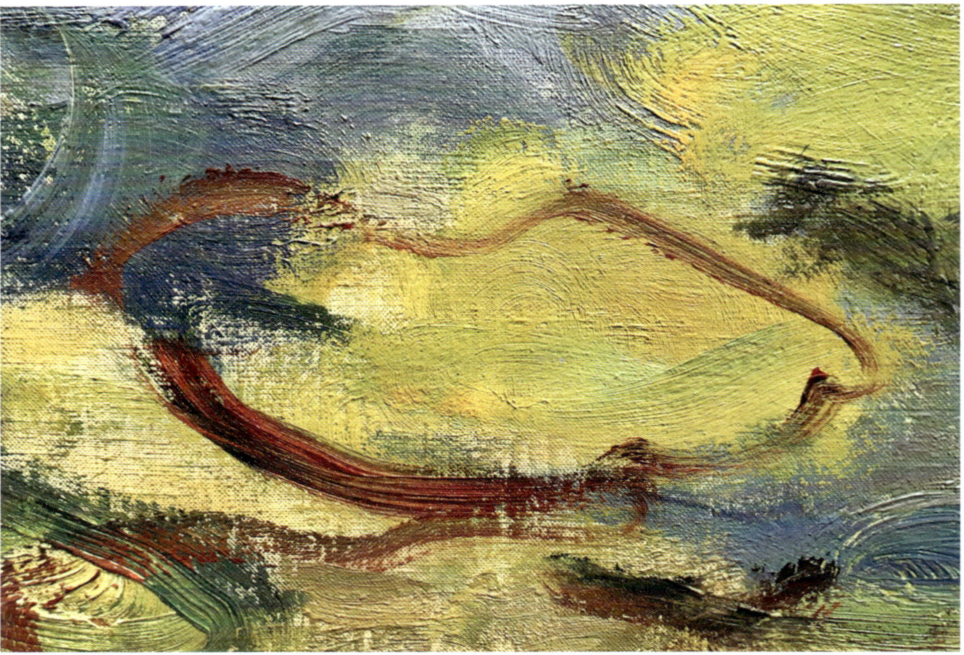

Fig. 67. Detail of lily-pad outlines in red lake in foreground of *Water-Lily Pond* (fig. 65)

The National Gallery's *Water Lilies* (fig. 63) is distinguished by its use of quiet pastel colors. The vibrant, fragmentary red dabs Monet applied for the water lilies in the upper left provide the brightest color accents. The panel imparts an overall foggy, vaporous atmosphere that Monet achieved by intentionally blurring the outlines of shapes reflected on the pond's surface. Its subdued, idiosyncratic coloring, coupled with its enormous size, suggests that the artist painted *Water Lilies* entirely indoors.

Water-Lily Pond (fig. 65) displays the most vivid colors and brightest reflections of the three paintings. The transient reflections of a sunny, blue sky with pink and yellow puffed clouds suggest that Monet painted this work out-of-doors, in the afternoon. Strong color contrasts and linear brushstrokes distinguish the thin, dangling leaves of the willow branches from clouds and other types of foliage mirrored on the water's surface. Monet adjusted hues to suggest the relative distance of the water-lily pads, using cooler shades to recede and warmer shades to advance. In the foreground, he outlined the lily pads in red lake to emphasize their close proximity to the viewer, while in the upper left he tinted them a cooler, pale green where they float beneath the shade of the weeping willow (fig. 67).

The artist expressed the physical presence of the sun-drenched water lilies in the upper left by pairing bold dabs and dashes of pure red for highlights with purple for shadows. He returned to cancel out some of the blooms with elongated strokes of green paint that convey the shifting position of the water-lily pads on the water's surface. Monet applied the green paint wet over dry, indicating that he had left sufficient drying time between laying in the blooms and adding the lily pads. By alternating strokes of pure green, blended yellow-green, or green and yellow paint mixed wet-in-wet on the brush, Monet employed a nuanced range of hues that expressed subtle distinctions between areas of light and shadow. After the yellow-green paint near the center of the image had dried, the artist partially concealed the water-lily pads with opaque applications of pale pink and blue paint to signify the shifting reflections of the bright, cloud-studded sky. Elsewhere the tangible forms of the water-lily pads superseded the reflections on the water's surface, floating above the dark green reflections near the pond's left bank and the pink and yellow clouds at center.

The dazzling lavender-blue reflections of the sky on the water's surface in the Met's *Water Lilies* inspires its rich, glowing colors. This distinctive lighting suggests that Monet began the painting outdoors in the late afternoon. Like *Water-Lily Pond*, the Met's painting exhibits sharp color distinctions that enhance the clarity of forms. In both works, Monet reinforced the shape of the water-lily pads using red lake outlines, but in the Met's *Water Lilies*—finished for sale—his handling of the green reflections and foliage is more nuanced. Monet reserved his brightest color for the water lilies in the upper left. Their red, coral, and gold tints, often mixed wet-in-wet on the brush and modulated with orchid-colored accents, reflect the oblique angle of the setting sun (fig. 68). Further back, Monet rendered a group of water lilies with cooler tints, mixing coral with white to suggest their relative distance. The artist created a dynamic interplay between the bright yellow lily pads that glimmer in the afternoon sun and the cooler green pads that appear in shadow (fig. 69). The reflection of the weeping willow at upper right, streaked with yellow, suggests the last rays of the afternoon sun highlighting its dangling branches.

Brushwork and Surface Texture

Contemplating his water-lily canvases, Monet once stated, "The crucial thing is the mirror of water, whose appearance changes constantly with the reflections of the sky."[70] Despite their shared compositions and artistic intentions, however, the surfaces of these three water-lily compositions represent completely different levels of paint application. Their close examination sheds light on Monet's variable ideas about finish. Throughout the development of these paintings, he focused his attention on the elliptical center field. The edges of the rectangular canvases were left unpainted until later stages. In the case of the Met's *Water Lilies*, as with the Kimbell's *Weeping Willow*, Monet filled the edges in with loosely applied, perfunctory brushwork before signing and dating the painting; similarly, he applied sketchy brushwork to the borders of *Water-Lily Pond* and the National Gallery's *Water Lilies* that matched each painting's general color but not its surface texture. In the absence of signature and date, the decision as to whether or not a painting is finished ultimately rested with Monet alone, but, as these cases suggest, his notions about completion seem always to have prioritized the central area of the painting. To Monet, the existence of unpainted or hastily filled-in edges were apparently insignificant details that didn't detract from his primary goal of capturing the ephemeral effects of light and color in his garden.

The National Gallery's *Water Lilies* has the most thickly layered and textured paint surface of these three examples. The heavily worked, opaque, encrusted surface completely obscures both the texture of the underlying canvas and the luminosity of the white ground. Monet built up successive layers of paint, applied wet over dry, over a prolonged period, allowing sufficient drying time between work sessions. The final surface reflects the texture of many underlying pentimenti—islands of leaves and flowers no longer visible underneath subsequent layers—evidence of the artist "using up and wasting a lot of paint." When Monet shifted the position of a water-lily pad, he made little effort to conceal his change of mind. Thus, the paint surface reflects not only the artist's final thoughts, but also his artistic process, recording his earlier struggles at capturing the transient appearance of light, color, and form. Monet's extensive use of lead white, a brittle paint, mixed into linseed oil, a fast-drying medium, in *Water Lilies* contributed to its encrusted, corrugated surface texture. As he selectively deposited new layers of paint

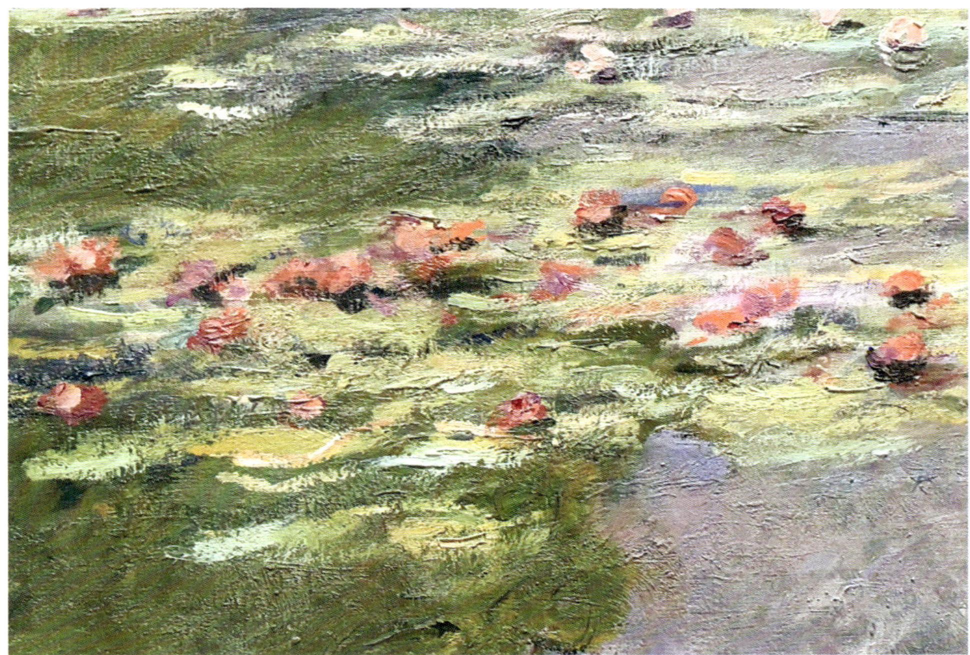

Fig. 68. Detail of wet-in-wet mixing of color in the Metropolitan Museum of Art's *Water Lilies* (fig. 64)

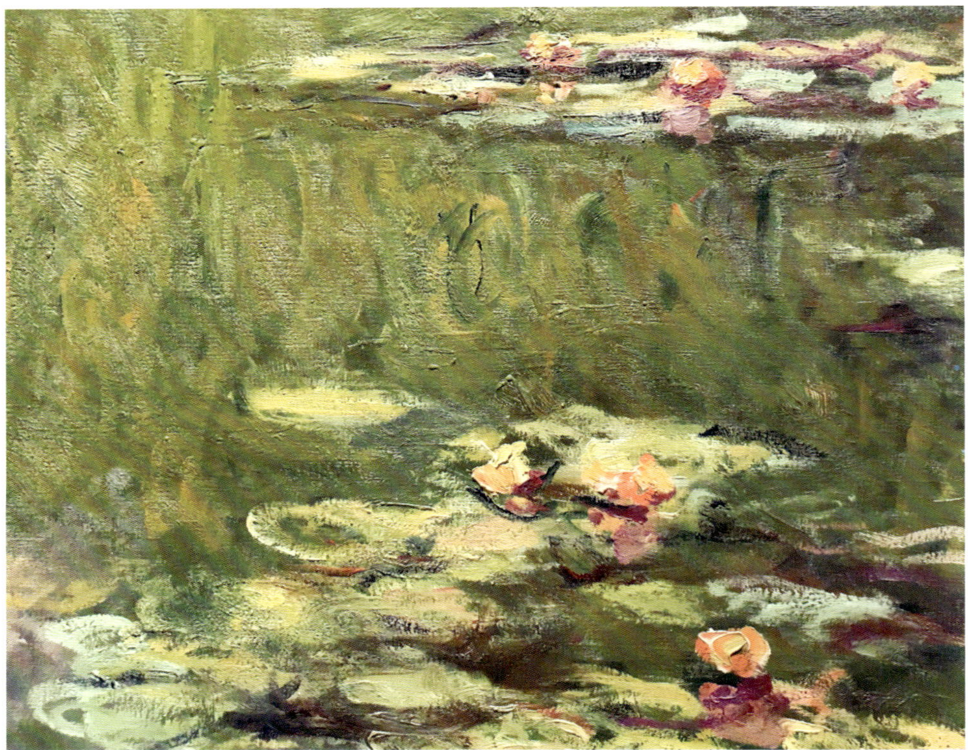

Fig. 69. Detail of the Metropolitan Museum of Art's *Water Lilies* (fig. 64) showing Monet's varied use of color in the water-lily pads to distinguish between light and shadow

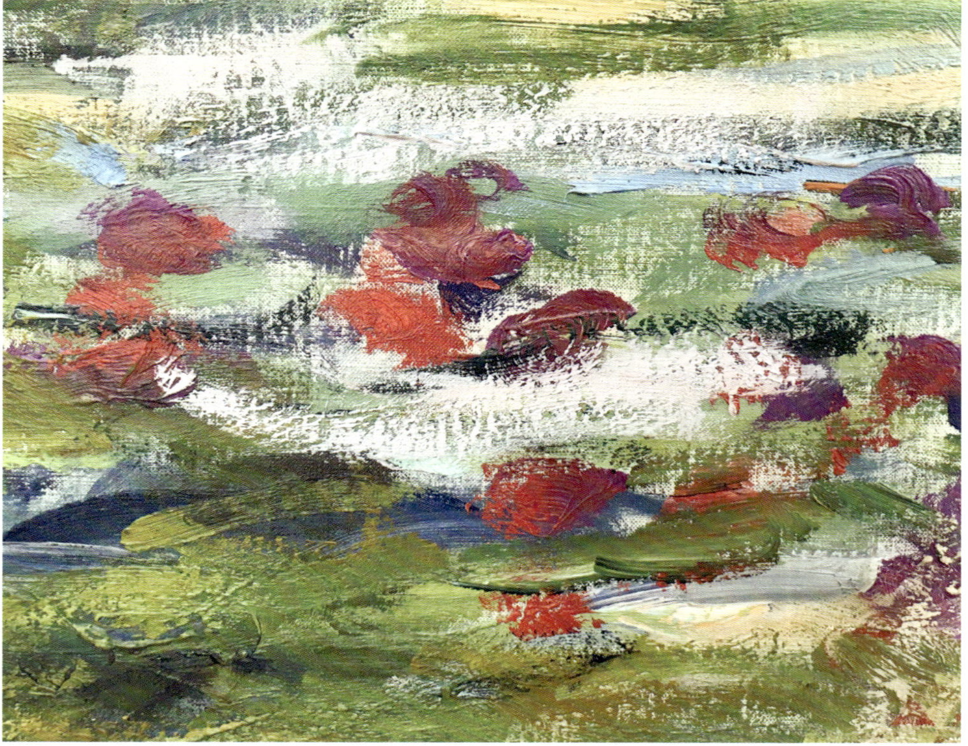

Fig. 70. Detail of *Water-Lily Pond* (fig. 65) reflecting the texture of canvas along with Monet's simple paint application for the water lilies

over the ridges of underlying brushstrokes, Monet built up a thickly ribbed texture that simultaneously suggests ripples of water on the pond's surface. His brushwork appears to carry additional meaning, as its distinctive texture transforms the paint surface into a low relief that catches light and casts shadow.

Whereas in the National Gallery's gigantic *Water Lilies* the artist intentionally obscured the boundaries between fleeting reflections and tangible matter, in the Met's more concentrated *Water Lilies* he used decisive, calligraphic brushwork to impart clarity to the forms captured in the bright afternoon sun. He placed equal emphasis on the physical presence of the water lilies and the transitory reflections of clouds and willow fronds on the pond's surface. However, he varied his facture to describe these different areas. The most heavily worked area of the paint surface surrounds the cluster of water lilies in the lower left, reflecting the build-up of numerous underlying pentimenti. But the eye is quickly drawn to the vivid hues of the crisply rendered water-lily blossoms, painted wet-in-wet, and the solid, graphic outlines of water-lily pads rendered in a rainbow of colors. These robust contours, imprinted with the bristles of Monet's brush, provide physical evidence of the force with which he applied these brushstrokes. He altered his technique, however, to portray the reflection of the lavender sky at the pond's center. Using dry brushwork that crumbled into tiny fragments as it was pulled across the underlying paint, he layered a swirling web of rose, lavender, and blue tints. Monet's choice of imprecise, whirling brushwork for the reflection creates the impression of clouds in motion. The elusive quality of these brushstrokes contrasts sharply with his decisive, thickly impastoed treatment of the water lilies.

The freshness of the surface of *Water-Lily Pond* exhibits the free, loose qualities of a large oil sketch. Nevertheless, it displays all the key components of other, more "finished" water-lily canvases in its portrayal of light, color, and reflections on its "mirror of water." Monet roughly blocked in much of the composition, leaving areas of the white ground and the tooth of the weave canvas exposed. Together, they form an integral part of the final image, emphasizing the physical presence of the canvas support (figs. 70, 71). The artist abstained from describing the water lilies in any detail, often rendering their forms using just a single color and simple dab of paint (fig. 70). Instead, he seemed to focus on the brilliant reflection on the water's surface at the center of the composition: the bright blue sky strewn with pink, yellow, and lavender clouds (fig. 71). He energized this area with swirling, imprecise brushstrokes that provide an effective contrast to the linear brushstrokes used for the reflection of dangling willow fronds at upper right. For all the sketchiness of the overall image, however, Monet achieved incredible textural variety in his manipulation of paint. Tendrils of impasto exist alongside dry brushstrokes that break up over areas of exposed canvas and thickly impastoed paint (fig. 71). Once again, the artist invested surface texture with meaning. By manipulating his brushwork, he distinguished between palpable and transitory forms.

Conclusion

Despite the challenges Monet faced towards the end of his career—the death of his wife and son, the tumult of war, the threats to his eyesight—he chose not to stagnate but continued to push himself as a working artist. As these limited case studies illuminate, the artist's late painting technique exhibited extraordinary flexibility in paint handling and invention. The different notions of finish reflected in these works were driven both by the intended purpose of each particular canvas (easel painting versus étude versus *Grandes Décorations*) and by Monet's response to the water-lily pond under fluctuating conditions of light, weather, season, and time of day. Thus, a more sketchily rendered painting, such as *The Water-Lily Pond* (fig. 65) could be considered as fully resolved as the more thoroughly worked *Water Lilies* (figs. 63, 64): in both, Monet successfully captured the color of light and transient reflections mirrored on the water's surface. Restricting his subject matter to his Giverny garden, itself a work of art of his own invention, Monet prioritized ephemeral qualities such as light and color over tangible forms. He appropriated the garden's flowers, trees, and water-lily pond to facilitate serious investigations of color, light, and reflection and to test the very limits of painting nature itself.

In challenging himself to depict the variable appearance of color in natural light, Monet adapted his practice. Seeking greater permanence of color, he altered his palette in his late years to adopt new, chemically stable pigments as they appeared on the market. However, Monet's late works emphasize the materiality of the paint as well as its color. The artist employed texture— including the use of exposed areas of primed canvas, visible pentimenti, and the layering of impastoed brushstrokes—to create distinct surfaces that worked hand in hand with color to describe the transient effects of light in nature. Monet's ambition to create *Grandes Décorations* for France was not achieved without years of struggle, worry, and self-criticism, in which the artist attacked and destroyed numerous paintings that fell short of his exacting standards. Monet's own modest description of his late technique—"I'm not performing miracles, I'm using up and wasting a lot of paint"—while hinting at his relentless ambition, belies the astonishing degree of technical inventiveness that he achieved in the last years of a long and storied career.

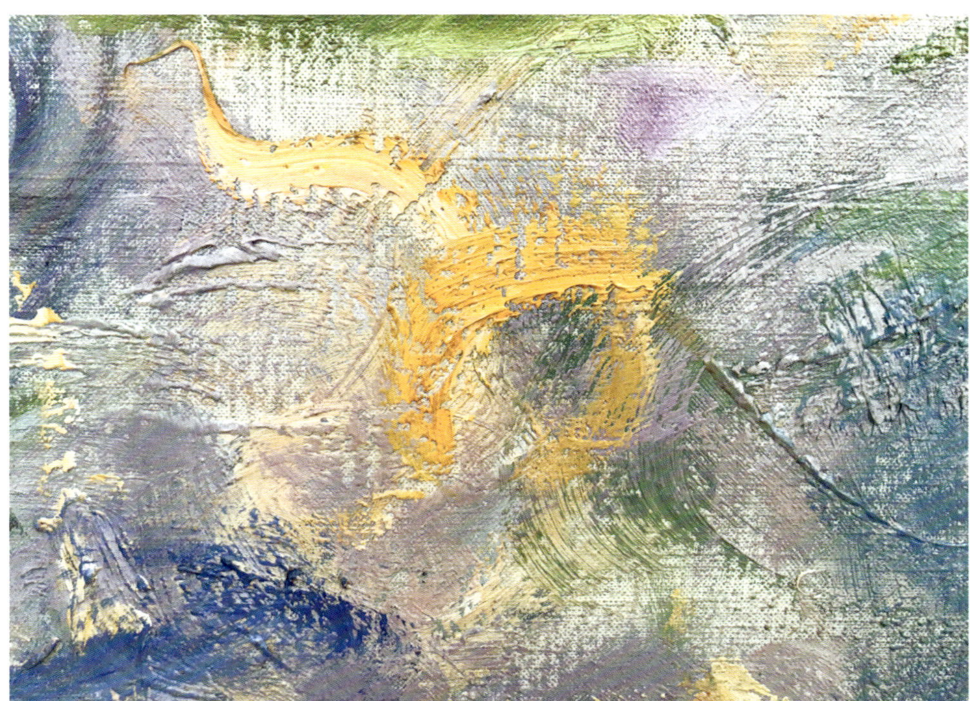

Fig. 71. Detail of *Water-Lily Pond* (fig. 65) reflecting the variety of Monet's paint application and the role of the canvas in the final surface

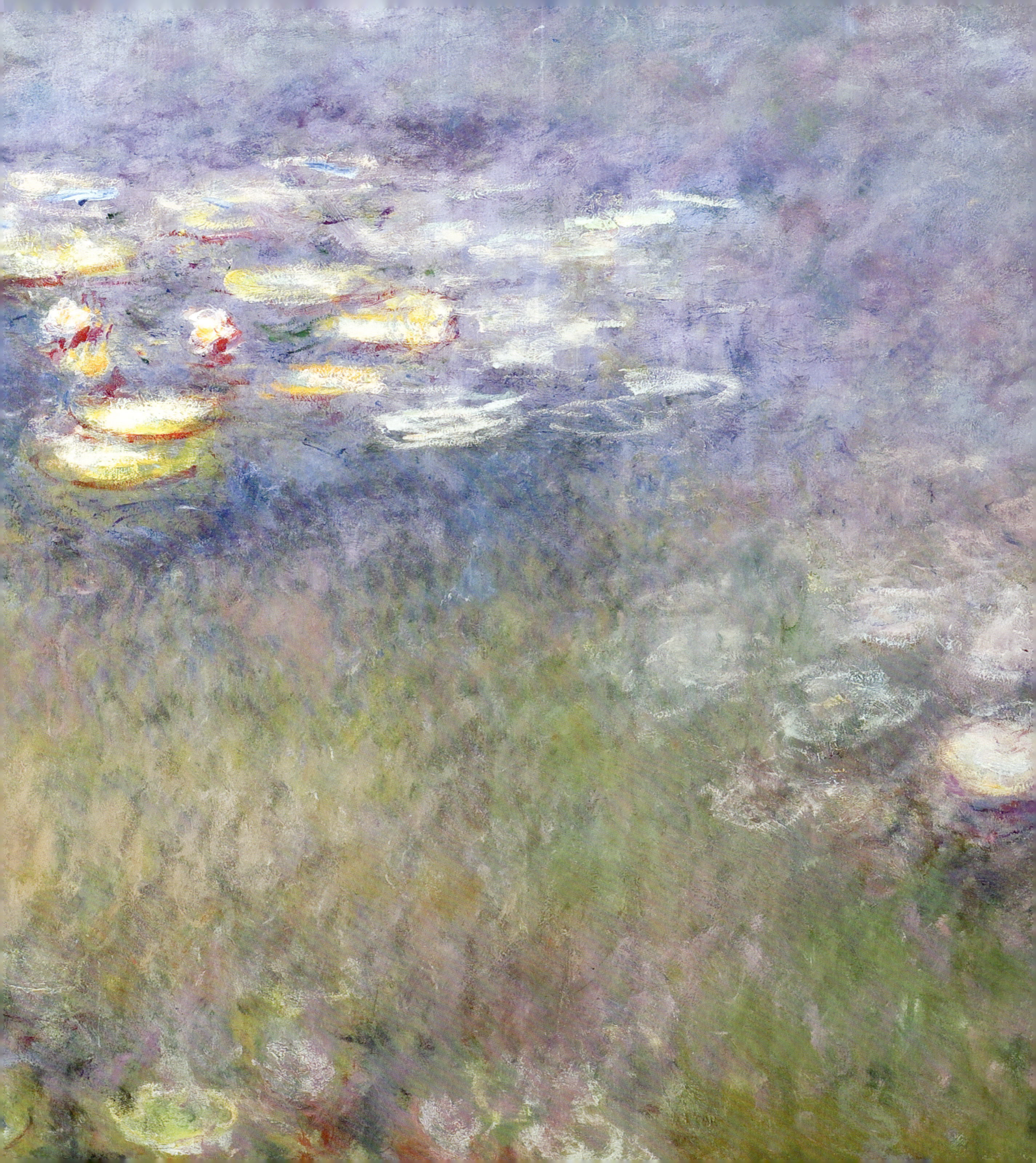

"My four best series": Monet's Panorama at the Hôtel Biron

Simon Kelly

Curator of modern and contemporary art, Saint Louis Art Museum

On his eightieth birthday, on November 14, 1920, Claude Monet told his aristocratic visitor, the Duc de Trévise, "I am bequeathing my four best series to the French State."[1] These twelve works from his *Grandes Décorations* paintings—the quadriptych, *Three Willows*, the triptychs, *Agapanthus* and *Clouds*, and the diptych, *Green Reflections*—represented the culmination of his painterly career (figs. 72–75).[2] They were photographed soon after for a forthcoming biography of Monet (figs. 76–79).[3] In the months and years to come, the precise number and configuration of canvases in Monet's gift would change, but the artist's commitment to the conditions of their installation remained constant. He had always been fascinated with creating decorative ensembles of his work. He thought, for example, of his *Grainstacks*, installed at the Durand-Ruel gallery in 1891, as a complementary whole rather than as individual paintings. Following the gift of his twelve panels, Monet focused on the project for a purpose-built rotunda to house these works (fig. 80). The critic Arsène Alexandre described this as a "Monet Museum."[4] It was to be constructed on the grounds of the Hôtel Biron as a counterpoint to the museum of works by the sculptor Auguste Rodin already there.[5] Monet's panels were to be installed in a panoramic space that would have looked forward to secular chapels like those of Mark Rothko in Houston—a building virtually the same size—or Ellsworth Kelly in San Antonio.[6] Although the project never came to fruition, it showcased a more inventive and ambitious approach to decoration than would be the case with the ultimate installation of his panels in the existing building of the Orangerie. In particular, it engaged with the important tradition of the panorama and, in effect, offered a blueprint for the reinvention of this medium.[7]

Recent decades have seen a growing interest in the medium of the panorama and its many possible meanings.[8] Michel Foucault explored the panoramic gaze as an instrument of social control in his work on the related prison structure, the panopticon.[9] Vanessa Schwartz has emphasized the panorama's central role within Parisian

Claude Monet, *Water Lilies* (detail), c. 1915–26, cat. 28

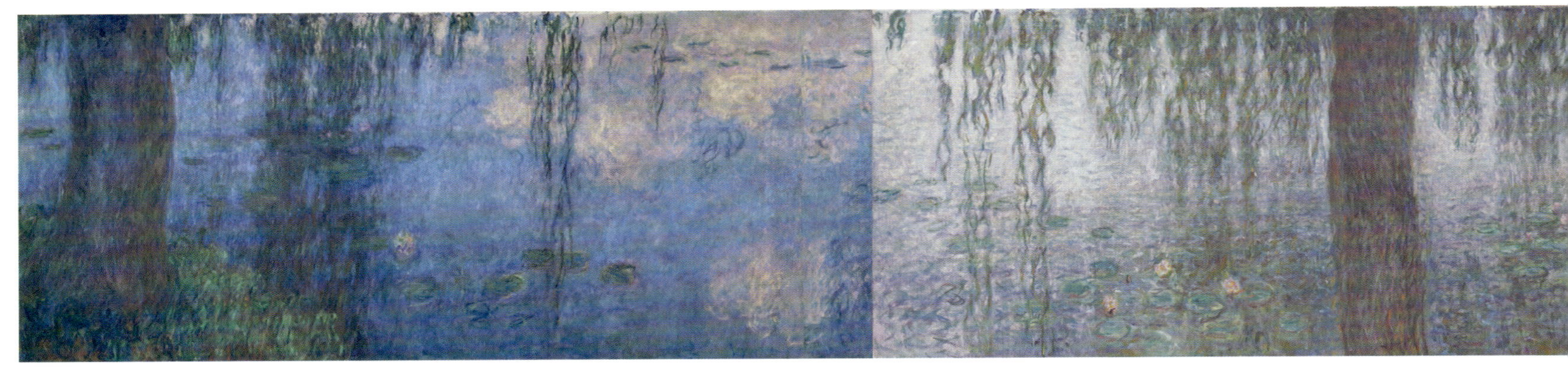

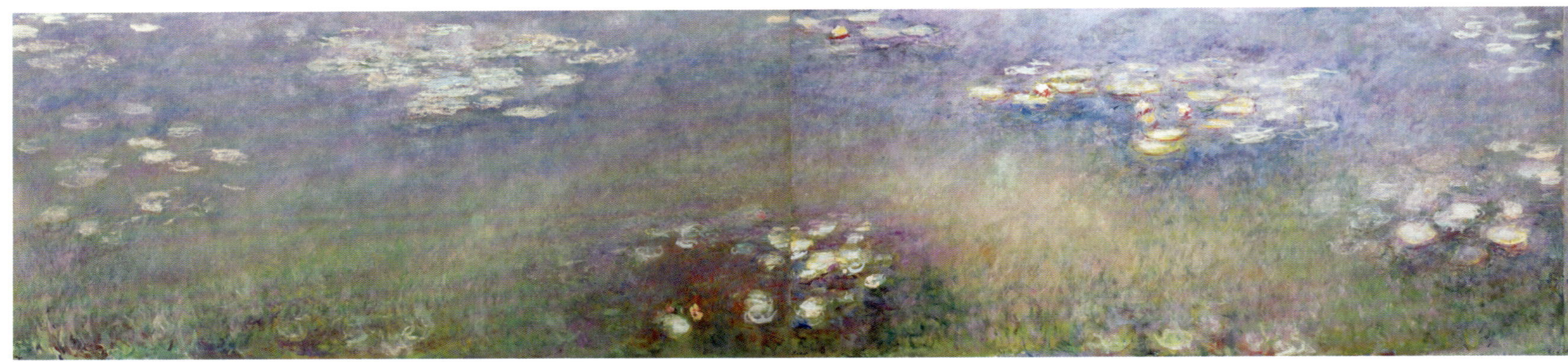

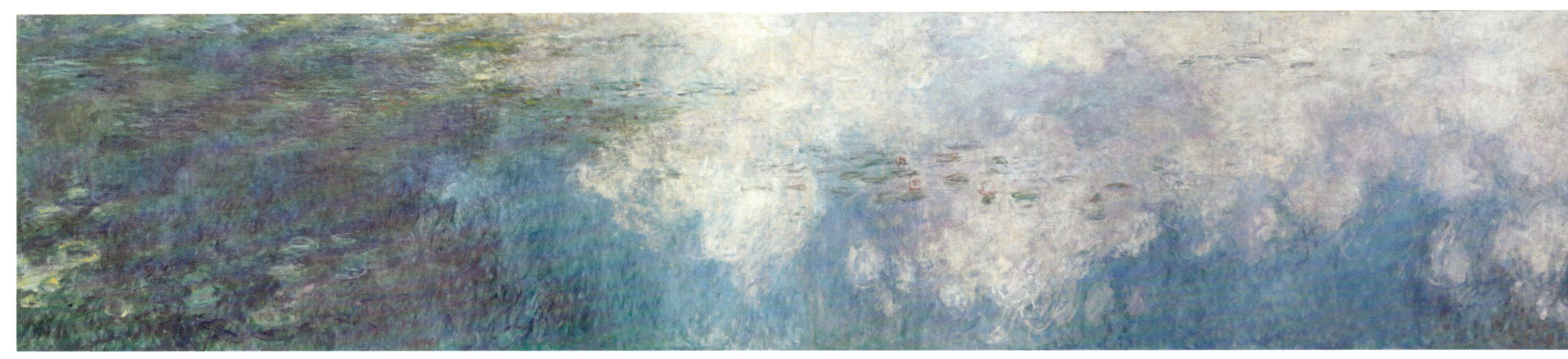

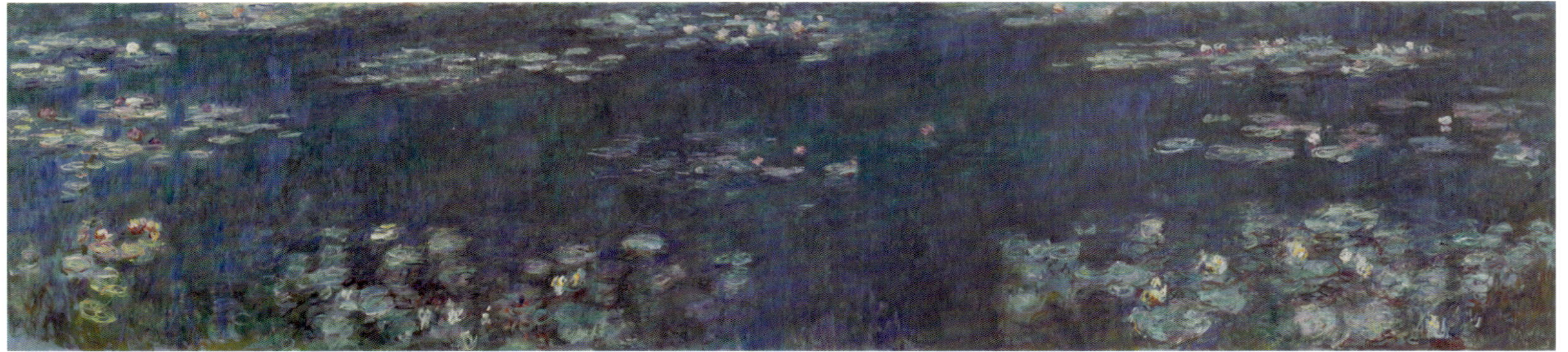

Fig. 75. Claude Monet, *Green Reflections* diptych (*Water Lilies: Green Reflections*), c. 1915–26. Oil on canvas, 78 ¾ x 334 ⅝ in. (200 x 850 cm). Room 1, east wall, Musée de l'Orangerie, Paris

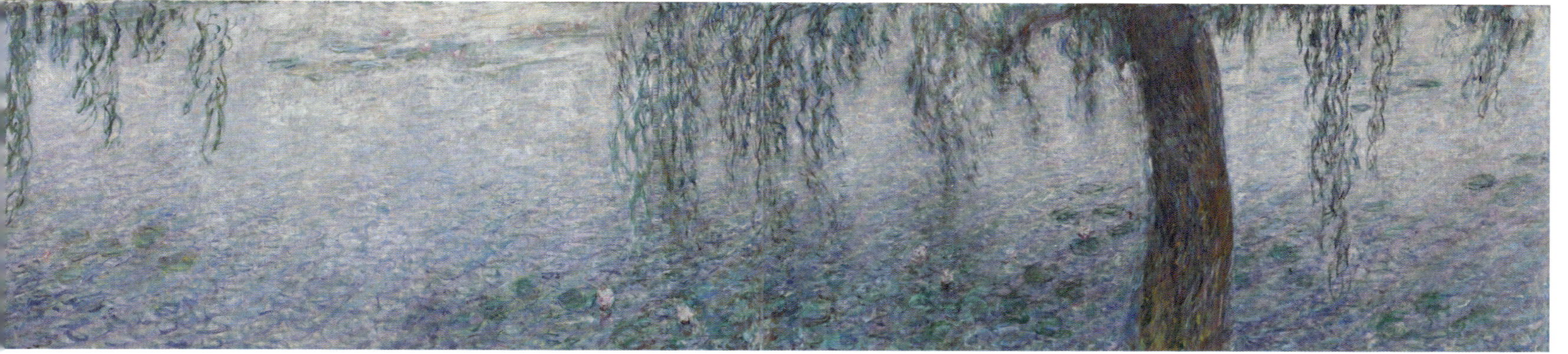

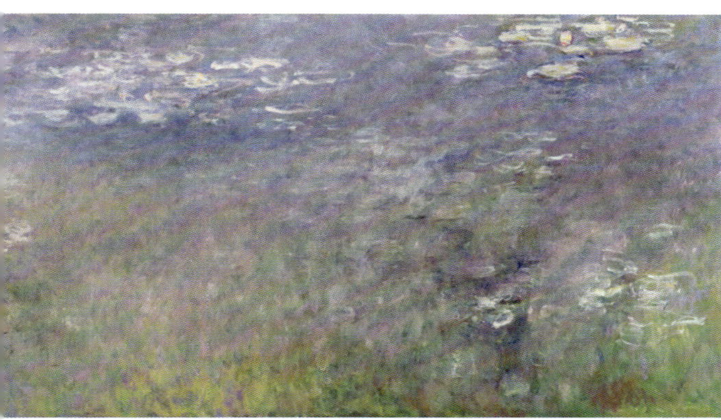

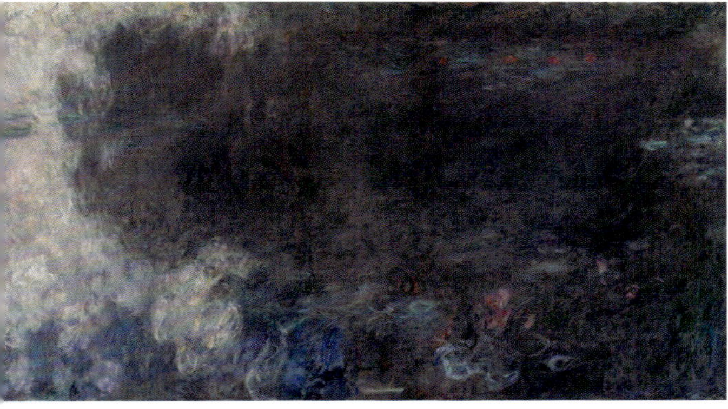

Fig. 72. Claude Monet, *Three Willows* quadriptych, composed of *Water Lilies: Morning with Willows* (left panel of triptych), c. 1915–26. Oil on canvas, 78 ¾ x 167 ¼ in. (200 x 425 cm). Room 2, north wall, Musée de l'Orangerie, Paris; and *Waterlilies: Clear Morning with Willows*, c. 1915–26. Oil on canvas, 78 ¾ x 502 in. (2 x 12.75 m). Room 2, south wall, Musée de l'Orangerie, Paris

Fig. 73. Claude Monet, *Agapanthus* triptych, composed of *Water Lilies (Agapanthus)*, c. 1915–26. Oil on canvas, 79 ¼ x 167 5/8 in. (201.3 x 425.6 cm). Cleveland Museum of Art. John L. Severance Fund and an anonymous gift, 1960.81; *Water Lilies*, c. 1915–26. Oil on canvas, 78 ¾ x 167 ¾ in. (200 x 426 cm). Saint Louis Art Museum. The Steinberg Charitable Fund, 134:1956; and *Water Lilies*, c. 1915–26. Oil on canvas, 78 ¾ x 167 ½ in. (200 x 425.4 cm). The Nelson-Atkins Museum of Art, Kansas City. Purchase: William Rockhill Nelson Trust, 57-26

Fig. 74. Claude Monet, *Clouds* triptych (*Water Lilies: Clouds*), c. 1915–26. Oil on canvas, 78 ¾ x 502 in. (2 x 12.75 m). Room 1, north wall, Musée de l'Orangerie, Paris

popular culture and spectacle in the final decades of the nineteenth century.[10] The panorama has been seen, too, as anticipating today's virtual reality by way of its creation of a controlled, immersive space.[11] In the last third of the nineteenth century, Paris was the world capital of the panorama, with numerous examples of the medium across the city. Highly illusionistic battle paintings—often from the Franco-Prussian War (1870–71)—were particularly popular. Monet would have had firsthand experience of the medium, notably the Panorama Reichshoffen (figs. 81 and 82), which occupied a large rotunda alongside the building that housed the seventh Impressionist exhibition in 1882. This re-created a battle from the Franco-Prussian War on an enormous scale, with a circumference of 328 feet, a diameter of 98 feet, and height of 41 feet. Its illusionism was increased by wax simulacra of dead soldiers placed on the ground between the spectators' viewing platform and the canvases. The memory of such a building undoubtedly provided a conceptual and architectural framework for Monet as he planned his own decorative space, even as he emphasized the difference of his own installation.

Monet's earliest documented interest in a decorative panorama for his *Water Lilies* came in 1897. The journalist Maurice Guillemot noted that he wanted to create "a round room whose walls . . . would be entirely occupied by a horizon of water spotted with these plants, walls of a transparency by turns green and mauve, the calm and the silence of dead waters reflecting the spread-out blooms."[12] Just over a decade later, Monet himself amplified this vision, imagining a drawing room decorated by a continuous grouping of water-lily paintings. "Carried along the length of the walls, enveloping the entire interior with its unity, it would produce the illusion of an endless whole, of a watery surface with no horizon and no shore."[13] Monet experimented with configurations of his paintings at Giverny. When the dealer René Gimpel visited in 1918, he found an arrangement of a group of Monet's mid-size water-lily pictures, "a dozen canvases placed one after another in a circle on the ground, all about six feet wide by four feet high, a panorama of water and water lilies, of light and sky."[14] Photographs of Monet's large Giverny studio also show his *Grandes Décorations* on casters that enabled the artist to move them around to form different arrangements.

On September 27, 1920, in a conversation with the directeur des Beaux-Arts, Paul Léon, Monet agreed to give his aforementioned twelve panels to the French state. The politician Georges Clémenceau, a friend of the artist, had been instrumental in prompting Monet to make this gift. It was accompanied by the proviso that the State would finance the construction of a building specially to house the paintings. Monet noted to the dealer Georges Bernheim, "they'll have to build the room as I want it, according to my plan, and the pictures will leave my house only when I am satisfied with the arrangements . . . I've painted these

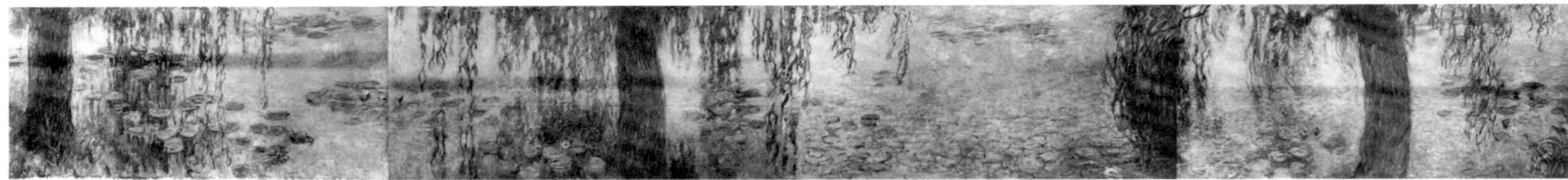

Fig. 76. Claude Monet, *Three Willows* quadriptych, photographed by André Marty for the Bernheim-Jeune gallery, February 1921

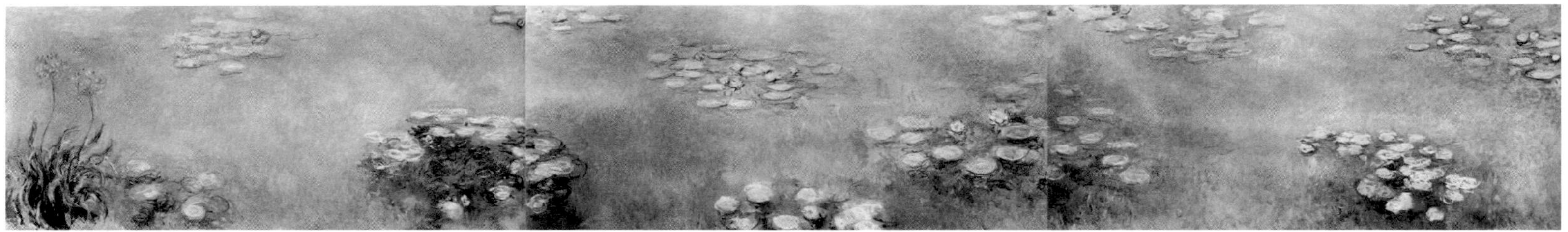

Fig. 77. Claude Monet, *Agapanthus* triptych, photographed by André Marty for the Bernheim-Jeune gallery, February 1921

Fig. 78. Claude Monet, *Clouds* triptych, photographed by André Marty for the Bernheim-Jeune gallery, February 1921

Fig. 79. Claude Monet, *Green Reflections*, photographed by André Marty for the Bernheim-Jeune gallery, February 1921. Two of these three canvases seem to have been used for the *Green Reflections* diptych.

pictures with a certain decorative aim, and I want it to be attained."[15] Monet added, "They will build on the Boulevard des Invalides side, where there is more daylight, and even there I'll be up against the light which has always defeated me." Monet was always thinking about the importance of natural light for his space, and he imagined the siting of his building in the northwest corner of the Hôtel Biron grounds, where it would receive morning light from the east across the open expanses of the gardens. The notion of a "Monet museum" alongside a "Rodin museum" was one that Monet wanted, aware as he was of constructing his legacy. He had long admired Rodin, the greatest French sculptor of the day, and the two men's joint retrospective exhibition, organized by the dealer Georges Petit years before, in 1889, had first secured Monet's national and international reputation. The men even nearly shared a birth date—they were born two days apart in November 1840.

Monet insisted that he should choose the architect for the building at the Hôtel Biron and picked out his friend Louis Bonnier, a well-known figure who had been made architect of the city of Paris in 1884 at the age of only twenty-eight.[16] Bonnier subsequently made his name with his Art Nouveau structures in the 1890s. He produced innovative designs, most notably a 200-foot-high structure with a spiraling ramp surrounding an enormous globe of the earth, which enabled visitors to imaginatively travel from the South Pole to the North Pole (fig. 83). This gave visual form to the ideas of the radical geographer Elisée Reclus but was ultimately never built. Another project, a bright red, modernist dome, housing Schneider armaments, shocked the public at the 1900 World's Fair. Bonnier was known for his use of new materials such as reinforced concrete. His architecture indeed represented a crucial link between Art Nouveau and the later constructions of Le Corbusier. Bonnier's avant-garde credentials were also evident in his network of artist friends, including the Belgian neo-Impressionist Théo van Rysselberghe, who painted his portrait (fig. 84), and the writer André Gide, whose villa at Montmorency he designed.

In 1920, Monet had known Bonnier for more

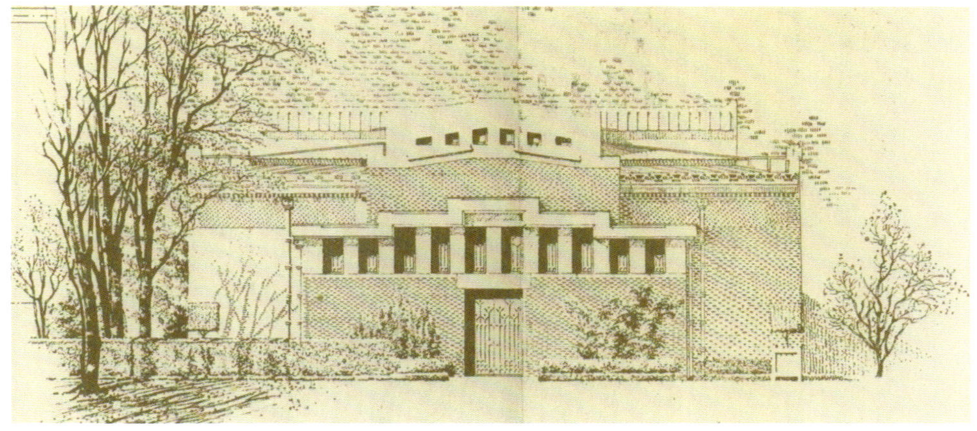

Fig. 80. Louis Bonnier, façade of Monet's pavilion, from the proposal "Pilot study for an exhibition pavilion to house a series of canvases by Monsieur Claude Monet," 1920. Archives nationales, France

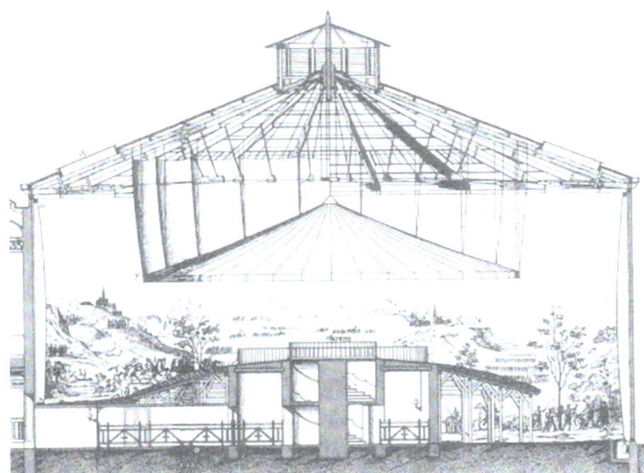

Fig. 81. Section of the Panorama Reichshoffen, 1882

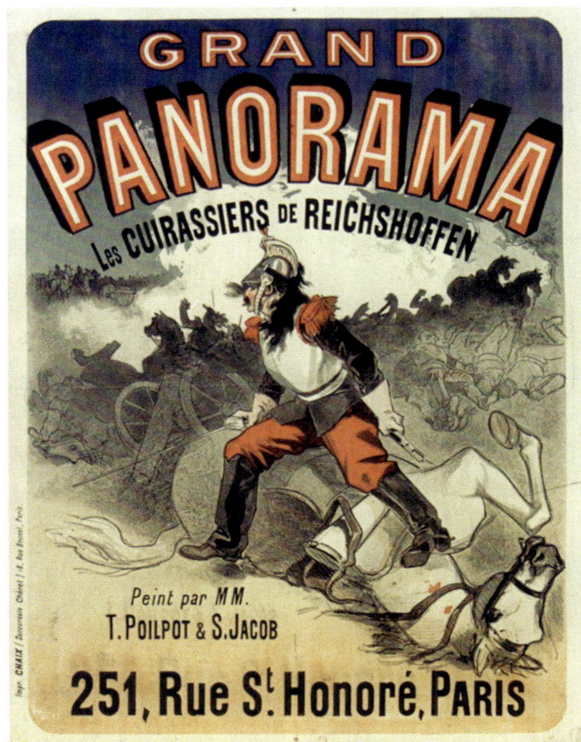

Fig. 82. "Grand Panorama: Les Cuirassiers de Reichshoffen," inaugural poster, 1881. Bibliothèque nationale de France, Paris

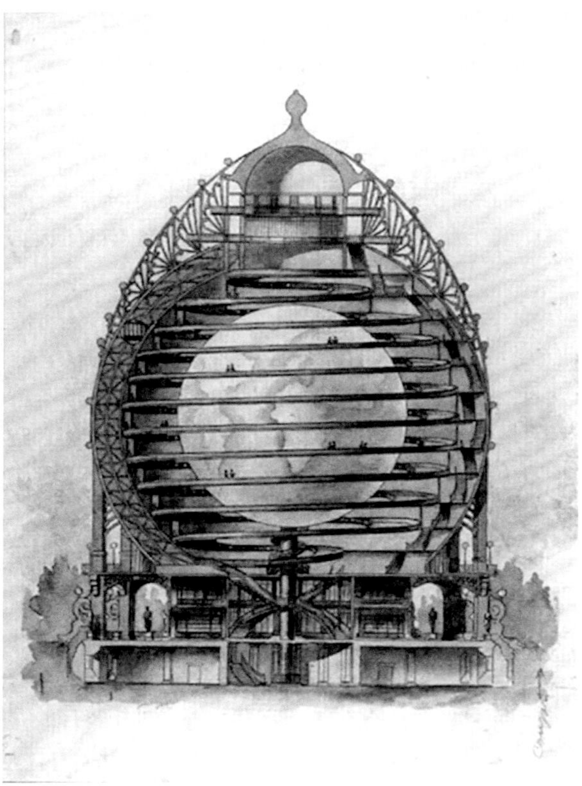

Fig. 83. Louis Bonnier, design for geographer Elisée Reclus's "Great Globe," c. 1897–98

than twenty years, having met him through the intermediary of his friend Ferdinand Deconchy, a landscape painter and Bonnier's brother-in-law.[17] Both Monet and Bonnier were independent figures and outsiders to the artistic establishment. Bonnier shunned the members of the Institut, while Monet refused the offer of entry to the same body.[18] Monet benefited from Bonnier's advice for the construction of his second studio at Giverny in 1899.[19] He again sought the architect's council for the building of his third studio space in 1915, sending three unpublished letters in which he was particularly concerned with the heating, intent as he was on working year-round on his *Grandes Décorations*.[20] Monet's involvement with Bonnier on this large, sky-lit studio with blind walls provided helpful context for their subsequent collaboration.

Monet and Bonnier first met to discuss the rotunda project at Giverny on October 3, 1920.[21] The artist wanted an elliptical building, with his paintings displayed in an oval space, and he remained committed to this.[22] Why did Monet want an oval? He never fully explained his reasons, but it is probable that he was seeking an original space that complicated and subverted the more conventional circular form of the traditional panorama. Throughout his career, Monet always wanted to differentiate his output from his peers. In this oval space, he seems to have wanted to explore in novel ways the effects of color, light, and space on perception. Bonnier, for his part, noted that an elliptical building would be expensive, involving "formidable costs."[23] Within two days, the architect had produced his first plans for the pavilion (unfortunately now lost) based on the artist's input.[24] The initial cost estimate for the 6,587-square-foot building was a substantial 790,000 francs.[25]

Monet's choice of panels was carefully thought out. According to Bonnier, the 56-foot-long *Three Willows* and the diptych, *Green Reflections*, were intended to be opposite each other on the two long walls of the oval (figs. 76, 79).[26] On the sides to left and right with the tighter curvature would be the two triptychs, *Clouds* and *Agapanthus* (figs. 77–78). We do not know the angle of the curvature of the ellipse, but it seems to have been quite subtle. The critic, Arsène Alexandre, a frequent visitor to Monet's studio, recorded a slightly different configuration of the panels in the most poetic description of the potential pavilion space. Alexandre, who was in the midst of writing Monet's biography, wrote that, at either extremity of the oval, would be the "diptych in blue" of *Green Reflections* and the "molten gold" of *Agapanthus*.[27] On the longer sides would be the *Clouds*, "silver and pink, of all the most tender freshness of morning" and the *Three Willows*, with its expanses of water and trunks rising "like dark votive columns."[28] From what we can infer of the color of these panels at this time, based on Alexandre's description, André Marty's photographs for Monet's biography (figs. 76–79), and technical analysis, Monet seems to have been experimenting with the placement of paintings on the longer walls with receding cooler blues.[29] On the shorter axes were panels with warmer and stronger colors and a greater number of flower blooms, which would have advanced in the visitor's sight. Monet may even have wanted to suggest—playfully—a circular space by the contrasting effects of these pictures. Alexandre emphasized that the low hanging of works just above the floor would enhance the immersive effect of the installation on the spectator, who would be "plunged fully into the great artist's passion for color and hundredfold dream."[30] Monet

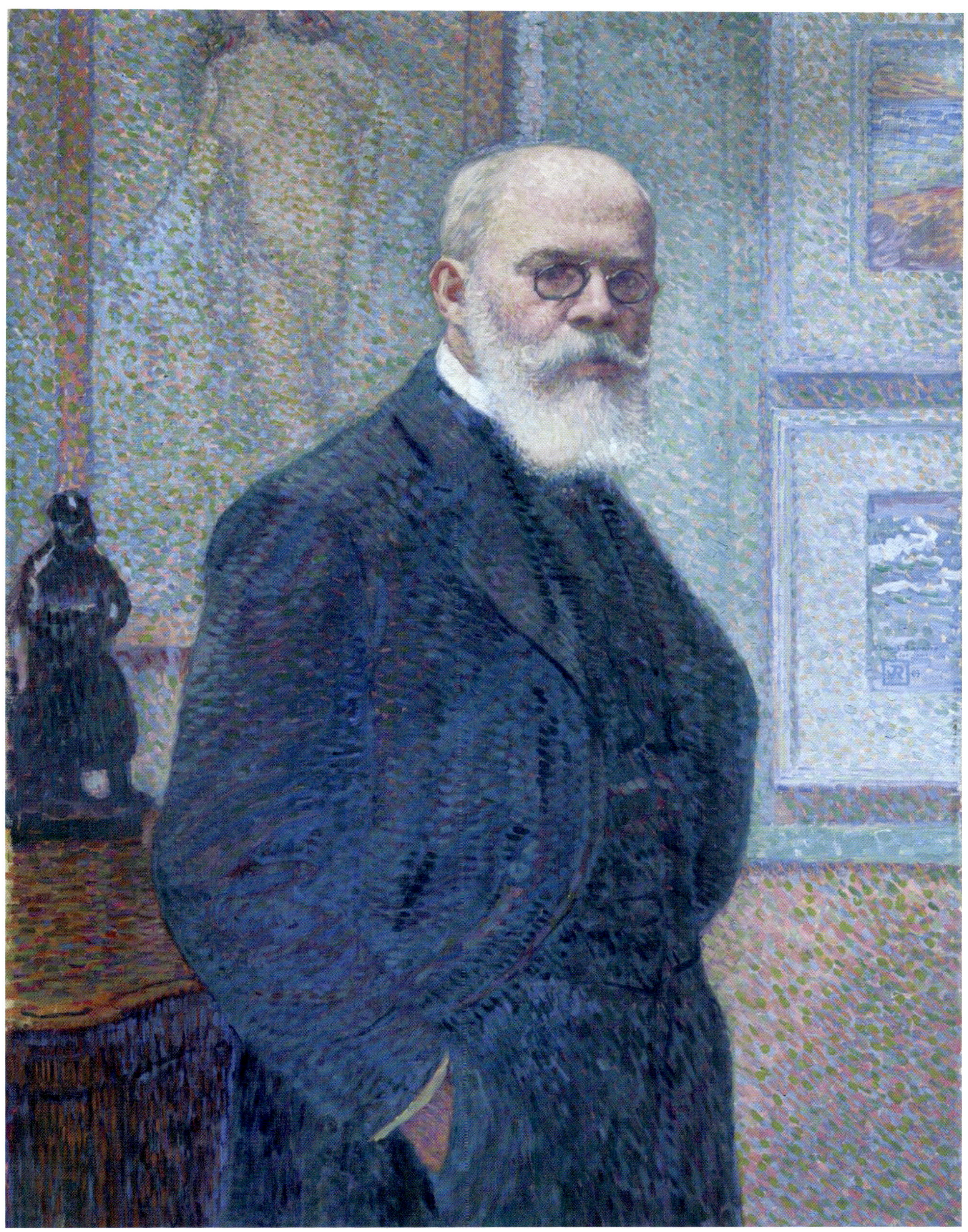

Fig. 84. Theodore van Rysselberghe, *Louis Bonnier*, 1903. Oil on canvas, 39 x 29 in. (100 x 73.5 cm). Museum of Fine Arts, Boston. Mary L. Cornille and John F. Cogan, Jr. Fund for the Art of Europe

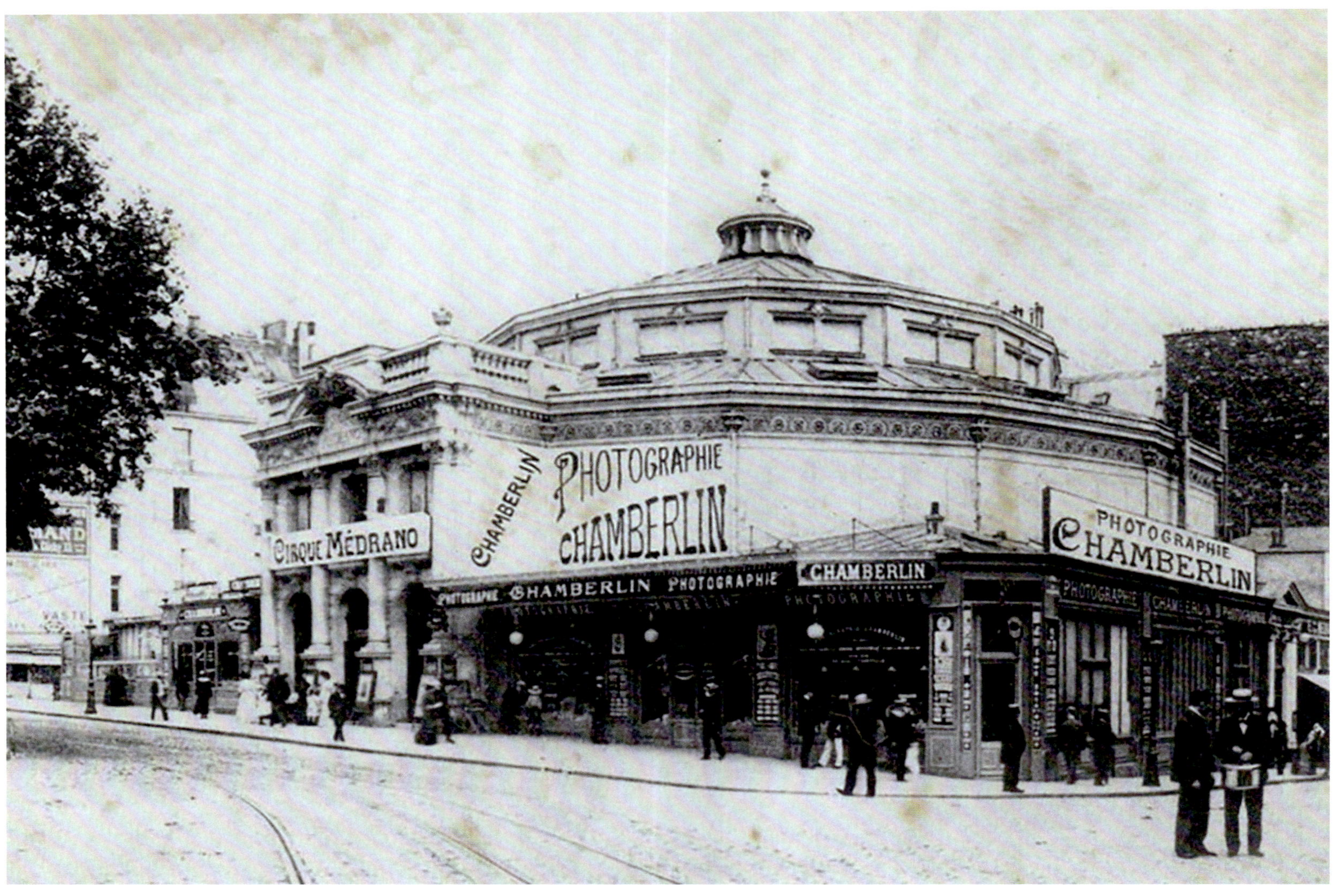

Fig. 85. The Cirque Médrano, Paris, c. 1898

was particularly pleased by Alexandre's review and wrote to the critic: "Your article is very beautiful."[31]

Another writer, the journalist François Thiébault-Sisson, who also visited Monet frequently at Giverny, offered further information on the installation.[32] He provided the first mention of additional "decorative motifs" that would be placed above gaps between the four series, as well as the installation of a "large composition" in the entry vestibule.[33] Thiébault-Sisson described a panorama of panels, placed alongside each other "to give the impression of a single canvas" and wrote that their color was "characterized by dark blue, pink and white, and green and gold harmonies."[34] He also employed the conceit of the spectator experiencing the effect of being on the island at the center of Monet's water-lily pond, surrounded by water. One of the reasons for Monet's attraction to an oval space may, indeed, have been its resemblance to his actual pond at Giverny.[35] In a later article, Thiébault-Sisson would add that Monet "had dreamed of a vast rotunda where his canvases would reside, like a panorama, in the wall."[36] Monet seems to have wanted to showcase a range of light effects, from morning in *Clouds* to what was probably sunset in *Agapanthus*. As the critic Marcel Pays later noted, the twelve panels were "a decorative ensemble, where every kind of enchanting light effect unfolds across the water from dawn to dusk, according to the hour."[37]

For Bonnier, Monet's insistence on an oval space only presented problems. The architect saw there a certain "indecision" in the choice of a type of oval that was "not very pronounced and comes too close to the circle."[38] A more dramatically stated ellipse would, however, increase the angle of curvature of certain canvases as well as further affect the amount of space for the viewer to step back. Bonnier also noted the extra complications and cost to the structure and roof for an elliptical form.[39] He argued instead for a more traditional circular building that would offer a uniform distance to step back and be cheaper to construct. Monet, for his part, continued to explore different options, probably looking at different types and curvatures of ellipses. Bonnier noted in his diary with some frustration on October 10, "Monet has a new idea every day."[40]

Monet's gift of his panels embodied his patriotism. One of the artist's friends, the writer Gustave Geffroy, described the earlier gift of the *Green Reflections*—part of the Hôtel Biron group—on Armistice Day of 1918 as a "bouquet of flowers" to the French nation.[41] In their patriotic intent, these twelve panels were comparable to the grand battle panoramas of the late nineteenth century. The Panorama Reichshoffen and others had celebrated French military valor in the wake of the Franco-Prussian War. However, Monet communicated his patriotism in a very different way. He was much affected by the events of World War I: a rail line carrying troops to the front ran directly between his gardens; his son Michel fought at the battle of Verdun; he could arguably even hear the guns on the front line from his Giverny studio. In his Hôtel Biron project, Monet sought to create a contemplative space that emphasized the regenerative force of nature in contrast to this recent horror. As such, it provided a direct contrast with traditional panoramas that memorialized and celebrated episodes of war.

In a conversation with the Duc de Trévise, Monet insisted that his gift of the panels to the State, at a time when dealers wanted to pay hefty sums for them, was conditional on "specifying [his] clear conditions."[42] He noted firstly the importance of a prestigious location in the center of Paris (rather than a remote area like the "slaughterhouses" on the outskirts of the city).[43] He also affirmed that he wanted a "quite specific, rounded form," an allusion to his experiments with an ellipse. He even quipped, "if we don't have that, why not be in a circus? We would only need Monsieur Loyal [the archetype of the Parisian ringmaster] with his whip."[44] For Monet, a circular space was comparable to a circus ring, where one would only require a ringmaster to complete the full effect. His comparison is illuminating in referencing this central aspect of Parisian popular culture. Like the panorama, circus rotundas covered the capital, notably the Cirque Medrano (fig. 85), which had been built in Montmartre in the late nineteenth century. As is well known, Monet's Impressionist colleagues Renoir and Degas represented this circus and its performers. Rather than embracing such an association, however, Monet seems to have been arguing that it would be debasing for

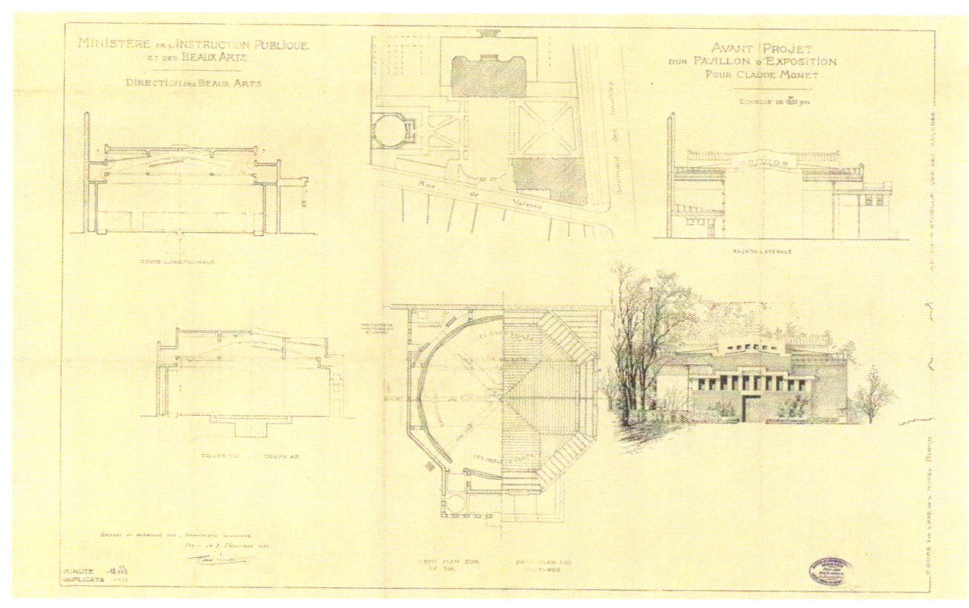

Fig. 86. Louis Bonnier, plans from the proposal "Pilot study for an exhibition pavilion to house a series of canvases by Monsieur Claude Monet," 1920. Archives nationales, France

his space to be similar to such a popular and raucous entertainment. He wanted his building to be a more meditative environment, a kind of secular chapel or "lay sanctuary."[45]

At the end of November 1920, Monet hosted a high-level official delegation who would have to approve the rotunda and its significant price tag. This was made up of André Honnorat, minister of public instruction, Paul Léon, directeur des Beaux-Arts, Raymond Koechlin, the collector, M. Sales, another government administrator, and Bonnier, the architect. Bonnier had already planned out a smaller and cheaper circular space and must have brought his suggestions to the meeting.[46] The architect left this gathering with the impression that the mercurial Monet was now supportive of this plan.[47] He worked on such a configuration and submitted a comprehensive proposal entitled "Pilot study for an exhibition pavilion to house a series of canvases by Monsieur Claude Monet" to Léon on December 18, 1920.[48] It contained drawn plans (fig. 86), cost estimates, and an explanation of the building's aesthetic.[49] Somewhat surprisingly, Bonnier does not seem to have shown them to Monet before submitting them. Nonetheless, his plans probably contained the essence of what Monet and his high-level visitors had approved in their discussions at the end of November.

Bonnier's plan showed a modernist building that was 4,779 square feet in size and that was to be built in the northeast corner of the gardens of the Hôtel Biron, close to the rue de Varenne, rather than on the northwest side as Monet had earlier stated he preferred. The architect's submission, in the Archives Nationales, provides unpublished details on materials and costs.[50] The framework of the building, including pillars, lintels, trusses, and floors, was in reinforced concrete; any visible elements of the concrete were coated in white cement.[51] The façade would be in white brick originating in Dizy, a town in the Marne département known for its brick production.[52] The crown of the building and the cornice would be made of stone.[53] Bonnier planned a wrought-iron entry door and grilles, providing elements of understated decoration that reflected his origins in Art Nouveau. In his submitted budget, amounting to 579,159 francs, the most expensive parts of the building were the brick and stonework (139,375 francs), the reinforced concrete (105,000 francs) and the ironwork, including "artistic wrought-iron" (62,968 francs).[54] The use of the modern materials, in particular reinforced concrete and iron, was crucial to the building's modernity.

Bonnier had used reinforced concrete in a school complex, built from 1908 to 1912, in the suburb of Grenelle in Paris, and he used it again extensively in the expansive interior nave of the swimming pool at Butte-aux-Cailles in the early 1920s. The façade of the latter building (fig. 87) resembles the planned façade for Monet's pavilion in its mix of brickwork and stone. Bonnier's interest in brickwork is also evident in his contemporary project for low-cost housing in the Parisian suburb of Ménilmontant: this used Dizy red and white bricks (fig. 88). In describing his aesthetic for the exterior of Monet's pavilion, Bonnier noted: "We have not sought for the planned building any effect that might be likely to undermine the architecture of the Hôtel Biron, but only a great simplicity, a discreet neutrality for the framing of the paintings by Claude Monet. Likewise, on the inside, no decoration with the same goal; at the very least, a certain refinement in the wrought-iron entry door."[55] The relationship of Bonnier's building with the Hôtel Biron (fig. 89) would subsequently become a subject of contention, but it could certainly be argued that its understated

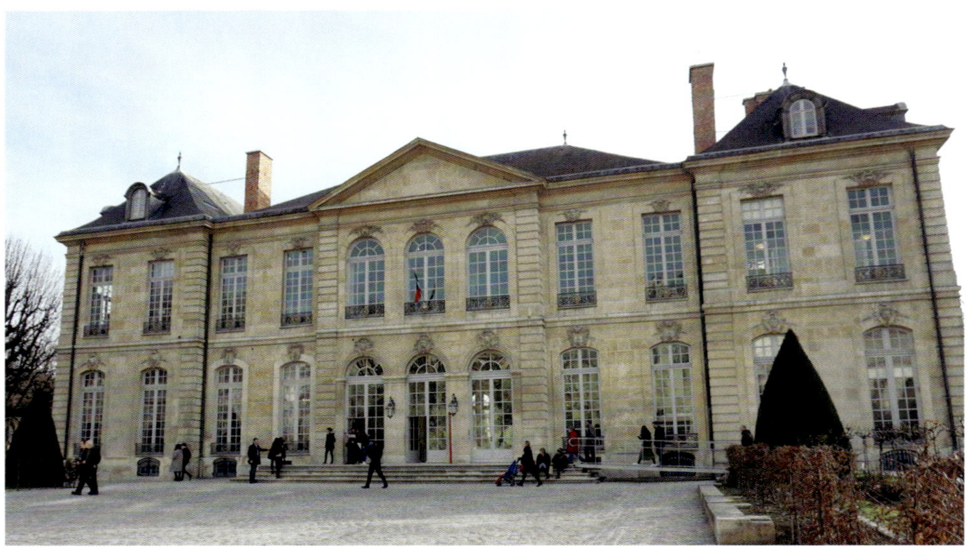

Fig. 89. Jean Aubert, Hôtel Biron, Paris, 1727–32

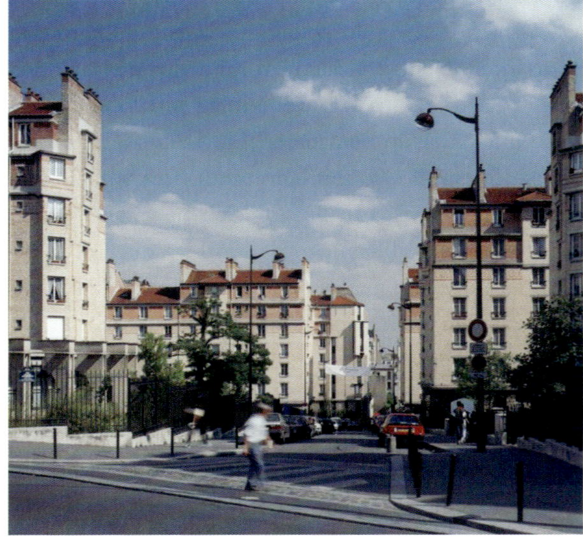

Fig. 88. Louis Bonnier, housing project in Ménilmontant, 1920–25

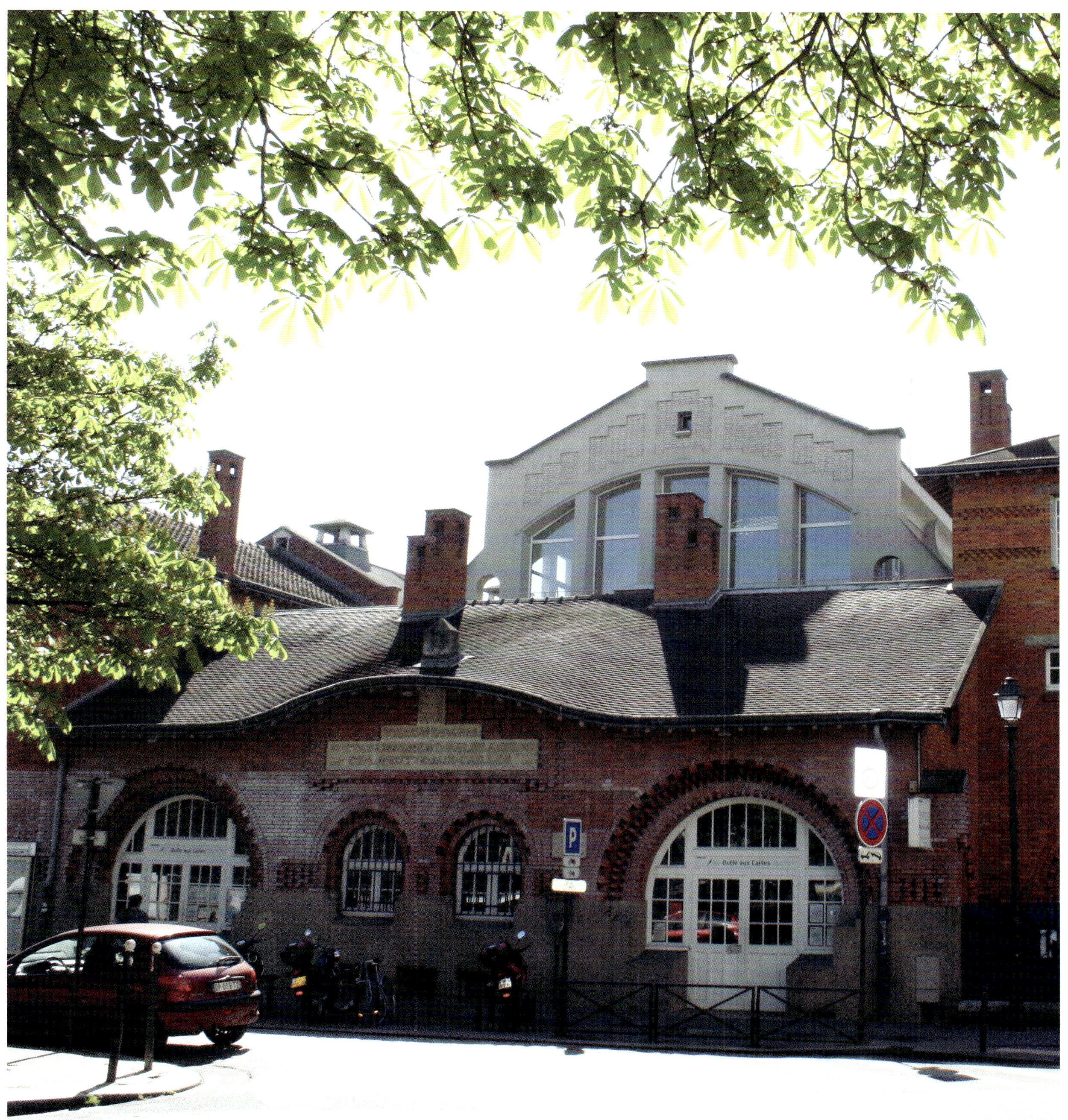

Fig. 87. Louis Bonnier, façade of the Butte-aux-Cailles swimming pool, 1920–23

rigor and geometry complemented the classicism of the older building, constructed in the 1720s during the reign of Louis XV.[56]

For the interior of the building, Bonnier designed an entry vestibule with a mosaic floor that would lead into the circular exhibition gallery with a wooden parquet floor.[57] There was also a heating system. Bonnier noted that the vestibule would be darkened to facilitate the transition between the outdoor light and that of the exhibition space, which was to be lit from above by a glass roof. He then described the exhibition space itself:

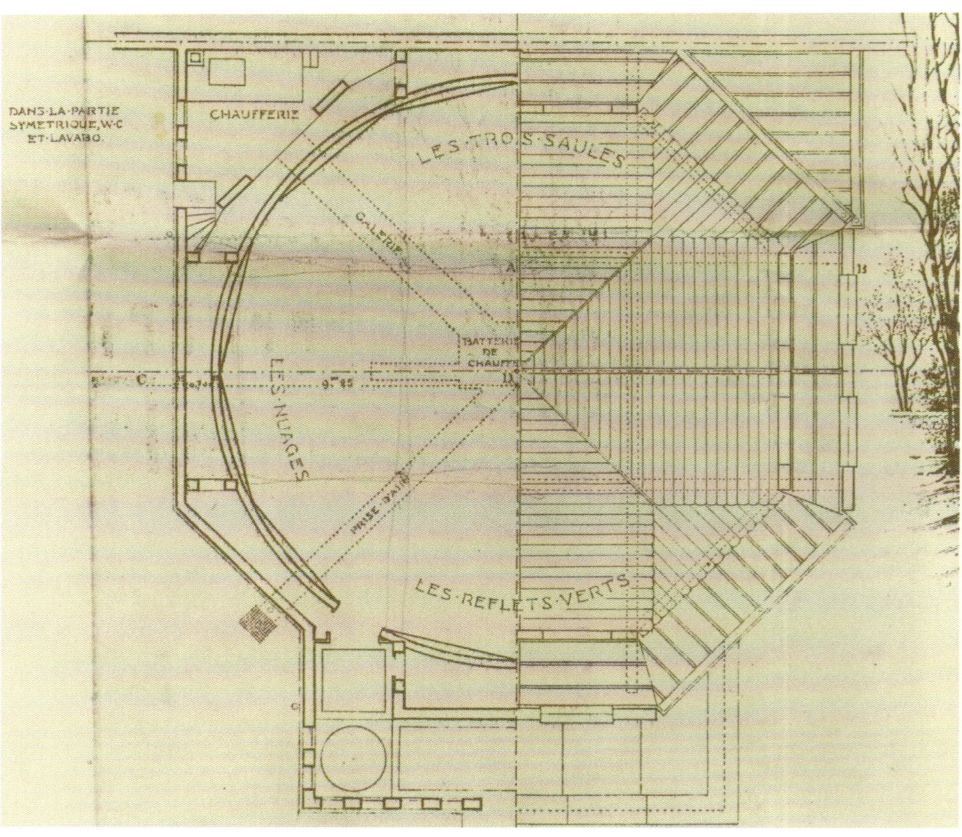

Fig. 90. Louis Bonnier, floor plan of the room, from the proposal "Pilot study for an exhibition pavilion to house a series of canvases by Monsieur Claude Monet," 1920. Archives nationales, France. The *Agapanthus* triptych is covered by the roof.

"The large exhibition room, with a distinctive shape, and true to the instructions provided by the program of M. Claude Monet, measures a radius of 25 meters and is laid out in a way that allows the view of the ensemble, with the necessary space to step back from all the canvases. The lighting is obtained by means of a glass roof above the room . . . The light is diffused by a vellum blind, placed under the entire glass surface."[58]

Bonnier's reference to the room's size was actually incorrect here, and his accompanying plan shows that it in fact had a radius of 9.25 meters (30 feet, 4 inches) (a diameter of 18.5 meters, or 60 feet, 8 inches) (fig. 90). His side elevations indicate that the walls were 18 feet high from the floor to the vellum blind. Above the blind was a space of a further 3 feet, 4 inches, to a horizontal glazed ceiling.[59] The exterior glass roof, at a diagonal angle, was some feet higher still. In the gallery below, the configuration of the panels remained the same as in the earlier oval plan. The visitor would enter the richly colorful space to be confronted by the *Three Willows*, the *Green Reflections* behind, the *Clouds* to the left, and *Agapanthus* to the right.[60] The panels were installed at an angle on independent screens rather than being glued to the walls as would be the case at the Orangerie. Again intense blues offset golds. Softer pinks and silvers complemented dark tree tones. The strong verticals of the willow trunks complemented the elegant and fragile curve of the agapanthus plant.[61]

Bonnier's side elevation showed the low position of the panels, hung close to the ground. Following Monet's instructions, he also indicated in his accompanying text that there would be an encircling frieze at the top of the exhibition walls (fig. 91).[62] Monet had, indeed, recently discussed his intentions for a frieze of garlands of wisteria.[63] He painted three wisteria panels that are strongly horizontal (cats. 29 and 30)—measuring 1 x 2 meters—and would have fit well with this plan, and the artist undoubtedly would have realized more had he constructed the rotunda. Monet represented the reflections of wisteria hanging from the trellis of his Japanese bridge. As such, he thought to create a kind of flower chain around the space, tapping into rococo eighteenth-century histories of floral motifs as decorative elements.[64] This foliage would have complemented the hanging fronds of the willow trees in the *Three Willows*. Monet's plan also related closely to Art Nouveau. Louis Comfort Tiffany created a stained glass wisteria frieze, which surrounded the dining room of his Laurelton Hall mansion, constructed in 1905 (figs. 92, 93). Monet may have known of this, and Bonnier, too, was familiar with Tiffany's work, having designed Siegfried Bing's *Maison de l'Art Nouveau* in 1895, which included several stained glass windows by Tiffany. Monet also produced five taller wisteria panels (1.5 x 2 meters) that may have been intended for the vestibule.

Monet's space engaged with the tradition of the panorama but also established significant differences. In contrast to the continuous circularity of the panorama (where the visitor generally ascended from below to the viewing platform in the center of the room), Monet's plan was interrupted by doors and gaps between panels. Interestingly, according to a comment made by his painter friend Albert André, Monet had considered having an entrance at the center of the room in order to create an unbroken flow of canvases around the room perimeter.[65] Unlike the panorama, where the spectator saw the scene on a viewing platform from a distance, the visitor was able to see Monet's panels not only at a distance but also close-up, at eye level, enabling a focus on paint texture. Whereas the panorama, as in a cinema today, placed the viewer in darkness against illuminated images, Monet's space was lit by even daylight. Compared with rotundas like the enormous Panorama Reichshoffen, it was also modest in scale. Nonetheless, for all these differences, Monet's space encouraged the spectator to engage in a panoramic gaze, seeing the range of panels in a single 360-degree experience.

Bonnier's plans for the rotunda were reviewed by the noted architect Charles Girault, inspecteur géneral des bâtiments civils, a conservative member of the Institut whose best-known building was the ornate Beaux-Arts Petit Palais that he had designed for the Exposition Universelle in 1900. His review was rapid and negative, and he delivered his report to the Counsel for Public Buildings on December 23, 1920. He complained of the "forbidding appearance" of Bonnier's building.[66] Here he contrasted Bonnier's stark concrete structure with the more conventionally elegant design of the Hôtel Biron's Louis XV architecture.[67] The potential expense of the new building—budgeted for 579,000 francs—was also put forward as a deterrent, especially as this was an expense that would have to be paid by the State. Girault also regretted that Monet had not considered employing the resident architect of the Hôtel Biron.[68] Although Girault's report was not favorable, he did make the suggestion that a mock-up wooden version of Bonnier's rotunda be constructed at the Hôtel Biron in the spring of 1921 and that the paintings be installed there for a trial period. However, his suggestion was not taken up, and the Counsel rejected Bonnier's proposal on December 23, 1920.[69] In making its decision, the Counsel noted "a complete lack of harmony between this construction and the façade of the Hôtel Biron" as well as the cost of the building at more than 1,200 francs per square meter.[70]

Despite this review, the pavilion still seems to have been under consideration in January 1921.[71] At the end of the month, Monet noted his belief that the State was reluctant to pay the cost of the rotunda at a million francs.[72] Based on Bonnier's budget, he seems to have been exaggerating the cost of the building. After discussion with Bonnier, it was finally the mercurial Monet who was ultimately responsible for dooming the pavilion plan.[73] On February 11, he wrote to Paul Léon, criticizing the circular gallery space and again

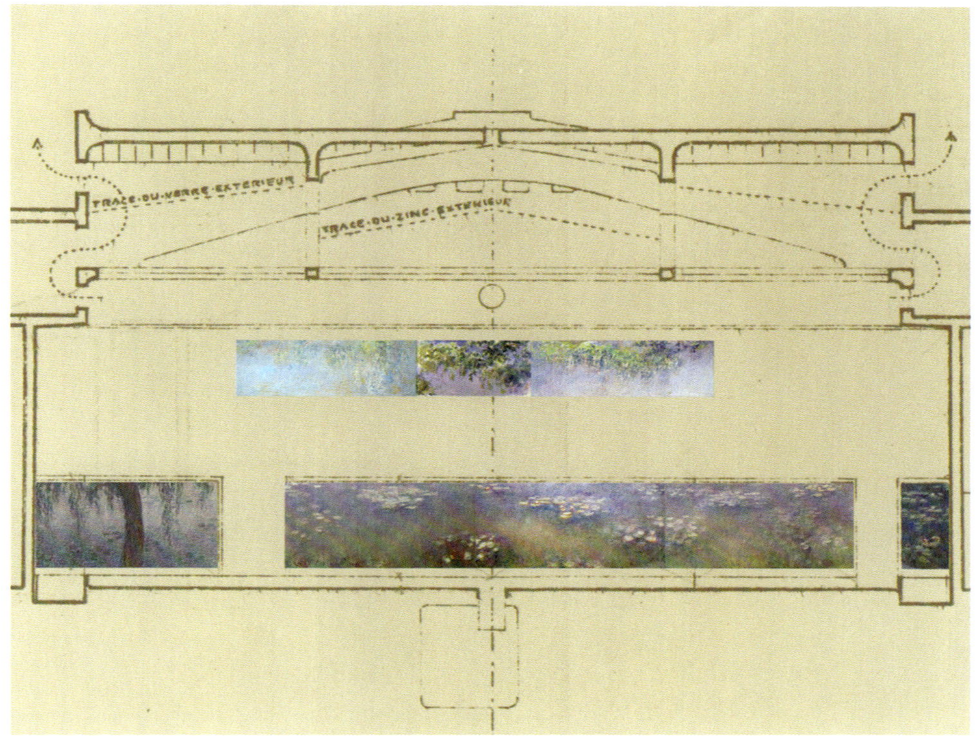

Fig. 91. Imagining of the interior of Monet's pavilion, based on Bonnier's longitudinal section

making the unflattering comparison to a circus ring: "I admit to being quite a bit disappointed by the too-regular form of the room that thus planned becomes a veritable circus, and I have real fear that it may not create a very good effect."[74] Monet then suggested that he would give fewer works, eight or perhaps ten, presumably because this would allow him to keep an elliptical structure for his paintings that could be housed in a smaller—and cheaper—space.[75] This

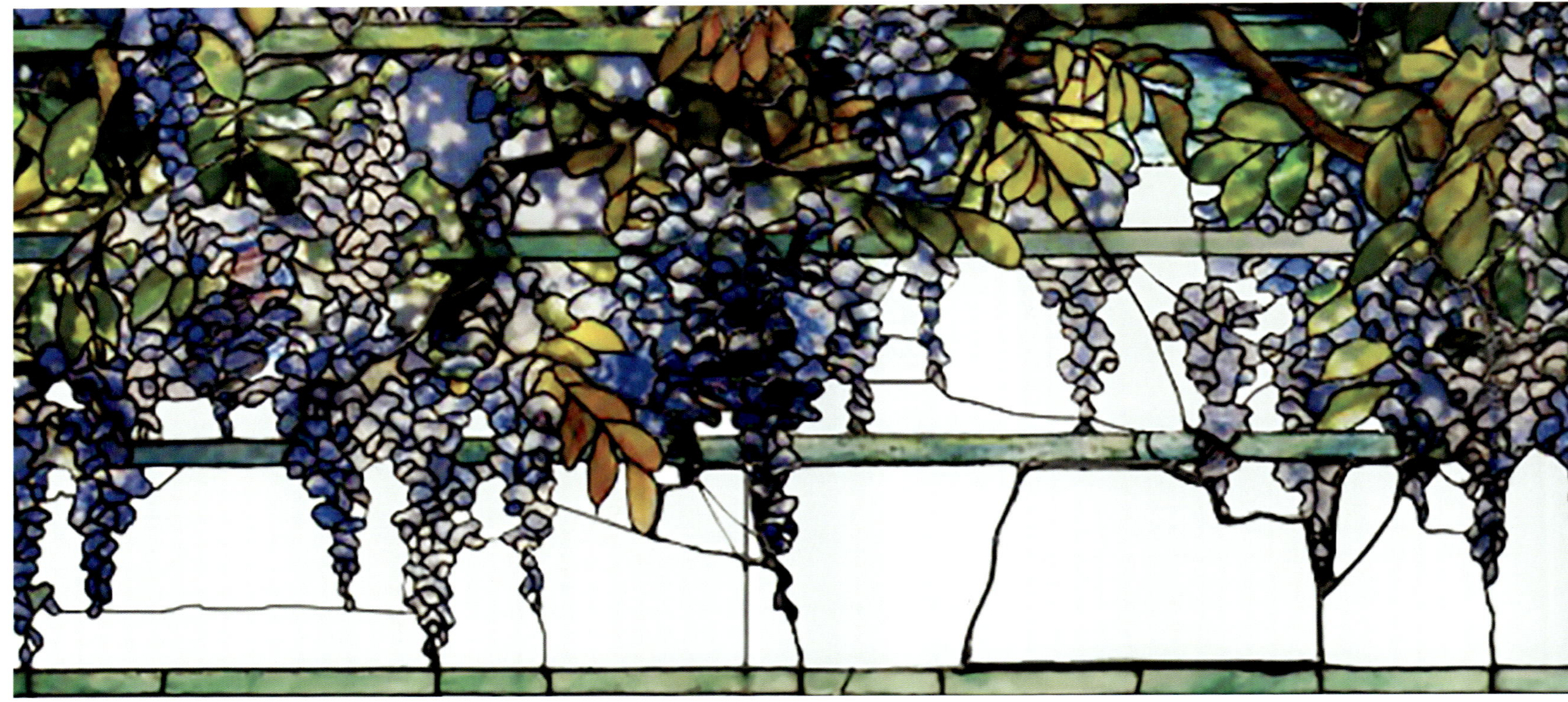

Fig. 92. Louis Comfort Tiffany, *Transom*, c. 1915. Leaded glass, 37 x 96 in. (94 x 243.8 cm). The Charles Hosmer Morse Museum of American Art, Winter Park, Florida

suggestion was, however, never realized. In April, an anonymous review in the bulletin of Monet's dealer, Bernheim-Jeune, described Bonnier's building as "a special construction made of reinforced concrete" that had been condemned by the Counsel "with a unanimous voice"; the principal concern was that the maverick Bonnier was not an "in-house" candidate.[76] The following month, Gustave Geffroy, Monet's friend and biographer, also spoke in favor of this pavilion that remained his preference for the display of the panels. He noted that "the proximity of Rodin and Monet would be most enlightening."[77] Geffroy went on: "The modernism of the art of Monet would support very well a boldly modern architecture in iron, cement, and ceramic."[78]

By now, however, another space had been proposed, namely the existing Second Empire building of the Orangerie. On April 6, Monet had visited the Orangerie with an official delegation including Clémenceau, Paul Léon, Léon Bérard, Bonnier, and Geffroy.[79] He initially agreed to this structure and encouraged Bonnier to start to produce plans.[80] Within weeks, he had changed his mind, even taking back the donation of the panels because he was unhappy with the narrow spaces of the Orangerie.[81] Looking back to the pavilion, he noted that he had always envisaged a purpose-built space, "a special room."[82] After further negotiations, Monet ultimately agreed to the Orangerie when the State agreed to extend the length of the exhibition galleries. Here he would install twenty-two panels in two galleries, the first measuring 67 feet, 9 inches x 40 feet, 8 inches, and the second 76 feet, 5 inches x 40 feet, 8 inches. Each of these spaces was longer than the circular gallery in Bonnier's pavilion but considerably narrower. The artist always seems to have considered the Orangerie a compromise. Monet wrote to Arsène Alexandre about Bonnier: "between us, I can assure you that I have only ever had praise for him [Bonnier], that I understand perfectly that he is inclined to force costs [lower] and that, if I chose him for M. P. Léon, it's because I know of no other architect."[83] In December, 1921, Bonnier sent Monet a set of plans (now lost) for the refurbishment of the Orangerie.[84] Yet, the State had now turned to another architect, Camille Lefèvre.[85] Monet acquiesced to this decision, effectively abandoning Bonnier.[86] The loyal architect's protracted work on the different structures for Monet's panel installations was thus ultimately

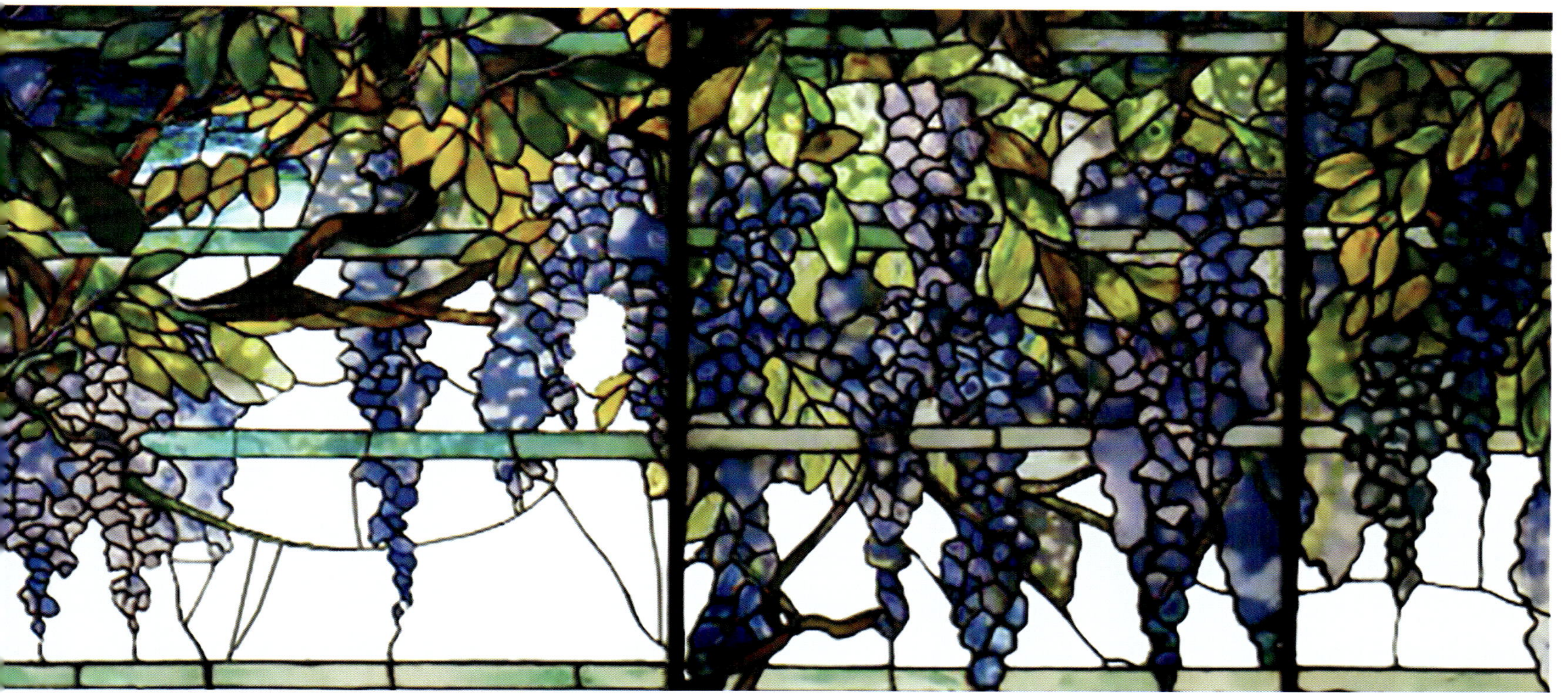

fruitless. There is no evidence of subsequent contact between the two men.

What then are we to make of Monet and Bonnier's aborted pavilion? Had it been built, it would have offered a new, avant-garde space to match the avant-garde quality of Monet's paintings. As Geffroy had noted, Bonnier's modern design and materials would have complemented Monet's experimental paintings. The artist's emphasis on abstract, painterly surfaces, the low-hanging pictures, and the absence of horizon line would all have contributed to an effect of immersion on the spectator. For all its differences, the purpose-built pavilion tapped into the history of the panorama to a greater extent than the long, narrow spaces of the Orangerie. It would have condensed the essential elements of Monet's whole *Grandes Décorations* project—reflections, willow trees, water lilies, and agapanthus—into one large space, as opposed to the diluted arrangement of panels across the two smaller rooms at the Orangerie. The artist's decorative frieze made the pavilion even more ambitious. Monet's pavilion at the Hôtel Biron would have reinvigorated the tradition of the panorama on the artist's own terms.

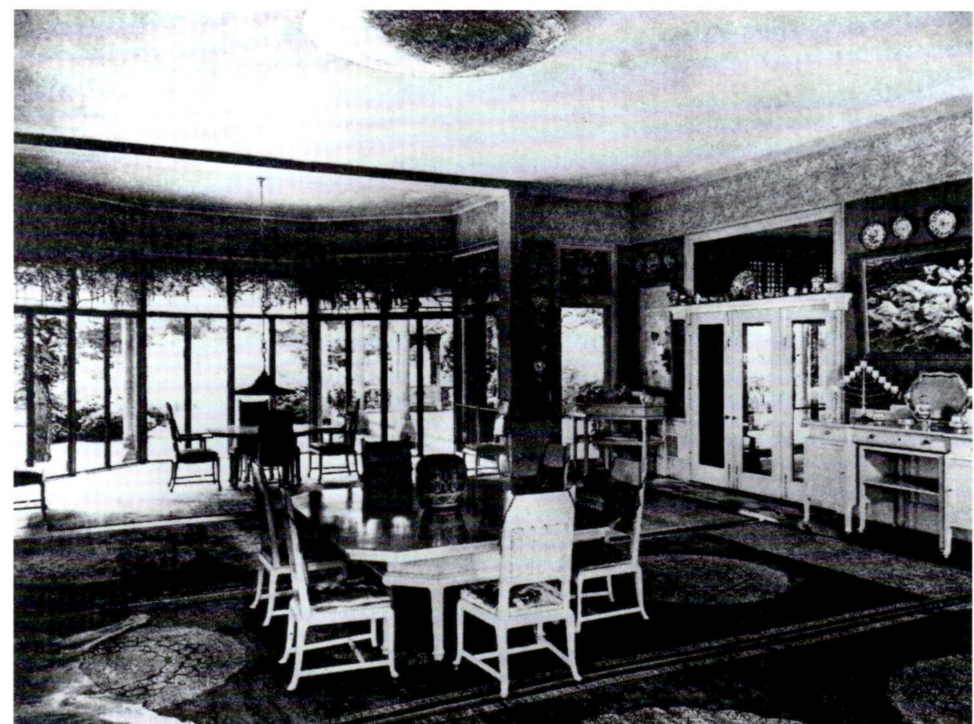

Fig. 93. Archival photograph of dining room with transom, Laurelton Hall (built 1902–5), Long Island, New York, c. 1925. Published in *Objects of Art . . . The Louis Comfort Tiffany Foundation*, public auction catalogue, Parke-Bernet Galleries, 1946

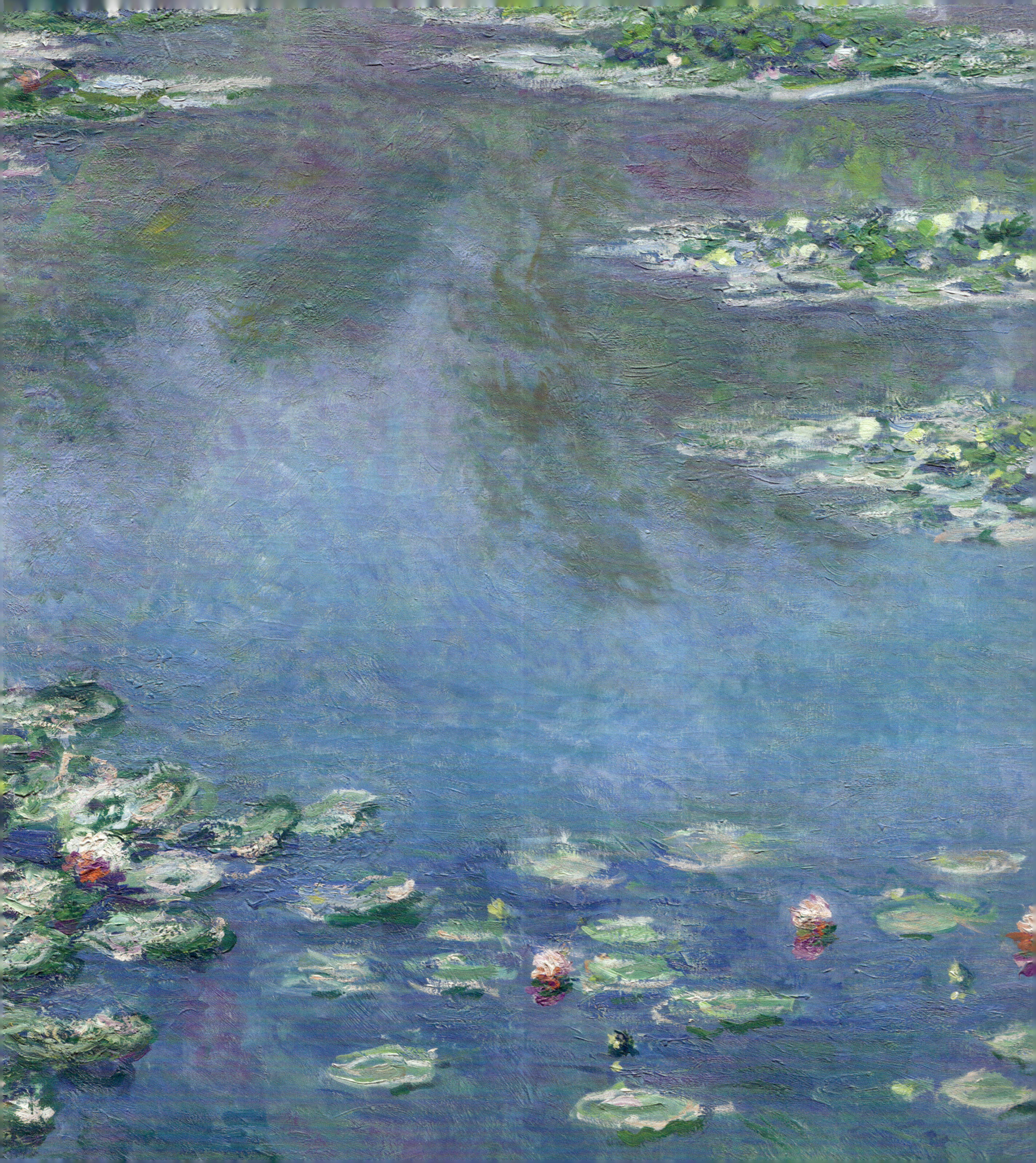

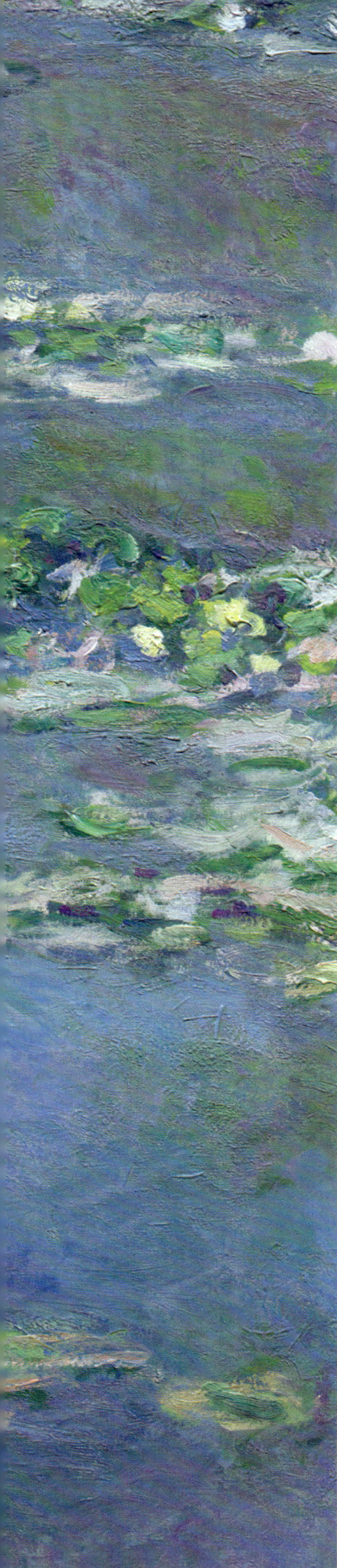

The Late Monet and His Critics: Water Lilies, "Cunning Mirrors on Paradise"

Emma Cauvin
PhD Candidate at Sorbonne University, Paris

> The shadow that you see is the reflection of your image:
> It is nothing in itself; it arrived with you and remains with you;
> With you it will go away, if at least you are able to go away!
> – Ovid, *Metamorphoses* 3.434–36

The Lake in the Garden of Enchantment

In 1909, when Monet exhibited his *Nymphéas, Séries de paysages d'eau* (*Water Lilies, Landscapes of Water*) for the first time at the Galerie Durand-Ruel (fig. 94), there was stupefaction: by making the horizon disappear, the painter destroyed the landscape genre as it had long been envisaged (fig. 95). His choice of subject—which may no longer surprise us, so well do we know it through the multiple reproductions of the *Water Lilies* over the years—was for the Paris public in the month of May 1909 a staggering innovation, the pure *idea* of the artist. Among the most distinguished critics to publish a reaction to the exhibition was Claude Roger-Marx, whose often-cited review appeared in the *Gazette des beaux-arts* in June 1909 (fig. 96). He began his review by evincing his visual and spatial reaction to the paintings. "One's first reaction to these 48 pictures is bewilderment," he wrote:

> In most of them, objections having little to do with painting are the cause of this malaise; they have to do more with the identity of the subject and the number of duplications and with the at first seemingly fragmentary aspect of these pictures. The paintings manifest an authority and independence, an egocentric quality that is offensive to our vanity and humbling to our pride.

Claude Monet, *Water Lilies* (detail), 1906, cat. 6

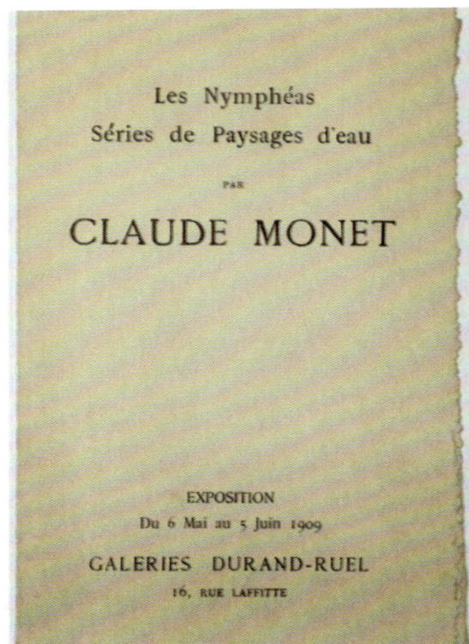

Les Nymphéas
Séries de Paysages d'eau

PAR

CLAUDE MONET

EXPOSITION
Du 6 Mai au 5 Juin 1909

GALERIES DURAND-RUEL
16, RUE LAFFITTE

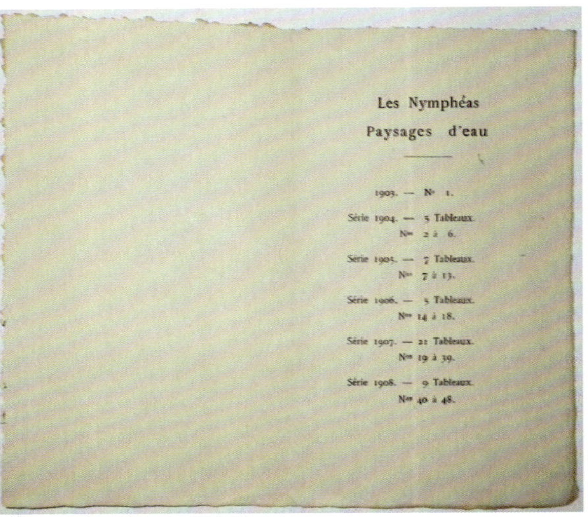

Les Nymphéas
Paysages d'eau

1903. — N° 1.

Série 1904. — 5 Tableaux.
Nos 2 à 6.

Série 1905. — 7 Tableaux.
Nos 7 à 13.

Série 1906. — 5 Tableaux.
Nos 14 à 18.

Série 1907. — 21 Tableaux.
Nos 19 à 39.

Série 1908. — 9 Tableaux.
Nos 40 à 48.

Fig. 94. Program from the 1909 exhibition *Les Nymphéas: Séries de Paysages d'eau*. Cover and interior with works listed in series by year. Martinez D. gallery, Paris

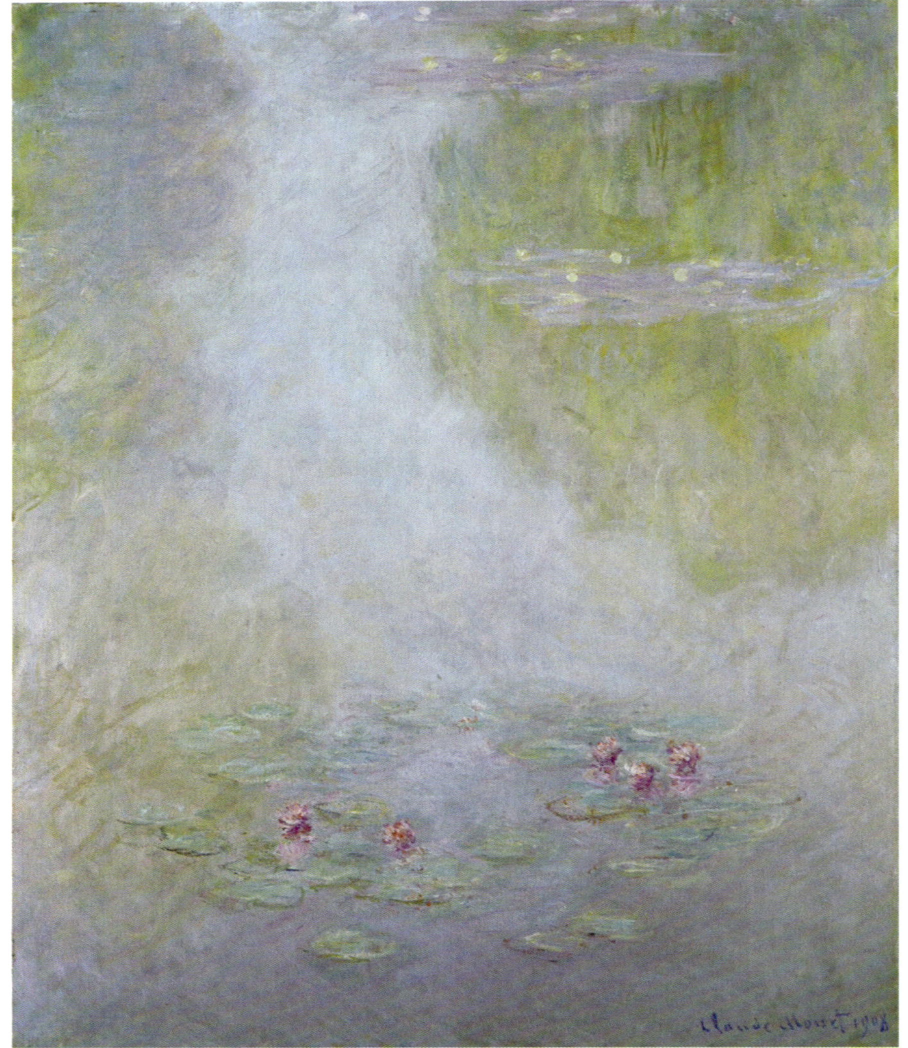

Fig. 95. Claude Monet, *Water Lilies*, 1908. Oil on canvas, 39 5/8 x 32 in. (100.7 x 81.3 cm). National Museum Wales. Bequest of Gwendoline Davies, 1952. NMW A 2480

> M. Claude Monet is interested in pleasing only himself. His exertions are directed at recording the multifaceted differences of the pleasures he experiences during the course of the day as he works in one single place: such are the apparently selfish goals of his art, and it suits him to subordinate everything to this end. The value of a theme lies in its potential for increasing the number of sensations aroused in the viewer and enriching their quality. His system is a familiar one, but M. Claude Monet has not heretofore undertaken to push its consequences quite so far.

Though apparently severe in his first reaction, Roger-Marx admired the paintings prodigiously. Their audacity was tempered by their sensuality. "No more earth, no more sky, no limits now," he wrote; "the dormant and fertile waters completely cover the field of the canvas; light overflows, cheerfully plays upon a surface covered with verdigris leaves." He went on to extoll the "magical evocation of the reflections," their "harmonious languor, gentle voluptuousness," and "the beneficence of daydreams." Though recognizing the works' poetic beauty, he was equally concerned with the ways in which they challenged perception and the depiction of the physical world in its dimensions on the planar canvas.[1]

Other critics, nowadays less well known, shared Roger-Marx's fascination with the ensemble, but took their interpretation of the images in other directions. Robert Kemp, for instance, asked his reader to:

> Imagine forty-eight canvases, of medium size, almost all square, all representing a section of the quiet surface of a pond on which float the broad leaves of water lilies, sometimes with flowers of yellow and red. Not a patch of sky above the water and no horizon; not a tuft of greenery. . . . – is this not a delightful poetic idea? Certainly! But how difficult to create![2]

The author was not yet the authority in the world of theater, music, and literature whose renown would earn him a chair at the Académie Française, but was just starting out as an art critic at *L'Aurore*. He recommended that readers hasten "to go see this prodigy" for "on this clear and sensitive mirror, the sky is nevertheless reflected, and foliage is mirrored. It is like the Platonic myth of the Cave. We don't see the real world; but we grasp what it looks like."[3] Such descriptions and comparisons were absolutely necessary to allow readers to picture something they could never have imagined in painting. Accordingly, using a pseudonym, Marie de Régnier (fig. 98), novelist, poet, and playwright, invented a world by means of the *Water Lilies,* where she herself, a spectator, was transformed, so as to participate in this "fairy tea party" in which flowers became "cups and saucers":

> Imagine several rooms where paintings hang, paintings so luminous, so limpid, so transparent that after a quarter of an hour you have the sensation of being in the water, of being an inhabitant of ponds, of lakes and of pools, of being a siren with blue-green hair, a naiad with fluid arms, a nymph with cool legs, or a green frog singing in the evening with a voice crystalline and yet throaty, a little frog sitting on the wide pads of the water lilies, its little bottom the color of jade.[4]

The writer's sense of wonder, a sort of regression sending her back to the boundless imagination of childhood, was so strong that at the end of her visit she concluded that what she had seen was "painting by an elf or a sprite, an inhabitant of woods or springs," with colors "stolen from nature and not mixed by human hand. It's very curious, very surprising, and very beautiful."[5] Her emotion was shared by Louis de Fourcaud, art historian, poet, and musician, who, in an article entitled "M. Claude Monet et le Lac du Jardin des Fées" (M. Claude Monet and the lake of the fairies' garden), thanked the painter for the "beautiful hours of dreams" offered by the exhibition of "something unexpected and desired, intimately poetic and absolutely real": "That little pond, stippled with corollas, with no more horizon than that legendary Sargasso Sea and more mirages than words could ever evoke. . . . We cannot pull ourselves away from it."[6] The critic chose his metaphor to perfection, evoking that sea southeast of Bermuda, grassy with algae, endless and with no shore, said to trap ships, which could never leave it—for in fact, all of the critics noted how spectators seemed bewitched in front of *Paysages d'eau,*

LES « NYMPHÉAS » DE M. CLAUDE MONET[1]

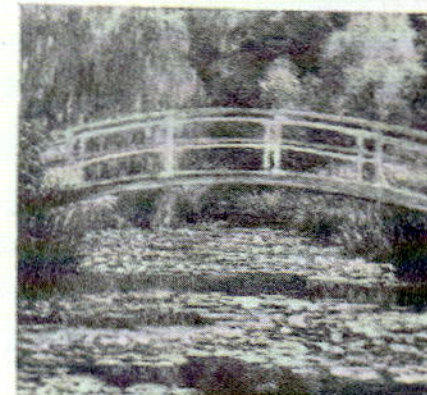

LE BASSIN AUX NYMPHÉAS PAR M. CLAUDE MONET (SÉRIE DE 1900)

On voudrait, avant de transcrire ses impressions, en remonter le cours et les ordonner pour mieux les définir. Le premier sentiment éprouvé devant ces quarante-huit ouvrages est celui d'une surprise désorientée. Chez la plupart, des objections, étrangères à la peinture, révèlent ce malaise : elles tiennent à l'identité du sujet et au nombre des répliques ; elles tiennent à l'aspect fragmentaire que semblent d'abord revêtir ces tableaux. Il y a là une affirmation d'autorité et d'indépendance, une suprématie du moi, qui offensent notre vanité et humilient notre orgueil. M. Claude Monet n'a souci que de se satisfaire; il dépense sa peine et trouve son plaisir à différencier les jouissances éprouvées, le long du jour, au regard d'un même site ; telles sont les fins, égoïstes en apparence, de son art, et il sied que tout s'y subordonne : un thème vaut dans la mesure où il enrichit la vue de sensations plus abondantes et plus précieuses. Le système nous était connu; mais M. Claude Monet ne s'était pas encore avisé d'en pousser aussi loin les conséquences.

Que le dôme des meules s'arrondisse au ras de la plaine; que les peupliers dressent leur haie et fusent dans l'air à intervalles égaux ; que tel portail gothique offre ses sculptures au flamboiement de la lumière; que la falaise surplombe l'océan ou que la Seine enlace de ses bras l'îlot boisé; que, dans le parc, les nénuphars hérissent la face du bassin paisible; à Londres, qu'un pont enfonce ses

1. Exposition à la galerie Durand-Ruel, du 6 mai au 12 juin.

Fig. 96. The first page of Claude Roger Marx's review of "Les 'Nymphéas' de M. Claude Monet" in the *Gazette des beaux-arts*, June 1909

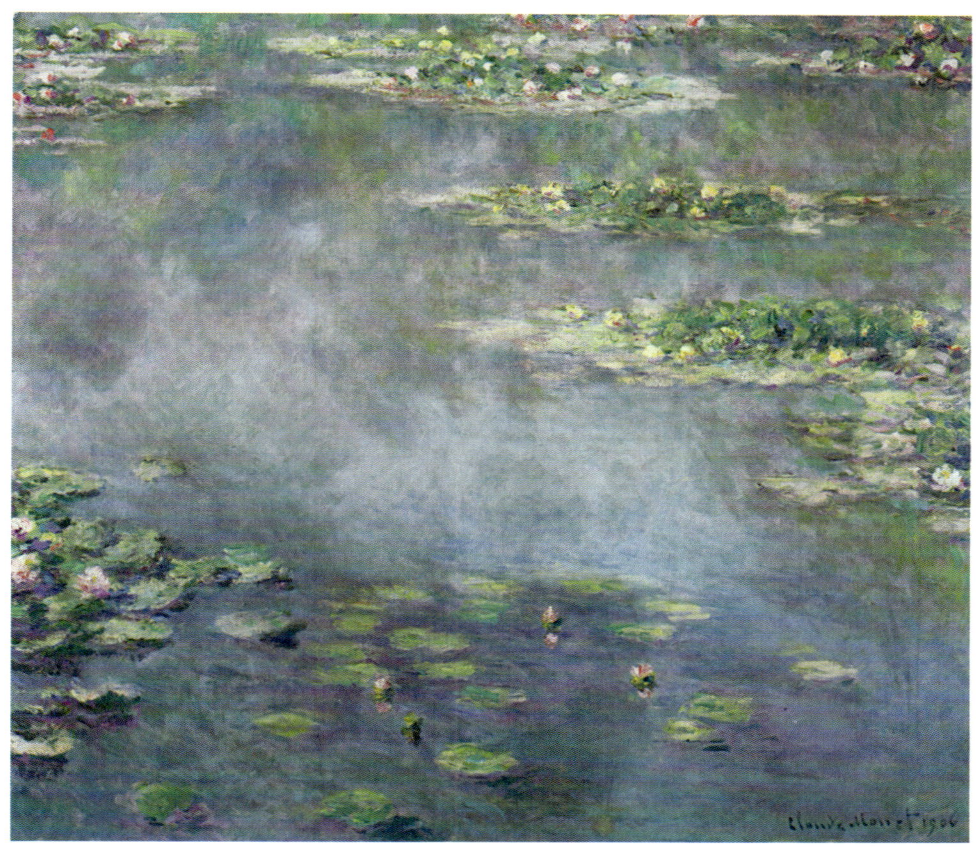

Fig. 97. Claude Monet, *Water Lilies*, 1905. Oil on canvas, 31 7/8 x 39 ½ in. (81 x 100.5 cm). Private collection, courtesy of Sotheby's, New York

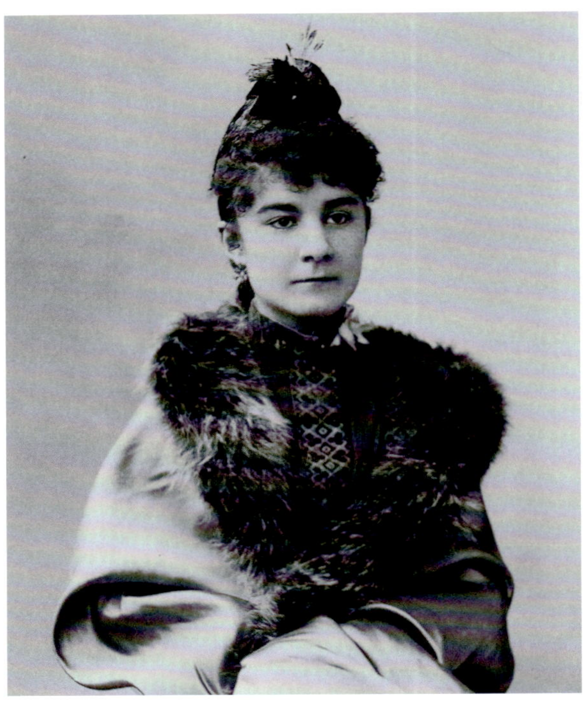

Fig. 98. Marie de Régnier, April 18, 1889. Photograph by Paul Nadar

by their presence not in front of a simple canvas whose surface would invite formal or aesthetic observation, but in an *environment*—that is to say, by an experience not just contemplated, but lived.

The works seemed to open a door into a re-enchanted world in which everyone would play delightedly at make-believe: the Platonic cave, damp and nymphic expanses of water populated with frogs, the Sargasso Sea—the ponds of Giverny once again came alive, even becoming "living" water according to the anthropomorphism of Lucien Descaves, who wrote to Monet to share his admiration after he had visited the exhibition, proud to be "a little bit his friend." The journalist and novelist left it "dazzled, full of wonder," saying he had seen "in painting, living water, as animated as the face of a happy young woman," water whose mysteries had been revealed to him, "water where all of the hours of the day are written, like lines on a human forehead."[7] Then too, Maurice Étienne Legrand, a writer and poet also known by the pseudonym Franc-Nohain, related his experience of being subjugated, as if suspended outside reality:

> As you look at these marvels, you are frightened to speak, to smile, to breathe. Assuredly, all of this is a spell that will be broken at the least noise. You have the feeling that you are there secretly, that you are looking at something that is forbidden for men to see; and you leave in silence, as gullible as a child, convinced that in the depths of a half-open sky, you have surprised a garden favored by the gods.[8]

The spell cast by Monet, the "illusionist," the magician, thus makes the viewer regress to the most "gullible" period of his existence—childhood. Indeed, this criticism of the painter's work drives the conscious suspension of disbelief any person needs to appreciate any work of fiction to its most "immersive" extreme: by constantly using the vocabulary of astonishment and marvel, the critic reverts to the status of a child, for whom these two states are normal emotions, though lost to the adult because of his rational, measured apprehension of the surrounding world. The painter's innovative choice of point of view from which the world is represented is no longer the simple "window open upon nature"[9] that Émile Zola had perceived in Impressionism at its beginnings; it offers the critics instead a boundless "magic mirror."[10] As Arsène Alexandre notes, "no horizon is given in these paintings, which have no beginning and no end other than the limits of the frame, easily extended by the imagination as far as it wishes."[11] If the subject and the

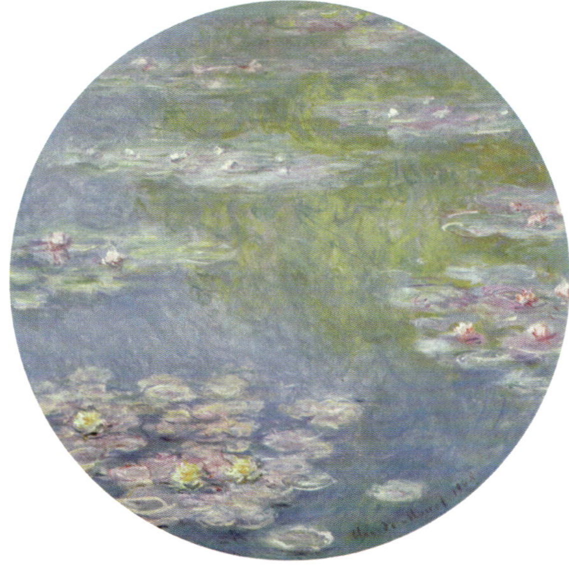

Fig. 99. Claude Monet, *Water Lilies*, 1908. Oil on canvas, diam. 31 ½ in. (80.01 cm). Dallas Museum of Art, gift of the Meadows Foundation, Incorporated. 1981.128

framing chosen by Monet became progressively more constrained, eventually abandoning the Japanese bridge that looked over the pond and its banks with their plants and flowers to show only the water's surface, their abandonment paradoxically increased the suggestive potential of the work tenfold, opening up in all directions the singular imagination of each viewer.

The sense of marvel born of contemplating the *Paysages d'eaux* falls more largely within a change in critical thought regarding Monet, parallel to the one made by the artist in the course of the 1890s: he appeared to progressively detach himself from the "frank" representation of the real, the naturalism that Zola had desired for Impressionism. The color effects explored in his series, and particularly in those dedicated to the cathedral in Rouen (fig. 100), demonstrated to the public how, for Monet, the "object" painted was no longer his subject: it was the versatility of light and atmosphere that took over the object that interested him. From then on, the series became variations on the same theme: to paint them the painter played with reality, a reality that most often was a little too drab or looked a bit too much like itself. The outrageousness of the colors and their less-than-likely combinations were pointed out. Although Monet had consciously communicated an image of himself as a painter who worked exclusively *sur le motif*, outdoors, rotating canvas after canvas on his easel—eventually giving rise to the belief that he had "a marvelously sensitive retina, a temple with an eye against which a tangle of nerves snuggled, like a magic telegraph communicating with every nuance of the air"[12]—from this moment on, he began to take liberties with reality. Thus came distancing, interiorization, idealization: "More and more overcome by a dream-like feeling," the painter moved closer to "a profoundly idealistic vision."[13] "This is painting for women . . . They cannot contest it, it's too pretty: nature doesn't provide that."[14]

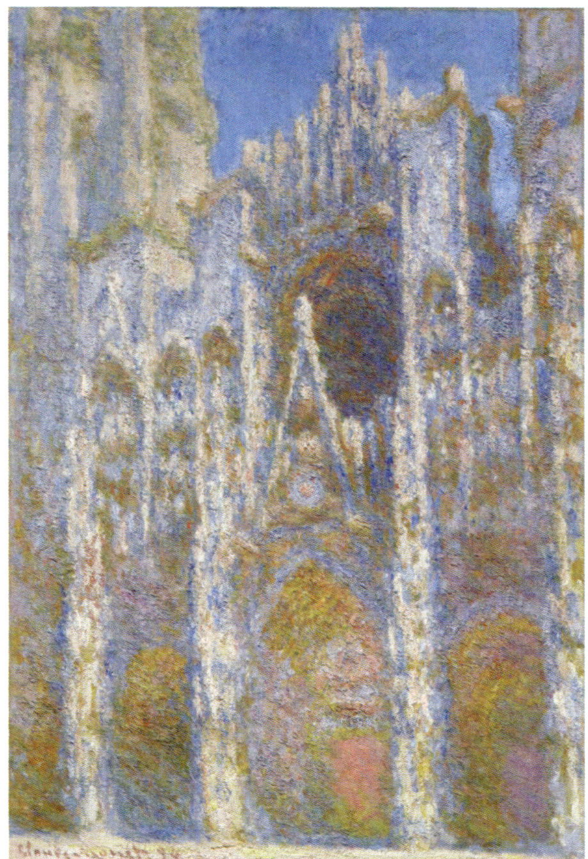

Fig. 100. Claude Monet, *Rouen Cathedral, Façade*, 1894. Oil on canvas, 39 5/8 x 26 in. (100.6 x 66 cm). Museum of Fine Arts, Boston. Juliana Cheney Edwards Collection. 39.671

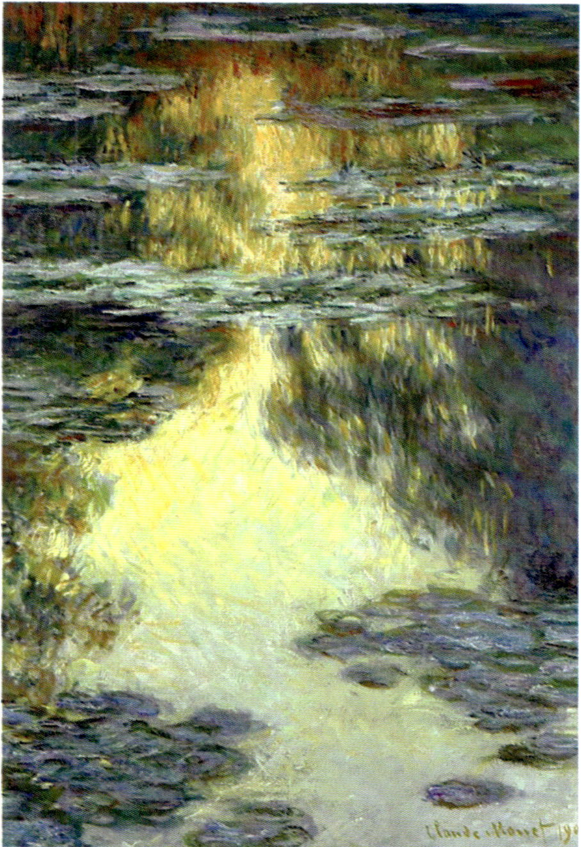

Fig. 101. Claude Monet, *Water Lilies*, 1907. Oil on canvas, 41 ¾ x 29 in. (106 x 73.5 cm). Gothenburg Museum of Art, Sweden. Bequest of Gerda Sigvaldason, 1988. GKM 2232

Thus it was in the space shaped by Monet between the real and his ideal, between motif and canvas, that those who gave enthusiastic evaluations of his work in an almost systematic fashion chose to speak of it, using the vocabulary of enchantment and of magic. After 1909, the instances only multiplied: first he was "a magician,"[15] a "great magician,"[16] a "Japanese magician,"[17] or a "wizard without equal"[18]; then the designer of "porticos to a land of enchantment,"[19] creator of a garden "of all the colors of enchantment,"[20] inventor of "a fairyland of atmosphere,"[21] or of a "vast fairyland."[22] The two notions—enchantment and magic—are pertinent to what the perception of his work would become, since both of them share the quality of being rooted in reality—but with a slight twist—bending our tangible points of reference. Enchantment and fairies almost always involve the introduction of a foreign being or element, surprising when *in* the real, whereas magic, as a discipline, involves playing with the rules that govern the physical world: the laws of gravity, appearance and disappearance, the separation or reconstitution of mass or bodies. When the impossible or the unexpected suddenly appears to interrupt reality, we are enchanted because of the break with the banality of the everyday. Magic is rare—as are the colored visions of the painter of Giverny, who saw cathedrals, cliffs, haystacks, and the reflections in his pond in blue, pink, orange, green, red, mauve, or yellow. The strangeness of these *Paysages d'eau*, which resides even in their title (how, by definition, could a landscape be made only of water?) thus leads Franc-Nohain to pose a question: "Can these even be called paintings? Obviously, they're hung on a wall and have had frames put around them. But might this not also be the window display of an extraordinary fabric merchant, or even of those cunning mirrors onto Paradise . . . ?"[23] Cunning is the dexterity or intelligence with which the prestidigitator hides the mechanisms of his trick so as to offer the spectator the sensation that what he is seeing is "real," that he is in the presence of the impossible: to submerge him in a reinvented real governed by new rules set by the magician himself—for Monet had no intention of painting by the rules of the pictorial tradition against which he constantly fought.

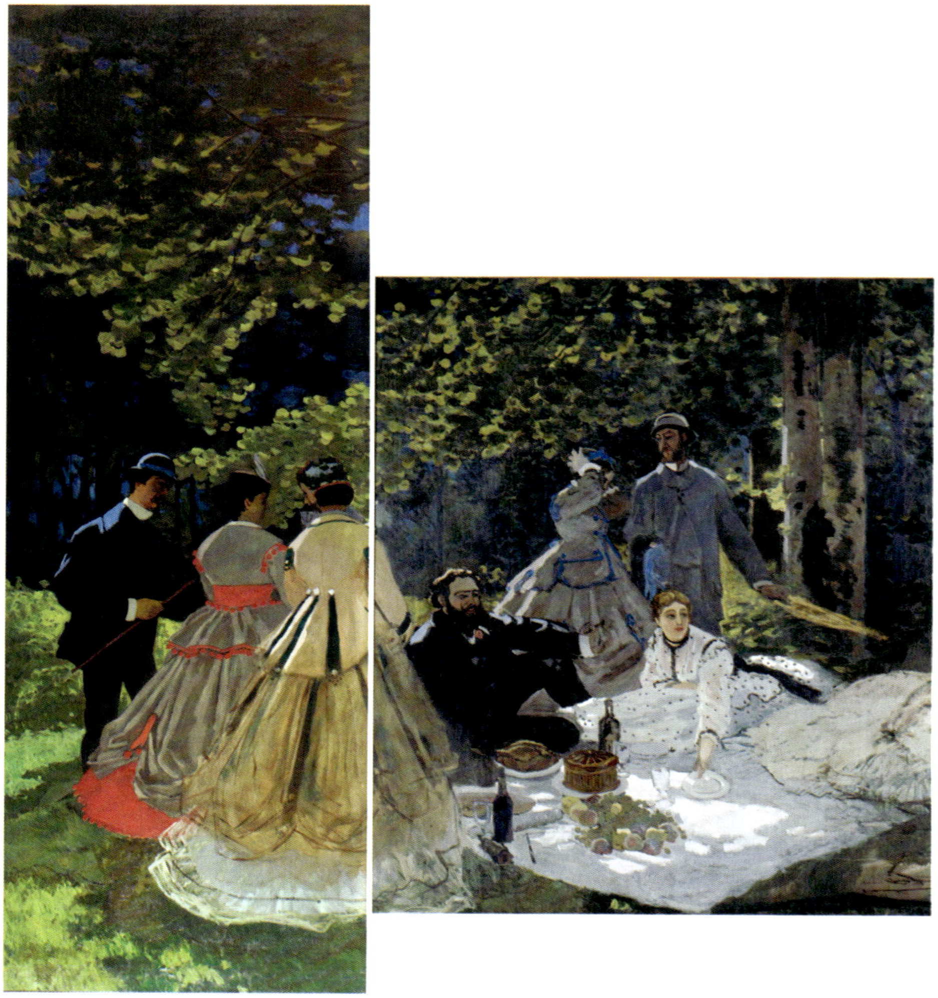

A Kind of Evaporation of Things

It was in the wake of the *Paysages d'eau*, this act of painting *against* the tradition, that the subsequent reception of Monet's work—until his death in 1926 and in the years following—must be understood. After the *Paysages d'eau*, the painter dedicated himself to a series of canvases depicting Venice, which he visited in 1908 with his wife Alice, who then died in 1911. His son died prematurely three years later. It was at this period, in the course of 1914, that the painter concocted his insane plan: he would give his *Nymphéas* the physical dimensions reserved since the seventeenth century for prestigious canvases, the most respected "grand" history paintings; and he would multiply his paintings one after the other. It was perhaps not a coincidence that Monet had begun his career by experimenting with such grandiose formats in the *Déjeuner sur l'herbe*, a canvas more than 4 x 6 meters, which he intended for the Salon of 1866 but finally abandoned (fig. 102). In 1914, as war threatened and he mourned the successive deaths of intimates, the despairing painter decided to confront a final challenge: an immoderate amplification of his pond, giving his "jewel," his "mirror of black bronze"[24] proportions that would trivialize the spaces of that Salon where he had been so shabbily treated. He was in a race against time in the form of his age: "I am speaking here as if I had lots [of time] ahead of me, which is pure folly—as is having undertaken such work at my age, launching myself into gigantic constructions. Yes, it's insane, completely insane."[25] Then when, at last, he offered his work to—or imposed it on—France in 1918 as a celebration of victory, and even while he

Fig. 102. Claude Monet, *Luncheon on the Grass (Déjeuner sur l'herbe)* (two extant panels), 1865–66. Oil on canvas, left panel: 164 5/8 x 59 in. (418 x 150 cm); central panel: 97 7/8 x 85 7/8 in. (248.7 x 218 cm). Musée d'Orsay, Paris

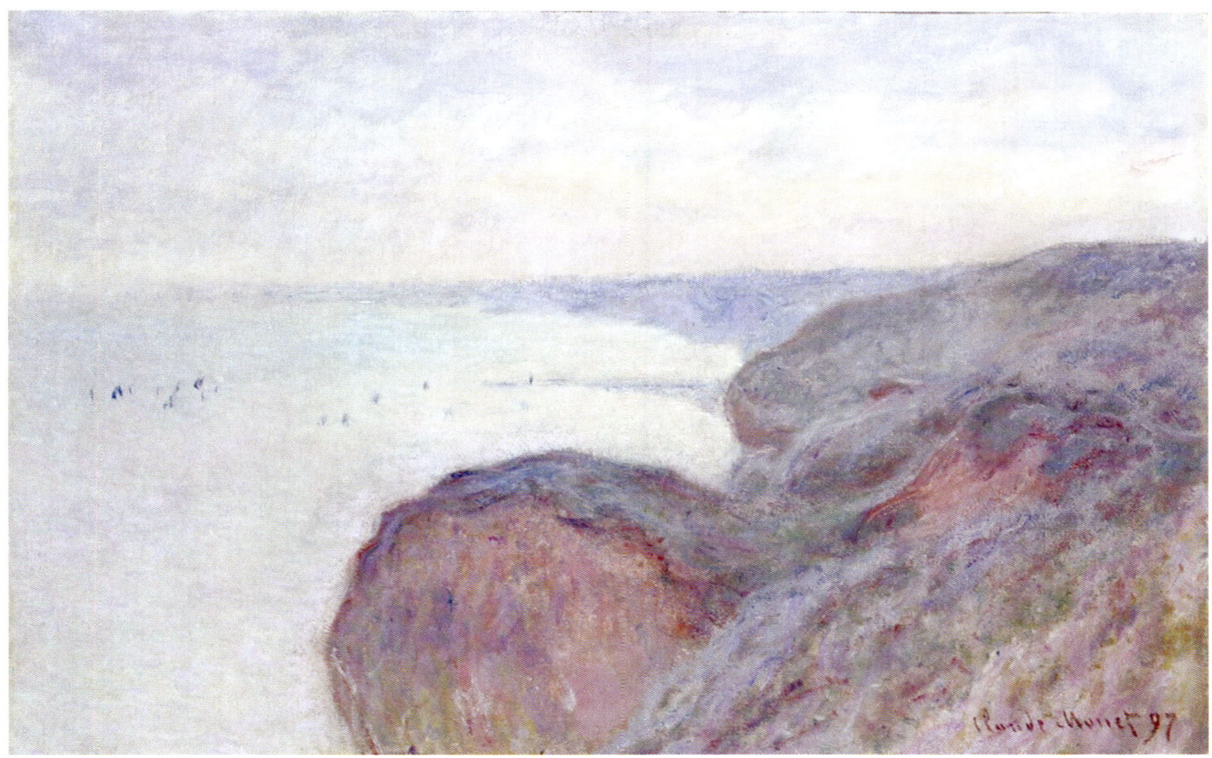

Fig. 103. Claude Monet, *Steep Cliffs near Dieppe*, 1897. Oil on canvas, 25 5/8 x 39 ½ in. (65 x 100.5 cm). The State Hermitage Museum, St. Petersburg, Russia. Entered the Hermitage in 1948; handed over from the State Museum of New Western Art, Moscow; originally in the Sergei Shchukin collection. ГЭ-8992

was supported and encouraged by his faithful friend and intermediary, Georges Clémenceau, who was committed to seeing the project come to fruition, Monet still battled with himself. The painter devoted himself exclusively, even obsessively, to his project, but could not make up his mind to surrender it to the eye of the public. In keeping with his wishes, the immense panels of the *Nymphéas* would finally be on view at the Musée de l'Orangerie only after his death in 1927.

The artist, as he continuously touched and retouched his canvases in the privacy of his studio at Giverny, was nervous about the reaction of critics to his masterpiece, and he was right to be so: their attitude had very clearly become harsher when writing of Monet's painting. Gustave Geffroy, an important critic, biographer, and friend of the painter, persisted in defending him, explaining that at the turn of the nineteenth to the twentieth century, Monet had managed to "create a 'painting of the air' that very much seems to have never been so successfully done before"[26] (fig. 103) and now saw in his canvases "a sort of evaporation of things, a vanishing of contours, a delightful contact between surfaces and the atmosphere." But this pictorial evolution was not to everyone's taste. Thus, we see Louis Dimier, in his *Histoire de la peinture française au XIX*ème *siècle (1793–1903)*, published in 1914, judging that Monet had "exhausted himself looking for light in a uniform whiteness, dabbed on in little fat blobs of paint, with shadows thrown across the canvas which utterly wreak havoc on the painting." Referring to the series paintings of the 1890s, the author argued that "to make up for an effect that evaporates, he adds all the iridescence that his informed eye discovers in the rays of daylight, and by applying his principle to excess, slides into pure extravagance" (fig. 104).[27] Dimier, representing the Action-Française militant-monarchist Right, considered that all the best of France pre-dated 1789; for him, Monet surely represented the deplorable essence of any revolution: the *dispersion* of what had been *concentrated*. The concentration represented by tradition, patterns, and continuity (but also the powers of the monarchy) was dilapidated by the republic which divided them up. Atomized artistically by Impressionism with its scattered brushstrokes and freedom in choosing a subject—with Monet this meant

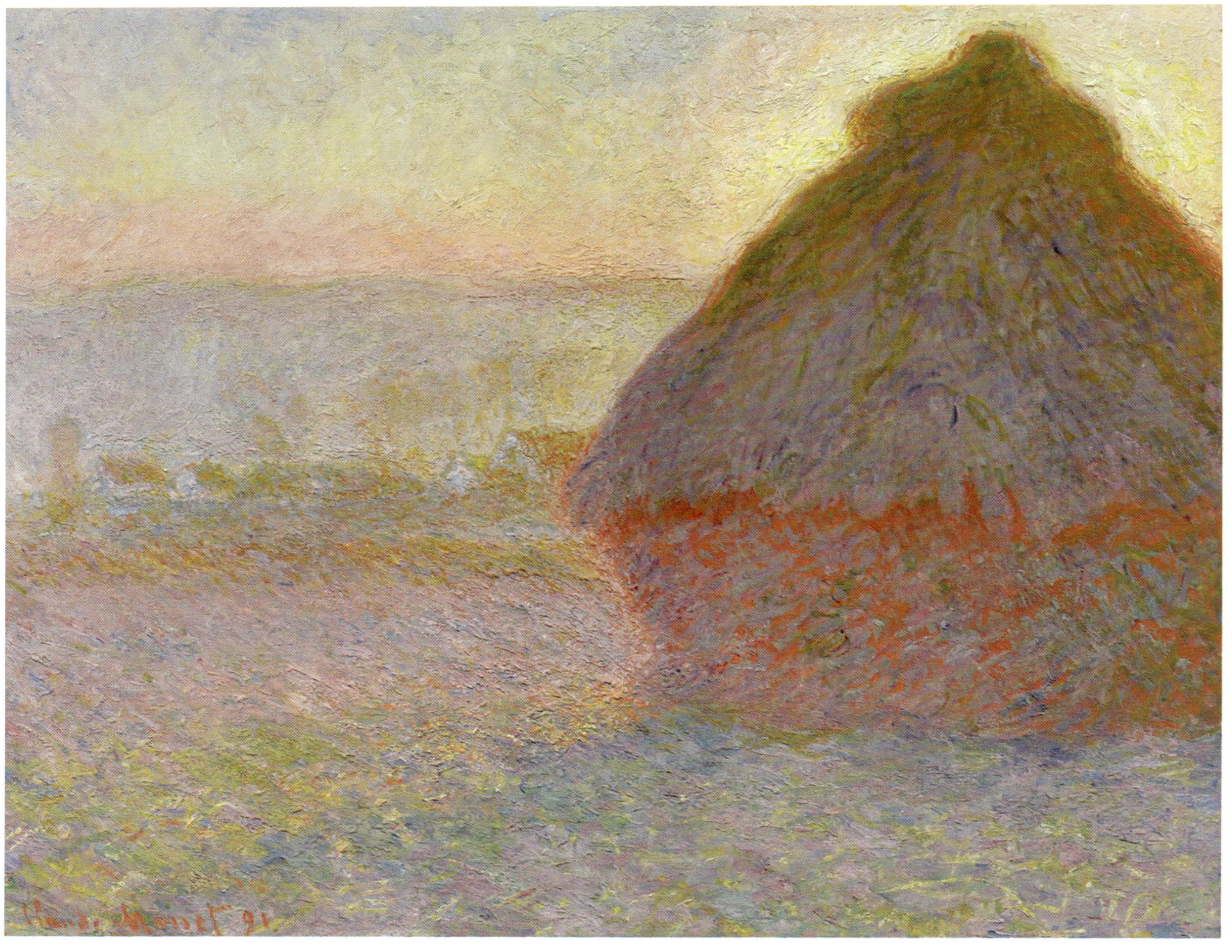

Fig. 104. Claude Monet, *Grainstack (Sunset)*, 1891. Oil on canvas, 28 7/8 x 36 1/2 in. (73.3 x 92.7 cm). Museum of Fine Arts, Boston. Juliana Cheney Edwards Collection. 25.112

"evaporation"—this resulted in the disappearance that, in the eyes of Dimier, always signified loss.

Others expressed similar criticism, among them André Michel, curator of the Department of Sculpture at the Louvre, who as early as 1896 wrote that Monet's canvases, "exasperated syllogisms," were the product of the "logic of a maniac, carrying the development of a theme to a painful, pathological tension." According to him, the "process had something of the exasperated and the morbid" in it, and "after such an effort and such an astonishing attempt at the impossible, such an abuse and a disarticulation of its processes, oil painting has nothing more to say."[28] This curator, a Protestant and, increasingly, a nationalist republican, greatly preferred Puvis de Chavannes (fig. 105), who embodied "the melancholy of the modern soul," Jean-François Millet, or Camille Corot (fig. 106) "in all the innocence and purity of his heart, alone against Nature . . . without preoccupying himself with the system, with a theory *for* or *against*."[29] Michel's exceptional, peremptory virulence with regard to Impressionism, and Monet in particular, was due to the fact that he found in them

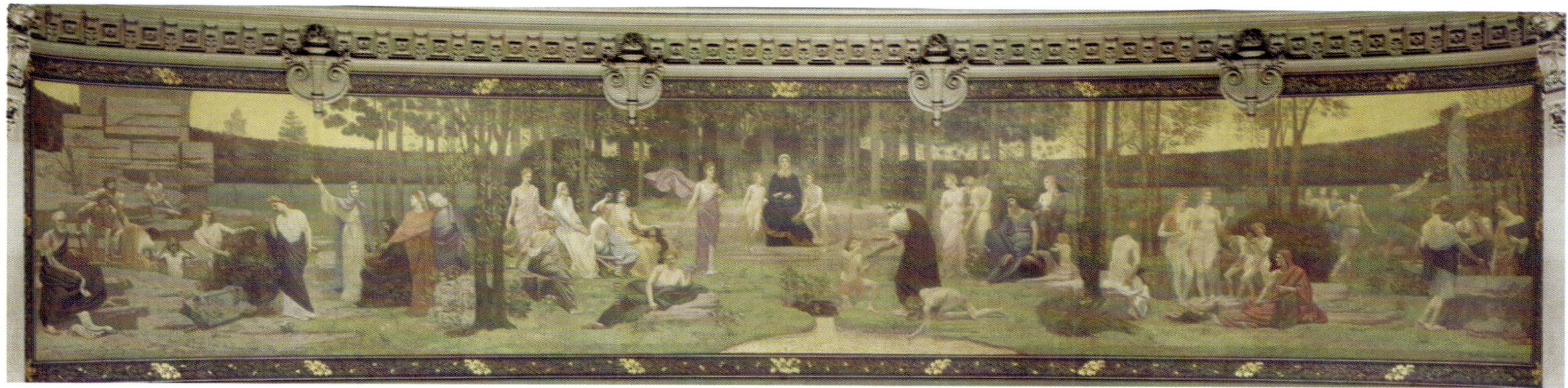

Fig. 105. Pierre Puvis de Chavannes, *The Sacred Wood*, 1887–89, fresco. Mural in the Grand Amphitheatre of the Sorbonne, Paris

both deprivation—concerning subject matter (the disappearance of nature)—and destruction—that of painting itself, the profession it represented as well as its pictorial tradition. In the language the critic employed, the practice of the painter of the *Cathédrales* morphed into a sickness, a sort of bacteria devouring the "sincere" mimetic tradition that Michel so loved. When he took up his pen in 1912 to write of Monet's vision of Venice, it was to describe it as "more chimerical than any other" for "whatever pretext would suffice for him. The monuments of Venice don't interest him."[30]

Henry Marcel, Administrateur Général de la Bibliothèque Nationale, said exactly that when in *Peinture française au XIXème siècle* he wrote that Monet's London, "a gigantic city, depicted by a new Turner, was no longer anything but the prodigious apparition of a dream." The artist "spiritualized . . . shapes released from all the constraints of weight, volume, substance," summoning forth "insubstantial mobilities."[31] Still, if these authors thus gave a particularly ethereal image to Monet's painting in generalist works of art history, this means that the authors as well as the public admitted that the history of painting did indeed include a chapter on the dissolution of its subjects, the consequence of Impressionism, and more particularly the end result of the art of Monet.

Breaking Down the Object to Its Total Destruction

Monet's ability to move away from the real, from all forms of naturalism, to abstract representation so as to give it over to the power of the imagination or to the meditation of the spirit[32]—everything that the critics cited here loved about *Paysages d'eau*—represented everything about the painter that was beginning to be pointed at, then frankly detested, in other circles. What differentiates the authors of these two critical trends should also be underlined: those making up the first belonged to literary and musical milieus, were interested in what was going on in theater and poetry, and were themselves writers. These most certainly rejoiced as they stood before the *Nymphéas,* finding in them unexpected beauty and infinite meanings (philosophical, narrative, sensory, and even musical). On the other hand stood traditional art historians and curators, who made themselves the guardians of an opposing pictorial tradition that saw it as a duty to exclude Monet, precisely because his progressive

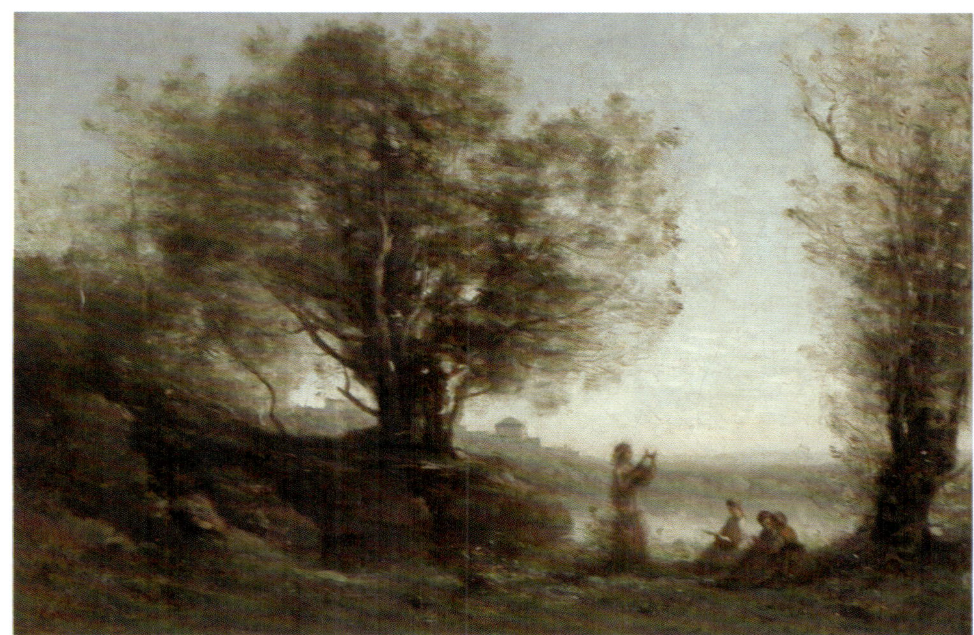

Fig. 106. Jean-Baptiste-Camille Corot, *Orpheus Lamenting Eurydice*, c. 1861–65. Oil on canvas, 16 ½ x 24 in. (41.9 x 61 cm). Kimbell Art Museum, Fort Worth

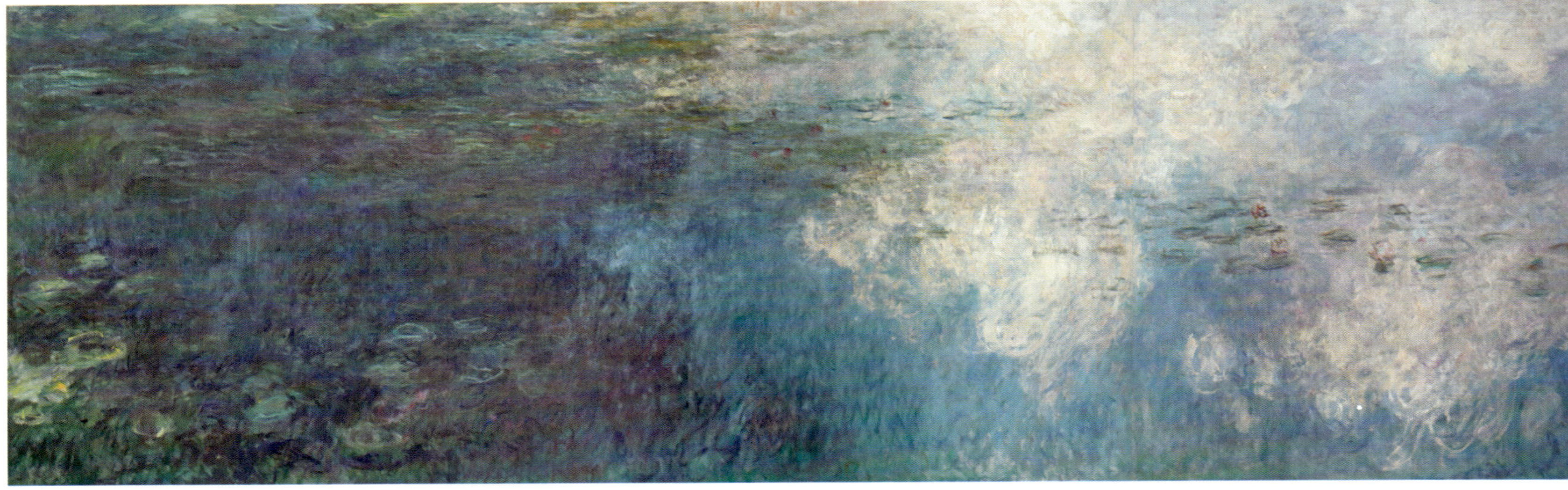

Fig. 108. Claude Monet, *Water Lilies: Clouds*, c. 1915–26. Oil on canvas, 78 ¾ x 502 in. (2 x 12.75 m). Room 1, north wall, Musée de l'Orangerie, Paris

"evaporation" of subject cut all ties to the past. The radical innovation of the painter, which led him to more and more abstract canvases, horrified them.

René Schneider is another example of this second category, writing after the opening of the Musée de l'Orangerie and the revelation to the Parisian public of what it contained. A professor of art history at the Faculté de Lettres de l'Université de Paris who had written his thesis on the classical aesthetics of the neoclassical theorist Quatremère de Quincy,[33] Schneider undertook the writing of *L'art français, XIXème et XXème siècles. Du réalisme à notre temps* in 1930. Did the death of the painter permit him to make a case even more brutal than the previous arguments? The disappearance of subject matter at Monet's hand was exemplified, as Schneider saw things, in the *Rouen Cathedrals*, which "oozed decay in grey, blue and violet."[34] As evidence, Schneider used one of the panels at the Musée de l'Orangerie (fig. 107) to stand for the "technical experiments" of the painter, "an end in themselves in the mind of a practitioner who . . . cheerfully shut himself off inside the circle of pure art." Impressionism became responsible for a "lyricism" in French painting that maintained only the most fragile links with the real, which kept only the "reflection and fragrance of things but soon led to absolute disregard of subject: the real, precise and observed."[35] Obviously, with his "completely insane" project, underway at Giverny for over a decade, Monet had gone too far: art for art's sake, a disdain for the real, is indeed the menacing tendency of painting preoccupied only with itself, with its own gestures—that is to say, abstract painting. This is a strange idea for those of us who clearly recognize the surface of a pond and its floating water lilies in the last panels of the painter; to understand, we must try to go back to the artistic place and time of his astonished contemporaries. The immense scale of the work exhibited at the Orangerie was comparable to only two things: to painted décors, even if the isolation and autonomy of the panels exhibited alone in the two elliptical rooms of the museum are antithetical to a "decorative" status; or to frescos and other large works, first royal, then public commissions, the enormity of which assured them status as works of art, though not, as before, as history paintings with suitably classical subject matter.

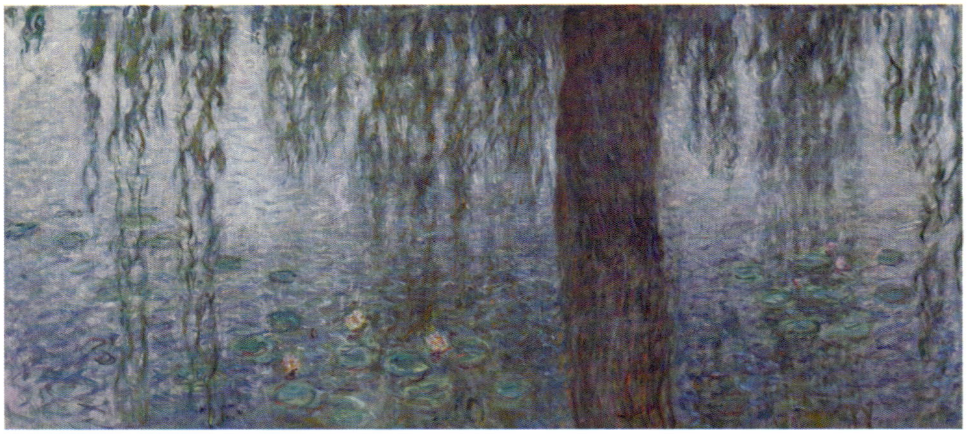

In addition, what was aesthetically admissible in the classic easel formats of the *Paysages d'eau* in 1909

Fig. 107. Claude Monet, *Waterlilies: Clear Morning with Willows* (detail of left panel), c. 1915–26. Oil on canvas, 78 ¾ x 502 in. (2 x 12.75 m). Room 2, south wall, Musée de l'Orangerie, Paris

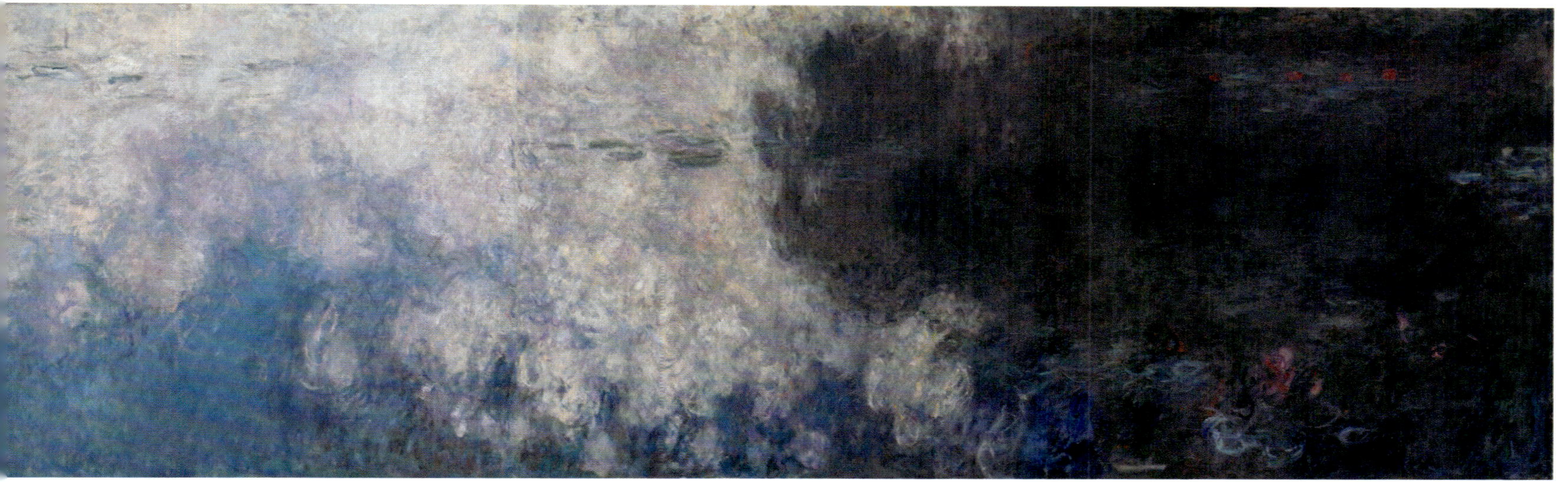

became shocking in 1927 over the immense surfaces of the Orangerie panels: Monet's brushstrokes had widened, thickening and growing before the eyes of viewers who—if they took the trouble to look closely—could distinguish nothing more than a chaos of colors mixed with no regard for one of the basic lessons of art: that drawing must preside over composition (fig. 108). Here, painting seemed to have been definitively set free. Thus in an article in the *Intransigeant* of May 18, 1927, announcing the opening of what was then referred to as the "Musée Claude Monet," was it said that the painter "worked for more than twenty years to complete his painted poem," but that he "unfortunately retouched his work up to just before his death and his last repaintings are not successful."[36] Camille Mauclair, a critic who was more and more hostile to modernity in the arts, openly displayed the same verdict, despite his affection for the painter: "What can be said with all justice is that Monet—magnificent individual dreaming only of satisfying his passion—made an attempt at a pictorial "raid," one hardly possible to carry out without ending up with the unintelligible, [since] an excess of analysis finishes by breaking down the object to its complete destruction."[37] Even Arsène Alexandre (fig. 109), admirer and friend of Monet, seems for once to have lost his enthusiasm:

> But we cannot precisely affirm that the retouching improves this powerful symphony. . . . The painter tried playing the prodigious virtuoso, seeing what color without form could give materially. It can go no further without going beyond suggestion itself.[38]

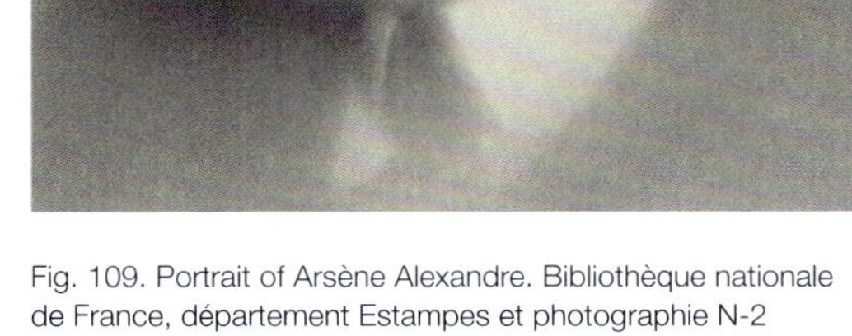

Fig. 109. Portrait of Arsène Alexandre. Bibliothèque nationale de France, département Estampes et photographie N-2

Condemnations, always of the same kind, followed one another everywhere. The art historian Louis Gillet tried to defend Monet against one of his sharpest detractors, François Fosca, claiming that the *Grandes Décorations* were the greatest abstract work in existence, limpid as far as what abstraction then meant for the public: art able to transmit an emotion (of which it is the heart and the reason for existing—its only justification) and which, in order to exist, preferred to separate itself progressively from the meaning that immediately accompanies the recognizable "object." Suggestion can procure a range of emotions that is wider than the closed meaning of the faithful imitation, and this is where abstract painting is similar to music and poetry:

> Ever since pure painting and pure poetry have been spoken of, ever since attempts have been made in the arts to separate what is feeling, expression, music, and to isolate each from the terrestrial elements of the poem; ever since a plastic art has been sought out, a language

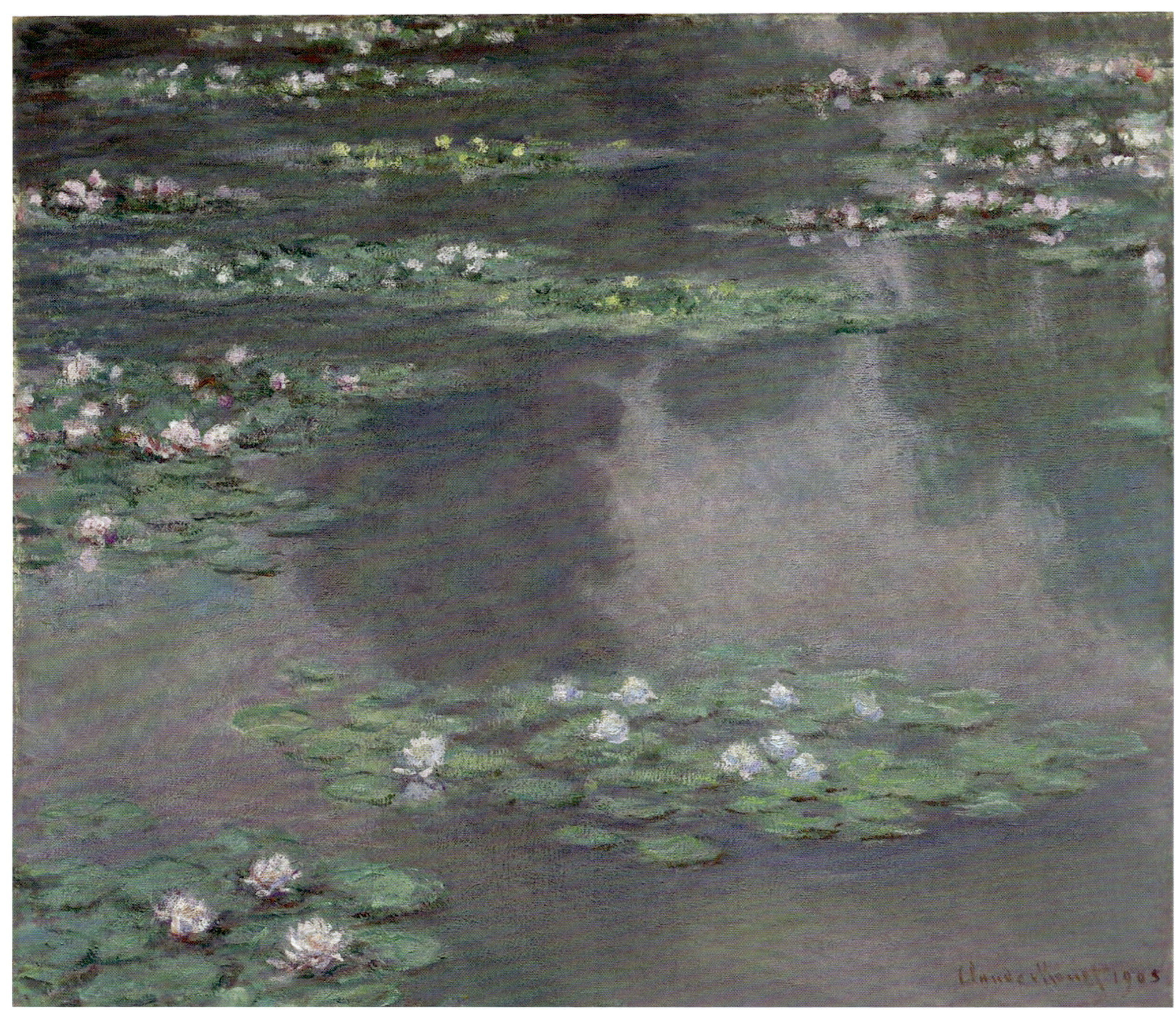

Fig. 110. Claude Monet, *Water Lilies*, 1905. Oil on canvas, 35 ¼ x 39 ½ in. (89.5 x 100.3 cm). Museum of Fine Arts, Boston. Gift of Edward Jackson Holmes. 39.804

removed from all distinct representation that moves, as the heart is moved by a piece of Persian faïence, by the charm of a rug, without taking into consideration the moral content of the thing painted or described; ever since we have tormented ourselves trying to invent an art that imitates nothing but is satisfied with evoking [and] is nothing but allusion, suggestion, symbol, I don't believe that a formula superior to that of Claude Monet's *Nymphéas* has been found.[39]

For Fosca, however, this was the heart of the problem. In the monograph he devotes to Monet, he asserts that the exemplary nature of the work is meant as a warning, since "from time to time, when painting becomes too abstract, or too dried out, young artists will come to ask Monet for advice." They will then become "aware of the error to which [his] temperament leads."[40] The author further explains that "[I] estimate, for myself, that the art of Monet represents a sort of expedition, a raid, on the extreme outermost reaches of painting,"[41] employing the same words as Mauclair. The word "raid," used by both of them, says much about how the last *Nymphéas* were perceived: Monet's approach was a *rapid* incursion into *enemy* territory—an unfamiliar place, unexplored, dangerous, one where no one should "set foot,"[42] to use Fosca's terms. Abstraction was also a form of violence (the term is from military vocabulary) characterized by its rapidity—just like the painter's brushwork. In his conclusion, Gillet concedes to Fosca a fear about the future: "The work—one of the most daring ever attempted in painting—would it be understood? With intrepid audacity, the master here pushed his principle to its logical conclusion."[43]

So, what fear does Monet's "intrepid audacity" speak of? What was the danger that the painter stood up to? To use the terms of the curator André Michel, long before the *Paysages d'eau* were radicalized into the *Nymphéas* at the Musée de l'Orangerie, "good sense protests; there is an obscure feeling that by pursuing forever and only these changing and disappointing shades [of color], painting would lose itself in nothingness" (fig. 110).[44] But the good sense that "closes off all dialectical paths of escape, defines a homogenous world where one is at home, sheltered from the upset or loss of the 'dream,' "[45] as Roland Barthes calls it, is indeed also what agonizes over "nothingness," that is, all that is foreign, unfamiliar, uncertain. Isn't it just that fear of nothingness expressed by Michel that finally corroborates the powerful feeling of immersive absorption that the *Nymphéas* even now provoke in the viewer (fig. 111)? Not being afraid of drowning in them necessitates the ability to still *be moved* when faced with art and this, in the unsettled period between the two wars, which can be described artistically as a return to order, declined. At the heart of it, these "cunning mirrors on Paradise" were indeed the object of a slightly magical trick; they caused the critics to see not the crepuscular reflections in the pond at Giverny but those of their own preoccupations—their sorrows and worries, their hopes and imaginary worlds. In them, each one was confronted with his own depths: in the face of this "immeasurable nothingness"[46] some felt only a "painful malaise, a desperate need to set themselves free,"[47] whereas others could "dream of the poetry of the world."[48]

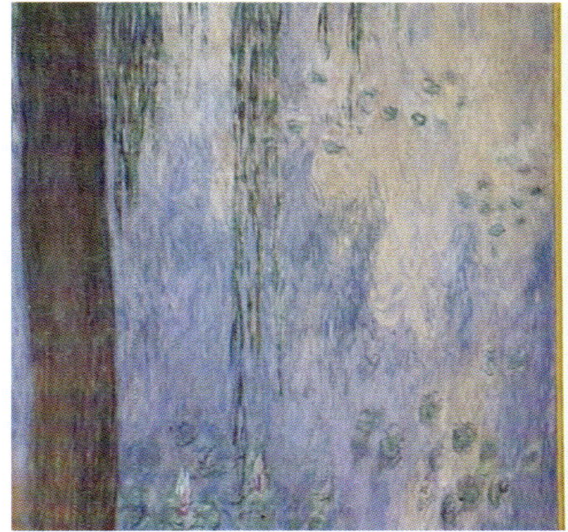
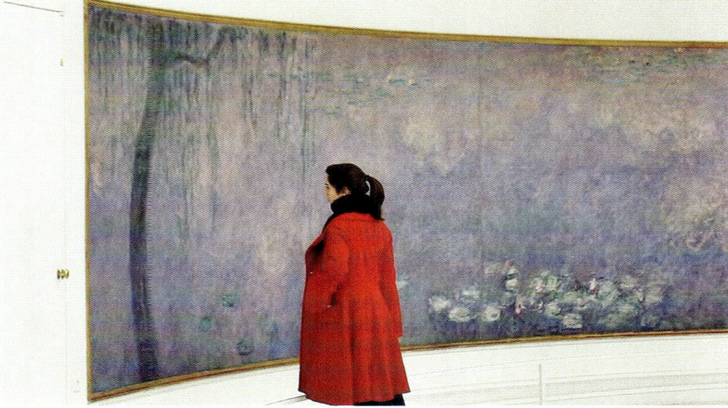

Fig. 111. Visitor looking at Monet's *Water Lilies* in the Musée de l'Orangerie, 2011

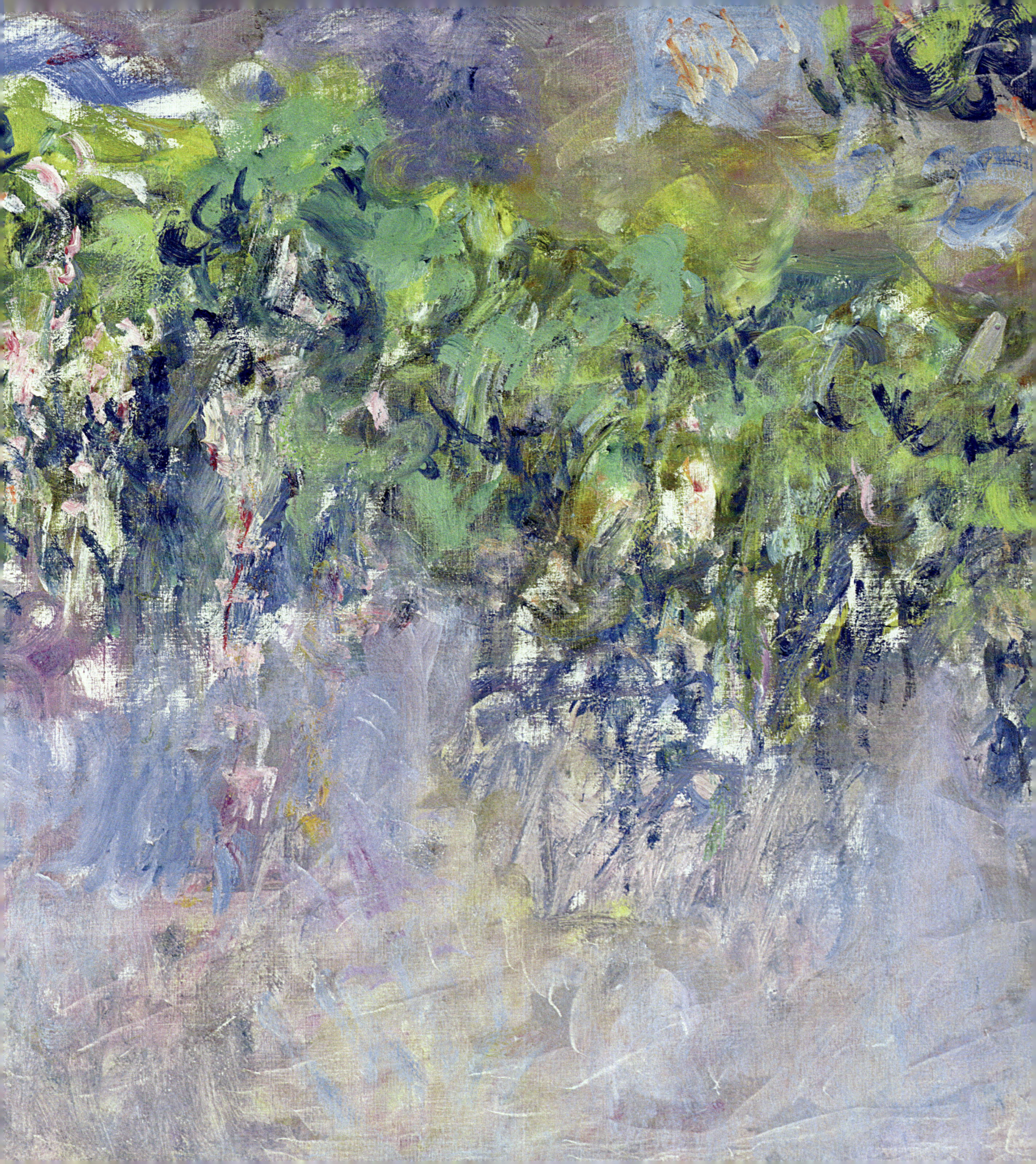

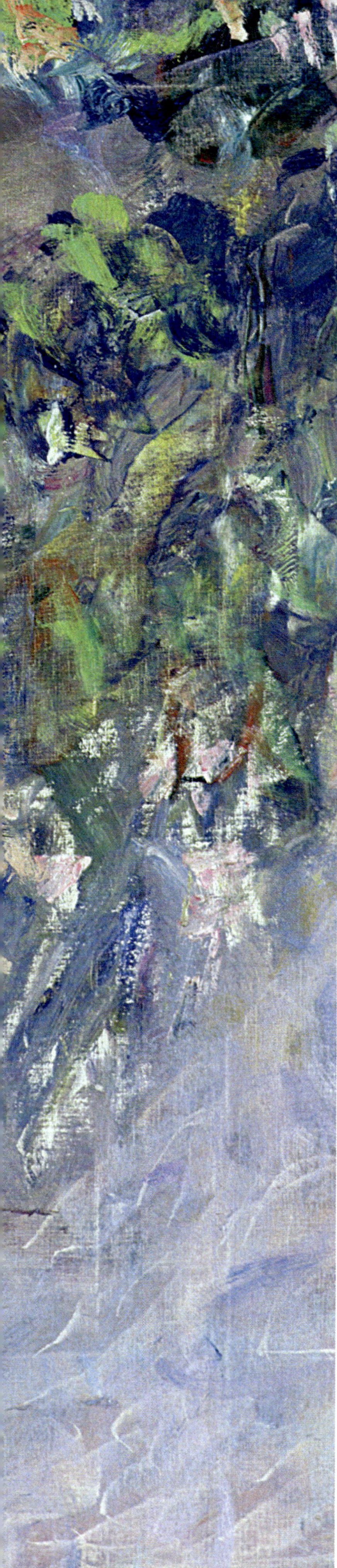

The *Grandes Décorations* from Claude to Michel Monet (1914–1966)

Marianne Mathieu

Senior curator at the Musée Marmottan Monet, Paris

On November 12, 1918, to celebrate the end of the First World War, Claude Monet sent a letter to his closest friend, the Président du Conseil, Georges Clémenceau: "My dear and great friend, I am on the eve of finishing two decorative panels that I want to sign on Victory Day, and I am addressing myself to you to ask that you act as intermediary in my giving them to the State. It is little enough, but it is the only way I have to participate in the victory. I want these to be placed in the Musée des Arts Décoratifs, and I want you to be the one who chooses them."[1]

Beginning in 1914, Monet had frenetically devoted himself to a series of monumental paintings focused on the theme of his water garden at Giverny. To undertake this titanic project, the artist had built a third studio on his property, this one measuring 275 square meters—just over 900 square feet—and equipped with a system of pulleys allowing him, despite his advanced age, to manipulate enormous canvases by himself. Aside from sketches measuring roughly 2 x 2 meters painted *sur le motif* (in nature), this series as a whole is composed of very unusual formats: for free-standing canvases, panels 2 meters high and either 6 or 4.25 meters wide, or sometimes 3 meters wide for those forming diptychs or triptychs.

Having been informed that Monet had been mulling over the design of "a circular room whose picture rail below the plinth would be entirely occupied by a horizon of water dotted with . . . vegetation"[2] since the beginning of the century, Clémenceau, in the days that followed the initial letter, convinced the artist to proceed to a larger gift, one that materialized his dream: the construction of a room with measurements tailored to his panels, a kind of Musée Monet.[3] Since the project was particularly costly, Clémenceau—at the end of his political life—suggested that the greatest possible discretion be exercised until the negotiations with the State bore fruit.

Claude Monet, *Wisteria* (detail), 1919–20, cat. 30

It must be said that when the war ended, curiosity about Monet's work—not seen by the public since his exhibition of Venetian scenes in 1912—was at its height. Recent work by the person then considered the undisputed master of French painting naturally kindled the interest of dealers. In November 1918, the Galerie Bernheim-Jeune, which had organized the Venice exhibition, offered to buy a monumental canvas.[4] "Impossible," replied Monet. "I use each one for the others."[5] On January 21, 1919, however, the painter turned over to Bernheim and the Galerie Durand-Ruel five easel paintings: views of the garden ponds, their facture dramatic and already marked by the effect of the painter's cataract problems (fig. 112).[6] This did not prevent Monet from selling them for a great deal of money. The largest formats (between 131 x 110 centimeters and 120 x 89 centimeters) sold for 20,000 French francs (FRF), the smallest (73.5 x 100 centimeters) for 18,000,[7] a sum that was more than thirty percent over the selling price for the very sought-after *Paysages d'eau* shown in 1909 at Durand-Ruel.[8] Numerous nonprofessionals also appeared on the scene. In February 1920, even though the donation project had not yet been made public, the painter confided to the dealer René Gimpel that Doctor Gosset was interested in his large formats: "[He] wanted several of them for a property he was building in the country. I told him," the artist continued, "that I would only let him have them if he placed them in full light. People are starting to make offers, but I don't think I'll sell them. I'll work on them until I die; that will help me get through life; work already helped me get through the terrible hours of war."[9]

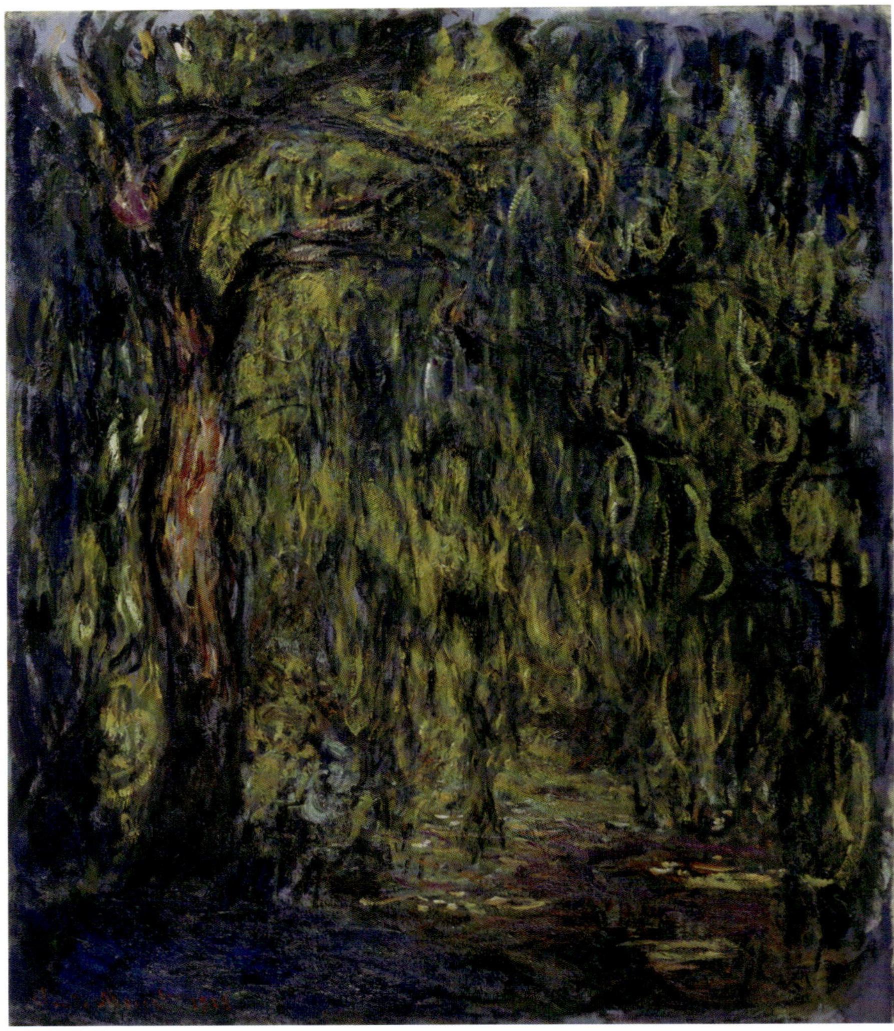

Fig. 112. Claude Monet, *Weeping Willow*, 1918. Oil on canvas. 51 5/8 x 43 1/2 in. (131.1 x 110.3 cm). Columbus Museum of Art, Ohio. One of the paintings Monet sold to Bernheim-Jeune and Durand-Ruel in 1919

His American clientele—to whom Monet owed a great deal of his success—also turned up. In June 1920, the richest man in Chicago, Martin A. Ryerson (fig. 113, who already owned sixteen Monets, obtained an "audience" at Giverny through the intermediary of Joseph Durand-Ruel. Ryerson was an eminent member of the Board of Trustees at the Art Institute of Chicago and, with Bertha Palmer and Clarence Buckingham, had founded its Impressionist collections. On this occasion, he was representing the interests of the Institute, which was undergoing impressive expansion. Accompanied by Frances Hutchinson, the wife of the president of the Art Institute, and also, according to the newspaper *Le Temps*,[10] by a curator and an architect, Ryerson apparently offered to buy thirty or so panels—or the majority of the monumental production—to exhibit on the first floor of the Art Institute "in premises designed by the artist."[11] Privileging France with no doubt whatever as the beneficiary of the donation, Monet declined his offer, impervious to the $3,000,000 that he allegedly was to be paid for them,[12] an extravagant sum corresponding to FRF 42,615,000 at the rate of exchange of the time,[13] or nearly eight-and-a-half times the total value of Monet's estate (FRF 5,038,308) at the time of his death![14]

The Japanese art lover Kojiro Matsukata was more fortunate (fig. 114). Son of a Japanese prime minister from the Meiji period and an alumnus of Yale University, Baron Matsukata was a leading figure in naval construction. Working out of Kobe, he manufactured infrastructure for ships delivered worldwide, including ready-to-be-finished "stock boats," and established himself as the principal supplier to both the British and the French during World War I. As of 1916, he regularly traveled to England, France, and the United States, taking advantage of his visits to form a large art collection. Recommended by Léonce Bénédite, the former director of the Musée du Luxembourg and first curator of the Musée Rodin, he was received at Giverny on September 13, 1921, with two compatriots, the Renaissance historian Yukio Yashiro and a student, Eisaku Wada. The latter confided a summary of the day's events to his diary, still not well known outside Japan. Monet, whose proposed donation to the State had been public for almost a year, opened to his visitors the doors of his studio, of which the young Wada gave a description:

> Of an impressive size. A space of about six *ma* by eight *ma*,[15] no, surely more. Incredibly high ceiling. Metallic frame structure. At the four corners of the room, round holes have been pierced, to evacuate toward the outdoors the hot air blown around by the fan. The place is also equipped with radiators to heat in winter. There were several panels of painted murals on the theme of the water lilies. Some were independent, others constituted a continuous whole over about five panels. The whole forming a total length of nearly 24 meters, with a height of nearly 5 *shaku*.[16] Each panel was of the same height, but some measured one *jô*, others eight *shaku*, still others up to 3 meters wide. All showed beautiful colors, emanating a powerful effect and bold touch."[17]

There is no doubt that, like Wada, Matsukata particularly appreciated the recent work by the painter, as evidenced in this passage:

> Leaning against the wall [of the studio salon], a recent work, the latest in progress, of an incredible boldness. It would seem that it represents a pond, the shadows of the trees reflected on the surface of the water, but the outlines of the shapes were only sketched, barely suggested. However, there was a beauty in the colors that went beyond everything he has painted up to now. Monet asked me what I saw there. 'A symphony of color,' I answered, 'that must be apprehended as music would be.' 'Entirely,' he approved, enchanted to have someone opposite him who understood his intentions."[18]

It was probably because Matsukata wanted to create the first museum of Western art in Tokyo—to be called the "Museum of Shared Pleasures"—that in May 1922, only a month after designating nineteen panels as destined for the Orangerie,[19] Monet agreed to sell Matsukata eighteen canvases, including three recent works: *Weeping Willow* (cat. 44), a *Water Lily* of 2 x 2 meters (fig. 115), and, above all, a large canvas of 2 x 4.25 meters, *Water-Lily Pond, Weeping Willow Reflections* (fig. 116).[20] The sale of the monumental panel was mentioned even in the American press. The weekly *American Art News*, which had been able to interview Matsukata in January, titled its article "Monet Gets $85,000 for a Single Canvas" and retraced the event, stating that "a short while ago Claude Monet was the recipient of a check for 800,000 francs which he said was sent to him by 'a Japanese collector of Western art' (who could have been no other than Matsukata) with the request for a picture selected by the artist himself according to his own pleasure."[21]

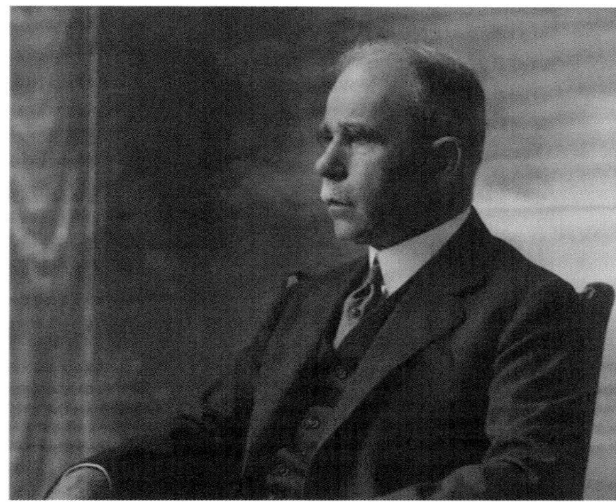
Fig. 113. Martin A. Ryerson. University of Chicago Photographic Archive. Gift of Mrs. E. Philip Miller

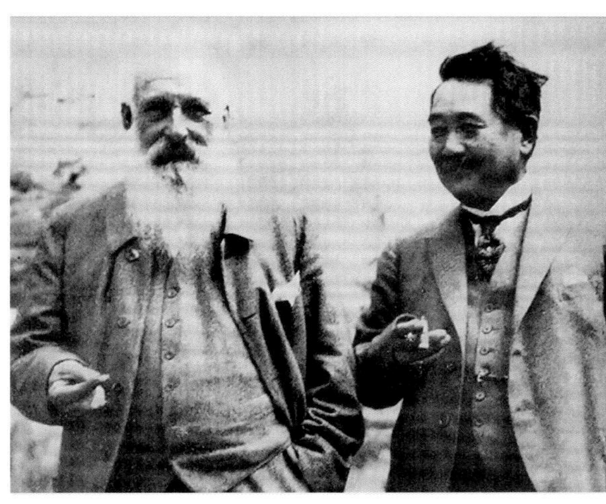
Fig.114. Claude Monet and Kôjirô Matsukata, 1921

What the weekly said was true: *Water Lily Pond, Weeping Willow Reflections* would have been not only the largest but also the most expensive work ever sold by the artist. The price set by the art lover—intentionally compared by the journalist to a Renaissance art patron—was two-and-a-half times higher than Monet's rates in 1922.[22] It was incomparable to the "friend's price" (FRF 25,000) for which Picasso sold his *Demoiselles d'Avignon* to the couturier Jacques Doucet in 1924 (hoping that, thanks to the latter, it would enter the Louvre);[23] and, despite inflation,[24] it was also superior to the $30,000[25] that Doctor Barnes gave Henri Matisse in 1930 for *The*

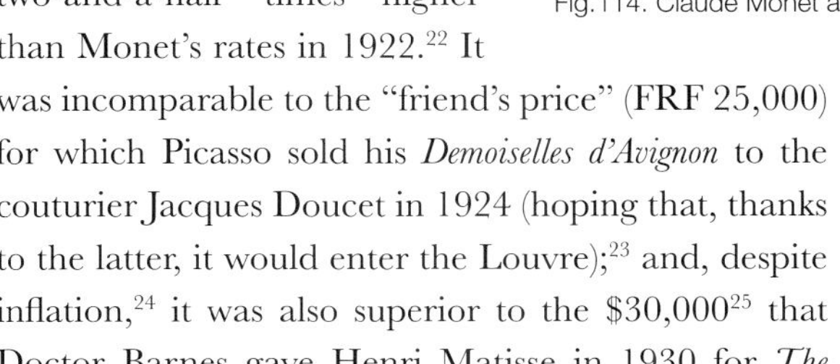

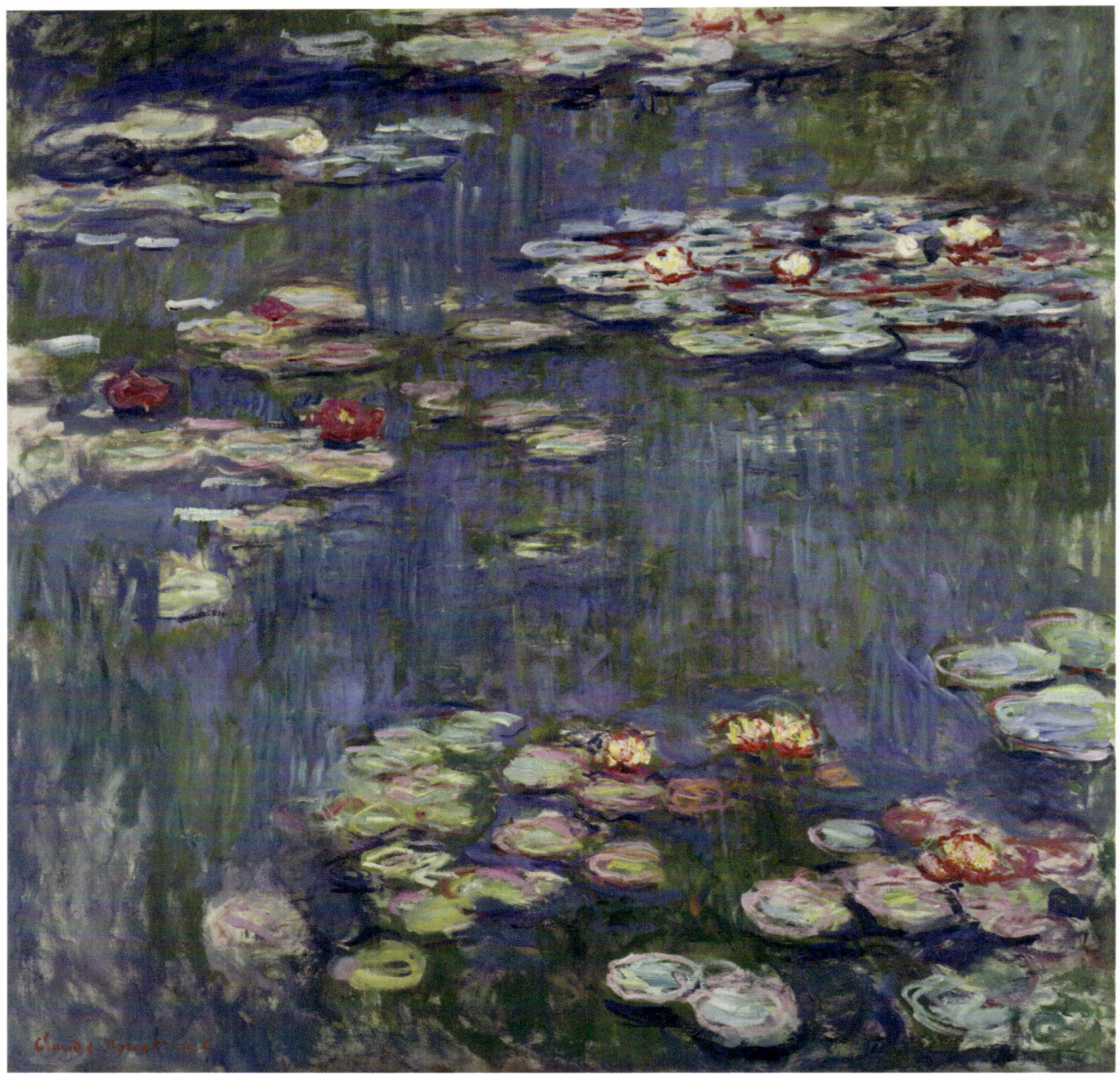

Fig. 115. Claude Monet, *Water Lilies*, 1916. Oil on canvas, 79 x 79 1/8 in. (200.5 x 201 cm). The National Museum of Western Art, Tokyo. Matsukata Collection, P.1959-0151

Dance II, a decorative fresco of 4 x 13 meters! First stored at the Hôtel Biron, then in Normandy during World War II, after the Liberation of Paris, Monet's panel, along with the rest of the Matsukata collection, was impounded by the French administration as the property of an enemy alien. It was at this period that *Water Lily Pond, Weeping Willow Reflections* was lost to view. Known only through photographs, it was rediscovered and recognized by the author, rolled up and two-thirds ruined, in the reserves of the Louvre on September 26, 2016. France has transferred the painting to the National Western Art Museum in Tokyo, which has the core of the Matsukata holdings. Despite its condition, the painting offers a unique testimony: it is the sole monumental panel that left Giverny during Monet's lifetime, and thus the only one to be signed and dated, the inscription miraculously preserved in red in the lower left of the damaged canvas: Claude Monet 1916 (fig. 117).

Despite the interest of dealers and collectors in the teens and twenties, after the death of Monet in 1926, the situation changed. No longer was there a group of chosen collectors trying to convince a living legend to sell recent, never-before-seen canvases at any price. With the inauguration of the *Water Lilies* at the Orangerie of the Tuileries in 1927, Monet's ultimate work was finally made public (fig. 118). From then on, it could be compared with

Fig. 116. Claude Monet, *Water-Lily Pond, Weeping Willow Reflections,* 1916. Oil on canvas, 78 ¾ x 167 ⅜ in. (200 x 425 cm). The National Museum of Western Art, Tokyo. Matsukata Collection (as temporarily faced with tissue paper during restoration)

the art of its time. A few days after the inauguration, the Polish-French critic Waldemar-George wrote: "This ensemble of paintings, which everyone has been talking about for the last few years, but in reality, very few people had seen, was not only representative of a style and a period, but also of a whole conception of art."[26] And it was indeed this approach—founded on vision, light, and color—that aroused hostility from some avant-garde groups, especially in Cubist milieus. The judgment of the artist André Lhote on the subject is uncompromising: "there is only light for the painter of color . . . one has only to see—at the Orangerie—where the love of this phenomenon led Claude Monet: to artistic suicide."[27] In a sentence that became famous, the author Paul Morand declared: "The *Water Lilies* are not a condemnation of Impressionism, as the Ecole des Beaux-Arts has hastened to say: it's old age, it's technique, it's Monet after Monet, and it's also, after Vétheuil, Giverny. We know that—with the exception of the Treaty of Versailles—the *Water Lilies* are the ugliest gift a Statesman has ever given to France."[28]

As a result, the way Monet was portrayed broke in two. On the one hand, the painter of the years 1870–90, leader of Impressionism and one of the great masters of the late nineteenth century, was celebrated. On the other, the Orangerie *Water Lilies* and the whole of his late work stood condemned. It was at this period that a notion implicitly imposed itself: that of the "last Monet," eminently pejorative since it qualified the work of a

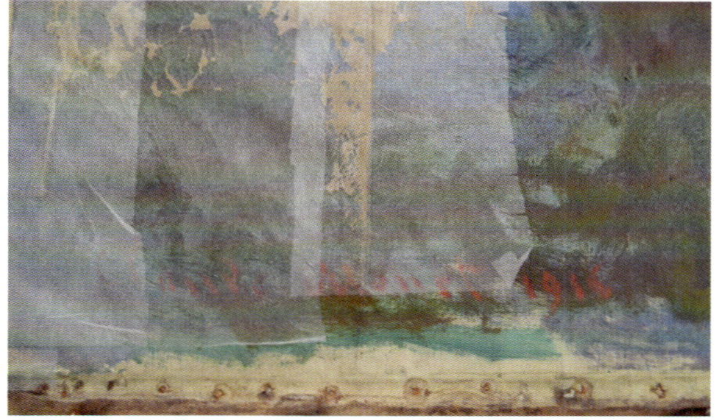

Fig. 117. Detail of Claude Monet's signature on *Water-Lily Pond, Weeping Willow Reflections*

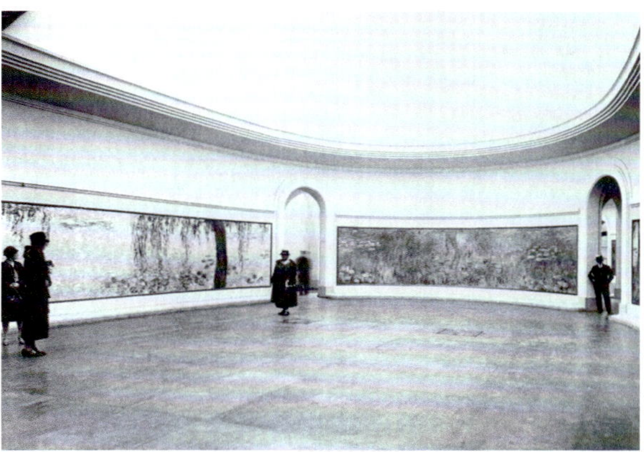

Fig. 118. The exhibition of Monet's *Water Lilies* in the Musée de l'Orangerie, 1930

painter who many considered had died to the world of art in 1914.

This situation was not limited to France; it was general, finding a particularly pointed echo in the United States.[29] Immediately after his death, Monet the Impressionist was celebrated in America. In 1927, four commemorative exhibitions were organized by the museums of Baltimore and Boston, the Art Club of Philadelphia, and the Galerie Durand-Ruel in New York. In 1929, the Havemeyer bequest to the Metropolitan Museum of Art in New York—where Matisse joyfully noted, "one finds the whole of the history of art"[30]—was of a scope comparable to that of the Caillebotte bequest, transferred the same year from the Musée du Luxembourg to the Louvre. Early collectors of Impressionist works in the United States, Louisine and Horace Havemeyer had reserved eight of their most beautiful Monets for the institution, with powerful results. "The representation," *The Arts* considered, "is so complete, joyous and instructive that it becomes really a matter of indifference to the Metropolitan Museum whether it acquires further Monets or not."[31] But the Havemeyer paintings—the early *Green Wave* and *Bathers at La Grenouillère* (fig. 119), the 1880s *Bouquet of Sunflowers* and *Chrysanthemums*, and, from the nineties, *Haystacks (Effects of Snow and Sun)*, *The Four Trees*, *The Houses of Parliament (Effect of Fog)*, and *The Water Lily Pond*—were all painted before 1900. Accordingly, all the art of Monet seemed to be limited to this period.[32] Not only was his work approached from a restrictive angle, but it was considered a thing of the past, having no relevance for the future.

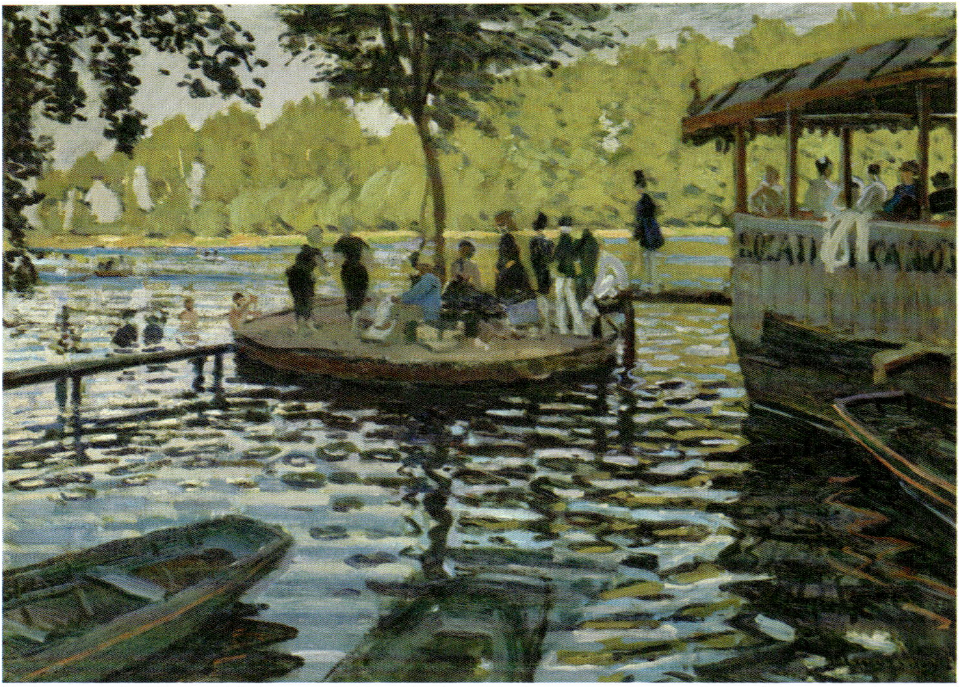

Fig. 119. Claude Monet, *Bathers at La Grenouillère*, 1869. Oil on canvas, 29 3/8 x 39 ¼ in. (74.6 x 99.7 cm). The Metropolitan Museum of Art, New York. H. O. Havemeyer Collection, Bequest of Mrs. H. O. Havemeyer, 1929

On the subject, the inauguration of the Museum of Modern Art (MoMA) is edifying. "The first museum of modern art in the world," according to its charismatic director, Alfred H. Barr, Jr., opened its doors in New York in 1929.[33] While waiting to receive its first collections, it organized temporary exhibitions, borrowing from museums and private collectors. To situate contemporary artistic creation within its context, the first event[34] was dedicated to the French artists who "had initiated the modernist movement."[35] Among them, according to the schema he elaborated as early as 1936, Barr included Cézanne—established as the Father of Modernity since his discovery by the future Cubists in 1907—as well as Gauguin, Seurat, and Van Gogh. Not only was Monet not included, but he was criticized. In his preface, Barr placed Cézanne in opposition to Monet (and Pissarro): "when Monet and Pissarro were working their way toward the impasse of Impressionism, Cézanne was concerning himself with those problems of composition and form which Daumier, Delacroix, and Courbet had previously rediscovered."[36] Until the 1950s, Monet figured only as an exception in the exhibitions at MoMA and was featured there as a foil to modernity. This was the case in 1931 for the memorial exhibition of the collection of Lizzie P. Bliss, one of the founders of MoMA and its vice president. Out of the 149 works displayed, two-thirds were promised to MoMA and founded its permanent collections. Twenty-two Cézannes, including the iconic *Bather*, eight works by Degas, three Renoirs, and even a Pissarro were left to the new museum. The only Monet present, *The Manneporte near Étretat*, was reserved for the encyclopedic museum, New York's Metropolitan. Astonishingly, Monet is also only represented by one work in the traveling exhibition *A Brief Survey of Modern Painting*, organized by Barr using reproductions and traveling to thirty-three American cities beginning in October 1932. In the catalogue, a canvas entitled *Summer*, now known as *Fields in the Spring* and in the Staatsgalerie Stuttgart (fig. 120), was described as a "typical Impressionist picture,"[37] while of the late work of the painter, Barr wrote: "Monet continued to paint as an Impressionist during his long career of sixty-five years. But with him were associated three greater artists—Degas, Renoir and Cézanne—who soon broke away from Impressionism because," Barr argued, "they felt it too insubstantial, too lacking in structure, like shimmering clothes unsupported by a body of flesh and bones."[38]

Thus, on both sides of the Atlantic, Monet's Orangerie *Water Lilies* were deemed contrary to the dominant aesthetics of the time and placed outside a certain accepted version of the history of art. Artists and critics, to say nothing of the public, became uninterested in late Monet, as we have seen.[39] This was also the case for collectors and galleries. Durand-Ruel concentrated on works from 1865 to 1888 in the exhibition *Claude Monet*, shown during November and December of 1935. The following year, Paul Rosenberg took his turn, selecting canvases executed between 1891 and 1912. The large panels—henceforth assimilated into the "decoration" category, and thus considered a minor art—aroused no interest. On the contrary, from here on the larger the work, the less it was sought after. In this way, *Water Lily Pond* (Wildenstein number 1893 [W. 1893])—one of the rare canvases measuring 1 x 2 meters foreshadowing the *Grandes Décorations* sold during the artist's lifetime—was cut down the middle to form two approximately 1 x 1 meter canvases. The half that was signed and dated "Claude Monet 1919" by the painter himself was put on the market during the period (fig. 121).[40]

This situation could not but have an effect on the administration of Claude Monet's estate and its settlement upon his sole legatee, his younger son and only direct descendant, Michel Monet (fig. 122). At the death of the artist, Michel inherited more than five hundred works. The whole included the private collection assembled by his father (around 120 items) and nearly 390 works by the master's hand: two hundred of these were late paintings, including nineteen monumental panels. Having no source of revenue other than the sale of this "painting-capital,"[41] each year Michel relinquished a part of his inheritance by selling to dealers such as Paul Rosenberg, the Bernheims, the Durand-Ruels, Jacques Seligmann & Cie., and Wildenstein & Co. There is little documentation on these transactions. An inventory drawn up by Germain Seligmann on March 24, 1935, and a book of accounts kept by Blanche-Hoschedé Monet, mentioning "the asking price" for works still at Giverny on June 28, 1937, furnish rare indications.[42] They hoped for FRF 200,000 ($8,000) for Renoir's *The Algerian Woman* (1870, now called *Madame Clementine Valensi Stora*, Fine Arts Museums of San Francisco), and the same for a large *Bather* by Renoir (1892, The Metropolitan Museum of Art, New York). Compared to the FRF 200,000[43] paid out in 1939 by the MoMA for the acquisition of *Les Demoiselles d'Avignon*, which Barr unhesitatingly described as "the most important painting of the twentieth century,"[44] these "studio prices" bear witness to the vitality of the market for "classic" Impressionism. This is also illustrated by the portrait *Madame Monet Stretched Out on a Sofa* (1875, Calouste Gulbenkian Foundation, Lisbon) by Renoir. Sold by Michel to Paul Rosenberg, it was resold to the art lover Calouste Gulbenkian for a princely £6,500 ($32,000).[45] Quite logically, Michel parted with the most sought-after canvases first. Between his father's death and the outbreak of the Second World War in 1939, in particular, he sold twenty-one major items from his father's collection. Aside from works by Renoir, Pissarro, Manet, Degas, Corot, and Morisot, Michel sold ten of the fourteen Cézannes collected by his father. Ironically, one of them, *Ginger Pot with Pomegranate and Pears* (1893, Phillips Collection, Washington D.C.) figured in the inaugural exhibition of MoMA in 1929;[46] another, *L'Estaque* (1879–83, The Museum of Modern Art, New York), in the exhibition celebrating the tenth anniversary of that institution.[47] The large 6 meter panels proposed at FRF 200,000 and the nearly 13 meter triptychs of the *Agapanthus* type (cat. 28) at FRF 400,000 remained

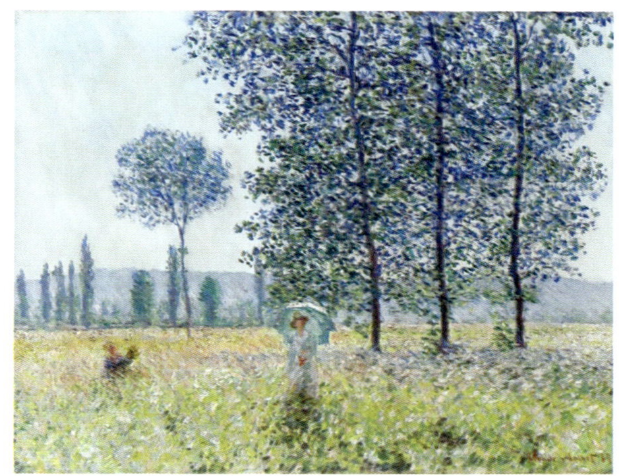

Fig. 120. Claude Monet, *Fields in the Spring*, 1887. Oil on canvas, 29 1/4 x 36 5/8 in. (74.3 x 93 cm). Staatsgalerie Stuttgart, Germany. Friends of the Staatsgalerie, 1906, GVL 16

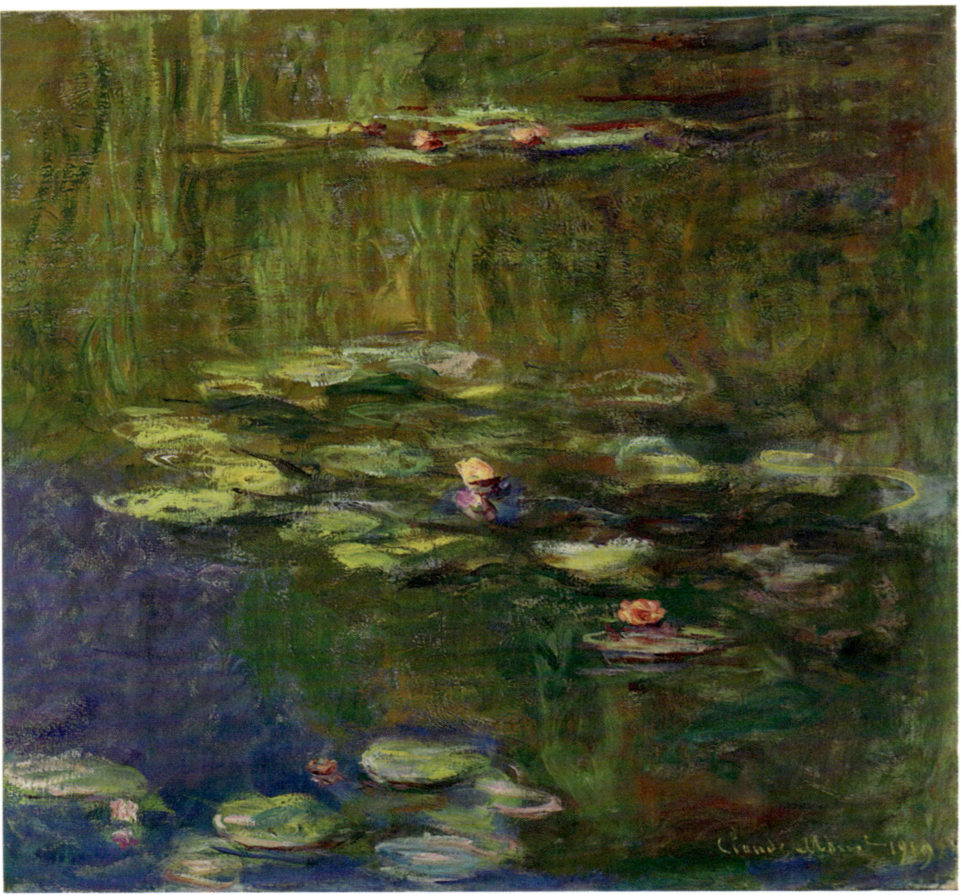

Fig. 121. Claude Monet, *Water-Lily Pond*, 1919. Oil on canvas, 39 1/4 x 40 3/4 in. (99.6 x 103.7 cm). Private collection. This is the right half of the original 1 x 2 meter canvas.

at Giverny along with other late works. It may be these that are referred to simply as "Numerous uninteresting paintings by MONET" by Seligmann in 1935.

The end of the Second World War signaled the beginning of a paradoxical period. Even as the Orangerie *Water Lilies* remained closed to the public in 1944 because of the damage caused to them by the bombings at the moment of the Liberation of Paris, and Monet's last pictorial legacy literally disappeared from the artistic landscape for several years, the very elements that would govern its reevaluation and the recognition of late Monet—a phenomenon known as the "Monet revival"—were falling into place.[48] The process went by way of the United States, coinciding with the emergence of its first great "school" of painting, that of Abstract Expressionism, its first generation represented by Jackson Pollock, Willem de Kooning, Mark Rothko, Mark Tobey, and Barnett Newman.

Two main elements connect the Abstract Expressionists to the revival. First, their esthetic principles, founded on the primacy of color and gesture—as witnessed in the drip paintings that Pollock was focusing on in 1947—served as a paradigm. Second, they were convinced that very large formats were the preferred vector for artistic expression. "Big pictures," Dorothy Miller wrote in the press statement for the *Exhibition of Large-Scale Modern Paintings* at MoMA in 1947, are, "at their best, assertions of the artist's self-confidence and esthetic convictions, affirmations of his belief in the importance of painting itself" (fig. 123).[49] All of these characteristics cannot but echo Monet's late work. Even if these correspondences are coincidental, they still struck certain critics. Reworking an idea put forth by Mayer Shapiro in 1937, the very influential Clement Greenberg—who had for a time criticized Monet's last phase—changed his mind, comparing the techniques of Impressionist painters and the "all-over" of the American Abstract Expressionists.[50] Gradually, Impressionism seemed to benefit from new-found public interest, with even MoMA publishing the first history of the group, under the signature of the extremely knowledgeable John Rewald.[51] Highly ranked artists such as Newman committed themselves to restoring "classic" Impressionism—and by extension Monet—to its rightful place alongside the founders of modernity. With the emergence of a new kind of painting, a new way of seeing was about to be applied to Monet.

The "Monet revival" was also taking place in Switzerland. Lucas Lichtenhan, art historian and curator of the Kunsthalle Basel, organized for his last exhibition at the Kunsthalle an Impressionist show, from September 3 to November 20, 1949. The organization of such events being particularly complex at the close of the war, the curator counted exclusively on loans from Swiss museums and collectors and from private European collections. In a letter dated June 4, 1949, Lichtenhan appealed to Michel Monet for his support. Michel's aid was major: he recommended that Lichtenhan contact Thadée Natanson to give a talk, as well as Durand-Ruel, who turned out to be one of the most important lenders to the exhibition. Michel also gave him direct support. On a visit by Lichtenhan to Giverny in late June or early July, the two men selected eighteen easel paintings and nine drawings and pastels for the show, most of them typically Impressionist, as requested by the curator. This took place just as Michel was about to address a complaint to the administrators of the national museums concerning the "lamentable state" of the Orangerie *Water Lilies*, deploring the "disgusting canopy" and the use of one of the rooms as a "junk room."[52] Against this background, he suggested that the Swiss historian present to the public for the first time certain flower panels from the same series, still at Giverny. In a much worse state than those at the Orangerie, the panels were dusty, and many had more than one hole, but this did not discourage Lichtenhan. In all likelihood, he heard in Michel's suggestion the condition that was implicit to his support, as well as seeing the possibility that he would be able to contribute to restoring the late work of an artistic giant to favor. With all of this in mind, it was decided to design the exhibition with two distinct sections. The ground floor of the Kunsthalle would present Lichtenhan's initial project—that is, the very sought-after easel paintings in their gilded frames—and in the separated Room X on the next floor, Michel would group the flower panels; not only were they less valuable, but at that stage, they were considering exhibiting them in their as-found state.

As Lichtenhan had been able to see only one 6 meter canvas the day of his visit, Michel would be responsible for making the selection. On July 12, the latter communicated his choices and sent his advice on how they should be hung:

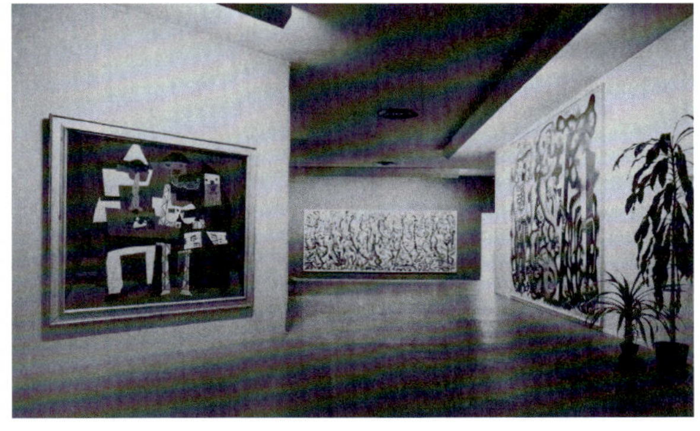

Fig. 123. Installation view of the exhibition *Large-Scale Modern Paintings* at The Museum of Modern Art, April 1–May 4, 1947. Photographic Archive. The Museum of Modern Art Archives, New York. IN346.7

> We were at Giverny yesterday, where we moved the large panels around, and I think I made a good choice. . . . I will send you 4 [panels] of 6 m, one of which is composed of two 3 m [panels] that must be placed end-to-end forming a magnificent whole. . . . You will see that this ensemble is marvelous; it must be placed on the same side as the 6 m that you saw. So you will have for each of the large sides of your room 2 panels of 6 m to which you can add other, smaller ones. I am sure that the effect will be most successful, even more so as the colors are varied. For the far end of the room, I'll send you a 4.50 m which you will also be able to surround with smaller formats. In short, I hope that you are satisfied, I've done my best to see to it.[53]

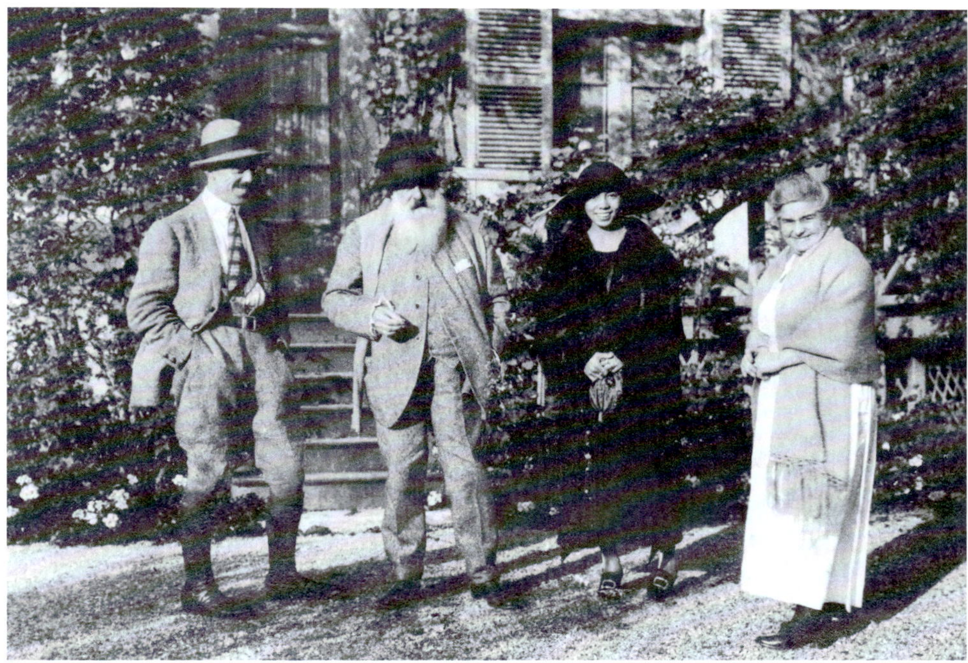

Fig. 122. Michel Monet, Claude Monet, Fukuko Naruse, and Blanche Hoschedé Monet, Giverny, 1921. Photo by Seliichi Naruse. Musée Marmottan Monet, Paris

Since the exhibitions organized by the Kunsthalle were in part commercial, Michel discreetly proposed the contents of Room X for sale, and a list was drawn up of "Sale prices for the Basel exhibition" (fig. 124). Fifteen pieces were valued according to their format. Paradoxically, the larger they were, the less expensive they were relative to their size. Thus the 6 meter panels were offered for FRF 2,000,000 ($6,000), while sketches of around 2 x 2 meters were proposed for between FRF 600,000 and 800,000 ($1,800–$2,400). The smallest formats, even if they were late works, were proportionally more expensive. This was the case for *Green Bridge* (100 x 115 centimeters), a work particularly affected by the artist's cataracts, for which FRF 1,000,000 ($3,000) was proposed—a sum that was nevertheless derisory compared to the insurance value of the highlight of the

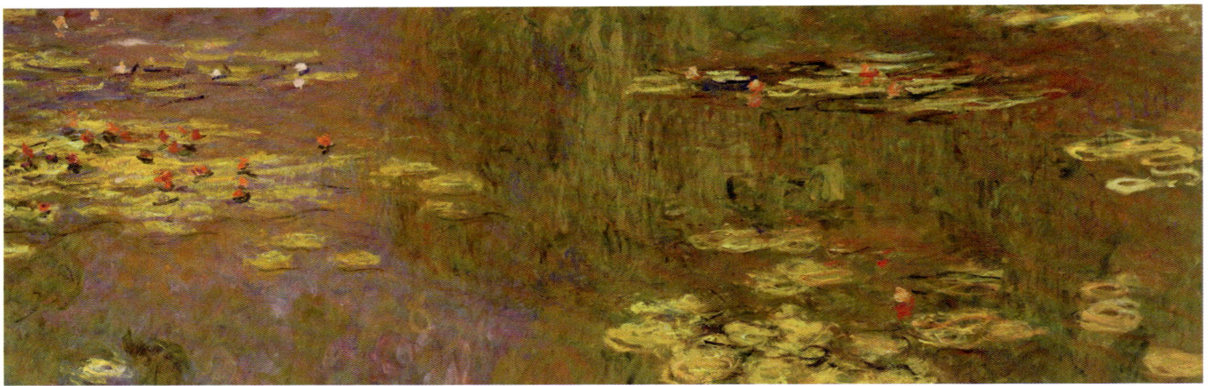

Fig. 125. Claude Monet, *Water Lilies*, c. 1915–29. Oil on canvas, 78 x 234 ⁷/₈ in. (198 x 596.6 cm). Carnegie Museum of Art, Pittsburgh. The first large panel by Monet in the United States

exhibition, also loaned by Michel, *The Beach at Trouville*, a still-smaller canvas (38 x 46 centimeters) painted in 1870 and insured for FRF 2,700,000 ($8,145). This value scale—attested to for the first time in official documents, backed up by evidence—illustrates the distortion of prices between works considered decoration and those thought of as "true" paintings, no matter the period of their creation. A single canvas, of a medium format and reproduced in the catalogue, was sold during the exhibition (W. 1789). The purchaser was none other than Walter Schiess, president of Basler Kunstverein, who acquired three other canvases of the same type from Michel after the event.[54]

While not one of the very large formats was sold, their display left a mark in the minds of certain viewers. At the inauguration of the exhibition, Lichtenhan denounced "the criticism of which these paintings have been a target, which has, on the one hand, frequently come to our ears, even in Basel; and in Paris, it is, at the very least, truly shameful to see the splendid isolation in which these canvases have been left—Monet's gift to the nation, condemned to sink forgotten in the depths of the furthest rooms of the Orangerie. On the other hand," he continued, "we were obviously obliged to tell ourselves that Monet, whose superior genius can be seen ever more clearly as time passes, did not, in all probability, work for more than a quarter of a century on the largest and most ambitious of his series without having a reason, and certainly not merely to see it finally ignored by the public."[55]

Prix de vente pour l'exposition à Bâle

Nymphéas

1)	Deux fleurs	73/100 cm	1.000.000
2)	Iris	120/100 cm	800.000
3)	Le pont vert	100/115 cm	1.000.000
4)	Nymphéas bleus	130/200 cm	700.000
5)	Nymphéas lilas-claire avec branches de saule pleureur	150/200 cm	600.000
6)	Nymphéas, calices jaune-vifs	200/200 cm	800.000
7)	Nymphéas, lumière bleu-violet	130/150 cm	600.000
8)	Glycines	100/200 cm	600.000
9)	Sept nymph. rouge-violets	130/150 cm	800,000
10)	Nymph. verdâtres a l'ombre d'un saule-pleureur	200/200 cm	700.000
11)	Les 3 grands formats de 6 m de longeur chacquun		2.500,000
12)	Nymph. jaunatres et lilas à tiges de roseaux	200/215 cm	800.000
13)	Nymph. rouges et blancs	200/425 cm	2.000.000
14)	Nymph. jaunes et bleuatres (reproduit au catalogue)	175/135 cm	700.000
15)	Crépuscule au lac des nymph.	200/600 cm	2.000.000

Fig. 124. Sale prices for the Basel exhibition. State Archives Basel-Stadt

The curator of the Kunstmuseum in Basel, Georg Schmidt, shared Lichtenhan's point of view, pleading on November 18, 1949, with the administrative board of the museum to acquire works, recounting that "The room [of the Kunsthalle] where the studies done by Monet for the Orangerie *Water Lilies* are exhibited is the sensation of the event dedicated to the Impressionists. The studies are clearly more spontaneous than the finished panels. Monet's late works are of prodigious interest for art history: on the one hand, they represent the ultimate consequence of Impressionism, and on the other, his turning toward Jugendstil." While waiting to decide, the board reserved two 6 meter panels (W. 1980 and 1983). The latter was finally acquired by the American collector Walter Chrysler directly from Michel Monet, in 1950 (fig. 125). Even if there is absolutely no doubt that the Basel exhibition was a milestone in the genesis of this acquisition, the precise circumstances of the purchase—of crucial importance, since it marks the entrance of the first large panel into the United States—have yet to be determined.

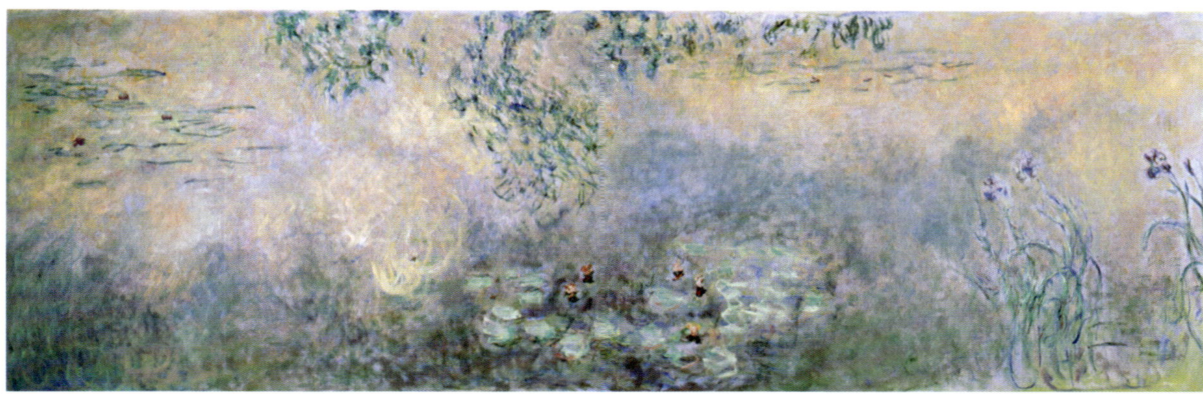

Fig. 126. Claude Monet, *Water-Lily Pond with Iris*, c. 1914/22. Oil on canvas, 78 3/4 x 236 1/4 in. (200 x 600 cm). Kunsthaus Zürich. Gift from Emil G. Bührle, 1952

This is not the case with the sales to Emil Bührle, an important Zurich collector and lender of seventeen paintings to the Basel exhibition.[56] In this instance, a key role was played by René Wehrli, director of the Zurich Kunsthaus beginning in 1950 and close to Bührle, who financed the construction of an extension to the Kunsthaus. Introduced to Michel Monet in all probability by the gallery owner Irma Hoenigsberg,[57] Wehrli visited Giverny for the first time in late April 1951.[58] Upon his return to Zurich, he reported to the Kunsthaus commission that he had seen "some late works by Claude Monet which might be available at rather advantageous prices. A large painting of water lilies about 2 x 5 m might be available for 2,000,000 francs [$6,000]. This would be," Wehrli went on, "an exceptional occasion in view of the new Kunsthaus."[59] He thus reserved four canvases.[60] The commission gave him "full authority" to select, with the aid of one of its members, the painter Max Gubler, a work that Bührle agreed to finance.[61] The sums necessary would be drawn from the "construction fund" set up by the patron, falling under the "Kunst am Bau"(literally, "art in building") provision that allowed one percent of the construction budget to be allocated for the acquisition of *ornamental* works. Thus it was as an architectural decoration that the Kunsthaus first sought out a late Monet painting.

After a second visit to Giverny conducted by Werlhi, Bührle, and most probably Gubler, the director chose to acquire a 6 meter panel, *Water-Lily Pond with Iris* (fig. 126), a choice ratified by the institution on October 4, 1951.[62] Contact with the son of the painter was renewed in view of organizing a Monet exhibition projected by the Swiss museum for 1952. Wehrli himself selected the large panels that would figure in it.[63] Among the late works presented, a diptych (W. 1964–1965) was acquired for the Kunsthaus. For himself, Emil Bührle bought two other panels: a 2 x 2 meter water-lily painting (W. 1804) and a 4.25 meter panel (W. 1979) that the Kunsthaus hoped someday to see in its collection.[64] The purchases took place on November 3, 1952.[65] Unfortunately, no documents exist that allow us to know the exact amount of the transaction. However, we do know that the Wintertur Kunstverein acquired in the same year a 2 x 2 meter panel (W. 1801) at the price asked at the 1949 exhibition ($1,800–$2,400).[66] Ironically, as a consequence of these numerous purchases, the Kunstmuseum in Basel—where the first exhibition had been held—became fearful that people would see "in every Swiss museum, similar, or even identical, works from the same master"[67] and renounced making its own acquisition.

Afterwards, the 1952 Monet exhibition traveled—in a reduced version—to the Galerie des Beaux Arts in Paris and then to the Gemeentemuseum in The Hague.[68] (It should be noted that at this time not one late Monet was to be seen in France, as the Orangerie was still closed to the public; this was not the case for the Dutch museum, which held a small selection of them.[69]) In the traveling exhibition was the 6 meter panel from the Kunsthaus Zurich. The work was insured for 30,000 Swiss francs (CHF) ($7,000) for the event, a modest sum compared to the $45,000 paid out by the Museum of Fine Arts, Boston, the same year for the *Portrait of Camille Monet in Japanese Costume* (*La Japonaise*). There is no doubt that of the three venues of the exhibition, Zurich was the most important. It was in Zurich—and not at the Orangerie in Paris—that the painter Ellsworth Kelly discovered the large *Water Lilies* by Monet. It was there that the artist began to share the interest shown in Impressionism by the second generation of American abstract painters, who drew part of their inspiration from the movement and were thus christened "abstract impressionists."[70] The same year, to mark the exhibition, or perhaps the reopening of the Orangerie, Tériade published in the magazine *Verve* André Masson's "Monet le fondateur" (*Monet the founder*), a key text establishing the Orangerie *Water Lilies* as a kind of Sistine Chapel of Impressionism and bestowing on Monet the title of the founder of modernism (fig. 127).

All the parameters were now set for Monet to finally enter the Museum of Modern Art in New York. Much more than *Poplars at Giverny, Setting Sun*, which was donated to the museum in 1951, it was the 1955 acquisition of a large-scale late panel that marked the takeoff of the "Monet revival." The work was selected in view of the stylistic traits that echoed (in reverse) the art of the American Abstract Expressionists; Alfred Barr himself did not hesitate to describe the new canvas as "abstract impressionist"[71] in the official documents, including those for arbitration.[72] Despite the difficulties proposed by the installation of such a work, a monumental canvas—a *Water-Lily Pond* (W. 1802) of 6 meters—was specifically chosen, the better to emphasize the link with the local school (fig. 128). The painting, shown in 1949 in Basel as number 214 in the catalogue, had doubled in price, reaching FRF 4,000,000 ($11,500). While there was a trend to higher prices for large panels, the curve did not reverse itself, and easel paintings—irrespective of period—were still worth more. Thus MoMA, and particularly Dorothy Miller, who had worked to have the large formats recognized as the vector "par excellence" of modern artistic expression, also agreed in 1956 to pay slightly more than $12,000 for a *Japanese Bridge* of 89 x 116 centimeters painted around 1920–22, though they considered the easel painting as "supplementing the large panel purchased the previous year."[73] (Even this sum, however, does not compete with the $45,000 paid to Knoedler by MoMA the same year to acquire *The Rose Marble Table* by Matisse, a slightly larger canvas from 1917.)

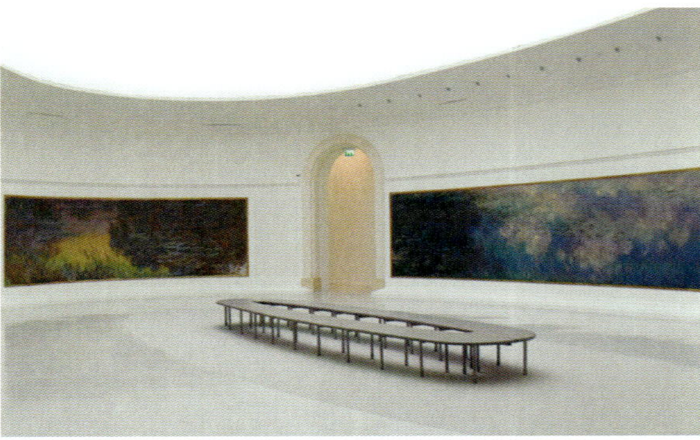

Fig. 127. The current installation of Monet's *Grandes Décorations* in the Musée de l'Orangerie, Paris

Some of the circumstances surrounding the acquisition of this first large panel by MoMA still need to be clarified. As attested in the museum archives, Walter P. Chrysler, Jr., the chairman of MoMA's library committee, informed Barr by April 1955 of the existence of numerous panels at Giverny.[74] It is widely thought that Katia Granoff (fig. 129), a gallery owner in Paris, may have introduced Chrysler to Michel Monet, but no known, convincing document corroborates Granoff's role.[75] On the contrary, when the Nelson Atkins Museum of Art, which had been interested since February 1956[76] in Monet's large panels, asked MoMA "who the person would be to contact in case we were interested in inquiring about them,"[77] the reply made no mention of her. "When we bought our Monet *Water Lilies* at this time last year," Alfred Barr himself responded, "there were still about a dozen canvases of this series to be seen in Monet's huge studio at Giverny. I believe most of them were available for purchase. You should get in touch with the artist [sic] son Michel Monet / Sorel-Moussel / (Eure et Loir) / France. He apparently has complete charge of his father's estate so that all arrangements can be made with him."[78]

A gallery owner of Ukrainian origin who arrived in Paris in 1924, Granoff, according to what her family remembers, was probably introduced to Michel Monet by André Barbier, a friend of the late painter and close friend of his son. This was quite an event. Of all the galleries that Michel had frequented—some of them since childhood—this new person was the first to interest herself in *late* Monet. Michel had always favored selling to professionals rather than private collectors. He found in Granoff a new prospective buyer as well as a woman committed to the rehabilitation of the last works of his father. The gallerist remembered her very first, instantaneous reaction to the "opaque layers of oblivion under which this [late] work had sunk, the distain of the public and dealers who judged it outdated, unsaleable, unwieldy. I knew all that, and yet I dove into the adventure insanely enamored of these water lilies of my soul."[79] The exact date of their meeting is unknown, but those close to her generally refer to the early 1950s as the time period. Never-before published documents—including correspondence and manuscript notes belonging to them—attest to important transactions beginning before January 1955.[80] In this archival material, Michel emerges as a businessman, favoring outright sales over consignments and revealing himself deliberately intractable on prices ("if you would like to go over there [Giverny] to see the blue Water Lily, I must tell you right now, and in the most formal fashion, that I will not give it to you for 1.2 [FRF 1,200,000], my very lowest price is 1.4 [FRF 1,400,000]. If then this is unacceptable to you, discussion is useless.").[81] At the very most lenient, he consented to terms for payment over time—the longest for a year—and respecting his terms was very likely a condition for further sales.[82] These "easier" terms allowed Granoff to buy a block of work and organize two seminal exhibitions in Paris. For the first one, *Les grandes evasions poétiques de Claude Monet (The Great Poetic Flights of Claude Monet)*, held June 1–July 30, 1956, we can match an I.O.U. dated the day of the opening, in which Granoff promises to pay FRF 27,000,000 at the end of July 1957.[83]

For the second exhibition, *L'étang enchanté de Claude Monet (Claude Monet's Enchanted Pond)*, held from May 24 to the annual summer closing in 1957, there are three documents that probably correspond. The first document, dated July 1, 1956, is a list headed "Large [panel]" and mentions seven canvases measuring 4 meters and two of 3 meters, "for an overall price of 27,000,000 francs"[84] to be paid, at the latest, at the end of July 1957. The other two documents,[85] both of them from July 9, 1956, refer, in the case of the first, to FRF 8,000,000 for three *Water Lilies* measuring 130 x 200 centimeters, and the other to "12,000,000 francs for an ensemble of some canvases of water lilies." If, given the absence of a stock register or exhibition catalogues, these documents provide only partial information, they at least allow us to measure the breadth of the financial risk undertaken by the gallery. Granoff would say that she committed herself "to the point of having risked everything to acquire them."[86] According to those close to her, to carry out her project she pawned part of her gallery stock[87] until the bank advanced her the necessary funds.[88] The dealer's audacity elicited Michel's respect: "I see that your iron will has overcome the resistance of those around you, since you managed to carry off the exhibition that you so much wanted," he wrote to her, before consequently reserving for her "the entire exclusivity to this period."[90]

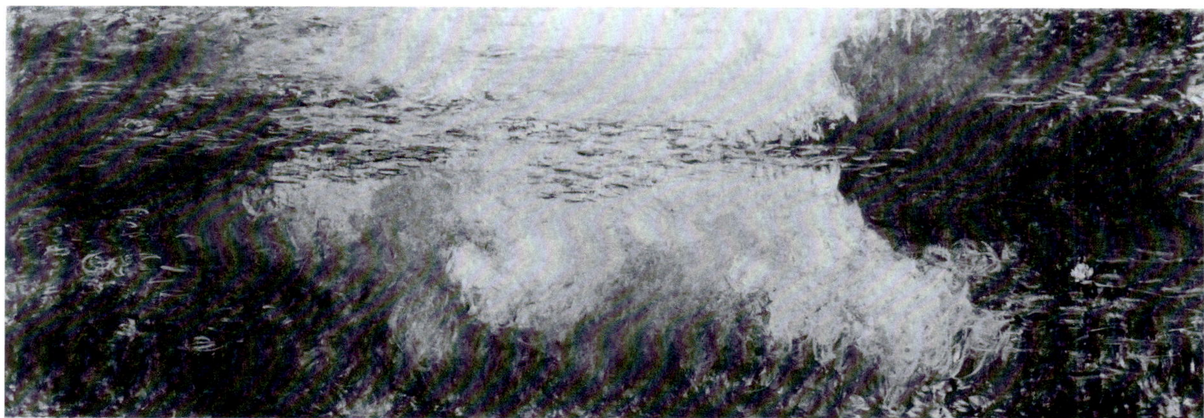

Fig. 128. Claude Monet, *Water Lilies*, 1914–26. Oil on canvas, 78 ¾ in. x 221 ½ in. (200 x 562.6 cm). Formerly in the Museum of Modern Art, New York. Mrs. Simon Guggenheim Fund. Destroyed by a fire in 1958

From this point on, Granoff can be considered as an essential figure in the "Monet revival." While few French collectors seem to have figured among her first clients, artists of all nationalities and American curators were present at the very beginning. The painter Sam Francis recalled that as of 1956 he had "seen at Katia Granoff's exhibition the last works by Monet—even canvases that were said to be unfinished but which for me seemed superb."[91] Hungarian-born painter Arpad Szènes remembered having lived thirty-four years in Paris, "without a thought for Monet . . . [when] in 1957, everything changed. At the time, I went almost every day

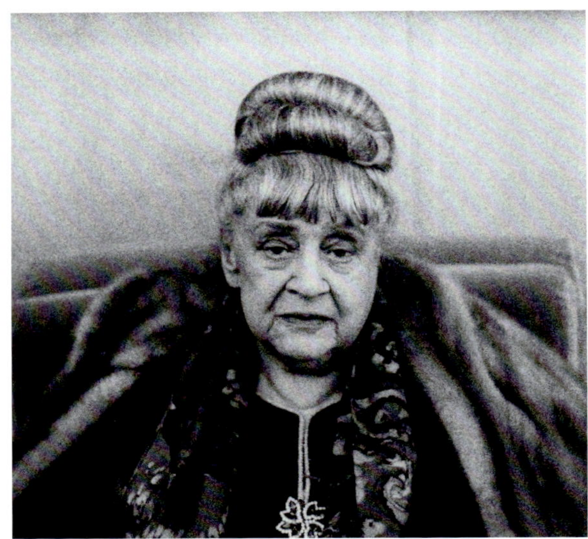

Fig. 129. Katia Granoff, 1964

to see the Monets at Katia Granoff's."[92] The indispensable Alfred Barr was also present at the beginning. At *The Great Poetic Flights of Claude Monet*, he acquired several canvases for American collectors, as well as a 180 x 200-centimeter *Water Lily* for MoMA,[93] with the Art Institute of Chicago opting for an *Iris* of a similar format. Granoff was even a presence in the United States, with the Knoedler Gallery serving as an intermediary; its directors bought two *Japanese Bridges* from her in April 1956,[94] then, for $139,280, the *Agapanthus* triptych in July of the same year (see cat. 28).[95] These works were presented in New York, in the exhibition that Knoedler dedicated to *Paysages d'eau*, from October 8 to October 27, 1956. It was from the latter that the Nelson Atkins Museum of Art and the Saint Louis Art Museum bought two of the three panels of the *Agapanthus* triptych in 1957. The canvases, at $40,000 each, were sold at a loss of about $7,000. But the situation changed quickly. The "Monet revival" made use of every possible means: major critical texts, the general press, and first-rate temporary exhibitions celebrating the Monet of the Orangerie and his links with contemporary American painting, which of late had firmly established its dominance in the art world. So it was not astonishing to see that MoMA, the day after a tragic fire destroyed its two *Water Lilies* on April 15, 1958, decided to replace them without delay. Questioned by the museum, Michel Monet's wife, Gabrielle, let it be known—in the words of Ann Temkin—that "the studio was now empty—all the paintings having been sold to Katia Granoff in Paris."[96] In turn, MoMA purchased two key pieces from the gallery: a single 6 meter panel for $83,000 (seven times the price paid three years before for a panel of the same size) and a triptych for $150,000 (fig. 130). Just two years later, The Cleveland Museum of Art paid $100,000 for the remaining single panel of the *Agapanthus* triptych, its price—against the $130,000 Knoedler had paid for the entire triptych—illustrating the explosion in the cost of late Monets.

Katia Granoff had won her bet. Conscious of the importance of Alfred Barr and, more widely, the United States in the rediscovery of late Monet, she presented as a thank-you a panel to MoMA (*Water Lily, Weeping Willow Reflections*, W. 1861)[97]:

> [M]y gift . . . comes from an thankful heart as I told you: first the American army freed the little French town of Manosque [where] we were refugees, my family and I, in 1944; secondly a certain Director of the Museum of Modern Art New York, Monsieur Alfred Barr, was he who first understood the importance of Monet['s] last period and opened the eyes of the public on it. It is a great merit only a justice to the greatest French painter of our time. I am very happy to be able to give you [this] extraordinary mysterious and beautiful painting, that you loved as soon as you saw it."[98]

Regularly presented in the French press as the woman who had acquired the contents of Claude Monet's studio, Granoff exhibited the work of the master

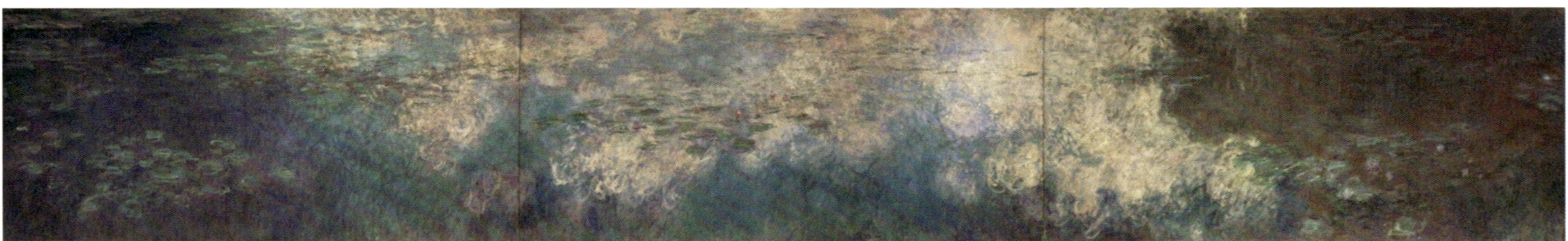

Fig. 130. Claude Monet, *Water Lilies*, 1914–26. Oil on canvas, 78 ¾ x 502 in. (200 x 1,276 cm). Museum of Modern Art, New York. Mrs. Simon Guggenheim Fund. 666.1959.a-c

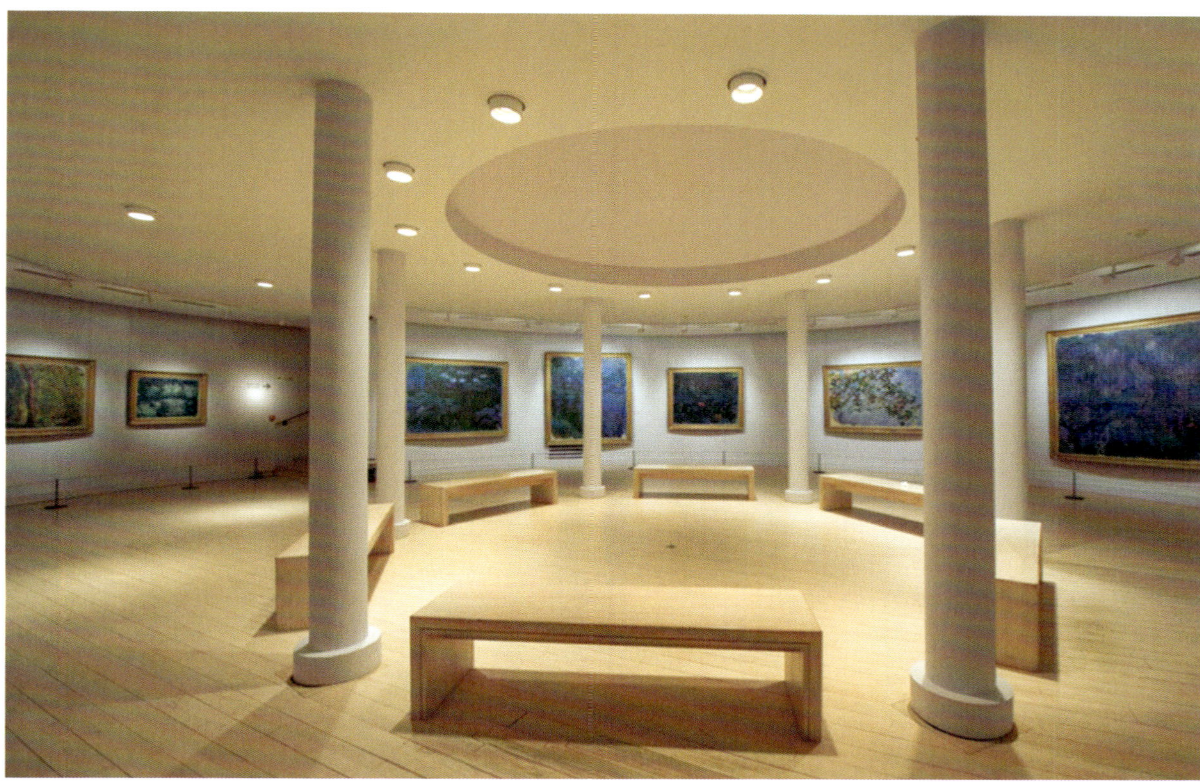

Fig. 131. Musée Marmottan Monet, Paris, with three paintings in this exhibition: *Weeping Willow*, cat. 40 (far left); *Water Lilies*, cat. 15 (center); and *Roses*, cat. 22 (second from right)

until her death. The last individual exhibition that she dedicated to him took place in 1965. The press spoke of the "abstract Monet,"[99] the works that Granoff "saved from destruction"[100] and that she kept in her "sanctuary-gallery."[101] At that date, with the exception of a two works—a triptych that today is the pride of the Fondation Beyeler and a painting now in the Chichu Art Museum in Naoshima, Japan—all the large panels issued from the series of *Grandes Décorations* already belonged to foreign museums. A certain part of the press was indignant. On June 23, 1965, the newspaper *Carrefour* had as its title: "'The Water Lilies Must Be Kept in France" and lamented:

> Alas! This incomparable work risks being split up, sold to some American museum or foreign collectors. Any country other than France would never give up such a marvel, born as it was on its soil. A special vote by parliament or a general subscription would allow for collection of the funds necessary for the purchase of these *Water Lilies*, supreme gift from the Old Man of Giverny to his country, the boldest exploit ever undertaken in painting. Why does not André Malraux take this affair in hand? Let him go contemplate the *Water Lilies* exhibited at the Galerie Katia Granoff! I am sure that he will feel a violent desire to keep them in France and will find the means to do so.[102]

Without ever being made public, the question was asked. On the subject, Granoff confided, "We resolved . . . not to buy anything more from him [Michel], knowing that he wanted to leave a bequest to benefit the museums. This decision came from my nephew Pierre Larock and the renouncement was hard for me."[103] As for André Malraux, in 1964, he let Michel know that he considered his inheritance a question of the patrimony of the nation.[104] Refusing to leave his inheritance to the State, Michel—who was childless—in March of 1964 made the Musée Marmottan, an institution belonging to the Académie des Beaux-Arts, his sole legatee. On his death in 1966, the establishment received the world's premier stock of works by the leader of Impressionism, in the first rank of which a unique ensemble of twenty late works constitutes the core of this exhibition (fig. 131).

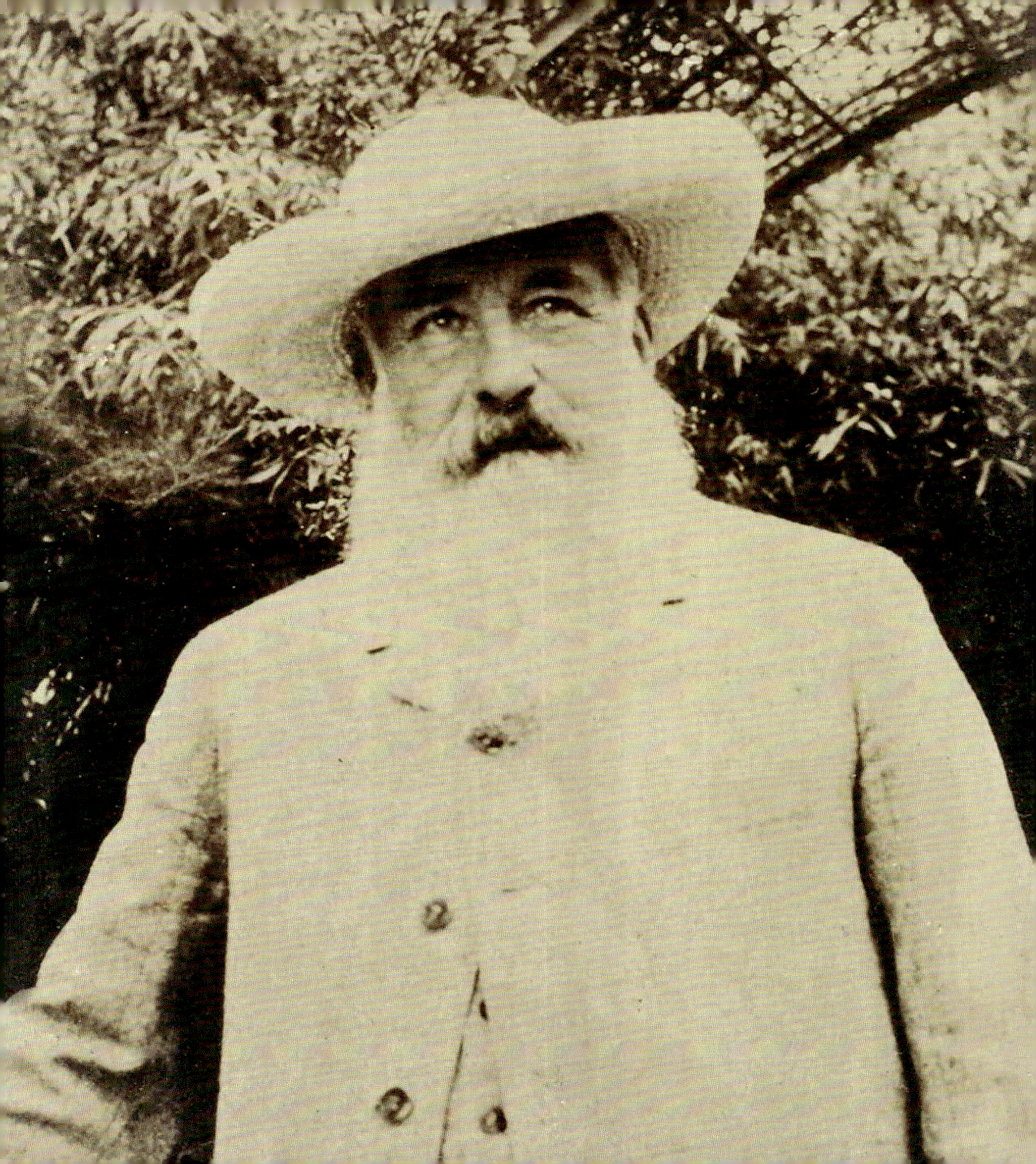

Claude Monet: A Summary Chronology, 1909–1926

This chronology is based on the exemplary account of the artist's life in abbreviated form compiled by Charles F. Stuckey for his great exhibition, *Monet 1840–1926*, presented at the Art Institute of Chicago in 1995. His chronology recorded and painstakingly documented events gathered from a wide variety of sources; since its publication, the information it provided has become part of the history of Monet and his milieu. Our debt to his research is gratefully acknowledged.

1909

After planting the first water lilies in his enlarged pond at Giverny in early 1902 and beginning his first *Water Lilies* paintings in the summer of 1903, finally, by May 1909, after two postponed exhibitions, Monet is ready for the first exhibition of forty-eight *Water Lilies* paintings at the Durand-Ruel gallery in Paris. The water-lily motif would absorb much of Monet's creative energy until his death.

On May 5, the artist travels to Paris to install the works and attend the opening. The paintings are hung throughout three rooms at the gallery. Among the variety of formats chosen, eleven of them are approximately square in shape and four are in tondo format.

The critics and public respond to the exhibition with high praise. Many journalists compare Monet's achievement to poetry or music, where the superimposition of what is near and far and what is below and above is simultaneously active in the compositions, and this is accompanied by an imaginative interplay of reality and reflection. A few journalists even regret that the ensemble of works will be dispersed instead of remaining intact as a great decorative triumph.

When Monet encounters Degas at the Gallery of Ambroise Vollard, the painter of dancers says to the painter of water lilies, "I only stayed at your exhibition for a second. Your paintings gave me vertigo."

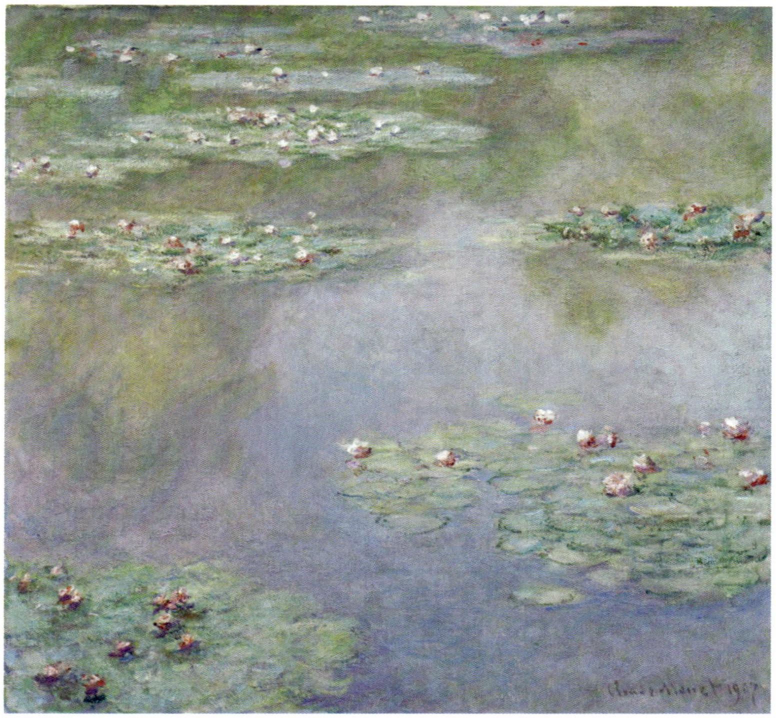

Fig. 133. Claude Monet, *Water Lilies*, 1907. Oil on canvas, 38 1/8 x 38 3/4 in. (96.8 x 98.4 cm). Museum of Fine Arts, Boston. Bequest of Alexander Cochrane, 19.170.

1910

Having suffered from bouts of poor health for over a year, Alice Monet is diagnosed with spinal leukemia in late February and immediately begins radiation therapy. By the summer, Alice enters remission, while Monet, desperate for a remedy to the chronic headaches that have plagued him for over a year, travels to Paris in the summer for a medical consultation.

Fig. 132. Claude Monet, Giverny, 1915. Photograph by Sacha Guitry. Gelatin silver print, aristotype, 4 x 3 in. (10.3 x 7.6 cm). Private collection. Courtesy of Christie's

In the late autumn, Alice's health worsens and Gustave Geffroy brings his friend Dr. Vasquez to Giverny to examine Alice.

1911

On May 19, Alice Monet dies, sending the artist into many months of mourning. She is buried next to her first husband, Ernest Hoschedé, and her daughter Suzanne.

In a moment of acute grief, Monet rereads his wife's letters and chooses to burn them all.

Monet's grief is debilitating. Clémenceau, Geffroy, Octave Mirbeau, and Renoir, concerned for their old friend, come in turn to Giverny to try to console and distract him.

1912

Twenty-nine of Monet's Venice paintings are exhibited at the Bernheim-Jeune Gallery in Paris from May 28 to June 8. Mirbeau, who had studied the works in Giverny the month before, wrote the catalogue preface. Among the critics well-disposed to the exhibition was the painter Paul Signac, who declared that the Venice paintings were Monet's best works in the last three decades.

Following the success of the Venice exhibition, Monet writes to Geffroy that Dr. Valude has diagnosed him with cataracts and has prescribed a treatment to slow the inevitable progression to total loss of sight. Describing his condition to his friend, he says: "the right eye no longer sees anything, the other is *also* slightly affected." However, the painter receives a second, more hopeful, medical opinion from Clémenceau, who is also a doctor. He writes Monet at the end of July, claiming, "You are in no danger whatsoever of losing your eyesight . . . the cataract on the bad eye will certainly soon ripen and then one could operate. But that is nothing, and the continuity of your eyesight is assured."

In November, Alice Monet's son Jacques Hoschedé organizes a sale of his mother's belongings; most of the items are sold to his step-father. Around the same time Jacques also sells eight unsigned Monet paintings that were, most likely, gifts from the painter to his wife. The paintings are sold to the Galerie Bernheim-Jeune, which sells them back to Monet.

Having suffered from a stroke in June, Jean Monet's health continues to decline. Monet buys a home for his son and his daughter-in-law, Blanche Monet in Giverny by selling the trout farm he had started in Beaumont-Le-Roger (Eure) two years earlier.

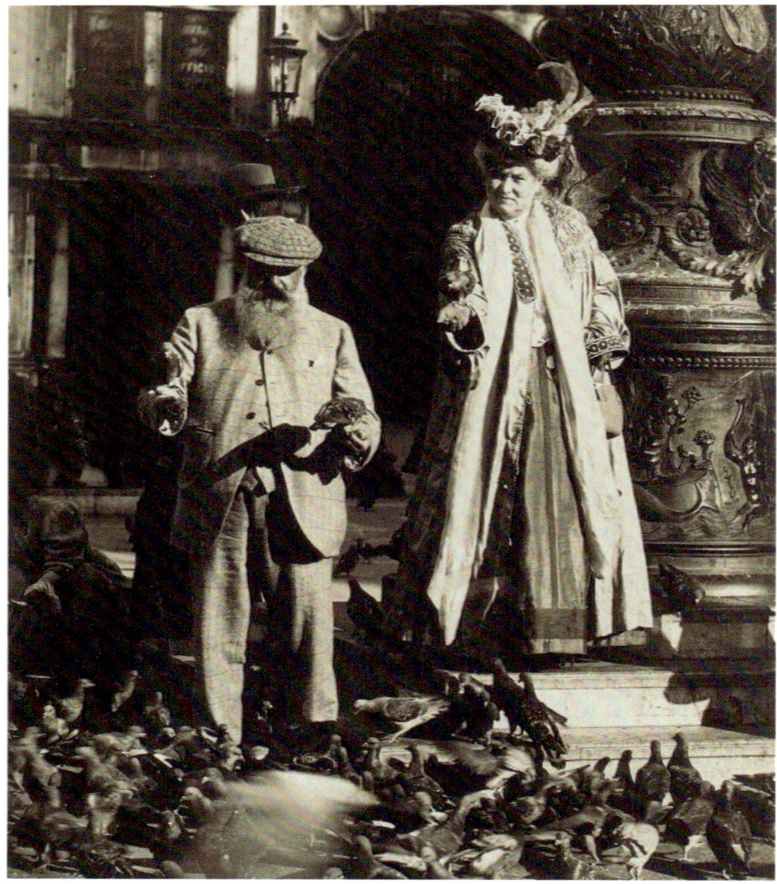

Fig. 134. Claude Monet and his second wife, Alice Hoschedé Monet, in St. Mark's Square, Venice, October 1908. Gelatin silver print on postcard, 5 3/8 x 3 3/8 in. (13.8 x 8.7 cm). Private collection. Courtesy of Christie's

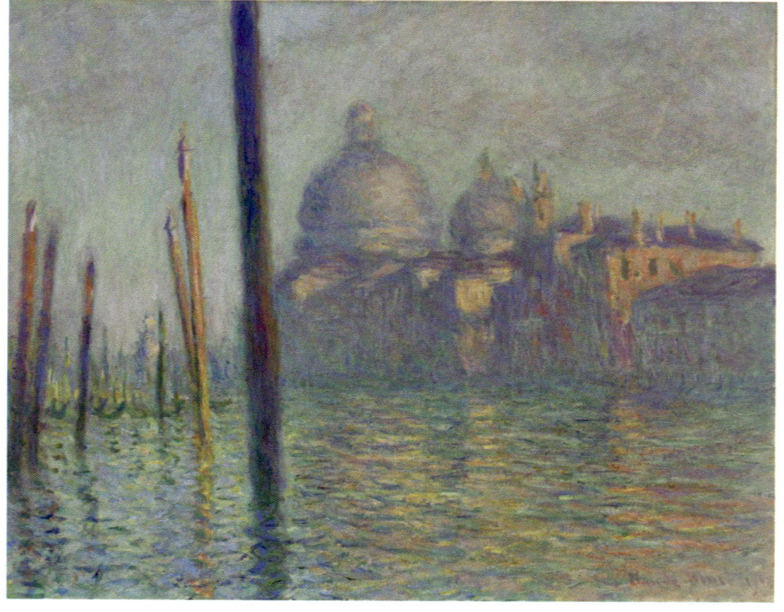

Fig. 135. Claude Monet, *Grand Canal, Venice*, 1908. Oil on canvas, 29 x 36 3/8 in. (73.7 x 92.4 cm). Museum of Fine Arts, Boston. Bequest of Alexander Cochrane, 19.171

1913

In the spring, Monet goes to Paris for another eye examination. Throughout the year, he consults a variety of doctors for their opinions on his cataracts, hoping that a specialist will be able to offer an alternative solution to surgery.

Monet's chief gardener, Félix Breuil, writes an article about Monet's garden, which is published with a preface by Georges Truffaut, the horticulturist and retailer, in the October issue of his magazine *Jardinage*.

In mid-November, Monet is interviewed by André Arnyvelde in Giverny for an article that is published in January of the following year in *Je sais tout*. During Arnyvelde's visit, Monet reveals that since his wife's death in 1911 he has hardly worked at all with the exception of the past two to three months. The article is accompanied by photographs of Monet in his studio-salon and at work on a recent painting (see figs. 8 and 9).

1914

At the year's beginning, Monet is bedridden with the flu. Jean Monet, confined to his own bed in the studio-salon of the Giverny house, grows weaker and weaker. On February 9, Jean dies. In March, while mourning Jean's death, Monet is called to Paris, where his other son, Michel, has undergone an operation.

Monet's reinvigorated interest in his mural project takes precedence throughout the summer, and he does not attend the opening of the inaugural exhibition of the collection of Count Isaac de Camondo at the Louvre. The display, including works by Degas, Monet, and Renoir, breaks the museum's policy to never exhibit works by living artists.

On June 29, Monet writes Durand-Ruel that he begins work in the morning at 4 a.m. and works throughout the day without his eyes bothering him.

Geffroy visits the painter in July to see the results of Monet's vigorous work over the last two months, and around this time, the writer Michel Georges-Michel and Clémenceau note that two enormous *Water Lilies* panels are under way.

On August 1, Germany declares war on Russia, and by August 24, there are one million troops marching on France. Jean-Pierre Hoschedé immediately enlists and leaves for the front. Concerned about German troops impending advance on France, Germaine Hoschedé Salerou, whose husband has also enlisted, leaves Giverny with her children. Monet considers sending many of his paintings to Paris to be stored for safety but decides to remain in Giverny with his son Michel and Blanche.

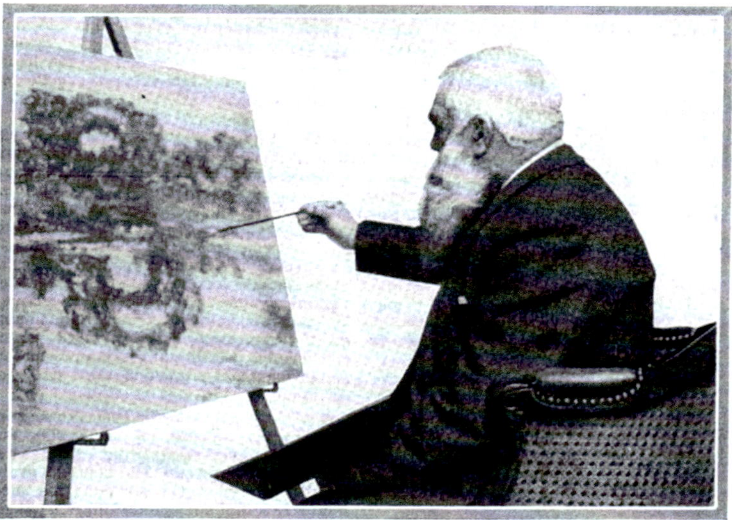

CLAUDE MONET AU TRAVAIL

On voit ici l'admirable peintre achevant une de ses plus belles toiles. C'est, dans la parure fastueuse jetée par l'été sur les parterres, la représentation éblouissante d'une tonnelle, toute irradiée de fleurs vives, de son jardin de Giverny.

Chez le Peintre de la Lumière (1)

"Je sais tout" interviewe Claude Monet

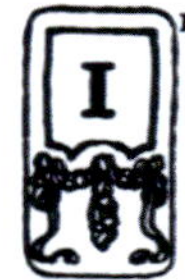

IL y a cinq kilomètres de la gare de Vernon au village de Giverny, où le peintre a depuis plusieurs années fixé sa vie. L'automobile que M. Claude Monet a bien voulu envoyer me prendre à la descente du train, à Vernon, m'emmène avec rapidité à travers la campagne. Voici l'Eure, avec le vieux pont dont quelques piles en ruines et couvertes de mousse émergent de la rivière, une église, une falaise crayeuse, des collines brunes où paissent des moutons... Au bout d'un chemin tournant et resserré, l'auto s'est arrêtée devant une vieille porte cochère de bois, peinte en vert, un peu vermoulue, et que surmonte un doux arceau de pierre. Cette porte franchie, je suis une courte allée qui longe une remise grande ouverte où sont trois automobiles; puis un pavillon rustique, blanc et rouge, dont le côté qui regarde l'allée semble n'être tout entier qu'une immense fenêtre. Cette fenêtre est celle de

(1) On va faire grand bruit autour de l'installation très prochaine au Musée du Louvre de la collection Camondo, collection composée en majeure partie, on le sait, d'œuvres des plus célèbres peintres impressionnistes: Manet, Claude Monet, Renoir, Degas, Sisley, Pissarro, Cézanne. Nous avons pensé qu'il serait intéressant de faire raconter par l'un de ces artistes (à présent tous entrés dans la gloire), et par celui-là même que l'on considère comme le plus glorieux d'entre eux, Claude Monet, l'histoire des luttes passionnées que l'impressionnisme eut à soutenir à ses débuts contre les peintres officiels et contre l'opinion. Notre collaborateur, M. André Arnyvelde, a rendu visite à l'illustre Claude Monet, dans sa propriété de Giverny, et c'est le récit de cette visite que nos lecteurs vont trouver ici.

29

Fig. 136."Chez le Peintre de la Lumière" article in *Je sais tout*, January 14, 1914

Fig. 137. Claude Monet, *Water Lilies*, 1914–26. Oil on canvas, 78 ½ x 235 ½ in. (199.5 x 599 cm). Museum of Modern Art, New York. Mrs. Simon Guggenheim Fund, 712.1959

In September, German forces are halted on the river Marne, just twenty-four miles (forty kilometers) from Paris. Mary and Frederick MacMonnies, American artists residing in Giverny, join the war effort and establish a fourteen-bed hospital on their property for wounded soldiers. Monet provides vegetables for the hospital from his garden. "I am back at work; it is still the best way not to think too much about current woes, even though I should be a bit ashamed to think about little investigations into forms and colors while so many people suffer and die for us," writes the painter to Geffroy at the beginning of December.

1915

Michel Monet joins the infantry, and his unit is deployed on April 2, leaving Blanche and Monet in Giverny with the household staff.

Monet continues to work on his murals, and in June, Mirbeau and Geffroy, along with the writers Lucien Descaves, Léon Hennique, and J.-H. Rosny, who are members of the Académie Goncourt, visit Giverny to see Monet's progress. Descaves later recalls seeing works of great size (1 x 3 and even 1 x 5 meters) in a studio space.

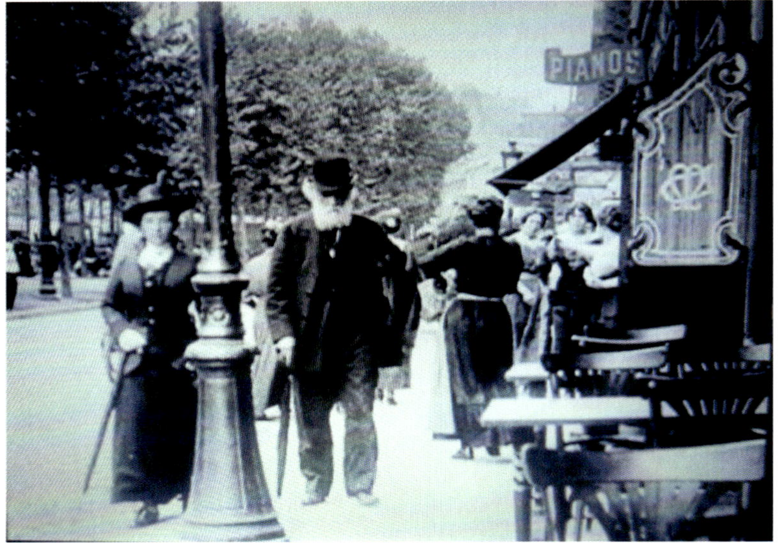

Fig. 138. Edgar Degas in Sacha Guitry's *Ceux de chez nous*, 1915

On another day in June, after lunch with the painter, Vuillard notes in his diary that the paintings by Monet that he has seen, like the Sistine ceiling, "suggest rhythm and color, all works linked by a majestic lyricism."

Due to the enormity of the murals, Monet estimates he will need at least five years to finish the project and an entirely new studio space, as the detached studio at the west side of the garden is far too small for the project he envisions. In July, Monet is officially granted a work permit to begin construction on a new studio in the northeast corner of his property, which he had recently extended by buying the adjacent land.

Maurice Lanctuit, a Vernon contractor, who oversees the demolition and construction, estimates the new studio will cost around 30,000 francs to build, not including the installation of central heating; the construction costs will be more than 50,000 francs.

Monet admits in August that he finds the vast new studio hideously ugly, yet the final result allows him the space and light he needs to gauge the surfaces and the dimensions of the paintings.

In late November, Monet attends the screening of a film by Sacha Guitry called *Ceux de chez nous* at the Variétés Theater in Paris with commentary provided by the filmmaker. The film is historically significant for its rare silent footage of France's greatest living artists, including Degas, Renoir, Rodin, and Monet, who is shown painting at his pond in the summer (see fig. 158).

1916

German troops attack Verdun, where Michel Monet is deployed. A four-month battle ensues, leaving 650,000 dead, but Michel survives and takes a few days leave in Giverny in late February.

At the urging of Etienne Clémentel, the wartime Minister of Commerce and Industry, Rodin donates his works to France in April. He stipulates that the State transform the Hôtel Biron into a Rodin museum, which the Chamber of Deputies and the Senate do not formally agree to until the end of the year.

In April, Monet asks Bonnard to visit him in Giverny to see the progress he has made on the murals. Photographs taken in 1916 show continuous panels of water lilies and willow trees. He embarks on other series as well, on a smaller scale: in May, he orders six stretched canvases measuring 1 x 1.5 meters and six measuring 1 x 1.3 meters from his art supplier.

In November, Monet writes to the Bernheim brothers agreeing to a visit from Matisse, since he should have put the final touches on his large "machines" (murals) by then. However, on December 12, Monet withdraws the invitation, saying he has no time for visitors: "Just now I have thrown myself into transformations on my large canvases . . . and my mood is foul."

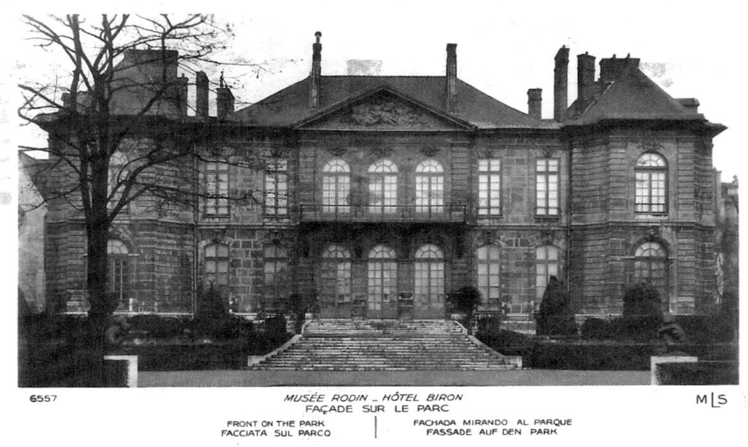

Fig. 139. Postcard of the Musée Rodin in the Hôtel Biron, c. 1937

1917

Interest in Monet's mural increases, and in February, Joseph Durand-Ruel writes to the artist that his brother Georges would like to have photographs of the decorations in order to market them to collectors and museums. A few days later, Monet writes to Georges Durand-Ruel in seeming agitation: "I have no photographs of the decorations and will make none until the work—which, by the way, does not always proceed as I would wish—is a little closer to being finished, at least in part . . . So for now it is useless to talk of sales and prices."

On February 16, Mirbeau dies, and Monet, who had visited his friend on his sickbed in late November the preceding year, grieves intensely for him.

In April, Monet donates a 1913 painting to an exhibition at the Georges Petit Gallery, Paris, where works are to be sold to benefit the Fraternity of Artists. At the end of the month, an official delegation asks Monet to paint the Rheims Cathedral, which has experienced heavy bombing since September 1914. In return for the painting, they offer to help Monet keep his car and to subsidize gas and coal. Monet is officially commissioned for the project—never realized—on November 1.

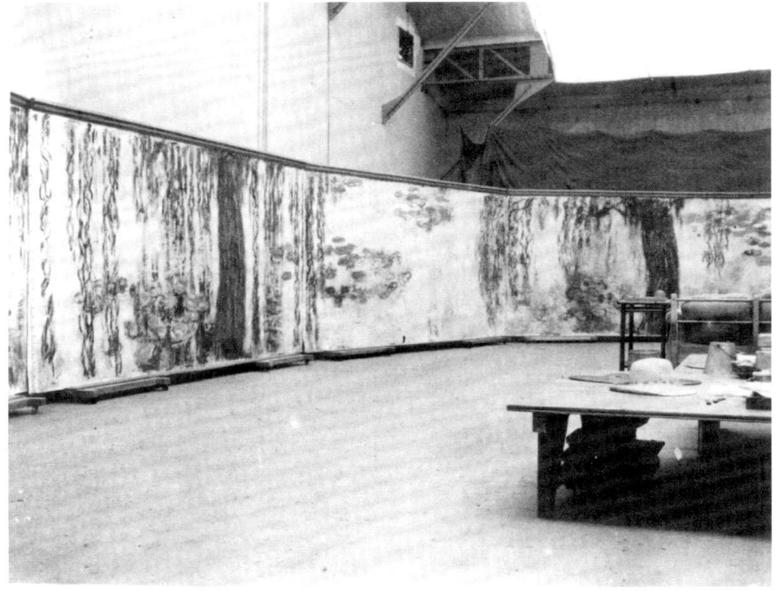

Fig. 140. Monet's third studio at Giverny with the *Grandes Décorations* in progress, November 11, 1917. Galerie Durand-Ruel, Paris

Monet writes to Joseph Durand-Ruel in August that he has been steadily working on his murals since late May 1917 and will continue rigorously through October when outdoor work in the garden will return to the studio. In November, Durand-Ruel's photographer documents works in progress at that time (see figs. 17–22).

1918

At the start of the year, Monet orders more flat brushes and stretched canvases from his art supplier and asks Clémentel to exempt him from wartime civilian rail freight restrictions so the large canvases can reach Giverny.

In early February, François Thiébault-Sisson writes an account of his visit to Giverny. According to him, Monet has completed eight of the projected twelve 2 x 4.5 meter works and has begun on the final four, which the artist estimates will take at least another year to complete if his eyesight does not fail him. Other canvases measuring 6 meters and 8 meters wide were also underway. This account is not officially published until 1927.

In the summer, while continuing work on his murals, Monet begins three new series at his water garden. One group consists of four easel-scale views of one end of the water garden (see cat. 31).

A second is a group of *Japanese Bridge* paintings on the 1 x 2 meter canvases ordered from his art supplier on April 30, extending over several years into a variety of formats (see cats. 32–38). The third series is a dozen easel-scale paintings of the *Weeping Willow* (see cats 39–44).

As he has done before, Monet moves his operations from garden to studio in October. He writes to Gaston Bernheim that he is now indoors for the winter. He also writes to ask Clémentel to help his paint supplier, who has run out of oil to make paints.

On November 12, the day after Armistice, Monet writes to Clémenceau, offering two new paintings, a *Weeping Willow* and a large decorative *Water Lilies* panel, as a celebration of the Allied victory. Monet stipulates that the paintings should go to the Museum of Decorative Arts in Paris. However, Monet's donation never occurs, perhaps because Clémenceau and Geffroy visit Monet on November 18 to persuade him to expand the scale of his proposed donation.

At the end of November, Joseph and Georges Durand-Ruel visit Giverny to purchase six more paintings, including two recently completed *Water-Lily Pond* compositions. At this same time, the Bernheim brothers also visit to buy two *Weeping Willow* paintings (one of them is cat. 43). Monet charges 20,000 francs for each easel-scaled work.

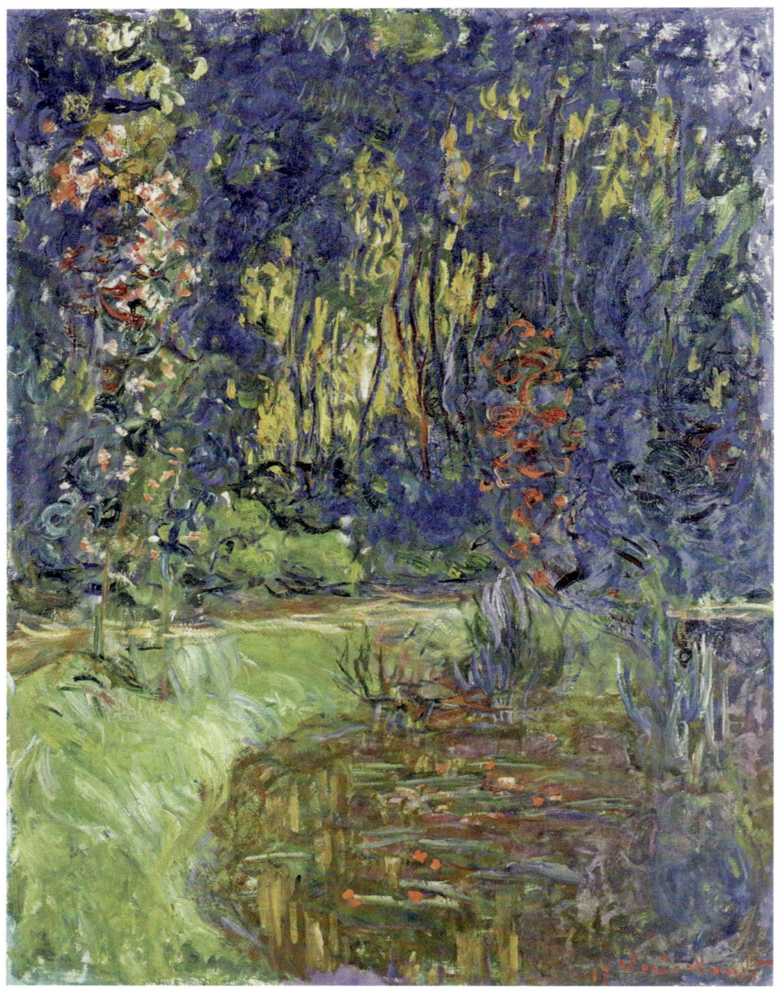

Fig. 141. Claude Monet, *Corner of the Water-Lily Pond*, 1918–19. Oil on canvas, 51 1/8 x 34 5/8 in. (130 x 88 cm). Private collection

1919

The year begins with a Monet-Rodin exhibition at the Bernheim-Jeune Gallery, Paris, and includes four 1918 paintings by Monet.

In the late summer, Monet sets aside the murals until the winter and works instead on a series of garden views on an easel-scale. The smaller scale proves difficult for the artist to return to after working on the large-scale murals, which he explains to Gimpel the following February: "I can't [paint on easel-scale canvases] anymore because I've become used to painting broadly and with big brushes."

The Bernheim brothers buy four 1 x 2 meter *Water Lilies* paintings in October or November, negotiating a half-share partnership for the purchase with Durand-Ruel in 1921.

Monet's eyesight continues to worsen, and he is forced to stop painting before he is able to finish suitably any of his recent works. On one of Clémenceau's frequent visits, he urges Monet to have an operation for his cataracts. Monet, who is concerned the procedure would lead to complete blindness, plans to contact Mary Cassatt, who recently underwent this operation.

On December 3, Renoir dies in Cagnes-sur-mer, in the south of France.

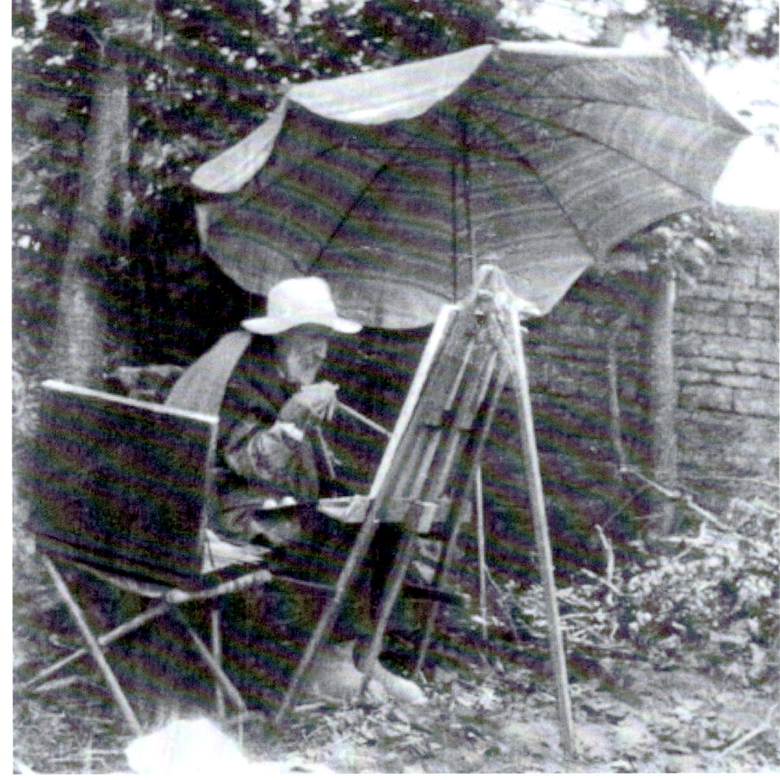

Fig. 142. Pierre-Auguste Renoir painting with his brush tied to his arthritic hands, 1919

1920

Hindered by his continually deteriorating vision and feeling discouraged with the progression of his paintings, Monet decides to help Geffroy with research for a biography commissioned by the Bernheim brothers. Eventually Geffroy decides against participating in the project and Thiebault-Sisson and Arsène Alexandre compete to replace him as author.

In March, Monet is troubled by the constant appeals from buyers. Among them is Léonce Bénédite, acting on behalf of Baron Kojiro Matsukata, who is acquiring works for a museum he plans to build in Japan.

On June 4, Monet agrees to meet with Joseph Durand-Ruel and a group of buyers from Chicago, including Mrs. Charles (Sara) Hutchinson (wife of the president of the Board of Trustees of The Art Institute of Chicago) and the collectors Mr. and Mrs. Martin Ryerson, who are considering the purchase of Monet's Water Lilies decorations for their museum; Monet does not accept their offer of a huge sum for the ensemble. (See Marianne Mathieu's discussion of this episode in her essay, "The *Grandes Décorations* from Claude to Michel Monet (1914–1966).")

During the summer, both Thiebault-Sisson and Alexandre attempt to intervene behind the scenes in Monet's ongoing negotiations with the

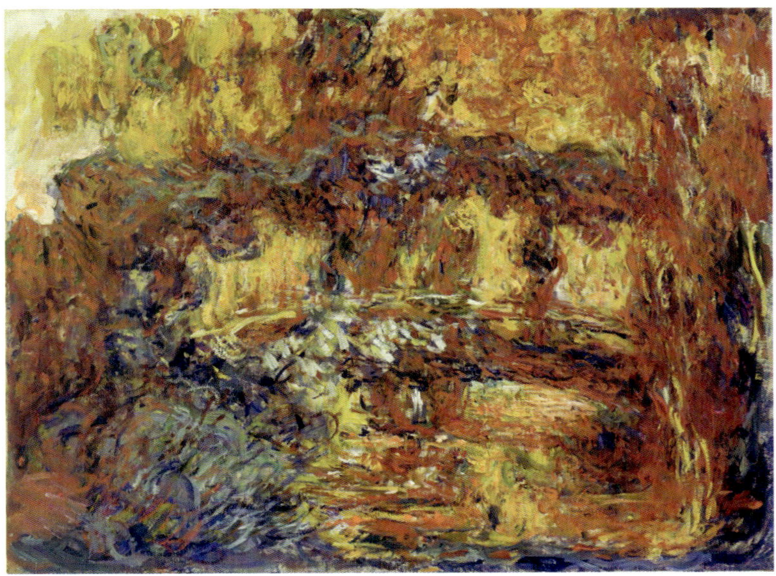

Fig. 143. Claude Monet, *The Japanese Footbridge*, c. 1920–22. Oil on canvas, 35 ¼ x 45 7/8 in. (89.5 x 116.3 cm). Museum of Modern Art, New York. Grace Rainey Rogers Fund, 242.1956

State for the water-lily donation. Monet assumes there will eventually be an agreement with the State; he writes to Clémentel in July asking for ten tons of coal for his studio: "If the State wants me to work for it, they must provide the means," he asserts.

On October 3, the architect Bonnier visits Giverny in October to discuss the pavilion that will house the *Grandes Décorations*, and two days later they settle on preliminary plans for a sky-lighted elliptical rotunda, as well as an alternative circular ground plan. At this point, four multi-panel compositions are part of the twelve-panel ensemble. (See Simon Kelly's essay "'My four best series': Monet's Panorama at the Hôtel Biron.") Shortly thereafter, Monet confirms to Georges Bernheim that he will donate twelve of his recent decorative paintings for installation in the gardens on the boulevard des Invalides side of the new Rodin Museum, on the condition that the building meets his expectations.

On November 13, Monet celebrates his eightieth birthday. The Duc de Trévise attends and writes an extensive account of this and another visit, which Monet reviews prior to their publication. This takes place in *La Revue de l'art ancien et moderne* only in January and February 1927.

1921

The year begins with a retrospective of forty-five paintings by Monet at Bernheim-Jeune Gallery from January 21 through February 2.

In the spring, Clémenceau encourages Monet to agree to the Orangerie of the Tuileries, a Second Empire structure near the Place de la Concorde, as a site for the *Grandes Décorations*; the building had recently been placed under the administration of the Luxembourg Museum. Monet visits the Orangerie with Leon Berard (Minister of Public Instruction and Fine Arts), architect Victor Blavette, Bonnier, Clémenceau, Geffroy, and Paul Léon on April 6. Monet also visits the Louvre on this day and tells Clémenceau that his favorite painting is Watteau's *Embarkation for the Island of Cythera.*

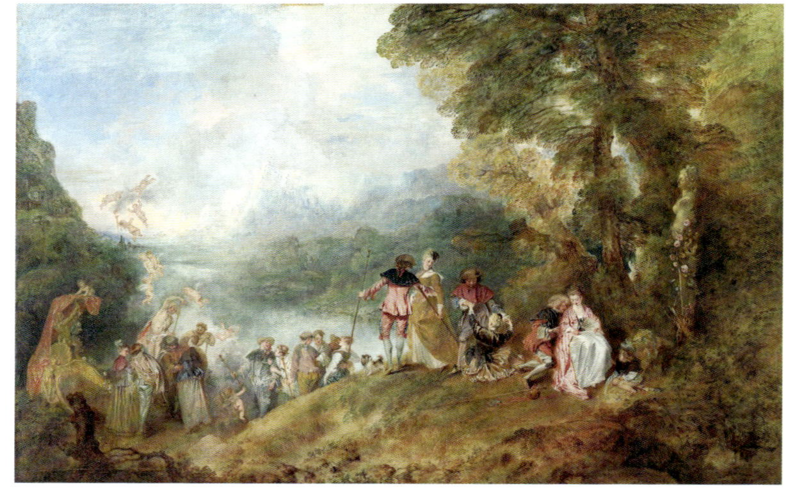

Fig. 144. Jean-Antoine Watteau, *The Embarkation for the Island of Cythera*, 1717. Oil on canvas, 50 3/4 x 76 3/8 in. (129 x 194 cm). Musée du Louvre, Paris, inv. 8525

By April 17, after settling upon the Orangerie, Monet writes to Léon, urging him to cooperate with Bonnier and hasten the building's renovation. However, on the April 25, Monet writes to Léon that he wishes to abandon his donation since his original installation intentions for the murals have to change due to the Orangerie's narrow space.

In early June, Clémenceau visits Giverny with Count Sanji Kuroki and his wife, Princess Matsukata; the collectors buy a 1907 *Water Lilies* painting.

Monet agrees to reconsider the Orangerie for his donation, but tells Alexandre, Léon, and Bérard that the space needs to be extended three or four meters, allowing him to extend the ensemble throughout two rooms instead of one.

Still awaiting confirmation from Léon, Monet sends an urgent letter to Alexandre on June 19 that if he does not receive a response from Léon about his latest request for an additional room in the Orangerie, he will strongly consider selling his Water Lilies Decorations.

Monet writes to Clémenceau in October outlining his proposal for the *Grandes Décorations* donation in the Orangerie. The painter now envisions a suite of eighteen panels to be arranged in two rooms, the second room housing his *Three Willows* composition and facing *Green Reflections*. To either side would be a 6 meter-wide panel.

Clémenceau discusses this plan with Léon, who agrees to Monet's two-room proposal. A few days later, Monet meets with Clémenceau, Léon, and Bonnier in Giverny on November 8 to discuss the donation plans, and the group settles on a list of twenty panels grouped into four compositions for each room. The Orangerie's renovation is expected to be completed by spring of 1922, giving Monet three to four months to continue working on the paintings indoors and outdoors in his garden.

By December, the budget for renovations is approved and Camille Lefèvre, the recently appointed architect to the Louvre, is hired as the architect for the project.

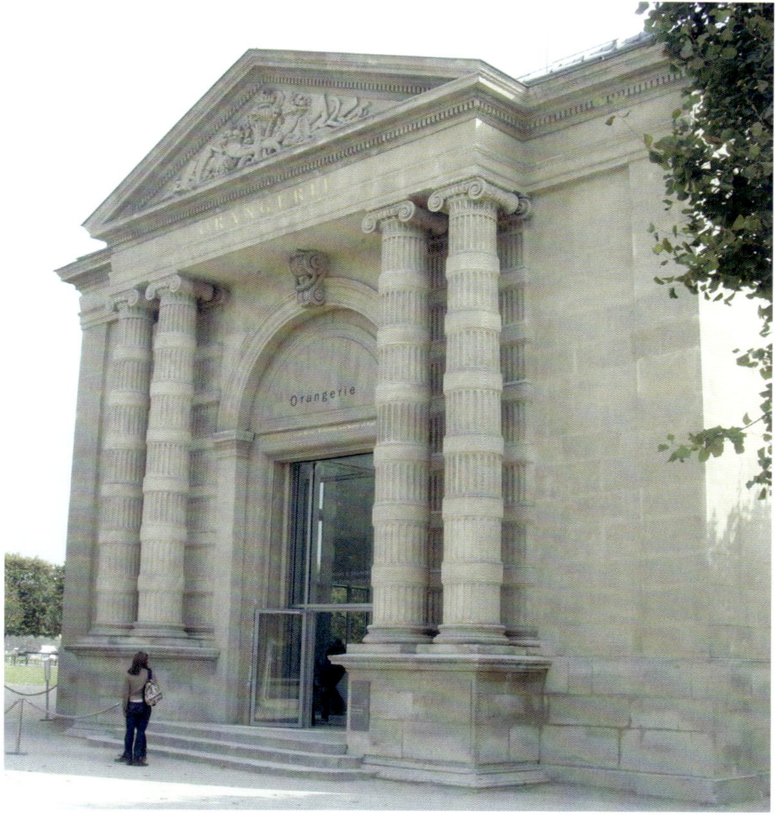

Fig. 146. The Musée de l'Orangerie, Paris

1922

The new Lefèvre plans, extending the amount of space accorded to the panels within the Orangerie, allows for the inclusion of twenty-two panels. April 12, Monet and Léon notarize a provisional act of donation in Vernon, which refers to the plans Lefèvre drafted in January. The paintings should be finished by April 1924 and the estimated cost to the State for renovations is 600,000 francs. The contract receives its final approval on December 4.

Monet's work rapidly slows in May, and he writes to Clémenceau that his eyesight is gone and he has stopped working. Clémenceau again urges that Monet consider an operation. Despite this encouragement, Monet says that he has ruined his decorations over the winter; that he is almost blind and unable to work, and that in a bout of frustration, he destroyed several of his large panels.

Again, desperate for a solution to the crisis of his failing eyesight, Monet goes to Paris in September for a consultation with Dr. Charles Coutela, a well-known ophthalmologist. His left eye, which sees better than his right, is still barely functional, so the doctor prescribes drops that are supposed to allow Monet to see two or three times better. He is eager to return to his murals before deciding if he should have surgery.

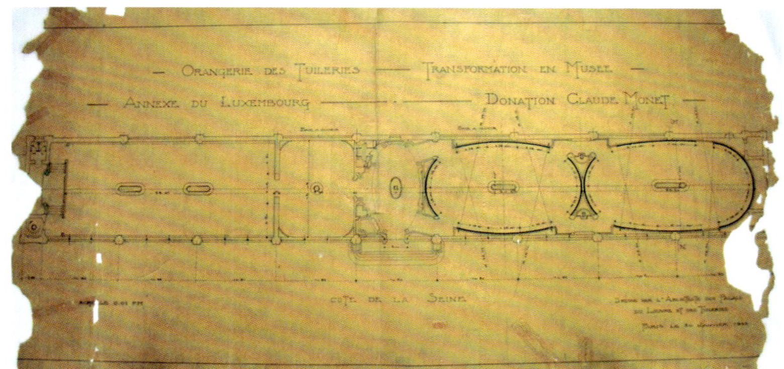

Fig. 146. Camille Lefèvre, plans for Monet's donation to the Orangerie, 1922

By October, Monet is back at work on many paintings of his garden. Joseph Durand-Ruel visits, recognizing many of the familiar motifs in the works, but exclaims at how "black and sad" they are and how they could hardly be marketed.

1923

After years of indecision, Monet agrees to undergo surgery to remove his cataracts at the Neuilly Clinic of Dr. Coutela. On January 8 or 10, he has the first surgery on his right eye. He reacts badly to the local anesthetic and is kept at rest for several days. The collector Kojiro Matsukata visits him. At the end of the month, he returns for a second operation on his right eye and again remains to recover for more than two weeks. Monet is discharged from the clinic to visit the Orangerie with Clémenceau and Léon on February 17, and then he returns to Giverny the next day.

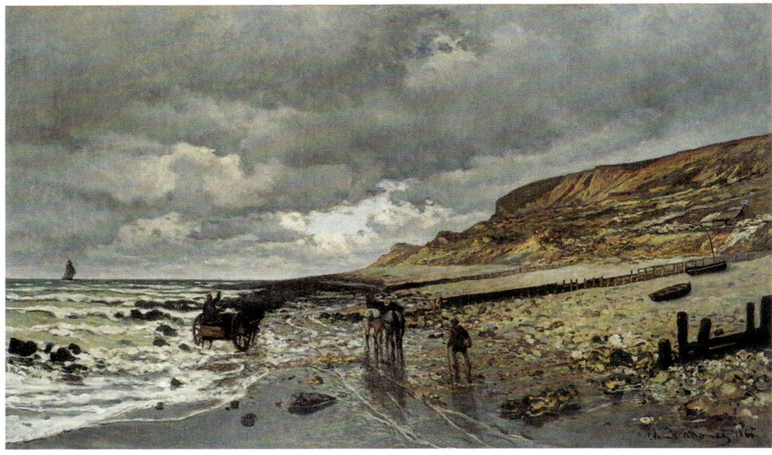

Fig. 147. Claude Monet, *La Pointe de la Hève at Low Tide*, 1865. Oil on canvas, 35 ½ x 59 ¼ in. (90.2 x 150.5 cm). Kimbell Art Museum, Fort Worth, AP 1968.07

In the spring, Clémenceau and Coutela visit Giverny with dark corrective eyeglasses for Monet and encourage him to consider a third operation on his left eye. Instead, Monet undergoes a third surgery on his right eye with Dr. Coutela; he has another bad reaction to the anesthetic and Coutela is apprehensive the procedure was unsuccessful, but when he examines Monet on July 20, he is pleased with his patient's progress.

During this recuperation, Georges Bernheim sends Monet two seascapes from the Salon of 1865 as a nostalgic diversion; one of them is the Kimbell Art Museum's *Pointe de la Hève, Low Tide* (fig. 147).

Throughout the autumn, Monet has difficulty acclimating to the effects of his new eyeglasses. Coutela provides another set of lenses to counter the intense yellow cast that Monet perceives, allowing the painter to return to his murals. He is still skeptical of an operation on his left eye and wants to know whether any other painter has had this treatment with successful results.

The Durand-Ruel brothers visit Giverny in October and are also surprised by Monet's most recent paintings in his garden with their "atrocious and violent" colors. Monet is even experimenting with a darker palette in his *Japanese Bridge* paintings.

1924

In January, sixty Monet paintings are exhibited at the Georges Petit Gallery, Paris, to benefit victims of a devastating September 1, 1923, earthquake in Tokyo. Twenty-four of the works belong to the Matsukata collection. Two are late works, including the *Water Lilies* and *Willow Reflections* (see figs. 116 and 148). Wishing to keep secret the nature of his recent largest work, Monet has Clémenceau urge Léon to insist that Bénédite not include the four meter panel.

In the spring, Coutela prescribes a new pair of glasses for Monet. The painter André Barbier acts as a liaison between Monet and the painter Maurice Denis's oculist, Dr. Jacques Mawas, a research scientist, who comes to Giverny and delivers the eyeglasses to Monet on June 6. However, in July, as Monet begins to work out-of-doors again, he complains that he sees only blue and must choose colors based on tube labels.

Unable or unwilling to stop tinkering, Monet is constantly refining his panels—to Clémenceau's frustration. Clémenceau writes angrily to Monet to chastise him for what the statesman perceives as childish and dishonorable behavior.

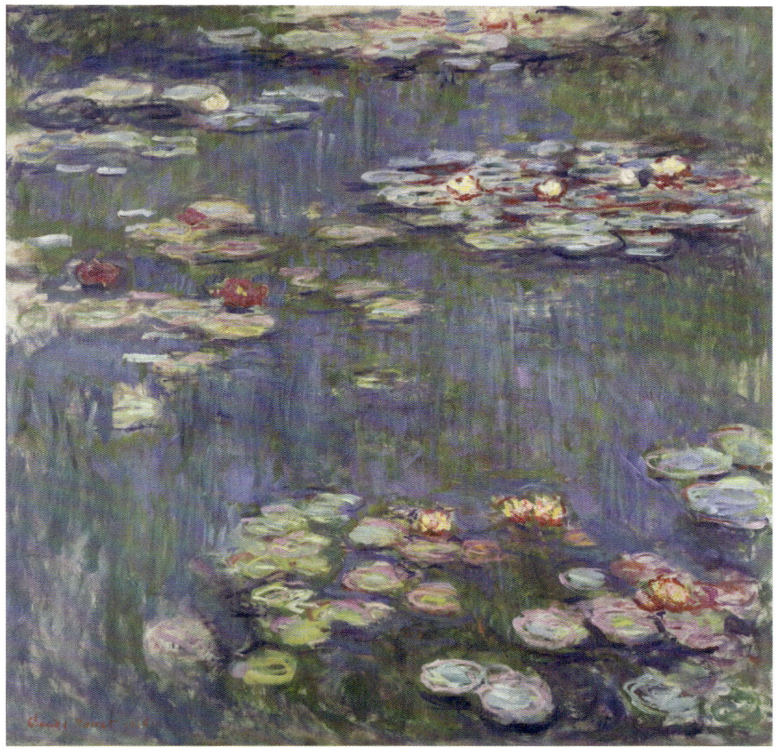

Fig. 148. Claude Monet, *Water Lilies*, 1916. Oil on canvas, 79 x 79 1/8 in. (200.5 x 201 cm). The National Museum of Western Art, Tokyo. Matsukata Collection, P.1959-0151

1925

At the start of the year, Clémenceau learns from Léon that Monet has revoked his donation. Clémenceau exclaims he will have nothing further to do with someone who breaks his word of honor to France and cancels a visit to Giverny. By February, Clémenceau writes to Blanche saying he no longer wishes to be involved with the donation and that Léon must be the one to talk to Monet.

After a month of no communication with Monet, Clémenceau realizes he needs to reestablish his friendship with the artist and returns to Giverny on March 22.

Monet writes to Mawas on March 25, apologizing for not having tried his newest glasses. "When a singer has lost his voice he retires; the painter operated on for a cataract has to give up painting, and it is this which I could not do. Excuse my candor."

Monet's eyesight improves, and he writes to Barbier on July 17: "I warn you in advance that I must be free at 10 a.m., being hard at work and with an unequaled joy, for, since your last visit [in April], my vision is completely improved. I am working as never before, satisfied with what I am doing, and if the new eyeglasses are still better, then I ask only that I live to be 100 years old."

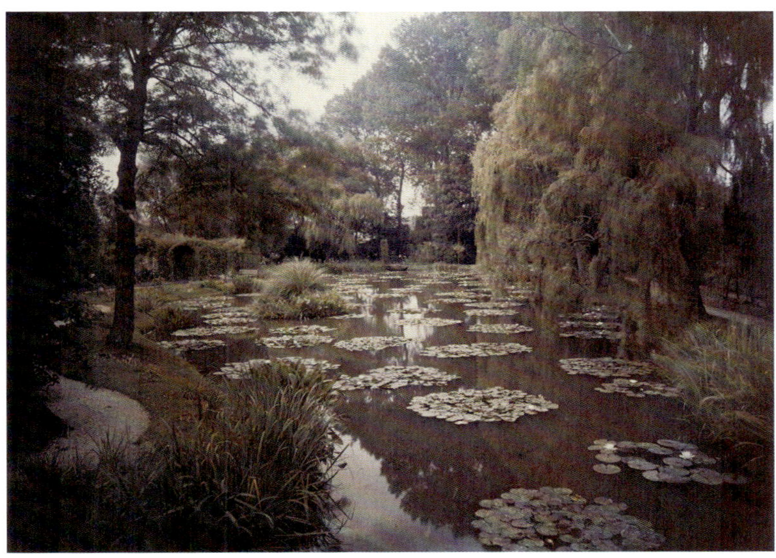

Fig. 149. Claude Monet's water-lily pond, 1920s, autochrome photo

After working diligently through the summer, Monet writes to Geffroy in the autumn that despite the variable weather, he can now return to his large panels before finally sending them off. He anticipates delivering the panels the following spring.

1926

On April 4, Clémenceau visits Giverny to tell Monet that their dear friend Geffroy had died that morning. Afterward, Clémenceau writes: "The human machine is coming apart at the seams. He is stoic and even gay at moments. His panels are finished and will not be touched again. But it is beyond his powers to separate them from himself . . . The poor Monet did not even find the strength to make a tour of his garden and the expense becomes such that he asked if it would not be best to give it up."

In the late summer, Dr. Rebiere tells Monet that an X-ray has revealed an incurable tumor on the painter's left lung. The diagnosis is pulmonary sclerosis.

Monet writes to Clémenceau on September 18: "You should know that if my powers do not return to the point where I can do what I want with the panels, I have decided to give them as they are, at least a part of them." He says that his medication has reinvigorated his appetite and helped him sleep again.

When Clémenceau visits Giverny on November 21, Monet talks about his garden and predicts that Clémenceau will see the flowers bloom next spring without him. On Clémenceau's next visit on December 2, Monet's condition has worsened significantly and confined him to his bed.

On December 5, with Clémenceau at his bedside, Monet dies around 1 p.m. He is buried in the family plot in the Giverny cemetery on December 8. Instead of a small family affair, without ceremony, as the artist had wished, there are large crowds and extensive press coverage. Artist Henri Vidal will recall that on a table in Monet's studio there was a volume of Baudelaire's poems open to "L'Étranger," a poem about a man who loves clouds more than anything else.

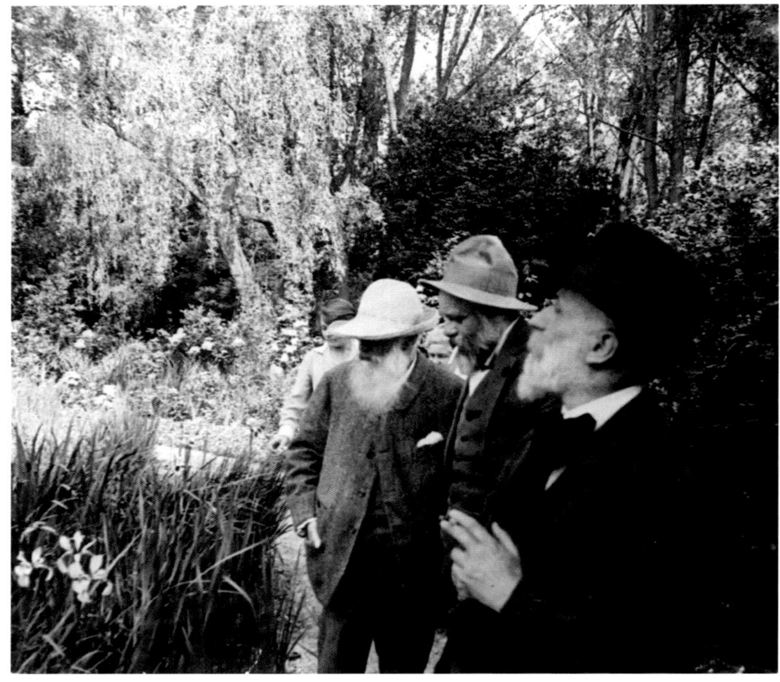

Fig. 150. Jacques Salomon, Édouard Vuillard, Ker Savier Roussel, Claude Monet, Blanche Hoschedé-Monet, and Madame Salomon at Giverny, 1926. Tinted and enlarged silver print, 6 1/4 x 77 1/4 in. (16 x 18.4 cm). Private collection

1927

Eighteen years after planting the first water lilies in his garden at Giverny, Monet's *Water Lilies* open for their first private showing on May 16, 1927, at the Orangeries, Paris. The official inauguration is on May 17 and is followed by a public opening three days later.

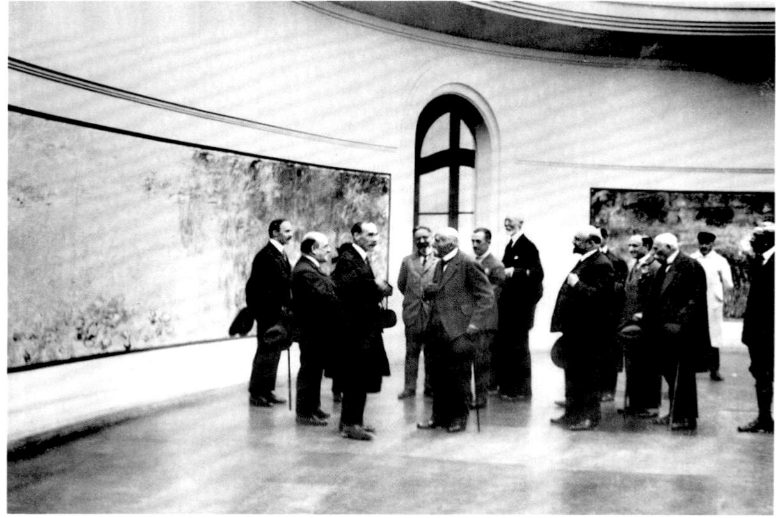

Fig. 151. The inauguration of Monet's *Grandes Décorations* in the Musée de l'Orangerie, May 17, 1927

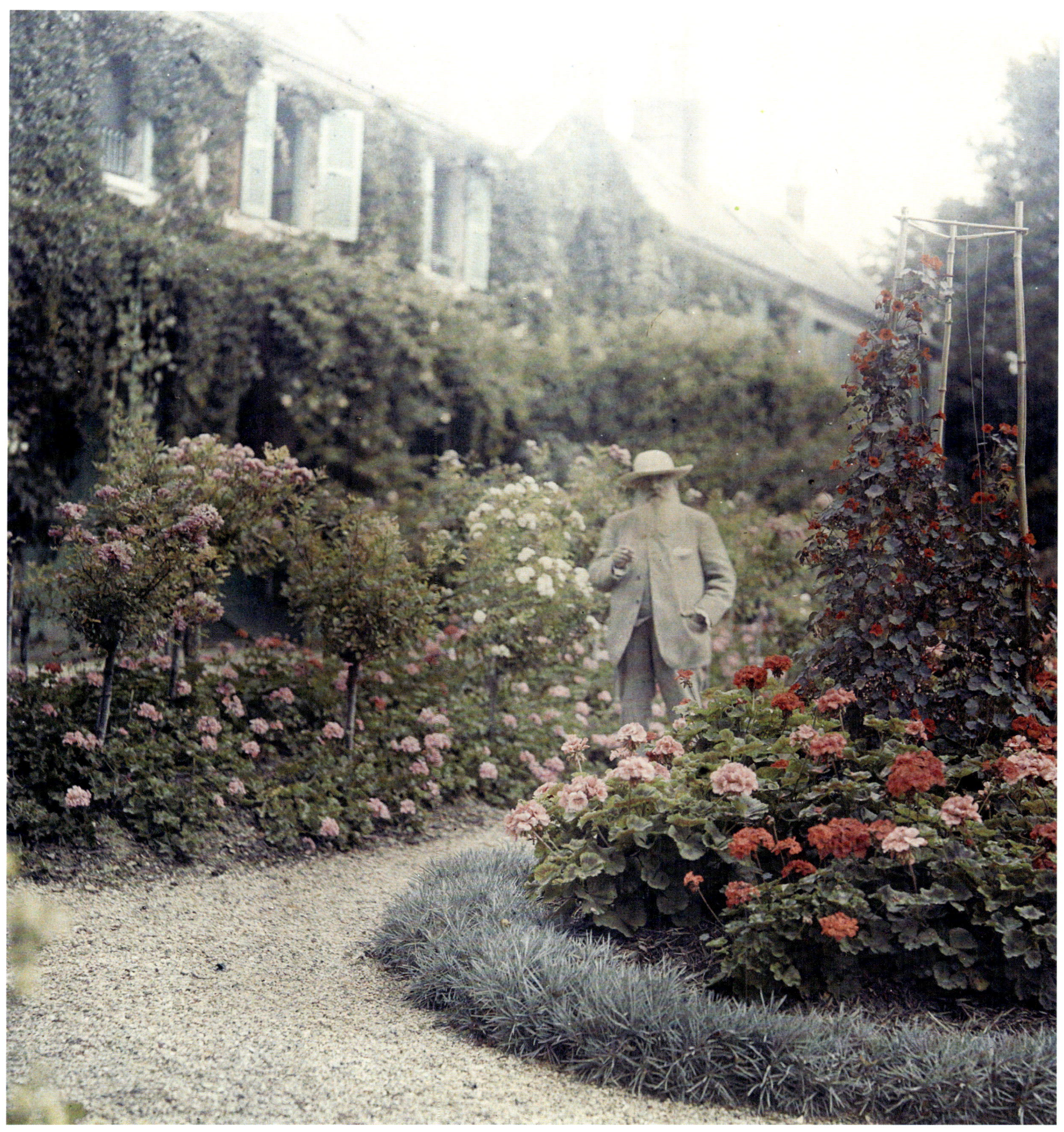

Fig. 152. Claude Monet in front of his house in Giverny, 1921. Autochrome, 7 x 9 3/8 in. (18 x 24 cm). Musée d'Orsay, Paris

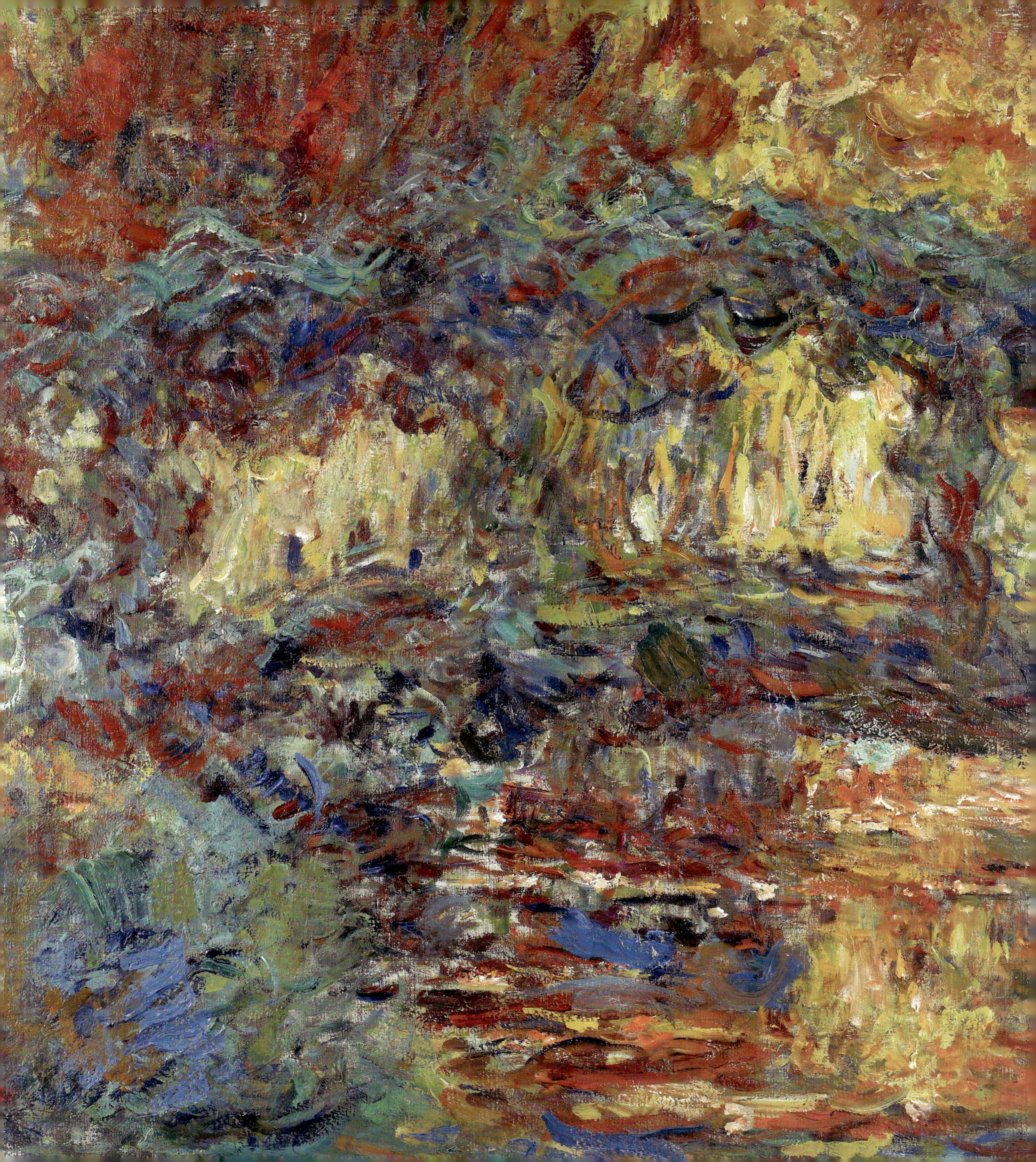

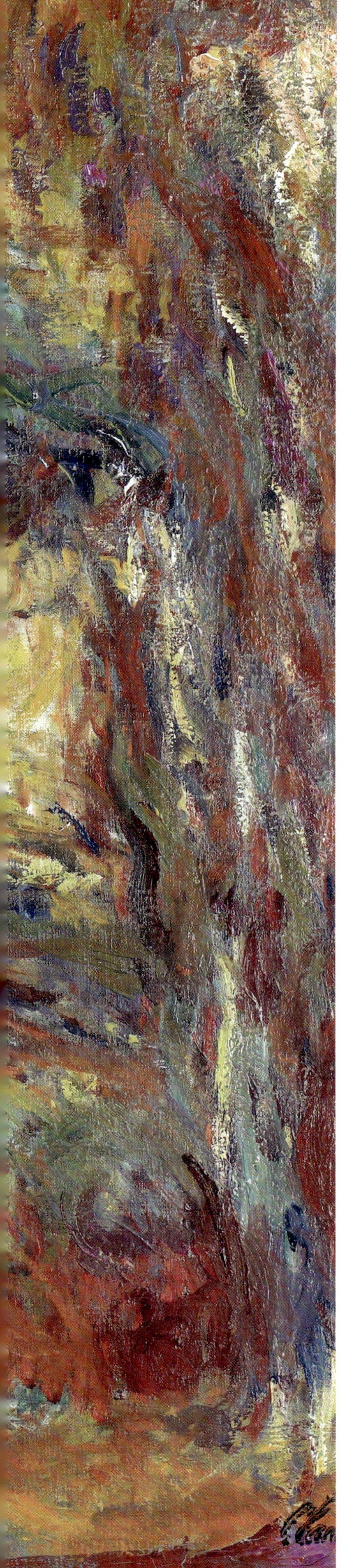

Catalogue

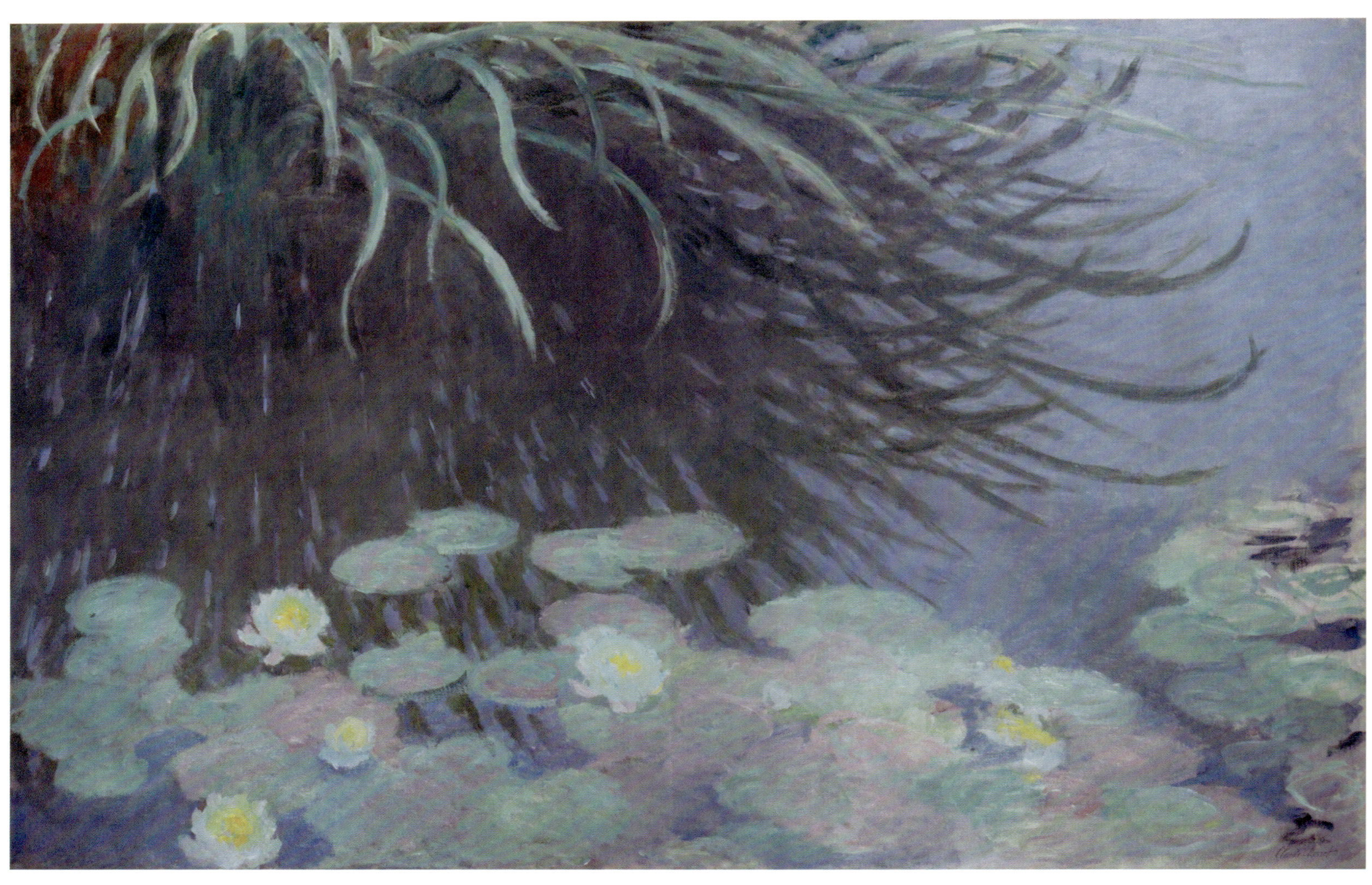

Cat. 1. *Water Lilies, Reflections of Tall Grasses*, 1897. Private collection. Courtesy Helly Nahmad Gallery, London

Monet and his assembled family—his own sons, his companion Alice Hoschedé, and her children—moved from Vétheuil in 1883 to the village of Giverny, into a farmer's house on the main street of the town. With the proceeds from the sales of his paintings growing greater every year, in 1890 Monet bought the house. Living for the first time ever in a house that he himself owned, he set about transforming the garden around the building into a true estate, planting extensive beds of flowers in the space to the south of the garden façade. A long allée of fir trees stretched from the house to the edge of the garden, where an east–west road marked the limit of Monet's property.

The public road and a parallel, minor railway line separated the garden around the painter's new house from a watery expanse of land that lay between the town and the Seine. Through the field flowed the Ru, a tiny tributary of the great river, barely more than a stream. In 1893, Monet bought part of this land, nearest the road, and proceeded to create a second garden there. If the first garden was rectilinear, the second garden was all curves; the central feature of the first garden was its long gravel allée, while the second centered on a marshy pond, created by flooding part of the land with water from the Ru.

By a few years later, the garden had filled out. The plants that the artist had ordered in 1894 from the nurseries at Latour-Marliac in southwest France had begun to mature. They included many species of reeds, grasses, and other watery foliage plants, as well as several varieties of *nymphéas,* the water lilies that were the firm's real specialty. These Monet had planted in the shallow pond, a vague hour-glass shape bordered by leafy banks. The painter, who had documented every garden he had inhabited—in Ville d'Avray, in Argenteuil, in Vétheuil—was struck by the impulse to document this new and, for him, exceptional garden feature, a sheet of water that mirrored the sky.

Though traditionally thought to have been painted after 1914, *Water Lilies, Reflections of Tall Grasses* (cat. 1) must be one of a group of some eight canvases Monet had completed by August of 1897, when they were seen by Maurice Guillemot, a journalist who had come to interview the painter for *La Revue illustrée.* His article, published in the spring of the next year, described the paintings the artist had shown him, all of which were devoted to the pond and its flowers, as "studies, large panels" with "the calm and silence of the still waters reflecting the opened blossoms" in tones that were "vague, deliciously nuanced, with a dreamlike delicacy."[1] Five canvases, among them the *Water Lilies* from Rome (fig. 153), are on average-sized stretchers, but three others, including cat. 1, are of a truly large format, measuring 130 centimeters in height by 150 or 200 centimeters in width.[2]

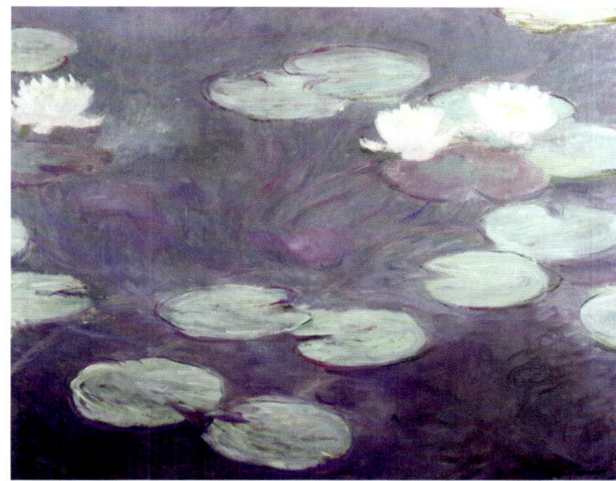

Fig. 153. Claude Monet, *Water Lilies*, c. 1897. Oil on canvas, 31 7/8 x 39 3/8 in. (81 x 100 cm). Galleria Nazionale d'Arte Moderna e Contemporea, Rome

The "still waters" of the pond made it possible for a mirrorlike effect to be captured; the rushes, almost *art nouveau* in their elegant curvature, are exactly reflected in the pond's limpid surface, and in their shadow the viewer can almost imagine seeing into the water's depths. One does expressly in fig. 153, where stems that anchor the water-lily pads play against each other underneath the water.

At the same time that he was undertaking his first studies of the water-lily plants he had so recently acquired, Monet was in the midst of painting the first of his series pictures devoted exclusively to the problem of reflection. Some of the *Poplars* he had shown in 1892 depended on reflection as a critical element, but their compositions were so varied that sky or tree or water could vie for compositional dominance. In 1896 and 1897, however, he began painting pictures like *Morning on the Seine* (cat. 2), in which reflection becomes the principal theme.

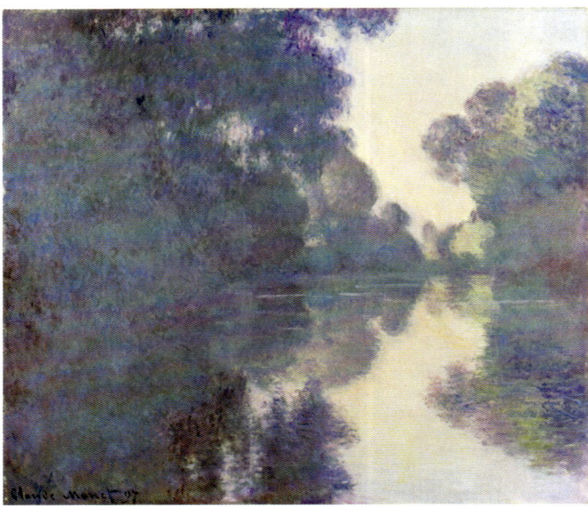

Fig. 154. Claude Monet, *Morning on the Seine Near Giverny*, 1896. Oil on canvas, 32 1/8 x 36 5/8 in. (81.6 x 93 cm). The Metropolitan Museum of Art, New York. Bequest of Julia W. Emmons, 1956

In the "*Mornings*," as the group is called, the artist took as his motif an unchanging perspective on a stretch of the River Seine, focusing on a distant bank of the bending river at the center of the canvas, the left side of the composition taken up by an overhanging tree and its reflection, which merge into one form. Although seen in perspective, the image is almost symmetrical on a horizontal axis, the top half of the painting almost identical to the bottom half. The reflection of the sky on the surface of the water takes the shape of a roadway—or perhaps another river—of light, dividing two masses of shadow. Monet worked on the series in the early morning, in his floating studio moored on the river near his house. On one such morning—after seeing the water-lily panels the previous afternoon—Guillemot followed him as he struck out, before dawn:

> His torso snug in a white woolen hand-knit, his feet in a pair of sturdy hunting boots . . . , his head covered by a picturesque, battered, brown felt hat with the brim turned down to keep off the sun, a cigarette in his mouth—a spot of brilliant fire in his great, bushy beard—he pushes open the door, walks down the steps, follows the central path through his garden, . . . crosses the road . . . , slips through the picket fence beside the railroad track . . . , skirts the pond mottled with water lilies, steps over the brook lapping against the willows, plunges into the mist-dimmed meadows, and comes to the river.
>
> There he unties his rowboat moored in the reeds along the bank, and with a few strokes, reaches the large punt at anchor which serves as his studio. The local man, a gardener's helper, who accompanies him, unties the packages—as they call the stretched canvases joined in pairs and numbered—and the artist sets to work.
>
> Fourteen paintings have been started at the same time—a study in scales, as it were—each the translation of a single, identical motif whose effect is modified by the time of day, the sun, and the clouds.
>
> This is where the Epte River flows into the Seine, among tiny islands shaded by tall trees, where branches of the river, like peaceful, solitary lakes beneath the foliage, form mirrors of water reflecting the greenery; this is where, since last summer [1896], Claude Monet has been working.

Guillemot underestimated the number of such canvases that Monet had begun by 1897, for more than twenty related canvases were in play. Many of these, such as *Morning on the Seine Near Giverny* (fig. 154), were worked on through many sessions and finished in the studio before being shown at the Galerie Georges Petit in June 1898. Others, such as cat. 2, preserved the loose and vivid application of paint that must have characterized them all in the early stages of their elaboration. These were retained by the artist in his studio; this example was purchased by Durand-Ruel in 1911. Such a painting, then, was present as a point of reference as Monet began to conceive the many compositions in which the pathway of light would be a dominant feature—both the vertical water lilies of 1907 (see cats. 7 and 8) and the panoramic waterscapes of 1917–19 (see cats 25–27).

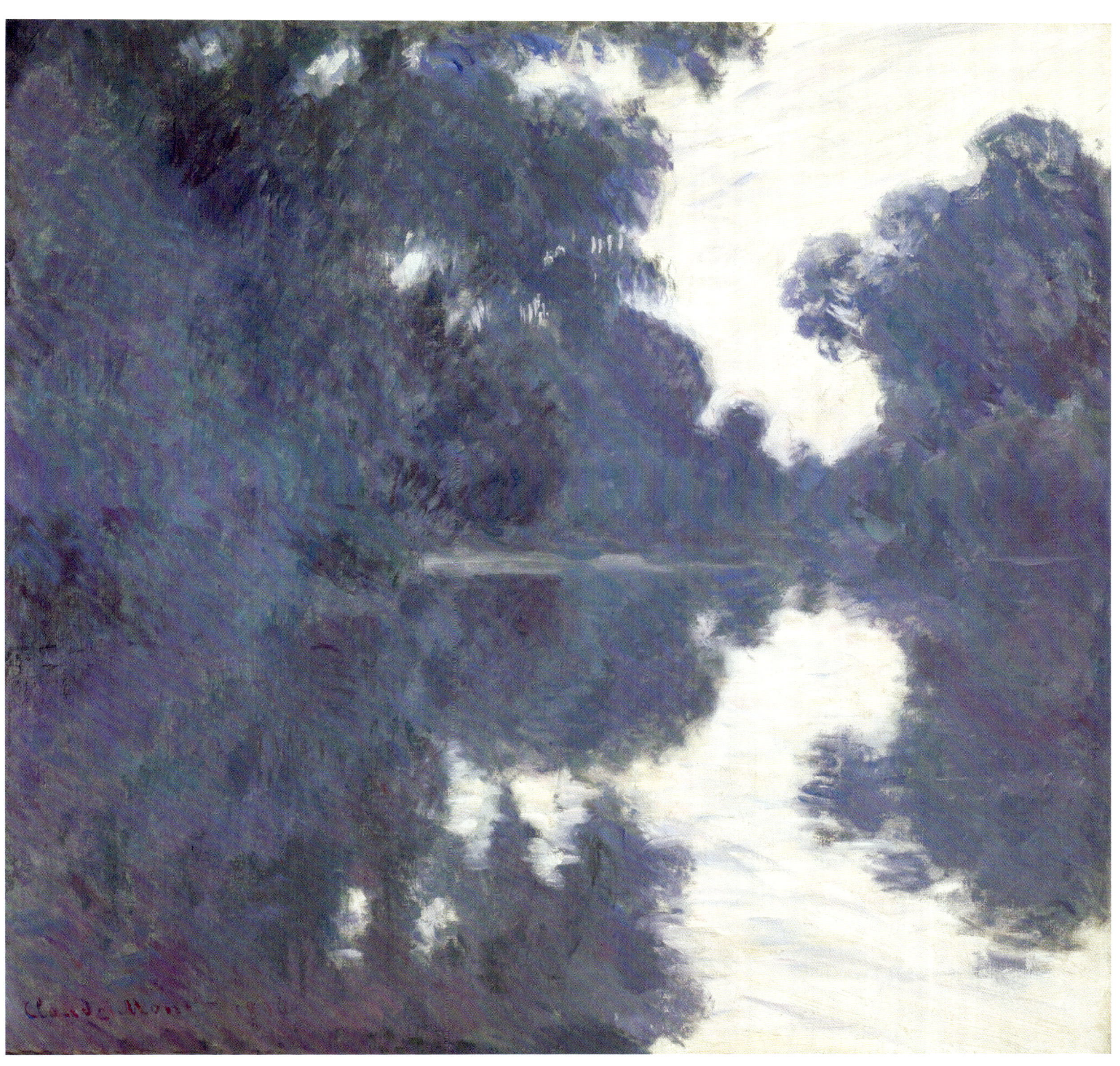

Cat. 2. *Morning on the Seine*, 1896. Private collection. Courtesy Sotheby's, New York

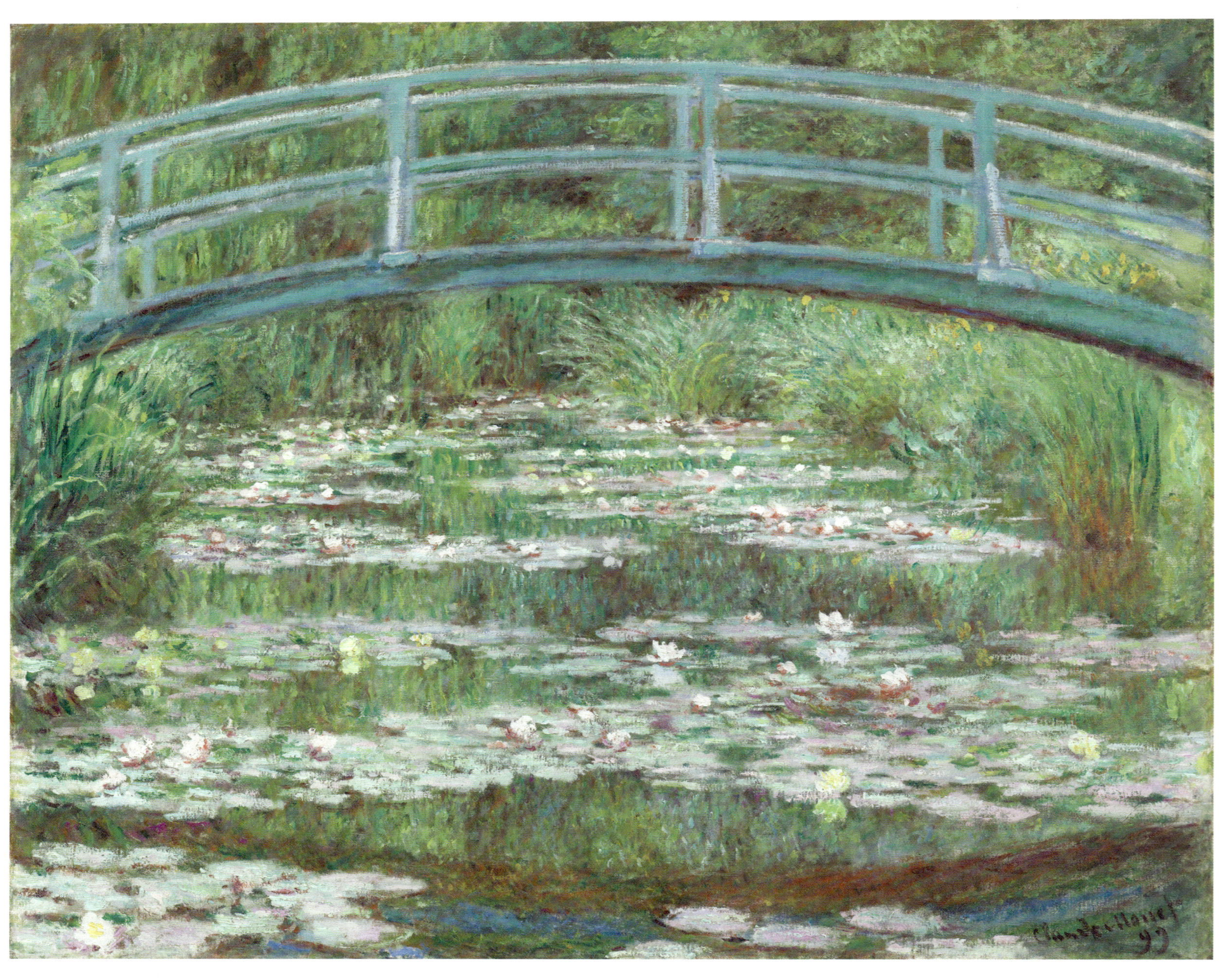

Cat. 3. *The Japanese Footbridge*, 1899. National Gallery of Art, Washington, DC

Maurice Guillemot, who visited Monet's garden in 1897, was among the earliest authors to describe what the painter had in mind. "Beyond the road and the unweeded path of the railroad track," he wrote, "along a brook flowing between the willows, Claude Monet has had a pool dug out, spanned by a wooden bridge in the Japanese style. . . . On either side are locks to allow a daily change of water. The locals were opposed at first, suspicious of this unfamiliar flower, claiming that the artist was poisoning the countryside, that their cows would no longer be able to drink."[1] The relatively small pond that Guillemot saw narrowed at its center so that it could be spanned by an arched wooden bridge, inspired by Japanese examples; the bridge was placed on axis with the long pathway leading out of the *clos Normand*, the orchard/garden within the walls surrounding Monet's house, on the other side of the road from the pond garden.

Though small, the pond presented an intriguing subject: one that Monet had both already explored and that he was cultivating—literally—for future use. "Upon that immobile mirror float water lilies, aquatic plants, unique species with broad, spreading leaves and disquieting flowers of a strange exoticism," Guillemot wrote.[2] Monet had first painted the bridge itself as early as 1895, in a series of paintings exploring his new garden, but the surface of the iris-bordered pond in those paintings is glassy smooth; no waterlilies, not even leaves, can be seen. Following on the close-up paintings—the large panels mentioned by Guillemot—from 1896 or 1897, the artist waited until 1899 to return to the pond as a subject. Then, in such works as *The Japanese Footbridge* (cat. 3), he began to set out the compositional device that was to become, in his late years, a central feature of his art.

In this painting, between the arch of the bridge and its reflection below, the artist frames a view facing east across the surface of the pond. As with the *Mornings*, the composition stretches into the distance, but here emerges a new spectacle: the mirror of the pond's surface is interrupted by receding clumps of flowers and foliage, floating like islands on the receding plane. The simplicity of the formula that made the *Mornings* so hypnotic has grown complicated, as the sensation of deep space is reinforced by the diminution of the size of the clumps and the converging lines of the banks of the pond. The bridge and its reflection act as a window surround, standing between the viewer and the distance—not defining inside and outside but near and far. Behind all these horizontal or arching interruptions, however, lies another element, difficult to discern at first: the pattern of verticals established by the trees in the distance and continued by the trees' reflection in the surface of the water. The mirror of the water brings the verticals nearly to the foreground, beneath and behind all the other elements that are seen not in reflection but directly.

In 1901, as he was developing his series of paintings of the Thames at London—leading up to their exhibition in 1904—Monet caused the pond in his garden to be enlarged, more than doubling its expanse, particularly to the east. In 1903, he returned to the pond as a subject, at first using such elements as a hanging willow bough to establish the viewer's position beneath a tree on the bank. By 1904, when he painted the Denver Art Museum's *Water Lilies* (cat. 4), he eliminated all points of reference in the foreground but maintained at the top of the canvas a strip of bank, covered with bushes and grasses, that established the limit of the pond. The pond, here, takes on a greater role than it had in 1899—not only is it physically larger in reality, it looms larger as an element, reflecting the massing of foliage of the trees that rise outside the viewer's focus, beyond the frame of the picture. Using tones of dark blue-green in the shadows and lilac in the highlights, Monet creates in the reflections a quiet ground for the sunny islands of leaves and flowers.

In the 1905 canvas from a Dallas private collection (cat. 5), the painter all but eliminates the bank, which appears as a sketchy fringe of leaves at the upper edge of the canvas. Here, the clumps of vegetation seem to retreat to the margins of the composition to give pride of place to the large reflection at center. The water's mirror reveals a weeping willow in shadow against bright patches of blue sky, setting up an energetic, almost jagged, pattern of dark and light that looks forward to the vigorous brushwork of a decade later.

By the time Monet painted the *Water Lilies* at the Art Institute of Chicago in 1906 (cat. 6), all vestiges of the distant bank had disappeared: the water's surface extends beyond the pictorial frame in every direction, and the relatively shallow reflection of foliage, coming short of half the depth of the composition, suggests that it is far away. Suffused with sunlight and with the dominant blue of the reflected sky, the composition is among the brightest and most coloristically intense of any of Monet's early water lilies. It is also among the most sophisticated in what might be called its choreography—the placement of the flowers across the canvas. This arrangement, it turns out, was the result of much repainting and refinement, as conservation studies of the painting have demonstrated. The artist corrected his placement of the pads, the leaves, and the flowers to achieve the balance he desired.[3]

In 1907, Monet abandoned the square or horizontal formats that he had used in earlier water-lily compositions and turned his canvases ninety degrees for a series of paintings in which vertical elements predominate. In each of these, reflected forms of trees are divided, left and right, by a band of lighter, reflected sky, cascading from the top of the image and expanding into a broad field of light at its lower edge. As he had done with the *Mornings*, Monet established a framework for these compositions: delicate horizonal elements placed against the vertical ground of reflected light and shadow establish a repeated pattern. Thus, clumps of lilies anchor both bottom corners; in the middle distance, halfway up the composition, a single clump spans the band of light between two shadows, against which other clumps rise towards the top of the image.

Having established this pattern, Monet could vary the color and density of each element in turn. In one painting, cat. 8, a close tonal range across the various hues of blue and green suggests a time of day, likely the morning, when there was a balance between light and shadow. Another presents a glowing sky between shadowy reflections, suggesting that the view was taken as the sun began to shine from the west; in yet other views from this angle the sky takes on the pink and orange hues of sunset.

The number and variety of these canvases is revealed by a photograph taken in March 1908 (fig. 155). Leaning in layers against each other and rising up the walls of Monet's studio are paintings from 1903 to 1907—the most recent are in the front row. Some have been fitted into the thin frames that the painter favored

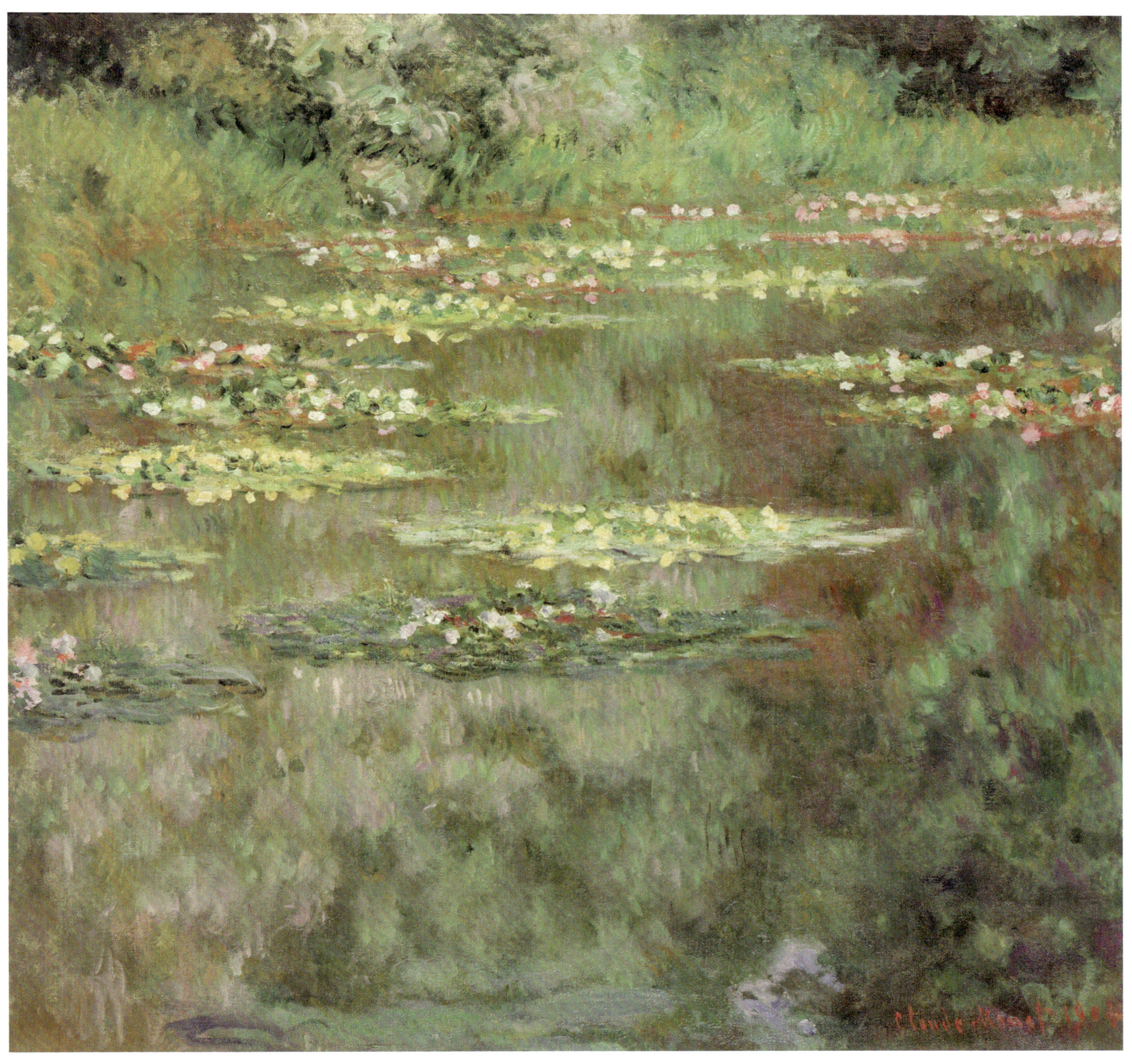

Cat. 4. *Water Lilies*, 1904. Denver Art Museum

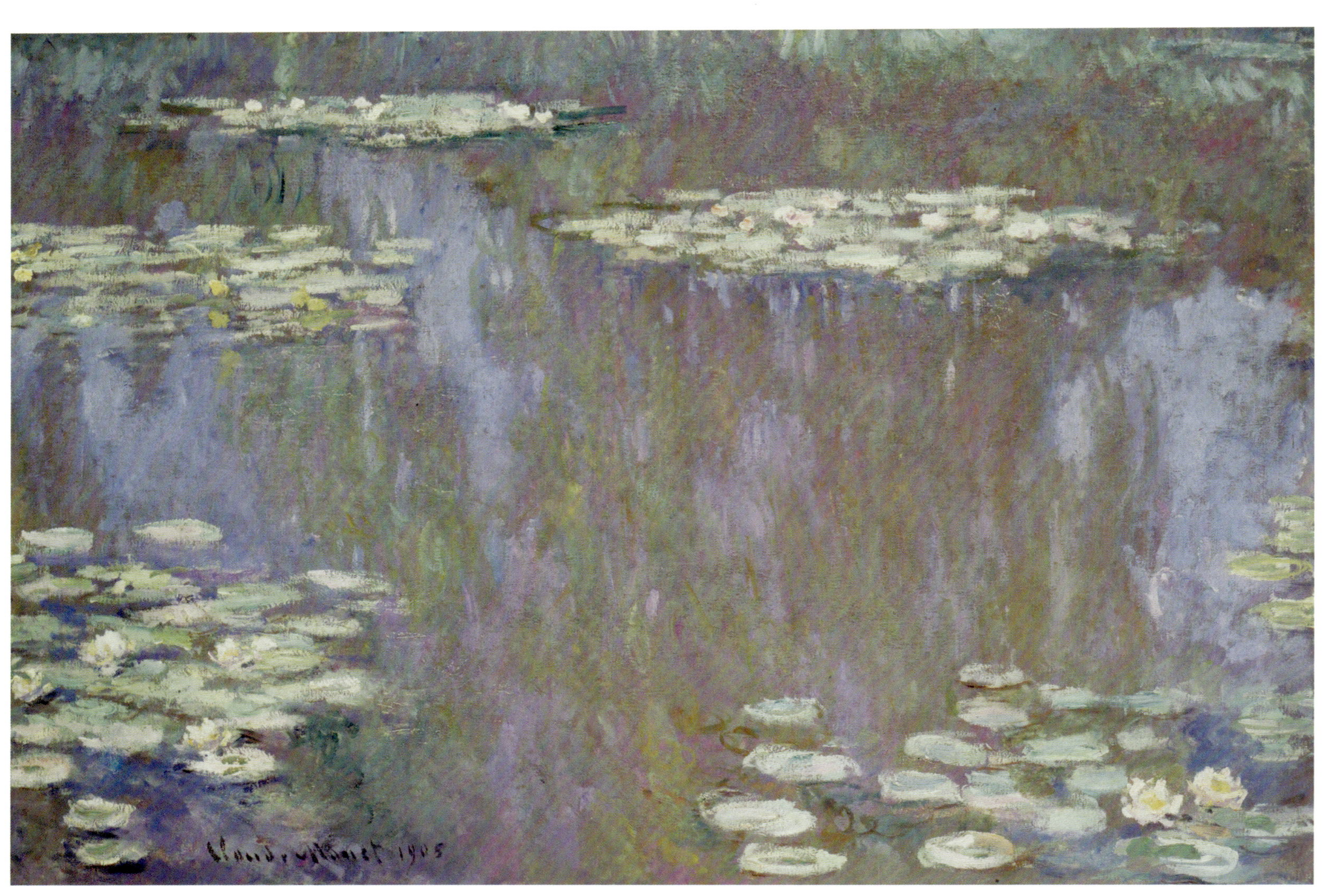

Cat. 5. *Water Lilies*, 1905. Private collection, Dallas

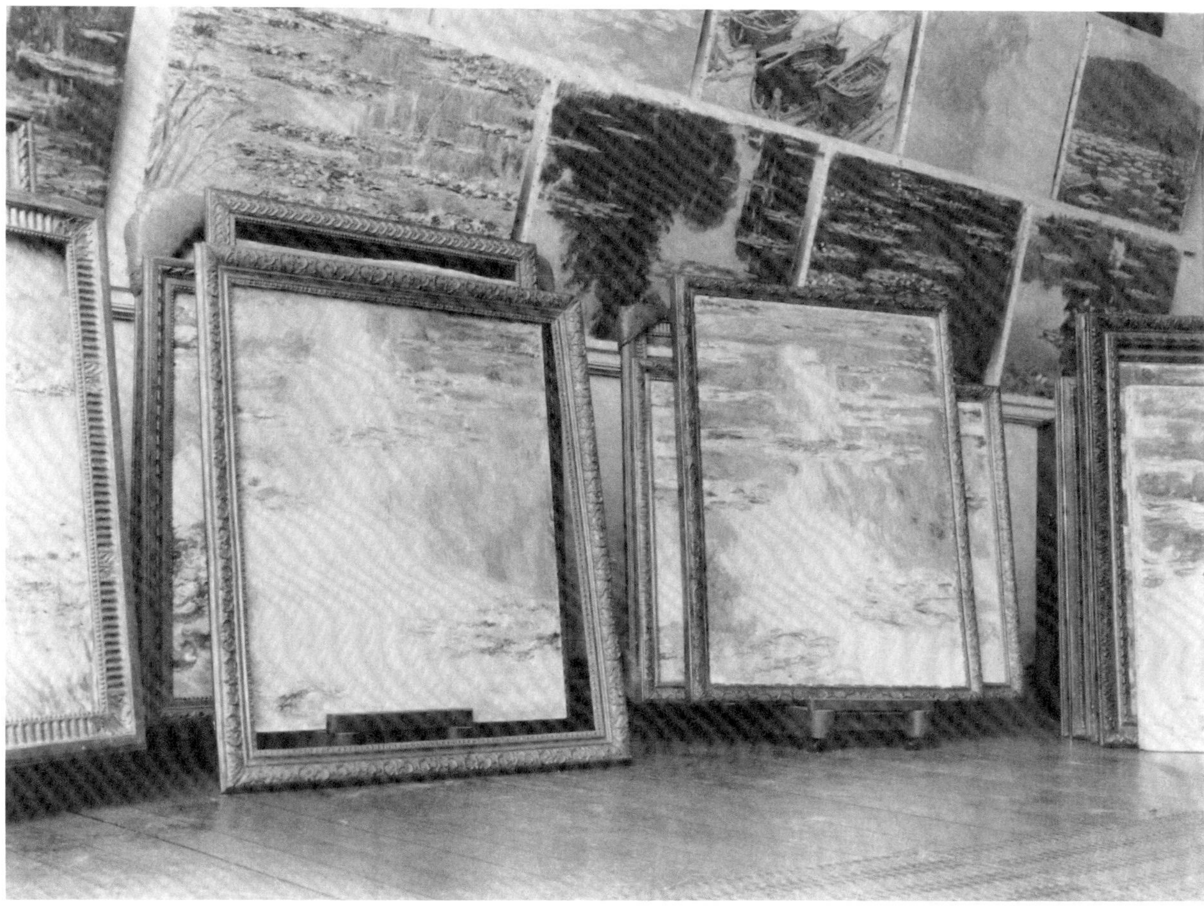

Fig. 155. Water Lilies paintings in Monet's studio in Giverny, March 1908. Galerie Durand-Ruel, Paris

for his series paintings at this time, an indication of how anxious the Durand-Ruels, who took the photograph, were (and had been) to schedule an exhibition of this latest group of works. This was not to occur in 1908: the artist again insisted on painting another summer's worth of canvases, the last of which were pale and diaphanous in contrast with the visual focus he had brought to the theme at the beginning of the campaign.

In May 1909, forty-eight of the water lilies, the *Nymphéas*, were exhibited at Durand-Ruel's gallery, with the subtitle *Paysages d'eau*—"lanscapes of water." Lauded by critics, the group seemed so coherent, in spite of the range of solutions to a common problem, that its inevitable dispersion seemed a shame. The idea of keeping the exhibition together as a unit was bandied—but was impractical, as the paintings had already begun to sell during the run of the exhibition.[4] But the suggestion that a group of such paintings might form an ensemble, already on Monet's mind for a decade, was firmly implanted by the close of the exhibition.

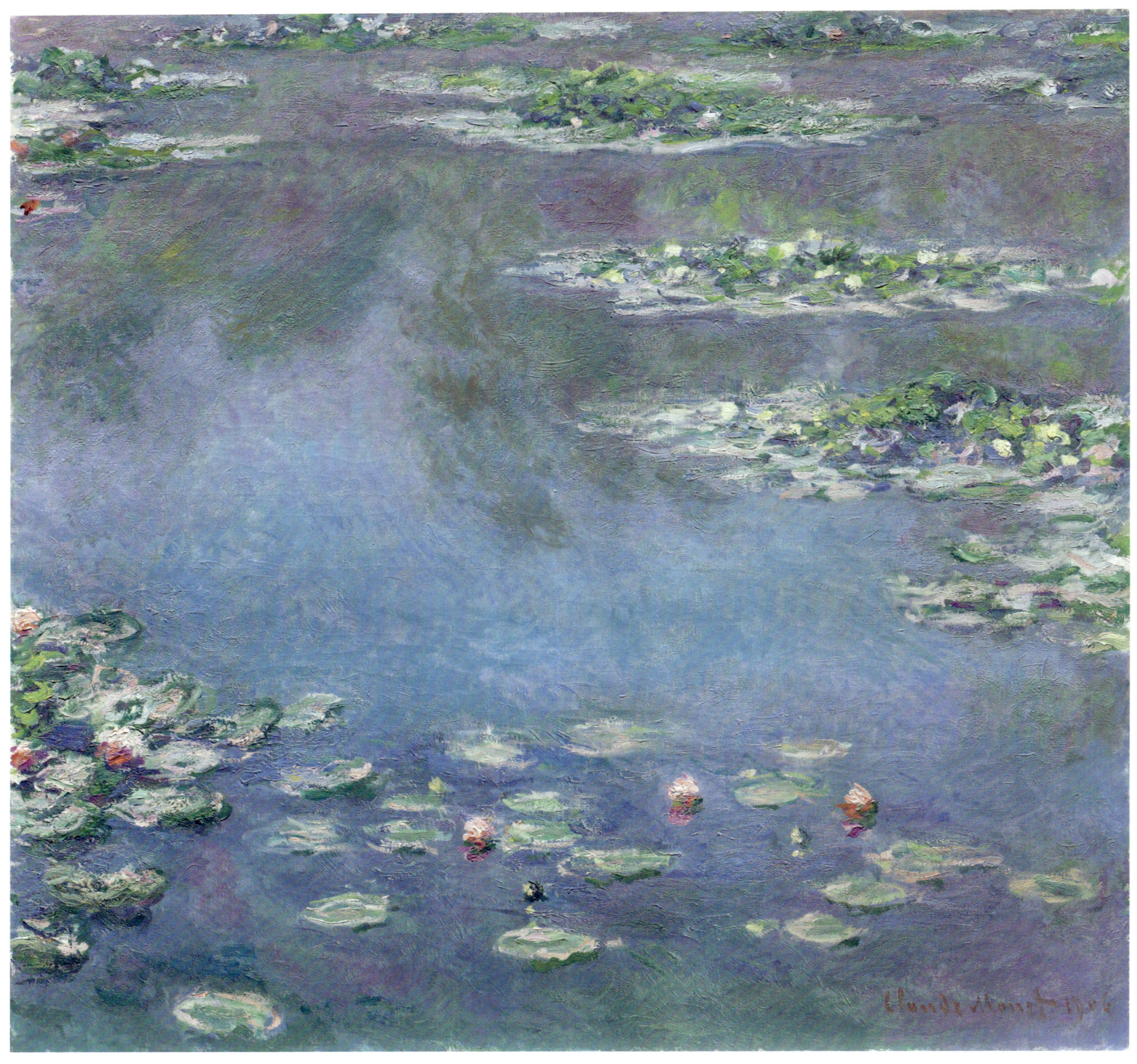

Cat. 6. *Water Lilies*, 1906. The Art Institute of Chicago

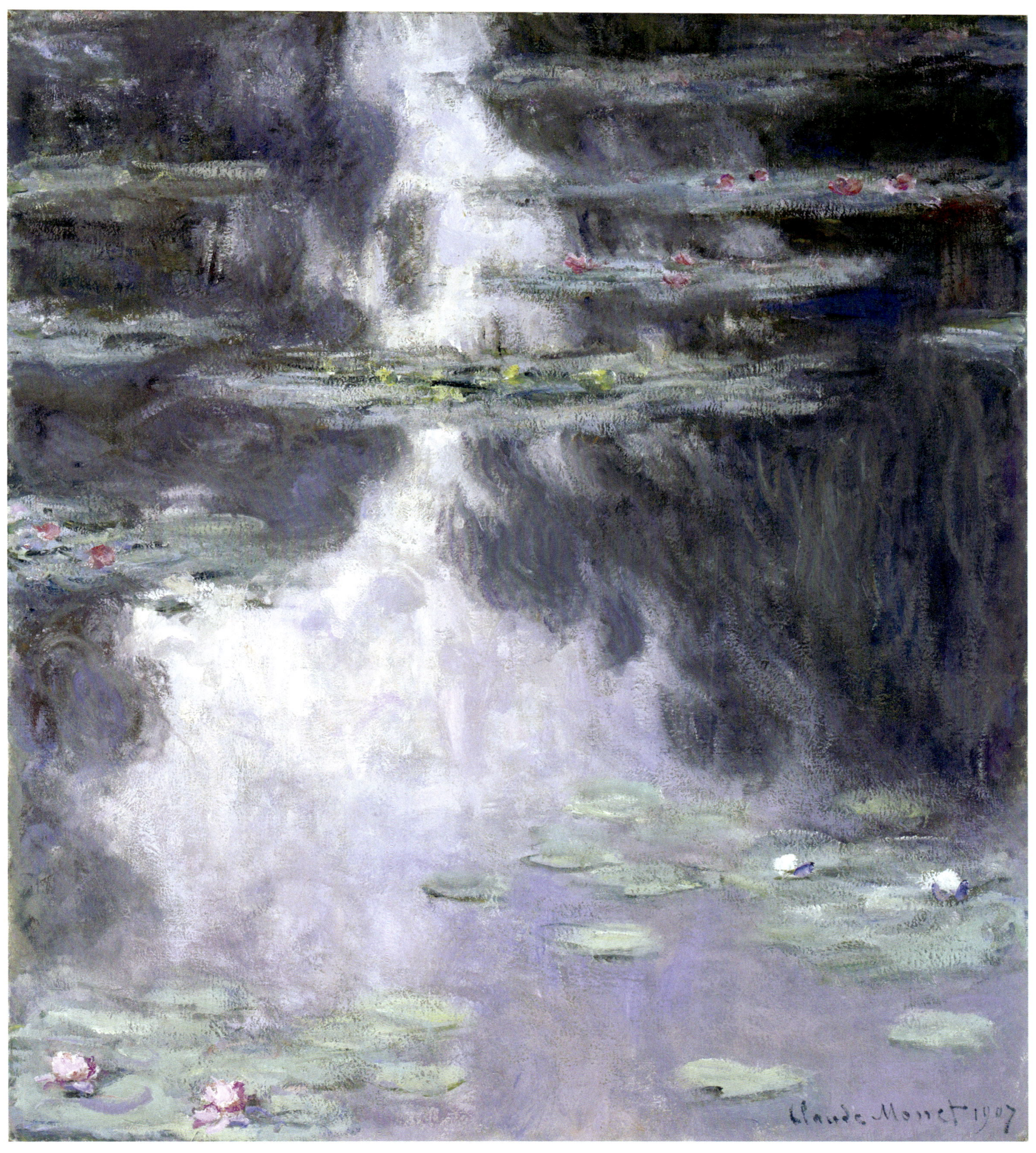

Cat. 7. *Water Lilies*, 1907. Museum of Fine Arts, Houston

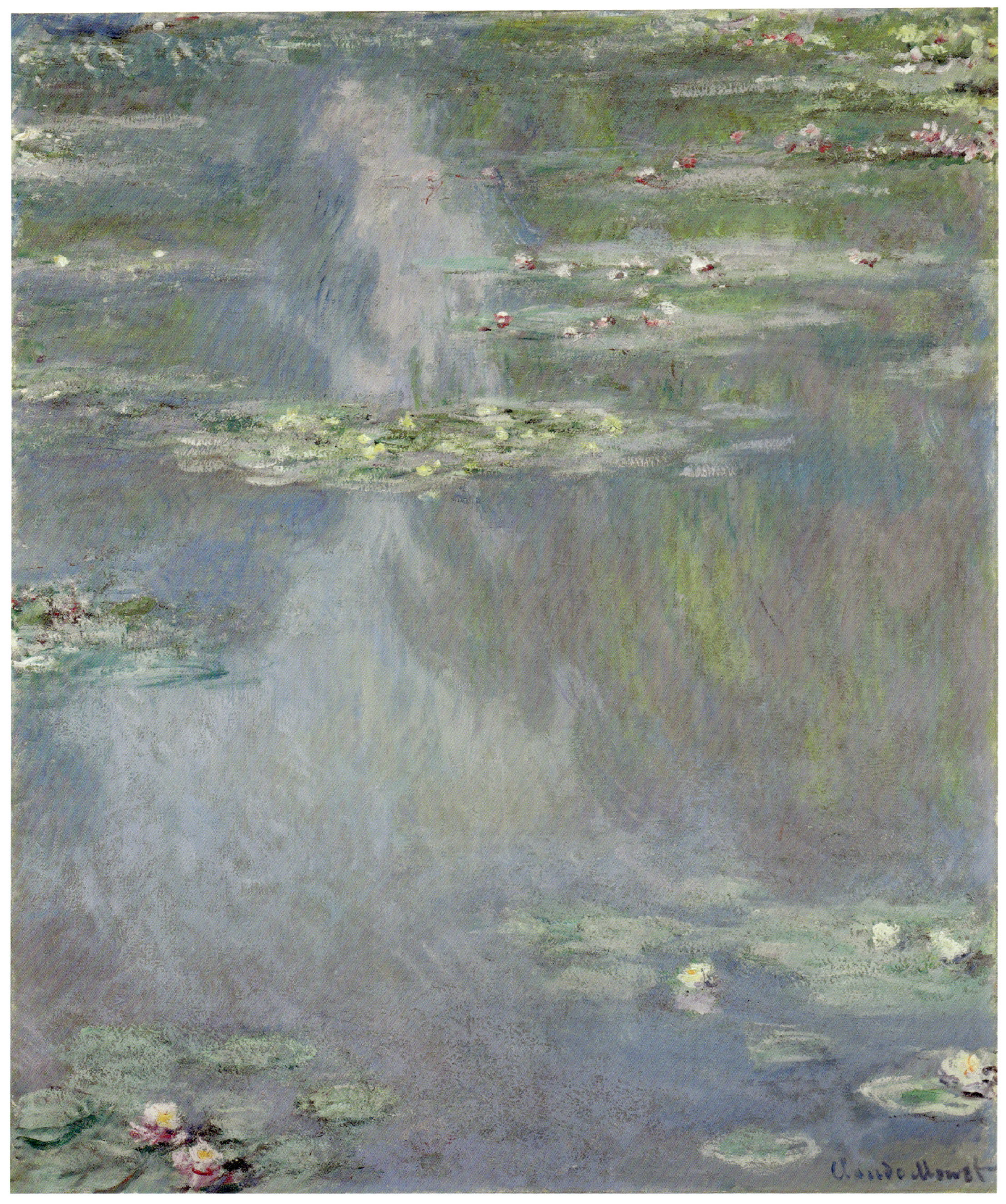

Cat. 8. *Water Lilies*, 1907. Private collection. Courtesy of Christie's, New York

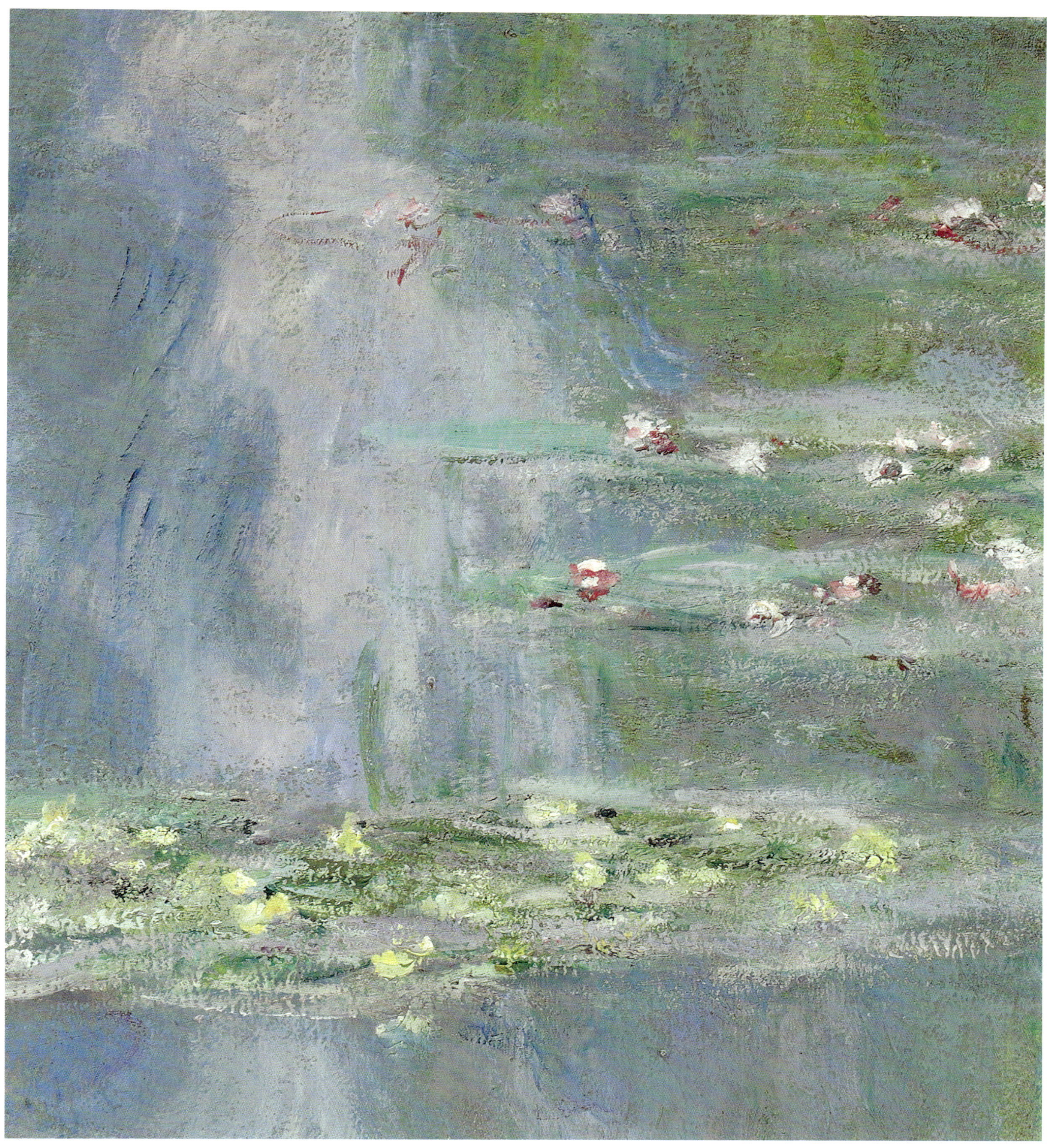

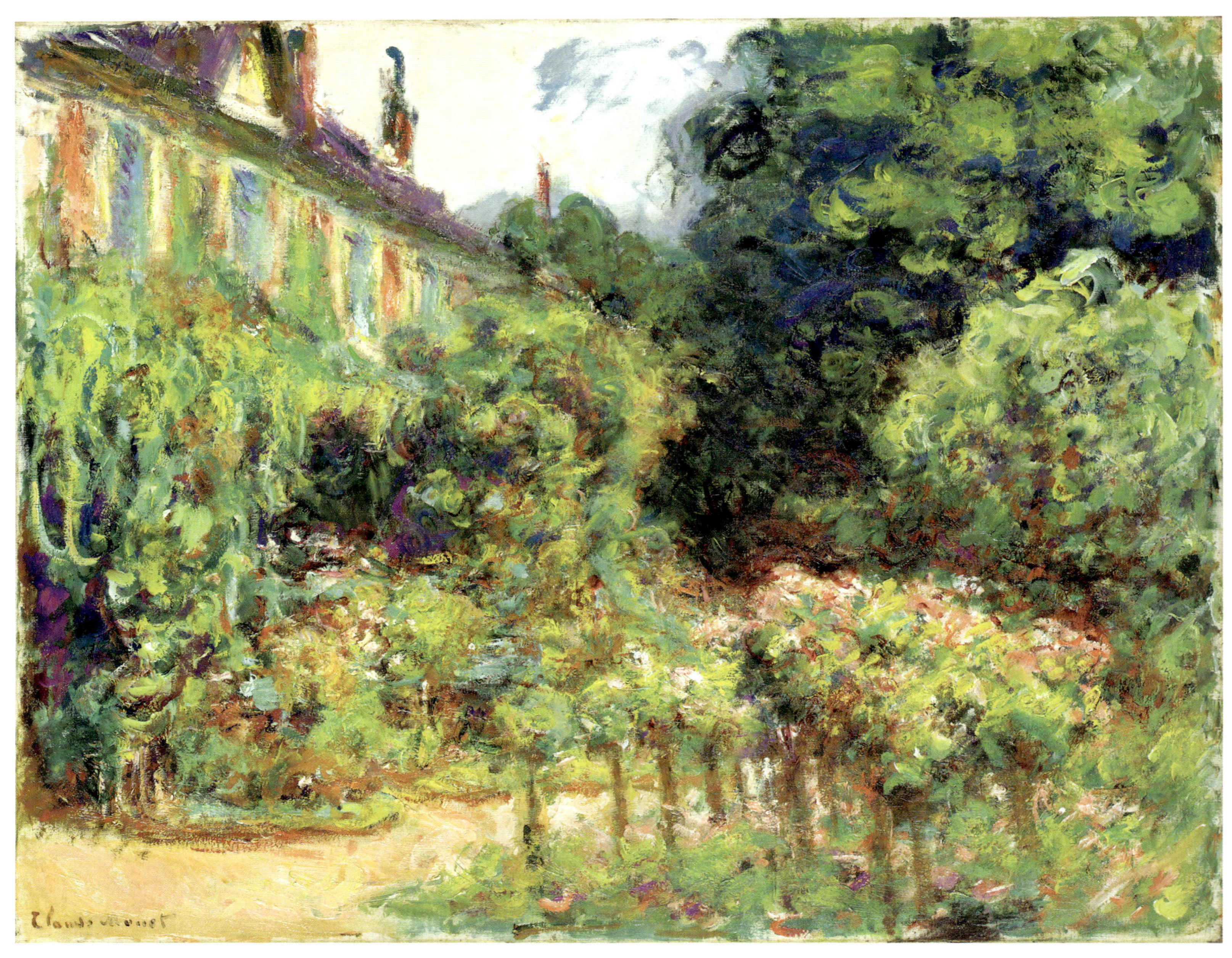

Cat. 9. *The Artist's House at Giverny*, 1913. Private collection. Courtesy of Christie's, New York

The spring of 1912 presented many difficulties to Monet. Still in mourning for his wife Alice, who had died a year before, he was obliged to finish the canvases he had begun in Venice on a trip they had taken in 1908. Though dissatisfied with the results, he persevered, and an exhibition of twenty-nine paintings opened at the Galerie Bernheim-Jeune, Paris, on May 28. On June 7, the painter wrote to Gustave Geffroy, "I know only that I do what I can to render what I feel in the face of nature and that, more often than not, in order to arrive at what I sense, I completely forget the most elementary rules of painting—if they exist, that is." Even while the exhibition of his Venetian paintings was underway in Paris, he lamented the present state of his abilities, despairing that he would forever "allow lots of faults to appear in order to fix my sensations."

At the end of June, he went back to work, but a few days later, he complained to Geffroy about being thwarted by bad weather. "I had returned to work, but now I have to give up what I'd done." Nature, he wrote, did not respond to man's desires and must be seized when there was a chance, "which isn't my case today, having stayed so long indifferent to everything."

In fact, during Alice's long illness—she fell ill in early 1909 and was diagnosed with spinal leukemia in February 1910—Monet painted little, unable to concentrate on much besides his wife's deteriorating health. The situation did not improve after her death. Despite his work on the Venetian canvases, Monet's output as a painter in 1912 and 1913 reflects the indifference "to everything" that he confessed to Geoffroy. Barely a handful of pictures are datable to the eighteen months between the late spring of 1912 and the spring of 1914, and little evidence allows us to fix precisely the time of the works we do know.

The Artist's House at Giverny (cat. 9) may be a painting from the summer of 1912, when the roses planted in beds in front of the house would have been in profuse bloom. Seen in perspective, the pink façade of the house, with its blue-green shutters, is almost completely covered in creeping vines, rendered with quickly placed, overscale versions of the "comma stroke" that had become Monet's hallmark in the 1880s. These strokes continue through the flowering plants and the rising mass of trees at right, hues of pungent blue- and yellow-green acting as the foil to bright spots of pink, red, and white; the roof of the house is rendered in a powerful purple, which is reintroduced here and there to bring light into the deepest shadows; and the sky is a roughly brushed combination of deep blue and white.

The painting's composition is strikingly similar to that of a painting that Renoir had completed in 1879, showing the rose beds at Wargemont, the country home of his friends M. and Mme. Paul Berard (fig. 156). The Berard's manor house was altogether grander than

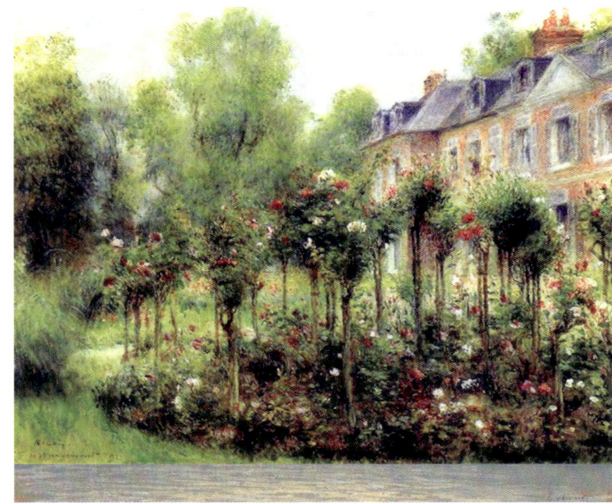

Fig. 156. Pierre-August Renoir, *Roses at Wargemont*, 1879. Oil on canvas, 25 5/8 x 31 7/8 in. (65 x 81 cm). Private collection

Monet's home, but its simple façade acted, as Monet's did, as an architectural backdrop for densely planted beds of roses. Renoir's precise manner made the spatial separation of each rose tree from the next very clear, playing with effects of space that the seventy-two-year-old Monet ignored. *Roses at Wargemont* had been exhibited in 1883 at Durand-Ruel. There is no evidence that Monet had seen it often, if at all; but it belonged to Charles Deudon, a Parisian collector who, like the Berards, was a collector of Monet's work. Perhaps a memory of the painting returned to Monet as he chose a spot from which to paint his house some thirty years later.[1]

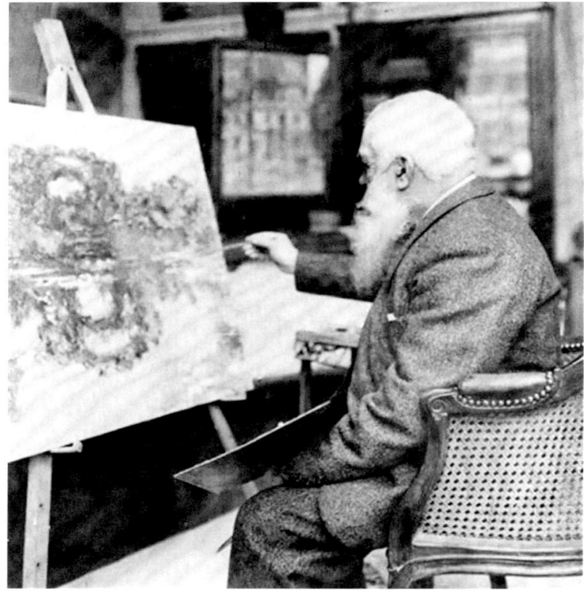

Fig. 157. Claude Monet painting *Flowering Arches, Giverny*, November 1913

Two versions of *The Artist's House at Giverny* are known; the other bears a signature and the date 1912, while the present example displays only the artist's name. Both were probably signed several years later—the dated canvas around 1920, when the artist contributed it to a benefit sale, and this example likely in 1924, when it was sold to Durand-Ruel. By the 1920s, Monet was inclined to forgetfulness even about his most recent work, and it is possible that the date was an approximation—it might equally date from 1913, the year in which he painted *Flowering Arches, Giverny* (cat. 10).

With this picture, Monet returned to painting his water-garden for the first time in five years. The subject is a construction of four metal arches, making a square "gazebo," covered over with flowering roses. This ornamental bit of architecture is located on the southeast end of the water-lily pond, and served as a point from which to launch the rowboat that his gardeners used to tend to the pond's plantings. To paint it, Monet stood on the opposite bank. Raising his point of view from the water's surface to scan the southern shore of the pond, he saw the profile of the arches rising above the vegetation separating the water garden from the open meadow beyond. The flanking trees, the background screen of green, and the arches are reflected in the pond's surface, much as the distant banks of the Seine had been reflected in the painter's *Mornings* of more than fifteen years earlier (see fig. 154). The reflection is all the more clear because no clumps of water lilies interrupt it—whether in reality or by the painter's choice.

There was always something slightly contrived about this painting and the two other versions of the composition that exist. It is exquisitely painted, with beautiful superpositions of opaque and transparent paints, yet the subject itself seems unusually delicate. Perhaps this is because, as Paul Tucker suggests, the paintings of the pergolas are tied, as were the *Japanese Bridges* of 1899–1900 (see cat. 3) to the aesthetics of the Far East, which in Monet's orbit would have been considered more contemplative; by contrast, the energetically painted views of the house would have corresponded to a more aggressive Western aesthetic.

But it is also possible that these paintings are as much the product of the studio as of *plein air* work. In November 1913, months after the flowers would have faded in Monet's garden, a photographer came to Giverny to take pictures for an article that would appear in January of the next year. Among them was a shot showing Monet seated in his studio, in a cane-backed eighteenth-century style chair, his palette in hand, and a long brush reaching out to touch the surface of *Flowering Arches, Giverny* (fig. 157). This unusual photograph, showing the painter at work on a canvas far from the motif, was captioned: "Here we see the admirable painter finishing one of his most beautiful canvases. It is, in the sumptuous adornment thrown by summer onto such parterres, the dazzling representation of an arbor, all radiant with vivid flowers, in his garden at Giverny."[2] Perhaps it is the disconnection between what Monet felt "in the face of nature" and what he could reasonably achieve in the studio that explains the curious hesitancy of this group of works.

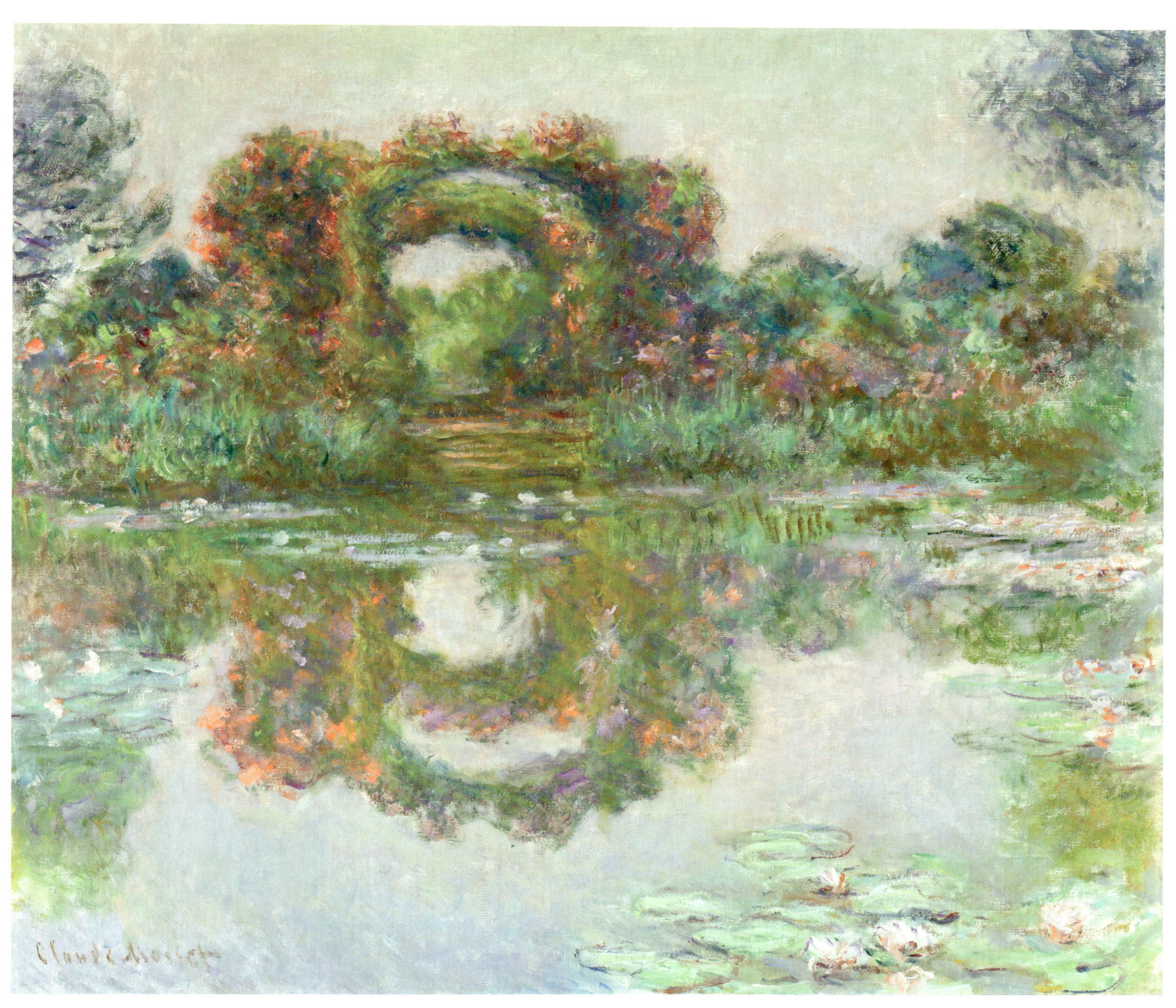

Cat. 10. *Flowering Arches, Giverny*, 1913. Phoenix Art Museum

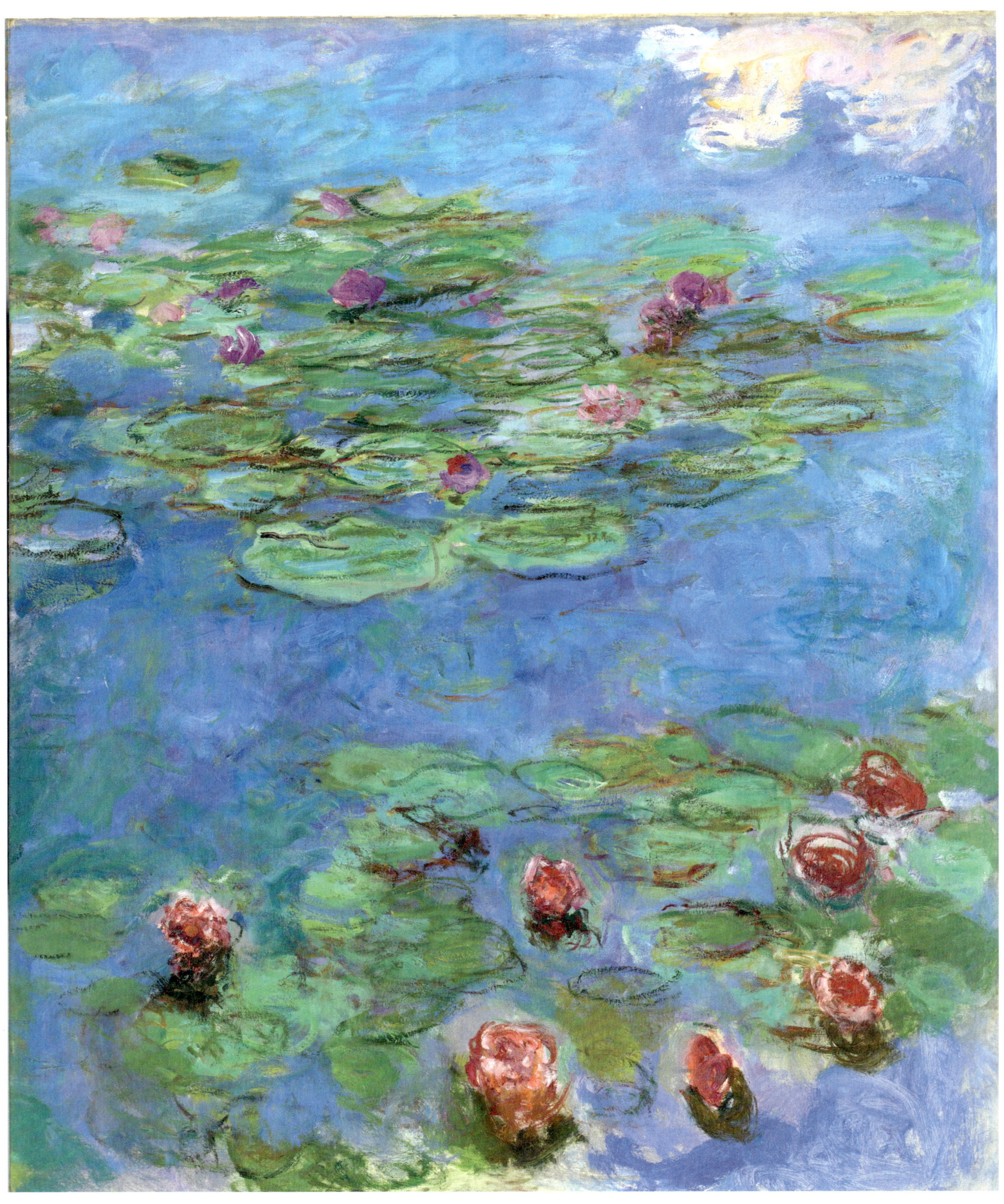

Cat. 11. *Water Lilies*, c. 1914–17. Fine Arts Museums of San Francisco

At first sight of the ravishing *Water Lilies* from the Fine Arts Museums of San Francisco, the viewer is immediately struck by its physical size, by the vigor and intensity of its surface, and finally by its intense color. Against a vast field of blue—the reflection of a bright summer sky, with one bright cloud—two gigantic clumps of water lilies are positioned, one spanning the very bottom of the canvas and the other in the top half, to the left. The first impression is that the flowers are life-size, but they are no longer the delicate blooms that Monet had painted in 1906 in the Chicago *Water Lilies* (cat. 6); these enormous flowers are composed of swift and sure arced strokes of deep red on a wide brush, which is then dipped into white and orange and pink mixtures on the palette to give the blossom volume, highlight and shadow. Looking at the largest flower at the bottom of the canvas, the viewer can count the number of times Monet's brush went from palette to canvas, reconstructing the sequence of movements in the imagination. A nearby leaf would have been made with even fewer marks—a few strokes of jade green overlaid with a deeper emerald color, the whole given greater form by broad outlines of deepest green and wisps of bright yellow.

Even at first glance, the viewer would know that this painting must have been painted by an artist filled with joyful energy, rapidly improvising the image on the canvas as a record of his sensations before the motif. This is exactly the spirit with which Monet was working in the summers of 1914 and 1915. In June 1914, he excused himself from not having replied to a critic's letter, saying that he was "in a high fever of working, and so absorbed, so tired at day's end, I don't have the strength to write. . . . I know it's bad, but work above all. I am overjoyed to be back at it."[1]

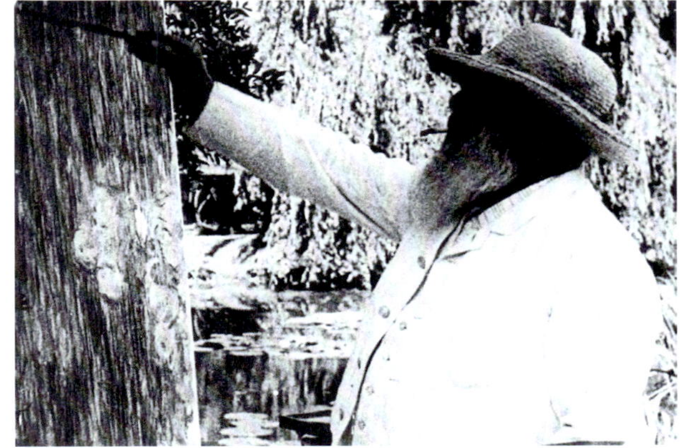

Fig. 158. Claude Monet painting *Water Lilies* outdoors, 1915. Still from a video produced by Sacha Guitry for his project *Ceux de Chez Nous* (*Those of Our Land*)

Since none of the works from Monet's exuberant return to painting in 1914 onwards bears a date, it is impossible to say exactly when a picture was made. The painter was filmed in 1915 in the act of painting a picture that resembles the three grouped here (fig. 158), and a photograph of Monet painting the Portland Art Museum's *Water Lilies* might be reasonably dated to the same time (see fig. 14). San Francisco's *Water Lilies*, in comparison, seems to be the closest echo of the paintings from the 1909 *Landscapes of Water* exhibition, for example the bright blue canvas from Chicago (cat. 6). Perhaps it is one of the paintings that was under way in 1914; it is possible that Monet's first forays onto this larger scale might have been, in fact, "enlargements" of the kind of composition with which he was already quite comfortable.

That might lead us to believe that the Portland canvas and the closely related painting in the collection of Diane B. Wilsey (cat. 13) were underway in 1915, as suggested by the photographic evidence. They are markedly freer in the application of paint—paint which is also much more liquid when brushed on, particularly in the long vertical strokes that describe the reflected branches and leaves of a weeping willow tree on the opposite bank. The depth of that reflection—it goes from bottom to top of the canvas—must mean that Monet has chosen to paint groups of flowers and leaves that are relatively far away from his own vantage point, mentally bringing them closer to his canvas to heighten their immediacy.

The brushwork itself brings the motif a greater sense of immediacy, as it seems to capture the gentle movement of the water and the breeze stirring the leaves of the tree. This is particularly noticeable in the Wilsey canvas, in which parallel wavy lines of green and blue hues seem to undulate throughout the field, wavering between being reflected leaves and underwater grasses. Here and in the Portland canvas the description of flowers and lily pads is also more abbreviated: four or five strokes might define a leaf, a few more a flower. This is Monet beginning to paint on a vast scale—the Portland canvas measures 160 x 180 centimeters, roughly 1 x 6 feet. The Wilsey canvas was originally even larger than its present size of 170 x 122 centimeters: before it was hit by shrapnel during the second World War, it measured 200 x 150 centimeters, the same format canvas that the artist used to paint cats. 14 and 15. Though altered in size, this painting—unlike most from this period—preserves its original physical appearance, beautifully showing the artist's much-prized matte paint surface.[2]

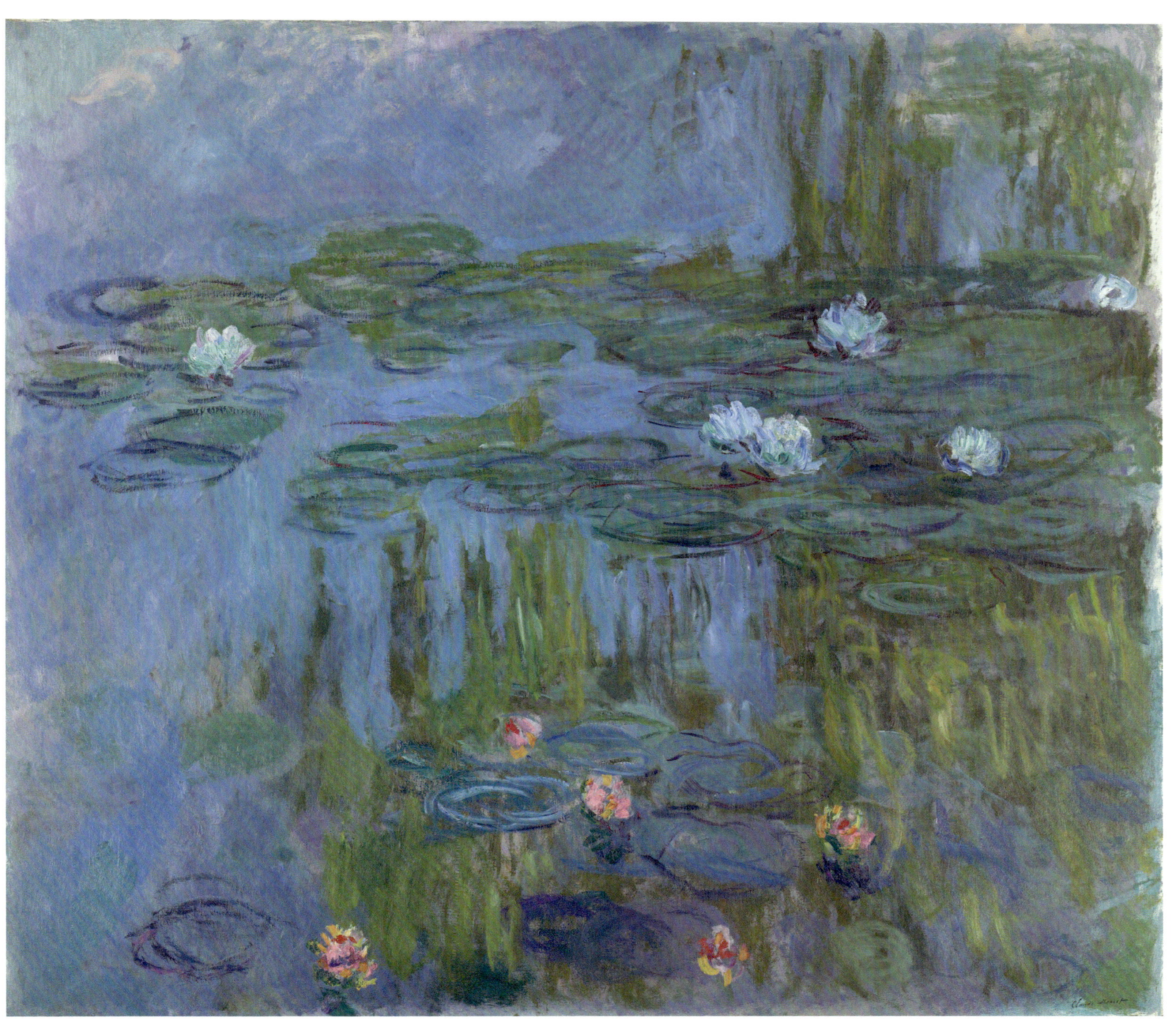

Cat. 12 *Water Lilies*, 1914–15. Portland Art Museum, Oregon

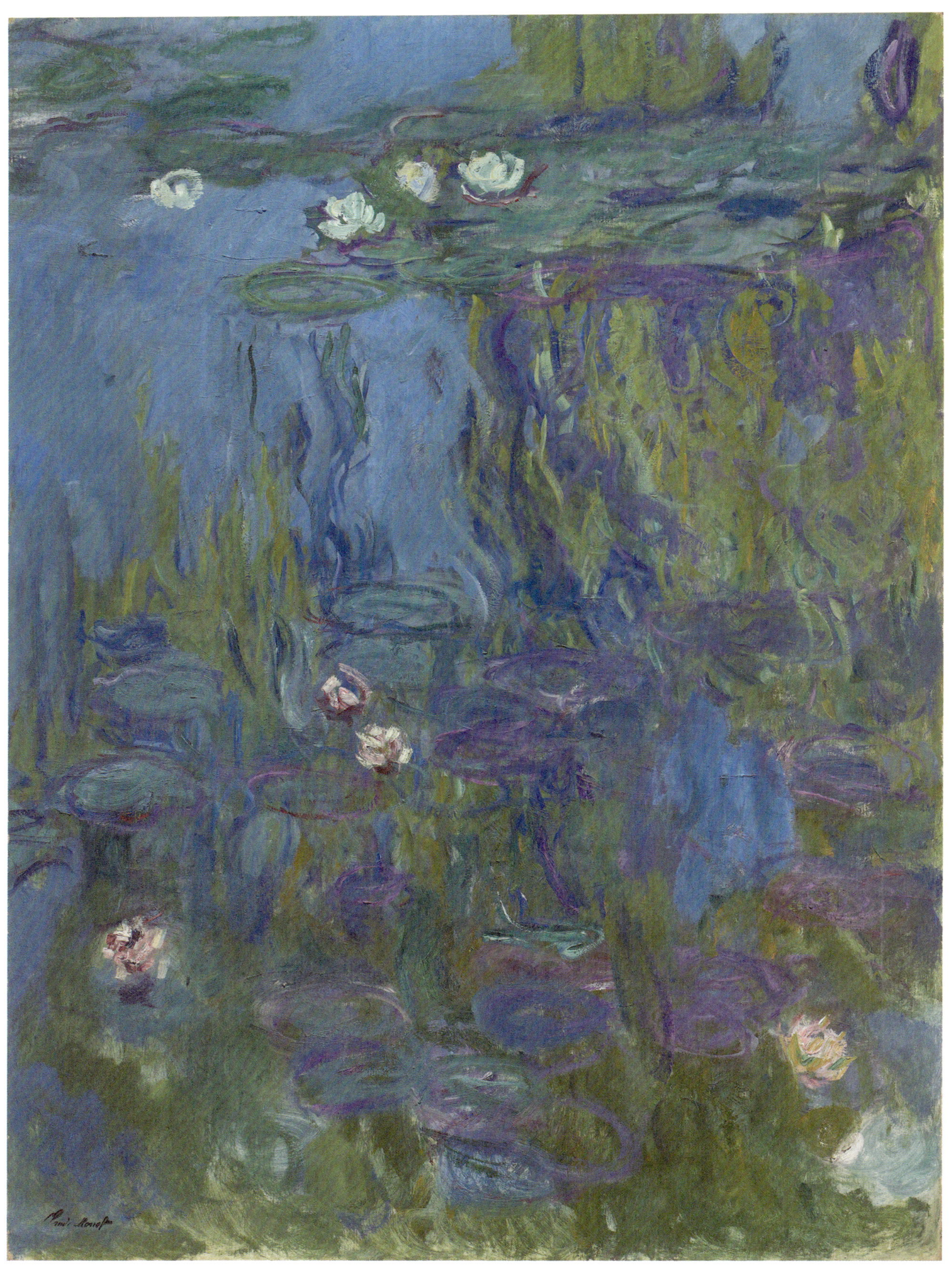

Cat. 13. *Water Lilies*, 1914–17. Collection of Diane B. Wilsey, San Francisco

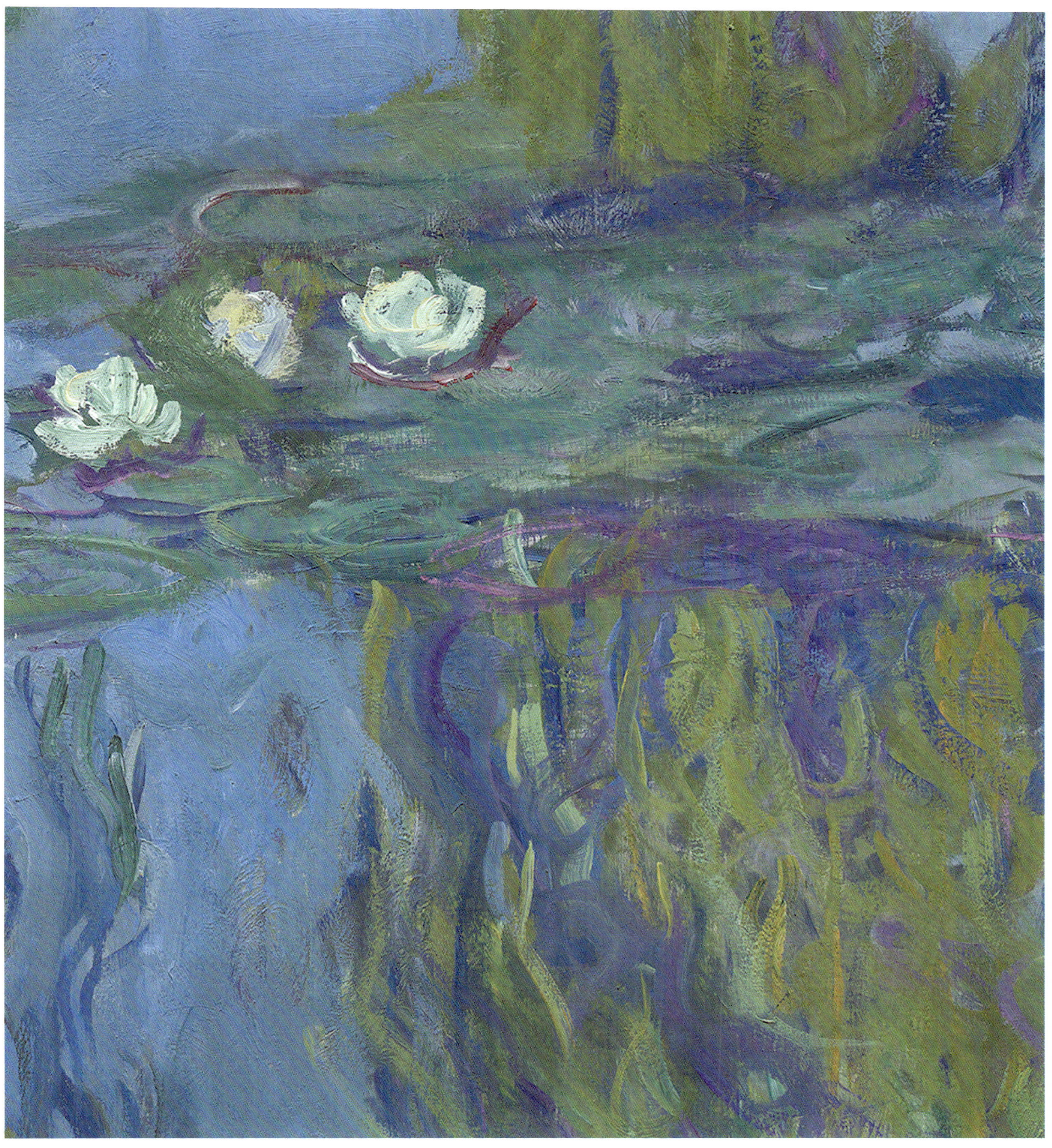

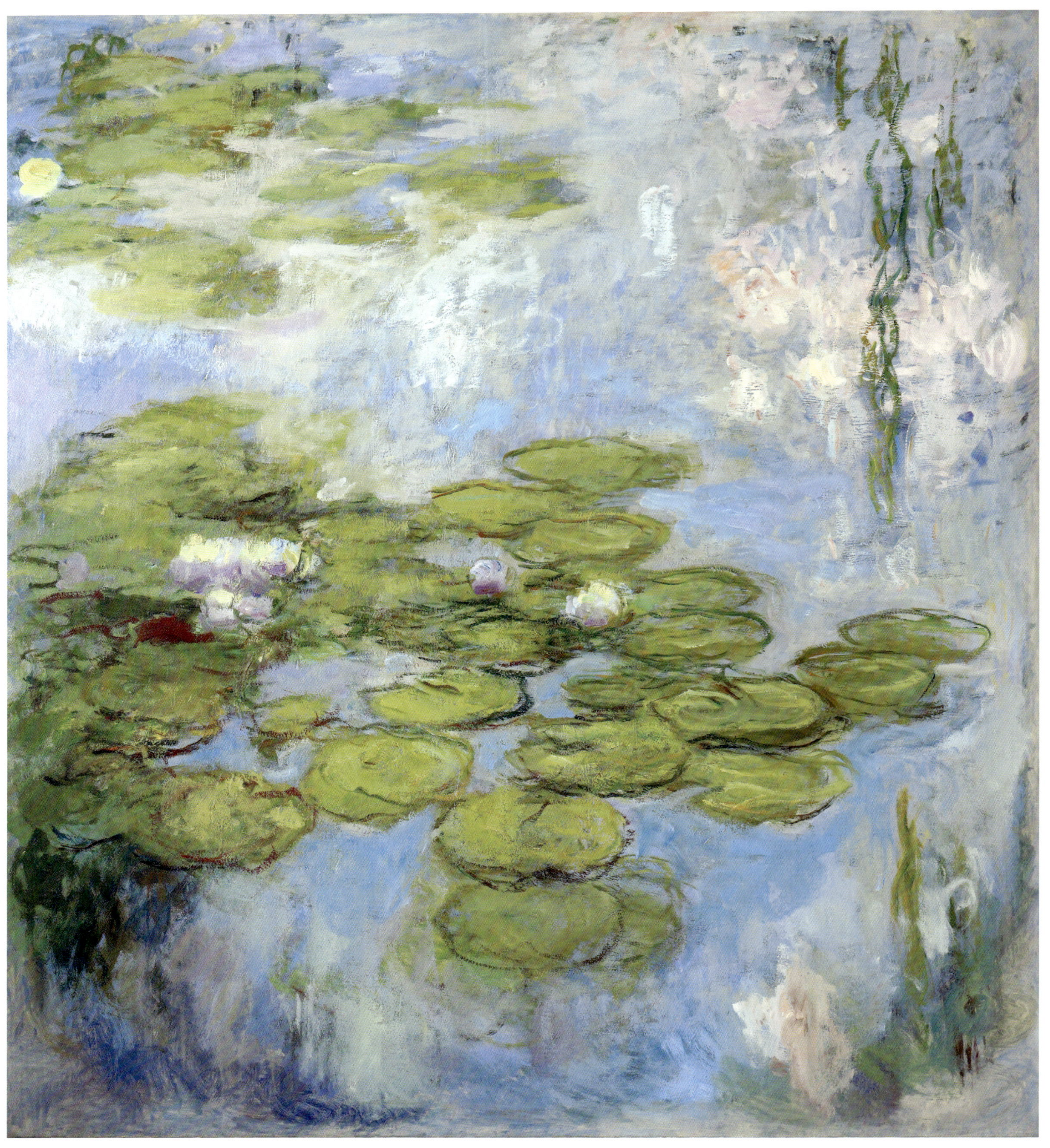

Cat. 14. *Water Lilies*, 1915–17. Fondation Beyeler, Basel, Switzerland

Over the course of the years 1915 and 1916, Monet was steadily at work—at least in fine weather—on the large-scale *plein-air* paintings that he would use to compose the even larger *Grandes Décorations* under way in the newly constructed studio designed to accommodate them. The largest paintings made beside the pond seem to be the several canvases measuring 2 x 2 meters. Some, such as the panels from the Fondation Beyeler and the Musée Marmottan Monet exhibited here, measured 1.5 meters in width (cats. 14, 15). In these paintings, we see the artist further exploring the same subjects as he had previously treated, but with a subtle difference. Here the point of view has shifted slightly, and Monet looks down onto the water just beside the bank where his easel is standing. No longer do the reflections of willow branches descend from the top of the painting; they rise from the bottom of the pictorial frame, encroaching on the reflection of a mass of blue sky to the upper right in both compositions.

These large studies are part of a series of some eight similar works painted around the biggest willow tree in the water garden, located on the south bank of the pond, to the west of the Japanese bridge. The tree itself is depicted twice in the series, in one canvas at the Musée Marmottan Monet and in another belonging to a private collection (fig. 159). All of these are distinguished by the fact that they show not only the reflections of the tree's branches but also the branches themselves, descending in greater or lesser profusion into the picture space from the top margin of the composition. In cat. 14, the leaves are visible in the top right corner; their reflection is in the lower right corner. In cat. 15, the reflection is dominant, and the descending tendrils are just a few leaves, which seem to merge with the greater reflection of the tree at upper left.

In some of the paintings in the series, Monet concentrates on the willow leaves themselves, but in the majority of them, as here, he includes a slice of the grassy bank where the willow stood. The inclusion of these elements—either at lower left or right—allows them to be positioned in a row with one of the portrayals of the tree trunk to create a continuous picture of a tree trunk at center and open water to either side (fig. 160). The studies of the tree trunk seem to have directly inspired the trunk at the extreme left of the *Three Willows* quadriptych (see fig. 72), which was almost finished by the end of 1917 (see figs. 17–22). In that more or less direct quotation from the studies, there is no open water to the left, but as there are no canvases that correspond to the other two tree trunks in the quadriptych, it might be reasonable to assume that the two extant studies were the models for all three trunks, simply modified and differently aligned to suit the painter's compositional needs as the larger painting progressed.

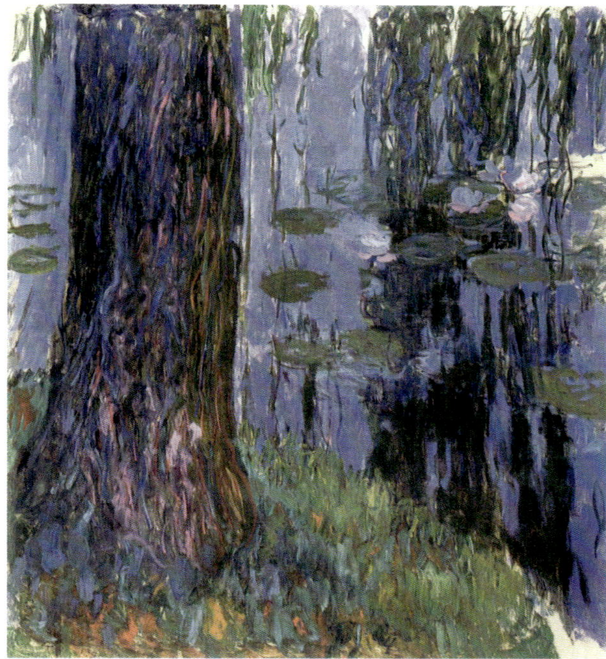

Fig. 159. Claude Monet, *Weeping Willow and Water-Lily Pond*, 1916–19. Oil on canvas, 78 3/4 x 70 3/4 in. (200 x 180 cm). Private collection

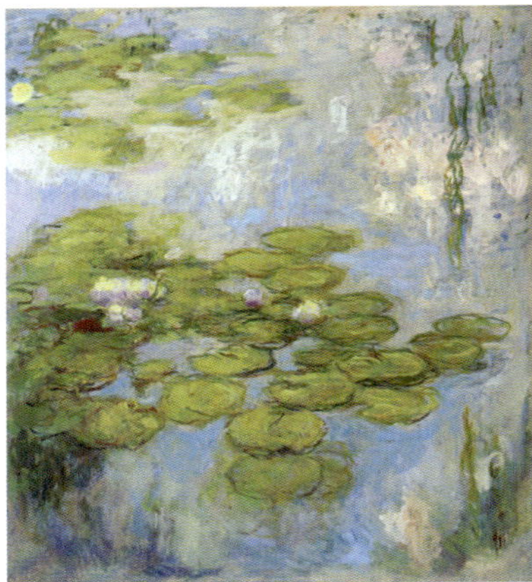 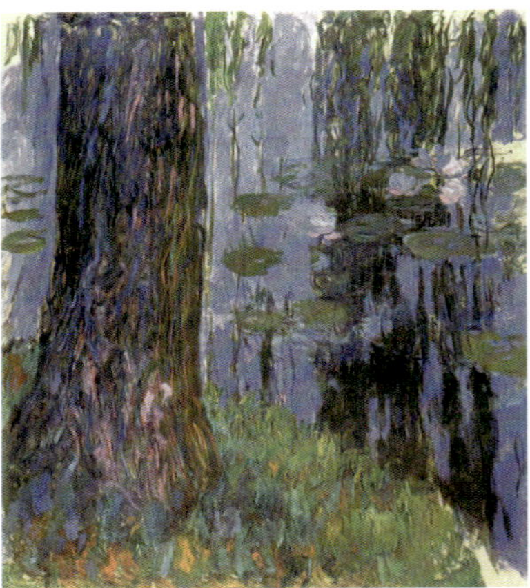 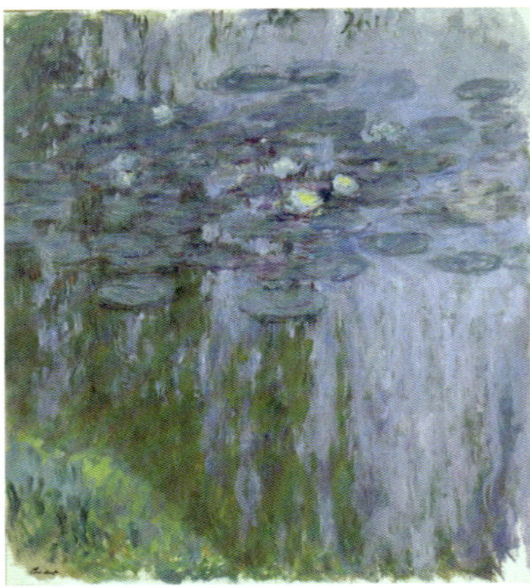

Fig. 160. *Water Lilies* (cat. 14), *Weeping Willow and Water-Lily Pond* (fig. 159), and *Water Lilies* (cat. 15) aligned with the tree in the center

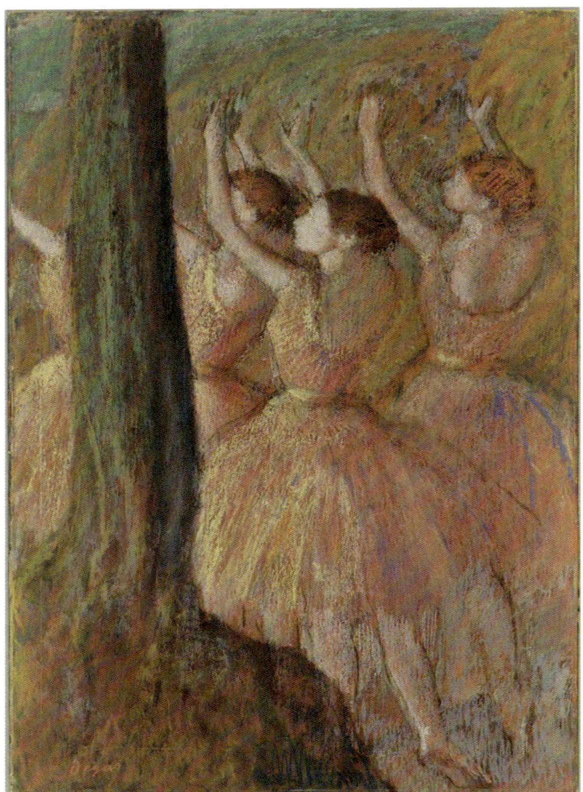

Fig. 161. Edgar Degas, *Dancers in Rose*, c. 1900. Pastel on paper, 33 1/8 x 22 7/8 in. (84.1 x 58.1 cm). Museum of Fine Arts, Boston. Seth K. Sweetser Fund

The Marmottan painting (cat. 15) might well have inspired the center of the leftmost segment of the quadriptych, where descending leaves touch their rising reflection in the pond. The boldly painted water lilies in the Beyeler canvas (cat. 14) do not find an equivalent in the larger mural panel, but the sunny clouds at upper right are similar to the clouds in the same left-hand segment of that painting.

Monet decided to focus in this series on the element of a large tree trunk rooted in the earth at the bottom of the pictorial frame, its upper reaches unseen as it rises beyond the pictorial frame above. The device is one he had used repeatedly in the 1880s—painting pine trees beside the Mediterranean Sea—and in the 1890s—painting poplars on the banks of the Epte near his Giverny home. Here, though, in the context of creating a decorative scheme, the trunk is both more solid—like a portrait—and more abstract—like a large dark band between bands of light.

Seen this way, the trunk has both a symbolic and purely decorative function, being both a stand-in for the painter himself and a shape giving balance to the composition by virtue of its width and tonality. Monet's colleague in the origins of Impressionism, Edgar Degas, sometimes used a tree in this way—as a purely abstract device, as a very real depiction of a painted flat at the edge of a stage, and as an allusion to the men who stood backstage—technicians, admirers of the dancers, and an artist. The tree in *Degas's Dancers in Rose* (fig. 161), a large pastel from the later 1890s, is a case in point: its trunk is rooted in a fictive hillock and bends slightly as it rises towards the theater's fly loft above the stage. Beyond it, a group of dancers are shown in ethereal pink, like Monet's water lilies or light-struck clouds. *Dancers in Rose*, as it happens, was purchased from Degas by Durand-Ruel and was in the dealer's backroom stock in 1909, when forty-eight of Monet's *Nymphéas* were on exhibition in the gallery's public spaces.[1]

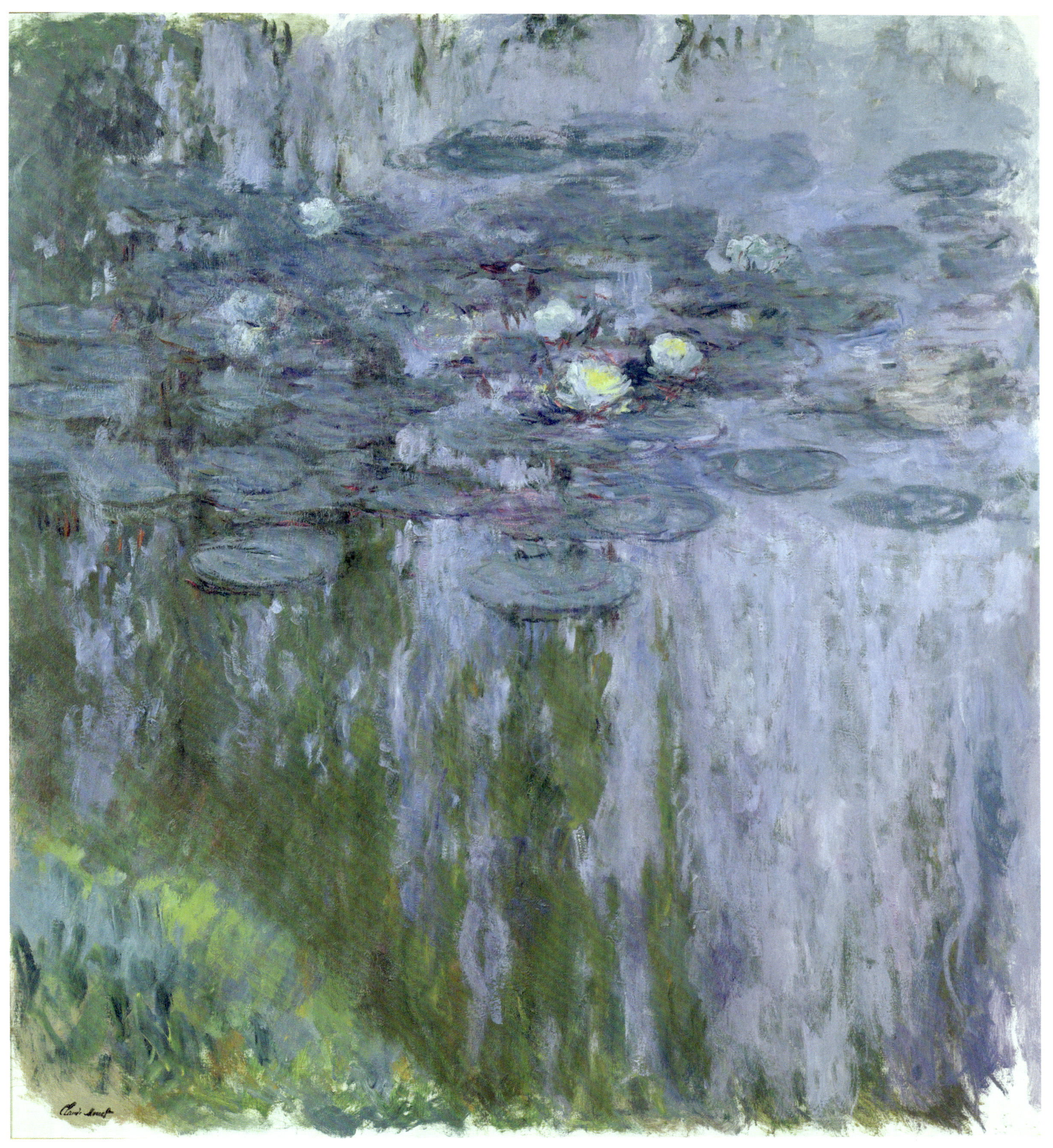

Cat. 15. *Water Lilies*, 1915–17. Musée Marmottan Monet, Paris

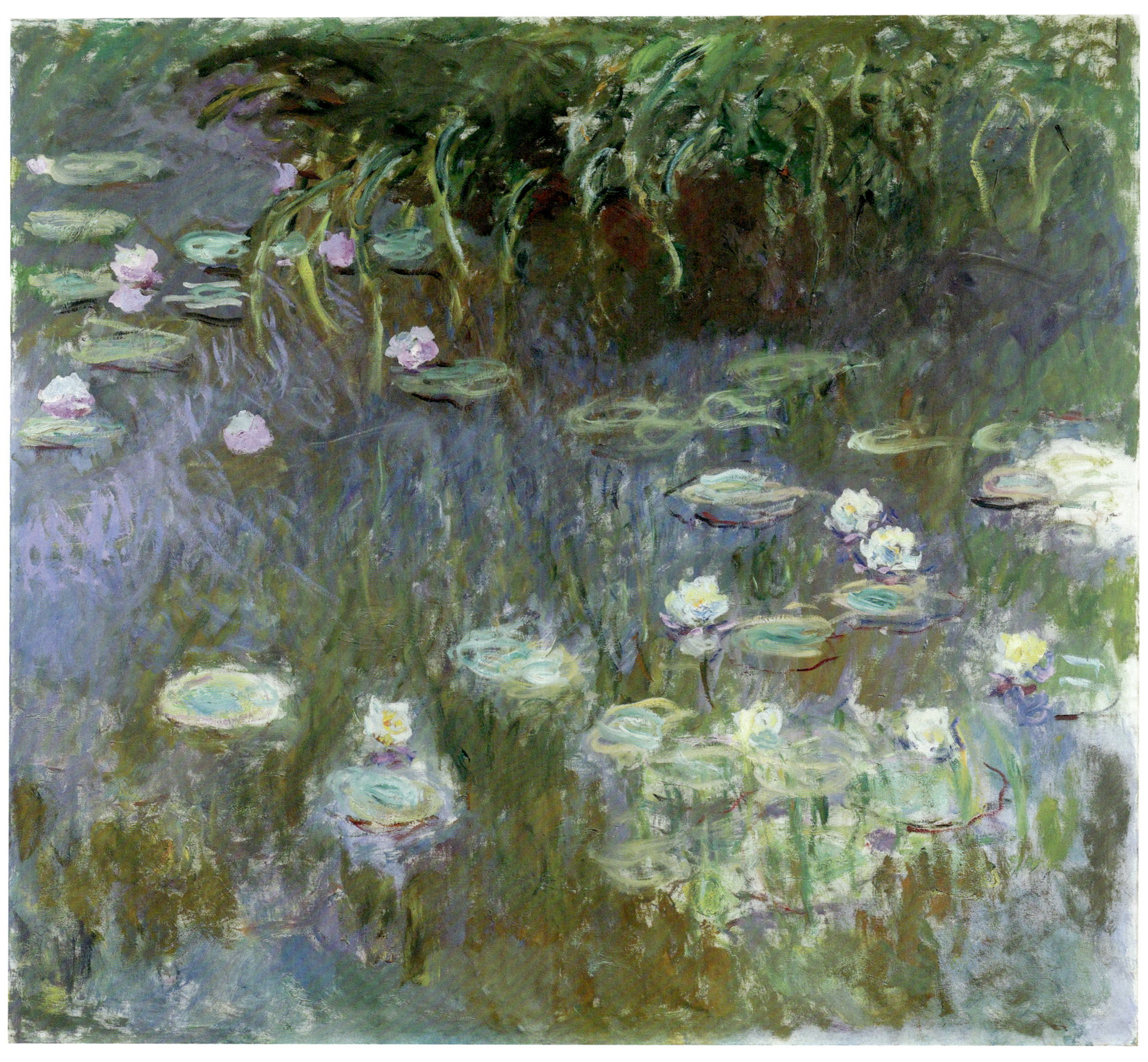

Cat. 16. *Water Lilies*, c. 1921–22. Toledo Museum of Art, Ohio

The Toledo Museum of Art's *Water Lilies* is one of the most resplendently beautiful of all the paintings of the square format made in connection with Monet's work on the *Grandes Décorations*. At the top of the canvas, the leaves of waterside plants curve languorously into the composition, reminiscent of the leaves Monet had painted in the 1890s (see cat. 1) but conceived with a new nervous intensity. In their shadow, the pond surface is a deep green tinged with dark red, but as the reflection broadens it becomes a gentle pattern of alternating blue and yellow-green, the mirror image of the willow boughs and sunlit sky above. On this shifting ground, the painter cast leaves and flowers as if at random; they are not shown in clumps but as single leaves and individual blooms, some casting their own reflections in the water's surface. These leaves are painted in lighter, more tender green, sometimes outlined in pale yellow mixed with violet, at other times given a slender shadow in deep purple-red. With flowers like glints of white, yellow, and violet light, the overall effect is opalescent.

In its overall composition, the painting corresponds to the left-most panel of the quadriptych entitled *Morning*, in the first room of the Orangerie installation.[1] What is more, it corresponds with this panel in its measurements. Instead of being the standard 200 x 200 centimeters, these panels are the same slightly wider, at 212 (Orangerie) and 213 (Toledo) centimeters. While this difference might seem an accident, in fact it may be important.

In 1922, the American opera singer Marguerite Namara came to Monet's vast third studio to give a recital and was photographed there with Monet seated beside her (fig.162). Behind Namara are the two panels that make up the composition in the Orangerie that is called *Water Lilies, Reflections of Trees*, each of which measures 425 centimeters in width.[2] This is one of the standard widths that Monet used in diptychs and triptychs (an example is the panel in this exhibition, cat. 28). With two exceptions, every wall in the Orangerie is made up of some combination of panels at 200 x 425 centimeters.

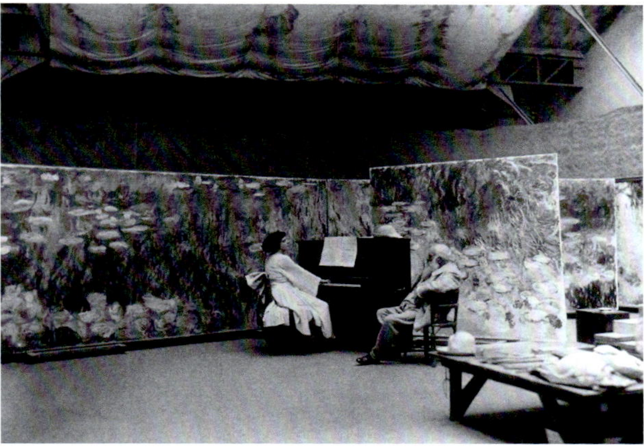

Fig. 162. Marguerite Namara and Claude Monet in his third studio at Giverny, 1922

The two exceptions are the unusually wide single panel *Sunset* in the first room, incorporating in one 6 meter composition the design prepared as a diptych, now at the Kunsthaus, Zurich.[3] The other exception is *Morning*, which consists of two 425-centimeter panels joined at the center, and with, at either end, a "half-panel" measuring 212.5 centimeters in width. In the photograph taken in 1922, the left-hand Orangerie half-panel can be seen on its mobile easel just behind the seated Monet. It is not displayed as part of the four-picture grouping that would be mounted on the wall at the Orangerie, but as if a separate painting. It has long been understood that the canvas and the half-panel at the right end of the grouping were painted to extend on either end an already existing diptych of the same size as *Water Lilies, Reflections of Trees*.[4] That extension would only have been necessary, however, after the decision was taken to install Monet's mural decorations in the Orangerie—that is, after 1921.

Allowing for the differences that stretchers and measuring can occasion, the left-hand panel of *Morning* and the Toledo canvas are virtually twins. But of all the large panels considered to be preparatory for the *Grandes Décorations*, none is more than 200 centimeters in width. That the Toledo canvas is unique in this regard, and that it and the Orangerie painting are the same dimensions, implies that they were not only painted on matching canvases, but that they were also invented at the same time, after 1921, when the need for a 212-centimeter panel first arose. Thus, as in the case of the two sunset compositions of equal size—one in the Orangerie and the other, less finished, in Zurich—Monet seems to have painted two virtually identical compositions, then took one of them to a slightly greater level of finish and joined it, after 1921, with an extant composition, the whole destined for inclusion in the *magnum opus*. In this analysis, the Toledo canvas must be interpreted not as an early study for, but as a contemporaneous version of, the compositional segment now at the Orangerie.

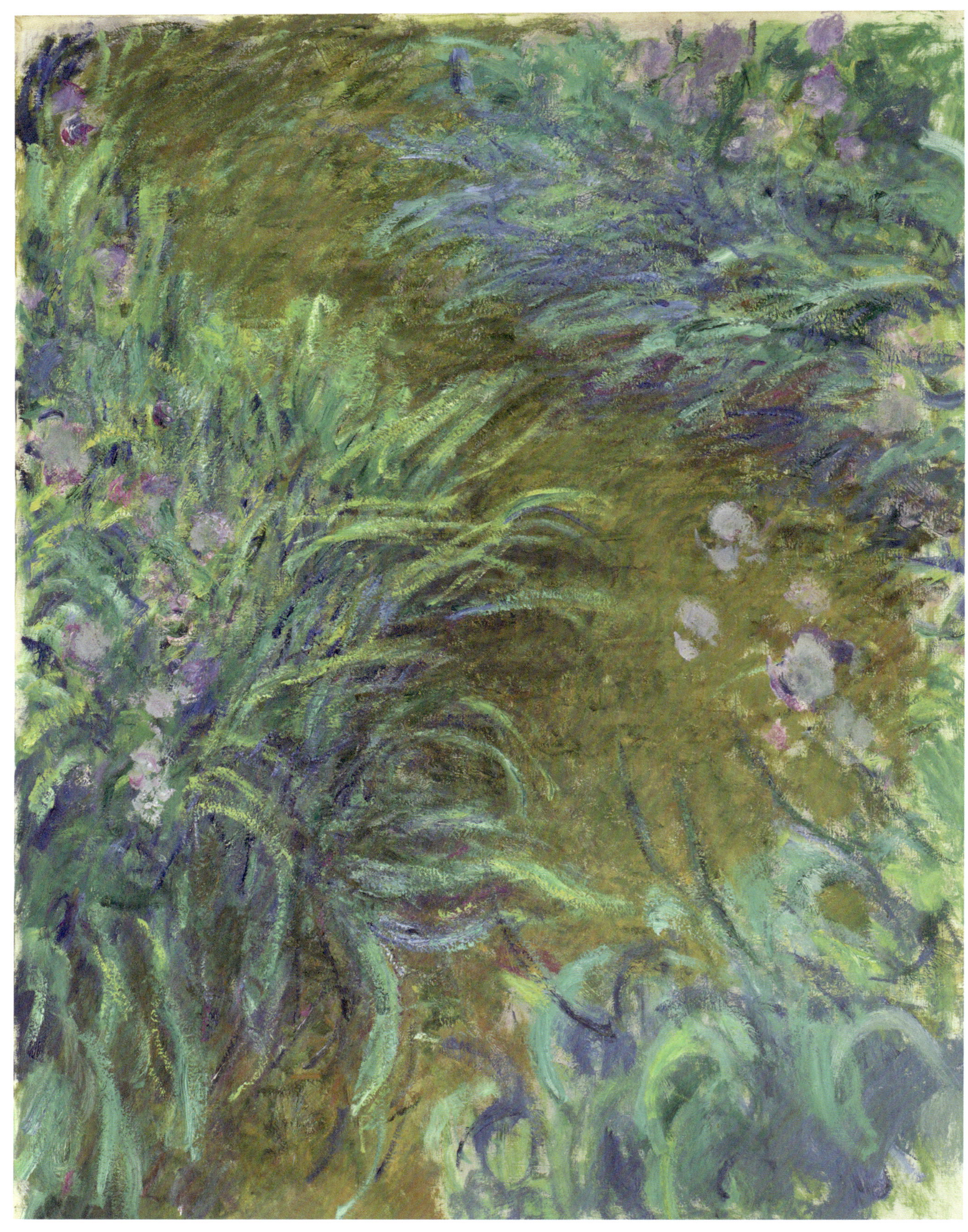

Cat. 17. *Irises*, c. 1914–17. The National Gallery, London

Next to water lilies, Monet's favorite garden flower was the iris. He planted them in profusion in the *Clos Normand*, the former orchard beside his house, where he depicted them in a series of paintings completed in 1900–1901.[1] He showed them scattered here and there beneath blossoming apple trees, planted beside meandering paths, and massed in large rectangular beds parallel to the long allée that divided the garden into two halves. But they also appeared in the pond garden. As he wrote to Roger-Marx in 1909, explaining the subject of his *paysages d'eau:*

> It's a water feature that I created about 15 years ago, about 200 meters around and fed by a tributary of the River Epte. It's bordered with iris and aquatic plants in the framework of a various trees, though they are mostly poplars and willows, including several weeping willows. It's in this spot that I previously painted *nymphéas* with a Japanese-style bridge.

"I once dreamed of doing a decoration with these water lilies for a theme," he continued, "a project that I may realize someday."[2]

In the *Grandes Décorations* that he did realize, among those that were installed at the Orangerie, irises are nowhere to be found—at least not their blossoms. Among the large panels that might have been candidates for the Orangerie, one, a 6 meter single canvas in Zurich, features purple iris in its right-hand corner. But a multitude of 2 meter tall pictures of irises were painted, measuring 150, 180, or 200 centimeters in width. Of these, some might have been developed as the right-most panel in the Orangerie *Morning*, but there no blooms are shown.[3] Of the others, none is a likely candidate for amalgamation in a large horizontal composition, since in each a winding path bordered by irises is the central motif.[4]

The *Irises* at the National Gallery, London (cat. 17), is among the compositions centered on this path, which here is painted in shades of ocher and green. To either side, the iris foliage is rendered in a range of hues, from deep blue to cool and warm greens to delicate highlights of yellow. Though the subject is peaceful, even lyrical, the painted surface is bold and energetic, with stroke after stroke of dry paint building up thick-knit layers of textured color. The fact that these plants grow on either side of a path, rather than beside the water, makes it likely that *Irises* was painted not in the water garden but in the western half of the *Clos Normand*, perhaps near where fruit trees still grew. With this in mind, it may be possible to guess at the variety of iris represented. In a 1913 article, Monet's head gardener, Félix Breuil, named the varieties of iris that were planted at Giverny in dry soil; these included some that were vivid or pale yellow—the cultivars *neubronner* and *flavescens*, one species, *germanica*, that appeared in many colors, and two cultivars—*pallida* and *stylosa*—that tend towards the blue-violet color Monet shows in the London painting.[5]

A sixth iris mentioned by Breuil, *Mme. Claude Monet*, is now known only by its name and the fact that it was introduced by Louis Denis, a hybridizer, in 1916. It is worth noting that Denis and Monet were among the more important sponsors of the First International Conference on Irises, held in Paris at the end of May 1922. Among the many French participants in the conference is listed "Claude Monnet," but the painter cannot have been in attendance, as his eyesight was so poor in spring 1922 that no journey to Paris to hear papers read at a conference would have been contemplated. Among the foreign visitors to the conference were a large number of English and American specialists and representatives of the American Iris Society, the London Horticultural Society, and a similar organization in Palermo. The person who came the farthest to the conference must have been the unnamed director of the *Jardin botanique, Tokio*—likely the Koishikawa Botanical Gardens of the University of Tokyo.[6]

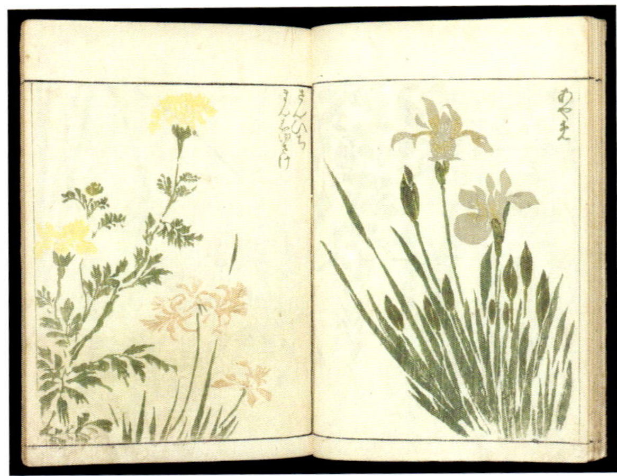

Fig. 163. Kitao Masayoshi, *Sôka ryakuga shiki* ("method of drawing flowers"), woodblock print book

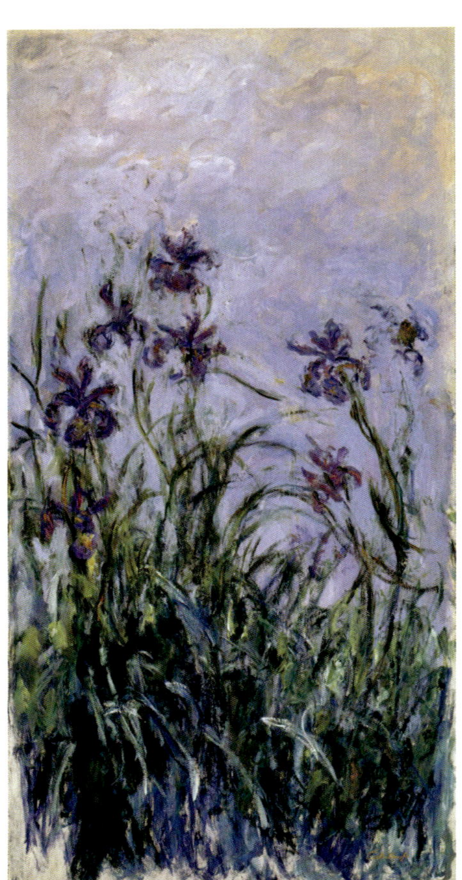

Fig. 164. Claude Monet, *Purple Irises*, 1914–17. Oil on canvas, 78 3/4 x 39 1/2 in. (200 x 100.3 cm). Private collection

That a Japanese horticulturist should come to an international conference on irises in Paris accords perfectly with the association between irises and the Far East, particularly Japan, that prevailed in French culture at the turn of the twentieth century. As Catherine Hug and Monika Leonhardt have noted, however, "the general, rather indiscriminate, fascination with things Japanese" meant that "new plants like tree peonies and particular varieties of iris were often described as 'Japanese,' although they actually came from other countries."[7] Still, the choice of iris varieties for the banks of the water-lily pond, a construction that was linked to Japan from its beginnings on account of the its bridge, is consistent with this association. Furthermore, Monet would have known the iris woodcuts of such artists as Hokusai and Hiroshige (see fig. 170), and, in addition to the prints that he displayed on the walls of his dining room, he had a large collection of bound woodblock books, including the *Sôka ryakuga shiki* ("method of drawing flowers") by the artist Kitao Masayoshi (fig. 163).

Such Japanese sources seem to be the direct inspiration for *Yellow Irises*, recently acquired by the National Museum of Western Art, Tokyo. The subject of the painting is almost certainly the *iris manieri* mentioned by Beuil, who praises it as "one of the most beautiful varieties to line the banks with. The flowers are lemon-yellow, are borne on stems one meter long, and open in June–July out of tufts of lancet-shaped leaves."[8] In Monet's depiction of the plants, the overall effect is one of flatness and pattern-making, resulting from the placement of the blossoms in a seemingly random order, atop tall stalks that rise from foliage that is rooted at the very bottom of the picture frame.

The extreme vertical shape of the canvas—200 x 100 centimeters, the format Monet usually used as a horizontal—contributes to its decorative aesthetic. A similar composition, with purple iris as a color contrast to yellow, might almost be a pendant panel (fig. 164). Monet had certainly used flowers before as decoration, and was even used to painting them in tall and narrow formats, necessitated when he decorated the paneled doors of Paul Durand-Ruel's salon.[9] But in composing a painting of iris that was taller than he was, Monet might not have been thinking of a decoration in a wall. His point of reference might have been the vaunted tradition of the Japanese folding screen, best exemplified by the famous *Irises* of Ogata Kōrin, each panel of which is only slightly more narrow in format than Monet's canvas (fig. 165). Though Monet almost certainly did not know this very screen, such works had been in his consciousness for fifty years when the time came to paint *Yellow Irises*.

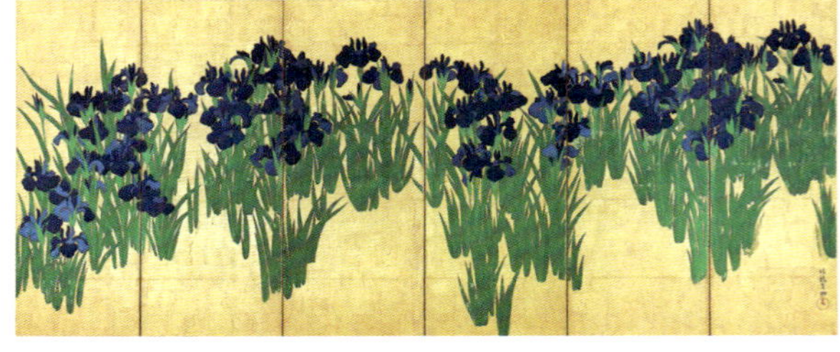

Fig. 165. Ogata Korin, *Irises* (one from a pair of six-panel screens), Edo period, early 18th century. Ink and color on gold-foil paper, 59 1/2 x 141 1/4 in. (151.2 x 358.8 cm). Nezu Museum, Tokyo

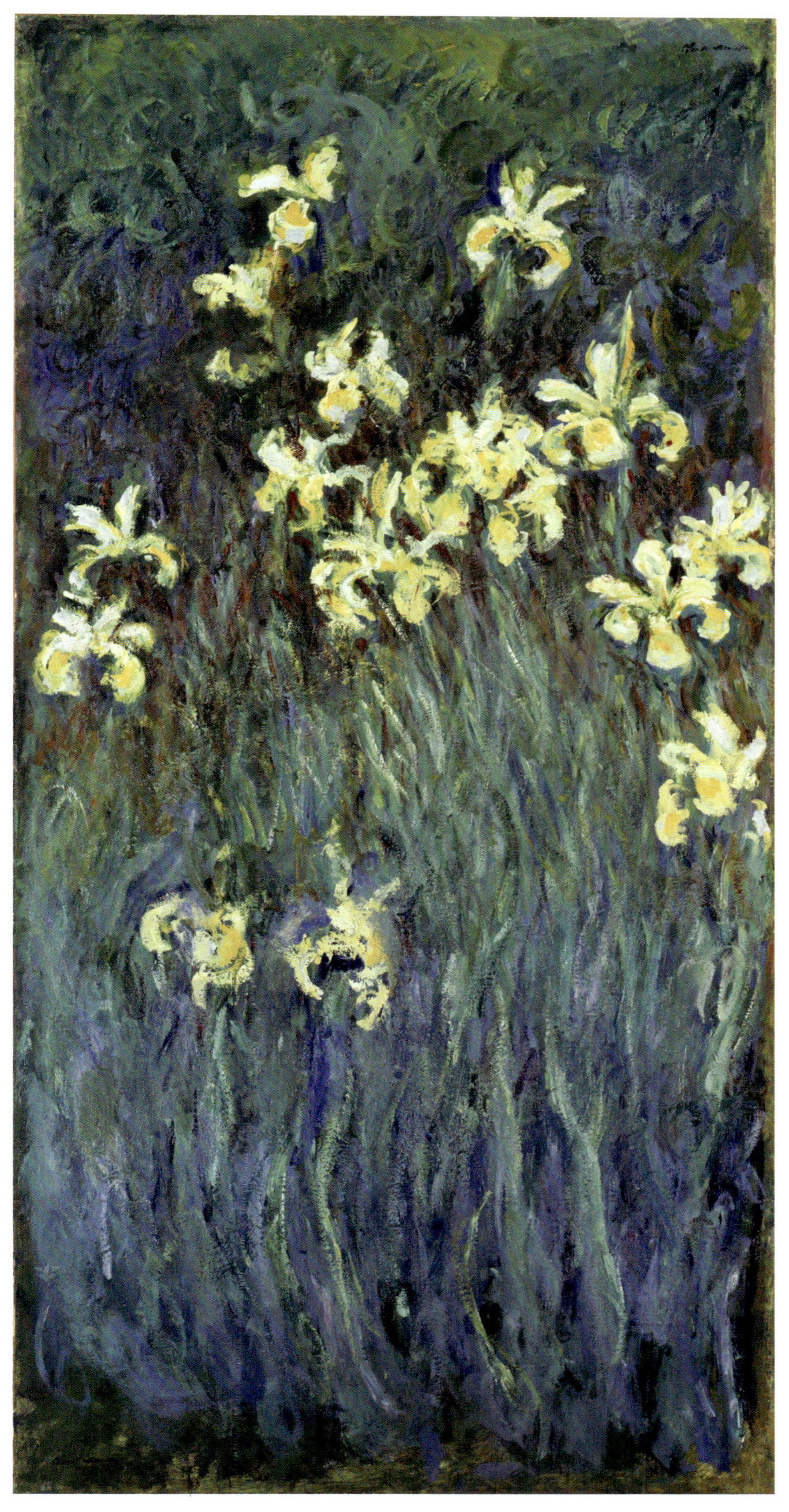

Cat. 18. *Yellow Irises*, c. 1914–17. The National Museum of Western Art, Tokyo

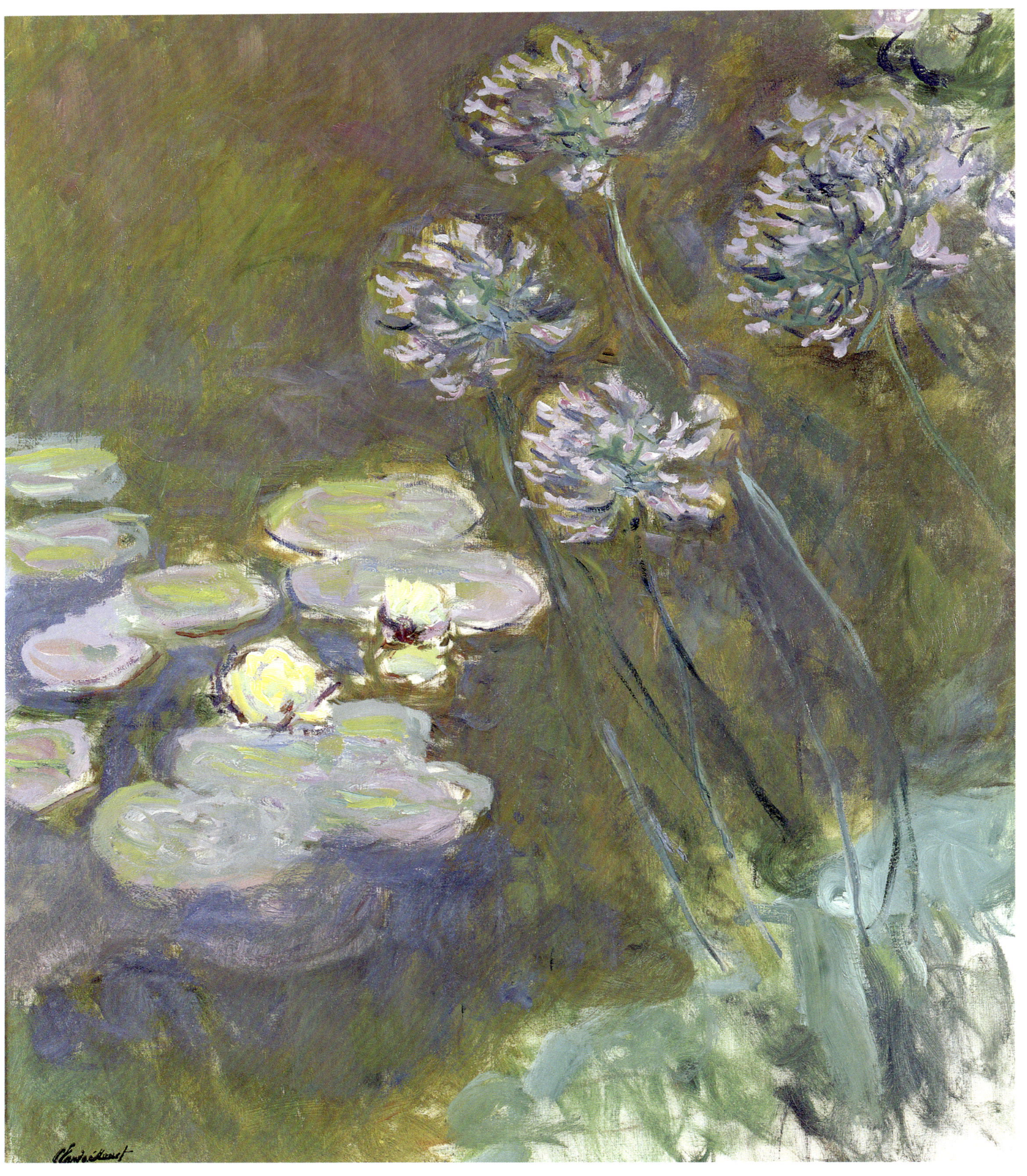

Cat. 19. *Water Lilies and Agapanthus*, 1914–17. Musée Marmottan Monet, Paris

Japanese anemone, aster, columbine, aubrietia, acanthus, wolfsbane, monkshood, bugloss, plume poppy, centaury, border bluebells, delphinium, leopard's bane, globe thistles, sea holly, fleabane, blanket flower, elecampane, sunflower, day lilies, iris, gladiolus, crocus, oxeye, lupins, plumbago, rose mallow, black-eyed Susan, sea lavender, lilies, poppy, beardtongue, various gentians, daffodil, tulip, sage, ox-eye daisies, hydrangeas, roses, sea daffodils, cranesbill geranium, ordinary and collerette dahlias, polygonum, Sweet pea, nasturtium, simple poppy, simple flowering garden aster, Californian poppy, foxglove, morning glory, malope, snapdragon, ornamental tobacco, simple poppy, marigold, yellow horned poppy, tree mallows.

This is the list of plants in Monet's garden—only the flowering ones—as recorded by his stepson Jean-Pierre Hoschedé in his memoir of life at Giverny, published in 1960.[1] The list, as long as it is, is limited to the plants that grow in dry soil; though there are varieties of irises and day-lilies that thrive in moist conditions, "sea holly" is a misnomer, being a spiny plant resembling a thistle, "sea daffodils" require well-drained, sandy soil, and "sea lavender" can tolerate salty soil but thrives in herbaceous borders.

The artist was passionately interested in plants. In the 1860s, he had often depicted his aunt's garden at Sainte-Adresse, in the 1870s and early 1880s he had cultivated gardens in the houses he rented at Argenteuil and Vétheuil, and of course he had transformed the Giverny house's *Clos Normand*, a practical everyday garden, into a painter's paradise. Proud of his "modest garden, which is, it's true, rather pretty at times," he was liberal with advice to others.[2] In 1914, he undertook to help his friends Sacha Guitry and Charlotte Lysès improve the garden at their home, writing to the latter:

> You would be so kind as to authorize me to order for you some rose plants at Nonin's and at Clark's, because time is passing; I'll arrange it so that the orders will be delivered as quickly as possible, and I will come to Yainville bringing along the plants that I want to give you at the present time and will get it all planted for you. If this suits you, I am at your service to make sure there is a start to the plantings in time for Good Friday.[3]

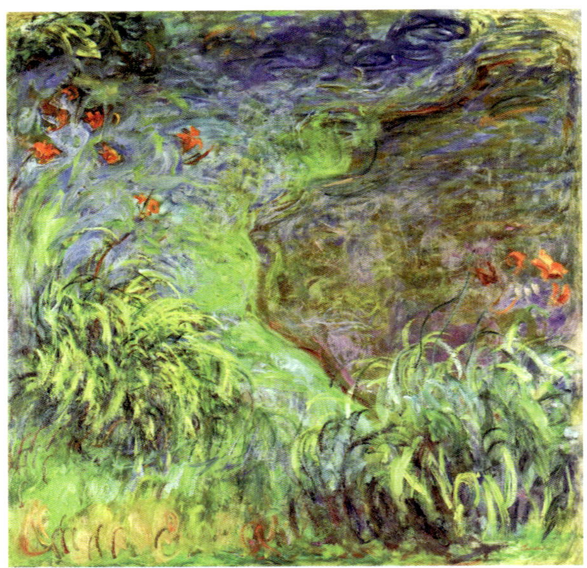

Fig. 166. Claude Monet, *Day Lilies at Water's Edge*, 1914–17. Oil on canvas, 78 3/4 x 78 3/4 in. (200 x 200 cm). Private collection

He wrote to Julie Manet, the daughter of his friend Berthe Morisot, excusing himself for being late in a reply, explaining that "we were in full flood conditions and, perfectly egotistical, I could think of nothing but my garden and my poor flowers all covered with mud."[4] He urged a correspondent to hurry to Giverny "because in just a while there's going to be a stopping time for blooming. After spring flowers, next the roses are going to come to an end," he cautioned. But, he noted, "you will always see the water lilies in full bloom."[5]

From his youth, Monet had painted studies of single types of flowers in still lifes—sunflowers, chrysanthemums, gladioli—but after 1914, he undertook a series of individual studies of different species planted in his garden, concentrating on the pond-garden and its water-loving plants. Among these are the agapanthus that were planted on the bank of the pond. The *Agapanthus* exhibited here is one of three studies executed on 200-centimeter tall canvases (this version has been reduced in size, having suffered damage while still in the studio). The blue-flowered *lis du Nil* or Nile Lily, actually a native of South Africa, provided a subject for highly decorative canvases, as had the yellow iris (see cat. 18). The flower was also to be included on the edge of one of the triptychs of the *Grandes Décorations*, a composition to which it gave its name, though all traces of the flower were eventually painted out (see the essay by Simon Kelly in this volume).

The day lily, or Hemerocallis, was not so frequently painted by Monet, though in cat. 20, showing the flower alone beside the pond, he clearly relished the opportunity to study this example. The plant is painted extremely swiftly, in long, looping strokes of paint against the white ground, areas of which are clearly visible throughout. The main body of the plant seems to have been painted all in one sitting, with colors mixed on the brush and applied wet-on-wet, resulting in underlying strokes sometimes lending their color to those that come later. The brownish background was filled in around the flower; only in this section does there seem to be any paint chattering over already dry work. So vivid was Monet's enjoyment of this exercise that he expanded the study in a 2 x 2 meter study, executed with equal speed and bravura (fig. 166). This ambitious painting seems to stand alone among the large square studies in showing water and bankside in equal measure. To make the flowers of the day lily seem even more vivid, Monet played with nature, streaking the grassy bank behind the lilies at left a rich blue.

Blue plays an important role in one of a group of studies of iris beside the pond, traditionally and admittedly speculatively, dated to the 1920s.[6] In its colors and in the fluidity of its brushwork it recalls the London *Iris*. Here, however, the composition is less anchored, and there is a noticeable joy in toying with the viewer's sense of perspective and reflection: reason tells us that we are looking down on clumps of iris and seeing clouds reflected in the pond, but at first glance the point of view seems to be that of a fish—looking up through the leaves at the sky. There is no such doubt in the depiction of rose branches that must have been painted in the garden on the other side of the road (cat. 21). Closest to the house Monet's roses were trained to stand upright (see fig. 182). This, on the contrary, is a free-floating group of vines, perhaps breaking away from a trellis, since they are shown against the sky. At once delicate and almost expressionistic, they are both Rococo and modern, leaping nymphs from Fragonard captured by Matisse.

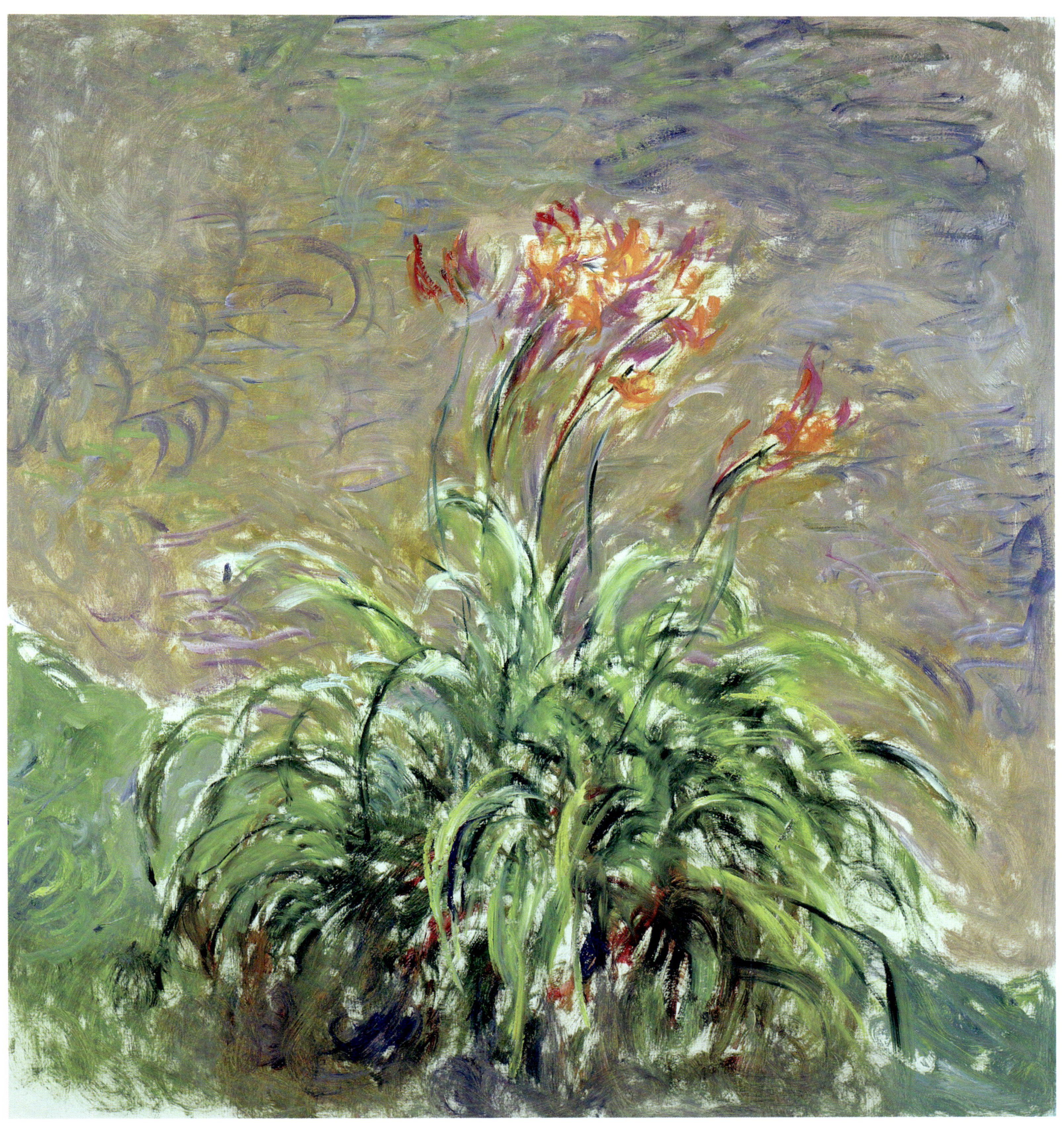

Cat. 20. *Day Lilies*, 1914–17. Musée Marmottan Monet, Paris

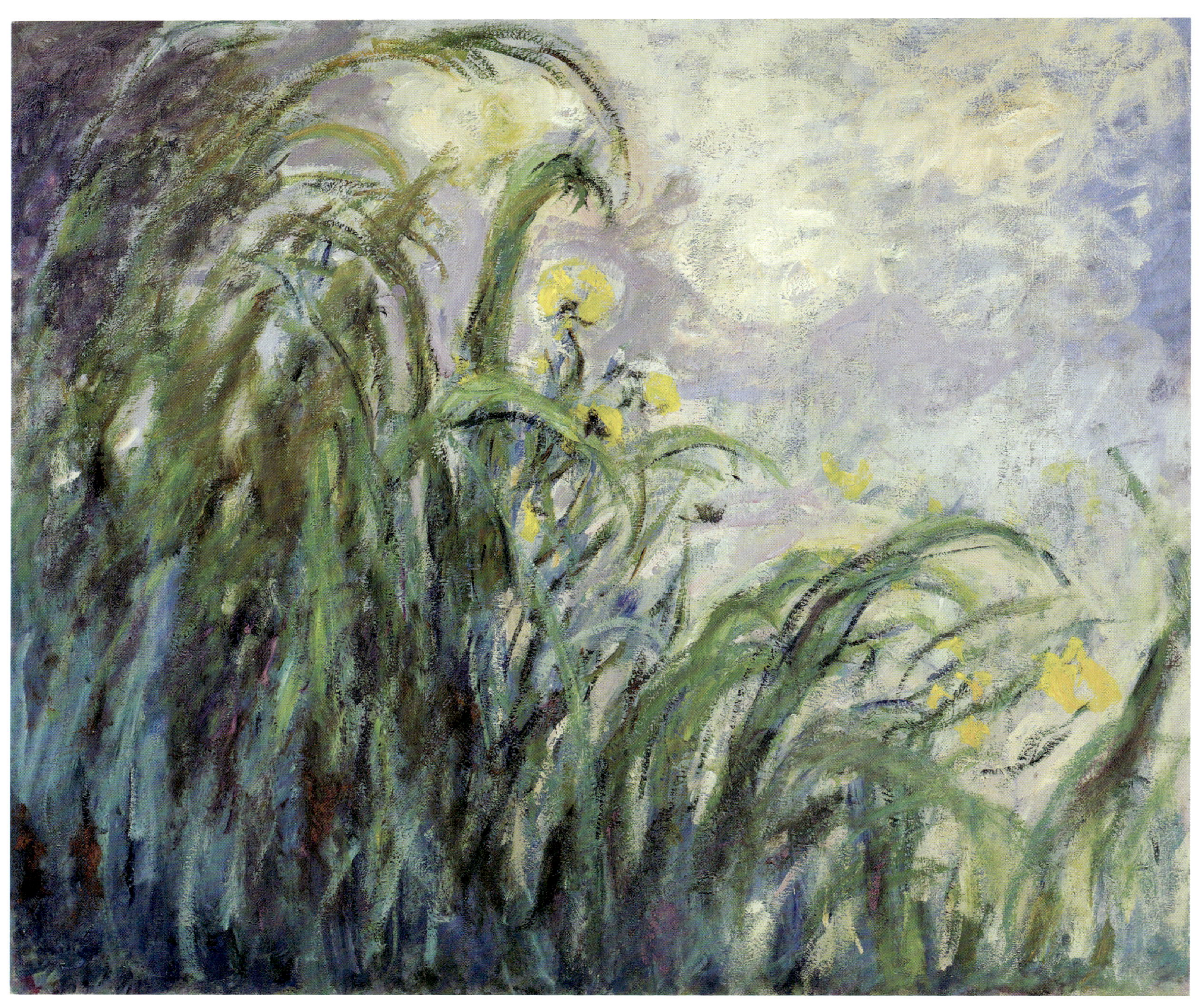

Cat. 21. *Yellow Irises*, 1917–19. Musée Marmottan Monet, Paris

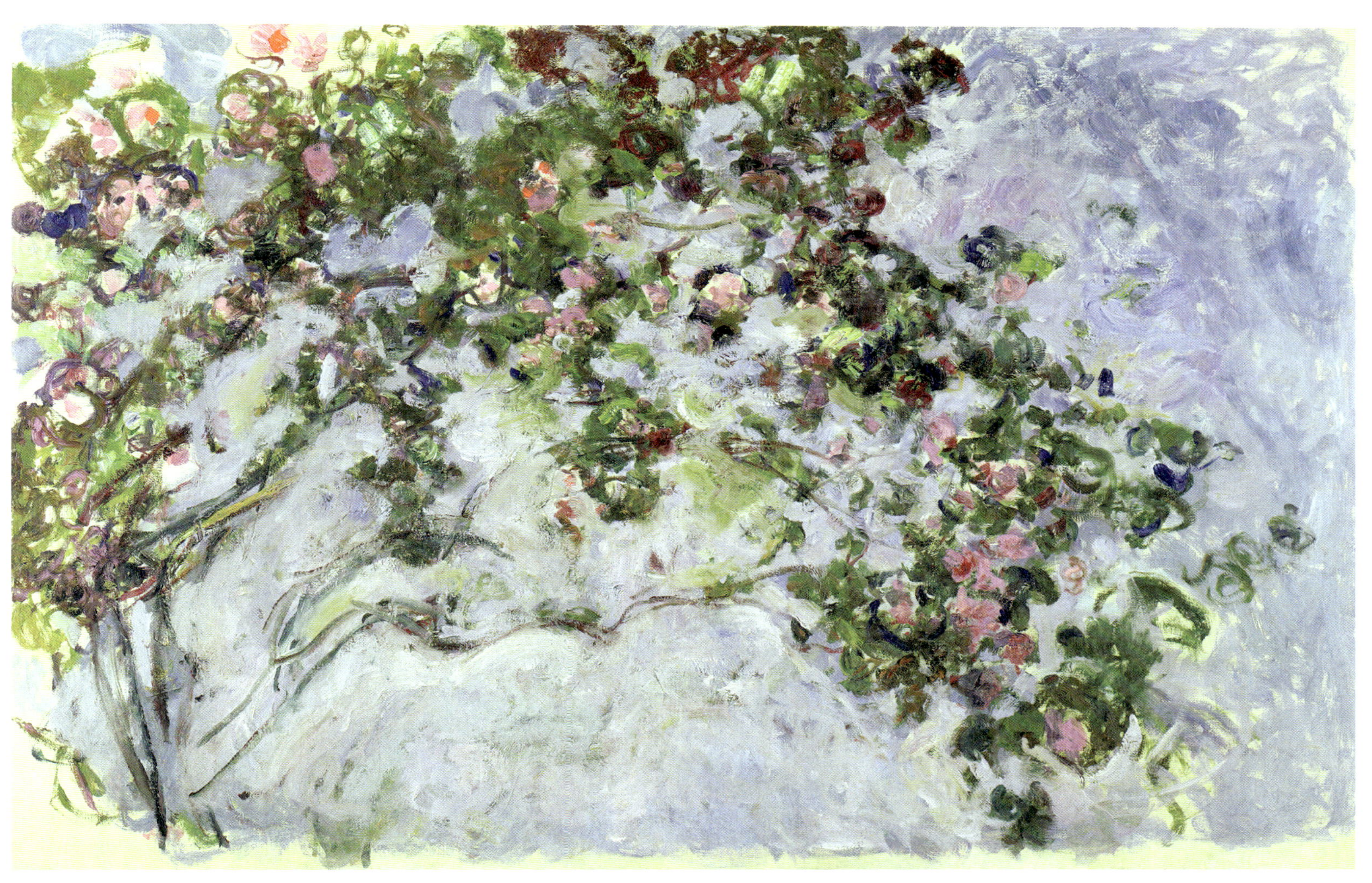

Cat. 22. *Roses*, 1925–26. Musée Marmottan Monet, Paris

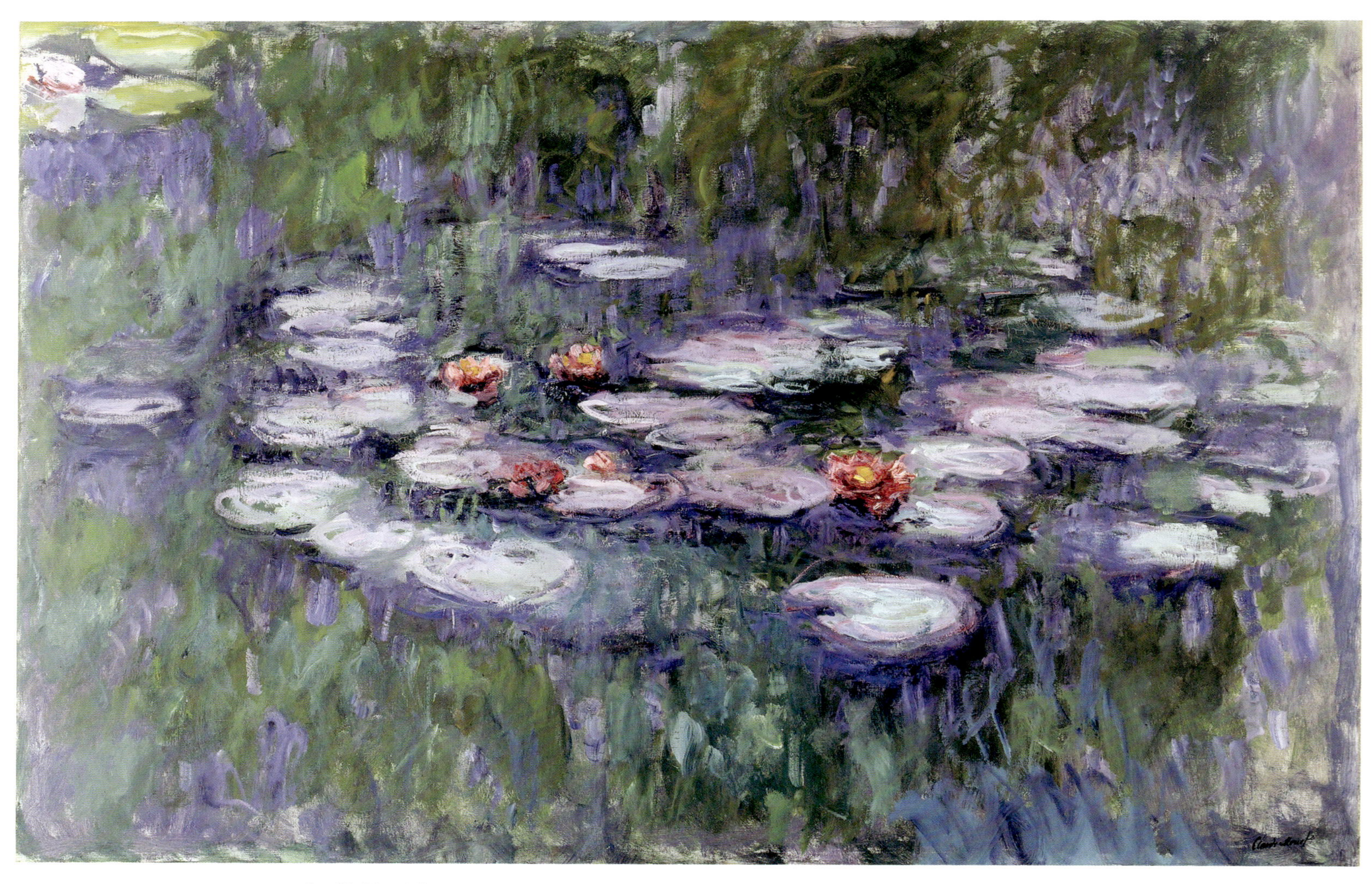

Cat. 23. *Water Lilies*, c. 1916–19. The Tobin Theatre Arts Fund. Courtesy of the McNay Art Museum, San Antonio

In parallel with his large-scale studies and the even larger panels of more than four meters in width, sometime after 1916 and continuing into 1919, Monet began to experiment with somewhat smaller pictorial formats. These were still generally twice as large as the *Nymphéas* he had shown at Durand-Ruel, but the majority were less than one quarter the size of the largest panels. In April 1916, he ordered from his color merchant in Paris, Barillon, located just south of the Boulevard de Clichy in the section of Paris called the *Nouvelle Athènes,* a total of twelve canvases, six of which were 200 x 150 centimeters, and six of which were 200 x 130 centimeters. These, along with canvases measuring 200 x 180 centimeters, provided a range of tall verticals useful for a variety of compositional needs—*Irises*, for example, is painted on a 200 x 130-centimeter canvas.

Eighteen months later, as we know from one surviving letter, he was in touch again about grades and types of canvas, and then, after a lapse of several months, he wrote back to Madame Barillon with a sense of urgency. Beginning by settling his account with the firm, he went to the question of his needs:

> I would like for you to quickly get started making 20 stretchers at 2 meters by 1 meter, of which 10 should be covered from [canvas] piece No. 1 and 10 with from No. 2. I will let you know, when you tell me that these frames are ready, whether or not you should send them already stretched or if you should send your worker again. On this subject, a would like to point out that for his last session you charged me for two days, though he was finished in one. I must tell you that I cannot use one of the 4 meter canvases, because the screws in the stretcher, not having been screwed in properly, threaten to pierce the canvas, it's most annoying. Do please tell me how long it will take to prepare the 20 stretchers.[1]

The two letters written in 1916 and 1918 specifying canvas sizes are the only documents that give a hint as to the dating of a whole series of paintings of water lilies that measure two meters in width. There must have been other orders, of course, since no communication survives to say when and how the stretchers for the largest panels—the ones measuring 4.25 meters, which Monet shortened to 4 meters—arrived. There

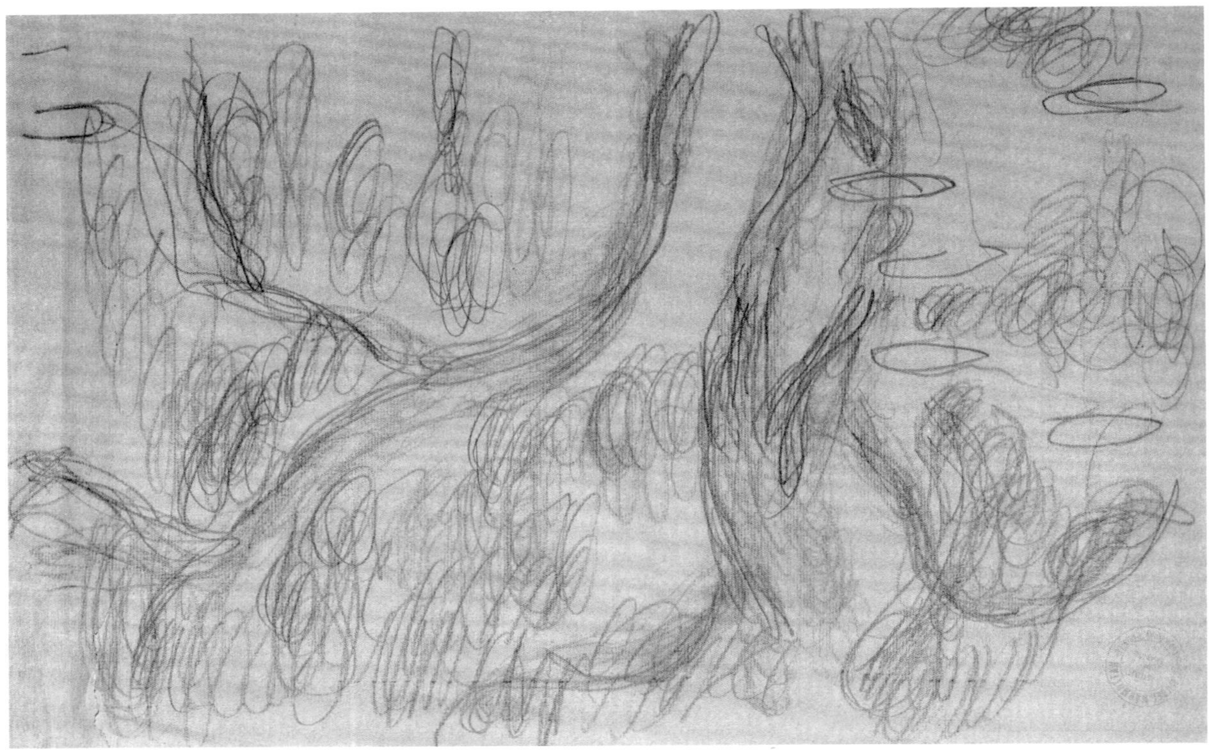

Fig. 167. Claude Monet, *Willows and Reflections*, 1916–19. Pencil on gray wove paper, 11 3/4 x 18 1/2 in. (30 x 47 cm). Musée Marmottan Monet, Paris

are at least twelve views of the pond executed on the canvases measuring 200 x 130 centimeters, of which Monet procured six in 1916. Three of this size are exhibited here: two called *Water Lilies*, from the Tobin Theatre Arts Foundation and the Metropolitan Museum of Art (cats. 23 and 24), and one called *Water-Lily Pond*, from the Art Institute of Chicago (cat. 27).

The first two of these were grouped by Daniel Wildenstein with others that feature the eccentric reflection of one of the pondside willows. Monet did one of his rare compositional drawings to explore this idea, presumably before embarking on the paintings (fig. 167). The circular "hatchings" and the parallel strokes of the pencil that he uses to fill the interstices between the meandering limbs are then transformed into daubs and parallel strokes of paint, glimmers of yellowish light in the Metropolitan's painting and four- and five-stroke patches of color in the Tobin canvas.

The 2 x 1.3 meter format is very nearly the "golden ratio," in which the longer side is about 1.6 times the shorter—a rectangular shape honored by tradition as having an aesthetic harmony appropriate to, for example, traditional landscape subjects. It was also very nearly—but not quite—one of the standard canvas sizes established to make framing easier, a tradition to which Monet had usually adhered before 1914. What Monet ordered in 1918, however, was something very different, appreciably narrower than the narrowest standard size, which was generally conceived for seascapes. The twenty 1 x 2 meter canvases the artist needed with such urgency were a quarter the size of the 2 x 4 meter panels that he was placing side by side to create the vast horizontal spans of the *Grandes Décorations.*

Once he got the canvases, Monet seems to have put them to use immediately on a series of paintings of the water-lily pond. Taking his position on the eastern end of the pond and looking towards the Japanese bridge, he took inspiration from the 1907 *Nymphéas* in the way he used a bright reflected sky as a curving pathway between dark masses of reflected trees (compare cats. 7 and 8). Using this succession of dark-light-dark as a sort of formula for organizing the compositions, he was free to react to changes in the motif and to experiment, to some extent, with capturing changing effect of light in the way that he had done at Rouen's cathedral, in his boat studio for the *Mornings* (see cat. 2), or the 1907 vertical water lilies. The scale of the 1 x 2

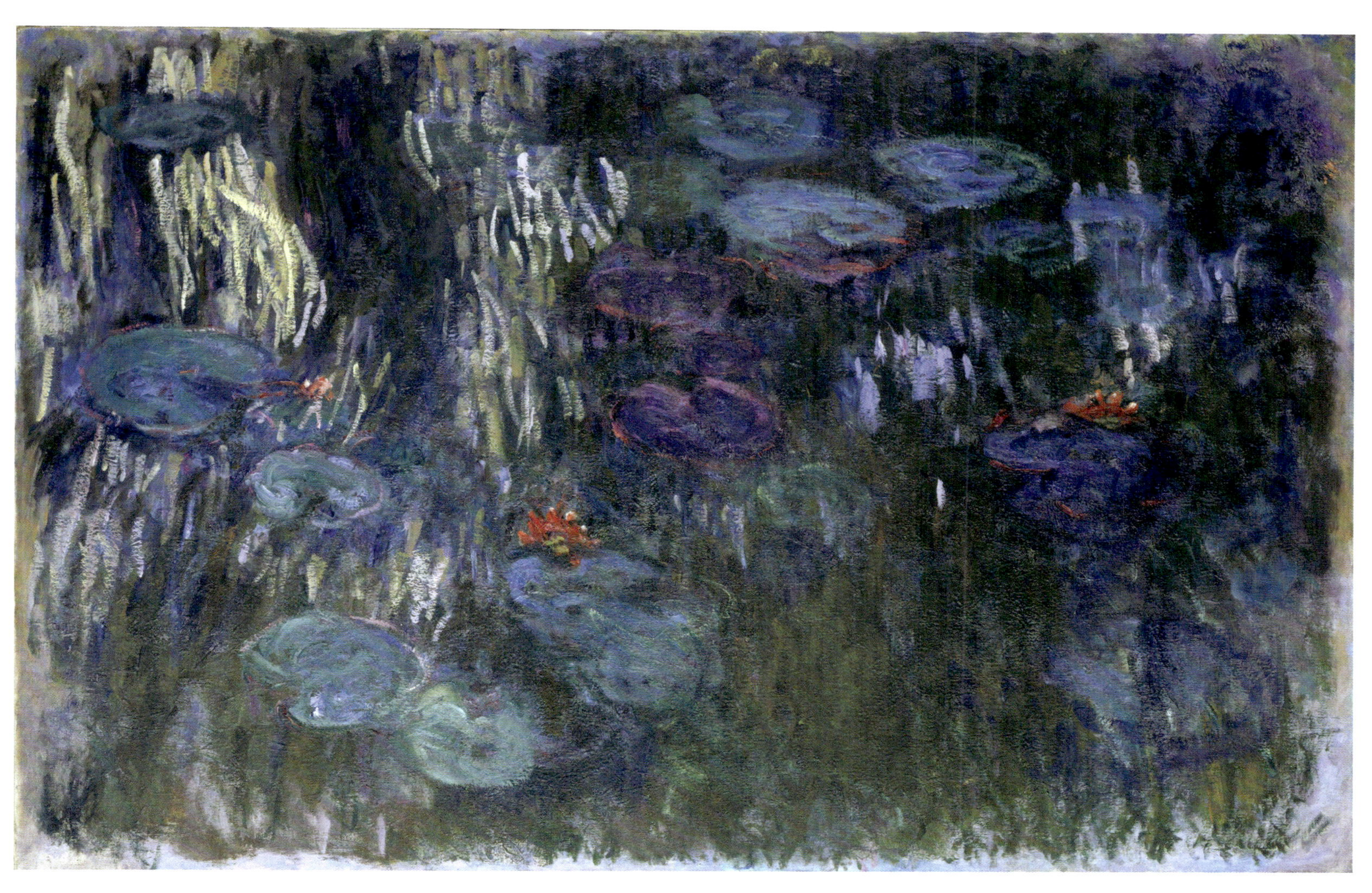

Cat. 24. *Water Lilies*, 1916–19. The Metropolitan Museum of Art, New York

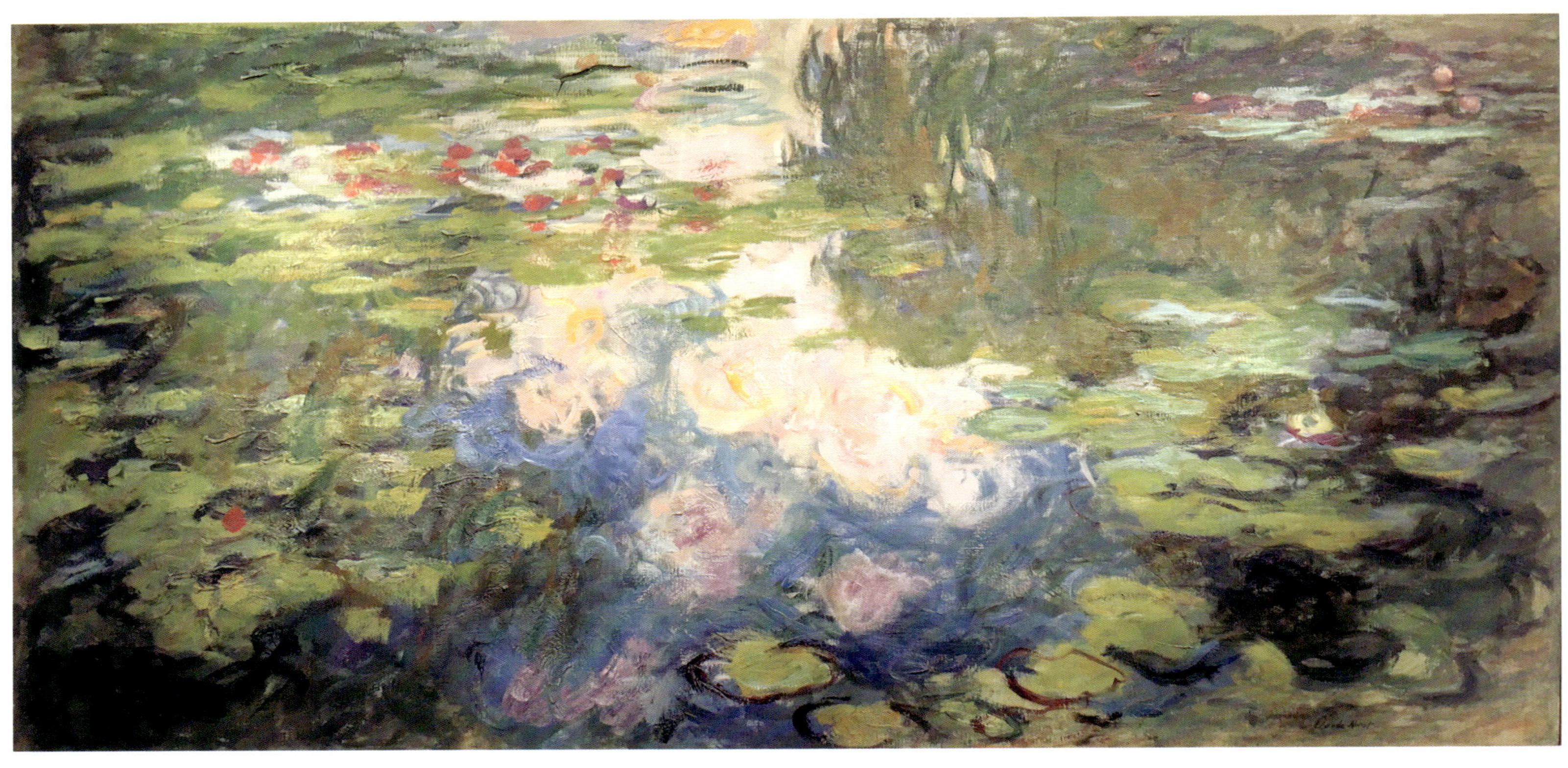

Cat. 25. *Water-Lily Pond*, 1917–19. Private collection. Courtesy of Benjamin Doller, New York

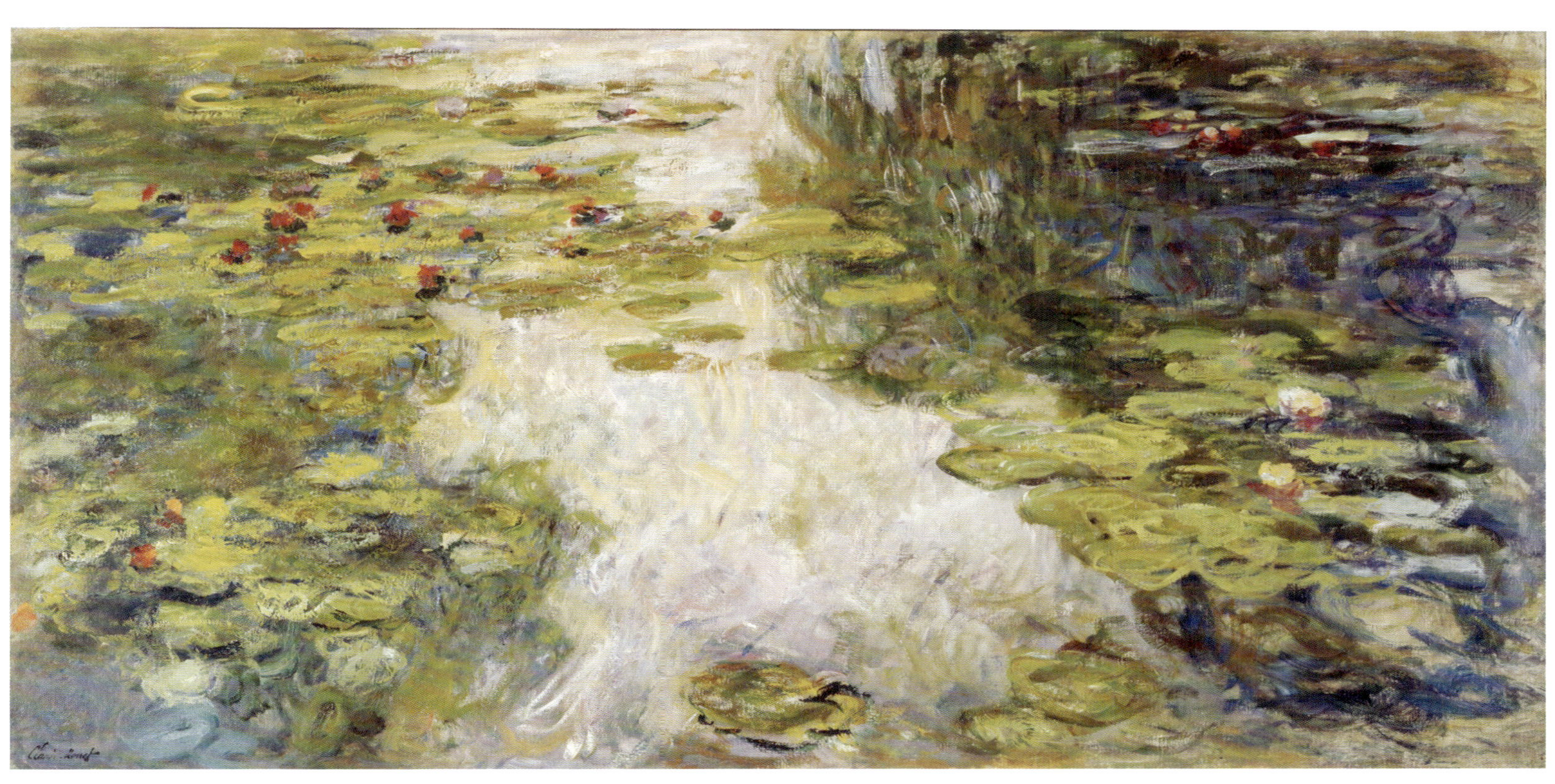

Cat. 26. *Water Lilies*, 1917/19. Honolulu Museum of Art

meter canvases made them relatively easy to transport to the garden, and their numbers made the theme and variations process, once so familiar, a pleasure. As he explained to René Gimpel, an art dealer associated with the Bernheim Jeune gallery:

> I work on the paintings all day. They bring them to me one after the other. In the atmosphere a color reappears that I had found and sketched on one of the canvases yesterday. Quickly I am passed the painting and I try my best to put down this vision definitively, but usually it disappears as quickly as it came into view to make room for another color already rendered several days before on another study which is almost instantly placed before me . . . and so on all the day.[2]

A comparison of two *Water-Lily Ponds* exhibited here, one from a private collection (cat. 25) and the other from the Honolulu Museum of Art (cat. 26), demonstrates both the shift that the motif might present and the differences in Monet's treatment of the phenomena. In the former, the brightness of the day meant that the white clouds in the sky were almost blinding; perhaps this is why Monet worked so quickly, setting down the effect in large, looping strokes for the clouds and bold patches for the foliage in the foreground. In the second, the day is more muted, the sky more uniform, and a certain calm prevails, giving time for a more detailed—but still summary—treatment of the leaves and flowers.

Gimpel had visited Monet in mid-August 1918, only a few months after the canvases had been delivered, but Monet had been productive over the course of the high blooming season. When he entered Monet's large studio, it was not the huge canvases on rolling easels that most intrigued him; instead, he was struck by:

> a strange artistic spectacle: a dozen canvases placed one after another in a circle on the ground, all about six feet wide by four feet high: a panorama of water and water lilies, of light and sky. In this infinity, the water and the sky had neither beginning nor end. It was as though we were present at one of the first hours of the birth of the world. It was mysterious, poetic, deliciously unreal.[3]

As Charles Stuckey has pointed out, the uniformity of these compositions would prevent them from actually being arranged as a panorama, and they are not explicitly tied to the themes or effects at play in the large panels. But one group of the 2 meter *Water-Lily Ponds*, including both the larger and more narrow formats, bears a close relationship to one of the single 4.25 meter panels not chosen for the Orangerie, a painting in the collection of the National Gallery of London (see fig. 63). The diaphanous treatment of the water surface and the choice of a very yellow green as a dominant color note make that painting almost a larger version of such paintings as the one from the Art Institute of Chicago (cat. 27) or the picture that Monet donated to the Musée des beaux-arts, Nantes, in 1922. That painting, signed with a wobbly hand, was certainly misdated by the artist to 1917.

The four paintings from the series that Monet signed at the time are securely dated 1918; they were sold to the Bernheim-Jeune gallery, who subsequently sold half ownership to Durand-Ruel (see fig. 24). The gallery certainly had hopes of being able to sell the larger water lilies, and perhaps the partners thought the acquisition of four adventuresome pictures might have made Monet well disposed to an offer. Exhibited both in Paris and in New York, the paintings did not find ready buyers, one apparently remaining in stock until the 1950s. One of the four was cut in half sometime before 1944, presumably to make a painting that, at 1 x 1 meters, resembled the classic *Nymphéas.*

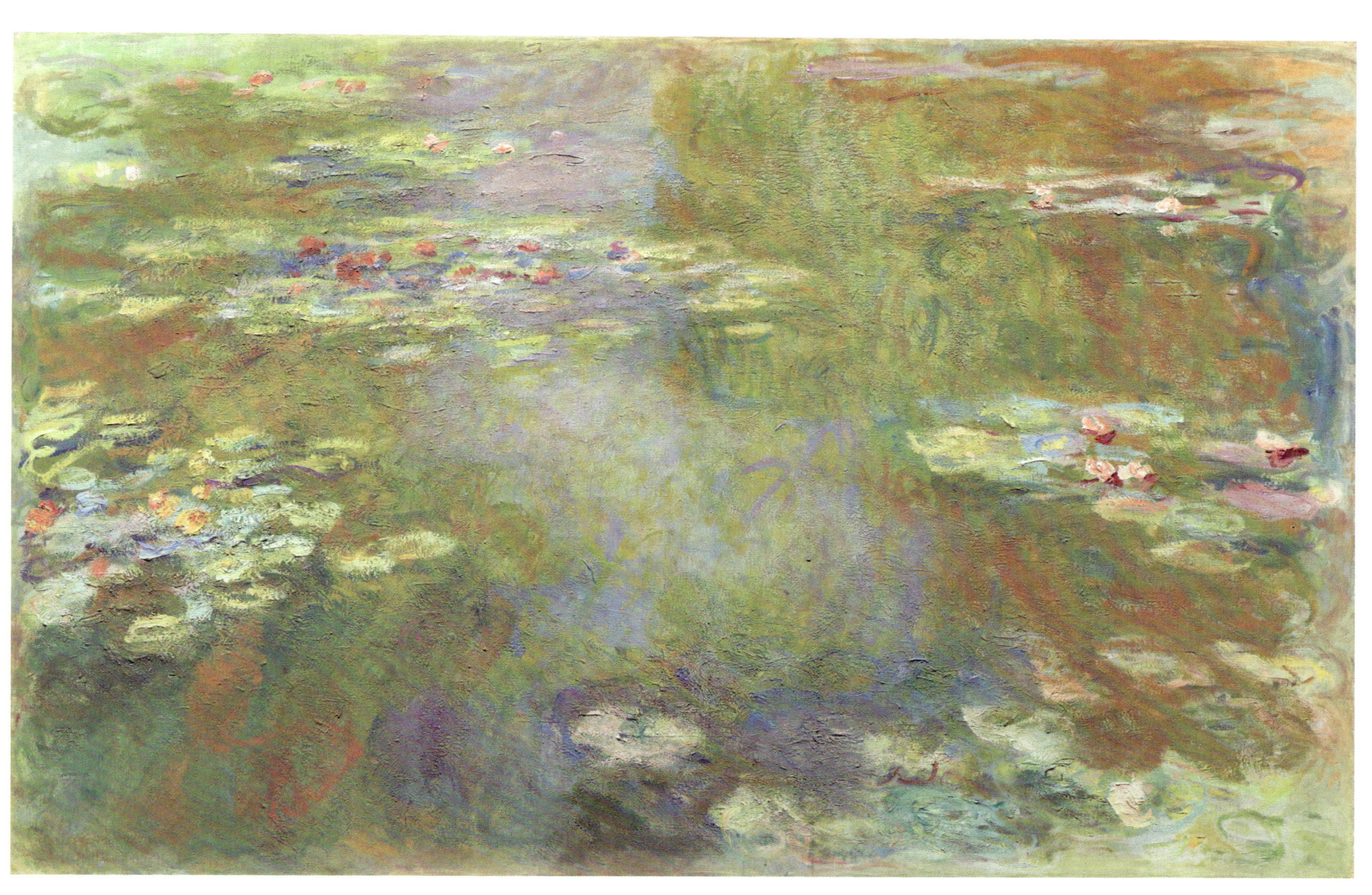

Cat. 27. *Water-Lily Pond*, 1917/19. The Art Institute of Chicago

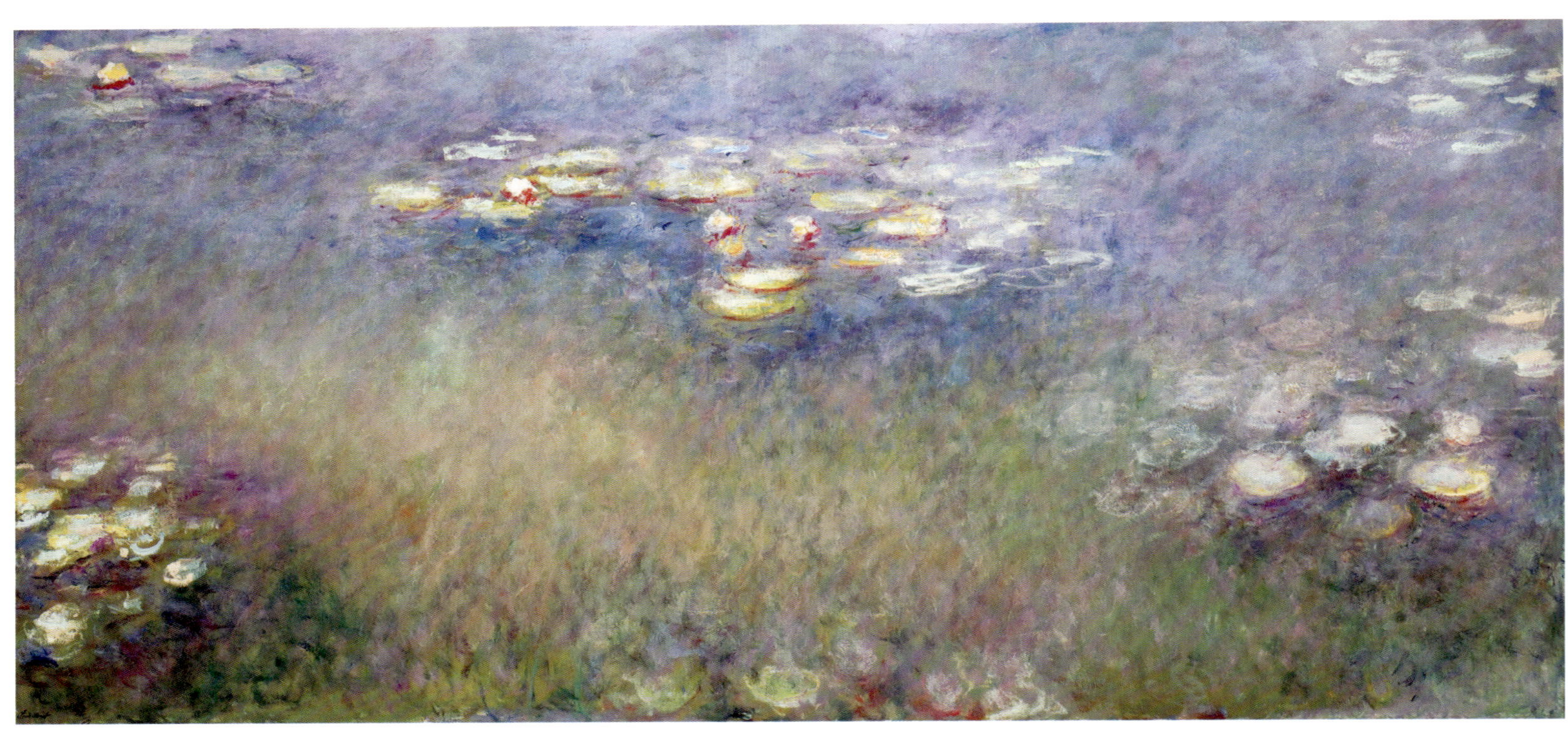

Cat. 28. *Water Lilies (Agapanthus)*, c. 1915–26. Saint Louis Art Museum

This majestic canvas, measuring some fourteen feet in width, is the central panel of one of the finest of the *Grandes Décorations*; lent by the Saint Louis Art Museum, it is also the largest painting in *Monet: The Late Years*. The artist was at work on the panel by the autumn of 1917, and work probably continued on it into 1926. The panels that joined together to form the complete composition are at the Cleveland Museum of Art (left) and the Nelson-Atkins Museum, Kansas City (right; see fig. 73). Together, because of the former inclusion of distinctive agapanthus plants in the lower left corner, the 3-panel composition was christened "The Agapanthus Triptych." As befits its central placement, the Saint Louis panel is the most symmetrical of all the panels, its top centered on a clump of water lilies and leaves painted in tones of white, yellow, and red against a field of blue; a few leaves float directly beneath it at the lower edges of the painting. At upper left and right are two smaller clumps of flowers and leaves; at lower left and at center right are two more groupings, slightly disturbing the otherwise perfect equilibrium of the arrangement.

Simon Kelly has thoroughly analyzed the origins and development of the triptych, and in this volume has discussed the history of Monet's plans for it as one of the critical panels in the first scheme for an architectural installation of the *Nymphéas* decorations (see his essay in this volume.)[1] That scheme, for a circular pavilion, was abandoned finally in favor of a larger and more exhaustive presentation in two rooms of the Orangerie in the Tuileries Gardens. One component of that first scheme—a component that remained at an investigative phase, was the creation of a frieze to supplement the great water-lily panels, a frieze on the theme of the wisteria vines that Monet had planted on a trellis appended to the original Japanese bridge. Two of the most ambitious paintings that survive from this exploration, both from the Musée Marmottan Monet, are exhibited here (cats. 29 and 30); each panel measures one meter high by three meters wide—wider by half than the very horizontal paintings he had been devoting to the water-lily ponds.

As Kelly points out, the *Agapanthus* painting has undergone a complex evolution, luckily documented photographically at several stages. Two of these are securely dated. In the group of six photographs surveying the paintings in process on November 11, 1917, the Cleveland and Saint Louis panels are the last paintings on the right side of the 180-degree panorama (see figs. 17–22). In 1921, Bernheim-Jeune photographed the entire triptych for publication in a book they were planning on Monet (see figs. 76–79). At an unknown time, a candid photograph was taken of Monet with Georges Clémenceau beside the painting, which is shown in raking perspective behind the two men. The date of this document is uncertain, but it might plausibly be sometime between the 1917 and 1921 photographs, given the study canvas placed beside it, most closely tied to the 1921 state of the painting (see fig. 44).

Juxtaposition of the historical 1917 and 1921 photographs, showing the left and center triptych panels, together with a photograph of the present state of the two, reveals the extent of Monet's revisions of the canvases over the course of nearly a decade (fig. 168). Isolated images of the two panels, lifted from the 1917 views and corrected for perspective suggest a composition far more inchoate than it would later become. The agapanthus plant that gives the triptych its name is visible at left; a dark form within the right-hand panel (the Saint Louis canvas) might be supposed to represent a deep shadow or perhaps a view into deeper water—though it is equally possible that the color the 1917 film rendered as a dark shadow might have been a much lighter tone.[2] By 1921, the sharp contrasts had been softened, and a seeming smoothness pervades the panorama. Subsequently, Monet continued to develop that canvas, for instance by greatly subduing the contrast and rendering much less powerful the circular clump of leaves and flowers that spanned the seam between the two panels.

What can be certain in looking at the evolution of the painting is that in its final form it has achieved an ethereal chromatic sophistication that transcends many of the panels that were in the end selected for the Orangerie. Every stroke of color is placed beside another that bears a particular relationship to it, whether as a contrasting note or as a note that brings reassurance or support to the other. This sophistication of the interrelationships of colors calls to mind the famous passage in the poet Rainer Maria Rilke's 1907 letters to his wife describing his reactions to paintings by Cézanne. Rilke was then working as a secretary to Monet's close friend Auguste Rodin, so was conversant with Monet's works, presumably including the water lilies that were being painted in that year. Though focused on a portrait in the Cézanne memorial exhibition, there is no passage in any of the criticism of Monet's work there comes closer to evoking the effect of paintings such as this one—extending to the poet's evocation of "the evening glow of water" and the "green of the Nenuphar's covering-leaves."[3]

> *It's as if every part were aware of all the others*—it participates that much; that much adjustment and rejection is happening in it; that's how each daub plays its part in maintaining equilibrium and in producing it: just as the whole picture finally keeps reality in equilibrium. Everything . . . has become an affair that's settled among the colors themselves: a color will come into its own in response to another, or assert itself, or recollect itself . . . intensifications and dilutions take place in the core of every color, helping it to survive contact with others . . . reflections (whose presence in nature always surprised me so: to discover the evening glow of the water as a permanent coloration in the rough green of the Nenuphar's covering-leaves) play the greatest role: weaker local colors abandon themselves completely; contenting themselves with reflecting the dominant ones: In this hither and back of mutual and manifold influence, the interior of the picture vibrates, rises and falls back into itself, and does not have a single unmoving part.

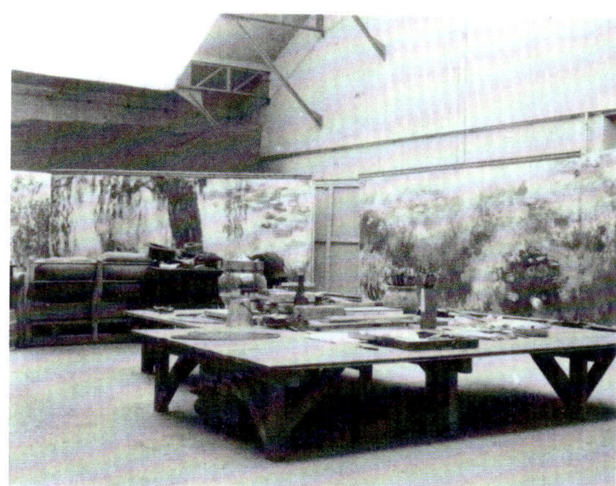
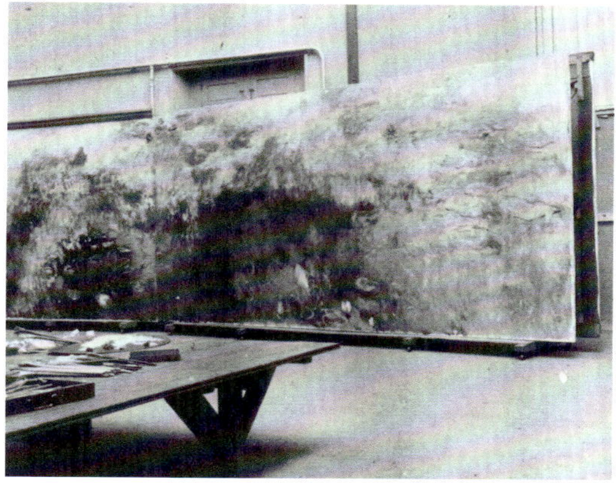
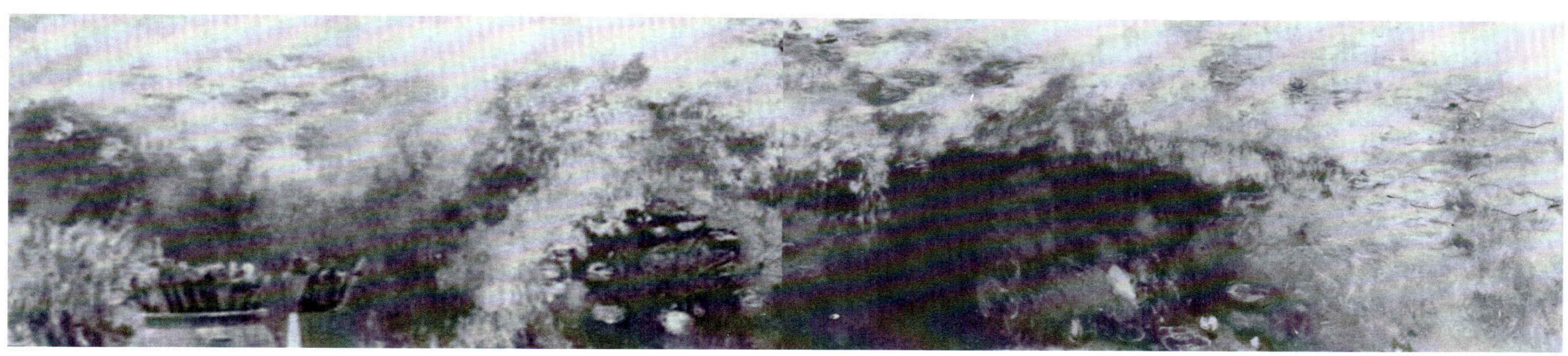
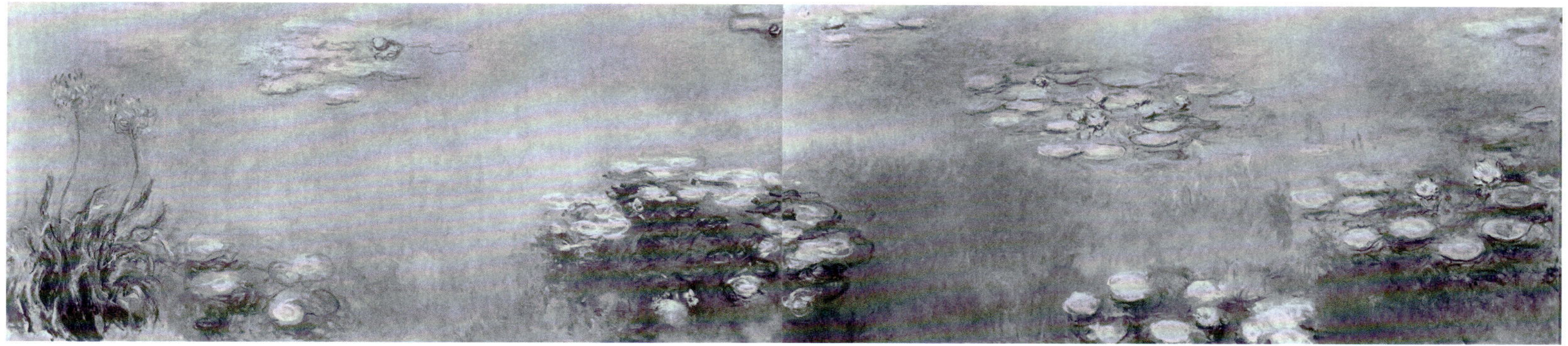
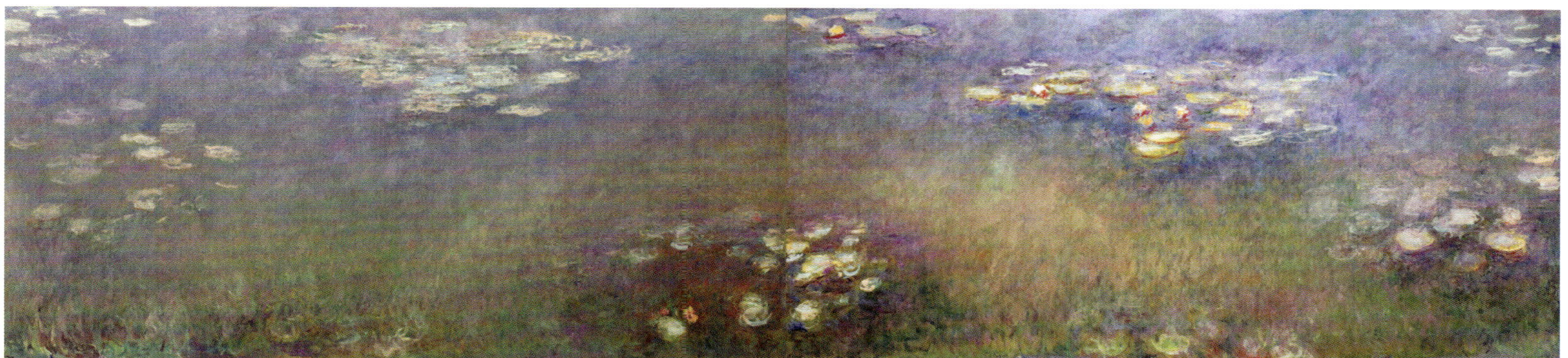

Fig. 168. The evolution of the left and central panels of Claude Monet's *Agapanthus triptych*, from the Durand-Ruel photographs of 1917 (with the paintings extracted and corrected for perspective) (see figs. 21, 22), to the Bernheim-Jeune photograph of 1921 (see fig. 77), to the final composition (left panel: *Water Lilies (Agapanthus)* from the Cleveland Museum of Art; central panel: cat. 28; see fig. 73)

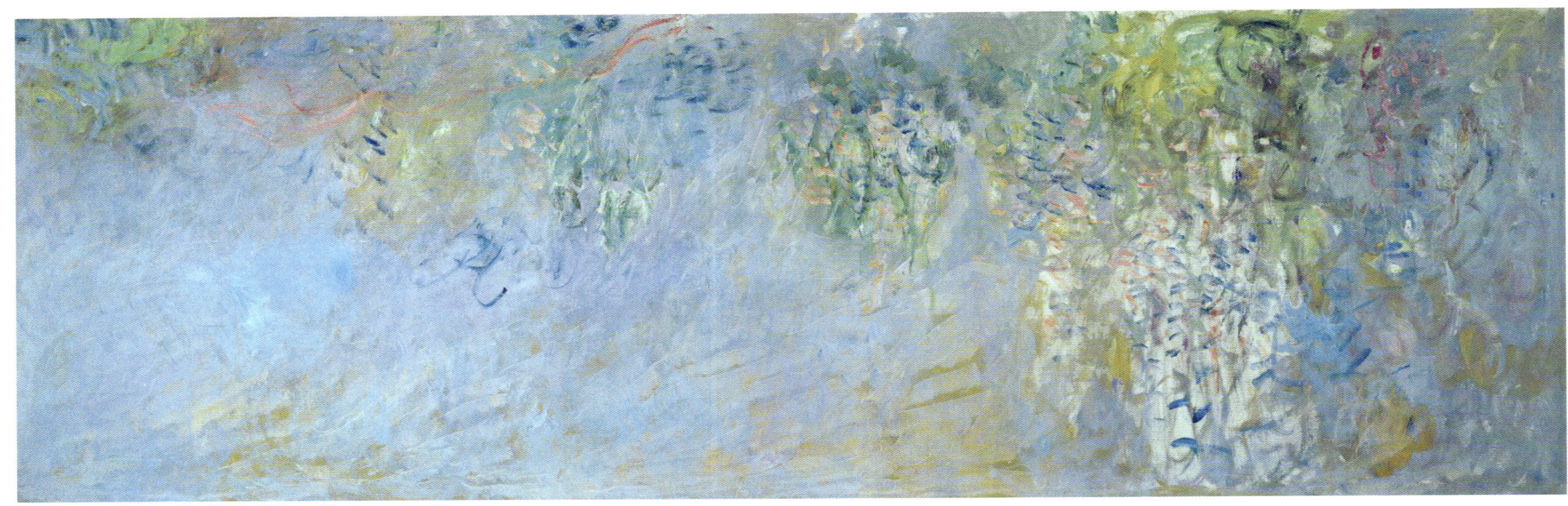

Cat. 29. *Wisteria*, 1919–20. Musée Marmottan Monet, Paris

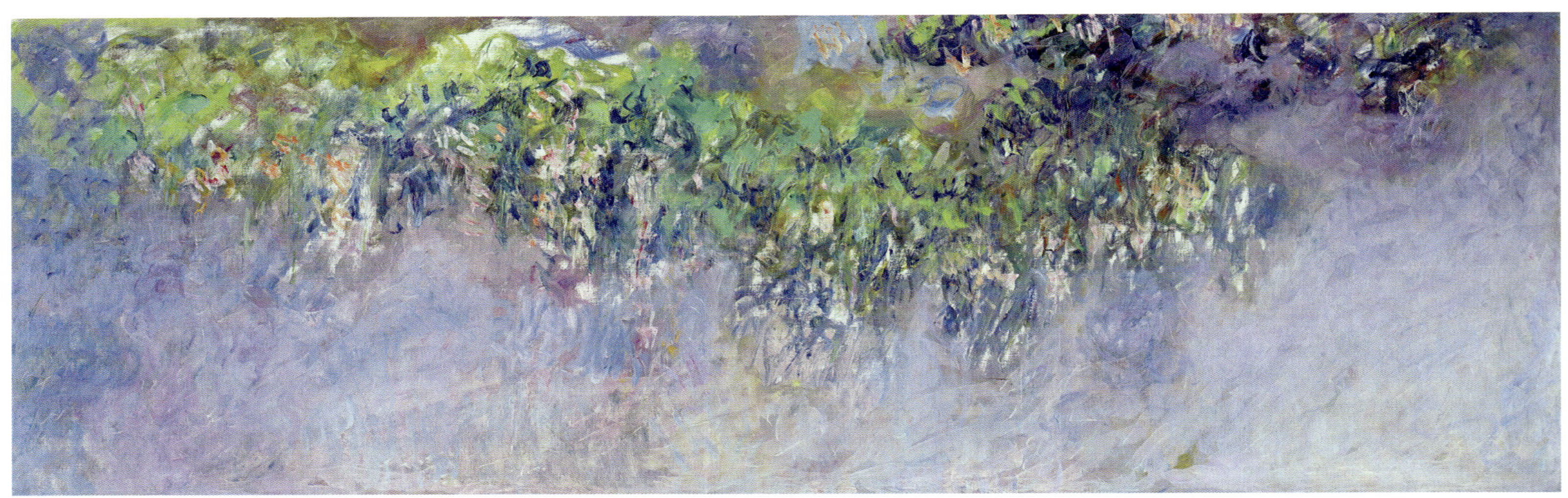

Cat. 30. *Wisteria*, 1919–20. Musée Marmottan Monet, Paris

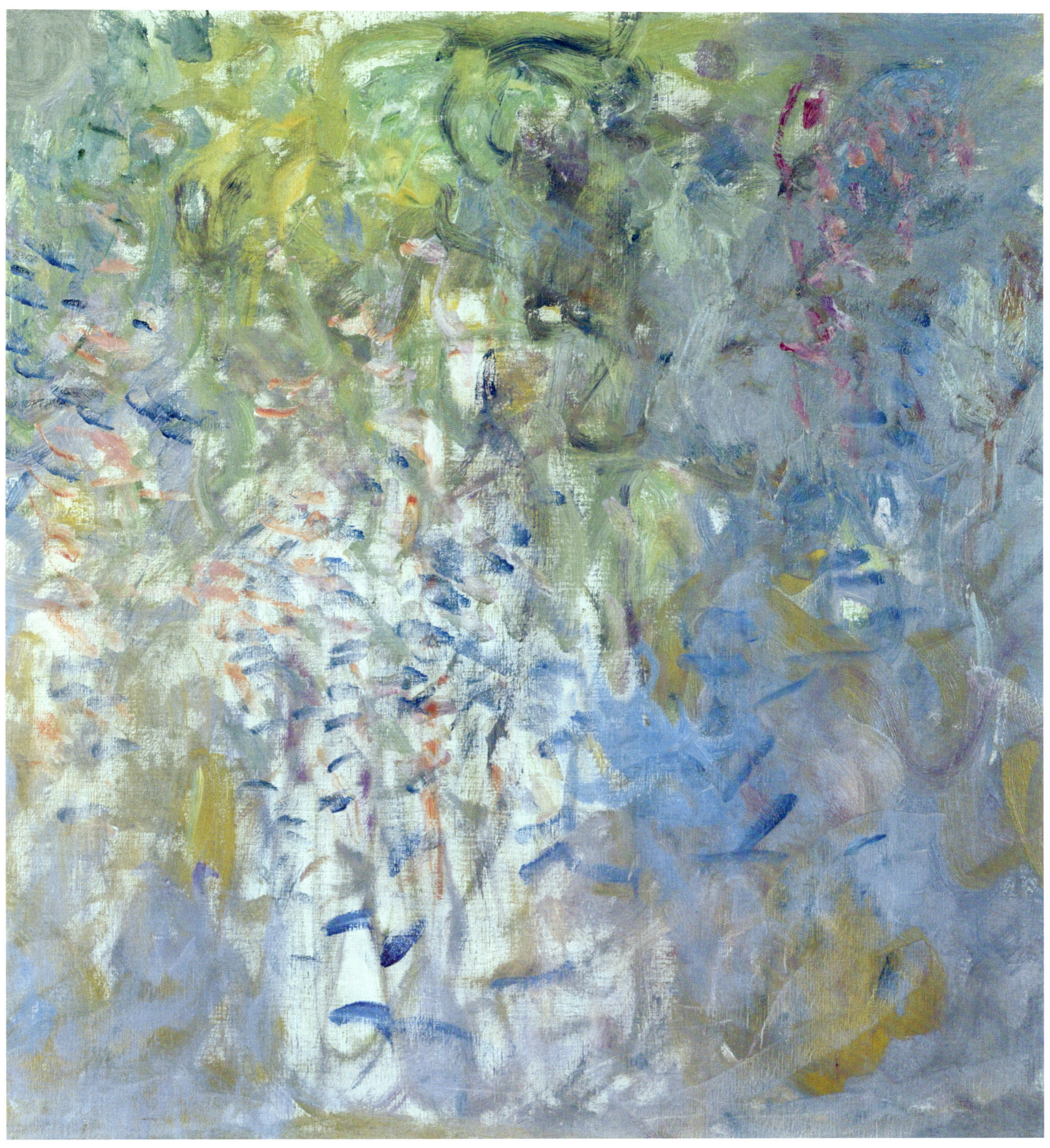

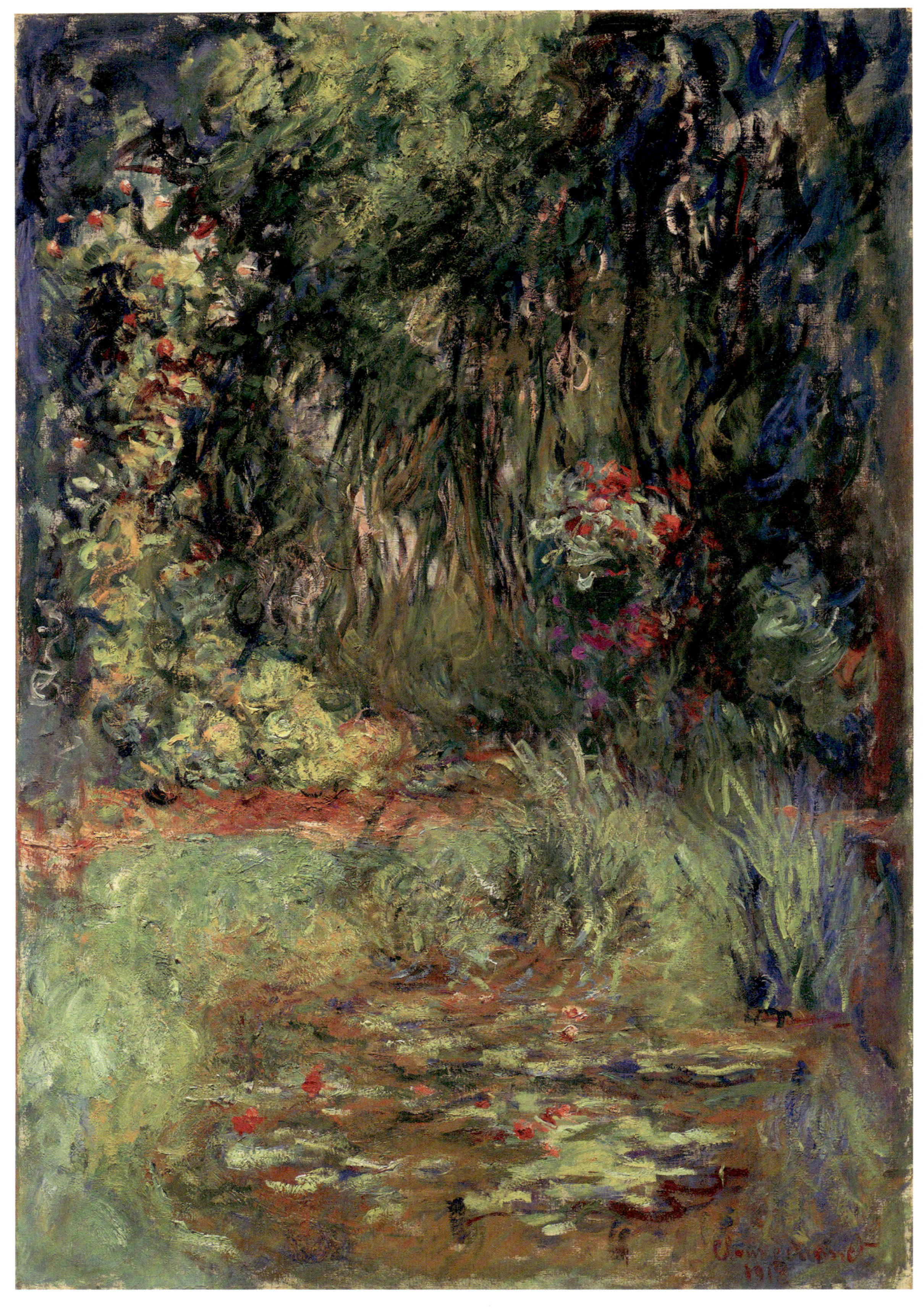

Cat. 31. *Corner of the Water-Lily Pond*, 1918–19. Private collection

This resplendent painting is one of four views of the extreme east end of the water-lily pond, near where the diversion of the River Ru could be controlled by a sluice gate, allowing Monet's gardeners to regulate the water level in the pond and to give it enough circulating water to maintain freshness.[1] It is a part of the garden that might have been easily overlooked, but in this group of paintings the artist set out to make something of a subject composed of many elements. With an appropriately wide range of brushstrokes, sometimes short and staccato, sometimes long and curling, sometimes blunt and thick, sometimes long and thin, Monet enumerates the elements of the motif. There is the lily-strewn pond in the foreground; clumps of grasses at the water's edge and their reflections; a tree covered in climbing roses at the far left, with bushes closer to the ground beneath; a screen of trees marking the end of the garden, through which light is trying to break; the leaves of those trees, glossy in the sunlight; and finally one standard rose bush, posed beside the path like a dazzling young lady, acting as a bright focal point against the trees beyond, their trunks deep red and blue, their shadowed leaves vivid blue and dark green.

The degree of attention paid to the elements that are *not* the pond is striking in this series. We can be relatively sure that the group was completed in the heady summer of 1918, one of the most productive moments in Monet's later career, particularly rich in the production of easel paintings such as this one. The series as a whole would seem to declare Monet's intention to lift his gaze from the surface of the pond and its reflections, or to stand back from the flattened, decorative treatments of individual plant subjects. In this painting, he shows the components of his garden in classic perspective, with a perceptible horizon line in the center of the canvas—adopting the view on the garden landscape that informed his *Flowering Arches* of just five years earlier (cat. 10) but with a wholly new approach to technique. It would not be wrong to say that *Corner of the Water-Lily Pond* marks a new development in Monet's late career, for from 1918 on, while the decorations advanced, he would paint dozens of paintings of the garden beyond, or beside, or above the water-lily pond.

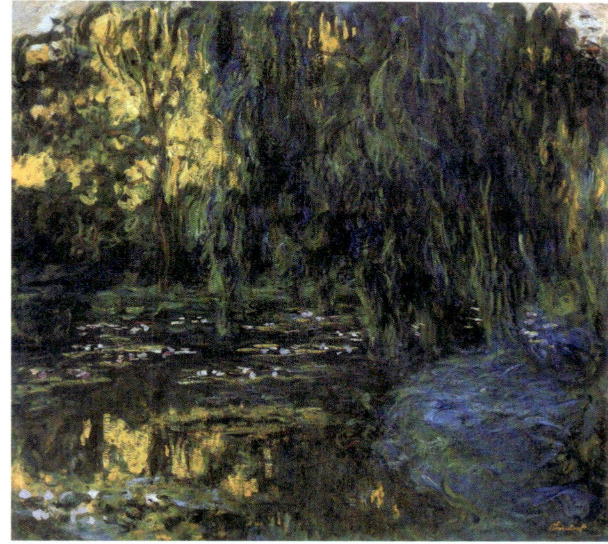

Fig. 169. Claude Monet, *View of the Water-Lily Pond with a Willow*, 1917–19. Oil on canvas, 55 1/8 x 59 in. (140 x 150 cm). Private Collection

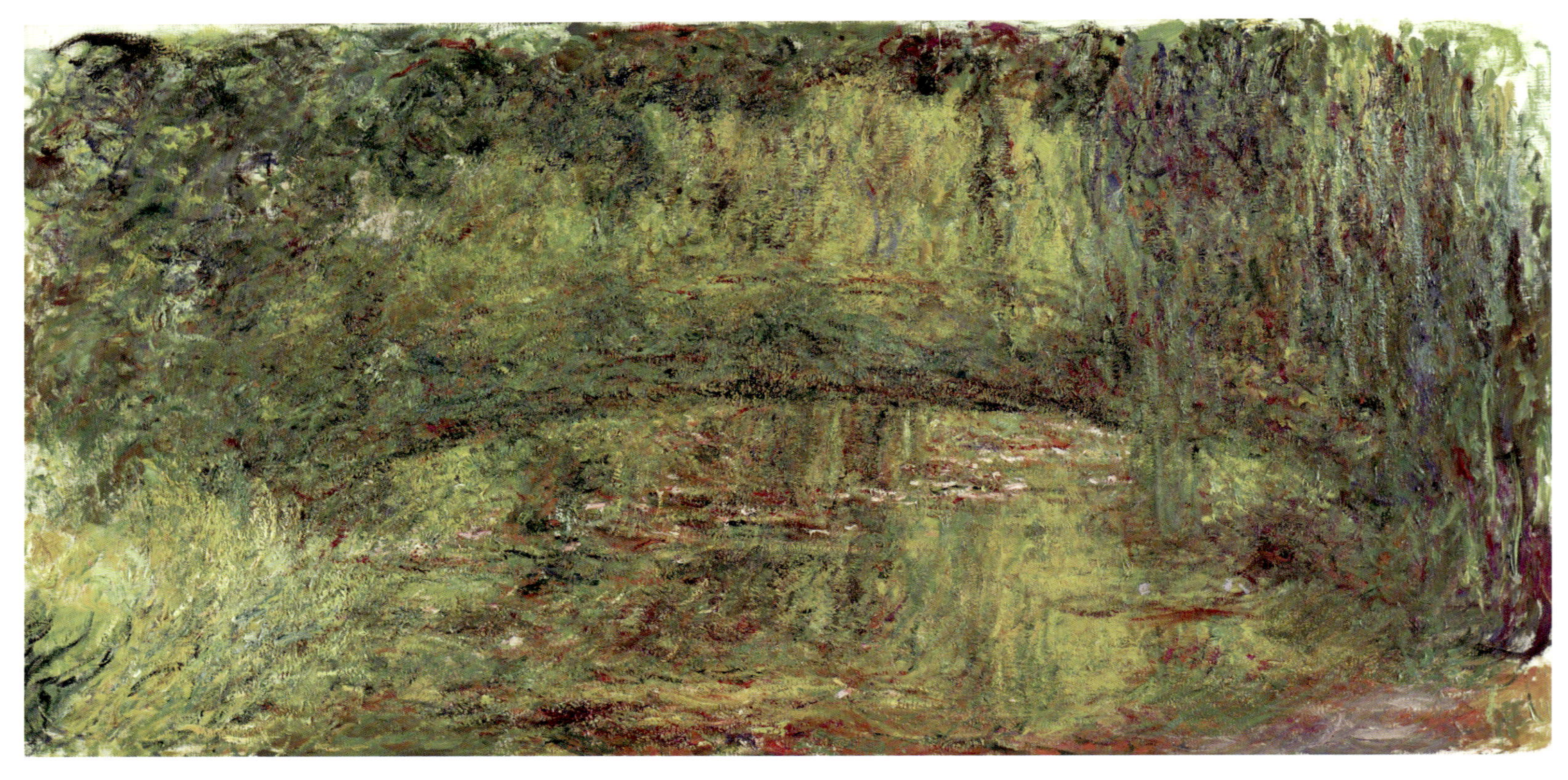

Cat. 32. *The Japanese Bridge*, 1918. Musée Marmottan Monet, Paris

Nearly twenty years after he had embarked on his first series of depictions of the Japanese bridge, around 1918, Monet began work on another group of images of the structure, the most significant and recognizable architectural element in his garden. Over the course of five or six years, he was to complete some twenty-two of these—and there may have been more, among the many canvases known to have been destroyed by the painter. Seven examples are exhibited here, ranging from 2 meter views of the bridge to one measuring less than half that size; their colors shift from bright greens and yellows through rich oranges, reds, and purples to deep blues and emerald greens.

The painter's inspiration in choosing to build such a bridge in the garden was likely the type of wooden bridge in use in Japan for centuries and made famous in the West through the prints of such artists as Katsushika Hokusai, whose *Under the Mannen Bridge at Fukagawa,* 1830–32, is a typical example (see fig. 170). Monet's friend James Whistler had, between 1872 and 1875, used this form as a point of reference in his distorted image of *Old Battersea Bridge*; Monet had at the same time played slyly with connoisseurs' awareness of such imagery when he depicted a bridge in Argenteuil under repair following the Franco-Prussian war.[1] When designing the pond in the 1890s, a bridge was an obvious feature to add, an extension in the lower garden of the axis established in the rectilinear *Clos Normand* to the north, and a point of reference to the Japanese aesthetic that would prevail in the asymmetrical, naturalistic water garden that would soon be planted with water lilies.

The first of canvases showing this motif appeared in 1895, but it was not until 1899 that the series of twelve views of the bridge and the water-lily pond beneath it were completed (see cat. 3).[2] The 1899 paintings were marked by their symmetry and, in general, by the absence of bank at either side of the canvas. In a further four views, executed in the next year, Monet shows the mass of foliage on the north bank from which the bridge springs. In such works as *The Bridge over the Water Lily Pond* (fig. 171), this compositional choice disturbs the equilibrium the earlier group possessed, making for a dynamic imbalance that accompanied a slight change in facture; the brushwork in the later paintings, particularly in the grasses at the left of the frame, is also more lively, and the choice of a more slanted light gives the picture a greater sense of excitement.

Sometime before 1905, Monet decided to alter the bridge, adding a pergola or trellis in metal on which he could train wisteria vines (see cats. 29 and 30).[3] The arc of the trellis followed that of the bridge, and four verticals supported it on either side, creating three evenly spaced openings when the bridge was seen laterally. By the next decade, the structure was covered with leaves and, in late spring, with blossoms. Monet was photographed beside the bridge on many occasions; one view, taken from the west, shows the ways in which the bridge acted as a means of establishing scale in the garden, both in nature and in representations, as the openings framed distant views of trees, and the tunnel

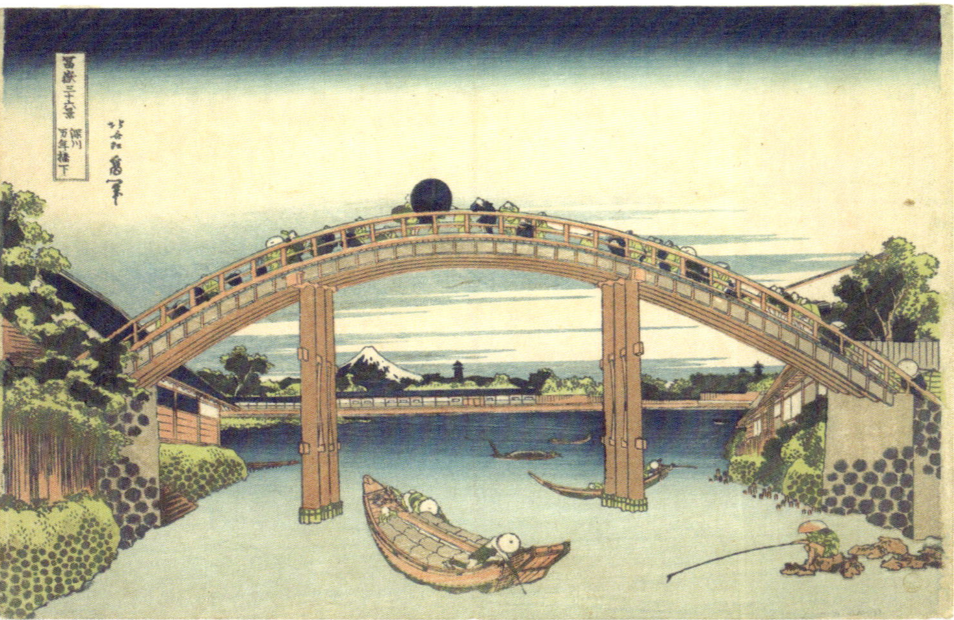

Fig. 170. Katsushika Hokusai, *Under the Mannen Bridge at Fukagawa*, from the series *Thirty-six Views of Mount Fuji*, c. 1830–32. Polychrome woodblock print, 10 1/8 x 15 1/4 in. (25.7 x 38.6 cm). The Metropolitan Museum of Art, New York. Rogers Fund, 1922

beneath the arc revealed the disappearing north bank of the pond (fig. 172). Whether in 1899–1900 or after 1918, Monet invariably depicted the bridge from this point of view, as is evidenced in the latter group by the strong presence of the tall weeping willow above the bridge at right, on the south side of the pond.

It is thought that Monet began work on the *Japanese Bridge* paintings in 1918, perhaps starting with three of the very horizontal canvases he had used for the *Water-Lily Pond* series. Two of these large panels, from the collection of the Musée Marmottan Monet (cats. 32 and 33), accommodate the double-square format of the support by stretching the bridge and flattening its arc. The surface of these canvases bears witness to many sessions of work, as layer upon layer of pigment is applied using brushes of various sizes. In the first of them, the repeated sessions of work seem to have overloaded the canvas with paint, so that the artist risks losing the focus that he would bring, for example, to the second. In the latter painting, the tangle of foliage that moves from the sprightly water grasses at lower right through the tendrils of the wisteria vines to the long and wavering lines of the willow branches is painted with great fluidity and mastery.

Only one of the later *Japanese Bridges* was signed and sold during Monet's lifetime. The Kunstmuseum Basel's canvas (cat. 34) was sold by the artist to the Bernheim-Jeune gallery in November 1919. As in many of the pictures in the series, the corners of the Basel painting had been left unpainted during the working sessions, and it was at the very end, most likely, that they were filled in; the fact that the date 1919 is painted in dark blue paint on top of a still-wet and lighter stroke of blue-green suggests that these were truly "finishing touches." This painting is among the most riotously composed of any of the later *Bridges*; its sale at the end of 1919 confirms that the loose finish of the canvases that remained in Monet's possession should not necessarily be interpreted as a sign of incompleteness.

The order in which these unruly paintings were begun or completed is unknown. The 1918 purchase of a large number of 1 x 2 meter canvases suggests a beginning point; the 1919 sale of the Basel painting gives another marker of time. Knowing the artist's previous practice of beginning a large number of canvases of one theme at more or less the same time and allowing them to evolve over months—his *Rouen Cathedrals*—or even years—the *Mornings*—it might be that many of the canvases were roughed in sometime before 1919. But how long the artist kept working on the group is unknown.

A large number of the compositions are marked by the intense mix of colors usually associated with the sunset, but which must, in this case, be linked to very early morning (cats. 35, 36). Facing east, Monet would have waited for the moment when the sun began to fill the corner of the garden with golden, almost flaming light, before it rose high enough to light the near side

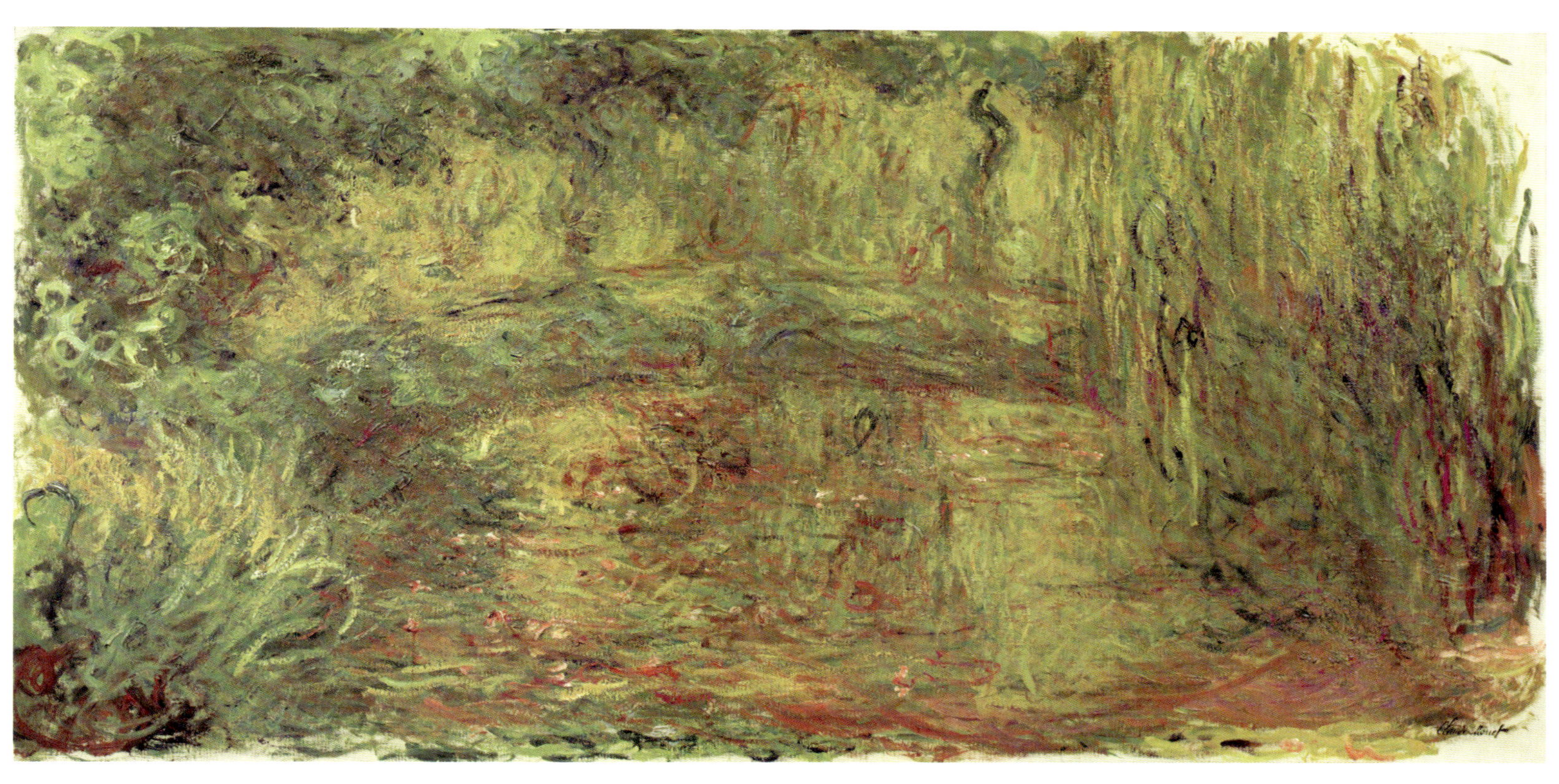

Cat. 33. *The Japanese Bridge*, 1918. Musée Marmottan Monet, Paris

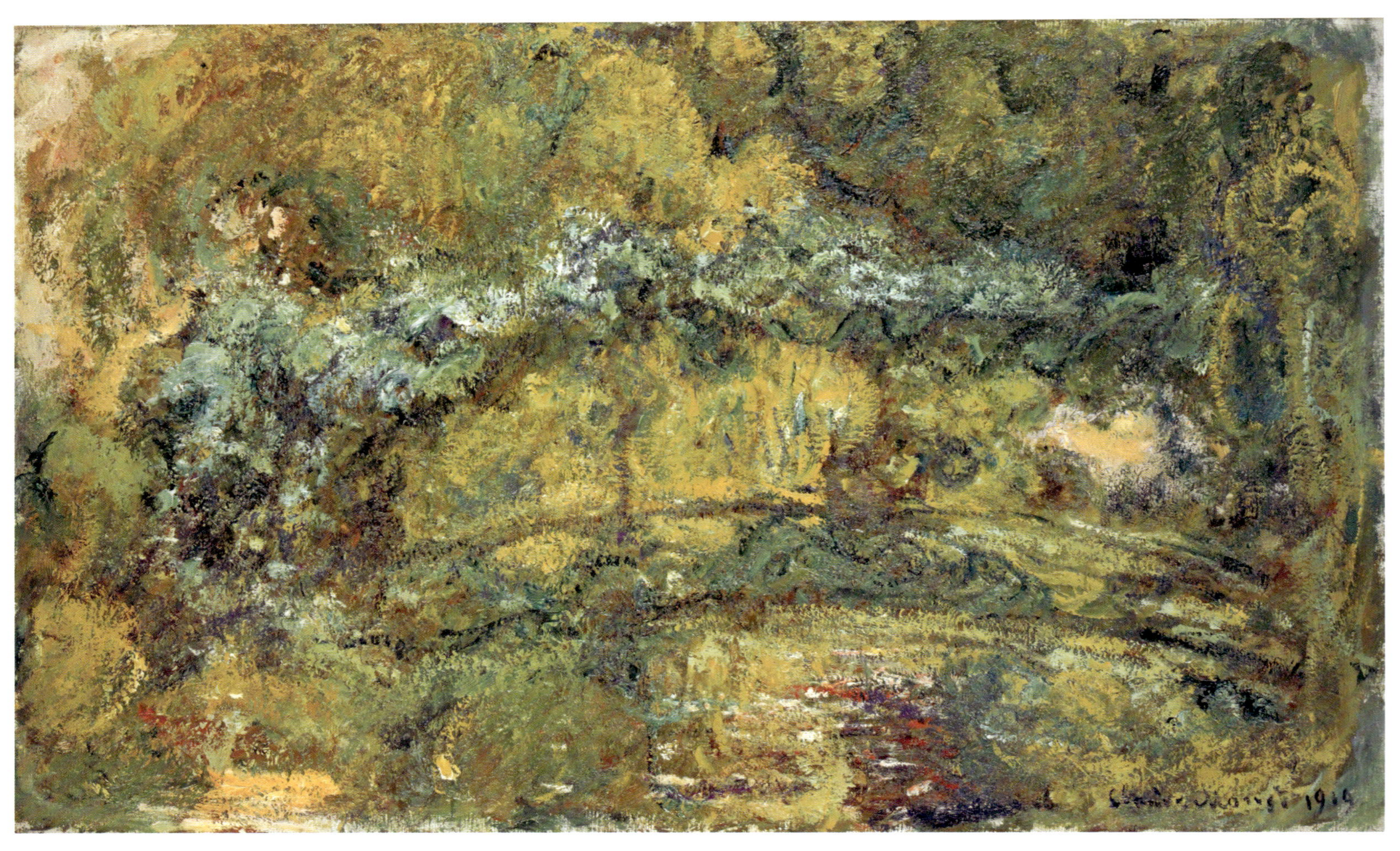

Cat. 34. *The Japanese Bridge*, 1919. Kunstmuseum Basel, Switzerland

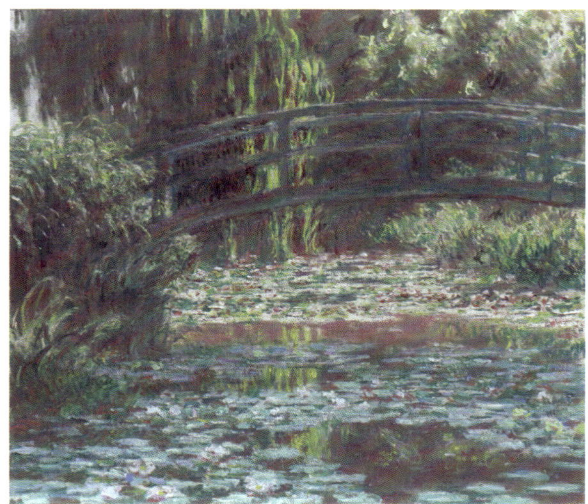

Fig. 171. Claude Monet, *Water-Lily Pond*, 1900. Oil on canvas, 35 3/8 x 39 3/4 in. (89.8 x 101 cm). The Art Institute of Chicago, Mr. and Mrs. Lewis Larned Coburn Memorial Collection, 1933.441

of the bridge, which is still in shadow. In some (cat. 37) the sun has risen high enough to bathe the vines on the bridge in light, reducing the sharp contrasts of light and dark that made the other pictures so intense. In all of these, however, the colors seem somewhat unnatural, as if real effects had been pushed to a dramatic extreme. Whether this is a deliberate decision on Monet's part or whether it is a result of the changes in his perception of color due to his cataracts can only be guessed at. If, as seems likely, the painter's eyesight did play a role in the effects of color that we now see in the canvases, then perhaps the shift in color from hot to cool—as, for example, in the blue-green canvas from the Fondation Beyeler—can be attributed to the overwhelming perception of blue that Monet experienced after his second cataract surgery. In these scenarios, what we now see on the canvas must be the result of Monet's careful attention to the hues of his paints and their placement on his palette, which would allow him to make a picture that reflected what he saw, knowing that what he saw as he looked at his canvas was certainly different from what his audience would see.

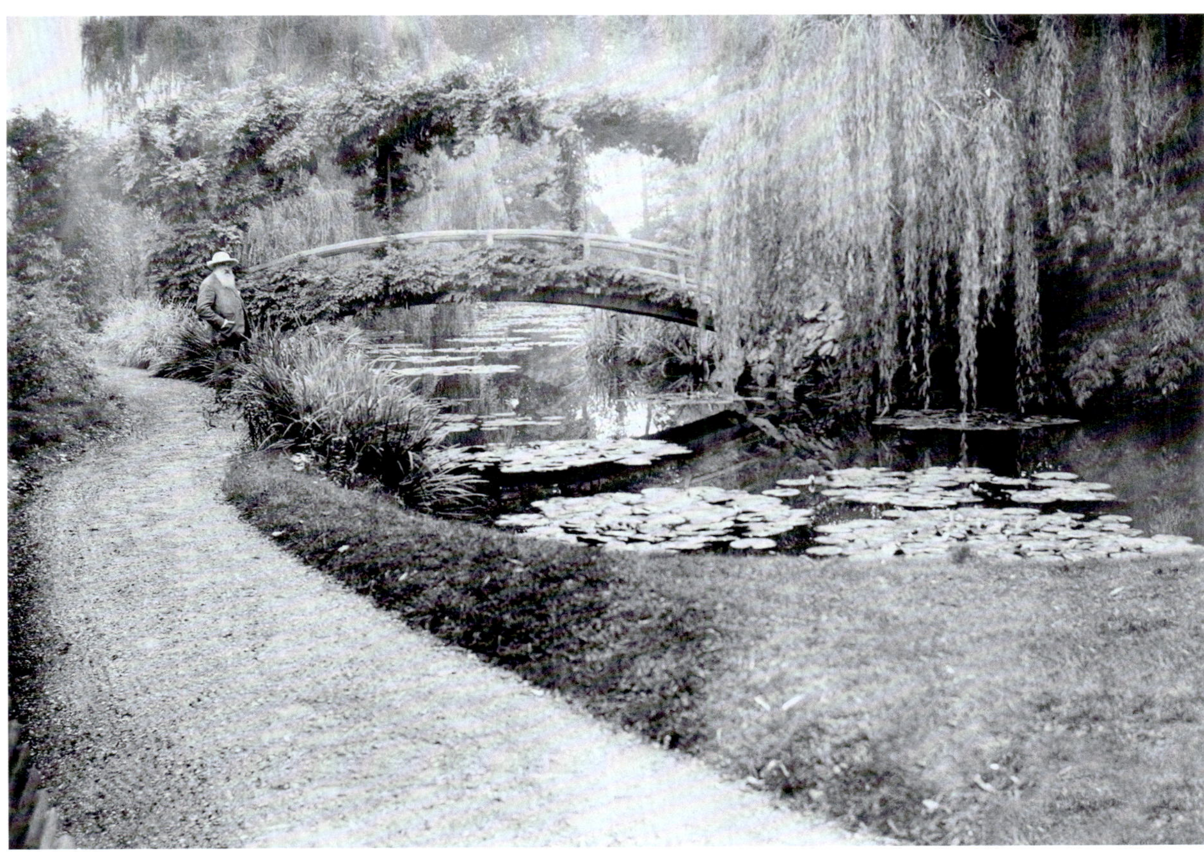

Fig. 172. Claude Monet near the Japanese bridge in his garden at Giverny. Private collection

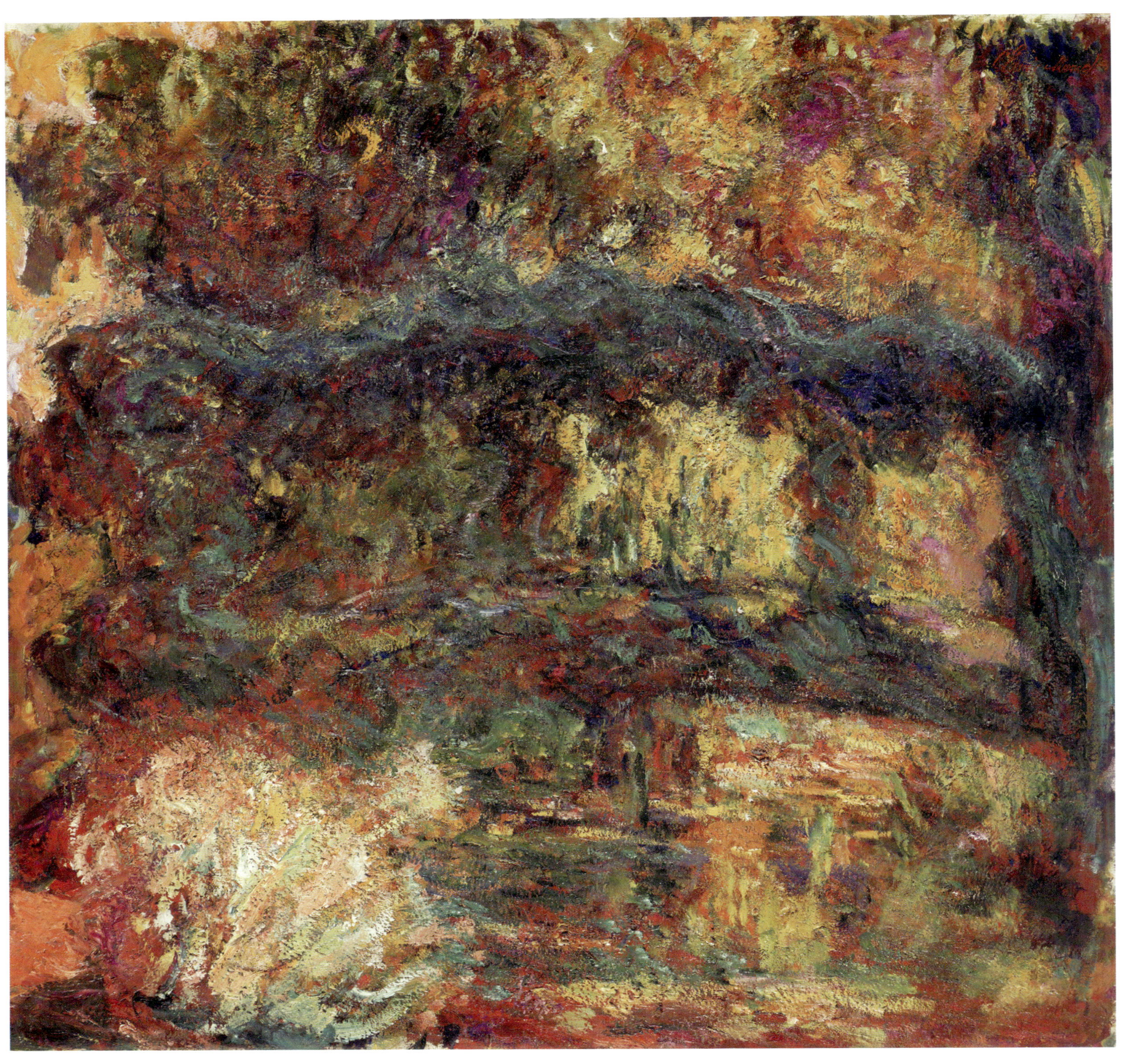

Cat. 35. *The Japanese Bridge*, 1918–26. Philadelphia Museum of Art

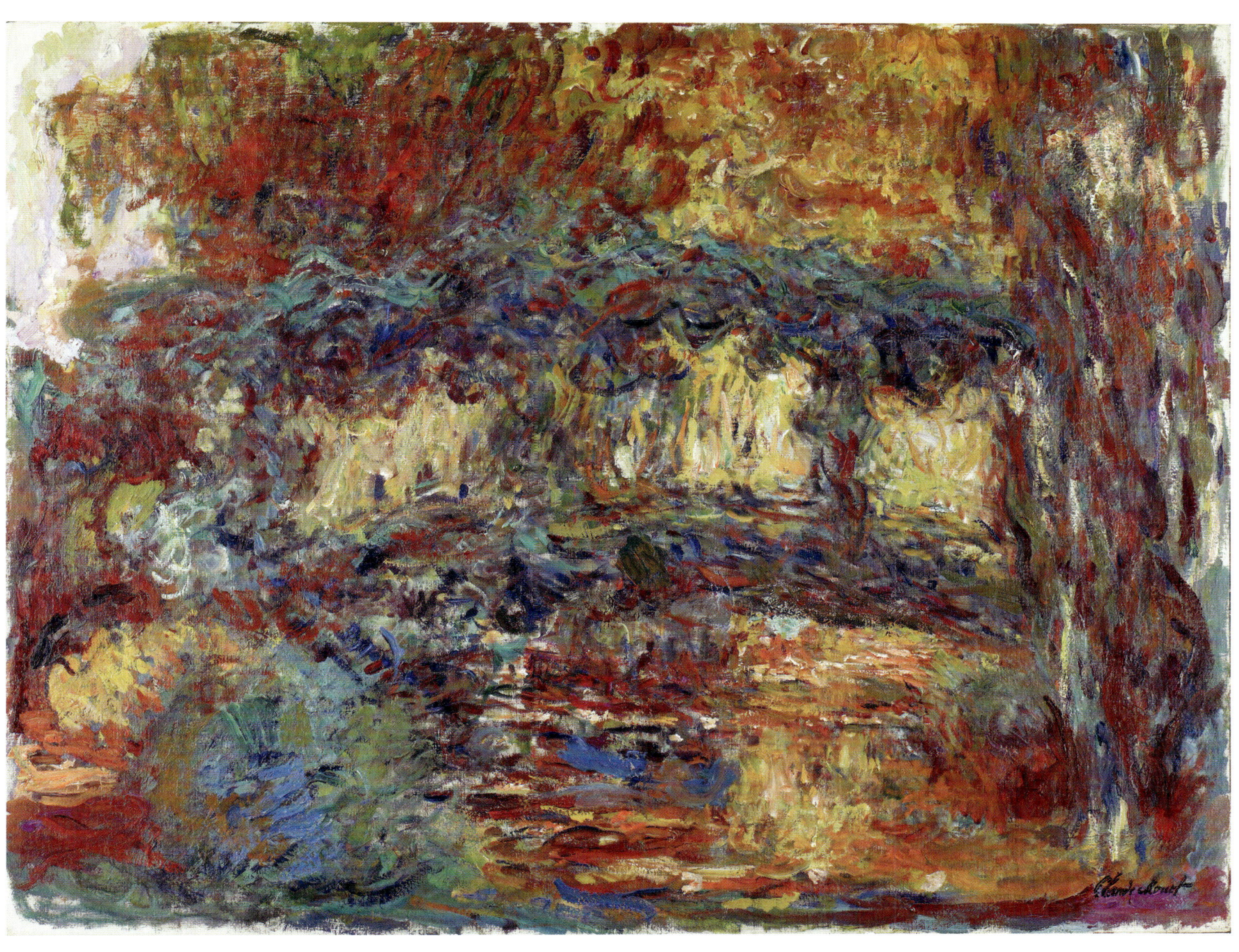

Cat. 36. *The Japanese Bridge*, c. 1923–25. Minneapolis Institute of Art

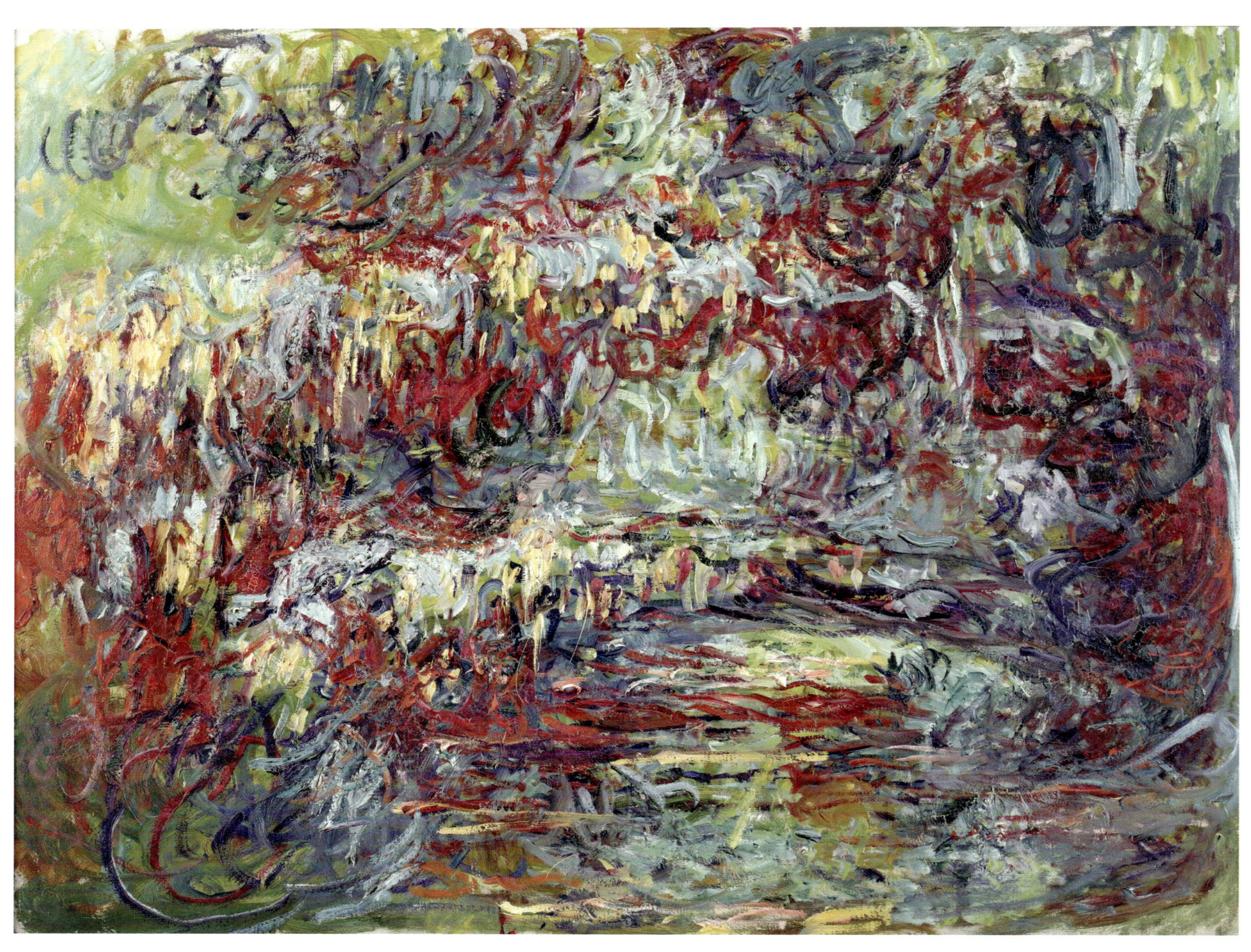

Cat. 37. *The Japanese Bridge*, 1918–24. Musée Marmottan Monet, Paris

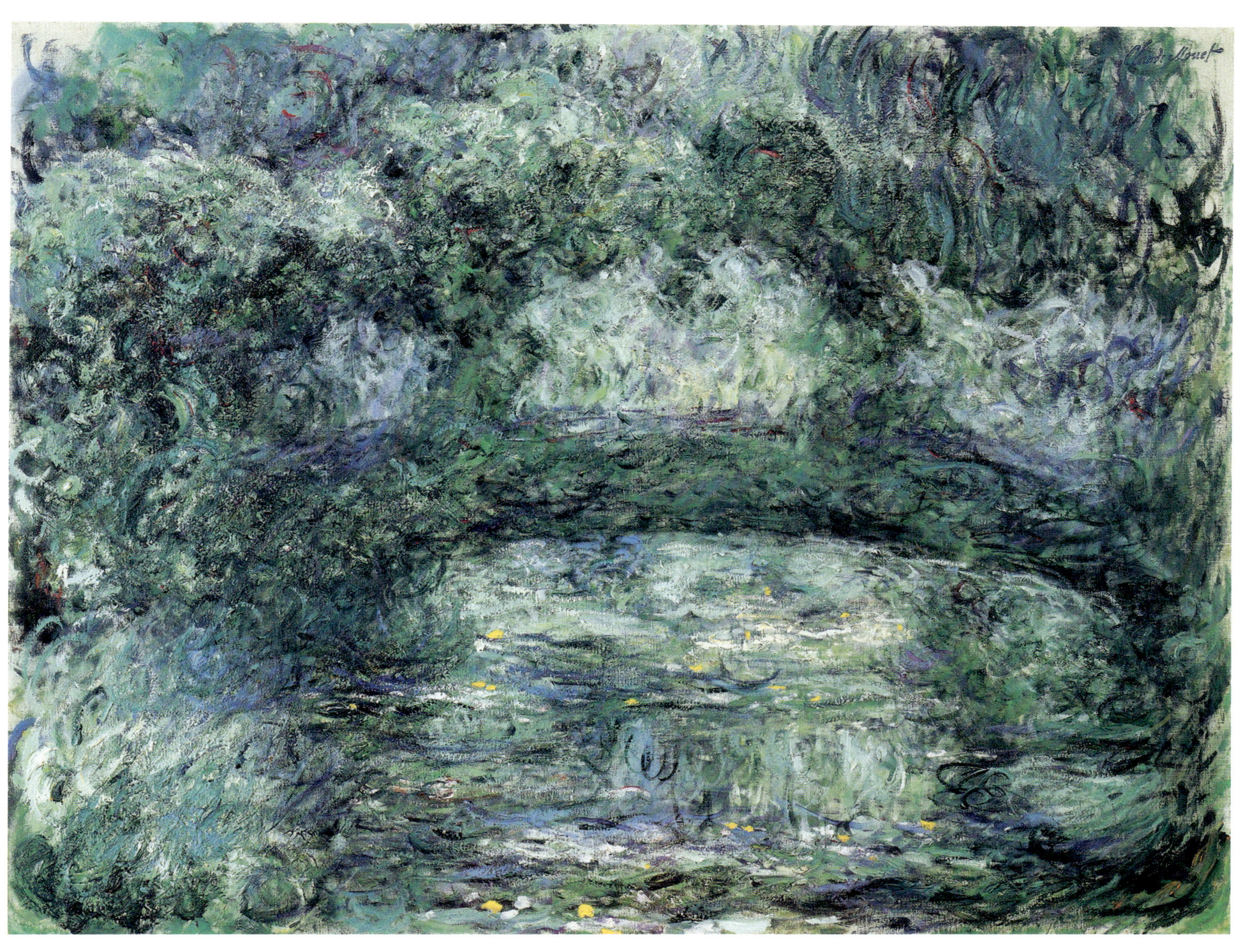

Cat. 38. *The Japanese Bridge*, 1918–24. Fondation Beyeler, Basel, Switzerland

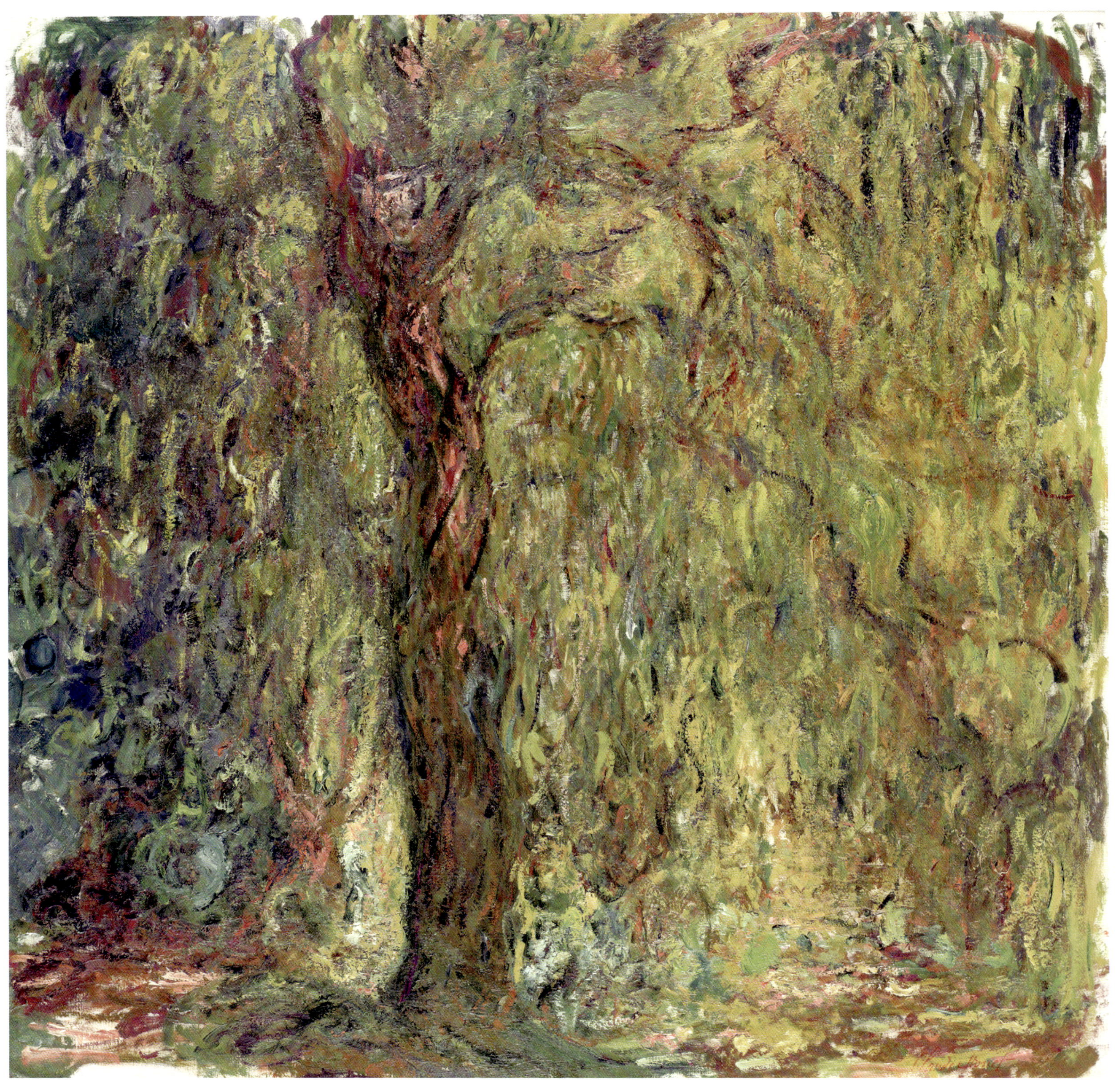

Cat. 39. *Weeping Willow*, 1918–19. Musée Marmottan Monet, Paris

In 1918, the war that was being waged at the eastern front for nearly four years suddenly became more perilous for anyone living in Paris or the Île-de-France, as the German army broke through the Allied lines and fought westward, stopping only forty miles from Paris. Cannons shot shells into the city over that distance, and airplanes dropped bombs onto Paris streets. The atelier and the collection of Edgar Degas, who had died in the previous year, was being sold at auction; shelling interrupted the bidding, with buyers fleeing the sales room.[1] Bombs fell perilously close to the Durand-Ruel gallery, where many canvases by Monet (not to mention by other Impressionists) were in store.

The painter stayed at Giverny throughout the war, accompanied only by his stepdaughter (and daughter-in-law) Blanche Hoschedé Monet. The rest of his extended family had moved away from the zone that was considered at risk. Had the German army ever reached the city, this would certainly have included any town along the River Seine to the west, including Giverny.

Paradoxically, the summer of 1918 was one of the most fertile periods in the late life of Monet. Inspiration and energy seem to have caught hold of the seventy-seven-year-old painter, and over the course of just a few months he had begun several series that would continue to be perfected over the autumn. In addition to the two meter *Water-Lily Ponds* (see cats. 23–27), these included the early works in his second, late series of views of the Japanese bridge (see cats. 32–38) and an extraordinary series of ten canvases devoted to an entirely new theme, the *Weeping Willow*. Six of these are gathered together here.

The weeping willow trees were an important feature of the water garden from its beginnings. In his 1909 letter to Roger-Marx, Monet characterized the trees by saying that they were "dominated by poplars and willows, including several weeping willows."[2] In August 1912 a "horrible cyclone" had struck the garden. "My weeping willows, of which I was so proud, are pillaged, their branches stripped away; the most beautiful of them wrecked," he wrote.[3] Their trunks and branches punctuated one of the first of the *Grandes Décorations* to be completed (see fig. 72) And of course their branches, in reflection, became the perfect foil for the floating water lilies, establishing the vertical axis in most of his paintings and reminding the viewer that the horizon line was well beyond the upper limit of the pictorial space.

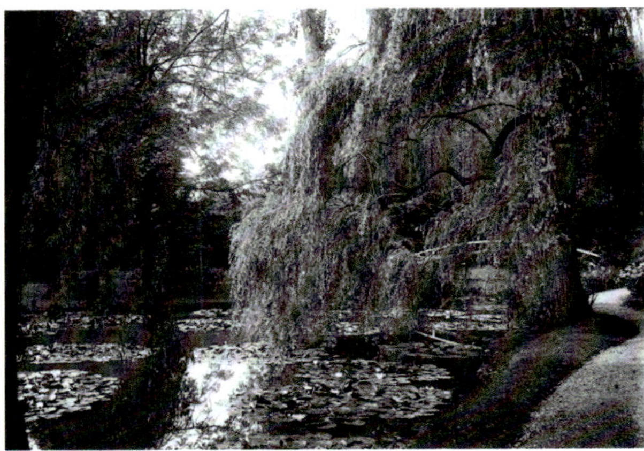

Fig 173. The water-lily pond with weeping willow, Giverny. Photograph Collection Georges Truffaut. Courtesy Société Clause

In the new series, however, the willow became the entire subject of the composition. The motif must be the enormous willow that stood on the north shore of the pond, one of two that rose to the left as the visitor entered the garden gate. A photograph taken before the trellis was added to the Japanese bridge shows the subject tree at right and the trunk of a second willow at extreme left (fig. 173). Setting his easel between the gate and the principal motif, Monet saw what was a one-sided tree, almost all its branches spreading craggily out over the water and few extending on the other side over the path. In each of the canvases from the Musée Marmottan Monet (cats. 39–41) and in the Kimbell Art Museum painting (cat. 44), the trunk of the second willow can be spied along the pathway that Monet shows to the left of the principal trunk. Two other canvases (cats. 42 and 43) shift the trunk of the nearer willow to the left margin of the picture space, masking the second tree from view.

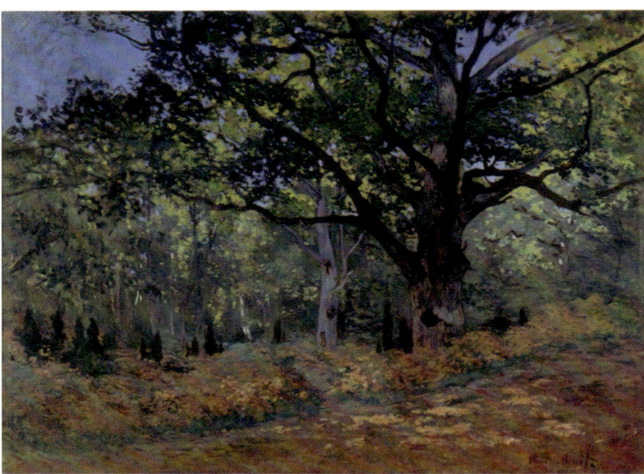

Fig. 174. Claude Monet, *The Bodmer Oak, Fontainebleau*, 1865. Oil on canvas, 37 7/8 x 50 7/8 in. (96.2 x 129.2 cm). The Metropolitan Museum of Art, New York. Gift of Sam Salz and bequest of Julia W. Emmons, by exchange, 1964, 64.210

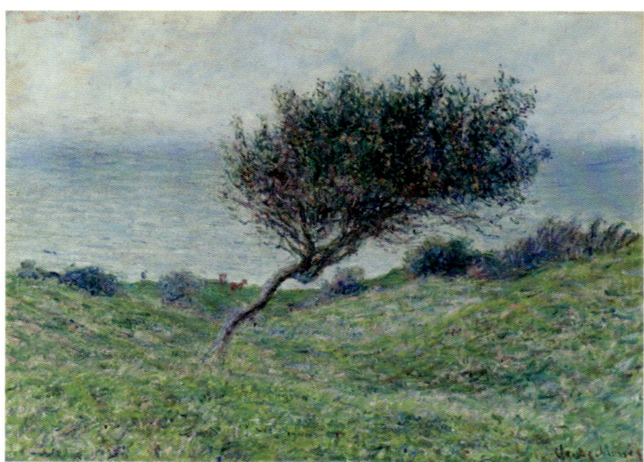

Fig. 175. Claude Monet, *Seacoast at Trouville*, 1881. Oil on canvas, 23 7/8 x 32 in. (60.7 x 81.3 cm). Museum of Fine Arts, Boston. The John Pickering Lyman Collection. Gift of Miss Theodora Lyman. 19.1314

It is impossible to know for certain the evolution of the series, but it is tempting to place the smaller of the canvases first, to be followed by the larger in the group (for instance, cats. 42 and 43). What is known for certain is that two of the canvases, the painting from the Columbus Museum of Art (cat. 42) and another in a private collection, were signed, dated 1918, and sold to the Galerie Bernheim-Jeune in December of the same year.[4] The others, as of early 1919, were in Monet's studio and may have been worked on at any time thereafter. An exception is the Kimbell Art Museum painting, which appears in a photograph taken about 1921, in a frame leaning against an easel to Monet's left (see fig. 29). At some point, its empty corners were filled in by the artist, who signed the painting 1919 and, in 1922, sold the painting to the Japanese collector Baron Matsukata.[5]

The weeping willow—in French, *saule pleureur*—has been used in gardens since its importation from the China in the eighteenth century. In the nineteenth century, the trees became associated with mourning and were often planted in cemeteries. As Ross King has recently shown, this association was current in Monet's culture, whether in the fanciful anthropomorphic studies of plants by the caricaturist Jean-Jacques Grandville, the Romantic verse of Alfred de Musset, or in the poetry of Monet's own friends.[6] That Monet should turn to a subject of mourning in 1918, four years into a conflict that even then showed little sign of coming to a close, was entirely appropriate. When Monet sent his second son to the army in 1914, he was still mourning the death of his first born in the months before war began. Since then, the enormous loss of life on all sides had reached numbers unprecedented in the history of war. In the past, Monet's references to current events, though certainly many, had never been overt; by taking up a theme in which weeping was forever associated, he was making a overt statement of sympathy and sorrow.

As Paul Tucker has proposed, he may also have been making a very personal statement, seeing in the willow tree a personification of himself, both as weathered artist and as mourner.[7] Assigning personality to specific trees had been a trope in French painting of the Generation of 1830—Corot had painted, for example, a famous tree in the Forest of Fontainebleau that was commonly known as "Le Rageur," the raging one, because it told "the story of the assaults it has withstood from wind and lightning."[8] Among Monet's early masterpieces is the 1865 *Bodmer Oak* (fig. 174), a mighty tree standing in the forest that had been given the name of Karl Bodmer, one of the painters who most portrayed Fontainebleau, and particularly this tree. In the 1880s, whether on the coasts of Normandy, at Antibes, or in the valley of the Creuse, Monet had from time to time singled out a tree for special attention. In the view of a *Seacoast at Trouville*, for example, a lone tree dominates the composition as if it were sitting for a portrait; like the artist, it is buffeted by the coastal winds and rains, suffering them, however, without the complaints the painter so often voiced (fig. 175). At the end of 1918, having turned seventy-eight, Monet was only starting to complain in earnest about his advancing age, beginning to feel himself, like the willow tree, time-worn and increasingly bowed with care.

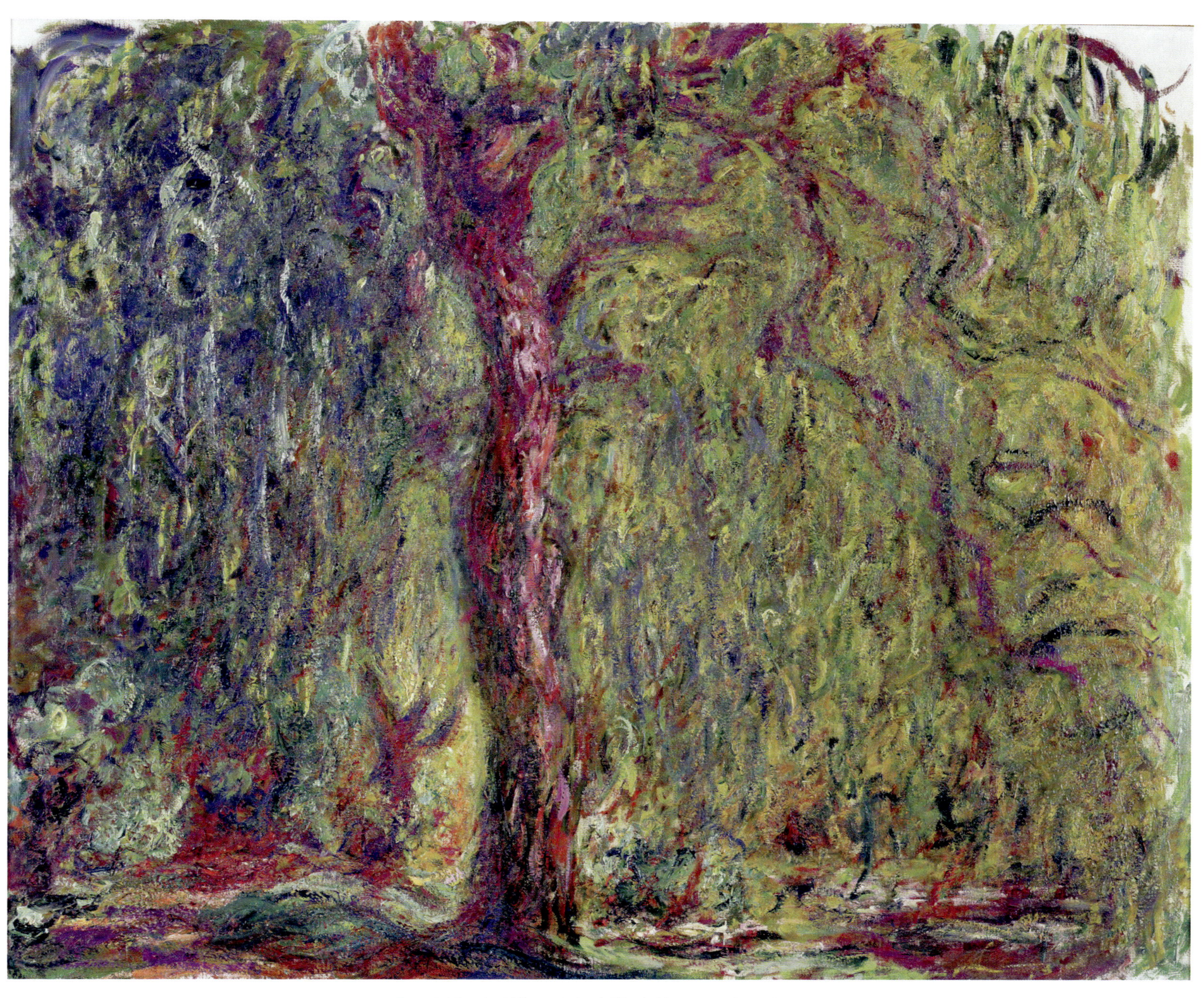

Cat. 40. *Weeping Willow*, 1918–19. Musée Marmottan Monet, Paris

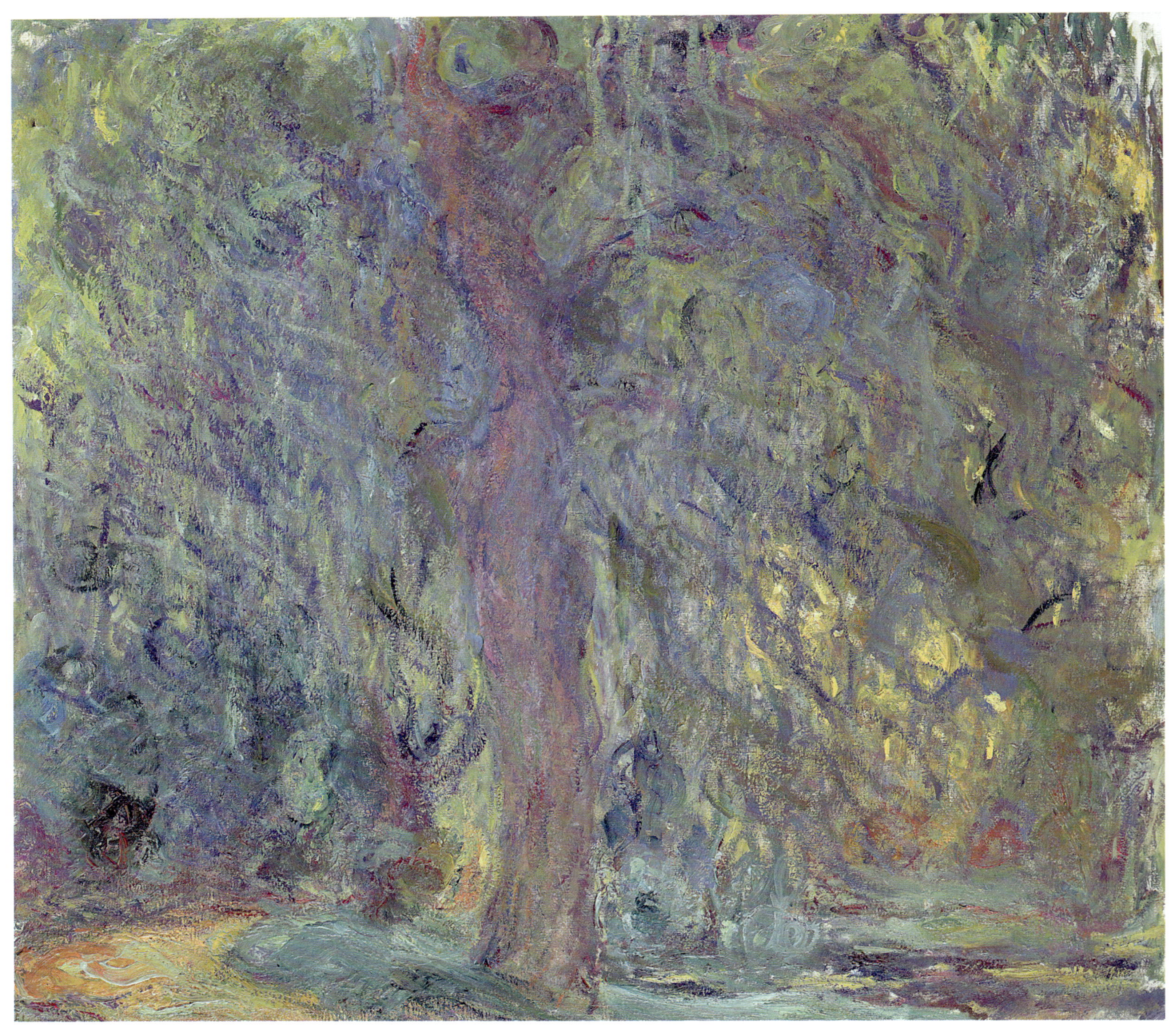

Cat. 41. *Weeping Willow*, 1918–19. Musée Marmottan Monet, Paris

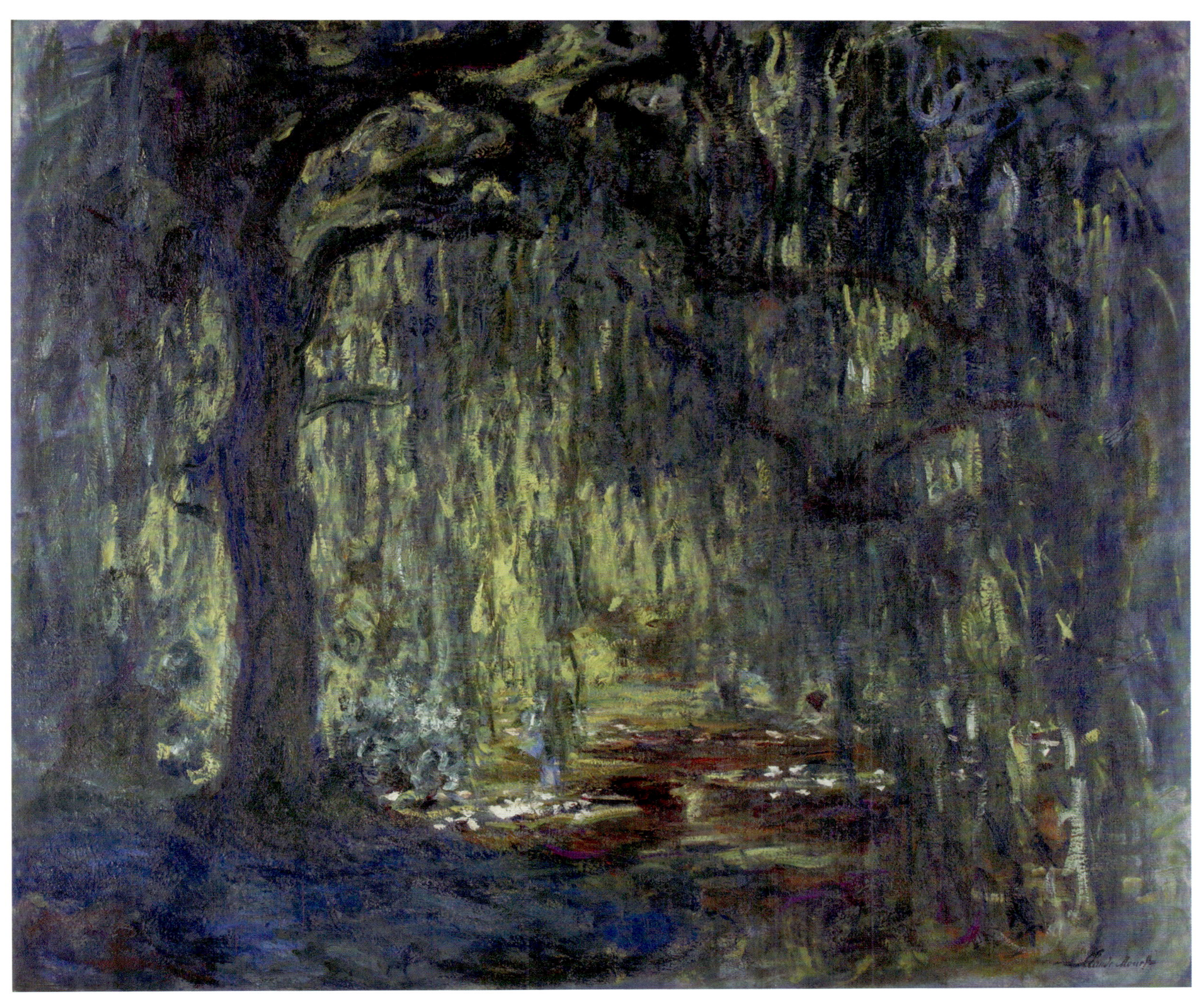

Cat. 42. *Weeping Willow*, 1918. Private collection, London

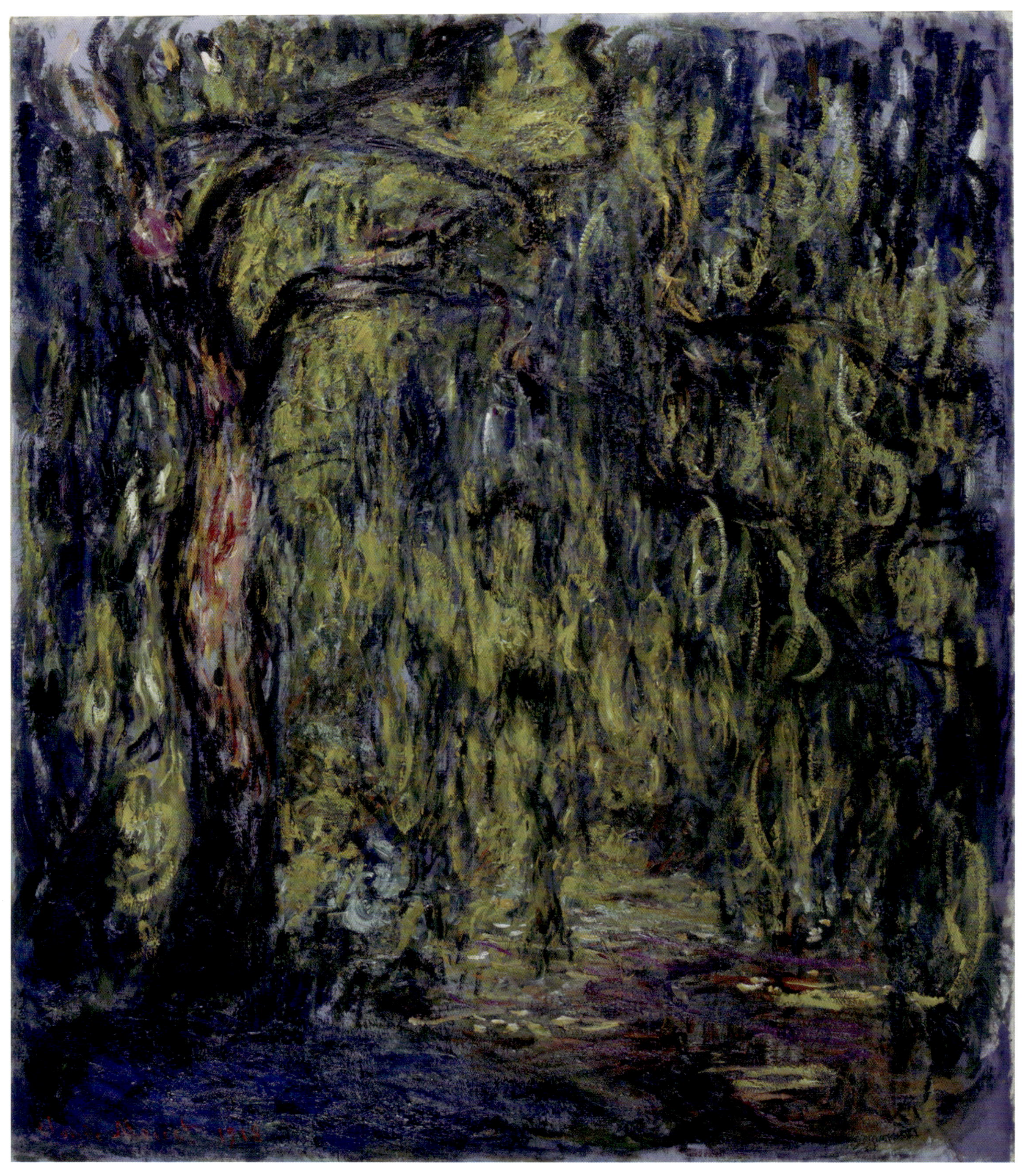

Cat. 43. *Weeping Willow*, 1918. Columbus Museum of Art, Ohio

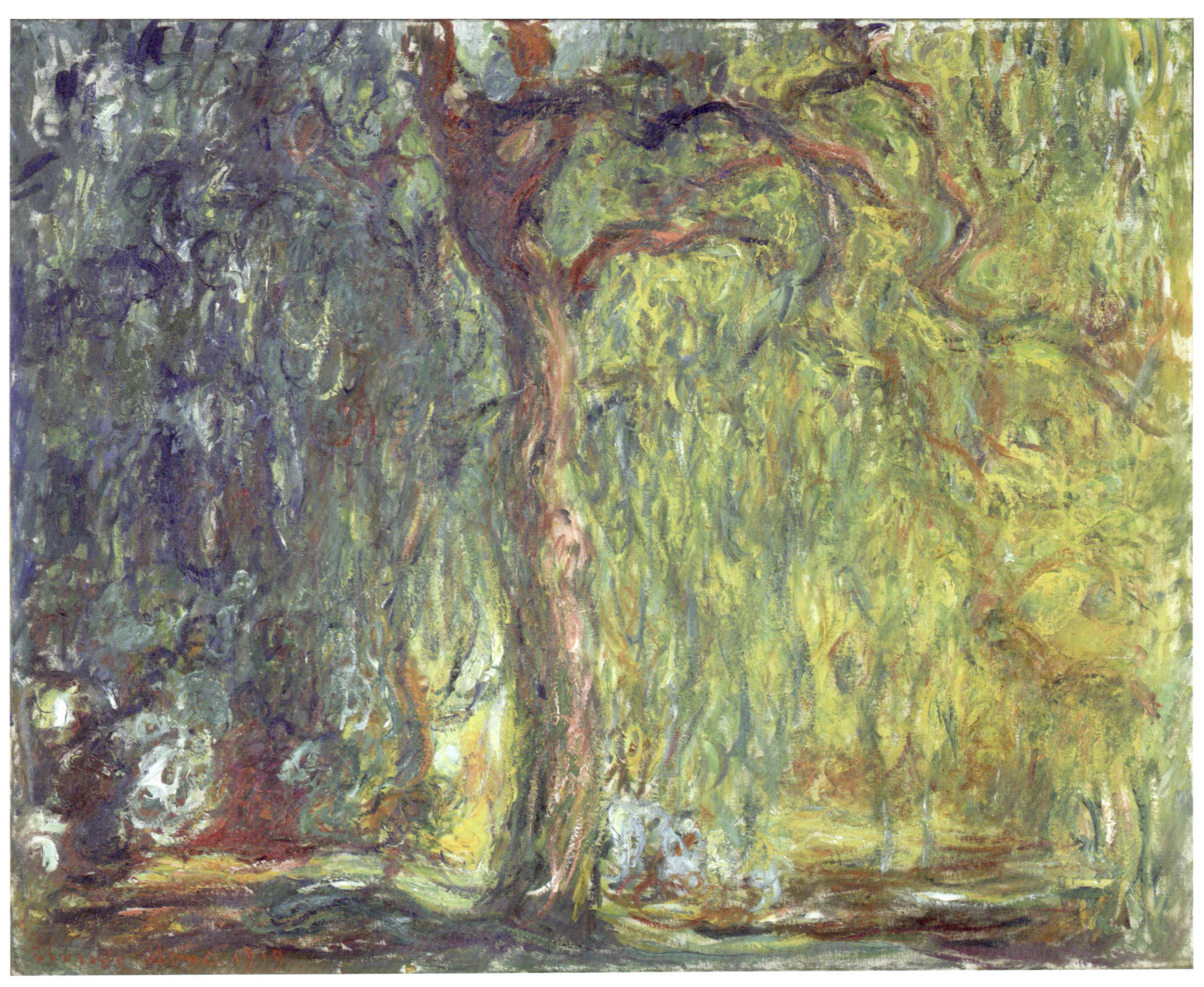

Cat. 44. *Weeping Willow*, 1918–19. Kimbell Art Museum, Fort Worth

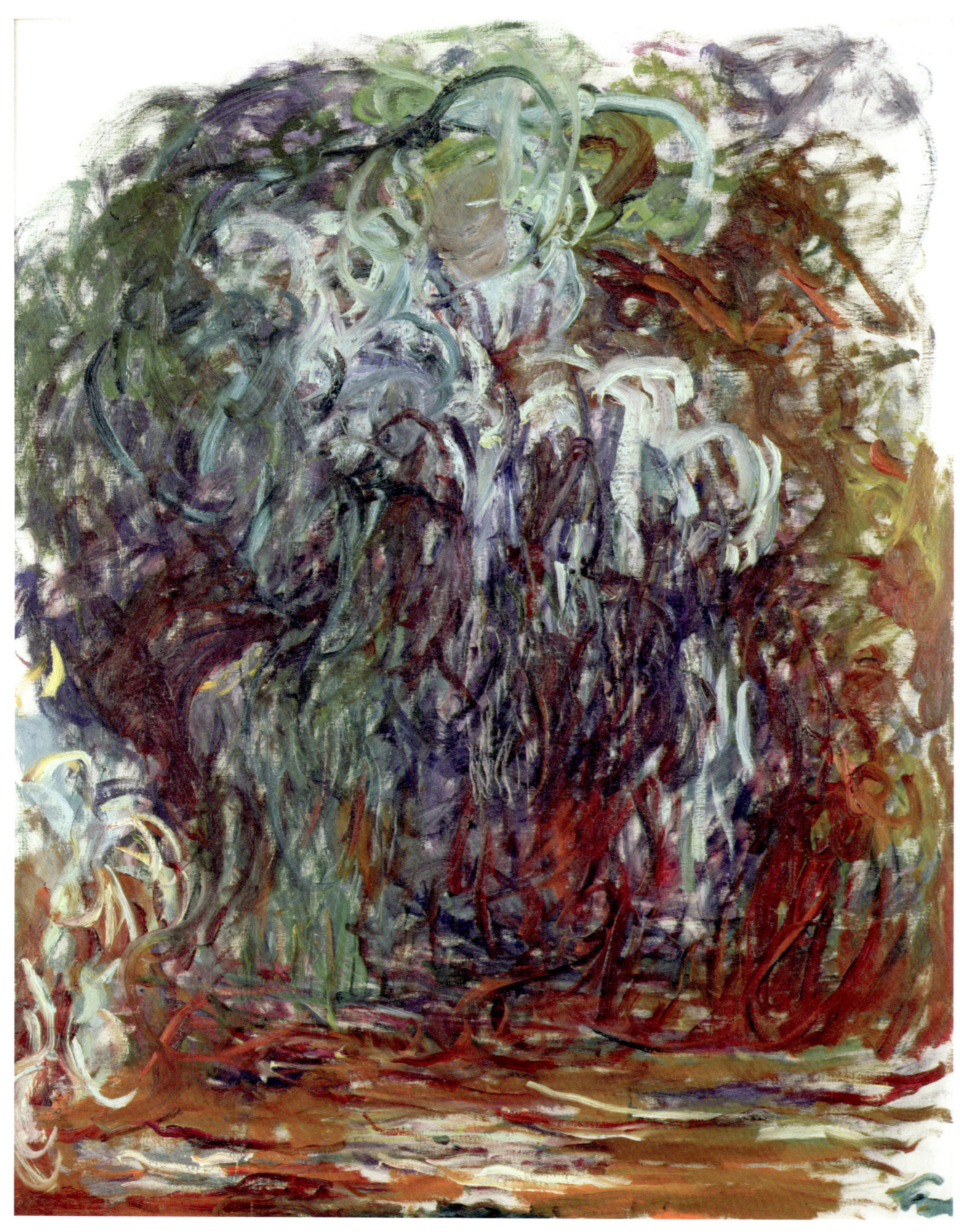

Cat. 45. *Weeping Willow*, 1921–22. Musée Marmottan Monet, Paris

On his visit to Monet's studio in 1920, for the painter's eightieth birthday, the Duc de Trévise spied some "vast and disconcerting studies" consisting of "skeins of related hues that no other eye could have untangled, bizarre assortments of bodiless wools."[1] It is likely that he was referring to a variety of paintings, including the *Japanese Bridge* series (cats. 32–38) and the group showing the *Path Under the Rose Arches* (cats. 47 and 48). But the image of tangled skeins of colored wool seems particularly appropriate to three canvases that show the branches of a weeping willow tree.

In this group Monet focused on just the branches of the tree, letting virtually every other point of reference back away from the central motif or sink into the shadows. In each canvas, a tuft of grasses anchors the left-hand corner, with the slightest hint of a tree trunk in shadow beyond; in each, a series of parallel lines of contrasting tones suggests the reflective surface of the water; in each, a series of darker strokes at upper left and right suggests more distant foliage. But the principal and central subject is the welter of branches, rendered in related but often unnatural hues.

The canvas at the Musée Marmottan (cat. 45) is the most naturalistic of the three, as the painter used varying tones of green and blue, applied in long, decisive strokes, to describe the swaying branches. This canvas is also the most thinly painted, retaining large areas of bare white ground. A second version at the Musée d'Orsay (cat. 46) is painted on a canvas that had been recycled by the artist. It had originally been used 90 degrees to the right, to sketch the trunk of a weeping willow, placed in roughly the same position as the trees in the Marmottan and Kimbell paintings; the canvas is the same size as cat. 41. A horizontal line across the leaves shows in reproduction where the trunk lies beneath, and the texture of the now-horizontal branches can be perceived here and there with the naked eye. In the Orsay painting, as in one in a private collection (fig. 176), Monet chose to use intense, saturated hues not only to paint the brilliant reflections on the leaves and the water but also in the shadows, bringing mysterious infiltrated color into the deepest recesses of the pictorial space.

These paintings, because they are few in number and have been, relatively speaking, so little exhibited, are among the most surprising to contemporary audiences. Inevitably viewers new to seeing them think of abstract painting of the twentieth century. It is tempting to see in Monet's swirling "skeins" of paint the visual ancestors of the flying pigments that, layered on each other, made up the complex surfaces

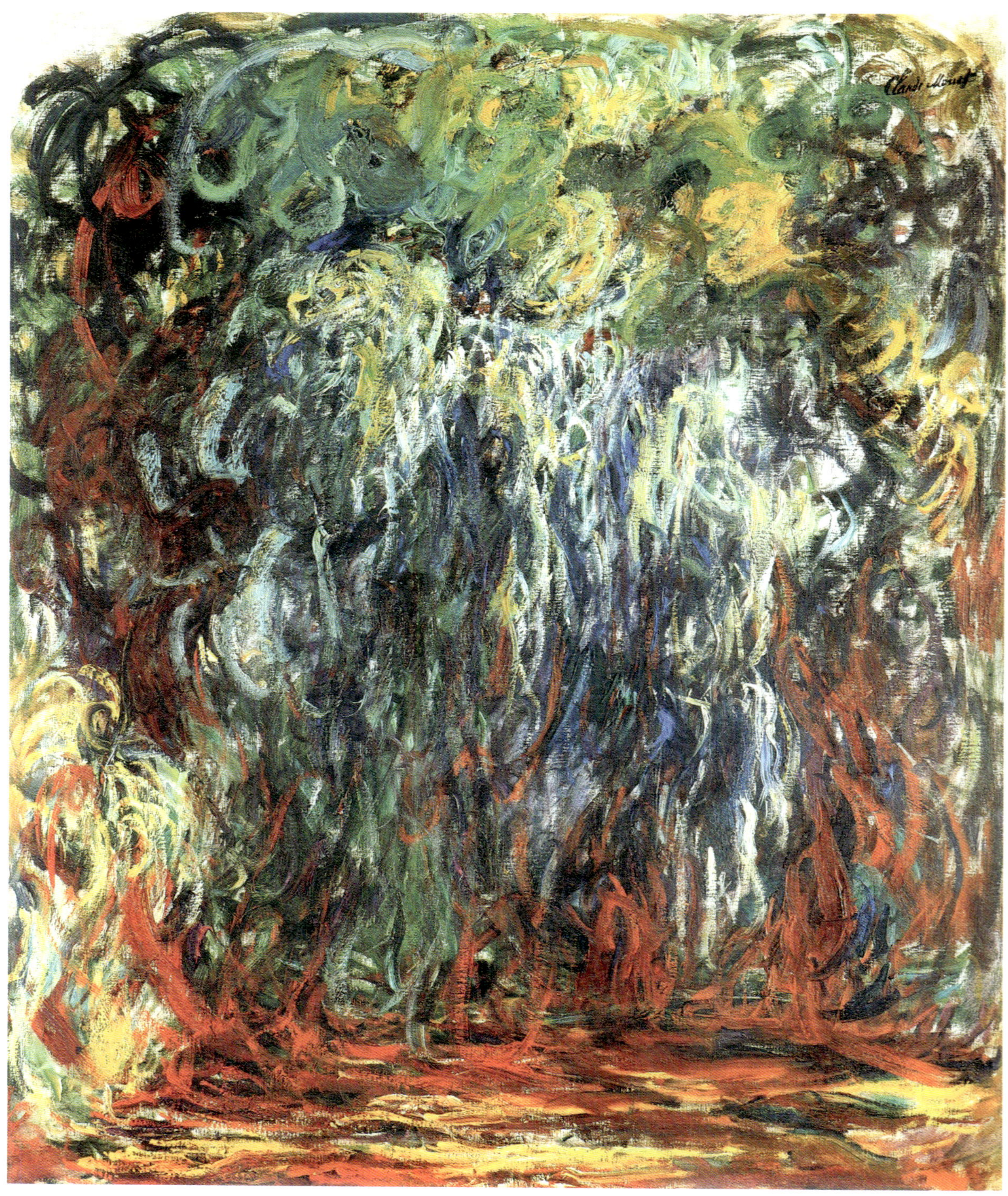

Fig. 176. Claude Monet, *Weeping Willow*, 1918–20. Oil on canvas, 47 1/4 x 39 1/2 in. (120 x 100 cm). Galerie Larock-Granoff, Paris

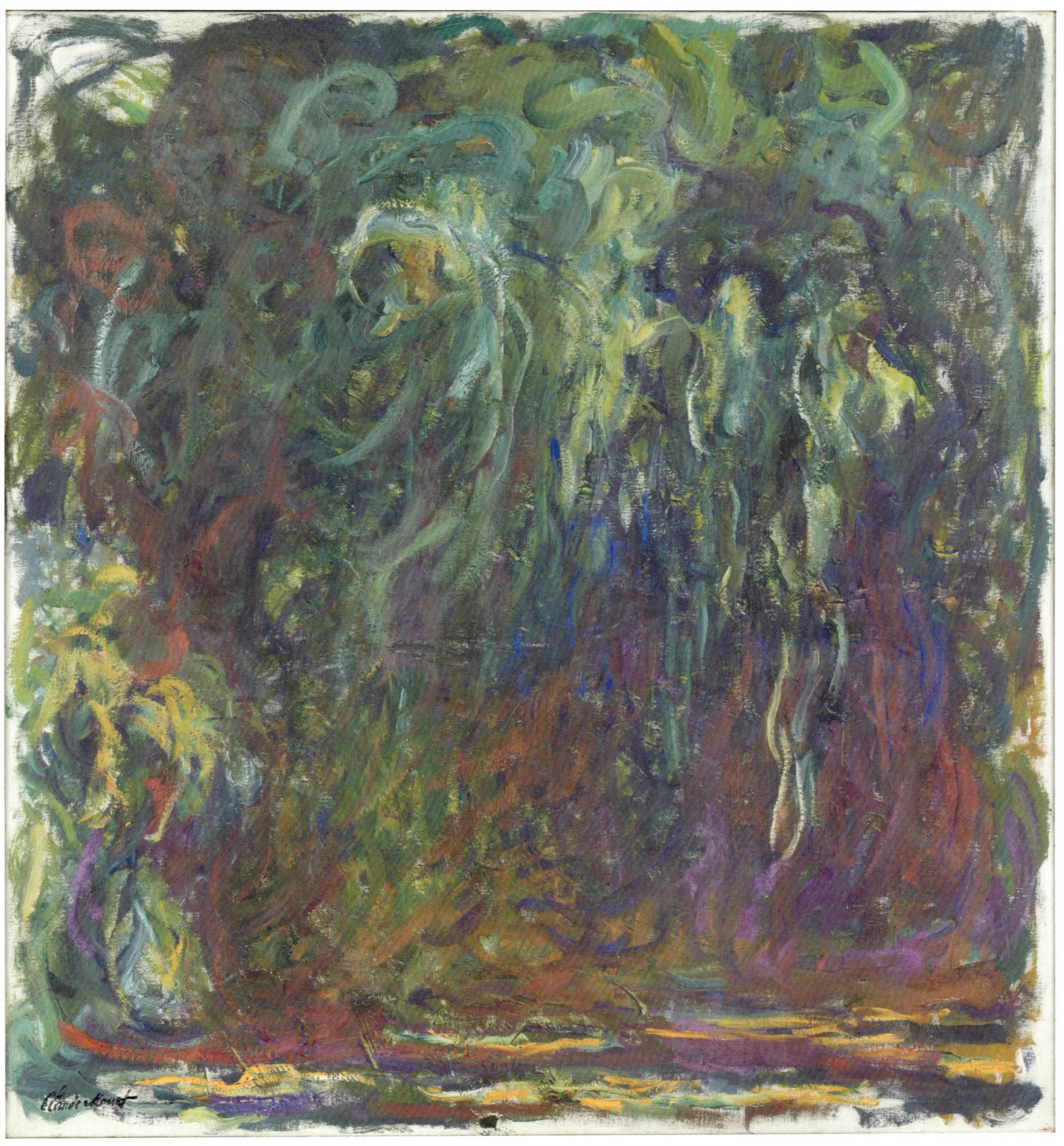

Cat. 46. *Weeping Willow*, 1920–22. Musée d'Orsay, Paris

Fig. 177. Clyfford Still, *PH-255*, 1955. Oil on canvas, 69 x 93 1/2 in. (175.3 x 237.5 cm). Clyfford Still Museum, Denver. © Clyfford Still/ARS, NY

of Jackson Pollock's drip paintings. In their insistent, jagged verticality they remind modern audiences of the impenetrable spaces of Clyfford Still's abstract paintings of the 1950s (fig. 177). But these resemblances are only superficial: neither Pollock nor Still could ever have seen one of these paintings. One painter, though, Joan Mitchell, took up residence in the orbit of Monet, settling in Vétheuil, Monet's home before he moved to Giverny, in 1967, little more than forty years after the older painter's death. Working indoors rather than *en plein air*, and notoriously unwilling to connect her own work with Monet's, Mitchell grumbled "that no one would mention his name to her if it weren't for the 'unfortunate coincidence' of her residing on avenue Claude Monet and gazing out on the same Seine vista that he himself beheld a century earlier."[2] But Mitchell was connected through friendship to members of Monet's family, and was certainly aware of the paintings that had been bequeathed to the Académie des Beaux-Art by the artist's son Michel in 1970. And by the time she had completed her 1990 diptych *Taillade,* Monet's garden at Giverny had been restored and open to the public for a decade (fig. 178).

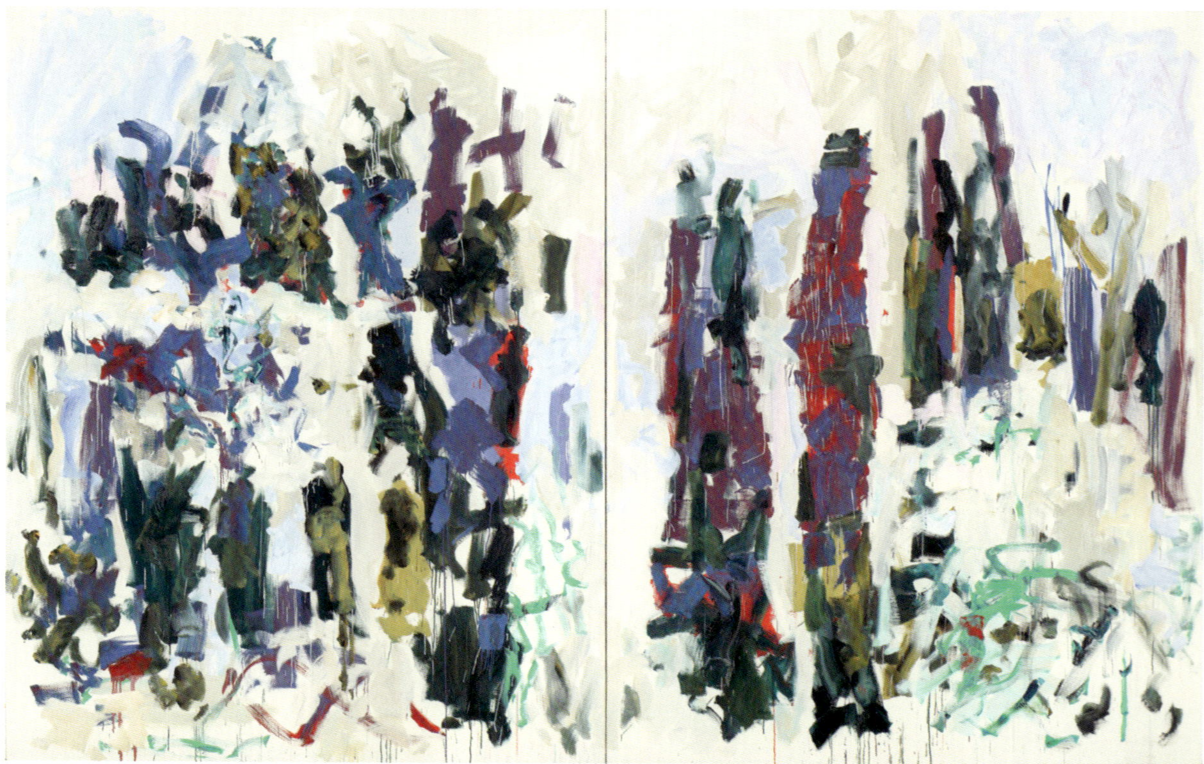

Fig. 178. Joan Mitchell, *Taillade*, 1990. Oil on canvas, 102 1/4 x 158 in. (259.7 x 401.3 cm). Museum of Modern Art, New York. Gift of Galerie Jean Fournier, Enid A. Haupt Fund, and Helen Acheson Bequest (by exchange), 365.1990.a-b. © Estate of Joan Mitchell

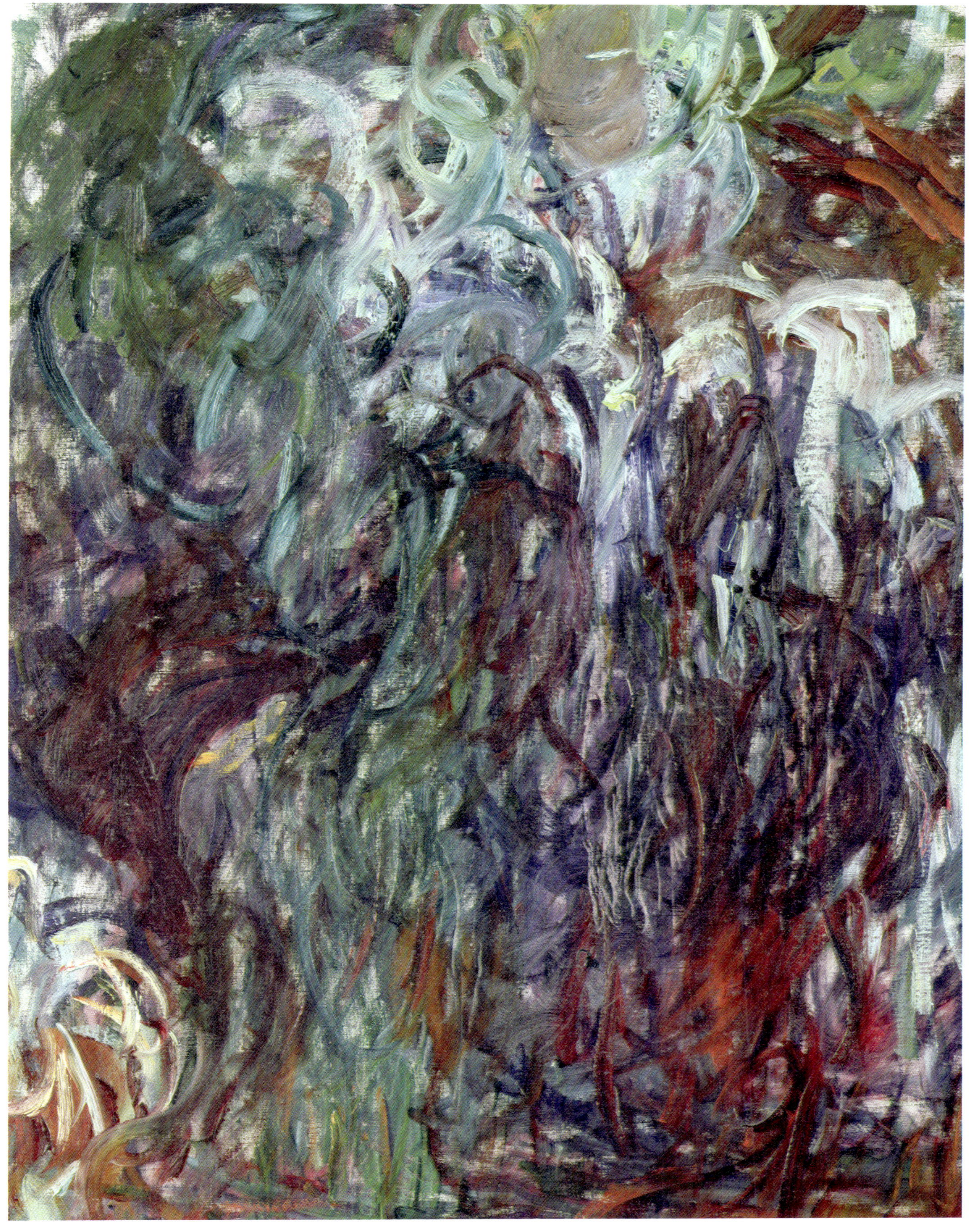

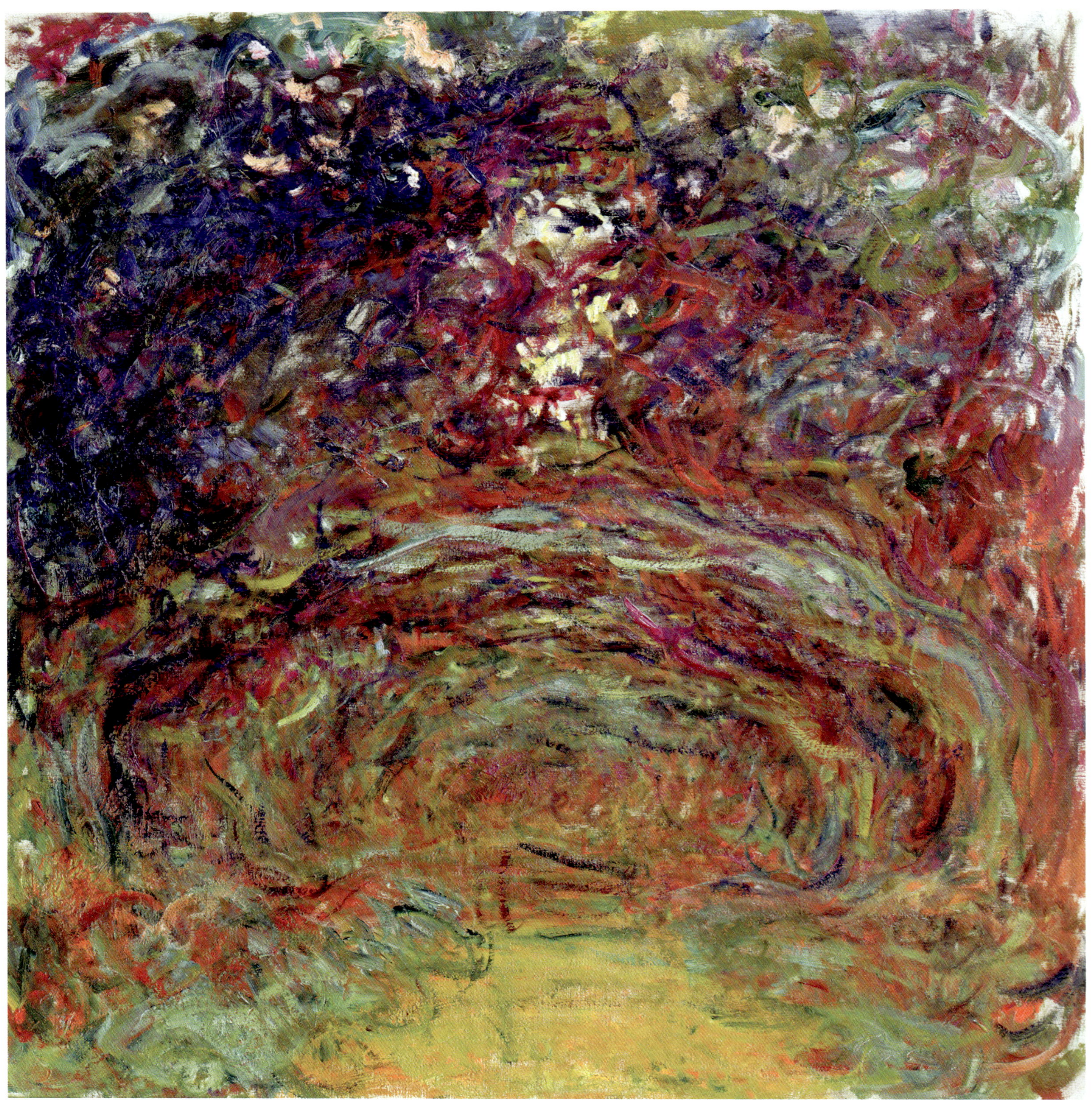

Cat. 47. *Path under the Rose Arches, Giverny*, 1920–22. Musée Marmottan Monet, Paris

One of the features that present-day visitors to the *Clos Normand* of Monet's house in Giverny first notice is the succession of metal arches that span the gravel path linking the house with the gate of the property giving onto the road. These were put in place to support climbing roses in the first decade of the century—though they do not appear in the first group of pictures the artist painted looking north towards the house from a position near the end of the path. In *A Pathway in Monet's Garden, Giverny*, 1902, the sunlit facade of the house is spied in the distance, its pink stucco and contrasting shutters covered with green vines (fig. 179). The fir trees on either side of the path close their branches together to block any view of the sky above, and as a result the light on the path is dappled, the shadows on the pink gravel glowing with tints borrowed from the flowers that line the path.

Though a pair of large trees stand at the house end of the allée nowadays, the fir trees are no longer there; they were mostly cut down during Monet's lifetime. While some photographs of the pathway show arches and tree trunks in alternation (fig. 180), the latter are no longer visible in photographs taken somewhat later—though specialists on the garden have not reached a consensus on when.[1]

Surely the trees—or at least several of the ones that stood at the northernmost end of the path—must have been still in place when Monet painted a second, late series of seven pictures of this view, in which the arches are placed against a deep and dark background that reaches to the top of the pictorial frame. In both the examples exhibited here, patches of lighter tone suggest the sky shining between two masses of foliage. In the first, the golden yellow pathway leads up to a series of abbreviated parallel lines that stand in for the steps and porch of the house; in the second, bands of orange and purple alternate to describe light falling from above and shadows cast by the arbors. The first painting is fluid, smooth, a mass of strokes—the "skeins of related hues that no other eye could have untangled" mentioned by Trévise. The second painting, by contrast, is more densely worked, with bold touches of coral pink indicating not only the pathway but also the flowers blooming above.

In their overall composition, with parallel arched shapes fitted into a relatively square format, as well as in their tangled strands of vines—and brushstrokes—the views of the *Path under the Rose Arches* closely resemble the paintings of the Japanese bridge (cats. 32–38). As Wildenstein has noted, these may be the pictures that Joseph Durand-Ruel was referring to when he wrote, in 1922, that Monet "has painted a large number of canvases in his garden; the motifs are similar, with a few modifications, to those which we already know, they are less brutal than his *Décorations*, but they are quite dark and sad."[2] Their

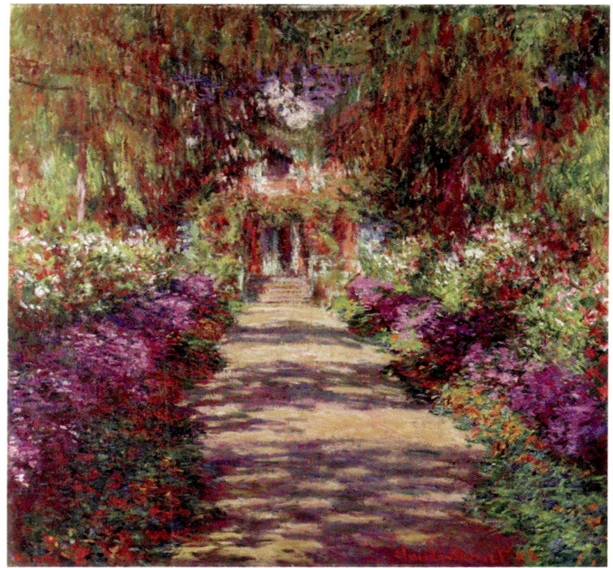

Fig. 179. Claude Monet, *A Pathway in Monet's Garden, Giverny*, 1902. Oil on canvas, 35 x 36 1/4 in. (89 x 92 cm). Oterreichische Galerie Belvedere, Vienna, Austria

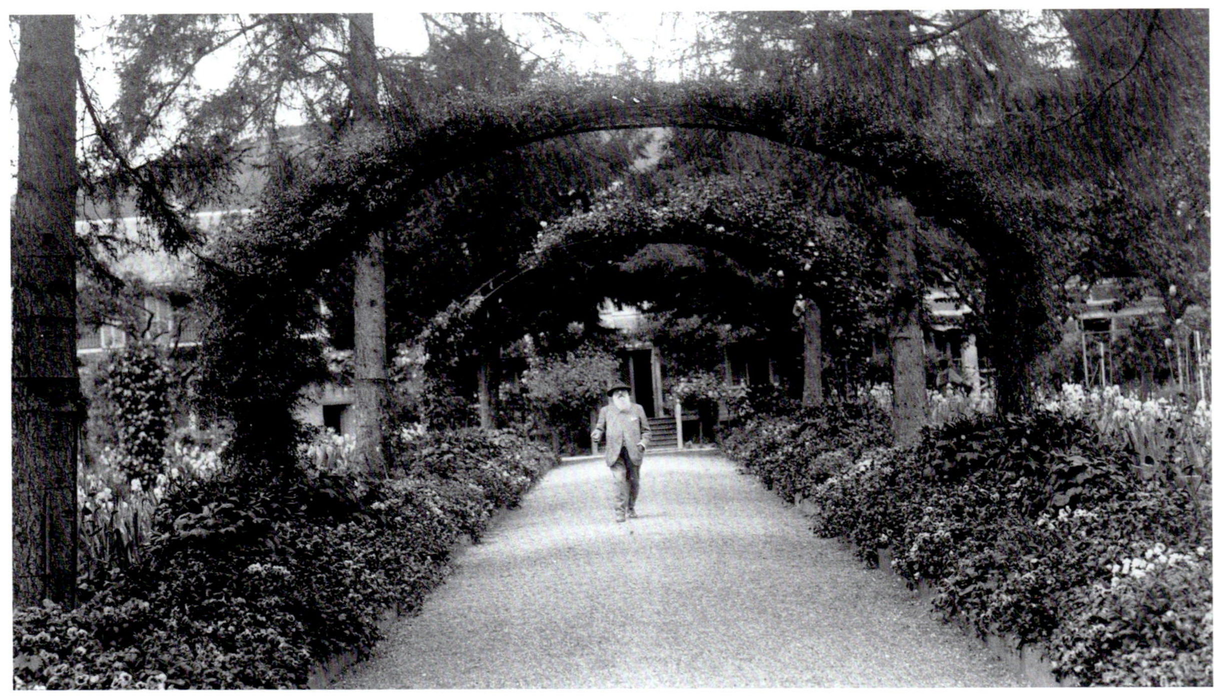

Fig. 180. Claude Monet under the arch of roses, Giverny

suggestion of a pathway to nothingness, the approach to an abyss, makes them nearly a century later remain the most challenging of Monet's late easel paintings.

In recent years, the photographer Abelardo Morell, known for his contemporary experimentation with the idea of the *camera obscura*, has created works in a series, *After Monet*. Balancing the pursuit celebrated views with a method that distorts the processes of plein-air painting, the artist uses a view-finder mounted atop a tent to project the image of one of Monet's sites onto the very ground where the artist must have stood to paint the view in his own time, and photographing that projection. One of the photographs (fig. 181) records on the gravel of the path in the *Clos Normand* the view of the house seen through the rose arches; something of the broken patterns established by Monet's daubing brush are repeated in the texture of the path itself. Minus the consciousness of Monet's infirmity, the view of a modern tourist mecca nonetheless manages to touch on something of the denial of easy patterns of sight that parallel the challenges Monet faced in his time.

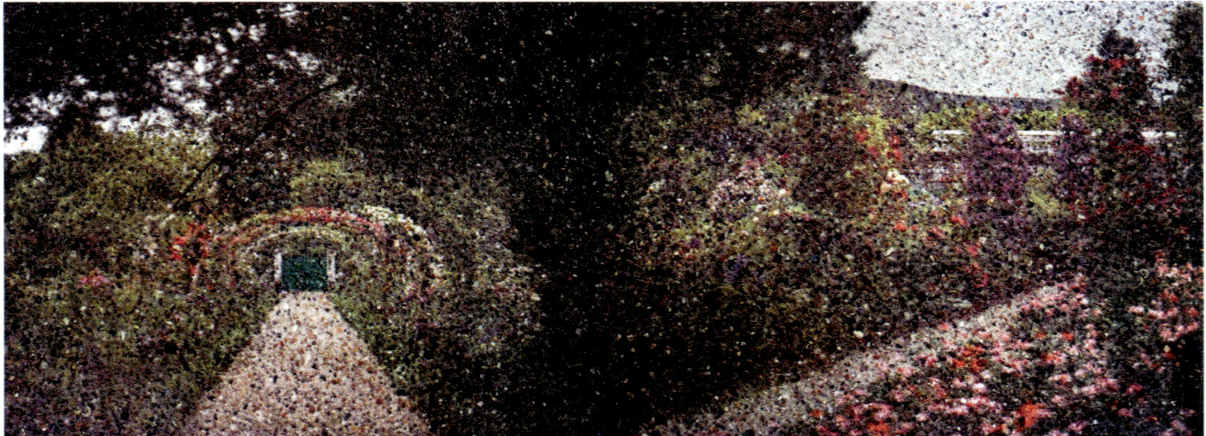

Fig. 181. Abelardo Morell, *Tent-Camera Image on Ground: Two Paths in Monet's Garden*, 2015. Photograph by Abelardo Morell. Courtesy of Edwynn Houk Gallery

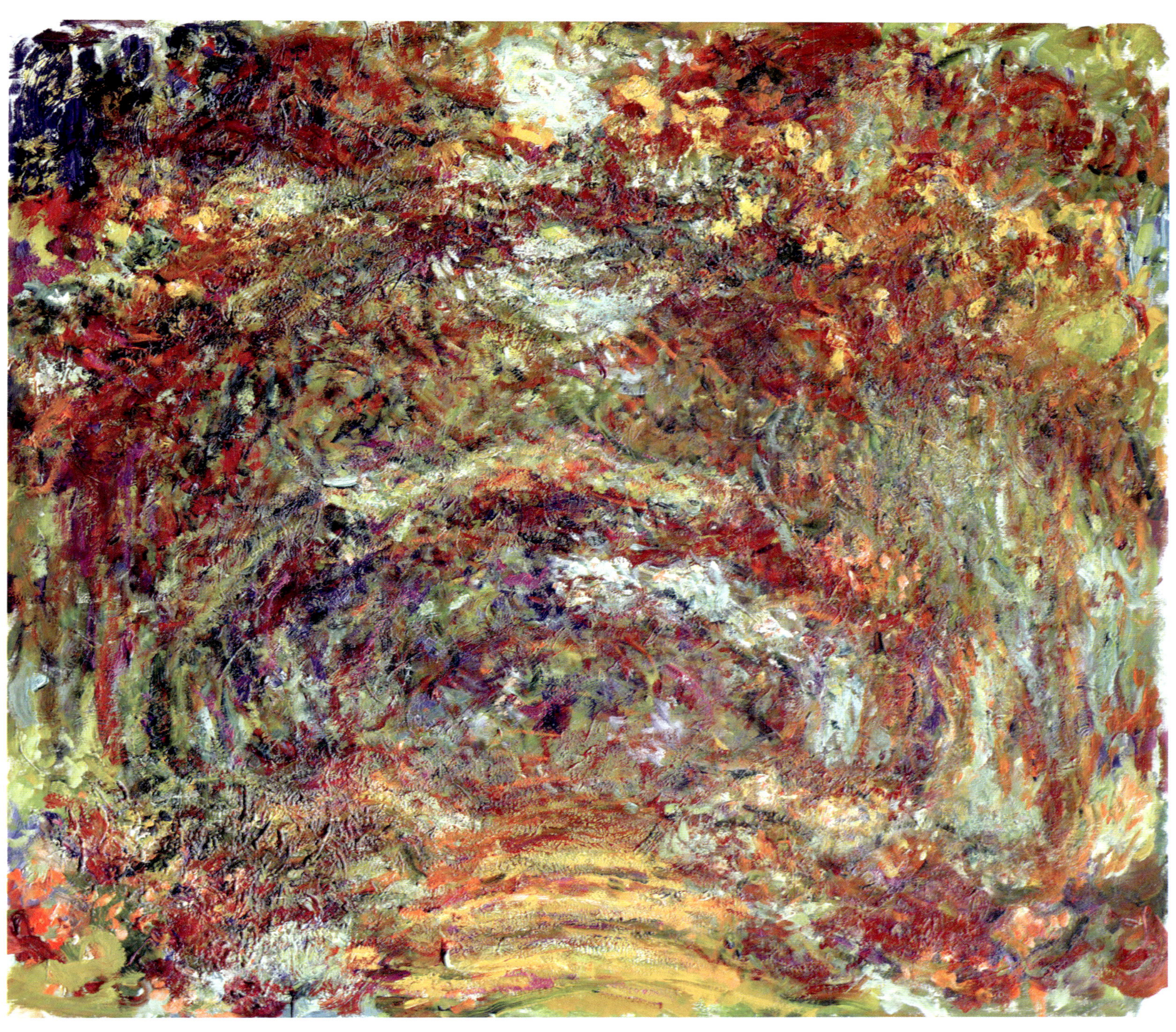

Cat. 48. *Path under the Rose Arches, Giverny*, 1920–22. Musée Marmottan Monet, Paris

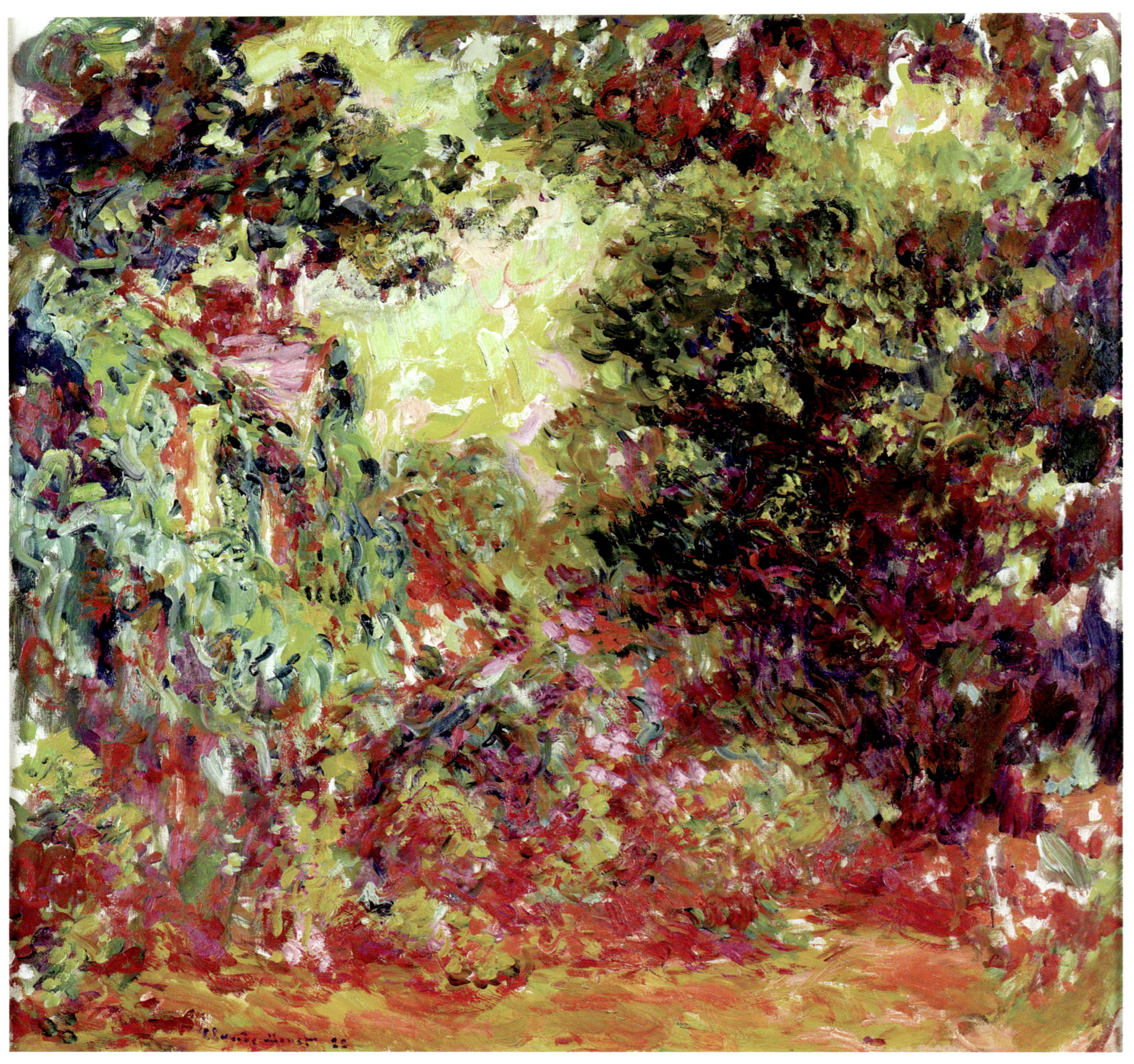

Cat. 49. *The Artist's House Seen from the Rose Garden*, 1922–24. Musée Marmottan Monet, Paris

Monet continued to adjust and perfect the *Grandes Décorations,* we know, into 1926. But the last of the easel paintings that he was to entertain were probably begun in 1924 and continued into 1925, and largely finished before the end of that summer. These consist of two groups of views of his house seen from the garden. One of these series was to number ten paintings in all, none of them progressing much past the stage of a laying in of a preliminary design, an *ébauche* in studio parlance. One of these is to be seen framed on the left wall of the late photograph of the studio-salon (see fig. 30). In some of these, the house is seen looking straight at its façade, rounded forms of blooming rose bushes framing the distant building. Others showed the house (or perhaps another structure) from a greater distance still—focusing on the outline of its roof.

Another group of paintings numbered eight in all, of which four are presented here. Comparison of them with an autochrome photograph of Monet in front of his house, generally thought to date from about 1922, may help clarify what these radical images represent. In the first of these paintings (cat. 49)—dominated by tones of bright and dark green, pink, gold, and bright and dark red—as in the photograph, the house itself is seen in perspective, the gable above the front porch and its peak covered in creeping vines. Chimneys are silhouetted against the sky, and at right a lush and rounded tree screens the front of the garden from the end of the path. Those elements, as outlines, are relatively easy to recognize; much more difficult to interpret, but for the aid of the photograph, is the mass of color in the lower half of the painting. By comparison, we can imagine that the grouping of pink dots at the center of the picture might be the individual blossoms of one of the standing roses that are in the bed behind where the painter is standing in the photograph. By extension, then, the other shapes in the foreground should be interpreted as part of the garden plan, heavily planted in annuals—geraniums, climbing nasturtiums, and the like.

This painting is the only one of the nearly twenty late views of Monet's house to be signed. It is inscribed, in very small, rather delicate letters, *Claude Monet 22* at the lower left. While Wildenstein has accepted this date at face value, it can also be argued that the paintings signed in this rather tentative way—some of them dating back to the 1870s—were not signed when they were completed but instead at a later date, sometimes much later. Nothing can prove for certain that the date is incorrect, but it might be better to look on it as a *terminus post quem* rather than the year in which the series was finished.

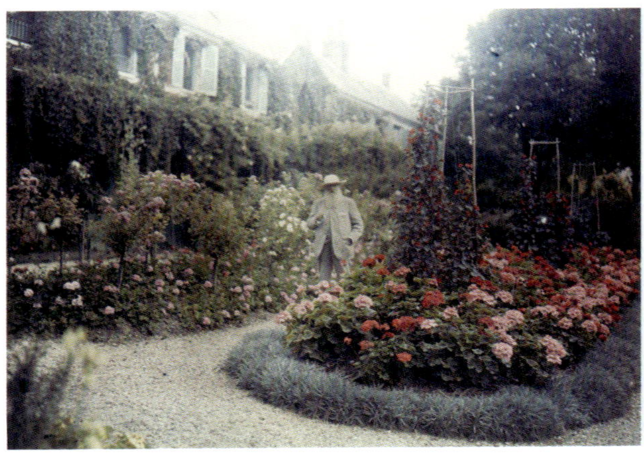

Fig. 182. Claude Monet in front of his house in Giverny, 1921. Autochrome, 7 x 9 3/8 in. (18 x 24 cm). Musée d'Orsay, Paris

Though the sizes of these four paintings differ slightly within a relatively similar range of measurements, and though their compositional gambits are essentially the same, the manner in which each picture is painted is extraordinarily different from painting to painting. Cat. 49 is rendered with small, generally rounded strokes of paint, daubed on top of each other, certainly over more than one session of work, but with many instances where dots and dashes of quite wet paint bump up against each other. Considerable amounts of white ground peek around the liquid paint, giving the surface of the painting a lively, brilliant quality. While also painted with relatively thin paints, cat. 50—dominated by the color blue—preserves a drier, more powdery surface, suggesting, perhaps, that as with his large scale decorations, Monet sometimes liked to use in easel pictures paint that had been laid on blotters to remove some of its oil binders.

The fiery views that close the group, cats. 51 and 52, are remarkably similar in the way in which paint was applied to the canvas. In both, curling, looping, weaving strokes of rich paint create jumbles of marks that bring a kind of melting, formless quality to the architecture and landscape elements. The difference between them resides most obviously in their color: while in cat. 51 the hues are dominated by red, orange, and yellow, cat. 52 adds to those colors significant amounts of green and blue, to give to its composition a range of hues closer to the most jewel-like of the paintings of the Japanese bridge. While these colors are associated with sunset, the artist is facing firmly to the east, which must mean that he is observing these intense colors early in the morning or, of course, that his eyes are perceiving colors that he had never seen before.

The closest parallel to this group of paintings, using architecture as a motif, would probably be the remarkably varied views that Monet had painted of the Houses of Parliament in advance of his Thames exhibition in 1904. Certainly nothing that he had attempted while studying the cathedral at Rouen (see fig. 183) could compare to these rude shifts of intense color, not to mention the garish manipulation of paint.

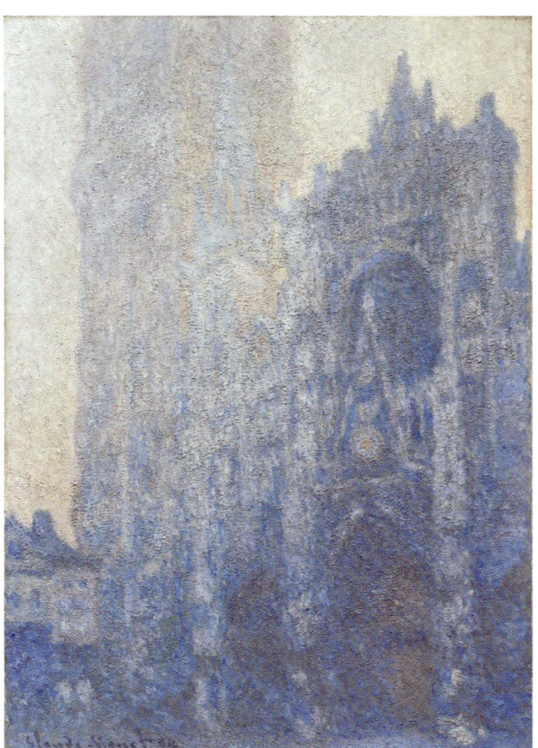

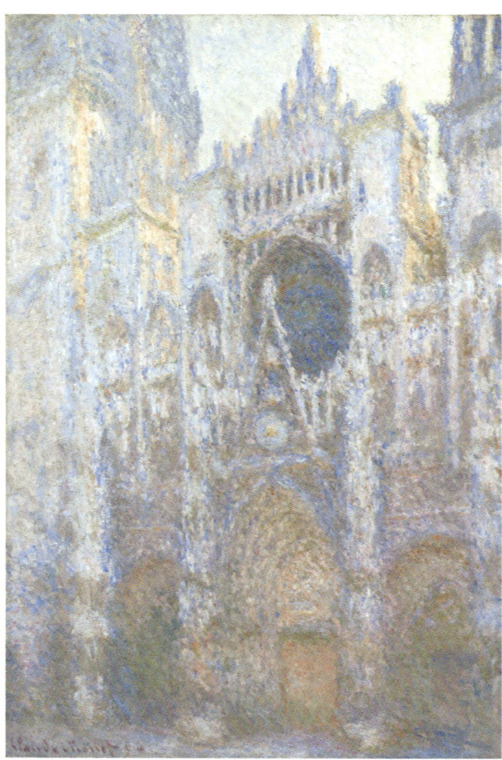

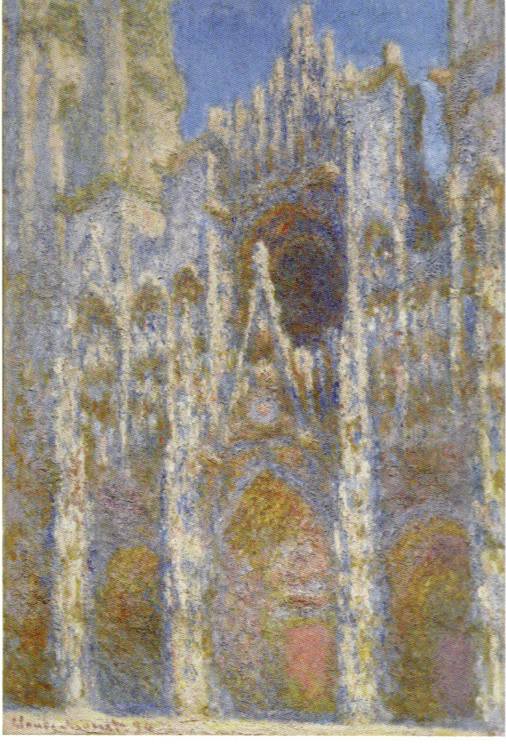

Fig. 183. Claude Monet, works from the *Rouen Cathedral* series, 1894, oil on canvas. Left: *Rouen Cathedral Façade and Tour d'Albane (Morning Effect)*, 41 3/4 x 29 1/8 in. (106.1 x 73.9 cm). Museum of Fine Arts, Boston. Tompkins Collection—Arthur Gordon Tompkins Fund. 24.6; center: *Rouen Cathedral, West Façade*, 39 3/8 x 25 7/8 in. (100.1 x 65.9 cm). National Gallery of Art, Washington, DC. Chester Dale Collection. 1963.10.49; right: *Rouen Cathedral, Façade*, 39 5/8 x 26 in. (100.6 x 66 cm). Museum of Fine Arts, Boston. Juliana Cheney Edwards Collection. 39.671

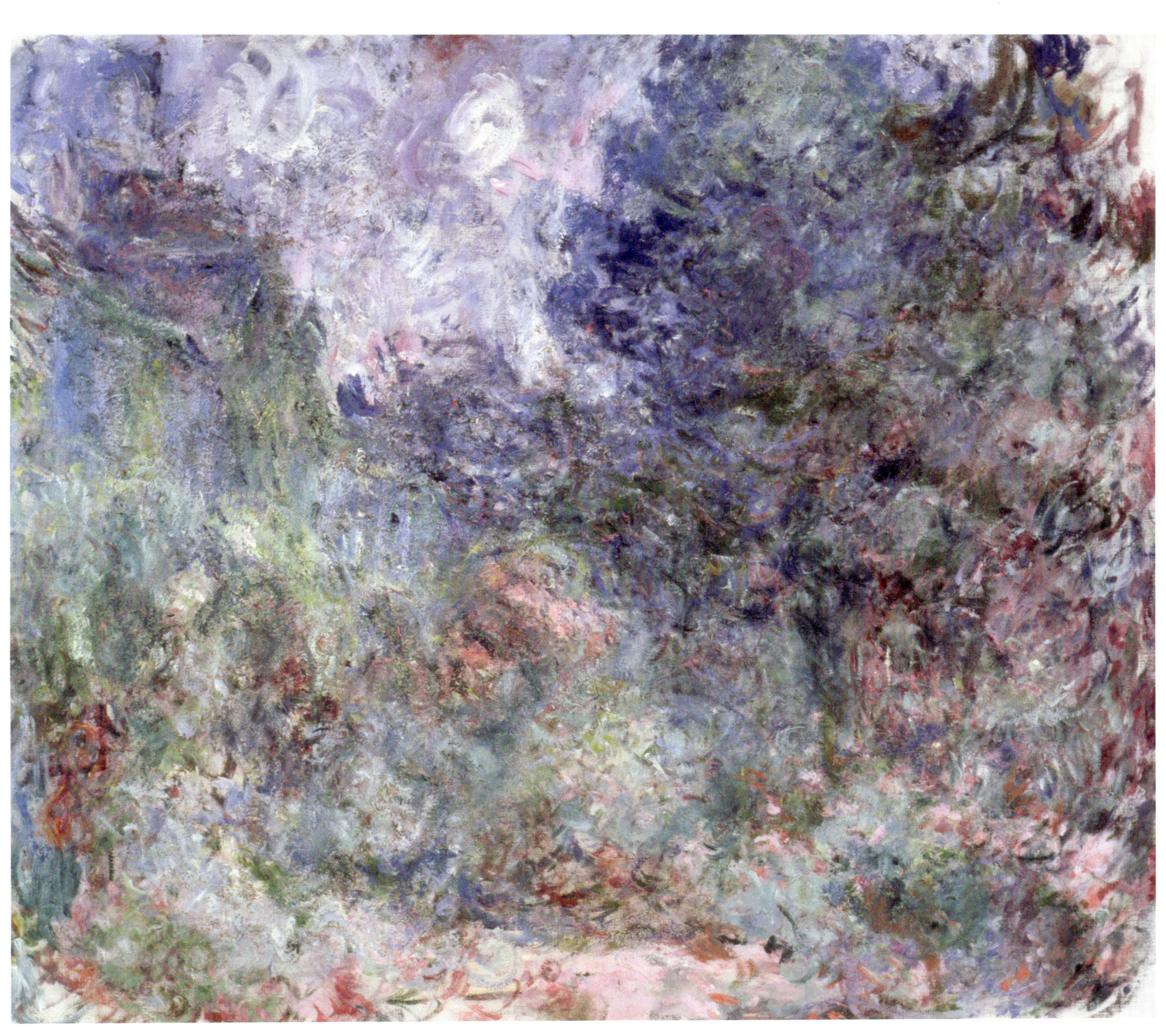

Cat. 50. *The Artist's House Seen from the Rose Garden*, 1922–24. Musée Marmottan Monet, Paris

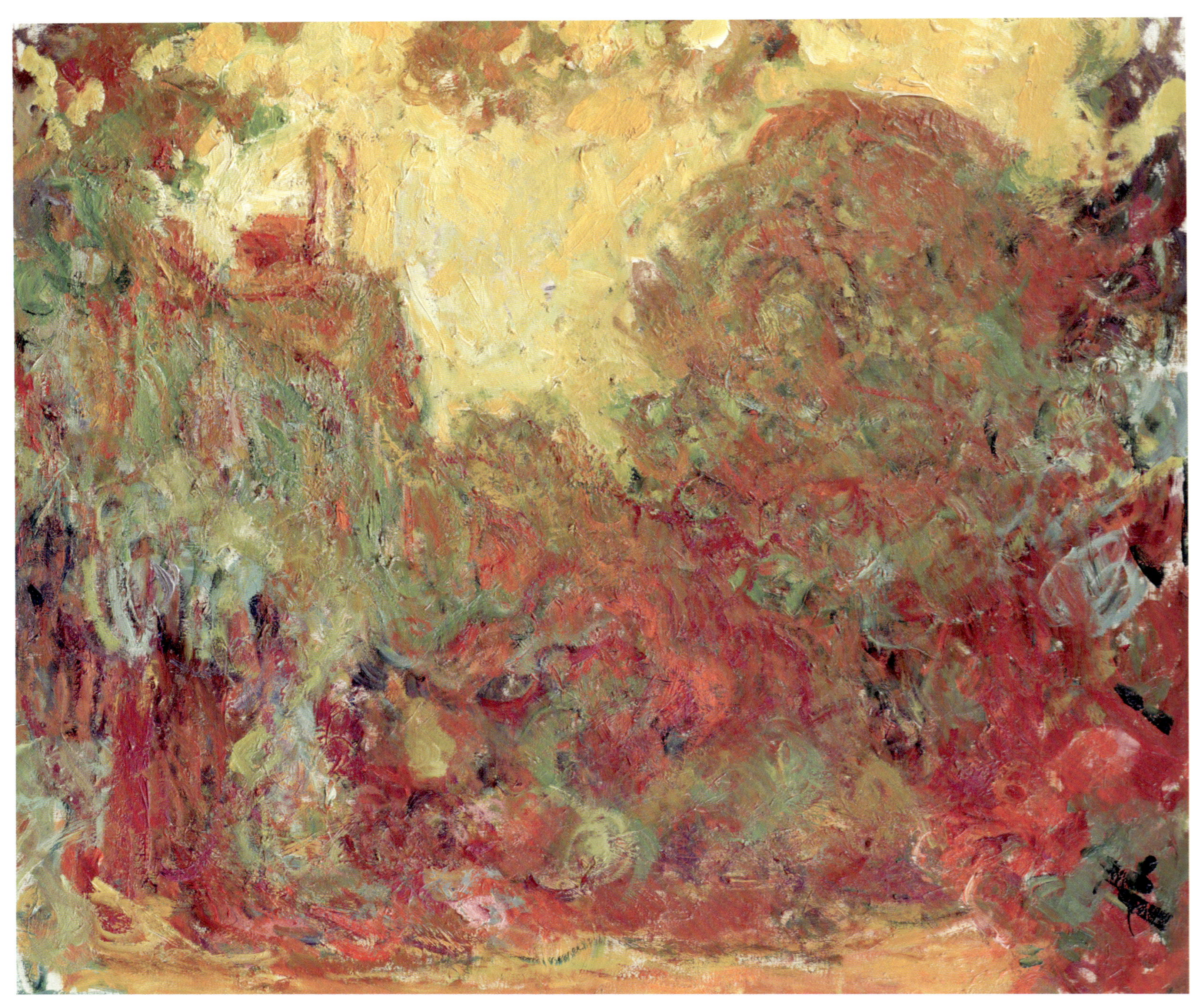

Cat. 51. *The Artist's House Seen from the Rose Garden*, 1922–24. Musée Marmottan Monet, Paris

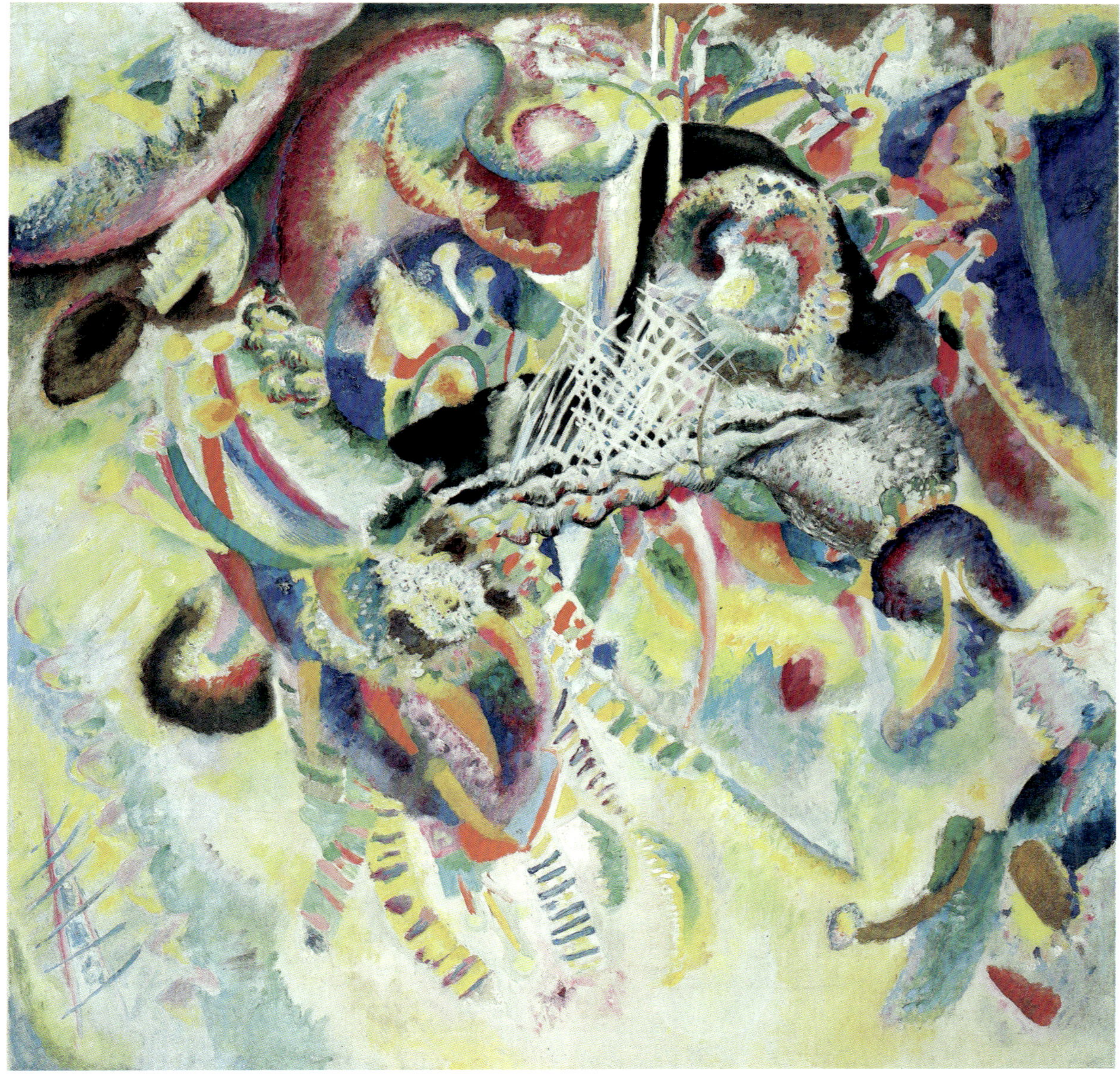

Fig. 184. Wassily Kandinsky, *Fuga*, 1914. Oil on canvas, 51 x 51 in. (129.5 x 129.5 cm). Fondation Beyeler, Riehen/Basel, Bayeler Collection

But the principles that the artist had established for himself at Rouen—that of establishing one unchanging vantage point and waiting for the conditions of light and climate and time to alter the immobile motif, are still being held to some thirty years later. Operating within that strict set of rules respecting the motive, however, the old man was to achieve something so audacious as to rival the most inventive abstractions of a younger generation—the likes of Wassily Kandinsky, for instance, whose brightly colored paintings, loosely suggestive of both natural and man-made phenomena, were seen as revolutionary in a way that the final work of an aging Impressionist never could have been understood (fig. 184).

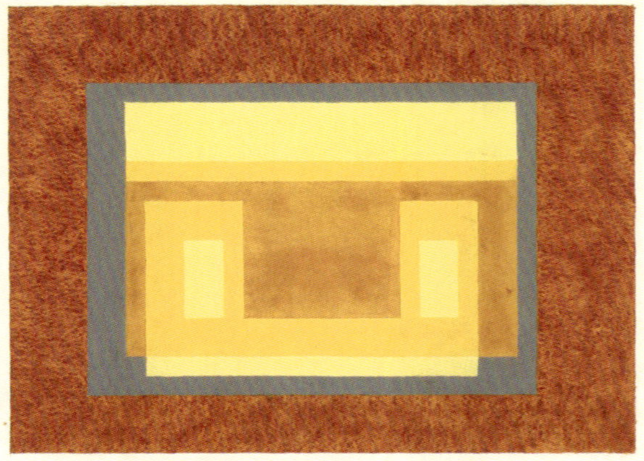

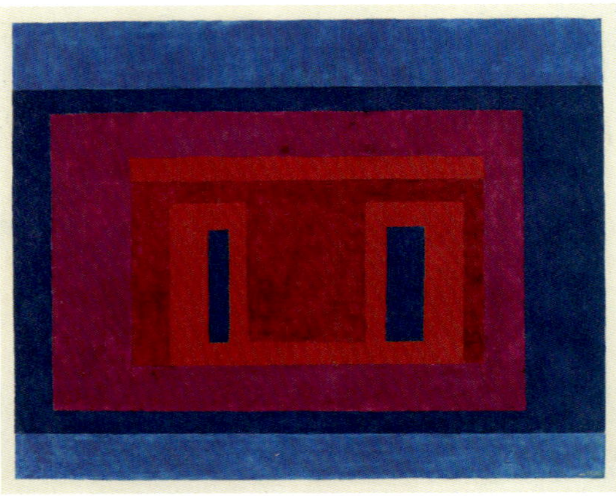

Fig. 185. Josef Albers. Top: *Variant/Adobe*, 1947. Oil on blotting paper (mounted on paper board), 16 1/2 x 22 3/8 in. (41.9 x 56.8 cm). The Josef and Anni Albers Foundation, Bethany, Connecticut. Bottom: *Variant/Adobe*, 1948–51. Oil on Masonite, 14 x 17 in. (35.6 x 43.2 cm). The Josef and Anni Albers Foundation, Bethany, Connecticut

The invention, so to speak, of a serial method has, in critic's eyes, given to Monet a kind of retrospective respect. The idea of taking a shape and methodically repeating it in different combinations of colors—as an artist like Josef Albers was to make a career-long strategy (fig. 185)—could justify Monet in some quarters in a way that the more romantic reaction to the apparent physical abandon of his lush surfaces could not. But all of these backwards reflections on what Monet's work might signify for posterity meant nothing to Monet, in the end. In 1858, at the age of seventeen, he had sent his first oil painting to an exhibition, eagerly seeking the opinion and the approval of others. In 1918, at seventy-seven, he had held out the beginnings of a remarkable gift to humanity, but he would make the gift, still, with confidence in the rightness of his own views. Monet, the old man, was poised to begin his last great period of intense innovation and creativity. He looked ahead, it is true, to an uncertain future, but counted on some time at least remaining to him, not to reinvent modern painting for history's sake, but to reinvent and revive his own painting, on his own terms, and if need be, for himself alone.

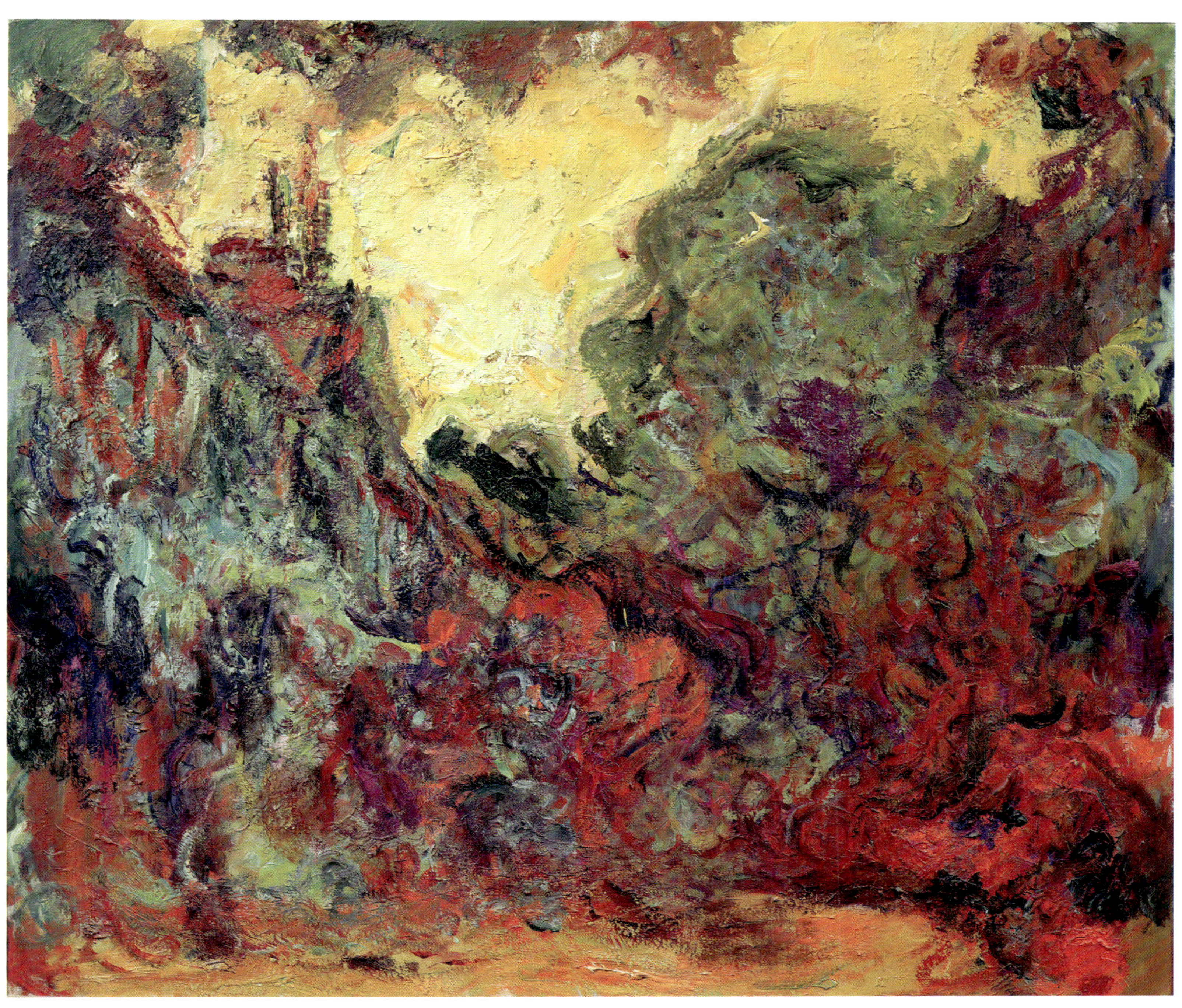

Cat. 52. *The Artist's House Seen from the Rose Garden*, 1922–24. Musée Marmottan Monet, Paris

Notes

Introduction: The Reinvention of Monet

1. Monet to Gustave Geffroy, April 30, 1914, quoted in Wildenstein 1985, vol. IV, 390, letter 2116.
2. Monet to Félix Fénéon, June 1, 1914, quoted in Wildenstein 1985, vol. IV, 390, letter 2119.
3. Marcel Proust, "Splendors," *Le Figaro*, June 15, 1907, quoted in Stuckey 1985, 250.
4. Monet to Gustave Geffroy, December 7, 1909, quoted in Wildenstein 1985, vol. IV, 378, letter 1908.
5. Monet to Julie Manet Rouart, September 12, 1911, quoted in Wildenstein 1985, vol. IV, 382, letter 1978.
6. Monet to Gustave Geffroy, May 30, 1914, quoted in Wildenstein 1985, vol. IV, 390, letter 2116.
7. See Charles F. Stuckey in Stuckey 1995, 242.
8. I am grateful to Philippe Piguet, who pointed out an October 1897 letter from Jean-Pierre Hoschedé to his mother suggesting that Monet should buy a camera for his son Michel. This would suggest that the photograph would have been made no earlier than 1898, and perhaps as late as 1905.
9. See George T. M. Shackelford et al., *Monet: The Early Years* (exh. cat., Fort Worth: Kimbell Art Museum, 2016), cats. 31, 32. Wildenstein numbers 134, 135.
10. Monet to Paul Durand-Ruel, June 29, 1914, quoted in Wildenstein 1985, vol. IV, 390, letter 2123.
11. Monet to Gustave Geffroy, July 6, 1914, quoted in Wildenstein 1985, vol. IV, 390, letter 2124.
12. Wildenstein numbers 63/1 and 63/2, 67.
13. Monet to Jean-Pierre Hoschedé, August 19, 1915, quoted in Wildenstein 1985, vol. IV, 392, letter 2155.
14. Stuckey 1995, 240, 244, 247.
15. Ibid., 247.
16. See Wildenstein 1996, IV, 972, Room 1, panels 2a–c.
17. See Wildenstein 1996, IV, 972, Room 2, panels 4a–c.
18. Monet to Sacha Guitry, December 14, 1916, quoted in Wildenstein 1985, vol. IV, 395, letter 2208.
19. See Stuckey 1995, 250.
20. For a discussion of the armistice and Monet's offer, see King 2016., 185–93.
21. Cat. 10 is Wildenstein number 1779; cat. 43 is Wildenstein 1869; the four *Water-Lily Ponds* are numbers 1890, 1891, 1893, and 1894; cat. 34 is number 1916.
22. Monet to Geffroy, November 19, 1919, quoted in Wildenstein 1985, vol. IV, 403, letter 2326.
23. See Suzanne Pagé et al., *Pierre Bonnard, l'oeuvre d'art, un arrêt du temps* (exh. cat., Paris: Musée d'Art Moderne de la Ville de Paris, 2006), 150–57.
24. See King 2016, 387.
25. Thiébault Sisson in 1928, in Stuckey 1985, 292.
26. This painting is Wildenstein number 1922.
27. Quoted in Wildenstein 1996, op. cit., IV, 938. The paintings are Wildenstein numbers 1953–58.
28. Monet to Barbier, July 17, 1925, quoted in Stuckey 1995, 255.
29. See Charles F. Stuckey and Robert Gordon, "Blossoms and Blunders: Monet and the State." *Art in America* 67, nos. 1 and 5 (Jan.–Feb. and Sept. 1979), 102, 117–25, 109–25; see also King 2016, who recounts over several chapters the details of the ongoing negotiations.
30. Stuckey 1995, 256.
31. Duc de Trévise, quoted in Stuckey 1985, 319.
32. For the reaction to Monet's work in the 1950s, see Michael Leja's essay on "The Monet Revival and New York School Abstraction" in Paul Hayes Tucker in Paul Hayes Tucker, George Shackelford, and MaryAnne Stevens, *Monet in the 20th Century* (New Haven and London: Yale University Press, 1999), 98-108. See also Cécile Debray et al. *Nymphéas: L'abstraction américaine et le dernier Monet*, (exh. cat., Paris: Musée de l'Orangerie, coedited with Musée d'Orsay, 2018). For examples of exhibitions that have examined Monet's work vis à vis contemporary art, see *Monets Vermächtnis Serie - Ordnung und Obsession [Monet's Legacy. Series - Order and Obsession]* (exh. cat., Hamburg: Hamburger Kunsthalle, 2001-2002), Jeremy Lewison, *Turner Monet Twombly: Later Paintings* (exh. cat., Stockholm: Moderne Museet, and tour 2011),and *Monet/Kelly* (exh. cat., Williamstown: Clark Art Institute, 2014), with essays by Yves-Alain Bois and Sarah Lees.
33. Claude Roger-Marx, "M. Claude Monet's Water Lilies," *Gazette des Beaux Arts*, June 1909, as cited in Stuckey 1985, 267.

"Color is my day-long obsession": Monet's Late Painting Materials and Techniques, 1914–1926

1. Monet made this remark shortly after the death of his second wife, Alice Hoschedé, in 1911, as quoted in K. E. Sullivan, *Monet: Discovering Art* (London: Brockhampton Press, 2004), 76.
2. Wildenstein 1985, letter 2065 to Geffroy, April 27, 1913: Monet's remark to Gustave Geffroy in the summer of 1920, as referenced by Paul Hayes Tucker in Paul Hayes Tucker, George Shackelford, and MaryAnne Stevens, *Monet in the 20th Century* (New Haven and London: Yale University Press, 1999), 60.
3. King 2016, 3.
4. The new pavilion was built on the northwest corner of Monet's property in Giverny. Ibid., 4.
5. Ibid., 4.
6. He was a member of the National Assembly of France.
7. Near Place Pigalle (123). See also Charles F. Stucky, "Chronology, 1914–17," in Stuckey 1995, 247–48.
8. Charles F. Stuckey and Robert Gordon, "Blossoms and Blunders: Monet and the State," *Art in America* 67, no. 1 (January–February 1979): 108.
9. King 2016, 109.
10. In 1917, Joseph-Durand-Ruel, the son of Monet's gallerist Paul Durand-Ruel, photographed Monet in his studio. There is also a fifty-minute film of the artist painting by his pond in 1915, produced by Sacha Guitry, entitled *Ceux de Chez Nous*.
11. King 2016, 9.
12. Ibid., 161.
13. Ibid., 103.
14. Anthea Callen, *The Art of Impressionism: Painting Technique and the Making of Modernity* (Yale University Press: New Haven, 2000), p. 127. Since Monet suffered from cataracts, he needed significant protection from glare while engaged in the act of painting.
15. See Anthea Callen, *Techniques of the Impressionists* (QED Publishing Ltd: Secaucus, New Jersey, 1982), 142. See also George T. M. Shackelford, *Monet: The Early Years* (Kimbell Art Museum: Fort Worth, 2016), 144. Although Monet generally preferred to work alone, during the late summer of 1869, Monet and Renoir spent a great deal of time together near Bougival in north central France. This was a period when both artists were living a "hand-to-mouth" existence. Renoir, who was staying with his parents at the time, sometimes provided bread for Monet and his first wife, Camille, when they had nothing to eat. Monet and Renoir occasionally painted side by side that summer. They both painted still lifes of the same vase of flowers and also simultaneously painted views of La Grenouillère, a popular restaurant and leisure establishment on the banks of the Seine River that featured swimming and boating.
16. In late October of 1922, visitors to Monet's studio had observed shreds of torn painting hanging from their stretchers, while elsewhere a pile of canvases were placed beneath a table, waiting to be burned. In July 1926, the artist informed one of his collectors that, during the past two weeks, Blanche had assisted Monet in destroying about sixty paintings. Blanche used a knife to free the paintings from their frames before Monet directed his staff to burn them. Clémenceau once estimated that Monet ordered the

destruction of some five hundred of his late paintings. Gimpel, 318–19, and Anon., 1927; Wildenstein IV, 146, as referenced in Stuckey 1995, 257.
17. Wildenstein 1985, vol. IV, 93–94 and letters 2349, 2355, and 2357, as referenced in Stuckey 1995, 250. See also James G. Ravin, MD, "Monet's Cataracts," *JAMA*, vol. 254, no. 3 (July 19, 1985): 394.
18. Robert Herbert, "Method and Meaning in Monet," *Art in America* 67, no. 5 (September 1979): 102.
19. Stuckey 1995, 249.
20. *American Magazine of Art* (March 1927), as quoted in King 2016, 152.
21. René Gimpel, *Diary of an Art Dealer*, trans. John Rosenberg (New York: Farrah, Straus and Giroux, 1966), 57–60.
22. Ibid., 59.
23. Ibid., 104. Early in his career, the artist began purchasing hand-ground paints from Maison Edouard, alleged to be the best in Paris and favored by other Impressionists. After Edouard's retirement in 1867, Moisse, one of his successors, continued to market colors under the owner's name before opening his own shop in 1904.
24. Stuckey 1995, 248.
25. From François Thiébault-Sisson, 1927, quoted in Stuckey 1985, 293.
26. Ibid.
27. Ibid., 249.
28. Ashok Roy, "Monet's Palette in the Twentieth Century," in *National Gallery Technical Bulletin*, vol. 28 (London: National Gallery, 2007): 58–68.
29. See John Twilley, "Report on the Palette and Paint Handling of Claude Monet's *Weeping Willow*," submitted to the Kimbell Art Museum on July 18, 2018. Cobalt arsenate occurs in both the National Gallery and Kimbell paintings, in spite of Roy's listing it as cobalt phosphate in footnote 2 of the pigment table in the National Gallery article, evidently an error in editing since the author lists the pigment as cobalt arsenate in the table itself.
30. Monet's use of cobalt blue in *Weeping Willow* was described in e-mail correspondence from John Delaney to the author on June 11, 2018.
31. Letizia Monico, et. al., "Degradation Process of Lead Chromate in Paintings by Vincent Van Gogh Studied by Means of Spectromicroscopic Methods. Part. 5. Effects of Nonoriginal Surface Coatings into the Nature and Distribution of Chromium and Sulfur Species in Chrome Yellow Paints," *Analytical Chemistry* 86, no. 21 (2014): 10804–11.
32. Ibid.
33. Ashok Roy, 1991, letter to Anne Dumas.
34. Twilley, "Report," 2.
35. See Roy, "Monet's Palette," 65: the following pigments were identified in *Irises*, c. 1914–17: lead white, cobalt violet, ultramarine, viridian, cadmium orange, zinc/barium yellow, cadmium yellow, cobalt blue, and rose madder lake. See also John Twilley, "The Palette and Paint Handling of Claude Monet's *Weeping Willow*," July 18, 2018. The full palette in *Weeping Willow* is as follows: lead white, viridian, red lake, vermilion, zinc potassium chromate yellow, barium chromate yellow, cadmium yellow, cadmium orange, cadmium red, cobalt arsenate violet, cobalt blue, French ultramarine, and minor zinc oxide including occasional zinc soap formations. E-mail correspondence, John Twilley to author, July 2[illegible], 2018.
36. David Bomford, Jo Kirby, John Leighton, and Ashok Roy, *Art in the Making: Impressionism* (London: National Gallery in association with Yale University Press, 1990).
37. Roy, "Monet's Palette," 61.
38. Twilley, "Report," 2–3.
39. Ibid. It occurred even when zinc-containing colors, such as chromate yellow, were not present.
40. Ibid. These occurred particularly in organic-rich, white areas.
41. Twilley, "Report," 2. The red lake samples in *Weeping Willow* contained a substantial amount of phosphate, as opposed to the alumina lake with residual sulfate found in *Irises*. The *Weeping Willow* samples also contained alumina, but with a high and varying amount of both phosphate and sulfate.
42. Ibid.
43. Probic, "Exploring Late Monet."
44. Bomford, Kirby, Leighton, and Roy, *Art in the Making*, 200–201; Paula Dredge, Richard Wuhrer, and Matthew R. Phillips, "Monet's Painting under the Microscope," *Microscopy and Microanalysis* 9 (2000): 139–143.
45. As stated earlier, Monet applied a second, cooler layer of lead white ground over the creamier, commercially applied priming, possibly to adjust its tonality.
46. Roy, "Monet's Palette," 61. See also Conservation file, Monet, *Irises*, 1914–17, oil on canvas, 200.7 x 149.9 cm, National Gallery Scientific Department.
47. Callen, *The Art of Impressionism*, 105.
48. Roy, "Monet's Palette," 61–62.
49. Ibid.
50. Ibid.
51. Callen, *The Art of Impressionism*, 101.
52. Richard Newman, Head of Scientific Research, Scientific Research Lab, Museum of Fine Arts, Boston, Analytical Report dated December 18, 2018, of Claude Monet, *Weeping Willow*, 1918–19, Kimbell Art Museum, AP 1996.02, SR project number: 2018-142. See Table I: Media analysis.
53. Ibid., 1, 3.
54. Richard Newman analyzed the four samples of paint from Monet, *Weeping Willow* by pyrolysis gas chromatography-mass spectrometry with TMAH derivatization.
55. E-mail correspondence between Richard Newman and the author on December 18, 2018. There is also the possibility, however, that both the conifer resin and beeswax result from a later treatment, such as lining.
56. Bomford, Kirby, Leighton, and Roy, *Art in the Making*, 72.
57. Ibid., 74–75. Monet's *Bathers at La Grenouillière*, 1869, *The Beach at Trouville*, 1870, and *The Gare Saint-Lazare*, 1877, all contained mixtures of linseed oil and poppy oil, while Monet's *Lavacourt under the Snow*, c. 1879, contained a mixture of walnut oil and poppy oil.
58. Bomford, Kirby, Leighton, and Roy, *Art in the Making*, 73.
59. Marion Boddy-Evans, "Is Walnut Oil a Good Medium for Oils?" ThoughtCo.com. Updated March 20, 2018. https://www.thoughtco.com/walnut-oil-as-medium-for-oils-2578595.
60. Callen, *The Art of Impressionism*, 101.
61. Twilley, "Report," 16.
62. Anthea Callen, "The Unvarnished Truth: Mattness, 'Primitivism' and Modernity in French Painting, c. 1870–1907," *The Burlington Magazine*, vol. 136, no. 1100 (Nov. 1994): 738–46.
63. Stuckey 1995, 256.
64. Conservation files at the National Gallery note than a thin layer of MS2A was applied to the surface of *Water Lilies*.
65. Callen, "The Unvarnished Truth." Monet observed that that the ancients didn't varnish their paintings and that discolored varnish had caused the Rembrandts in the Louvre to yellow. See also Gimpel, *Diary of an Art Dealer*, 75.
66. Callen, *The Art of Impressionism*, 211.
67. The triptych remained in Monet's studio for nearly three decades after his death; the three panels are now in the Cleveland Museum of Art, the Saint Louis Museum of Art, and the Nelson Atkins Museum of Art, Kansas City. Simon Kelly, *Monet's Water Lilies: The Agapanthas Triptych* (Saint Louis: Saint Louis Art Museum, 2011), 10.
68. Stuckey 1995, 249.
69. Ravin, "Monet's Cataracts," 394.
70. From *La Revue de l'art ancient et modern*, June 1927, as quoted in King 2016, 41.

"My four best series": Monet's Panorama at the Hôtel Biron

Thanks to Robert Gordon for his careful reading of a draft of the essay. Thanks also to Sylvie Patry for her invitation to present an initial version of this paper at the symposium, "Ils ont continué Monet. La reception américaine des Nymphéas" at the Musée d'Orsay on May 30–31, 2018. All translations are by the author unless otherwise noted.

1. See Duc de Trévise, "Le pèlerinage de Giverny," *La revue de l'art ancien et moderne*, v. LI, no. 283 (January–May 1927): 131.
2. *Three Willows* was subsequently divided by Monet and consists, from left

to right, of the left panel of *Morning with Willows* and the triptych *Clear Morning with Willows*, both of which are now in the second room of the Orangerie. *Clouds* is probably the triptych of the same name in the first room of the Orangerie. *Green Reflections* is probably the diptych of the same name, also in the Orangerie's first room. See Wildenstein 1996, vol. IV, 318–19. Monet subsequently removed *Agapanthus* from his gift to the French state, and this triptych remained in his studio at his death. The central panel was sold to the Saint Louis Art Museum in 1956, the right panel to the Nelson-Atkins Museum of Art in 1957, and the left panel to the Cleveland Museum of Art in 1960. See Simon Kelly, *Monet's Water Lilies: The Agapanthus Triptych* (Saint Louis: Saint Louis Art Museum, 2011).

3. The paintings were photographed by André Marty in February 1921 for the Bernheim-Jeune gallery with a view to their inclusion in Arsène Alexandre's forthcoming biography of Monet. See Gordon and Forge 1983, 236–41, and Wildenstein 1985, vol. IV 318–19. Monet subsequently reworked several of these panels, complicating subsequent identification, notably of *Clouds* and *Green Reflections*.
4. Arsène Alexandre, "L'épopée des Nymphéas," *Le Figaro* (October 21, 1920).
5. Monet's rotunda project was first discussed in detail in Robert Gordon and Charles F. Stuckey, "Blossoms and Blunders: Monet and the State," *Art in America* 67, no. 1 (January–February 1979): 102–117, and Charles F. Stuckey, "Blossoms and Blunders: Monet and the State, II," *Art in America* 67, no. 5 (September 1979): 109–125. See also Gordon and Forge 1983, 236–41. Wildenstein next provided a valuable and detailed account, drawing not only on Monet's correspondence but also on Bonnier's diary notes Wildenstein 1985, IV, 93-100; An abbreviated and translated version of this appears in Wildenstein 1996, I, 413-419. Pierre Georgel published important correspondence by Bonnier from the Musée Marmottan Monet in his 1999 exhibition catalogue *Monet, le cycle des Nymphéas* (Paris: Editions de la Réunion des musées nationaux), 225–26. See also Paul Hayes Tucker, *Claude Monet: Life and Art* (New Haven and London: Yale University Press, 1995), 215–18. For recent discussions, see Kelly, *Monet's Water Lilies*, and Félicie Faizand de Maupéou, "Du peintre à l'architecte. La mise en exposition des *Nymphéas* de Monet à l'Orangerie des Tuileries," *In Situ*, no. 32, 2017 (July 27, 2017). https://doi.org/10.4000/insitu.14862. This article draws not only on these existing sources but also on unpublished areas of Bonnier's submission to the Direction des Beaux-Arts in December 1920; these are now housed in the Archives Nationales in Paris.
6. The Rothko chapel measures 56 x 59 feet and is thus a little smaller than the dimensions of Monet's rotunda.
7. John House makes the comparison to the panorama, focusing on the Panorama Mesdag, in "Monet: The Last Impressionist?" in Paul Hayes Tucker, George Shackelford, and MaryAnne Stevens, *Monet in the 20th Century* (New Haven and London: Yale University Press, 1999), 11–12.
8. Stephan Oettermann, *The Panorama: History of a Mass Medium* (New York: Zone Books, 1980); Bernard Comment, *The Panorama* (Reaktion, 1999); and William Uricchio, "A 'Proper Point of View': The panorama and some of its early media iterations," *Early Popular Visual Culture*, 9:3 (2011): 225–38.
9. Michel Foucault, *Discipline and Punish: The Birth of the Prison* (New York: Vintage Books, 1979), 317, note 4.
10. Vanessa R. Schwartz, *Spectacular Realities: Early Mass Culture in Fin-de-Siècle Paris* (Oakland: University of California Press, 1998), 149–78.
11. Oliver Grau, *Virtual Art: From Illusion to Immersion* (Cambridge, Mass.: MIT, 2003).
12. Maurice Guillemot, "Claude Monet," *La revue illustrée* 13 (March 15, 1898), unpaginated. Transl. by Steven Levine in Steven Z. Levine, *Monet, Narcissus, and Self-Reflection* (Chicago and London: University of Chicago Press, 1994), 178. Although the article was published in 1898, Guillemot's visit to Giverny had taken place the previous summer.
13. Claude Monet, quoted in Roger Marx, "Les Nymphéas de Claude Monet," *Gazette des Beaux-Arts* 4, 1 (June 1909): 523–31.
14. René Gimpel, "August 19, 1918," in *Diary of an Art Dealer*, trans. John Rosenberg (New York: Farrah, Straus and Giroux, 1966), 60.
15. October 9, 1920. Gimpel, *Diary*, 150.
16. For Bonnier's career, see Bernard Marrey, *Louis Bonnier, 1856–1946* (Mardaga: Collection Architectes, 1988).
17. For Monet's broader interest in picturing architecture, see Richard Thomson, *Monet and Architecture* (London: National Gallery Company, 2018).
18. In spring 1919, painter Ernest Laurent, friend of Seurat and others, encouraged Bonnier to present his candidacy to the Institut. Bonnier refused. He described the Institut in his "Souvenirs" as a "bloc enfariné" (block covered with flour). See Marrey, *Louis Bonnier*.
19. Claude Monet to Louis Bonnier, August 24, 1899, in Aguttes auction sale (June 12, 2013). Livres, Affiches et Vieux Papiers (Hotel des Ventes de Neuilly, Neuily-sur-Seine), lot 334. https://www.aguttes.com/html/fiche.jsp?id=3065428&np.
20. Claude Monet to Louis Bonnier, July 21, 1915; Claude Monet to Louis Bonnier, July 22, 1915; Claude Monet to Louis Bonnier, August 14, 1915. See Aguttes sale, ibid., lot numbers 335–37.
21. On September 28, following Monet's directions, the directeur des Beaux-Arts, Paul Léon, called Bonnier to ask him to be the architect for the project.
22. He later referenced "la forme ovale que j'ai toujours voulue." Monet to Clémenceau, October 31, 1921.
23. Wildenstein 1985, IV, 96.
24. Louis Bonnier to Monet, October 5, 1920. D55 in "Documents manuscrits," in Georgel, *Monet, le cycle des Nymphéas*, 225.
25. Louis Bonnier to Monet, January 27, 1921. D56 in ibid., 226.
26. Louis Bonnier to Monet, October 5, 1920.
27. Alexandre, "L'épopée des Nymphéas," transl. Gordon and Forge 1983, 234–35.
28. Ibid.
29. Our knowledge of the color of Monet's canvases at this time depends largely on contemporary accounts, notably that of Alexandre. Marty's photographs (figs. 5–8) show the panels' configuration but obviously do not confirm their actual color. Recent cross-section technical analysis has, however, added to our knowledge. The triptych that Monet changed the most is *Agapanthus*, and cross sections taken from the right panel of *Agapanthus*, in the Nelson-Atkins Museum of Art, have shown that the colors were originally more intense and more in line with Alexandre's comparison to "molten gold." Monet reworked the canvas in more pastel tones at some point between 1920 and 1926. See Mary Schafer and Johanna Bernstein, "The Evolution of Monet's *Water Lilies*: A Technical Study," in Kelly, *Monet's Water Lilies*. Other panels, like *The Three Willows* and *Green Reflections*, seem to have changed less and probably retain a color palette close to that in 1920.
30. Alexandre, "L'épopée des Nymphéas," transl. Gordon and Forge 1983, 234–35. Alexandre's report was based on close collaboration with the artist, with whom he corresponded regularly in the fall. He had also orchestrated the meeting with Léon in late September to set up the State purchase of the works.
31. Monet compared his satisfaction with Alexandre's article with his disappointment "in recent days" by unnamed "certain articles, shocking by their useless and misplaced gossip." Alexandre's description does, however, describe only two tree trunks (rather than three) in the *Willows* panels.
32. François Thiébault-Sisson, "Art et Curiosité: Un don de M. Claude Monet à l'État," *Le Temps* (October 14, 1920). Thiébault-Sisson (1856–1936) knew Monet well and had published an important interview with him. Despite Monet's growing irritation with this critic, his account was probably largely accurate, since he visited the artist at Giverny on two occasions in late September and early October (Wildenstein 1985, vol. IV, letters 2372 and 2373).
33. Thiébault-Sisson, "Art et Curiosité." The critic also noted "the relatively narrow gaps" between the series.
34. Ibid.
35. Thanks to Robert Gordon for this suggestion.

36. François Thiébault-Sisson, "Les Nymphéas de Claude Monet à l'Orangerie des Tuileries," *Revue de l'art ancien et moderne* (June 1927): 52.
37. "un ensemble décoratif où, de l'aube au crépuscule, s'épanouissent, selon les heures, toutes les féeries des lumières sur l'eau." Marcel Pays, "Les Nymphéas de Claude Monet," *Excelsior* (May 16, 1921).
38. "peu accentuée et se rapproche trop du cercle." Louis Bonnier to Claude Monet, October 5, 1920 in Georgel, *Monet, le cycle des Nymphéas*, 225.
39. Louis Bonnier to Claude Monet, October 5, 1920. Ibid., 225.
40. On October 27, 1920, Bonnier noted, "Not a minute to write for 15 days—worked every night on Ménilmontant and on Cl. Monet. I've finished as regards what concerns me." Wildenstein 1985, IV, 97, fn 887.
41. Gustave Geffroy, *Claude Monet: sa vie, son temps, son oeuvre* (Paris: G. Crès & Cie, 1922), vol. 2, p. 190.
42. Trévise, " Le pèlerinage de Giverny." At the very same time, Monet, the canny businessman, was selling his early large-scale painting *Women in the Garden* to the State for the very large sum of 200,000 francs. This sale also indirectly tied Monet to the donation of his twelve panels.
43. Ibid. Monet was probably referencing here the abattoirs at La Villette in the suburbs of Paris.
44. Ibid.
45. "Sanctuaire laic," Georgel, *Monet, le cycle des Nymphéas*.
46. Bonnier produced a "summary descriptive estimate" (*devis descriptif sommaire*) for the building in a document dated November 25, 1920, that he included in his submission to Léon in December.
47. Bonnier later said that he understood Monet had approved the circular form "for lack of anything better." Louis Bonnier to Monet, February 9, 1921, in Georgel, *Monet, le cycle des Nymphéas*, 225. After the meeting, he also noted, ""The whole project has to be restarted Wildenstein 1985, IV, 97.
48. Louis Bonnier, "Avant Projet d'Un Pavillon d'Exposition pour une série de toiles de Monsieur Claude Monet," Paris, Archives Nationales, F 21-6028.
49. Bonnier's submission contained "une feuille de dessins," "une notice explicative," "un devis descriptif sommaire," and "un devis estimative."
50. Louis Bonnier, "Devis descriptif sommaire," in "Avant-Project d'un Pavillon d'Exposition," Archives Nationales.
51. "L'ossature du batiment, comprenant les piliers, les linteaux, fermes, le plancher vitré, le plancher de visite dans les combles, est en béton armé. Toutes les parties vues du béton armé seront enduites en ciment blanc." Ibid., 3.
52. "Façade, en brique blanche de Dizy, jointe en creux, au ciment, dégageant l'arête." Ibid., 3.
53. "Couronnement des murs, linteaux, corniche en pierre no. 6." Ibid., 3.
54. Louis Bonnier, "Devis estimatif." These numbers were later amended by Camille Lemonnier.
55. Louis Bonnier, "Une notice explicative" in "Avant Projet d'Un Pavillon d'Exposition." See Kelly, *Monet's Water Lilies*, 30–31 and 49, fn. 49.
56. Its restrained quality contrasted with the neo-Gothic chapel, designed by Juste Lisch and built on the grounds of the Hôtel Biron in the mid-1870s.
57. Louis Bonnier, "Devis descriptif sommaire," p. 2.
58. Louis Bonnier, "Notice explicative," in Kelly, *Monet's Water Lilies*, 31 and 49, fn. 50.
59. This space was intended to help with removing effects of oblique light: "L'eclairage est obtenu au moyen d'un plafond vitré placé au-dessus de toute la salle, sauf une bande pleine en plafond de 1.00 de largeur, courant le long des murs et destiné à supprimer tout jour frisant." Bonnier, "Notice explicative."
60. Even though the *Agapanthus* triptych is not noted in Bonnier's plan (since covered over by the ceiling in the mock-up), it is clear that it was the fourth decorative piece intended for the Hôtel Biron. Bonnier often referred to the *Agapanthus* in his correspondence. See, for example, Bonnier to Monet, October 5, 1920, and Bonnier to Monet, February 9, 1921. See Georgel, *Monet, le cycle des Nymphéas*, 225–26, and Kelly, *Monet's Water Lilies*, 49–50.
61. Monet would later paint out the agapanthus, heightening the flatness of his composition.
62. "salle d'exposition et vestibule d'entrée, frise à la partie haute." Louis Bonnier, "Devis descriptif sommaire," 7.
63. Trévise suggested a flowered frieze at the top of a gray-walled gallery with the water lilies below, to which Monet responded: "That's exactly my idea: I am even going to show you the first garlands of this frieze; I am composing it with wisteria." (*C'est exactement mon idée; je vais même montrer les premières guirlandes de cette frise; je le compose avec glycines*). See Trévise, " Le pèlerinage de Giverny," 130–31. Monet's interest in wisteria may have referenced his association with Rodin, since the flower had long been associated with friendship.
64. For Monet's interest in the rococo, see Paul Hayes Tucker, *Monet in the 90s*, 147.
65. Albert André, interviewed in Francis K. Hutchinson, "An Afternoon with Monet," in *Bulletin of the Garden Club of America* (September 1921): 9. Although published later, this article by Hutchinson recorded a visit that she made with Martin Ryerson and his wife to Monet's Giverny studio in early June 1920.
66. "l'aspect rebarbatif." "Rapport fait au Conseil [Conseil général des Bâtiment Civils] de Mons. Ch. Girault, Membre de l'Institut," December 23, 1920. Paris, Archives Nationales, MS F 21-6028.
67. Ibid. Bonnier noted on January18, 1921, that his building was "pas assez Louis XV" (notes of Bonnier). See Wildenstein 1985, IV, 98.
68. Ibid.
69. Committee letter signed by the President, Nénot, and the Secteratry, E. Aube. December 23, 1920. Paris, Archives Nationales, MS F 21-6028.
70. "un manque d'harmonie complet entre cette construction et la façade de l'Hôtel Biron." Ibid.
71. On January 6, 1921, a second architect, Camille Lemonnier, worked to provide an updated estimate for the "pavilion," now in fact increasing it to 626,073.95 francs.
72. "On a fait un devis d'un million . . . Mais c'est beaucoup trop cher . . . Les économies s'imposent à l'heure actuelle." Monet to Marcel Pays in Marcel Pays, "Un grand maître de l'Impressionisme—Une visite à M. Cl. Monet dans son ermitage de Giverny," *Excelsior* (January 26, 1921). Contradicting his stated preference elsewhere for an oval room, he told Pays that he had his gifted his twelve panels to the State for a "circular room" (*salle circulaire*).
73. Bonnier's January 27 letter to Monet indicates that the artist was aware of the circular rotunda plan by that time. Faced with Monet's unwavering position, the ever-accommodating Bonnier pledged, despite his reservations, to examine again the oval space. He wrote to Monet on February 9, 1921: "nothing is lost other than time and I am absolutely ready to restart a new project, wishing above all to make you happy (*rien n'est perdu que le temps et je suis tout prêt à recommencer un nouveau projet, désireux avant tout de vous donner satisfaction*). See Georgel, *Monet, le cycle des Nymphéas*, 226. On February 10, Bonnier privately noted, "Cl. Monet does not want the 2nd project already submitted to P. Léon." See Bonnier, "Notes from his granddaughter," in Wildenstein1985, IV, 98, fn 908.
74. "J'avoue être quelque peu déçu par la forme trop regulière de la salle qui ainsi prévue devient un véritable cirque et j'ai bien peur que cela ne soit pas d'un très bon effet." Monet to Paul Léon, February 11, 1921.
75. Ibid.
76. "d'une voix unanime . . . quelqu'un "de la maison." Anon., "Le Musée des Nymphéas," *Le Bulletin de la Vie Artistique* (April 15, 1921): 230.
77. "Le meilleur des enseignements." See Geffroy in an interview with Marcel Pays in Marcel Pays, "Les Nymphéas de Claude Monet," *Excelsior* (May 16, 1921).
78. "Le modernisme de l'art de Monet supporterait fort bien une architecture hardiment moderne de fer, de ciment et de céramique," Ibid.
79. "This morning, rendez-vous with Clémenceau, Monet, Bérard, P. Léon, Geffroy, Blavette. We are moving forward with the Orangerie." Notes of Bonnier, April 6, 1921, in Wildenstein 1985, IV 99.
80. "I count on your goodwill to give every opportunity to M. Bonnier so that he can put together a plan within a short period based on the instructions that I have given to him . . ." Monet to Paul Léon, April 17, 1921.
81. Monet to Paul Léon, April 25, 1921.

82. "une salle spéciale." Monet to Paul Léon, April 25, 1921.
83. "Au sujet de M. Bonnier, je puis assurer, entre nous, que je n'ai jamais eu qu'à me louer de lui, que je reconnais parfaitement qu'il est porté à forcer les prix et que, si je l'ai désigné à M. P. Léon, c'est que je ne connais pas d'autre architecte." Monet went on, "If the Administration thinks it is in its interests to speak to another, that is its business and has absolutely nothing to do with me . . ."(*Si l'Administration juge de son intérêt de s'adresser à un autre, cela est son affaire et tout à fait en dehors de moi . . .*). Monet to Arsène Alexandre, June 19, 1921.
84. Monet to Paul Léon, December 19, 1921.
85. "*There will be no more difficulties. No more Bonnier.* Paul Léon has just named a new architect of the Louvre who will act according to his 'directions.'" Clémenceau to Monet, December 14, 1921, in D 61, Georgel, *Monet, le cycle des Nymphéas*, 227–28.
86. Monet notified Bonnier about the change in architect. See Monet to Paul Léon, December 22, 1921.

The Late Monet and His Critics: *Water Lilies*, "Cunning Mirrors on Paradise"

1. Claude Roger-Marx, "M. Claude Monet's Water Lilies," quoted in Stuckey 1985, 255–63.
2. F. Robert-Kemp, "Un peu d'art. L'exposition des Nymphéas," *L'Aurore*, May 11, 1909, 1.
3. Ibid.
4. Gérard d'Houville Marie, "Lettres à Émilie," *Le Temps*, May 18, 1909, p. 2.
5. Ibid.
6. Louis de Fourcaud, "M. Claude Monet et le Lac du Jardin des Fées," *Le Gaulois*, May 22, 1909, 1.
7. Letter from Lucien Descaves, May 30, 1909, quoted in Gustave Geffroy, *Claude Monet, sa vie, son oeuvre* [1922] (Paris: Macula, 2011), 376.
8. Franc-Nohain, "Les Fleurs sur l'Eau," *La Vie Parisienne*, May 22, 1909, 378.
9. "Eh oui! Voilà un tempérament, voilà un homme [Monet] dans la foule de ces eunuques. Regardez les toiles voisines, et voyez quelle piteuse mine elles font à côté de cette fenêtre ouverte sur la nature." Émile Zola, "Les réalistes au salon" in *Mon Salon*, 1866, quoted in Geffroy, op. cit., 62.
10. "With his water landscapes, where seasonal flowers are seen in the soft, mannered enchantment of light filtered by space, Claude Monet shows us a magic mirror in which we have not yet looked, where his painter's genius is resplendent, smiling with the beauty of the earth and sky." in Geffroy, op. cit., p. 369.
11. Arsène Alexandre, "La vie artistique. Les Nymphéas de Claude Monet," *Le Figaro*, May 7, 1909, p. 5.
12. Georges Rodenbach, L'Élite: écrivains, orateurs sacrés, peintres, sculpteurs (Paris: Fasquelle, 1899), p. 253.
13. Georges Rivier, *Le Journal des arts*, June 2, 1909, quoted in Marianne Alphant, *Monet, une vie dans le paysage* [1993] (Paris, Hazan, 2010), p. 665.
14. Jules Renard, *Journal*, May 11, 1909, quoted in ibid.
15. Marthe de Fels, *La vie de Claude Monet* (Paris: Gallimard, 1929), p. 218.
16. André Michel in *Les Débats*, June 5, 1912, quoted in Geffroy, op. cit., p. 386.
17. Louis Vauxcelles, Histoire générale de l'art français, de la Révolution à nos jours. Tome I, La Peinture, la gravure, le dessin (Paris: Librairie de France, 1922), p. 157.
18. François Thiébault-Sisson, "L'exposition Claude Monet," *Le Temps*, January 3, 1921, p. 3.
19. Georges Clémenceau, *Claude Monet, les Nymphéas* (Paris: Plon, coll. Nobles vies, Grandes oeuvres, 1927), p. 94.
20. Ibid., p. 50.
21. Louis Gillet, "1909," in Louis Gillet, *Trois variations sur Claude Monet* (Paris: Plon, 1927), p. 12.
22. Édouard Mortier duc de Trévise, "Le pélerinage à Giverny" [1920], *La Revue de l'Art ancien et moderne*, Tome LI, January–May 1927, p. 130.
23. Franc-Nohain, op. cit.
24. Louis Gillet, "1926," in Louis Gillet, op. cit., p. 92.
25. To Jean-Pierre Hoschedé, August 19, 1915, LW 2155.
26. Geffroy, op. cit., p. 319. He was referring to the canvases made at "Dieppe et de Pourville, comme dans les toiles du Bras de la Seine à Giverny," done in 1896 and 1897.
27. Quoted in Geffroy, op. cit., p. 391.
28. André Michel, *Notes sur l'art moderne* (Paris: Armand Colin, 1896), p. 260–62.
29. Ibid.
30. André Michel in *Les Débats*, June 5, 1912, quoted in Geffroy, op. cit., p. 386.
31. Ibid., p. 392.
32. "Un moment la tentation m'est venue d'employer à la decoration d'un salon ce theme des nymphéas: . . . cette pièce aurait offert l'asile d'une meditation paisible au centre d'un aquarium fleuri." Roger Marx, "Les 'Nymphéas' de Claude Monet" (1909), in Roger Marx, *Maitres d'hier et d'aujourd'hui* (Paris: Calmann-Lévy, 1914), p. 293.
33. René Schneider, *L'esthétique classique chez Quatremère de Quincy (1805–1823)* (Paris: Hachette, 1910).
34. René Schneider, *L'art français, XIX*[ème] *et XX*[ème] *siècles. Du réalisme à notre temps* (Paris: Henri Laurens, 1930), p. 99.
35. Ibid., p. 90.
36. Anonyme, "Le musée Claude Monet est ouvert," *L'Intransigeant*, May 18, 1927, p. 1.
37. Camille Mauclair, *Les musées d'Europe: le Luxembourg* (Paris: Nilsson, 1927), p. 155.
38. Arsène Alexandre, "La vie artistique. Les Nymphéas," *Le Figaro*, May 19, 1927, p. 2.
39. Louis Gillet, "1926," in Louis Gillet, op. cit., p. 107.
40. François Fosca, *Claude Monet* (Paris: Artisan du Livre, 1927), p. 94.
41. Ibid.
42. "Dans un tableau de Monet, on ne saurait jamais où poser les pieds avec sécurité." In ibid., p. 61.
43. Louis Gillet, "1926," op. cit., p. 111.
44. André Michel. *Notes sur l'art modern* (Paris: Armand Colin, 1896), p. 262.
45. Roland Barthes, *Mythologies* [1957] (Paris: Points, coll. Essais, 2014), p. 94.
46. Geffroy, op. cit., p. 407.
47. Edmond Sée, "Devant les paysages d'eau,"*Gil Blas*, May 20, 1909, p. 1.
48. Geffroy, op. cit., p. 407.

The *Grandes Décorations* from Claude to Michel Monet (1914–1966)

1. Wildenstein 1985, vol. IV, 401. Georges Clémenceau was Président du Conseil twice, from 1906 to 1909 and from 1917 to 1920.
2. Maurice Guillemot, "Claude Monet," *Revue Illustrée*, year 137, no. 7 (March 15, 1898): n.p.
3. Wildenstein 1985, vol IV, 89, and Pierre Georgel, *Monet, le cycle des Nymphéas*, exh. cat., Musée de l'Orangerie, Paris, May 6–August 2, 1999 (Paris: RMN, 1999), 47.
4. Galerie Bernheim-Jeune, Paris, *Monet Venise*, from May 28 to June 8, 1912.
5. René Gimpel, *Journal d'un collectionneur, marchand de tableaux* (Hermann, 2011), 113.
6. According to the Durand-Ruel archives, Durand Ruel acquired only W. 1781 and W. 1779. The following numbers were acquired jointly (50/50) by Bernheim and Durand Ruel: W. 1868; W. 1869; W. 1880. On January 27, 1921, Monet turned over five other canvases to the joint (50/50) ownership of the two gallerists: W. 1890, W. 1891, W. 1893, W. 1894, and W. 1916.
7. Durand-Ruel Archives, stock register from January 21, 1919: Three works were acquired jointly (50/50) by Durand Ruel and Bernheim: W. 1868 (stock DR 11409; stock BJ 23368), FRF 20,000; W. 1869 (stock DR 11408; stock BJ 21367), FRF 20,000; W. 1880 (stock DR 11411; stock BJ 21379), FRF 20,000. Durand Ruel by itself acquired the two remaining paintings, W. 1879 (stock DR 11410), FRF 20,000; and W. 1781 (stock DR 11413), FRF 18,000.
8. According to the Durand Ruel Archives, in 1909, the purchase price for the water landscapes oscillated between FRF 14,000 (nos. 3, 6, 15, 28, 30, and 32 from the exhibition catalogue *Monet, Les Nymphéas Séries de Paysage d'eau*, Galerie Durand Ruel, Paris, from May 6 to June 5, 1909, and FRF 15, 000 (nos. 7, 8, 9, 10, 11, 13, 22, 21, and 23 in the same catalogue).

9. Gimpel, 1963, op. cit., 202.
10. Thiébaut Sisson, "Un don de M. Claude Monet à l'Etat," *Le Temps*, October 14, 1920, n.p.
11. Ibid.
12. According to the *Chicago Daily Tribune*, quoted in Simon Kelly, *Monet's Waterlily, The Agapanthus Triptych*, exh. cat., 2011, 29.
13. In 1920, the rate of exchange dollars-to-francs was 1 dollar for 14.2050 old francs according to MeasuringWorth.com.
14. "Formule pour déclaration de mutation par décès de M. Claude Monet," quoted in Marianne Mathieu, "De Monet Collectionneur à Monet donateur," in *Monet collectionneur*, exh. cat., Marmottan, Paris, 2017 (Hazan: Paris, 2017), 234.
15. The *ma* is an outmoded unity of length, corresponding to the size of a tatami, or about 1.80 meters. According to Wada, the surface of Monet's studio would have been approximately 11 x 15 meters (NdT).
16. The *shaku* is an outmoded unity of length, equivalent to 30.3 cm. 10 *shaku* make up a *jô* (NdT).
17. "Journal de Wada Eisaku (August 16, 1921–February 7, 1922)," *Kindai Gasetsu (Peintures et discours de la période modern)*, 21–22, September 13, 1921, translated from Japanese to French by Camille Ogawa for ALTO International.
18. Ibid.
19. Certificate of donation by M. Claude Monet to the French State, dated April 12, 1922, listing in detail the nineteen Orangerie panels.
20. Letters from Claude Monet to Léonce Bénédite, dating from May 4 and 25, 1922, Wildenstein 1985 IV, no. 3061 and 3063.
21. "Monet Gets $85,000 for a Single Canvas," *American Art News*, May 6, 1922, p. I.
22. According to the Durand-Ruel archives and for the exhibition "Exhibition of Paintings by Claude Monet," Durand-Ruel, New York, the asking price for the panels treating the same theme but nearly four-and-a-half times smaller (or 1 x 2 meters) was $10,000. These were *Water-Lily Pond* (no. 10 in the catalogue / W. 1890) and *Water-Lily Pond* (no. 12 / W. 1892).
23. Annie Cohen-Solal, "Un jour ils auront des peintres. L'avènement des peintres américains Paris 1867–New York 1948," (Gallimard, 2000), p. 343. For the history of the work, painted in 1907 and now in the Museum of Modern Art, New York, see this same article.
24. According to the site MeasuringWorth.com, the franc-dollar exchange rate doubled from 1922 to 1930. In 1922, $1 was equal to FRF 12.130; in 1930, $1 was equal to FRF 25.4780.
25. Yves Alain-Bois (dir.), *Matisse in the Barnes Collection*, vol. 3, p. 32.
26. Waldemar-George, "La Revue mondiale," May 15, 1927, quoted in *Nymphéas: L'abstraction américaine et le dernier Monet*, exh. cat., Musée de l'Orangerie, Paris, 2018, coedited with Musée d'Orsay RMN, p. 52.
27. André Lhote, "Monet et Picasso," *Nouvelle Revue Française*, 1932, quoted in Michel Hoog, *Les Nymphéas de Claude Monet au musée de l'Orangerie* (Paris: Réunion des Musées Nationaux: 1989–2006), 72.
28. Paul Morand, *L'Art Vivant*, September 1, 1929, quoted in Ibid, p. 54.
29. On the subject of Monet's reception, see Eric M. Zafran, "Monet in America," in *Claude Monet (1840–1926): A Tribute to Daniel Wildenstein and Katia Granoff*, (exh. cat. New York: Wildenstein, 2007), 80–151.
30. L. Sherwin, "For Art, Matisse Says Remain in New York, Don't Go to Paris," *New York Evening Post*, September 22, 1930, quoted in Cohen-Solal, "Un jour," p. 353.
31. Mather, Franck Jewett, Jr., "The Havemeyer Pictures," *The Arts* (March 30): 444–83, quoted in *Splendid Legacy. The Havemeyer Collection*, exh. cat., 1993, p. 33–36.
32. Louisine Havemeyer, who bought Monets up until 1917 and whose thirty canvases were then considered the most representative group of Monet's art in private hands, possessed no piece later than 1903! On this question, see *Splendid Legacy*, op. cit.
33. Alfred Barr papers, *A New Art Museum*, p. 72, quoted in Cohen-Solal, "Un jour," p. 303.
34. *The Museum of Modern Art. First Loan Exhibition*. New York, November 1929. *Cézanne, Gauguin, Seurat, Van Gogh*, November 7–December 7, 1929.
35. Letter from Alfred Barr to Abby Rockefeller, August 23, 1929, MOMA archives, New York, dossier "Early Museum History," quoted in Cohen-Solal, "Un jour," p. 303.
36. *The Museum of Modern Art. First Loan Exhibition*. New York, November 1929. *Cézanne, Gauguin, Seurat, Van Gogh*, exh. cat., 1929, 19.
37. In the catalogue, the work—also known today as *Under the Poplars, Effect of Sun* (W. 1135)—was dated by error 1874. In reality, it was signed and dated "Claude Monet 1887," lower right.
38. Alfred H. Barr, Jr, *A Brief Survey of Modern painting*, exh. cat., 1932, 4.
39. The Orangerie *Water Lilies* in 1937 were visited by fewer than 6,000 people a year.
40. Sale "Tableaux Modernes," Hôtel Drouot, salesroom no. 6, Wednesday, May 17, 1944, lot no. 77.
41. Draft of a letter from Michel Monet to M. le Directeur des Contributions Directes in Chartres. Archives of Me Bourdon, notary in Abondant (Dossier Michel Monet/declaration of revenues).
42. Document belonging to the Archives of the History of Art, The Getty Center for the History of Art and the Humanities, Los Angeles; and household accounts of Blanche Hoschedé Monet. Musée Marmottan Monet, Paris, inv. 5136.2013.5.
43. Olivier Widmaier Picasso, *Picasso. Portraits de famille* (Éditions Ramsay, 2002), p. 76.
44. Quoted in Cohen-Sola, "Un jour," p. 349.
45. Invoice from the Galerie Paul Rosenberg to M. C. S. Gulbenkian, April 10, 1937, archives of the Calouste Gulbenkian Foundation, Lisbon.
46. *The Museum of Modern Art. First Loan Exhibition*. New York, November 1929. *Cézanne, Gauguin, Seurat, Van Gogh*, exh. cat., 1929, no. 25. *Still Life*, private collection Josef Stansky, reproduced.
47. *Art in Our Time: 10th Anniversary Exhibition: Painting, Sculpture, Prints*, May 10–September 30, 1939, no. 58 (loaned by William S. Paley).
48. 1952 is the date usually accepted for the reopening of the Orangerie *Water Lilies* Room (On this point see *Nymphéas, l'abstraction américaine et le dernier Monet*, exh. cat., 2018, Paris, Musée de l'Orangerie, ed. Musée d'Orsay, RMN). The correspondence collected in the Archives Nationales in the Dossier "Musée de l'Orangerie des Tuileries," call number 20144795/57 makes the case for an earlier date. See letter from Pierre Rollin to Yvon Delbos, July 12, 1949: "It seems to me that 'les Nymphéas,' given so generously by Claude MONET to the State, should be better called to the attention of visitors." Also see the article by A.-H. M., "À propos de Claude Monnet (sic). Son véritable lieu de naissance – Les 'Nymphéas,' " in *Le Parisien libéré*, September 13, 1947. This question deserves further study.
49. MoMA Archives.
50. Mayer Shapiro in Marxist Quarterly (I,1), 1937, quoted in *Nymphéas, l'abstraction américaine et le dernier Monet*, op. cit., 82; and Clement Greenberg, "The Crisis of the Easel Picture," *Partisan Review* 15, no. 4 (April 1948): 481–84, retranscribed in *Nymphéas, l'abstraction américaine et le dernier Monet*, 96.
51. John Rewald, *History of Impressionism*, 1946, MoMA.
52. Letter from Michel Monet to M. Delbos, Ministre de l'Education Nationale, July 19, 1949. Archives Nationales, Dossier "Musée de l'Orangerie des Tuileries," call number 20144795/57.
53. Archives for the Canton of Basel, PA 888a N 6 (1) 424 1949/6, letter from Michel Monet to Lichtenhan, dated July 12, 1949.
54. Quoted in Christian Geelhaar, "Les Nymphéas de Claude Monet, des créations pour l'avenir" in *Claude Monet / Nymphéas*. (Impression-Vision: Seghers, 1986), 11.
55. Quoted in ibid., 10.
56. The author thanks Lukas Gloor for his help and refers the reader to Lukas Gloor, "La collection d'Emil Bührle, La collection d'art international: inventaire complet," in *Manet, Cézanne, Monet, Van Gogh . . . Chefs-d'œuvre de la collection Bührle*, exh. cat., Fondation de l'Hermitage, Lausanne, 2017 (Bibliothèque des arts), 170–192.
57. Interview with René Wehrli and Hiroo Yasui dated June 21, 2001, recounted in "The European Monet Revival of the 1950s and 1960s and the Role of Katia Granoff," in *Monet Later Works: Homage to Katia Granoff*, exh. cat. 2001–2.

58. Minutes from the Kunsthaus Zurich Commission from April 27, 1951. Kunsthaus Zurich Archives.
59. Extract from ibid., kindly translated from German to French by Lukas Gloor.
60. Ibid.
61. Minutes from the Kunsthaus Zurich board meeting dated July 9, 1951. Kunsthaus Zurich Archives.
62. Minutes from the meeting of the commissioners of the Kunsthaus collection dated October 4, 1951. Kunsthaus Zurich Archives.
63. According to the correspondence exchanged between Wehrli and Michel Monet in the exhibition dossier "Monet 1952," Wehrli went twice in April 1952 to Giverny to prepare the exhibition. Kunsthaus Zurich Archives.
64. Minutes from the meeting of the commissioners of the Kunsthaus collection dated June 10, 1952. Kunsthaus Zurich Archives.
65. Letter from the Kunsthaus to Michel Monet, November 3, 1952. Exhibition dossier "Monet 1952." Kunsthaus Zurich Archives.
66. Interview with René Wehrli and Hiroo Yasui dated June 21, 2001, reported in "The European Monet Revival of the 1950s and 1960s and the Role of Katia Granoff," op cit.
67. Geelhaar, op. cit., 11
68. Kunsthaas, Zurich, from May 10 to June 15, 1952; Paris, Galerie des Beaux-Arts from June 19 to July 19, The Hague, Gemmetemeuseum from July 24 to September 2, 1952.
69. See note 48.
70. On the subject of the genesis of the term Abstract Impressionist, see Anne Montfort, "Monet en héritage: la construction d'un récit," in *Nymphéas, l'abstraction américaine et le dernier Monet*, op cit.
71. *New Acquisition Exhibition*, November 29, 1955–February 19, 1956. Checklist with notes by Alfred H. Barr Jr, MoMA Archives, p. 5.
72. Micheal Leja, "The Monet Revival and New York School Abstraction," in *Monet in the XXth Century*, 1998–99, p. 98–108.
73. Ann Temkin and Nora Lawrence, *Claude Monet Water Lilies*, Museum of Modern Art, 2009, 27.
74. Ibid., 18.
75. Ibid., 25, quoting Wildenstein 1996, vol. IV 1 ,030.***
76. Letter from Milton McGreevy to Laurence Sickman, February 11, 1956: "When John McAndrew was here the other night, he told me of a recent purchase of a large picture of water lilies by Mr. Monet which was bought from his son, or at least his heir, by the Museum of Modern Art and John said there were three other panels. I think they are eighteen feet long and I suppose four or five feet high and are supposed to be very similar to the several panels which are in the Orangerie in Paris. It seems to me that it would be desirable to get in touch with the Museum of Modern Art and find out about these and see if it would be practical for us to acquire one of them." Archives of the Nelson Atkins Museum of Art (Acquisition dossier for W. 1977).
77. Letter from Patrick J. Kelleher (Curator of European Art, William Rockhill Nelson Gallery of Art Atkins Museum of Fine Arts) to Andrew C Ritchie (Director of Painting and Sculpture at MoMA), April 12, 1956. Archives of the Nelson Atkins Museum of Art (Acquisition dossier for W. 1977).
78. Letter from Alfred H. Barr Jr to Patrick J. Kelleher, April 24, 1956. Acquisition file for W. 1977.
79. Katia Granoff, *Œuvres completes* (Christian Bourgois Editeur, 1980), 93.
80. Letter from Michel Monet to Katia Granoff, January 14, 1955. Archives of the Galerie Larock Granoff ("Unless there is some unforeseen reason we cannot, we will come to Paris next week and stop by your gallery on Wednesday the 19th to put our signature on your canvas.")
81. Extract from an unpublished letter from Michel Monet to Katia Granoff, March 28, 1955. Archives of the Galerie Larock Granoff.
82. Letter from Michel Monet to Katia Granoff, March 31, 1955. Archives of the Galerie Larock Granoff: "This is to inform you that I received your letter of yesterday and the check . . . As of today therefore, the only thing that is due is the bouquet of suns . . . As far as the Water Lily you are interested in is concerned . . . As you will collect it only after the bouquet has been paid for, I don't see any necessity for us to meet." Letter from Michel Monet to Katia Granoff, July 17, 1955, Archives of the Galerie Larock Granoff: "For form's sake, as we never know what the future holds for us, I would be grateful if you would confirm for me in writing that you owe me the sum of 11,000,000 to be paid within one year."
83. Katia Granoff, handwritten IOU, June 1, 1956. Archives of the Galerie Granoff Larock.
84. Ibid.
85. Katia Granoff, two handwritten IOUs, July 9, 1956, Archives of the Galerie Larock Granoff.
86. Katia Granoff, *Œuvres complètes*, 95.
87. Interview by the author with Marc Larock, October 3, 2018.
88. "in the last few years, Jean-Paul Crespelle remembered that in 1952 Katia Granoff, whose intuition was equaled only by her taste, borrowed several hundreds of thousands ("old" francs) from banks to buy from Michel Monet canvases by Claude Monet that seemed in a state of neglect . . ." extract from André Renaudin, "Claude Monet, cinquante ans après," in *Précis analytique des travaux de l'Académie des sciences, belles lettres et arts de Rouen*" (Académie des Sciences, Belles Lettres et Arts, Imp. de P. Periaux, 1976), 201.
89. Unpublished letter from Michel Monet to Katia Granoff, September 19, 1957. Archives of the Galerie Larock Granoff.
90. Katia Granoff, *Œuvres complètes*, 97.
91. Sam Francis, interview with André Parinaud, 32.
92. *Claude Monet / Nymphéas*, op. cit., 1986, 155.
93. Temkin and Lawrence, *Claude Monet Water lilies*, 25–27.
94. The Japanese bridges are numbered A 6356 and A 6357 and were acquired in a single lot in April 1956 for the sum of $8,380.
95. Stock registers from the Galerie Knoedler. The paintings in the *Agapanthus* triptych are numbered A6418, A6419, and A6420 and were acquired in a single lot on July 20, 1956.
96. Temkin and Lawrence, *Claude Monet Water lilies*, p. 31.
97. Sold by MoMA, the work today is at the Kitakyushu Municipal Museum of Art.
98. Letter from Katia Granoff to Alfred Barr, July 16, 1958, quoted in Rona Roob, "Fire and Waterlilies" in *From the Archives*, June 1958, 25.
99. Jean Paul Crespelle, "Parmi les Nymphéas, Un Monet abstrait chez Katia Granoff place Beauvau," *France soir*, June 13, 1965.
100. A. W., "Les 'Nymphéas' de Monet et les émaux de Jean Serrière," *Journal de l'amateur d'art*, June 25, 1965.
101. "In the footsteps of R.P. Piquet," in *Le déporté*, August–September 1965.
102. F.E., "Pour que 'Les Nymphéas' soient conservés à la France," *Carrefour*, June 23, 1965.
103. Katia Granoff, *Œuvres complètes*, 95–96.
104. On the Michel Monet bequest to the Musée Marmottan, Marianne Mathieu, "De Monet collectionneur à Monet donateur," in *Monet the Collector* (New Haven and London: Yale, 2018), 234–59.

Catalogue

Cats. 1–2, pp. 108–11

1. Maurice Guillemot, "Claude Monet," *La Revue illustrée*, March 15, 1898, quoted in Stuckey 1985, 200.
2. The smaller canvases are Wildenstein numbers 1501 (Los Angeles County Museum of Art), 1502 (Private Collection), 1504 (Musée Marmottan Monet), 1507 (Rome), and 1507 (Private Collection). One larger canvas, W. 1508, is known to be from this early group. This, *Water Lilies, Reflections of Tall Grasses* (W. 1782), and I believe another traditionally dated to after 1914, W. 1783 (Musée Marmottan Monet), would be the "large panels" that Guillemot saw. On the basis of style, I also believe that two paintings thought to be from the 1890s were actually painted later; these are W. 1503 and W. 1506, both in private collections.

Cats. 3–8, pp. 112–21

1. Guillemot 1898, quoted in Stuckey 1985, 200.
2. Ibid.

3. Kimberley Muir, "*Cat. 44. Water Lilies, 1906 : Technical Report*," in *Monet Paintings and Drawings at the Art Institute of Chicago*, ed. Gloria Groom and Jill Shaw (Art Institute of Chicago, 2014), para 12.
4. Tucker et al., *Monet in the 20th Century*, op. cit., 150.

Cats. 9–10, pp. 122–25
1. See Guy-Patrice Dauberville et al., *Renoir: catalogue raisonné des tableaux, pastels, dessins et aquarelles* (Paris: Éditions Bernheim-Jeune, 2007).
2. André Arnyvelde, "Chez le peintre de la lumiere." *Je sais tout* (Jan. 15, 1914), 29.

Cats. 11–13, pp. 126–31
1. Monet to Félix Fénéon, June 17, 1914, in Wildenstein 1985, vol. 4, 390, letter 2121.
2. For more on this topic, see Claire Barry's essay in this volume.

Cats. 14–15, pp. 132–35
1. Information from the Museum of Fine Arts, Boston, curatorial files and online catalogue of works at www.mfa.org.

Cat. 16, pp. 136–37
1. Wildenstein 1996, vol. IV, 975, First Room, painting 4a–d.
2. Wildenstein 1996, vol. IV, 972, First Room, painting 1.
3. *Water-Lily Pond, Evening*, Wildenstein 1964–65.
4. See Stuckey 1995, 253.

Cats. 17–18, pp. 138–41
1. See Wildenstein numbers 1620–26.
2. Monet to Claude Roger-Marx, June 1, 1909, in Wildenstein 1985, vol. IV, 377, letter 1893.
3. See Wildenstein numbers 1831, 1832, and 1833.
4. See Wildenstein numbers 1828, 1829 (cat. 17), and 1830.
5. Beuil's list is noted in Catherine Hug and Monika Leonhardt, "Claude Monet the Gardener," in *Monet's Garden* (exh. cat., Kunsthaus Zurich, Hatje Cantz Publishers, 2004), 140, and enumerated in note 79.
6. See *Les Iris cultivés : Actes et comptes-rendus de la 1re Conférence internationale des Iris, tenue à Paris en 1922* (Paris, Société nationale d'horticulture de France, Commission des Iris, 1923. Monet's sponsorship, 9; participants, 5. I wish to thank Anner Whitehead for bringing this publication to my attention.
7. See Catherine Hug and Monika Leonhardt, op. cit., 132.
8. Ibid.
9. See Wildenstein numbers 919–54.

Cats. 19–22, pp. 142–47
1. Quoted in in Catherine Hug and Monika Leonhardt, "Claude Monet the Gardener," in *Monet's Garden* (exh. cat., Kunsthaus Zurich, Hatje Cantz Publishers, 2004), 125; original given 146.
2. Monet to Madame Cathelineau, June 29, 1914, in Wildenstein 1985, vol. IV, 390, letter 2122.
3. Monet to Charlotte Lysès, March 31, 1914, in Wildenstein 1985, vol. IV, 390, letter 2112.
4. Monet to Julie Manet-Rouart, February 6, 1910, in Wildenstein 1985, vol. IV, 378, letter 1912.
5. Monet to Madame Cathelineau, June 29, 1914, in Wildenstein 1985, vol. IV, 390, letter 2122.
6. See the discussion of assigning dates to these works in Wildenstein 1996, IV, 839.

Cats. 23–27, pp. 148–55
1. Monet to Madame Barillon, April 30, 1918, in Wildenstein 1985, vol. IV, 399–400.
2. R. Gimpel, quoted in Stuckey 1985, 307.
3. Ibid.

Cat. 28, pp. 156–61
1. Simon Kelly, with Mary Shafer and Johanna Bernstein, *Monet's Water Lilies: The* Agapanthus *Triptych* (Saint Louis: Saint Louis Art Museum in association with the Univeristy of Washington Press, 2011).
2. As evidence of this pitfall, see two sets of photographs of the doors Monet painted for Durand-Ruel. In the photograph of a sunflower still life in situ—the earlier of the photographs—the petals of the flower read as black; a more recent photograph, still in black and white, confirms that the petals are pale, presumably yellow, as would be expected. See Wildenstein 1996, vol. II, 347, in connection with number 926.
3. Rainer Maria Rilke, *Letters on Cézanne* (New York: Farrar, Straus, and Giroux, 2002) 71-72.

Cat. 31, pp. 162–63
1. The other paintings are Wildenstein numbers 1878, given by Monet to the museum in Grenoble in 192; 1879, like this painting sold to Bernheim Jeune in January, 1919, and now in the Musée d'art et d'histoire, Geneva; and 1881, which was sold by the artist's son at an unknown time and is in a private collection.

Cats. 32–38, pp. 164–73
1. Whistler's *Nocturne: Blue and Gold–Old Battersea Bridge* is at Tate Britain, N01959. Monet's views of the Argenteuil bridge under repair are Wildenstein numbers 194 and 195. See *Monet: The Early Years* (Fort Worth: Kimbell Art Museum, in association with Yale University Press, 2016), cat. 50.
2. For the paintings from 1895, see Wildenstein numbers 1392, 1419, and 1419a. For the 1899 canvases, see numbers 1509–20.
3. See the reference for summer 1905 in Charles F. Stuckey's chronology in Stuckey 1995, 238.

Cats. 39–44, pp. 174–81
1. See Ann Dumas in Ann Dumas, Gary Tinterow, et. al, The Private Collection of Edgar Degas (Exh. cat., The Metropolitan Museum of ARt, 1997), 7.
2. Monet to Roger-Marx, June 1, 1909, in Wildenstein 1985, vol. IV, 377, letter 1893
3. Monet to Gaston or Josse Bernheim-Jeune, August 5, 1912, in Wildenstein 1985, vol. IV, 396, letter 2024a.
4. Wildenstein numbers 1868 and 1869.
5. See Wildenstein no. 1976
6. King 2016, 176.
7. See Paul Tucker in *Monet in the 20th century*, op. cit., 76–77.
8. See Emile Michet, quoted in Michael Pantazzi, Vincent Pomarède, and Gary Tinterow, Corot (exh. cat., New York: The Metropolitan Museum of Art, 1996), 87.

Cats. 45–46, pp. 182–87
1. Quoted in Wildenstein 1996, vol. IV, 930 (variant translation).
2. Deborah Solomon, "In Monet's Light," *New York Times*, November 24, 1991.

Cats. 47–48, pp. 188–91
1. See the succession of photo-postcards reproduced in Marina Ferretti Bocquillon et al., *Monet's Garden in Giverny: Inventing the Landscape* (Giverny: Musée des Impressionnismes, 2009), 122, in which the trees gradually disappear.
2. Joseph Durand-Ruel to his son, Pierre, October 19, 1922, quoted in Wildenstein 1995, IV, 916.

Selected Bibliography

Adhémar, Hélène, Anne Distel, and Sylvie Gache-Patin. *Hommage à Claude Monet (1840–1926)*. Exh. cat., Grand Palais, Paris, 1980.

Alexandre, Arsène. "La vie artistique. Les Nymphéas de Claude Monet." *Le Figaro*, May 7, 1909.

Alexandre, Arsène. "La vie artistique. Les Nymphéas," *Le Figaro*, May 19, 1927.

Alphant, Marianne. *Monet, une vie dans le paysage.* Paris, Hazan, 2010

Aspects of Monet. A symposium on the Artist's Life and Times. Published under the direction of John Rewald and Frances Weitzenhoffer from a symposium organized in Paris in September 1981. New York: H. N. Abrams, 1984.

Becker, Christoph, et al. *Monet's Garden*. Exh. cat., Kunsthaus Zurich, Hatje Cantz Publishers, 2004.

Bocquillon, Marina Ferretti, et al. *Monet's Garden in Giverny: Inventing the Landscape*. Exh. cat., Musée des Impressionnismes, Giverny, 2009.

Bomford, David, Jo Kirby, John Leighton, and Ashok Roy. *Art in the Making Impressionism*. Exh. cat., National Gallery, London, 1991.

Callen, Anthea. *The Work of Art: Plein Air Painting and Artistic Identity in Nineteenth-century France*. London: Reaktion Books, 2015.

Callen, Anthea. *The Art of Impressionism: Painting Technique and the Making of Modernity.* New Haven: Yale University Press, 2000.

Clémenceau, Georges. *Claude Monet: Les Nymphéas*. Paris, 1928.

Debray, Cécile, et al. *Nymphéas: L'abstraction américaine et le dernier Monet*. Exh. cat., Musée de l'Orangerie, Paris, 2018.

Fosca, François. *Claude Monet*. Artisan du Livre, Paris, 1927.

Geffroy, Gustave. *Claude Monet: sa vie, son temps, son œuvre*. Paris: G. Crès, 1922.

Gordon, Robert. "The Changing Inspiration of Monet: The Lily Pond at Giverny." Connoisseur (Nov. 1973), 154 -65.

Gordon and Forge 1983: Gordon, Robert and Andrew Forge. *Monet*. New York: Abrams, 1983.

Greenberg, Clement. *Art and Culture: Critical Essays*. Boston: Beacon Press, 1961.

Greenberg, Clement. "Towards a Newer Laocöon." *Partisan Review* 7 (July–August 1940): 296–310.

Groom, Gloria, and Jilll Shaw, eds. *Monet Paintings and Drawings at the Art Institute of Chicago.* Art Institute of Chicago online summary catalogue, 2014.

House, John. *Monet: Nature into Art*. New Haven and London: Yale University Press, 1986.

Levine, Steven Z. *Monet and his Critics*. New York and London: Garland Publishing, 1976.

Mathieu, Marianne, et al. *Monet the Collector* Yale, New Haven and London, 2018.

Muir, Kimberley, Inge Fiedler, Don H. Johnson, and Robert G. Erdmann. "An In-depth Study of the Materials and Technique of Paintings by Claude Monet from the Art Institute of Chicago." *ICOM-CC 17th Triennial Meeting Preprints*, Melbourne, Sept. 15–19, 2014.

Pays, Marcel. "Une visite à Claude Monet dans son ermitage de Giverny." L'Excelsior (Jan. 26, 1921).

Roger Marx, Claude. "Les Nymphéas de M. Claude Monet." Gazette des Beaux-Arts, 4th ser., 1 (June 1909), 523-31.

Roy, Ashok. "Monet's Palette in the Twentieth Century," in *National Gallery Technical Bulletin*, vol. 28. London: National Gallery, 2007, 58–68.

Seitz, William C. *Claude Monet: Seasons and Moments.* Exh. cat. The Museum of ModernArt, New York, 1960.

Stuckey 1985: Stuckey, Charles F. ed. *Monet: A Retrospective.* New York: Hugh Lauter Levin Associates, Inc., 1985.

Stuckey 1995: Stuckey, Charles F. with Sophia Shaw. *Claude Monet: 1840–1926.* Exh. cat., Art Institute of Chicago, 1995.

Thiébault-Sisson, François. "Claude Monet, les années d'épreuves." *Le Temps* (26 November 1900). Reprinted in *Claude Monet, Mon histoire, recueillie par Thiébault-Sisson*, Paris: L'Échoppe, 1998.

Thiébault-Sisson, François. "Les Nymphéas de Claude Monet à l'Orangerie des Tuileries." *La revue de l'art ancien et moderne*, vol. 52 (June 1927).

Trévise, Duc de. "Le pèlerinage de Giverny." *La revue de l'art ancien et moderne*, vol. 51, no. 283 (January–May 1927).

Truffaut, Georges. "Le Jardin de Claude Monet." Jardinage (Nov. 1924), 55-59.

Tucker, Paul Hayes. *Claude Monet: Life and Art.* New Haven: Yale University Press, 1995.

Tucker, Paul Hayes. *Monet in the '90s: The Series Paintings.* Boston: Museum of Fine Arts, 1990.

Tucker, Paul Hayes, George Shackelford, and MaryAnne Stevens, *Monet in the 20th Century.* New Haven and London: Yale University Press, 1999.

Wildenstein 1985: Wildenstein, Daniel with Rodolphe Walter, France Daguet, Madeleine Manigler, Michèle Paret, et al. *Claude Monet: biographie et catalogue raisonné.* 5 vols. Lausanne and Paris: La Bibliothèque des arts, 1974–1991.

Wildenstein 1996: Wildenstein, Daniel with Nicole Castais, Annie Champié, Marie-Christine Decroocq, Elisabeth Raffy, et al. *Monet, or, The Triumph of Impressionism.* 4 vols. Köln: Taschen; Paris: Wildenstein Institute, 1996.

Checklist of Works in the Exhibition

Cat. 1
Water Lilies, Reflections of Tall Grasses
c. 1897, oil on canvas
51 $\frac{1}{4}$ x 78 $\frac{3}{4}$ in. (130 x 200 cm)
Private collection
Courtesy Helly Nahmad Gallery, London
W. 1782

Cat. 2
Morning on the Seine
1896, oil on canvas
35 x 36 $\frac{1}{4}$ in. (89 x 92 cm)
Private collection
Courtesy Sotheby's, New York
W. 1436

Cat. 3
The Japanese Footbridge
1899, oil on canvas
32 x 40 in. (81.3 x 101.6 cm)
National Gallery of Art, Washington, DC
Gift of Victoria Nebeker Coberly, in memory of her son John W. Mudd, and Walter H. and Leonore Annenberg, 1992.9.1
W. 1517

Cat. 4
Water Lilies
1904, oil on canvas
34 $\frac{5}{8}$ x 36 in. (88 x 91.5 cm)
Denver Art Museum
Funds from the Helen Dill bequest, 1935.14
W. 1666

Cat. 5
Water Lilies
1905, oil on canvas
28 $\frac{3}{4}$ x 41 $\frac{3}{8}$ in. (73 x 105 cm)
Private collection, Dallas, in honor of Kay Fortson
W. 1678

Cat. 6
Water Lilies
1906, oil on canvas
35 $\frac{3}{8}$ x 37 in. (89.9 x 94.1 cm)
The Art Institute of Chicago
Mr. and Mrs. Martin A. Ryerson Collection, 1933.1157
W. 1683

Cat. 7
Water Lilies
1907, oil on canvas
36 $\frac{1}{4}$ x 31 $\frac{7}{8}$ in. (92 x 81 cm)
Museum of Fine Arts, Houston
Gift of Mrs. Harry C. Hanszen, 68.31
W. 1703

Cat. 8
Water Lilies
1907, oil on canvas
39 $\frac{3}{8}$ x 32 in. (100.1 x 81.2 cm)
Private collection
Courtesy Christie's, New York
W. 1707

Cat. 9
The Artist's House at Giverny
1912–13, oil on canvas
28 $\frac{3}{4}$ x 36 $\frac{1}{4}$ in. (73 x 92 cm)
Private collection
Courtesy Christie's, New York
W. 1778

Cat. 10
Flowering Arches, Giverny
1913, oil on canvas
31 $\frac{3}{4}$ x 36 $\frac{1}{4}$ in. (81 x 92 cm)
Phoenix Art Museum
Gift of Mr. and Mrs. Donald D. Harrington, 1964.231
W. 1779

Cat. 11
Water Lilies
c. 1914–17, oil on canvas
65 $\frac{3}{8}$ x 56 in. (166.1 x 142.2 cm)
Fine Arts Museums of San Francisco
Museum purchase, Mildred Anna Williams Collection, 1973.3
W. 1799

Cat. 12
Water Lilies
1914–15, oil on canvas
63 $\frac{1}{4}$ x 71 $\frac{1}{8}$ in. (160.7 x 180.7 cm)
Portland Art Museum, Oregon
Museum purchase, Helen Thurston Ayer Fund, 59.16
W. 1795

Cat. 13
Water Lilies
1914–17, oil on canvas
66 $\frac{1}{2}$ x 48 $\frac{1}{2}$ in. (169 x 123.2 cm)
Collection of Diane B. Wilsey, San Francisco
W. 1799

Cat. 14
Water Lilies
1915–17, oil on canvas
78 $\frac{3}{4}$ x 70 $\frac{7}{8}$ in. (200 x 180 cm)
Fondation Beyeler, Basel, Switzerland
Beyeler Collection, Inv. 03.2
W. 1854

Cat. 15
Water Lilies
1915–17, oil on canvas
78 $\frac{3}{4}$ x 70 $\frac{7}{8}$ in. (200 x 180 cm)
Musée Marmottan Monet, Paris
Michel Monet Bequest, 1966, inv. 5119
W. 1855

Cat. 16
Water Lilies
c. 1921–22(?), oil on canvas
79 x 84 in. (200.7 x 213.3 cm)
Toledo Museum of Art, Ohio
Purchased with funds from the Libbey Endowment, Gift of Edward Drummond Libbey, 1981.54
W. 1804

Cat. 17
Irises
c. 1914–17, oil on canvas
79 x 59 in. (200.7 x 149.9 cm)
The National Gallery, London
Bought, 1967, NG6383
W. 1829

Cat. 18
Yellow Irises
c. 1914–17, oil on canvas
78 $\frac{3}{4}$ x 39 $\frac{3}{4}$ in. (200 x 101 cm)
The National Museum of Western Art, Tokyo
Purchased, P.1986-0002
W. 1826

Cat. 19
Water Lilies and Agapanthus
1914–17, oil on canvas
55 $\frac{1}{8}$ x 47 $\frac{1}{4}$ in. (140 x 120 cm); originally 78 $\frac{3}{4}$ x 51 $\frac{1}{8}$ in. (200 x 130 cm)
Musée Marmottan Monet, Paris
Michel Monet Bequest, 1966, inv. 5084
W. 1821

Cat. 20
Day Lilies
1914–17, oil on canvas
59 x 55 $\frac{1}{4}$ in. (150 x 140.5 cm)
Musée Marmottan Monet, Paris
Michel Monet Bequest, 1966, inv. 5097
W. 1818

Cat. 21
Yellow Irises
1917–19, oil on canvas
51 $\frac{1}{8}$ x 59 $\frac{7}{8}$ in. (130 x 152 cm)
Musée Marmottan Monet, Paris
Michel Monet Bequest, 1966, inv. 5095
W. 1839

Cat. 22
Roses
1925–26, oil on canvas
51 $\frac{1}{8}$ x 78 $\frac{3}{4}$ in. (130 x 200 cm)
Musée Marmottan Monet, Paris
Michel Monet Bequest, 1966, inv. 5096
W. 1963

Cat. 23
Water Lilies
c. 1916–19, oil on canvas
51 $\frac{1}{4}$ x 78 $\frac{3}{4}$ in. (130.2 x 200 cm)
The Tobin Theatre Arts Fund
Courtesy of the McNay Art Museum, San Antonio
W. 1863

Cat. 24
Water Lilies
1916–19, oil on canvas
51 $\frac{1}{4}$ x 79 in. (130.2 x 200.7 cm)
The Metropolitan Museum of Art, New York
Gift of Louise Reinhardt Smith, 1983, 1983.532
W. 1858

Cat. 25
Water-Lily Pond
1917–19, oil on canvas
39 3/8 x 78 3/4 in. (100 x 200 cm)
Private collection
Courtesy Benjamin Doller, New York
W. 1897

Cat. 26
Water Lilies
1917/19, oil on canvas
39 1/4 x 79 1/8 in. (99.7 x 201 cm)
Honolulu Museum of Art
Purchased in memory of Robert Allerton, 1966, 3385.1
W. 1895

Cat. 27
Water-Lily Pond
1917/19, oil on canvas
51 1/2 x 79 1/2 in. (130.2 x 201.9)
The Art Institute of Chicago
Gift of Mrs. Harvey Kaplan, 1982.825
W. 1889

Cat. 28
Water Lilies (Agapanthus)
c. 1915–26, oil on canvas
78 3/4 x 167 3/4 in. (200 x 426.1 cm)
Saint Louis Art Museum
The Steinberg Charitable Fund, 134:1956
W. 1976

Cat. 29
Wisteria
1919–20, oil on canvas
39 3/8 x 118 1/8 in. (100 x 300 cm)
Musée Marmottan Monet, Paris
Michel Monet Bequest, 1966, inv. 5123
W. 1903

Cat. 30
Wisteria
1919–20, oil on canvas
39 3/8 x 118 in. (100 x 300 cm)
Musée Marmottan Monet, Paris
Michel Monet Bequest, 1966, inv. 5124
W. 1904

Cat. 31
Corner of the Water-Lily Pond
1918–19, oil on canvas
51 1/8 x 34 5/8 in. (130 x 88 cm)
Private collection
W. 1880

Cat. 32
The Japanese Bridge
1918, oil on canvas
39 3/8 x 78 3/4 in. (100 x 200 cm)
Musée Marmottan Monet, Paris
Michel Monet Bequest, 1966, inv. 5079
W. 1911

Cat. 33
The Japanese Bridge
1918, oil on canvas
39 3/8 x 78 3/4 in. (100 x 200 cm)
Musée Marmottan Monet, Paris
Michel Monet Bequest, 1966, inv. 5077
W. 1913

Cat. 34
The Japanese Bridge
1919, oil on canvas
25 7/8 x 41 7/8 in. (65.6 x 106.4 cm)
Kunstmuseum Basel, Switzerland
Acquired in 1986 with a special loan from the Government of Basel and a contribution from the Max Geldner Foundation, Inv. G 1986.15
W. 1916

Cat. 35
The Japanese Bridge
1918–26, oil on canvas
35 x 36 1/2 in. (88.9 x 92.7 cm)
Philadelphia Museum of Art
The Albert M. Greenfield and Elizabeth M. Greenfield Collection, 1974, 1974-178-38
W. 1930

Cat. 36
The Japanese Bridge
c. 1923–25, oil on canvas
35 x 45 3/4 in. (88.9 x 116.2 cm)
Minneapolis Institute of Art
Bequest of Putnam Dana McMillan, 61.36.15
W. 1931

Cat. 37
The Japanese Bridge
1918–24, oil on canvas
35 x 45 5/8 in. (89 x 116 cm)
Musée Marmottan Monet, Paris
Michel Monet Bequest, 1966, inv. 5106
W. 1933

Cat. 38
The Japanese Bridge
c. 1918–24, oil on canvas
35 x 45 1/2 in. (89 x 115.5 cm)
Fondation Beyeler, Basel, Switzerland
Sammlung Beyeler, Inv. 90.15
W. 1921

Cat. 39
Weeping Willow
1918–19, oil on canvas
39 ½ x 39 ½ in. (100.5 x 100.5 cm)
Musée Marmottan Monet, Paris
Michel Monet Bequest, 1966, inv. 5081
W. 1873

Cat. 40
Weeping Willow
1918–19, oil on canvas
39 ½ x 47 ¼ in. (100 x 120 cm)
Musée Marmottan Monet, Paris
Michel Monet Bequest, 1966, inv. 5080
W. 1875

Cat. 41
Weeping Willow
1918–19, oil on canvas
39 ½ x 43 ¼ in. (100 x 110 cm)
Musée Marmottan Monet, Paris
Michel Monet Bequest, 1966, inv. 5078
W. 1877

Cat. 42
Weeping Willow
1918, oil on canvas
51 ¼ x 60 in. (130 x 152 cm)
Private collection, London
W. 1870

Cat. 43
Weeping Willow
1918, oil on canvas
51 ⅝ x 43 ½ in. (131.1 x 110.3 cm)
Columbus Museum of Art, Ohio
Gift of Howard D. and Babette L. Sirak, the Donors to the Campaign for Enduring Excellence, and the Derby Fund, 1991.001.041
W. 1869

Cat. 44
Weeping Willow
1918–19, oil on canvas
39 ¼ x 47 ¼ in. (99.7 x 120 cm)
Kimbell Art Museum, Fort Worth
Purchased 1996, AP 1966.02
W. 1876

Cat. 45
Weeping Willow
1921–22, oil on canvas
45 ⅝ x 35 in. (116 x 89 cm)
Musée Marmottan Monet, Paris
Michel Monet Bequest, 1966, inv. 5107
W. 1943

Cat. 46
Weeping Willow
1920–22, oil on canvas
43 ¼ x 39 ½ in. (110 x 100 cm)
Musée d'Orsay, Paris
Donated by Mr. Philippe Meyer, 2000, RF 2000 21
W. 1942

Cat. 47
Path under the Rose Arches, Giverny
1920–22, oil on canvas
36 ¼ x 35 in. (92 x 89 cm)
Musée Marmottan Monet, Paris
Michel Monet Bequest, 1966, inv. 5104
W. 1938

Cat. 48
Path under the Rose Arches, Giverny
1920–22, oil on canvas
35 x 39 ⅜ in. (89 x 100 cm)
Musée Marmottan Monet, Paris
Michel Monet Bequest, 1966, inv. 5089
W. 1934

Cat. 49
The Artist's House Seen from the Rose Garden
1922–24, oil on canvas
35 x 36 ¼ in. (89 x 92 cm)
Musée Marmottan Monet, Paris
Michel Monet Bequest, inv. 5108
W. 1944

Cat. 50
The Artist's House Seen from the Rose Garden
1922–24, oil on canvas
35 x 39 ⅜ in. (89 x 100 cm)
Musée Marmottan Monet, Paris
Michel Monet Bequest, 1966, inv. 5103
W. 1947

Cat. 51
The Artist's House Seen from the Rose Garden
1922–24, oil on canvas
31 ¾ x 36 ¼ in. (81 x 92 cm)
Musée Marmottan Monet, Paris
Michel Monet Bequest, 1966, inv. 5086
W. 1946

Cat. 52
The Artist's House Seen from the Rose Garden
1922–24, oil on canvas
31 ⅞ x 36 ⅝ in. (81 x 93 cm)
Musée Marmottan Monet, Paris
Michel Monet Bequest, 1966, inv. 5087
W. 1945

Photography Credits

All image rights belong to the works' respective owners unless otherwise indicated.

© Agence de presse Meurisse, Bibliothèque nationale de France, Paris: Fig. 16

Albers Foundation / Art Resource, NY. © ARS, NY: Fig. 185

Image © Amgueddfa Cymru – National Museum Wales: Fig. 95

The Art Institute of Chicago / Art Resource, NY: Cats. 6 and 27

© Bibliothèque nationale de France, Paris: Figs. 31, 109

© Michele Brabo / Opale / Leemage / Bridgeman Images: Fig. 129

Bridgeman Images: Figs. 6, 12, 41, 73, 105, 112 122, 125, 164, 167, 179; cats. 4, 14, 28, 34, 36

Courtesy of Christie's: Figs. 35, 132, 134; cats. 8, 9

Photo © Christie's Images / Bridgeman Images: Fig. 121

De Agostini Picture Library / Bridgeman Images: Fig. 126

Image courtesy of John Delaney, senior imaging scientist, National Gallery of Art, Washington, DC: Fig. 45

Courtesy of Benjamin Doller, New York: Cat. 25

Photo Archives Durand-Ruel © Durand-Ruel & Cie: Figs. 5, 17–22, 40, 140, 155

Courtesy of Jérôme Faucheux: Figs. 27, 150, 182

Image courtesy of the Fine Arts Museums of San Francisco : Cat. 13

Galerie Larock-Granoff / Art Resource, NY: Fig. 176

© Getty Images: Fig. 162

Getty Images / Hulton Archive: Fig. 66

Courtesy Robert Gordon: Figs. 76–79, 90–91

Courtesy Helly Nahmad Gallery, London: Cat. 1

Courtesy of Heidelberg University Library, Germany: Fig. 96

HIP / Art Resource, NY: Figs. 4, 184; cats. 7, 18

© Ellsworth Kelly: Fig. 32

Erich Lessing / Art Resource, NY: Fig. 72, left panel

Photograph by Abelardo Morell / Courtesy of Edwynn Houk Gallery: Fig. 181

Digital Image © The Museum of Modern Art / Licensed by Scala / Art Resource, NY: Fig. 128, 130

Digital image © The Museum of Modern Art / Licensed by Scala / Art Resource, Ny. © Estate Joan Mitchell: Fig. 178

© The National Gallery, London / Art Resource, NY: Figs. 42, 63; p. 26; cat. 17

The Philadelphia Museum of Art / Art Resource, NY: Cat. 35

© Collection Philippe Piguet: Figs. 2, 3, 9, 11, 14, 28, 30, 37, 39, 44, 157

Image courtesy Phillips, New York: Figs. 149, 152

© The Milton Resnick and Pat Passlof Foundation: Fig. 33

© RMN-Grand Palais / Art Resource, NY: Fig. 102

© RMN-Grand Palais / Art Resource, NY. Photo: Gérard Blot / Hervé Lewandowski: Fig. 127

© RMN-Grand Palais / Art Resource, NY. Photo: Adrien Didierjean: Cat. 46

© RMN-Grand Palais / Art Resource, NY. Photo by Michel Urtado: Fig. 72, right three panels; figs. 74–75; 107–8

Réunion des Musées Nationaux, Paris : Fig. 8

Roger-Viollet, Paris / Bridgeman Images: Figs. 118, 172

Scala / Ministero per i Beni e le Attività culturali / Art Resource, NY: Figs. 10, 153

Scala / Art Resource, NY: Figs. 25–26

Photograph by Adrian Scottow: Fig. 111

Courtesy Société Clause: Fig. 173

Courtesy of Sotheby's: Fig. 97; cat. 2

© Clyfford Still / ARS, NY: Fig. 177

Photograph by Soichi Sunami: Fig. 123

Image courtesy of John Twilley: Figs. 49, 50, and 62

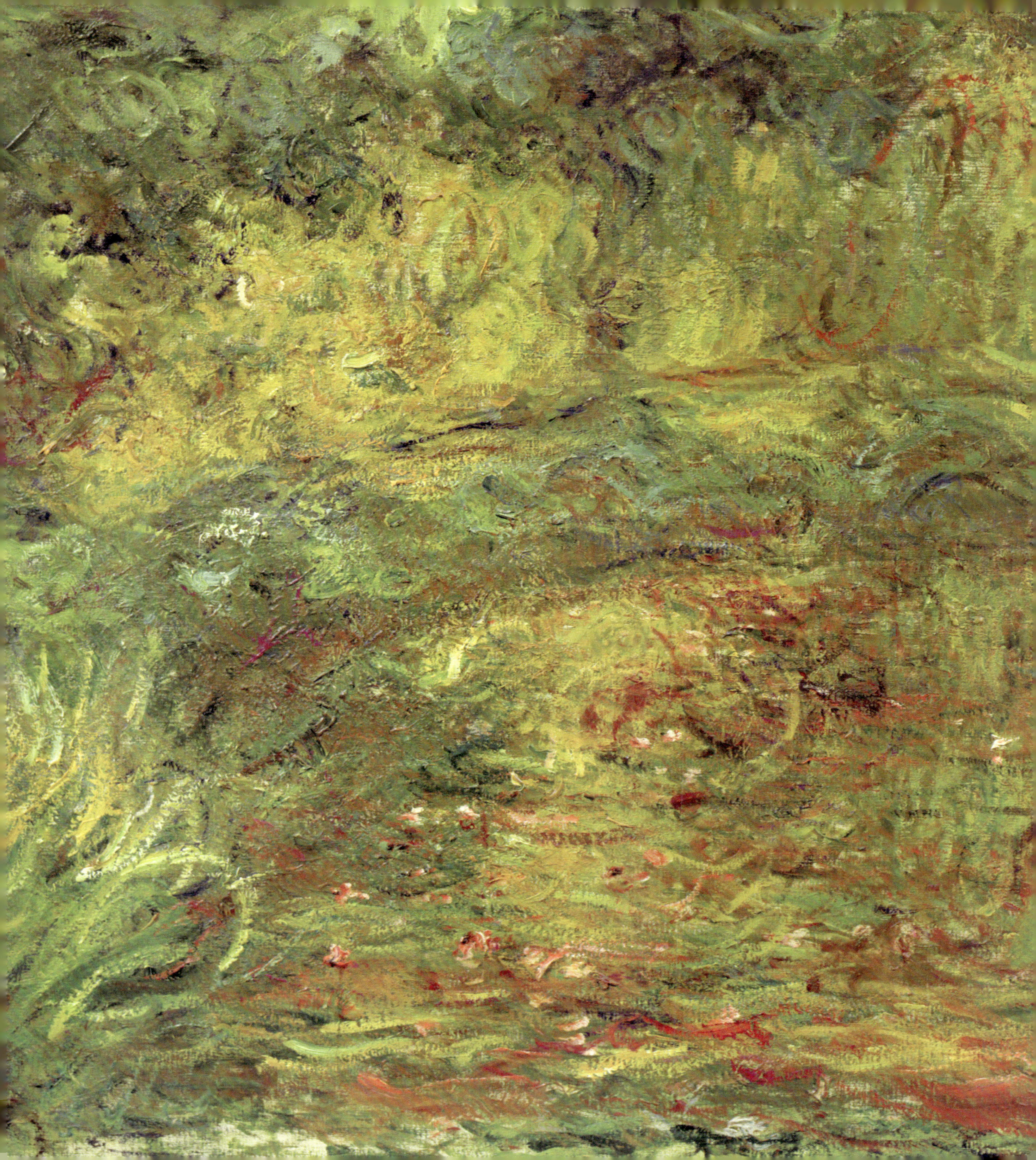